THE MANAGEMENT OF BUSINESS LOGISTICS

SIXTH EDITION

THE MANAGEMENT OF BUSINESS LOGISTICS

SIXTH EDITION

John J. Coyle
The Pennsylvania State University

Edward J. Bardi
University of Toledo

C. John Langley Jr.
University of Tennessee

WEST PUBLISHING COMPANY

Minneapolis/St. Paul • New York • Los Angeles • San Francisco

Cover Image: © Walter Wick/FPG International
Cover and Text Designs: LightSource Images, Minneapolis
Copyedit: Rebecca Pepper
Illustrations: Parrot Graphics
Composition: Parkwood Composition

WEST'S COMMITMENT TO THE ENVIRONMENT

In 1906, West Publishing Company began recycling materials left over from the production of books. This began a tradition of efficient and responsible use of resources. Today, 100% of our legal bound volumes are printed on acid-free, recycled paper consisting of 50% new paper pulp and 50% paper that has undergone a de-inking process. We also use vegetable-based inks to print all of our books. West recycles nearly 27,700,000 pounds of scrap paper annually—the equivalent of 229,300 trees. Since the 1960s, West has devised ways to capture and recycle waste inks, solvents, oils, and vapors created in the printing process. We also recycle plastics of all kinds, wood, glass, corrugated cardboard, and batteries, and have eliminated the use of polystyrene book packaging. We at West are proud of the longevity and the scope of our commitment to the environment.

West pocket parts and advance sheets are printed on recyclable paper and can be collected and recycled with newspapers. Staples do not have to be removed. Bound volumes can be recycled after removing the cover.

Production, Prepress, Printing and Binding by West Publishing Company.

 PRINTED ON 10% POST CONSUMER RECYCLED PAPER   **Printed with Printwise** ⊛
Environmentally Advanced Water Washable Ink

British Library Cataloguing-in-Publication Data. A catalogue record for this book is available from the British Library.

LIBRARY OF CONGRESS CATALOGING-IN-PUBLICATION DATA

Coyle, John Joseph, 1935–
      The management of business logistics / John J. Coyle, Edward J.
  Bardi, C. John Langley, Jr. — 6th ed.
          p.   cm.
      Includes bibliographical references and indexes.
      ISBN 0-314-06507-5 (hard : alk. paper)
      1. Business logistics. I. Bardi, Edward J., 1943–
  II. Langley, C. John, 1946–   III. Title.
  HD38.5.C69   1996
  658.7—dc20
                                                                                95-39258
                                                                                        CIP

Dedicated to Dr. Robert D. Pashek
Teacher, administrator, and friend

BRIEF CONTENTS

CONTENTS

PREFACE

Two recurring themes permeate the pages of our sixth edition—*challenge* and *change*. Perhaps a third theme should also be added, even though it is not stated as explicitly as the other two—*excitement*. Whether you view the current stage of logistics development as being exciting probably depends upon your perspective. Some individuals may lament the passing of the "good old days," because it is certainly not business as usual in logistics circles today. Much has changed, and change always brings some disruption. However, from the perspective of the authors, the overall net impact of the change has been beneficial to logistics professionals and their organizations. We also do not agree that the "old days" (prior to deregulation) were all that good. The present environment has more to offer and provides much more opportunity to be creative and innovative in meeting the challenges of the fast-approaching 21st century.

No one seems to disagree that tremendous changes have occurred in business logistics. The change has been revolutionary in many areas directly and indirectly related to logistics. We do not have to look any further than the transportation industry to see evidence of such change. The previous two editions of this textbook described the changes ushered in and made possible by the era of deregulation that was initiated by the deregulation of the airfreight industry in 1977. The transportation arena has continued to change, as documented in this edition. However, the change did not stop with transportation; warehousing, inventory practices, materials handling, and so forth have all changed dramatically.

Obviously, logistics is not the only area in business organizations that has felt the impact of the changing environment for business; it has cut across all functional areas. The forces of change will continue to drive us to adapt, thus providing opportunities for logisticians to play an important role in helping their organizations gain some competitive edge.

The forces of change also dictate the need for revision in textbooks. It was a challenge and something of a struggle to develop our strategy for revising this sixth edition. We decided to provide a new introductory chapter focusing upon supply chain management and also to use that concept throughout this edition. The supply chain focus of companies today offers tremendous opportunities (we said it again) to take cost out of the logistics system and yet to improve the effectiveness of that system.

Reducing cost and improving service would have been viewed as improbable at best when the first edition of this text was published twenty years ago. We usually talked about the trade-off of spending more to improve effectiveness. While that notion still applies today in some logistics situations, it is possible to both reduce cost and improve service in a number of instances. The supply chain approach has provided numerous instances in which this has been possible. As will be indicated in several chapters, there are many challenges in making the supply chain work effectively and efficiently, and it is not a panacea for success. However, there is no question that the supply chain focus can lead to improvements for companies. Supply chain management has probably been used in more paper titles at Council of Logistics Management (CLM) proceedings in recent years than any other term or concept.

Part I of this book now includes three additional chapters. Chapter 2 presents the traditional dimensions of logistics with some new twists. Chapters 3 and 4 focus upon inbound and outbound logistics, respectively, to reflect the importance of these two components of a logistics system. While the inbound system and the outbound system share some common logistics processes, they are each unique in certain respects. This uniqueness is stressed in Chapters 3 and 4.

Part II presents the various logistics processes, including *inventory* (Chapters 5 and 6), *warehousing* (Chapter 7), *materials handling* and *packaging* (Chapter 8), *transportation* (Chapters 9 and 10), and *order processing and information systems* (Chapter 11). Most of these chapter titles are similar to those used in the previous edition, but the reader will note significant revision of the chapter topics to reflect the changes that have taken place in logistics since the last edition.

Finally, Part III addresses strategic issues for logistics systems. Chapter 12 discusses a topic of critical importance, namely, *network design*. The supply chain concept, globalization, and the use of third parties have made network design a topic of special importance and a source of the lower cost and improved effectiveness mentioned above. ''Doing more with less'' has been the hallmark of some of the success stories in reconfigured networks.

Chapter 13 focuses upon *global logistics,* which had been covered in Part I in the previous edition. In reevaluating the material for this edition, we decided to move global logistics to the strategic issues portion of the text because of its overriding importance in setting the tone for the logistics environment of today.

Chapter 14 addresses the important issue of *organization* for logistics systems. The emergence of large third-party logistics companies with the related trend of outsourcing has made organizational issues a topic of continuing interest. Coupled with the impact of technology, corporate reengineering, and so on, it is easy to understand why we need to provide comprehensive coverage of the logistics organization.

Chapter 15, the final chapter, examines the leading edge logistics strategies companies need as they approach the 21st century. In many ways, this chapter serves as a convenient summary of the major points of focus in the previous chapters. A taxonomy of strategic efforts is presented that attempts to classify strategies according to whether they focus upon reducing cost, adding value, improving customer service, and so on. Not all strategies fit neatly into this framework, but many of them do.

As usual, the authors are indebted to many individuals at their respective institutions—Penn State, the University of Toledo, and the University of Tennessee. These individuals include but are not limited to Rosi Greaser, Bob Novack, Joe Cavinato, Jean Beierlein, Tom Hummer, and the thousands of students at Penn

State, Toledo, and Tennessee who provide continual feedback and input between editions.

A special note of thanks and gratitude is due to our wives, Barbara, Carol, and Anne, who have provided support and encouragement, but more importantly who have given up time that was due them from our schedules. Our children, John and Susan, Susan and Pamela, and Sarah and Mercer, who have made our lives more meaningful, also deserve mention, and now our grandchildren have added a new special dimension.

We extend appreciation to the members of our West Publishing team, who are professionals in every sense of the word: John Szilagyi, acquiring editor; Esther Craig, developmental editor; Mary Verrill, production editor; and Carol Yanisch, promotions manager.

Special thanks should be given to the following reviewers, who provided meaningful input that provided important help in creating the sixth edition:

Kathryn Dobie
University of Wisconsin—Eau Claire

Philip T. Evers
University of Maryland at College Park

Bruce Ferrin
Arizona State University

Kent N. Gourdin
University of North Carolina at Charlotte

Mary Collins Holcomb
University of Tennessee—Knoxville

Paul Murphy
John Carroll University

Richard Poist
Iowa State University

James P. Rakowski
Memphis State University

Skip Sherwood
California State University—Fresno

John J. Coyle
Edward J. Bardi
C. John Langley Jr.

PART I

THE LOGISTICS SUPPLY CHAIN

Corporate America has discovered a "new" weapon for building market share and increasing return on investment. It is not really new in the eyes of some logistics professionals, but logistics has captured the attention of senior managers in the upper echelons of U.S. companies. They have recognized the value-added role of logistics that can help to differentiate a product in the marketplace and effectively lower the cost of doing business for both buyer and seller.

There is an interesting twist to this new emphasis upon logistics in that the focus is upon the supply chain. In other words, there is a recognition that companies are usually part of a "pipeline" or supply chain that brings a product to the ultimate user. In its simplest context, the supply chain involves a company's vendors and direct customers. The supply chain perspective ultimately recognizes that all three parties are, in a sense, partners in bringing a product to market.

Part I of this text focuses upon the logistics supply chain. Chapter 1 presents an overview of the logistics supply chain, providing definitions, characteristics, and important perspectives about supply chain management.

Chapter 2 focuses upon the various dimensions of logistics. The chapter first examines the role and importance of logistics in the economy—a macro perspective. Then, logistics is discussed from an internal company (micro) perspective with an emphasis upon functional relationships. Finally, logistics is analyzed in terms of the major factors that affect logistics goals.

Chapters 3 and 4 examine the two major components of the logistics system—the inbound system (materials management and procurement) and the outbound system (distribution channels and customer service). These two chapters provide the foundation for Part II of the book, which discusses logistics processes.

Logistics Supply Chain Management

LEARNING OBJECTIVES

After reading this chapter, you should be able to do the following:

- Discuss the development and evolution of supply chain management.

- Understand why companies find a supply chain perspective important to improving their competitive position in the marketplace.

- Describe various definitions of supply chain management.

- Understand key characteristics of successful supply chains and how they differ from traditional approaches.

- Explain the objectives of effective supply chains.

- Understand the external or macro drivers of change that have influenced the development of supply chains.

- Describe the major strategic changes that firms have developed to respond to the macro change drivers.

BECTON DICKINSON COMPANY

"Build a better mousetrap and the world will beat a path to your door" is an often repeated phrase attributed to Benjamin Franklin. This may have been sound advice in the 18th century, but the Becton Dickinson Company feels that it is not sufficient for companies preparing to compete in today's global environment. Becton Dickinson does not manufacture mousetraps; rather, it is a world-class manufacturer and distributor of medical supplies and devices and diagnostic systems used by professionals in the medical field as well as by the general public. Becton Dickinson is located in Franklin Lakes, New Jersey, and is a multinational company with worldwide operations and global sales.

Becton Dickinson is proud of its products and its four business sectors, but it feels that good products are not sufficient today. It is the company's opinion that customers want these good products *when* and *where* they need them, *delivered* in the right quantity and in perfect condition at a competitive price.

To implement these customer requirements, a new operating division, designed to better respond to the company's distribution needs, has been established: Supply Chain Services. A focus upon supply chain management is not new at Becton Dickinson; rather, this is the latest organizational development in a continuum to be responsive to its customers' needs.

Becton Dickinson treats supply chain management the same way it does manufactured products; that is, the company supports it with the same level of research and marketing it gives a newly designed surgical blade. Supply chain management is viewed as being integral to the product's value. Brochures to distributors tout supply chain management in the same way that Becton Dickinson promotes the technical features of a new syringe.

Becton Dickinson's approach to supply chain management dates back to 1988, when the function was reorganized into a separate group reporting to the chief executive officer. Supply chain management has been credited with several operational improvements—reduced product cycle times, higher levels of order completeness, improved accuracy, and lower costs.

One Becton Dickinson overseas division has been able to reduce its inventories by 50 percent. Another division has seen its rate of complete order fulfillment jump from 50 percent to close to 90 percent. Another example is a joint effort with a key distributor that has led to a 36-percent reduction in inventory while improving the order fill rate from 94 percent to 98 percent.

Becton Dickinson's is not the standard approach. The traditional mind-set views logistics as a cost-cutting exercise characterized by arm's-length or even adversarial relationships with vendors and suppliers. By contrast, Becton Dickinson makes supply chain management a value-added product that requires a focus on growth, the customer, and partnerships with vendors. Along with its physical products, Becton Dickinson sells savings and convenience that result from reduced inventories and ordering times and improved flow of information between the company and its customers. Its supply chain services include refinement of the company's distribution center network, consolidation of shipments from various divisions, improved delivery schedules, and information services to link the whole process together. Most of Becton Dickinson's products are sold to distributors, who in turn sell to hospitals, laboratories, and clinics. Before 1988, distributors had to deal with each Becton Dickinson division individually. The supply chain management group was created to enable the company to present one face to its customers. The supply chain group supports the operating sectors and divisions with logistics and transportation, information technology, and marketing services. The inclusion of marketing within the supply chain group is significant. To provide good service, a company must know what customers want and need, and must market services and products as a valuable package.

Supply chain management is described by Becton Dickinson as "a strategic concept that involves understanding and managing the sequence of activities—from supplier to manufacturer to customer—that add value to the product supply pipeline." This definition is comprehensive and crosses traditional departmental bound-

continued on next page

LOGISTICS PROFILE

BECTON DICKINSON COMPANY *continued*

aries within companies. The concept requires a different approach, and that's the biggest obstacle to implementing effective supply chain management. Old mind-sets die hard. It's difficult to break out of the box of rigid habits.

Manufacturers are familiar with the idea of product platforms. Becton Dickinson likes to describe supply chain management in terms of "service platforms" that support a product by adding value in the eyes of the customer. When introducing a new product, a company progresses through market research, development, and pilot operation into full-scale operations and sales and marketing. At Becton Dickinson, supply chain management services go through similar steps. The product must be surrounded with basic services that customers expect and unexpected services that customers value. Those services must be surrounded by research and development, just like the physical product. To differenti-

ate itself, a good company is always seeking to add new value-added services.

Supply chain logistics encompasses more than logistics, product supply, or even integrated operations. Supply chain management should be viewed as "an integrating process, used to create and sustain competitive advantage based on the delivery to customers of basic and unexpected services." If the customer perceives that Becton Dickinson's supply chain management makes it easier to do business with the company, common sense dictates that the customer will be more inclined to buy Becton Dickinson's products.

While executives in the Becton Dickinson supply chain management group do not wear lapel pins proclaiming quality, they say that improved quality is the biggest payoff from supply chain management. When a company implements a true supply chain management concept, the whole operation works better, and quality is a natural result.

ADAPTED FROM: Joseph Bonnoy, "Supply Chain Management: Treat It Like a Product," *American Shipper* (February 1994): 39–42.

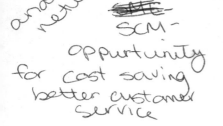

efficiency/ effectiveness

Supply chain management is an approach to analyzing and/or managing logistics networks that has captured the attention of many companies and their CEOs. The underlying rationale for this interest, and the vision of the proponents of supply chain management, is the opportunity for cost savings (efficiency) and/or better customer service (effectiveness). The ultimate objective is to improve a company's competitive position in the global marketplace and to sustain that position in spite of intensive competitive forces and rapidly changing customer needs. Logisticians who recognize the integral role that logistics can play on supply chain management take advantage of all opportunities to implement the appropriate changes in their structures and strategies. (The Becton Dickinson profile illustrates the key role that logistics supply chain management can play in today's market environment.)

The potential benefit to individual supply chains and/or industrywide supply chains is significant. For example, the National Grocery Manufacturers Association and other related groups have estimated that the package goods industry could save more than $30 billion per year by increasing the velocity of the inventory moving through the supply chain to the ultimate consumer.[1]

Before proceeding further, some background needs to be provided about the supply chain concept and the essential characteristics of supply chains.

DEVELOPMENT OF SUPPLY CHAIN MANAGEMENT: CONCEPTS AND DEFINITIONS

The underlying concepts and rationale for supply chain management are not brand new. They have evolved through several stages. In fact, logistics managers have been utilizing the underlying concepts of supply chain management for many years—systems analysis, value chain analysis, total cost/trade-off analysis, and related concepts. These concepts will be explored in more depth in Chapter 2.

The First Step: Physical Distribution

During the 1960s and 1970s, many companies both in the United States and world-wide focused attention upon what was defined as physical distribution or outbound logistics systems. They attempted to systematically manage a set of interrelated activities including transportation, distribution, warehousing, finished goods, inventory levels, packaging, and materials handling (see Figure 1–1) to ensure the efficient delivery of finished goods to customers.

outbound systems

It was an era of great challenge and change. There were many mitigating factors that caused companies to attempt to manage physical distribution more efficiently, including:

- *Product line expansion.* Many consumer product companies expanded their product lines not only in terms of additional brands of the same basic prod-

---

FIGURE 1-1   A View of Business Logistics in a Company

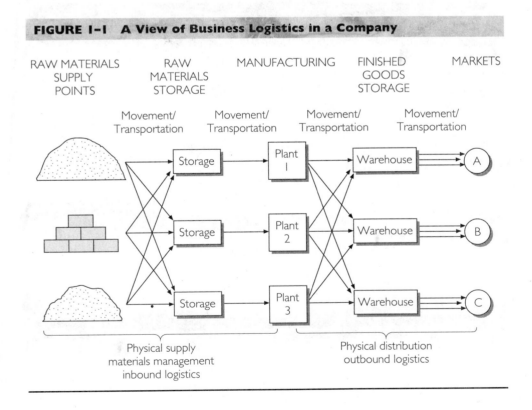

| RAW MATERIALS SUPPLY POINTS | RAW MATERIALS STORAGE | MANUFACTURING | FINISHED GOODS STORAGE | MARKETS |

Movement/ Transportation   Movement/ Transportation   Movement/ Transportation   Movement/ Transportation

Physical supply materials management inbound logistics

Physical distribution outbound logistics

uct, for example, soap, but also in the terms of the size, shape, color, and form in which you could purchase the product. This dramatic increase in the number of stock-keeping units (SKUs) led to higher inventory costs, order processing costs, and transportation costs, and increased the difficulty of forecasting demand. The underlying rationale for this expansion was to increase market share and recognize consumer segments and preferences. But there was an associated increase in manufacturing cost, especially physical distribution costs, that necessitated a different management approach. The multiple SKUs of essentially the same product made forecasting more difficult, led to more safety stock, and led to smaller, more costly transportation movements.

- *Rate increases.* The regulatory environment of the 1960s and 1970s gave rise to a steady increase in rates. Rate increases were approved by the Interstate Commerce Commission based upon any increased cost that carriers experienced through increased wages or other operating costs. The regulatory environment, which limited competition and approached ratemaking on a cost-plus basis, affected the transportation costs/rates of most shippers.
- *Higher-valued products.* As the U.S. economy changed during this period in response to internal and external factors, many manufacturers moved toward the production of higher-valued goods that were also less labor intensive. These higher-valued products also resulted in higher physical distribution costs, since inventory carrying costs, packaging costs, and transportation costs usually increase with higher-valued products.

As companies began to recognize the relationship between inventory cost and transportation cost from a systems/total cost perspective, they grouped these activities under a physical distribution manager. The rationale was the opportunity to reduce the total cost of physical distribution by managing the trade-offs from a systems approach.* For example, a shift to high-cost airfreight could lead to dramatic savings in inventory and warehousing by reducing stocking locations. Related activities such as packaging, materials handling, customer service, and so on were also evaluated for possible savings.

The Second Step: Integrated Logistics Management

logistics During the 1970s and 1980s, companies increasingly began to recognize the additional opportunities for savings by combining the inbound side (materials management) with the outbound side (physical distribution). The combining of the inbound side with the outbound side was described as business logistics or, simply, as the logistics system. (See Figure 1–1.) Initially, this provided potential savings by having a single transportation manager who could coordinate inbound and outbound transportation. After 1980, which ushered in deregulation, the opportunity to negotiate rates with carriers for both inbound and outbound movements provided volume to leverage for reduced rates and improved service. Companies also became aware of the opportunity to view the whole process, from raw materials to work-in-process inventory to finished goods, as a continuum that, managed from a systems perspective, could lead to more efficient operation. The inclusion

---

*The systems approach will be documented and discussed more fully in the next chapter.

of purchasing/procurement as part of the inbound logistics added significantly to the opportunity to reduce costs. The procurement process, which involves making decisions about how much to purchase (inventory quantities) and where to purchase (transportation), has a significant impact on inbound logistics. (See Figure 1–2 for additional opportunities for integrating inbound logistics.)

Again, there were a number of mitigating factors:

- *Deregulation of transportation.* Airlines were deregulated in 1977 (airfreight) and 1978 (passenger), followed by rail and motor carriers in 1980. The additional freedom of carriers to negotiate rates with shippers, serve new geographic points, and establish longer-term relationships with shippers led to the expansion of opportunities for shippers to use systems analysis and value chain analysis to lower costs or improve service in the logistics system of the firm.
- *Global competition.* Many of the foreign competitors of U.S. companies had introduced management practices such as just-in-time (JIT) production and inventory approaches and total quality management (TQM), which improved their total logistics systems (inbound and outbound). Recognizing the advantages in the marketplace, U.S. companies initiated similar practices in an effort to remain competitive in the domestic market and to expand into global markets.
- *Foreign sources of supply.* U.S. companies became increasingly dependent upon foreign sources of supply. This developed first with raw materials such as iron ore when domestic sources were depleted, but quickly spread to parts and other work-in-process inventory, which could be produced cheaper overseas. The longer pipelines had impacts on transportation cost and inventory and led to more focus on the total logistics system.

FIGURE 1–2 The Logistics Evolution

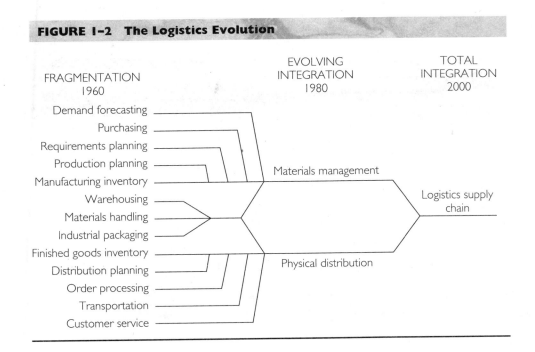

- *Economic factors.* The U.S. economy experienced a number of challenges during this period, including double-digit interest rates and a recession, which added to the need to manage logistics systems more efficiently and to carefully examine the potential trade-offs for savings.

Overall, the 1970s and 1980s were decades of great change in the U.S. economy. Businesses were forced to change in many ways to stay competitive. The organizational and management changes in logistics were a part of these fundamental changes.

The Third Step: Supply Chain Management

supply chain/logistics pipeline

During the 1980s and 1990s, a number of external factors, to be discussed later in this chapter, caused companies to expand their perspective on the logistics processes to include all of the firms involved in ensuring that the final customer received the right product, at the right cost, at the right time, in the right condition, and in the right quantity. From its narrowest perspective, this meant including the vendors and channels of distribution. (See Figure 1–3.) As this concept developed, it was referred to as the logistics pipeline or supply chain for somewhat obvious reasons. It was also based upon the partnerships/alliances that were developing between manufacturing companies and their suppliers/vendors, customers (read channels of distribution), and other logistics-related parties such as transportation and public warehousing companies. (Recall the importance of the vendor and customer partnerships for Becton Dickinson.)

efficient consumer response (ECR)

As was indicated previously, the supply chain or pipeline is a natural extension of the underlying logic for managing logistics as an important system or component of a single company. The trade-off/total cost and value chain types of analyses to be explored in the next chapter can be extended to the supply chain or pipeline. It is much more difficult to achieve an optimal strategy throughout the supply chain/pipeline because in the short run one or more members of the supply chain may find that their position is less optimal than it was previously. For example, efficient consumer response (ECR) is an attempt to increase the velocity of inventory in the package goods industry throughout the supply chain of wholesalers, distributors, and ultimately to consumers. To be successful, the ECR approach will have to eliminate most of the forward buying practices of large wholesalers and retailers, which have led to large inventory accumulations in that industry. The affected wholesalers and retailers have become accustomed to the promotional, end-of-quarter pricing discounts that increase their margin. How-

FIGURE 1-3 Logistics Supply Chain

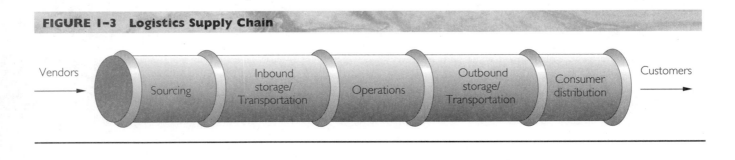

ever, the trade-off is the vast amount of inventory and the inefficient manufacturing patterns necessary for end-of-quarter sales spurts. The overall supply chain, however, can be more efficient with the ECR approach.

The potential associated with a supply chain/pipeline approach is tremendous from a savings perspective. The initiating study done for the efficient consumer response approach of the package goods industry, as indicated previously, estimated savings in excess of $30 billion per year, which could be used to lower the price paid by consumers for those products.[2]

It should be noted that the efficient consumer response example cited previously is not a complete supply chain but rather only the outbound side, from manufacturers to retailers. However, it encompasses many parallel, competing companies, making it a special challenge to implement to achieve the stated objectives. In other words, the package goods industry as a whole, including the manufacturers and the channels of distribution, have to cooperate to achieve the potential savings in the supply chain. The Becton Dickinson profile illustrated only one company's logistics supply chain, which should be easier to implement.

Another dimension of the supply chain concept is that companies can be part of several pipelines. For example, a manufacturer of steel could be part of the supply chain for autos, bicycles, filing cabinets, and so forth. Also, in a global sense, supply chains, not individual companies, compete with each other to deliver the best product at the best final cost for the ultimate consumer of the product and its related services.

Supply Chain Definitions. We will revisit the supply chain concept in later discussions. At this point, it may be helpful to present some definitions of a supply chain:

- An integrating philosophy to manage the total flow of a distribution channel from supplier to ultimate customer (Cooper and Ellram)[3]
- A strategic concept that involves understanding and managing the sequence of activities—from supplier to customer—that add value to the product supply pipeline (Battaglia and Tyndall)[4]
- Integrative management of the sequential flow of logistical, conversion, and service activities from vendors to ultimate consumers necessary to produce a product or service efficiently and effectively (Stenger and Coyle)[5]

All three definitions indicate the intercompany, boundary-spanning nature of the supply chain for the purpose of managing and/or coordinating the flow of material from raw materials through the final product, whether it be purchased by a consumer or by another industrial company that might use it.

boundary spanning

Efficiency and value-added (effectiveness) roles are important across the supply chain, as was indicated previously by the Becton Dickinson profile. The integration and coordination of this network of companies is a formidable task. Successful supply chain management is based upon the integration and management of three types of "flows" or basic processes—product, information, and cash. (See Figure 1–4.)

processes

The three basic flows of product, information, and cash exist among the members of the channel.[6] Information and cash would flow in both directions, whereas products would usually flow in only one direction, with the exception of those systems with reverse flows for product and parts returns. In fact, reverse product

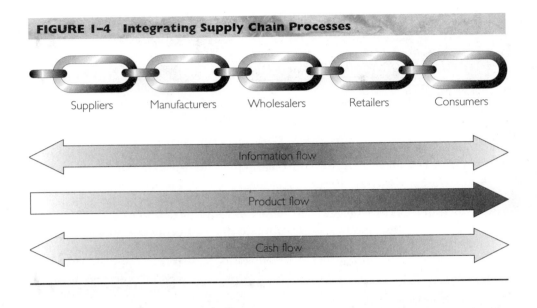

FIGURE 1-4 Integrating Supply Chain Processes

Suppliers   Manufacturers   Wholesalers   Retailers   Consumers

Information flow

Product flow

Cash flow

flows are likely to take on increasing importance in the future because of environmental protection and related issues.

visibility

Supply Chain Characteristics. One of the major challenges of supply chain management is to maintain the visibility of the inventory in the entire pipeline and to strive to minimize the uncertainty that leads to building safety-stock inventory or to nonoptimal pipeline practices such as forward buying. It would be useful at this point to examine the basic characteristics of supply chains compared to what could be considered traditional firm-oriented logistics systems. (See Table 1–1.) As noted in the first two items in Table 1–1, inventory, both from a management perspective

inventory

and from a flow perspective, is different in a supply chain. The level of inventory must be coordinated all along the supply chain to minimize inventory investment and cost. In the past, inventory was frequently pushed forward or backward, depending upon who had the most leverage in the supply chain. For example, when Chrysler initially introduced its JIT inventory program for inbound parts, its vendors dramatically increased their inventory levels to meet the Chrysler-imposed JIT delivery schedules. Pushing the inventory back to vendors did not lower inventory investment in the pipeline, it merely transferred it. The problem was resolved by providing vendors with more accurate and timely information about production scheduling to reduce uncertainty and to provide information about the inventory levels (provide visibility) that both Chrysler and its vendors had. The sharing of information about anticipated demand, orders, production schedules, and so on, forward and backward reduces uncertainty and leads to lower safety-stock inventory. Getting companies to share such important information is often a difficult hurdle to overcome. Companies are concerned about competitors finding out too much, which may reduce some competitive advantage.

As Table 1–1 indicates, the supply chain is optimized by focusing upon the final landed cost of the product.[7] Landed cost refers to the final, total actual cost to the customer at the point where they are going to use it, including the initial purchase price and delivery cost, inventory cost, and other costs. Companies are

TABLE 1-1 Comparison of Key Characteristics of Traditional Systems with Supply Chain

Factor	Traditional	Supply Chain
Inventory management	Firm focused	Pipeline coordination
Inventory flows	Interrupted	Seamless/visible
Cost	Firm minimized	Landed cost
Information	Firm controlled	Shared
Risk	Firm focused	Shared
Planning	Firm oriented	Supply chain team approach
Interorganizational relationships	Firm focused on low cost	Partnerships focused on landed cost

ADAPTED FROM: Ellram and Cooper, "Characteristics of Supply Chain Management and the Implications for Purchasing and Logistics Strategy," *International Journal of Logistics Management* 4, no. 2 (1993).

accustomed to focusing upon their own inherent cost and may not be aware of **landed cost** how their approach to doing business with their vendors or customers affects the landed cost of the final product. Not providing vendors with sufficient lead time information or requiring customers to buy in large quantities may increase their inventory costs, which are then passed along the pipeline to the final customer.

The sharing of information will continue to be a thorny issue, particularly in **sharing risk** cases where vendors and/or channel customers may also deal with competitors of a manufacturer. Some balance and judgment may be necessary, but shared information is a key ingredient to success. Risk is another characteristic likely to cause concern, since a supply chain perspective requires sharing of risk. One approach to sharing risk with third-party companies involves guaranteeing certain volumes of business over a stipulated period of time, which reduces the risk of losing business. Joint investment in assets is another method or approach to risk sharing.

Supply chain planning is becoming more popular in a number of industries, **supply chain planning** particularly in the automobile industry. Vendors have become more involved with auto manufacturers as the JIT programs have matured to the point where vendors have become part of the platform design teams and are providing engineering expertise in the development phase of the models. The consumer has also been brought into the picture in the auto industry through customer questionnaires and focus groups. The Ford Taurus was developed through customer survey research. Even the dealers, who make up the primary component of the distribution channel, have been playing a larger role in providing feedback for design and other customer service–related features.

Related to the joint planning just discussed are new organizational relationships **alliances** such as strategic alliances and partnerships. These relationships include, as was indicated previously, vendors, carriers, channel members, and third-party providers. The JIT environment tends to promote such relationships as companies reduce the number of their vendors and work more closely with them to achieve the cost and quality objectives necessary for success. There have been successes and there have been failures, but such organizational relationships will continue to blossom under the supply chain approach.

ON THE LINE

Customized Transportation Inc. Pushes Curve in Integrating Customers' Supply Chains

When BMW begins building 318i sedans at its new $400 million plant in Spartanburg, S.C., workers in blue smocks will deliver auto parts directly to the point on the assembly line where those parts are needed.

The blue-smocked workers will be employees, not of the BMW Manufacturing Corp., but of Customized Transportation Inc., the Jacksonville-based third-party logistics subsidiary of CSX Corp.

For CTI, the movement of parts directly to the assembly line points where BMW workers—in white smocks—will build them into 318i's, marks a new level of integration into a client's supply chain. While the practice is said to be common in Japan, the BMW plant is one of the first auto manufacturing plants in the U.S. where a logistics supplier will physically reach beyond the freight dock to the assembly line. (The Saturn plant in Springfield, KY, served by Ryder Dedicated Logistics, is another.)

Taking that final step is in keeping with the totality of services that CTI will be performing for BMW.

During its early stages—as it ramps up from producing four cars a day to an eventual 300 per day—the Spartanburg plant will rely on parts from Europe, particularly Germany. CTI will track and trace those parts and take physical control of them at the Port of Charleston. CTI's own trucks or hired truckers—depending upon who can do the job at the least expense—will dray containers to Spartanburg.

BMW plans to shift to U.S. suppliers while ramping up production. CTI will initiate the "milk" or "loop" runs that are the hallmark of its service to other car builders. On those runs, trucks pick up parts from numerous suppliers on tight schedules and deliver to the assembly plant only as many parts as are needed for planned production and, of course, just when they are needed.

"The concepts that have worked well in the automotive industry are now being embraced by other industries," says William C. Bender, who had been senior vice president–sales and marketing for Ryder/P-I-E and became president of CTI in 1983, when the company had revenue of less than $2 million and he was one of 20 employees. "The automotive industry had to emulate the Japanese. But the same pressures were not felt as intensely in other industries. Fortune 25 companies are now doing things from a total supply chain perspective."

The logistics manager for the facility says that inbound logistics as provided by CTI has given it a major advantage over the company's two main competitors in just a few months.

"They're quality focused," says this logistics manager. "They make fewer mistakes with probationary employees than we do with employees who have been here for 20 years."

CTI delivers 25 truckloads a day to the facility, most of which originates in an adjacent state. CTI also employs four tractor-trailers on 17 different loop runs that service 170 different suppliers, a number that will soon expand to 200. CTI has total inventory control for the 1,800 parts the plant now uses, a number that will be in the range of 2,500 later this year, and meters supplies to the plant. The company has been able to convert to returnable containers, with CTI making the returns, and has even found it possible to deliver finished goods to two distribution centers as CTI's backhaul. LTL tracking and bar coding by CTI are in the offing.

SOURCE: Jack Burge, "Customized Transportation Inc. Pushes Curves in Integrating Customers," *Traffic World* no. 7, vol. 238 (May 30, 1994): 21–23. Copyright 1994 by *Traffic World*. Reprinted with permission of The Journal of Commerce, May 30, 1994.

The reduced-supplier approach has also become the trend in dealing with carriers, to gain leverage and induce a win-win relationship. Increasingly, shippers are dramatically reducing the number of carriers from whom they purchase transportation service in an effort to lower rates by allocating higher, more regular, and more balanced volumes to carriers. With this approach, the carriers experience lower costs, which can then be passed on in the form of lower rates/prices. The carriers may also be able to give better service (be more reliable, purchase better equipment, etc.), which can lead to additional savings for shippers in such things as inventory.

Supply Chain Objectives. Successful supply chain integration appears to be based upon achieving three objectives:[8]

- Recognizing the final customer's service level requirements
- Deciding where to position inventories along the supply chain and how much to stock at each point
- Developing appropriate policies and procedures for managing the supply chain as a single entity

The first objective seems obvious, but it is sometimes omitted from business decisions. Final customer demand is the magnet that draws inventories through the channel. Successful manufacturing firms are able to identify who the customer is and what the customer wants and then coordinate inventory flows throughout their own locations as well as through the entire channel.

> **customer demand**

The second objective is a recognized basic operating principle of logistics management: what, where, and how much inventory is needed to satisfy customer and cost requirements. Traditional management practices would usually involve trying to minimize a company's own inventories by pushing them either backward to suppliers or forward to distributors. Supply chain management realizes that this concept might optimize a manufacturer's cost but definitely suboptimizes the channel's costs, which ultimately will affect the manufacturer.

> **inventory**

The third objective indicates that some type of coordinating mechanism should be present in the supply chain in the form of policies and procedures. This can be accomplished through the development of a comprehensive logistics organization in the manufacturer's firm or leadership farther down the supply chain.

> **coordination**

The overall set of characteristics and objectives for the effective supply chain management discussed above are highly interrelated, or synergistic. Nevertheless, they also represent objectives for achieving effectiveness that are very challenging, to say the least. It will not be feasible to take such a comprehensive approach in all instances. The next section examines the external forces that led to the evolution in logistics management described above.

EXTERNAL DRIVERS OF CHANGE

The 1980s have been described by some individuals as a decade of turbulence and change. It is likely that the change started in the late 1970s and has continued into the 1990s. But whatever the exact parameters of the period, a common set of external forces were driving the changes, and these forces affected not only logistics but also other functional areas in business organizations. This section reviews these major forces of change.

Changing Nature of the Marketplace

The U.S. domestic market has changed dramatically since 1980, but changes were starting to occur even before that time. Essentially, these changes have to do with the consumer market, where individuals have become increasingly more knowledgeable about products and much more demanding about price and quality. Consumers are no longer as loyal to product brand names. That is, they have learned that brand names do not necessarily signify quality, and they are not

> **price and quality**

willing to pay a higher price solely because an item is sold under a brand name. The price-quality trade-off is a more perceptible approach among consumers in today's marketplace.

time   Other factors are consumers' impatience with things that waste their time and their need for convenience and flexibility. The value of time is important in many ways to businesses (as will be discussed), but it is also very important to individual consumers. They increasingly have little or no tolerance for delays, especially if they perceive that some business is causing the delay by its inefficiency.

The need for convenience and flexibility is closely related to the time dimension. Consumers want to purchase goods and services at times convenient to their busy schedules, and they want to do so as quickly as possible. Purveyors of goods and services for consumers have had to respond to these pressures by providing expanded hours of service, in some instances even 24 hours a day, seven days a week. The convenience factor has also generated many changes in the way companies package their products and make them available. The "drive-in" concept so popular with fast-food restaurants and banks is an example of this trend.

Many of the changes in the consumer market are based upon the changing demographic trends in the United States. The increase in the number of dual-career families and single-parent families has contributed markedly to consumers' focus upon time, convenience, and flexibility and their intolerance for exceptions.

This changing consumer market has significant implications for logistics and supply chains. The logistics supply chain has to serve the businesses that operate in this environment. In fact, the demands of the consumer have become the same as those of the supply chain—reduced order cycle times and more convenient and more flexible delivery. Those requirements and others will be explored in subsequent sections. Suffice it to say that the need for a supply chain focus in logistics has been exacerbated by the demands placed upon those businesses that interface directly with consumers.

Changing Channel Structures and Relationships

Closely related to the changing consumer market are the major changes that have occurred in the channels of distribution for goods and services. The underlying trends involve the size, scope, and comprehensiveness of these channels. The result has been what some individuals refer to as the Wal-Mart or McDonald's effect.

large retailers   The newer, larger retailers not only have size in their favor, which gives them economies of scale to leverage, but they also are more sophisticated and demanding procurers who have been instigating changes in the supply chains that serve them. For many years, channels of distribution tended to be reactive (although there were always some exceptions, such as Sears). The manufacturers/producers set the pace and developed systems to meet the generic needs of the channel members.

proactive   The emergence of the new retailers like Wal-Mart, Toys-R-Us, Target, KMart, and McDonald's has produced channel members who are not willing only to react. They are proactive and are more likely to request change in the form of a customized or tailored logistics system. These large retailers have high expectations of companies from whom they purchase products. Also, because of their importance in terms of total sales, manufacturers have developed customized logistics strategies to maintain and/or increase their sales to these larger retailers.

An interesting dimension to this discussion is that efficient logistics is often the key ingredient in the success of the large retailing organizations. Their ability to sell at "everyday low prices" is often contingent upon their ability to operate an efficient logistics system that is in harmony with that of their vendors. The power and the leverage that the large retailing organizations have in package goods (Wal-Mart, KMart, etc.) and restaurants (McDonald's, etc.) are being duplicated in some other industries; for example, health care and banking.

logistics efficiency

Another aspect of the distribution of products to the consumer is the potential for new channels based upon technology, using a combination of the computer, television, and telephone system. The home shopping networks are an example of such an approach, but much is happening in this area. Catalogs are now becoming available on a CD-ROM that can hook up with a telephone to allow direct ordering. This menu-driven approach is also feasible for many other products and types of purchases, including grocery shopping. Technology will revolutionize distribution systems in the 21st century.

technology

Channels of distribution have had a major impact on logistics systems during the 1980s and into the 1990s, and it is safe to say that they have played a major role in shaping the supply chain systems that have developed, with their emphasis upon reduced order cycles, special pallet packs, direct store shipments, and so on.

Globalization of the Economy and Markets

The globalization of U.S. companies and the competitive pressure of foreign competitors in both domestic and international markets have had an impact upon large and small companies. This globalization of U.S. businesses has been a double-edged sword, providing both a threat and an opportunity. There is no doubt, however, that it is no longer business as usual, and companies have responded, in part, by copying some foreign business practices, including JIT inventory control, total quality management, and flexible manufacturing systems, as well as instituting other changes in their organizational structures to remain competitive.[9]

Globalization runs the gamut from foreign purchasing (sourcing) of raw materials and supplies and selective sales in international markets with extensive use of intermediaries to multifaceted international manufacturing and marketing strategies encompassing international production sites, multistaging inventory, and counter-trading product sales. The growing international dimension of both the inbound and outbound portions of supply chains has had and will continue to have a major impact upon the logistics and transportation requirements of companies. The complexity of logistics and transportation will increase because of the length (in distance and time) of the supply chains. The domestic transportation system will have to coordinate with international transportation companies.

complexity

While much attention has been focused upon the European Economic Community and the Pacific Rim countries, the recent events surrounding the North American Free Trade Agreement indicate that regional trade relationships with Canada and Mexico will also be changing dramatically.[10] In fact, much has happened already in terms of trade with Canada and Mexico. The peso crisis of 1995 had a negative impact upon trade with Mexico, but the long-range prospects are very good.

regional trading

The final economic and financial integration of the Western European countries will establish the largest single market area in the world. The combined GDP will be larger than that of the United States. There will be new distribution patterns internal to the integrated countries as well as the necessity for international transportation alliances. In fact, many U.S. transportation companies have already moved aggressively to establish partnerships to penetrate the European market.

distribution

The European Economic Community's goal of completely eliminating barriers affecting manufacturing and trade will have a significant impact on these countries. The complete removal of these barriers will also affect distribution and transportation patterns in Western Europe. Companies presently operating in the European Economic Community usually need to have plants and warehouses in each of the countries in which they wish to market their goods. With the elimination of trade barriers and tariffs among the various countries, a more regionalized approach, similar to that used in the United States, will be possible. In other words, because the countries involved are very small, a company could have a warehouse in one country from which it will distribute to several countries, using longer, more efficient transportation hauls and larger, more efficient warehouses instead of the current practice of having a warehouse in each country. Likely to have a dramatic impact in Western Europe, this regionalized approach may produce potential logistics savings not unlike those experienced in the United States during the 1980s.[11]

Globalization has increased the pace of change and will continue to do so during the balance of the 1990s. Decisions involving sourcing of supplies, manufacturing, assembly, packaging, and warehousing will have a global perspective, and the transportation system will play an important role in linking this all together. Partnerships or alliances of domestic and international carriers will play an increasing role. Intermodal partnerships offer special promise both on a global and domestic basis. Shippers will expect reliable and timely shipments despite the complexity of the global operations. One factor that has the potential of helping to resolve some of the problems of global operations is technology, which is discussed in the next section.

Technology

expert systems

Nowhere in day-to-day business operations is the force of technological change more apparent than in data processing and information systems. Major price breakthroughs in hardware and low-cost, user-friendly software have brought enormously powerful, low-cost computing support to the logistics integration process and to transportation providers.

The impact of changing computer technology on logistical practices has been far-reaching. Complex tasks such as truck routing and scheduling are now much more routine due to the use of desktop computers. Simulations of entire logistical systems can be developed to determine the optimal approach to achieving desired customer service performance. It is possible to simulate the knowledge of logistics experts and combine it with current data to develop new strategic alternatives. Such expert systems offer the promise of linking status and control information from material procurement to customer delivery of the finished product. The development and management of such a huge database would not have been possible a few short years ago.[12]

The information transmission part of the technological revolution is worthy of special note. Electronic Data Interchange (EDI) and bar coding have played a major role in the more efficient and effective management of the distribution process, but much more can be done to integrate the systems of vendors, customers, and transportation companies.[13]

information

Currently available systems such as bar coding are being improved and combined with data communication transmission to improve logistics control and manage inventory more effectively. With the advent of satellite transmission, a shipper/carrier can pinpoint the exact location and schedule of an individual package at any time as it moves through the logistics supply chain. Throughout the logistics infrastructure, carriers, warehouses, and special service providers are introducing much better information and control systems.[14]

The advances in technology have also spread to other parts of the logistics and distribution system. Automation in warehouses and terminals has advanced at a rapid rate with the development automated storage and retrieval systems as well as other sophisticated storage and conveyor systems. But perhaps the most important factor has been the creation of software packages that combine with the advances in communication technology to form integrated systems.[15] We are on the threshold of an era that will revolutionize the way we do business because of the advances in technology, and *the distribution process will probably be the most highly impacted area of business.* Technology will be the "glue" for effective supply chain management.

Interestingly, the adoption and use of the current technology is far from universal. Even technologies such as EDI have not been completely integrated into the supply chains of some major companies.[16] The same is true of some carriers who have not taken full advantage of the technology that is available. It seems likely that carriers that do not move forward with the available technology will be the business failures of tomorrow.

adoption

An interesting dimension of technology that is sometimes overlooked is that it has given rise to a form of economies of scale not envisioned previously. Large truckload carriers such as Schneider and J. B. Hunt have been able to expand in a market that has been viewed as an analogue for the pure or perfectly competitive market model. Such a market would usually preclude a company from becoming larger than its many competitors because of the lack of scale economies. J. B. Hunt and Schneider, as well as others, are examples of firms that have used the power of technology to make operations more efficient, which has provided a basis of efficiency and effectiveness that allows their operations to expand in scope and size.

Government Policy and Deregulation

Another force of change has been deregulation and changes in government policy. These have spurred a virtual revolution in the U.S. transportation system since 1980, resulting in many fundamental changes, some positive and some negative. Overall, it is probably safe to say that the cost and quality of transportation services have improved for many shippers since 1980. The deregulation started in 1977 with airfreight and continued in 1978 with the deregulation of air passenger movements. In 1980, railroads and motor carriers were also deregulated, which was a major political accomplishment.

economic regulation   In all four instances, economic regulation was drastically reduced. In other words, transportation companies became much more like other businesses in being able to adjust their prices and services quickly in response to the marketplace. Prior to 1980, a very complex, bureaucratic regulatory system required elaborate hearings to make relatively simple changes in transportation prices and services.[17]

While there has been a significant reduction in the area of economic regulation, there has been an increase in the amount of regulation, control, and policy in other areas, such as safety and the environment. Federal and state controls related to safety and the environment have increased in scope and complexity. The movement of hazardous materials, for example, has received increased attention.

reverse logistics systems   Concerns with gridlock (congestion) and pollution have led to increasing analysis of approaches to controlling the flow of traffic in urban areas, including required pooling and tolls. The reduction in waste materials and increased recycling have also received more attention. There is a growing interest among manufacturers in reverse logistics systems to support recycling and waste management. Overall, in the future we should see more legislation and policy related to safety and the environment that will affect the design and operation of logistics systems.

changes   It is virtually impossible to summarize all of the changes being driven by deregulation. In some cases, the number of carriers has increased dramatically; as is the case with motor truckload (TL) carriers, while in other instances the number of carriers has decreased as with the airlines, or there has been a shift toward more market concentration as with rail and motor less-than-truckload (LTL). The distinctions among common, contract, and private carriers have blurred. Transportation companies offer a greater variety of services with a more comprehensive set of service and pricing strategies. Transportation companies have changed dramatically since 1980, and the pace of change is accelerating. It should also be noted that deregulation in the communication industry and in the financial area has also affected logistics and transportation. Deregulation will continue to affect supply chains in the future, given the changes occurring in technology and related areas.

There are other drivers of change that could be discussed, but the five presented in this section have been the major driving forces shaping logistics practices and the development of the supply chain in logistics during the 1980s and 1990s. They will continue to help drive developments in logistics supply chains into the 21st century.

The next section briefly discusses some of the changes that have been implemented in logistics organizations and supply chains, providing additional insight into the dynamics of the developments in the supply chain. Later chapters will discuss these changes and strategies in more detail.

STRATEGIC CHANGES IN SUPPLY CHAINS

U.S. companies have been faced with many challenges and threats in the last twenty years. Some organizations did not respond to the new environment in a proactive manner, which has had serious financial implications. The successful companies responded to the more competitive global environment in a variety of ways.

Speed/Time

Most companies have recognized that time is a strategic variable that affects competitive success in the marketplace. Initially, the focus was upon product design and manufacturing, with the goal of shortening the lead time for the introduction of new models of existing product lines and completely new products. For example, in the automotive industry, the Japanese demonstrated the advantages of more flexible design and manufacturing strategies, which reduced the lead time to introduce a new model by more than 50 percent. Part of the U.S. auto industry's resurgence has been based upon this same factor, that is, reduced design times and more flexible manufacturing.

products

The emphasis upon time compression has spread to other areas, especially the logistics supply chain. Given the current emphasis upon reducing inventory levels and on JIT, materials requirements planning, and distribution requirements planning inventory practices, logistics will play an increasingly important role in the ability of distribution pipelines to meet the needs of "quick-response" logistics systems. Time has come to be recognized as a major source of competitive advantage. A reduction in lead time in responding to customer orders can reduce the customer's inventory and storage costs and help add value in the supply chain. Transportation carriers play a major role with faster, more reliable delivery schedules. For example, shippers' lower inventories and very short lead times will provide opportunity for airlines to compete with motor carriers for transporting more products. Federal Express and UPS have already demonstrated their competitiveness in selected product markets. This will be an area where companies will seek to lower costs and/or add value by reducing cycle/lead times in the supply chain, since the impact is so pervasive in lowering the overall costs of the supply chain.

logistics

Closely related to improved cycle times is the trend toward pull distribution systems as opposed to the traditional push systems, where products are produced in advance of demand and stored in warehouses. The traditional approach allows long production runs at a lower cost per unit but can dramatically increase inventory cost. There is presently much interest in quick-response manufacturing and in logistics systems that can respond after an order is placed.

Quality

Concurrent with the pressure for reduced lead times, there has been a significant trend to emphasize quality not only in the production of products but also throughout all areas in a company. The logistics pipeline has again become a major focal point of total quality management (TQM) programs, because in the final analysis it is the customer's perceived receipt of quality that is most important. The service areas that interface with the customer, such as transportation, have received increased attention with the recognition of their importance in this area. Purchasers of transportation services have increasingly higher expectations of consistent service levels.[18]

total quality management (TQM)

The synergistic impact of the time compression factor and quality expectations have led to carriers providing service deliveries and pickups to meet increasingly more narrow "windows," for example, 30 to 60 minutes. The rise in importance of companies such as Federal Express, UPS, RPS, CTI, and others reflects this combined trend. But all parts of the logistics system are feeling the affects of this pressure for timely, high-quality, and responsive service. Companies are analyzing their internal systems in terms of their quality needs and are sometimes turning to third-party logistics companies for a larger share of logistics services in order to lower costs and improve quality. The emphasis upon quality requires a continuing scrutiny and a commitment to make ongoing improvements. The payoff is lower cost and/or added value for customers.

Asset Productivity

inventory   Another factor that will continue to shape the logistics supply chain for the balance of the 1990s is an increasing concern among shippers about asset productivity. Inventory level reduction and inventory turnover improvement received most of the initial focus of the drive to improve asset productivity, as was indicated earlier. Recognizing that inventory investment was often the first or second largest current asset and that reduction in inventory levels could dramatically lower cost and improve return on capital led to a major effort to lower inventory costs in some U.S. companies.

facilities   Investment in fixed facilities such as warehouses has also been coming under scrutiny, with a definite trend toward decreasing private warehousing requirements through inventory reductions and/or increased use of public warehousing. This same focus has led to a more stringent evaluation of private motor carrier fleets and a subsequent reduction in the use of private motor carrier operations by many larger companies, especially for intercity movements.[19]

distribution pipeline   The drive to improve asset productivity has focused upon reducing not only internal inventories but also pipeline or supply chain inventories. Vendors and buyers have been cooperating and sharing data in an attempt to reduce inventories in the entire distribution pipeline. Procter & Gamble and Wal-Mart have received much attention in the business press for their efforts in this area, but there are numerous other examples.[20] Again, fast, responsive, and flexible transportation is a critical part of this vendor-customer relationship.

Reengineering the Organization

third parties   Another trend among U.S. corporations is a reexamination and evaluation of internal processes with the goal of minimizing transactional activities and emphasizing value-added activities. A manifestation of this reengineering has been the reduction of middle management in many companies. An outcome of the thinning of middle management ranks has been a trend toward outsourcing of distribution activities so that the company can focus more on core activities that add value. The development of third-party logistics companies that provide a range of distribution/logistics services on a contract basis to companies has been a response to such changes. A growing number of transportation companies have established third-party logistics companies that offer a range of logistics services including transportation (intercity and cartage), inventory management, warehousing, order processing, billing, and so forth. Some transportation companies have established third-party organizations that offer services to a broad base of users, while others have emphasized a particular niche such as the automotive industry, as in the case of Customized Transportation (CTI) of Jacksonville, Florida, described earlier.

Another dimension of the changing nature of organizational relationships that is quite important to the logistics supply chain is the practice adopted by shippers of reducing the number of carriers from whom they purchase transportation service to leverage their buying power. This practice is an outgrowth of deregulation and is also associated with the JIT philosophy of operations, which stresses win-win buyer-seller relations based upon long-term, high-volume, quality-based vendor commitments. The decrease in the number of carriers used by individual shippers has been dramatic, with some going from more than 1,000 to fewer than 100 carriers. Such relationships are viewed as partnerships (similar to the P & G–Wal-Mart relationship) where shippers and carriers share information that allows a win-win opportunity—lower rates and improved carrier efficiency.

carrier reduction

Customer Satisfaction

Another trend that is having an impact upon the logistics supply chain is the customer service/customer satisfaction emphasis of most companies. It has long been recognized that measures of service levels are important in evaluating performance. Some traditional measures have been length of order delivery cycle, order shipment time, percentage of orders shipped complete, and so on. Now the focus is more on the customer, with measures of service levels being aimed in that direction. For example, the very best companies utilize such measures as percentage of orders delivered on time, percentage of orders received complete (with no loss or damage), percentage of orders billed accurately, and so on. One result of this customer service focus is that transportation services receive more attention and transportation companies are frequently viewed as partners in providing higher levels of customer service. This has frequently necessitated sharing of data between shippers and carriers to develop the win-win type of relationship mentioned earlier.

measures of service levels

Another aspect of this focus on customer satisfaction is the level of customer service delineated by the very best companies. Reliability is viewed as the basic requirement, with employees given added flexibility to meet the special needs of customers. Employees are encouraged to act creatively to add value that will affect the customer's bottom line. Again, logistics can and will play an important role in this new era of customer service. Or perhaps a better way of stating the case is to say that the successful companies will be those that can offer customized and tailored services that are responsive to the needs of their customers, who will demand consistent, high-quality service so that they can maintain a competitive position in today's marketplace.

value

SUMMARY

- The implementation of logistics supply chain management by a growing number of companies has been based upon the promise of significant cost savings and the possibility of adding value for customers.
- The development of the supply chain perspective is actually a logical extension of several previous stages—physical distribution management and integrated logistics management.

- The focus upon physical distribution (first stage) was the outgrowth of several trends in the U.S. economy—product line expansion, rate increases, and the production of higher-valued goods.
- The logistics management phase (second stage) was based upon several new developments in the economy—deregulation of transportation, global competition, increased reliance upon foreign sources of supply, and a stagnant economy.
- The supply chain management approach was also shaped by several important economic and social factors in our economy—a changing consumer market, more powerful channels of distribution, advances in technology, global business strategy, and government policy and deregulation.
- A supply chain can be defined in several different ways, but the essence of a supply chain is the integrated management of the sequential flow of materials and associated activities from vendors through to the ultimate customer.
- The effective management of a supply chain requires certain key characteristics—pipeline coordination and seamless flows of inventory, focus upon landed cost to customer, sharing of information and risk, planning based upon a supply chain team, and strong partnerships or alliances.
- The successful implementation of a supply chain approach has usually encompassed important strategies, including reduction of order cycle time, quality management, increased asset productivity, new organizational approaches, and an emphasis upon customer satisfaction.

STUDY QUESTIONS

1. Why have companies increasingly focused upon managing logistics from a supply chain perspective?

2. The supply chain concept is not really a brand new idea. Do you agree or disagree with this statement? Why?

3. Discuss the factors that caused companies to attempt to better manage physical distribution activities.

4. What factors caused companies to broaden their perspective from physical distribution to integrated logistics?

5. Compare and contrast the several definitions of supply chains offered in this chapter.

6. Compare and contrast the key characteristics of traditional logistics systems with those that are supply chain focused.

7. Changes in the consumer market and in channels of distribution both had an impact upon logistics supply chains. In what ways were these two factors similar in their impact upon logistics supply chains? In what ways were they different?

8. How have developments in technology affected logistics?

9. Some individuals argue that globalization has been the single most important driving force behind supply chain management. Do you agree? Why or why not?

10. What changes have companies made to respond to the supply chain management concept?

NOTES

1. James A. Cooke, "Supply Chain Management—90s Style," *Traffic Management* (May 1992): 57–59.

2. Ibid.

3. Lisa M. Ellram and Martha C. Cooper, "Characteristics of Supply Chain Management and the Implications for Purchasing and Logistics Strategy," *International Journal of Logistics Management* 4, no. 2 (1993): 1–10.

4. A. J. Battaglia and Gene Tyndall, "Implementing World Class Supply Chain Management," unpublished paper.

5. Based upon a presentation by A. J. Stenger and J. J. Coyle of Penn State University.

6. R. A. Novack, "Integrating Logistics and Manufacturing," unpublished paper, Penn State University.

7. C. J. Langley and M. C. Holcomb, "Creating Logistics Customer Value," *Journal of Business Logistics* 13, no. 2 (1992): 3–8.

8. Novack, "Integrating Logistics and Manufacturing."

9. Donald Bowersox et al., *Leading Edge Logistics: Competitive Positioning for the 1990s* (Oakbrook, IL: Council of Logistics Management, 1990): 12–19.

10. L. M. Koestar, "NAFTA: A World Class Opportunity," *Transportation and Distribution Management* (February 1992): 42–44.

11. T. B. Gooley, "Countdown to the New Europe," *Traffic Management* 31, no. 9 (August 1992): 32–34.

12. E. Short and V. Traman, "Beyond Business Process Redesign," *Sloan Management Review* 34, no. 1 (Fall 1992): 7–21.

13. Short and Traman, "Beyond Business Process Redesign."

14. R. Bowman, "A Computerized Route to Better Distribution," *Distribution* 91, no. 5 (June 1992): 28–35.

15. R. L. Cook, "Expert Systems in Purchasing," *International Journal of Purchasing and Materials Management* (Fall 1992): 20–27.

16. M. Magnet, "Winners in the Information Revolution," *Fortune* 126, no. 12 (November 30, 1992): 110–117.

17. Donald V. Harper, "The Federal Motor Carrier Act of 1980: Review and Analysis," *Transportation Journal* (Winter 1981): 30–33.

18. E. S. Muller, "Climb Aboard the Quality Express," *Distribution* 91, no. 2 (February 1992): 34–37.

19. T. A. Foster, "Service is King for Private Fleets," *Distribution* 91, no. 7 (July 1992): 68–72.

20. S. Sherman, "Vendor Patronizing Pays Off for Pillsbury," *Modern Materials Handling* 47, no. 9 (May 1992): 47–49.

DIMENSIONS OF LOGISTICS

LEARNING OBJECTIVES

After reading this chapter, you should be able to do the following:

- Understand the role and importance of logistics in private and public organizations.

- Appreciate the impact of logistics on the economy and how effective logistics management contributes to the economy.

- Understand the value-added roles of logistics.

- Define logistics systems from several perspectives.

- Understand the relationship between logistics and other important functional areas in a company, including manufacturing, marketing, and finance.

- Discuss the important management activities in the logistics function.

- Analyze logistics systems from several different perspectives to meet different objectives.

- Determine the total costs and understand the cost trade-offs in a logistics system from a static and dynamic perspective.

EMC: SPEED AND QUALITY

Speed and quality in both product and logistics have played a major role in the success of EMC. The 14-year-old maker of high-availability computer storage and retrieval products broke into the ranks of the *Fortune* 500 in 1994, when its revenues reached $782 million.

The prompt movement of materials and speedy delivery of finished product are critical to sales in a competitive market. EMC's storage systems are made to order, with a turnaround time of four weeks between order placement and delivery. Smooth logistics operations ensure that parts will be moved on time and finished product delivered to the customer as promised.

Headquartered in Hopkinton, Massachusetts, EMC was established in 1979 as a supplier of add-on memory boards and expanded into the mid-range and mid-frame disk-storage products. At present, the company has become a leading supplier of disk-array technology. The cached disk arrays that have driven EMC's sales are basically electronic filing cabinets that hold large amounts of information for quick access. EMC's biggest customers are companies that manage huge databases like stock-brokerage houses, banks, and airlines. The company, by the way, doesn't make the guts of its machines. Instead it buys the components for its computer storage systems and assembles them at its two manufacturing plants in Massachusetts and in Cork, Ireland.

Dependent on suppliers for critical parts and operating with tight delivery windows, EMC has had to master supply chain coordination. Timely inbound shipments are necessary to complete production on schedule. Outbound deliveries must be handled expeditiously to meet customer schedules.

On the inbound side, the company looks to minimize the global movements of parts to feed its facilities. EMC tries to look for U.S. suppliers for its Massachusetts facilities and Irish suppliers for its Irish plant. "Ninety-five percent of parts for Ireland are sourced in Ireland," reports Kenn Farrell, vice president of supplier management. "We want to minimize the logistics nightmare and avoid shipping to Ireland."

The company seeks out quality suppliers, sourcing some $700 million worth of components. About 85 percent of those components come from a select group of 29 suppliers worldwide. "We come up with a supplier base that meets our needs. We look for technological capabilities as well as financial strength and geographic location," says Farrell.

At the same time that it's taking steps to get its product to market faster, EMC has made an effort to shorten its supply chain. In 1993, the company ended the year with nine days' worth of raw material in inventory, says Farrell. In the last quarter of 1994, EMC had only 3.5 days' worth of inventory on hand.

Close coordination with the suppliers has helped in this regard. EMC has worked with one supplier to transport disk drives in three days from Singapore to Hopkinton, Massachusetts.

Tight Delivery Windows

Delivery of the finished product can be tricky, however. For starters, purchasers of computer storage equipment often have narrow windows for installation. In a typical case, the buyer can only afford to shut down its computer system for a few hours Saturday night and then needs the storage system up and running by Sunday morning. "For our customers, we're often talking about the equivalent of life or death," says Michael L. Schoonover, senior vice president for operations.

Because EMC's storage products can weigh as much as a mid-size automobile, careful planning is required for the actual delivery of the more than 500 machines it ships throughout the world each quarter. In some cases, EMC has had to use cranes to deliver its system into a tall office building or remove façades to deliver product.

The company's customer-service and logistics staff works closely with EMC's group of core carriers to meet those delivery requirements. In fact, EMC's CEO, Michael Ruettgers, considers customer service to be every bit as critical as quality when it comes to making sales in

continued on next page

EMC: SPEED AND QUALITY *continued*

a competitive marketplace. "If our customer requests installation at 2 A.M., our truck is there," says Ruettgers.

Aside from its role managing inbound and outbound movements, logistics has proved vital for EMC's after-sale efforts. After all, EMC's customers cannot afford to have their computer storage systems down for an extended period of time. Yet EMC has tried to maintain minimal parts inventory and not invest in any bricks and mortar for warehousing.

Although supply chain management has proved critical to EMC's success to date, the logistics component of that chain may take on an even greater future role as overseas markets expand. At present, 60 percent of the company's sales come from the U.S. domestic market, while the other 40 percent are derived from overseas buyers. But Ruettgers believes that the two ratios will flip in the next few years.

When foreign countries become the major market for the company's products, extending the supply chain across the globe, logistics will become even more critical. "You'll not only have the difficulties of coordinating the domestic and international effort but also the coordination of parts and components coming in from international or multiple locations," he says. "Coordinating these things so people know when this stuff will be coming will be pretty important."

ADAPTED FROM: James Aaron Cooke, "CEOs Seize Logistics Opportunities," *Traffic Management* (March 1995): 29–34.

I n a famous article written in 1962 for *Fortune,* Peter Drucker discussed the logistics distribution area, using the title "The Economy's Dark Continent," and referred to distribution as a last frontier for significant cost reduction potential. In describing the situation at that time, Drucker made the following general observations:

> Distribution is one of the most sadly neglected but most promising areas of American business. . . . We know little more about distribution today than Napoleon's contemporaries knew about the interior of Africa. We know it's there, and we know it's big; and that's about all. . . . Most of our present concepts focus on production or on the stream of money and credit, rather than on the flow of physical goods and its economic characteristics. . . . To get control of distribution, therefore, requires seeing—and managing—it as a distinct dimension of business and as a property of product and process rather than as a collection of technical jobs.
>
> The industrial purchaser has to know his own business . . . he has to know what the product or supply he buys is supposed to contribute to his company's end results. . . . My purpose is to point to distribution as an area where intelligence and hard work can produce substantial results for American business. Above all, there is a need for a new orientation—one that gives distribution the importance in business design, business planning, and business policy its costs warrant.[1]

logistics potential   Reflecting back over the developments in logistics and transportation since 1962, one may be tempted to borrow the advertising slogan—"You've come a long way, baby." Logistics and transportation have indeed come a long way, and there are many signs of successful achievement. For example, the number of major manufacturing and service companies represented by individuals with titles of vice president or senior vice president of logistics, distribution, materials management, or supply chain has increased dramatically, as have the responsibilities and salaries of such individuals.[2] The membership of one of the best-known logistics organizations, the Council of Logistics Management, has swelled to more than 10,000 active members, and there are another 40,000 members who periodically attend the annual meetings of the organization.

In spite of the significant developments that have occurred in logistics and distribution since World War II, logistics is still in a period of growth and development, as depicted in Figure 2–1.[3] For many companies, 15 to 25 percent of the cost of their manufactured products goes to cover expenses incurred before an item gets to the production line or after it leaves the line (transportation, inventory, warehousing, packaging, and materials handling); for service companies, the costs are often higher. One U.S. automobile producer, for example, spent more than $3 billion on transportation alone in 1993.[4] (See Table 2–1.) **logistics cost**

The origins of the modern logistics concept in businesses can be traced to developments in military logistics during World War II. The recent Persian Gulf War again demonstrated the importance of logistics to a successful military effort. In fact, the Persian Gulf effort has been referred to as the "logistics war," and the importance of the integrated logistics pipeline or supply chain supporting the fighting effort was acknowledged repeatedly by the military and civilian leadership. The *integrated* logistics concept was obviously critical to the military's success in the Gulf War. The logistics supply chain has also been receiving increased attention in the private sector in the 1990s.[5] **origins**

One of the most widely used and most frequently cited definitions of logistics is provided by the Council of Logistics Management:

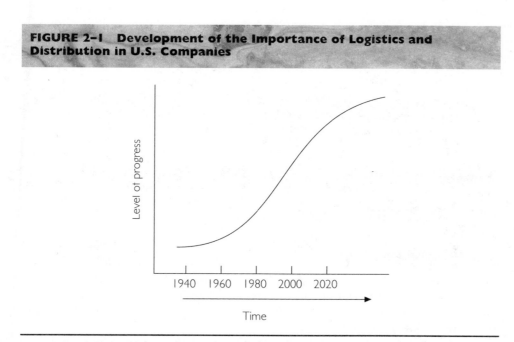

FIGURE 2–1   Development of the Importance of Logistics and Distribution in U.S. Companies

SOURCE: John J. Coyle, "Preparing Logistics for the 21st Century," in 1990 *Proceedings of Council of Logistics Management*, vol. II, (Oak Brook, IL: Council of Logistics Management, 1990): 2.

TABLE 2-1 Major Transportation Purchasers, 1993

Rank	Company	Purchasing Tab (in thousands)
1	General Motors	$3,750,000
2	Ford	3,250,000
3	Chrysler	1,700,000
4	IBM	800,000
5	Dow Chemical	750,000
6	DuPont	650,000
7	USX	628,000
8	Champion International	410,000
9	Xerox	404,000
10	PPG Industries	400,000
11	AT&T	400,000
12	Bethlehem Steel	360,000
13	LTV Steel	323,000
14	Union Carbide	300,000
15	Philips Electronics	250,000
16	Basf	225,000
17	Crown Cork & Seal	200,000
18	J. I. Case	172,000
19	Deere	170,000
20	Phillips Petroleum	125,000
21	Apple Computer	112,000
22	GTE	102,000
23	Honeywell	100,000
24	Raytheon	100,000
25	Maytag	100,000

SOURCE: Reprinted with permission of *Purchasing* magazine (November 1994): 66. Copyright © by Cahners Publishing Company.

Logistics is the process of planning, implementing and controlling the efficient, effective flow and storage of raw materials, in-process inventory, finished goods, services and related information from point of origin to point of consumption (including inbound, outbound, internal, and external movements) for the purpose of conforming to customer requirements.[6]

Implied in this definition is that the logistics process *provides a systems framework for decision making* that integrates transportation, inventory, warehousing space, materials handling systems, packaging, and other related activities that together encompass appropriate trade-offs involving cost and service from vendor to customer (supply chain).

Another definition suggests that logistics involves the efficient and effective management of inventory, whether in motion or at rest, to satisfy customer requirements or organizational objectives.[7] The important aspect of the latter definition is that transportation service is recognized as inventory in motion, emphasizing the fact that the true cost is more than the actual rate charged by the transportation company.

Another definition of logistics, sometimes called the layperson's definition of logistics, is the Seven Rs, which defines logistics as "ensuring the availability of the *right* product, in the *right* quantity and the *right* condition, at the *right* place, at the *right* time, for the *right* customer, at the *right* cost.''[8]   **Seven Rs**

The Seven Rs indicate the essential activities of logistics. They emphasize the spatial and temporal dimension (place and time, or movement and storage) and provide a basic understanding of the logistics area as referred to throughout this text. The Seven Rs also emphasize cost and service. Logistics managers must continually evaluate cost and service as they investigate changes for their logistics systems.

Another aspect of this definition is the importance of meeting customer re-   **quality** quirements. The focus upon the customer is essential for logistics, since logistics plays an important role in customer satisfaction. An additional element of the Seven Rs is the notion of quality. U.S. companies are increasingly recognizing that quality is important not only in the manufacture of a product but in all of the company's areas, especially logistics. EMC, the company profiled at the beginning of this chapter, has emphasized the Seven Rs in its rapid development since 1979.

The 1970s could be classified as the decade for products and markets, and the 1980s can be labeled as the decade for finance. Many individuals believe that the 1990s are the decade for logistics because gaining and maintaining access to a customer base and significant market share is the focus of strategic thinking and planning in large and small organizations. Logistics, particularly with a supply chain focus, can play an important role in helping achieve these strategic objectives. Again, EMC has capitalized upon good logistics to establish a competitive advantage in the market.

As was noted in the previous chapter, the 1980s was a decade of prosperity and   **change** growth, but it was also a period of turbulence and upheaval that changed the ways in which materials, products, and services move through the supply chain from vendors to manufacturers to customers. Of particular note have been the shifts in relationships among distribution channel members, especially the increased economic leverage of large retailers like Wal-Mart and Toys-R-Us and the growth in importance of the whole service sector. The increasing sophistication of all buyers, industrial and consumer, with their insistence on quality and value, has also contributed to the transformation. But the 1990s will be even more significant in terms of change in the U.S. economy and the distribution system that supports it.[9]

This chapter will focus upon the three major dimensions or environments of logistics. First, we will examine the external dimension to get some perspective on the importance of logistics in the economy. In other words, the discussion will emphasize the macro environment of logistics. Next is an overview of the internal firm or the micro environment for logistics. Here the focus will be upon the interrelationships between logistics and other functional areas in the firm, such as marketing, manufacturing, and financial control. The final dimension will also be internal, but the focus will be upon the logistics component and its internal relationships, including the supply chain.

LOGISTICS: THE MACRO PERSPECTIVE

The recession of 1991 was significant for a number of reasons, one of which was that new inventory practices such as just-in-time (JIT) and quick response (QR) appeared to have passed a major test. National data showed that because inventories had not been inflated during the more prosperous period preceding the recession, a modest increase in sales resulted in restocking—that is, new orders, after the recession.

In previous economic ups and downs, inventories would creep up to excessive levels during the "good times," and companies would then use up the inventories during the lean periods. The negative feature of this practice was that companies would not recall laid-off employees until the inventory levels came back down, prolonging the recession or the business cycle downturn. Economists sometimes call this a "double-dip" effect.

Since the end of the 1981–82 recession, inventories have not increased far out of line. In fact, as will be demonstrated in this chapter, inventory-to-sales ratios on a macro basis have declined.

new techniques   The best reason one can offer for this decline is that individual companies have adopted new inventory management techniques (such as JIT, MRP, QR, and DRP), which will be explored in depth in Chapter 3. U.S. manufacturers have adopted these measures in response to intense foreign competition. The new approaches to inventory management are an example of what companies can do to cut costs and ultimately increase profits.

We must emphasize two very relevant points here. First, logistics has an important impact on and a relationship to the overall economy (the macro level), and, as will be pointed out, inventories are not the only relevant economic factor. Second, important interaction occurs between micro-level and macro-level economic activities, so both need to be discussed.

In this section, we will first examine some macroeconomic data that show the importance of logistics in the economy and also, more important, demonstrate

TABLE 2-2   The Cost of the Logistics Supply Chain in Relation to Gross Domestic Product ($ billion except GDP)

Year	GDP ($ trillions)	Value of Business Inventory	Inventory Carrying Rate	Inventory Carrying Costs	Transporta- tion Costs	Administra- tive Costs	Total U.S. Logistics Cost	Logistics Percent of GDP
1981	$3.03	826	0.343	283	236	21	540	17.9
1982	3.15	824	0.309	255	240	20	515	16.3
1983	3.41	817	0.279	228	244	19	491	14.4
1984	3.78	882	0.291	257	250	20	527	14.0
1985	4.04	896	0.268	240	265	20	525	13.0
1986	4.27	893	0.261	233	271	20	524	12.3
1987	4.54	923	0.263	243	288	21	552	12.2
1988	4.90	996	0.267	266	313	23	602	12.3
1989	5.24	1,066	0.292	311	331	26	668	12.7
1990	5.51	1,099	0.272	298	354	26	678	12.3
1991	5.67	1,080	0.250	270	360	25	655	11.6
1992	5.95	1,093	0.228	243	379	25	647	10.9
1993	6.37	1,127	0.222	250	394	26	670	10.5

Inventory investment includes all business inventory, namely manufacturing, wholesale and retail trade, agriculture, mining, construction, utilities, and services defined by the Bureau of Economic Analysis, U.S. Department of Commerce.

SOURCES: *Survey of Current Business, U.S. Statistical Abstract,* U.S. Department of Commerce Methodology; J. L. Heskett, *Business Logistics,* 2d ed. (New York: Ronald Press, 1973).

the impact of improved logistics and transportation systems. The overview of the data will be followed by a more traditional discussion of the major economic impacts of logistics on the economy.

As Table 2–2 indicates, the total logistics costs of U.S. business was $670 billion in 1993, which represented 10.5 percent of the almost $6.4 trillion U.S. gross domestic product (GDP) in that year. While the actual cost of business logistics in the U.S. has fluctuated somewhat from year to year, the overall trend has been upward. However, the percentage of the GDP that consists of logistics has been steadily decreasing, from a high of 17.9 percent in 1981 to the 1993 level of 10.5 percent, as indicated by the last column in Table 2–2.

Many factors have contributed to the improved picture of macro-level logistics costs. Figure 2–2, which depicts the index of total logistics cost as a percentage of GDP, as well as showing inventory and transportation percentages separately, indicates that both sub-percentages have been decreasing. There appears to be no question that the deregulation of transportation that occurred from 1977 to 1980 provided a much more competitive environment, which has tended to lower transportation rates and to improve service. Improved transportation service, along with better inventory management practice, has helped to lower inventory costs.

deregulation

Table 2–3 shows a more complete breakdown of total logistics costs from 1994. Overall, transportation costs constitute the largest percentage (58%) of logistics

FIGURE 2–2 Index of Logistics Supply Chain Costs as a Percentage of GDP

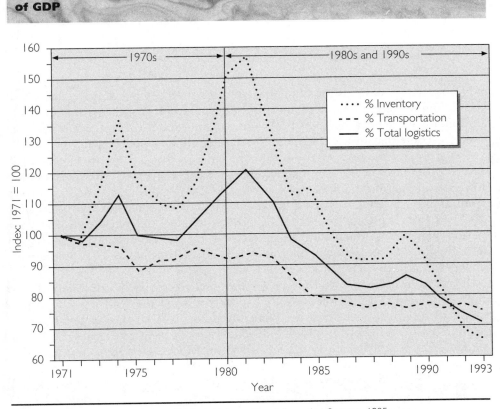

SOURCE: Reprinted with permission of Robert Delaney, Cass Information Systems, 1995.

TABLE 2-3 Components of 1994 Logistics Cost

Inventory Carrying Costs		$ Billions
Interest		53
Taxes, obsolescence, depreciation		161
Warehousing		63
	Subtotal	277
Transportation Costs		
Motor Carriers		
Public and for hire		96
Private and for own account		109
Local freight services		128
	Subtotal	333
Other Carriers		
Railroads		33
Water carriers		22
Oil pipelines		10
Air carriers		17
Forwarders		5
	Subtotal	87
Shipper Related Costs		5
Distribution Administration		28
	TOTAL LOGISTICS COST	$730

SOURCE: Cass Information Systems, in Thomas A. Foster, "It's About Time and Inventory," *Distribution* (July 1995): 8.

cost on a macro basis, as they usually do also on a micro, or company, basis. It is interesting to note the large share of the transportation cost that private and for-hire motor carriers garner, which obviously demonstrates the important role that motor carriers play in transportation for the logistics supply chain.

To provide some perspective on the efficiency of the U.S. logistics system, Figure 2–3 compares health care expenditures from 1971 to 1993 with logistics costs for the same period, both as a percentage of GDP. Health care costs have grown from about 7.5 percent of GDP to about 14 percent, while logistics costs have declined from close to 15 percent of GDP to about 9 percent during the same period. Figure 2–4, which compares indexes of the gross national product (GNP) and freight transportation expenditures, is further evidence of the dramatic changes that have occurred in recent years.

It has been estimated that motor carrier costs are currently $40 billion below their 1981 level and that rail costs are $10 billion below the 1981 level. Transportation of freight has declined to about 6.2 percent of GDP. Another dramatic decline has been in the inventory level. The ratio of inventory to sales during the period 1971 to 1993 decreased by 17 percent, which is a strong indicator that companies are using less inventory to support sales. As was indicated previously, improvements in transportation service offer part of the explanation, but the other part is better inventory management, with an emphasis upon reducing inventory levels. The improvement in the associated inventory velocity on turnover has had

FIGURE 2-3   Health Care Expenditures versus Distribution Costs/GDP

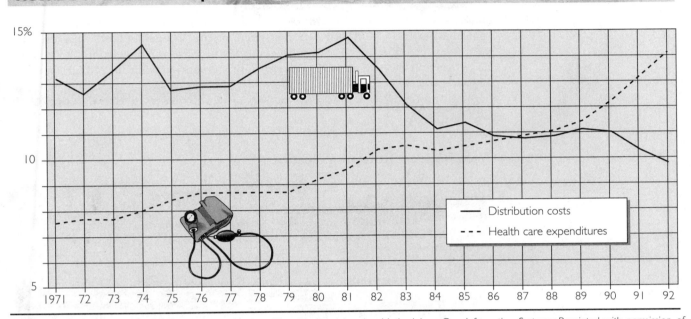

SOURCE: *Survey of Current Business and U.S. Health Care Financing Administration Methodology,* Cass Information Systems. Reprinted with permission of Robert Delaney, Cass Information Systems, 1995.

FIGURE 2-4   Index of the GNP versus U.S. Freight Expenditures

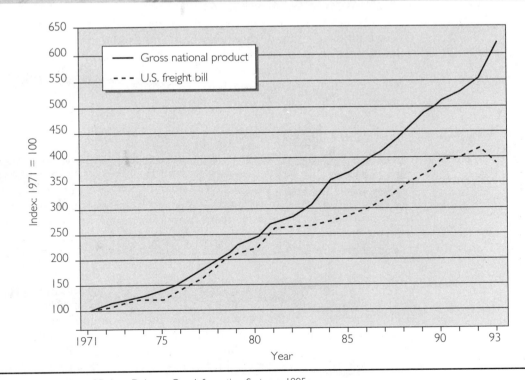

SOURCE: Reprinted with permission of Robert Delaney, Cass Information Systems, 1995.

a very positive impact upon the return on investment for companies, which is critical in today's competitive environment.

An in-depth study of four major industries—chemicals, electronics, foods, and pharmaceuticals—demonstrated that each of the industries had experienced a significant decline in the ratio of inventories to sales, ranging from a 23 percent improvement (foods) to a 37 percent improvement (chemicals), which supports the overall macro data discussed above.[10] Again, better management practices and a faster, more reliable transportation system have enabled these dramatic changes to take place.

Value-Added Role of Logistics

types of utility   As Figure 2–5 illustrates, four principal types of economic utility add value to a product or service. Included are form, time, place, and possession. Generally, we credit manufacturing activities with providing form utility, logistics activities with time and place utility, and marketing activities with possession utility. We will discuss each briefly.

what   *Form Utility.*   Form utility refers to the value added to goods through a manufacturing, production, or assembly process. For example, form utility results when raw materials are combined in some predetermined manner to make a finished product. This is the case, for example, when a bottling firm adds together syrup, water, and carbonation to make a soft drink. The simple process of adding the raw materials together to produce the soft drink represents a change in product *form* that adds value to the product.

In today's economic environment, certain logistics activities can also provide form utility. For example, breaking bulk and product mixing, which typically take place at distribution centers, change a product's form by changing its shipment size and packaging characteristics. Thus, unpacking a pallet of breakfast cereal into individual consumer-size boxes adds form utility to the product. However, the two principal ways in which logistics adds value are in place and time utility.

where   *Place Utility.*   Logistics provides place utility by moving goods from production surplus points to points where demand exists. Logistics extends the physical boundaries of the market area, thus adding economic value to the goods. This addition to the economic value of goods or services is known as *place* utility. Logistics creates place utility primarily through transportation. For example, moving farm produce by rail or truck from farm areas to markets where consumers need this produce creates place utility. The same is also true when steel is moved to a plant where the steel is used to make another product.

when   *Time Utility.*   Not only must goods and services be available *where* consumers need them, but they must also be at that point *when* customers demand them. This is called *time* utility, or the economic value added to a good or service by having it at a demand point at a specific time. Logistics creates time utility through proper inventory maintenance and the strategic location of goods and services. For example, logistics creates time utility by having heavily advertised products and sale

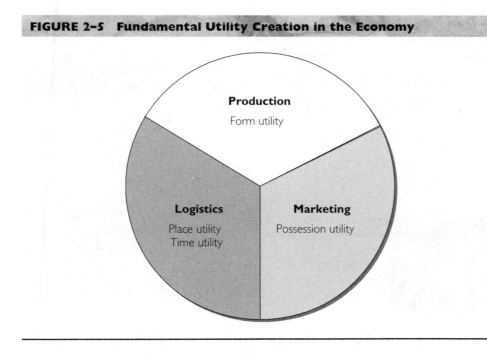

FIGURE 2-5 Fundamental Utility Creation in the Economy

Production
Form utility

Logistics
Place utility
Time utility

Marketing
Possession utility

merchandise available in retail stores at precisely the time promised in the advertising copy.

To some extent, transportation may create time utility by moving something more quickly to a point of demand. For example, substituting air transportation for warehousing adds time utility. Time utility is much more important today because of the emphasis upon reducing lead time.

Possession Utility.   This form of utility is primarily created through the basic marketing activities related to the promotion of products or services. We may define *promotion* as the effort, through direct and indirect contact with the customer, to increase the desire to possess a good or to benefit from a service. The role of logistics in the economy depends upon the existence of *possession utility,* for time or place utility make sense only if demand for the product or service exists. It is also true that marketing depends upon logistics, since possession utility cannot be acted upon unless time and place utility are provided.

why

Economic Impacts

Another important topic related to the macro, or external, environment is the economic impacts of logistics. This section highlights four major areas: economic development and specialization, variety of goods, effects on prices, and land values.

specialization or division of labor

Economic Development and Specialization. The emphasis upon production efficiency in the 19th and early 20th centuries resulted in considerable economic development in the form of production specialization. This tendency to specialize and to produce at lower costs was a normal development of economic growth as described by Adam Smith and other economists. We may question why labor specialization, potentially lowering costs and prices, did not advance more rapidly, or why the United States does not presently specialize more. We might also question why less-developed countries do not practice production specialization to aid in their economic development.

extent of the market

Adam Smith answered this question when he indicated that the extent of the market or the volume of demand for the product limits specialization or division of labor. In other words, an organization does not benefit from practicing specialization to a greater degree if the organization cannot sell the fruits of this specialization, the additional output, to consumers. The additional output would have no economic value unless the producer could move it from the production surplus point to the point or points of unfulfilled demand. Thus, logistics contributes to economic development by allowing firms to capitalize on comparative cost advantages in the production of goods and services by efficiently transporting goods to the market.

Variety of Goods. Another contribution of logistics is the volume and variety of goods made available to consumers in areas far from production or manufacturing points, and, frequently, long after the goods were manufactured or produced. We often take for granted that goods are available in a wide assortment at a desired time, but satisfying this demand very much depends upon all firms in the economy effectively performing movement and storage functions (logistics). The total of these logistics operations provides the link and storage network so crucial to the functioning of a modern and progressive economy. Eastern Europe, for example, faces a major challenge because it lacks a good logistics infrastructure.

Prices. By creating time and place utility, logistics activities in the economy also contribute to lower prices. For example, if logistics extends markets for goods in both time and space, transported goods may sell for prices lower than those of goods produced locally. Frequently, firms base lower prices upon the greater efficiency of large-scale production and the increased opportunity for trade-offs in the logistics system. As firms improve logistics systems from both a technical and managerial perspective, we are sure to observe numerous benefits in the form of lower prices and greater availability of goods.

Land Values. Logistics also affects other aspects of the economic system; for example, the transportation segment often affects land values when technical improvements occur. When a new major highway is built in an area, or when an existing facility is significantly enhanced, land values near the highway usually go up because of the increased accessibility to other areas.[11] The interchange areas of such highway facilities often attract manufacturing and storage facilities.

Logistics supply chains play a vital role in the economic development and continued economic growth of any economy. Efficient logistics systems add time (temporal) and place (spatial) value to goods and services provided by private and public organizations operating in the economy. Logistics supply chains also en-

ON THE LINE

CEOs Seize Logistics Opportunities

"Logistics remains one of the last frontiers to effect productivity gains and cost reductions as well as overall improvement in terms of competitiveness in the increasingly global marketplace," says Joe Nicosia, president of GATX Logistics, a third-party logistics company.

Smart chief executives are taking a second look at the once lusterless discipline of logistics. What they're finding are new ways to grow their business and satisfy customers.

A Chance to Make an Impact

In the past five years, the logistics function has taken on critical importance to several leading-edge companies' performance in the marketplace. Take Wainwright Industries, a maker of metal parts in St. Peters, Missouri, that won a Baldrige National Quality Award this year. A parts supplier to a wide range of industries, including automotive, Wainwright received the nation's highest award in large part because it responded to customer demands for faster order turnaround.

"The movement of material, both internally and externally, has a significant impact on (a manufacturer's) operation and subsequently a customer's operation," says Don Wainwright, CEO of the company. "Waste minimization and elimination in logistics supports our company business objectives of consistent profitability, quality performance, best-in-class processes, and associate job security."

Innovative companies like Viking Office Products also have turned to logistics to gain sales. Viking sells office products through catalogs to predominantly small and medium-size businesses. To gain an edge against super stores, Los Angeles–based Viking offers a value-added service: same-day delivery to customers.

"The logistics function of our business has become critical in today's competitive marketplace for office products," says Irwin Helford, president of Viking. "Delivering at the convenience of the seller is no longer acceptable. Our customers are small business offices that require complete, accurate, and effective delivery quickly. Therefore, during the past few years, we have implemented overnight delivery practically everywhere, and in six major markets, we deliver customer orders the same day, all at no charge."

SOURCE: James Aaron Cooke, *Traffic Management* (March 1995): 129–34. Reprinted with permission of *Traffic Management* magazine (March 1995). Copyright © by Cahners Publishing Company.

hance form and possession utility. In addition, logistics supply chains provide a wide variety of other economic, social, and defense impacts that are of major benefit to countries. In the next section, we will examine the micro dimensions of logistics.

LOGISTICS IN THE FIRM: THE MICRO DIMENSION

The second dimension of logistics is the micro perspective, which examines the relationship between logistics and other functional areas in a company—marketing, manufacturing/operations, finances and accounting, and others. Logistics, by its nature, focuses upon processes that cut across traditional functional areas, particularly in today's environment with its emphasis upon the supply chain.

Logistics Interfaces with Operations/Manufacturing

A classic interface area between logistics and manufacturing management relates to the length of the production run. We typically associate production economies

length of production runs

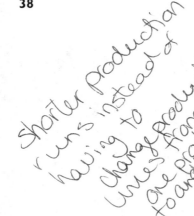

with long production runs with infrequent production line setups or changeovers. These can, however, easily result in excessive inventories of certain finished products and in limited supplies of others. Thus, the ultimate production decision requires management to carefully weigh the advantages and disadvantages of long versus short production runs. Many industries today tend toward shorter production runs and toward doing whatever it takes to reduce the time and expense normally associated with changing production lines from one product to another. This is particularly true for firms employing the just-in-time (JIT) approach to inventory and scheduling. The trend is toward "pull" systems, manufacturing/logistics systems where the product is "pulled" in response to demand as opposed to being "pushed" in advance of demand.

seasonal demand

The production manager is interested in minimizing the effects of seasonal demand for products. Fully anticipating such demand is not always possible, however; thus, having desired product quantities available when and where needed is not always possible. For example, cold weather and snow accumulation in various parts of the country easily influence sales of snow skis or snowmobiles. To keep costs low, to avoid overtime and rush situations, and to prepare for the sales schedule, production managers usually like to produce well ahead of the season and to produce a maximum amount. Such advance production may not be economically feasible because of inventory storage costs. However, production managers have to consider this problem in an attempt to keep production costs down. Therefore, the logistics department, in conjunction with production or manufacturing, must be prepared to accept seasonal inventory, which can start to accumulate three to six months before sales occur. For example, Hallmark Cards begins to accumulate Christmas items at its Kansas City warehouse during the summer months, so that the company will be prepared to ship to retailers and other customers during the fall.

supply-side interfaces

Since the logistics manager is responsible for the inbound movement and storage of raw materials that will feed the production line, logistics and production also interface on the supply side. A shortage or stockout situation could result in the shutdown of a production facility or an increase in production costs. The logistics manager should ensure that available quantities of raw materials and other production inputs are sufficient to meet production schedules, yet are conservative in terms of inventory carrying costs. Because of the need for this type of coordination, many firms today have shifted the responsibility for production scheduling from manufacturing to logistics management. The end result is a broadening of overall logistics responsibility.

protective packaging

Another activity at the interface of logistics and operations is packaging, which many firms treat as a logistics activity. In the context of either operations or logistics management, the principal purpose that packaging serves is to protect the product from damage. This is distinct from whatever value the package may have for marketing or promotional reasons.

foreign and third-party alternatives

The interface between logistics and operations is becoming more critical, given recent interest in the procurement of raw materials and other production inputs from foreign sources. Also, many firms today are making arrangements with third-party manufacturers, or "co-packers," to produce or assemble some or all of the firm's finished products. These arrangements are especially prevalent in the food industry, where many firms manufacture only food items to be sold under someone else's label.

Logistics Interfaces with Marketing

Logistics is sometimes referred to as the other half of marketing. The rationale for this definition is that the physical distribution part of a firm's logistics system is responsible for the physical movement and storage of goods for customers, and thus plays an important role in selling a product. In some instances, physical distribution may be the key variable in selling a product; that is, your ability to provide the product at the right time in the right quantities may be the critical element in making a sale.

This section briefly discusses the interfaces between logistics and marketing, activities in each principal area of the marketing mix. The material is organized according to the Four Ps of marketing—price, product, promotion, and place.[12] In addition, recent trends in the interface area between logistics and marketing will be discussed.

marketing mix

Price. From a logistics perspective, adjusting quantity prices to conform with shipment sizes appropriate for transportation companies may be quite important. Railroads, for example, publish minimum weight requirements for carload lots—for instance, 30,000 pounds. Motor carriers typically publish four or five rates that will apply to the same commodity shipped between two points depending upon the size (weight) of the shipment. The larger the size, the lower the unit rate charged. In other words, a price discount schedule for shipping larger volumes at one time applies because the transportation company experiences economy if the customer sends larger shipments.

carrier pricing

Companies selling products also typically provide a discount schedule for larger purchase quantities. If such discount schedules relate to transportation rate discount schedules in terms of weight, then the company may be able to save itself some money or save money for customers, depending on the sale terms. For example, if a company sells on a delivered-price basis (price includes transportation charges) and if its price schedule matches the transportation shipping requirements on a weight basis, the company should be able to get lower rates with larger purchases and thus save money. So when the company calculates the number of units that it wants to sell to a customer for a particular price, it should see how the weight of that number of units compares with the weight requirement for a transportation rate. In many instances, increasing the quantity purchased in order to produce a total shipment weight that will qualify for a lower per unit transportation weight becomes advantageous. Even if the firm were selling goods on an F.O.B. (free on board) point-of-origin basis (transportation charges paid by the buyer), this approach would enable the firm's customers to qualify for the lower rate and thus save money.

matching schedules

Although it is not always possible to adjust prices to meet rate breaks and to have a quantity convenient to deal with, organizations should investigate such alternatives. In some organizations, entire pricing schedules conform to various quantities the company can ship by motor and railroad or by other modes of transportation. Under the Robinson-Patman Act and related legislation, transportation cost savings are a valid reason for offering a price discount.

In addition, the logistics manager may be interested in the volume sold under different price schedules, because this will affect inventory requirements, replacement times, and other aspects of customer service. Although this is somewhat difficult to analyze, a firm may consider the logistics manager's ability to provide

volume relationships

sufficient volumes within an attractive price schedule. Such a situation may be particularly true when price specials generate extra sales at particular times of the year. The logistics manager must be apprised of such specials so that he or she can adjust inventory requirements to meet projected demand.

Product.   Another decision frequently made in the marketing area concerns products, particularly their physical attributes. Much has been written about the number of new products that come on the market each year in the United States. Their size, shape, weight, packaging, and other physical dimensions affect the ability of the logistics system to move and store products. Therefore, the logistics manager should offer input when marketing is deciding upon the physical dimensions of new products. The logistics manager can supply appropriate information about the movement and storage of the new products. In addition to new products, firms frequently refurbish old products in one way or another to improve and maintain sales. Very often such changes may take the form of a new package design and perhaps, different package sizes. The physical dimensions of products affect the use of storage and movement systems. They affect the carriers that a firm can use, equipment needed, damage rates, storage ability, use of materials handling equipment such as conveyors and pallets, exterior packaging, and many other logistics aspects.

It is very difficult to convey the frustration that some logistics managers experience when discovering a change in a product package that makes the use of standard-size pallets uneconomical, or that uses trailer or boxcar space inefficiently or in a way that could damage products. For example, when Gillette first introduced the Daisy razor, the logistics group did not learn until late in the game that they had to deal with light and bulky floor stand displays, with consequent low weight density. Not only would the floor stand displays not fit on the warehouse conveyors, but they had to be shipped at a rate that was 150 percent higher than the existing rate for the product itself. Gillette eventually corrected the situation, but it was an expensive lesson. These things often seem mundane and somewhat trivial to people concerned about making sales to customers, but they greatly affect an organization's overall success and profitability in the long run.

No magic formulas can spell out what firms should do in these cases, but we can keep in mind that interaction can allow the logistics manager to provide input about the possibly negative aspects of decisions. It may well be that logistics can do nothing and that the sale is most important. But often the logistics manager can recommend small changes that make the product much more amenable to a logistics system's movement and storage aspects while having no real effect upon the sales of the product itself.

consumer packaging   Another marketing area that affects logistics is consumer packaging. The marketing manager often regards consumer packaging as a "silent" salesperson. At the retail level, the package may be a determining factor in influencing sales. The marketing manager will be concerned about package appearance, information provided, and other related aspects; for a customer comparing several products on the retailer's shelf, the consumer package may make the sale. The consumer package is important to the logistics manager for several reasons. The consumer package usually has to fit into what is called the industrial package, or the external package. The size, shape, and other dimensions of the consumer package will affect the use of the industrial packages. The protection the consumer package offers also concerns the logistics manager. The physical dimensions and the protection aspects of consumer packages affect the logistics system in the areas of transportation, materials handing, and warehousing.

Promotion. Promotion is a marketing area that receives much attention in an organization. Firms often spend hundreds of thousands of dollars on national advertising campaigns and other promotional practices to improve a sales position. An organization making a promotional effort to stimulate sales should inform its logistics manager so that sufficient inventory quantities will be available for distribution to the customer. But even when logistics is informed, problems can occur. For example, when Gillette introduced the disposable twin-blade Good News razor, the company's original plan called for three consecutive promotions. The national launch promotion was to achieve sales of twenty million units. A following trade deal promotion was to net ten million in sales, and Gillette expected a third promotional campaign to net an additional twenty million—for a total of fifty million in sales. As it turned out, the first promotion sold thirty-five million— seventy-five percent over the plan. Needless to say, this placed quite a burden on the logistics group to try to meet the demand.

We should look beyond the obvious relation and analyze basic promotion strategies to see how they affect the logistics department. Marketing people often classify their promotion strategies into two basic categories: push or pull. What they are implying is that they try to either "push" the product through the distribution channel to the customer or "pull" it through.[13] We will discuss distribution channels subsequently in more detail. Briefly, they are the institutions that handle products after manufacture but before sale to the ultimate consumer. They include organizations such as wholesalers and retailers. **push versus pull**

Producers frequently compete to get distribution channels to give their products the sales effort they feel their products deserve. For example, a cereal producer may want to ensure sufficient space for its product on the retailer's shelf, or to ensure that wholesalers hold product quantities sufficient to satisfy retailers, believing that ultimately the final consumer demand for the product will influence the retailer and the wholesaler. By selling popular products, they improve their profitability. The higher the product turnover, the more likely they are to make a profit; the happier they are with a particular product, the more willing they are to give it space and a better position in the store. **channel competition**

Companies can attempt to improve their sales by *pulling* their product through the distribution channel with national advertising. Promotional advertising attempts to create or stimulate sales to customers and to get customers into the retail store asking for a product they have seen advertised in a magazine, have heard advertised on the radio, or, more likely, have seen advertised on television. The purchases will likely influence the retailer, and the retailer will influence the wholesaler, if any, from whom the retailer purchases. Some companies feel that the best approach in promoting a product is to pull it through distribution channels by directly stimulating demand at the consumer level. **pull strategy**

The other basic approach is the *push* method. Implied in the push approach is cooperation with the channels of distribution to stimulate customer sales—in other words, retailers or wholesalers possibly pay part of local advertising costs or have special store displays to stimulate sales. In cooperating with the wholesaler, a manufacturer may be able to offer retailers a special price at a particular time **push strategy** to stimulate product demand. The emphasis is upon having the distribution channel work with the company. This contrasts with the pull approach, wherein the company stimulates sales somewhat independently of the retailer by national advertising or by advertising a product on a broad regional scale.

logistics impact   We can offer many arguments both for and against these two approaches. In fact, some companies combine the two in their promotion efforts. From the logistics manager's point of view, however, push and pull are often different as far as logistics system requirements are concerned. The pull approach is more likely to generate erratic demand that is difficult to predict and that may place emergency demands upon the logistics system. Broad-scale national advertising has the potential to be extremely successful, but predicting consumer response to new products is often difficult. Such advertising may also strain the logistics system, requiring emergency shipments and higher transportation rates. Frequent stockouts may also result, requiring additional inventory. The Gillette situation is an example of such a case. On the other hand, a push approach may have a more orderly demand pattern. Cooperation with the retailer allows manufacturers to fill the "pipeline" somewhat in advance of the stimulated sales rather than quickly, on an almost emergency basis, as retailers and consumers clamor for some successfully promoted new product.

wholesalers versus retailers   *Place.*   The place decision refers to the distribution channels decision, and thus involves both transactional and physical distribution channel decisions. Marketers typically become more involved in making decisions about marketing transactions and in deciding such things as whether to sell a product to wholesalers or to deal directly with retailers. From the logistics manager's point of view, such decisions may significantly affect logistics system requirements. For example, companies dealing only with wholesalers will probably have fewer logistics problems than will companies dealing directly with retailers. Wholesalers, on the average, tend to purchase in larger quantities than do retailers and to place their orders and manage their inventories more predictably and consistently, thereby making the logistics manager's job easier. Retailing establishments, particularly small retailers, often order in small quantities and do not always allow sufficient lead time for replenishment before stockouts. Consequently, manufacturers may need to purchase time-sensitive transportation service at a premium price to meet delivery needs.

customer service   *Recent Trends.*   Perhaps the most significant trend is that marketers have begun to recognize the strategic value of place in the marketing mix, and the increased revenues and customer satisfaction that may result from high-quality logistical services. As a result, many firms have recognized *customer service* as the interface activity between marketing and logistics, and have aggressively and effectively promoted customer service as a key element of the marketing mix. Firms in industries such as food, chemicals, and pharmaceuticals have reported considerable success along these lines.

Table 2–4 shows the results of a comprehensive study undertaken to develop empirical evidence about the importance of customer service. The information shows that, in general, product was the marketing variable respondents perceived as most important. Price, customer service, and promotion followed in general order of importance. Although product and price were generally perceived by the

TABLE 2-4 Importance of Marketing Variables by Industry

	Food	Chemi-cal	Pharma-ceutical	Auto	Paper	Elec-tronic	Clothing/Textiles	Other Mfg.	Total Mfg.	Mer-chandise	Total Response
Product (quality, breadth of line, etc.)	34.8	33.0	36.9	26.8	23.2	41.3	34.7	32.6	33.2	32.9	33.3
Price (base price, competitiveness etc.)	25.8	34.8	29.4	29.8	35.8	26.5	22.0	33.7	30.0	27.9	29.9
Customer service	20.0	19.1	17.3	33.5	28.9	21.8	22.8	23.6	22.6	21.3	22.4
Advertising, promotion, sales effort	19.4	13.1	16.4	9.9	12.1	10.4	20.5	10.1	14.2	17.9	14.4
Total	100.0	100.0	100.0	100.0	100.0	100.0	100.0	100.0	100.0	100.0	100.0

NOTE: Survey respondents were asked to distribute 100 points among the marketing variables listed to indicate the importance of each in generating sales of product to the customer.

SOURCE: B. J. LaLonde, M. C. Cooper, and T. G. Nordewier, *Customer Service: A Management Perspective* (Ohio State University, Oak Brook, IL: Council of Logistics Management, 1988): 55.

participating industries to be more important than customer service, there were some notable exceptions. Specifically, automobile industry respondents ranked customer service most important; and paper and clothing/textile industry respondents ranked it second in importance.

Finally, firms are tending to place sales forecasting activity within the logistics area, rather than within the marketing area. This not only acknowledges that timely and accurate sales forecasting is important to the firm's logistics mission, but also highlights sales forecasting as another interface area between marketing and logistics.

sales forecasting

LOGISTICS INTERFACES WITH OTHER AREAS

In addition to manufacturing and marketing, logistics has important interfaces with other functional areas in any company. In fact, it is probably safe to say that logistics has some relationship to all areas of a company. Finance and accounting deserve special mention because of the role that logistics plays in managing such assets as warehouses and inventory. Inventory reduction, for example, has been an area where finance and logistics have interfaced to improve the return on investment and improve cash flow.

The recognition that CEOs have given to logistics as indicated in the On the Line feature of this chapter is also indicative of the far-reaching interfaces that logistics has in organizations today. In the next section we will examine in more depth the various activities that are a part of the logistics function.

LOGISTICAL ACTIVITIES

The logistics definitions discussed earlier indicate activities for which the logistics manager may be responsible:

- Traffic and transportation
- Warehousing and storage
- Industrial packaging
- Materials handling
- Inventory control
- Order fulfillment
- Demand forecasting

- Production planning
- Purchasing
- Customer service levels
- Plant and warehouse site location
- Return goods handling
- Parts and service support
- Salvage and scrap disposal

This list is quite comprehensive; some companies with well-organized logistics areas may not place responsibility for all of these activities within the logistics area. For example, companies having a physical distribution focus may not include procurement in their logistics organization.

Scope of Activities

The development of interest in logistics after World War II contributed to the growth in activities associated with logistics. Given the scope of this growth, it would be worthwhile to discuss these activities and their relationship to logistics.

Transportation. Transportation is a very important part of the logistics system. A major focus in logistics is upon the physical movement or flow of goods, or upon the network that moves the product. This network is composed of transportation agencies that provide the service for the firm. The logistics manager is responsible for selecting the mode or modes of transportation used in moving the raw materials and finished goods or for developing private transportation as an alternative.

transportation trade-off
Storage. A second area, which has a trade-off relationship with transportation, is storage. It involves two separate but closely related activities: inventory management and warehousing. A direct relationship exists between transportation and the level of inventory and number of warehouses required. For example, if firms use a relatively slow means of transport, they usually have to keep higher inventory levels and usually have more warehousing space for this inventory. They may examine the possibility of using faster transport to eliminate some of these warehouses and the inventory stored therein.

A number of important decisions are related to storage activities (inventory and warehousing), including how many warehouses, how much inventory, where to locate the warehouses, what size the warehouse should be, and so on. Because decisions related to transportation affect storage-related decisions, a decision framework to examine the trade-offs related to the various alternatives is essential to optimize the overall logistics system (discussed in detail in Chapter 9).

modal impact
Packaging. A third area of interest to logistics is industrial (exterior) packaging. The type of transportation selected will affect packaging requirements both for moving the finished product to the market and for the inbound materials. For example, rail or water transportation will usually require additional packaging expenditures because of the greater possibility of damage. In analyzing trade-offs for proposed changes in transportation agencies, logistics personnel generally examine how the change will influence packaging costs. In many instances, changing to a premium transport means, such as air, will reduce packaging costs.

Materials Handling. A fourth area to be considered is materials handling, which **efficiency** is also of interest to other areas in the typical manufacturing organization. Materials handling is important to efficient warehouse operation. Logistics managers are concerned with the movement of goods into a warehouse, the placement of goods in a warehouse, and the movement of goods from storage to order-picking areas and eventually to dock areas for transportation out of the warehouse.

Materials handling is usually concerned with mechanical equipment for short-distance movement; such equipment includes conveyors, forklift trucks, overhead cranes, and containers. Production managers may want a particular pallet or container type that is not compatible with logistics warehousing activities. Therefore, the materials handling designs must be coordinated in order to ensure congruity between the types of equipment used. In addition, the company may find it economical to use the same type of forklift trucks in the plants and in the warehouses.

Order Fulfillment. Another activity area that logistics may control is order fulfillment, which generally consists of activities involved with completing customer orders. Initially, one might question why the logistics area would concern itself directly with order fulfillment. However, one important physical distribution factor is the time elapsing from the time when a customer decides to place an order for a product until the time that those goods are actually delivered in a satisfactory condition, that is, the lead time.

For example, assume that the present system takes a total lead time of eight days for transmittal, processing, order preparation, and shipping. Order processing may take four days, and order preparation may take an additional two days, which means that the goods have to be transported to the customer in two days. The short delivery time may require a premium means of transportation. If order processing is considered part of the logistics system, then the company might examine improvements, such as using telephone calls and more computer equipment for processing, to reduce order processing time to two days or less. This would allow the firm to use much cheaper transportation and still get the goods to the customer within eight days. Looking from a time perspective or in terms of total lead time, we can see that order fulfillment is quite important to the logistics function.

Forecasting. Another activity important to the logistics area is inventory forecast- **inventory accuracy** ing. Accurate forecasting of inventory requirements and materials and parts is essential to effective inventory control. This is particularly true in companies using a just-in-time (JIT) or materials requirement planning (MRP) approach to control inventory. Logistics personnel should develop forecasts in those situations to ensure accuracy and effective control. Too frequently, forecasts developed by marketing staff reflect sales objectives rather than inventory requirements.

Production Planning. Another area of growing interest for logistics managers is **time perspective** production planning, which is closely related to forecasting in terms of effective inventory control. Once a forecast is developed and the current inventory on hand and usage rate are assessed, production managers can determine the number of units necessary to ensure adequate market coverage. However, in multiple-product firms, production process timing and certain product line relationships require close coordination with logistics or actual control of production planning by logistics. The integration of production planning into logistics is becoming increasingly common in large corporations.

Purchasing.   Purchasing, or procurement, is another activity that we can include in logistics. The basic rationale for including purchasing in logistics is that transportation cost relates directly to the geographic location (distance) of raw materials and component parts purchased for a company's production needs. In terms of transportation and inventory costs, the quantities purchased would also affect logistics cost. Including purchasing within the logistics area is primarily a matter of whether this more effectively coordinates and lowers costs for the firm. As was noted previously, a growing number of companies added purchasing to the logistics function during the 1970s and 1980s.

Customer Service.   Another area of importance is customer service. Customer service is a complex topic, and one that concerns other functional company areas. Customer service levels in many ways glue together other logistics areas. Decisions about inventory, transportation, and warehousing relate to customer service requirements. While customarily the logistics area does not completely control customer service decisions, logistics plays an extremely important role in ensuring that the customer gets the right product at the right place and time. Logistics decisions about product availability and inventory lead time are critical to customer service.

Site Location.   Another area that is important to logistics is plant and warehouse site location. We will discuss this activity at some length in a later chapter. A location change could alter time and place relationships between plants and markets or between supply points and plants. Such changes will affect transportation rates and service, customer service, inventory requirements, and possibly other areas. Therefore, the logistics manager is quite concerned about location decisions. In fact, plant location, as will be discussed in a subsequent chapter, is frequently as important as warehouse location. Transportation cost is frequently a very important factor in deciding on a location.

Other Activities.   Other areas may be considered a part of logistics. Areas such as parts and service support, return goods handling, and salvage and scrap disposal indicate the reality of logistical activities managed in companies producing consumer durables or industrial products. Here, a very integrative approach is necessary. Logistics offers input into product design as well as into maintenance and supply services, since transportation and storage decisions affect these areas. (The definitions of logistics and materials management implied the importance of such activities to systematic logistics management in such companies.)

APPROACHES TO ANALYZING LOGISTICS SYSTEMS

The analysis of logistics systems frequently requires different views or perspectives of logistical activities. The best perspective to take depends upon the type of analysis that is needed. For example, if a company wants to analyze the long-run system design of its logistics system, a view of logistics that focuses upon the company's node and link relationships would probably be most beneficial. On the other hand, if a company is evaluating a change in a carrier or mode of transportation, it should probably analyze the logistics system in terms of cost centers. In this section, we will discuss four approaches for analyzing logistics systems: materials management versus physical distribution, cost centers, nodes versus links, and logistics channels.

Materials Management versus Physical Distribution

The classification of logistics into materials management and physical distribution is very useful to logistics management or control in an organization. Frequently, the movement and storage of raw materials in a firm is very different from the movement and storage of finished products. For example, a steel company may move required raw materials of iron ore and coal by barge and large rail carload. Storage may require nothing more elaborate than land where these items can be dumped and piled for future use. On the other hand, the finished steel will very often be moved by motor carrier, and the storage will require an enclosed facility for protection against the elements and, perhaps, elaborate materials handling equipment.

The different logistics requirements that may exist between materials management and physical distribution may have important implications for the design of an organization's logistics system. Great differences may result in different logistics system designs for materials management and physical distribution. Companies may find it convenient to view their logistics system from these two perspectives, and somewhat different management approaches for each may result. Note that in spite of such differences, close coordination between materials management and physical distribution is still necessary.

Additional perspectives related to viewing logistics in terms of materials management/inbound logistics and physical distribution/outbound logistics deserve consideration. In fact, from the inbound and outbound requirements perspective, we may classify companies into four different types of logistics systems.

Balanced System. Some companies have a reasonably balanced flow on the inbound and outbound sides of their logistics systems. In other words, they receive supplies from various vendors in different locations and ship to various customers in different locations. Consumer product companies such as General Foods, Pillsbury, and General Mills typically fit this description. While these companies may emphasize the physical distribution or outbound side because of the importance of customer service, both inbound and outbound logistics are important.

Heavy Inbound. Some companies have a very heavy inbound flow and a very simple outbound flow. Aircraft companies such as Boeing and McDonnell-Douglas are good examples. They use thousands of parts manufactured by hundreds of vendors to assemble and produce a finished airplane. Once the airplane is finished and tested, the company simply flies it to the customer (Delta Airlines, for example), who ordered it two or three years before delivery. The process requires no warehousing, special transportation arrangements, or packaging. In contrast, the inbound side requires detailed scheduling, coordination, and planning to ensure that parts arrive in time. Varying lead times for parts from vendors present a complex logistics challenge. Auto manufacturers, using twelve thousand to thirteen thousand parts per car, also fit this model. Their outbound systems, while more complex than an aircraft company's, are not nearly as complex as their inbound systems.

Heavy Outbound.   Chemical companies like Dow offer a good example of a logistics system with heavy outbound flow. Inbound crude oil by-products, salt water, and other raw materials flow from a limited number of sources and frequently move in volume over relatively short distances. On the outbound side, a wide variety of industrial and consumer products are produced that need storage, packaging, and transportation to the final customer. Therefore, in a company with heavy outbound, the physical distribution side of logistics system is more complex.

Reverse Systems.   Some companies have reverse flows on the outbound side of their logistics systems. This is true of companies producing durable products that the customer may return for trade-in, for repairs, or for salvage and disposal. Companies that produce computers, telephone equipment, and copy machines have these characteristics. Companies that deal with returnable containers also fit this model. Increased concern with the environment will require more companies to develop reverse logistics systems to dispose of packaging materials on used products.

Cost Centers

We previously mentioned the management activities that many firms include in the logistics area, namely, transportation, warehousing, inventory, materials handling, and industrial packaging. We also emphasized the need to consider these activities as being highly interrelated. By looking at these activities as cost centers, one can analyze possible trade-offs between and among them that could result in lower overall cost and/or better service.

trade-offs   The breakdown of logistics into various cost centers or activity centers represents a second approach to logistics system analysis. Firms frequently analyze logistics systems by dividing them into cost or activity centers, since reducing total logistics costs and/or improving service most frequently will occur by trading off one activity center against another. For example, shifting from rail to motor carrier may result, because of faster and more reliable service, in lower inventory costs, which will offset the higher motor carrier rate. (See Table 2–5.) Another possibility might be increasing the number of warehouses, thereby raising warehousing and inventory costs but possibly reducing the cost of transportation and lost sales enough to lower total costs. (See Table 2–6.)

The activity or cost center perspective is very useful in reviewing various trade-offs for lower cost and/or improved service to the customer or plants. However, as Table 2–6 indicates, not every change results in lower total costs.

Nodes versus Links

A third approach to analyzing the logistics system in an organization is in terms of nodes and links (see Figure 2–6). The nodes are established spatial points where

TABLE 2-5   Analysis of Total Logistics Cost with a Change to a Higher-Cost Mode of Transport

Cost Centers		Rail	Motor
Transportation		$ 3.00	$ 4.20
Inventory		5.00	3.75
Packaging		4.50	3.20
Warehousing		1.50	.75
Cost of lost sales		2.00	1.00
	Total cost	$15.00*	$13.00*

*Costs per unit.

goods stop for storage or processing. In other words, the nodes are plants and warehouses where the organization stores materials for conversion into finished products or goods in finished form for sale to customers (equalization of supply and demand).

The other part of the system is the links, which represent the transportation network connecting the nodes in the logistics system. The network can be composed of individual modes of transportation (rail, motor, air, water, or pipelines) and of combinations and variations that we will discuss later.

From a node-link perspective, the complexity of logistics systems can vary enormously. One-node systems may use a simple link from suppliers to a combined plant and warehouse and then to customers in a relatively small market area. At the other end of the spectrum are large, multiple-product firms with multiple plant and warehouse locations. The complex transportation networks of the latter may include three or four different modes and perhaps private as well as for-hire transportation.

The node and link perspective, in allowing analysis of a logistics system's two basic elements, represents a convenient basis for seeking possible system improvements. As we have noted, the complexity of a logistics system often relates directly to the various time and distance relationships between the nodes and the links and to the regularity, predictability, and volume of flow of goods entering, leaving, and moving within the system.

TABLE 2-6   Analysis of Total Logistics Cost with a Change to More Warehouses

Cost Centers		System 1 Three Warehouses	System 2 Five Warehouses
Transportation		$ 850,000	$ 500,000
Inventory		$1,500,000	$2,000,000
Warehousing		$ 600,000	$1,000,000
Cost of lost sales*		$ 350,000	$ 100,000
	Total cost	$3,300,000	$3,600,000

*Expected cost, based upon probabilities, of not having stock/inventory available when customers want it.

FIGURE 2-6   Nodes and Links in a Logistics System

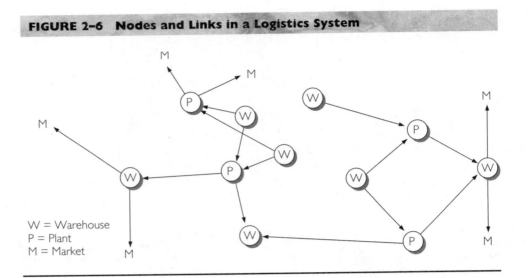

W = Warehouse
P = Plant
M = Market

Logistics Channel

A fourth approach to logistics system analysis is to study the logistics channel, the network of intermediaries engaged in transfer, storage, handling, communication, and other functions that contribute to the efficient flow of goods. We can view the logistics channel as part of the total distribution channel, which includes, in addition to the logistical flow, a transaction flow of specific interest to the marketing specialist.[14]

The logistics channel can be simple or complex. Figure 2–7 shows a simple channel in which an individual producer deals directly with a final customer. The control in this channel is relatively simple. The individual manufacturer controls the logistical flows since he or she deals directly with the customer.

Figure 2–8 presents a more complex, multi-echelon channel, with a market warehouse and retailers. The market warehouse could be a public warehouse. In

FIGURE 2-7   A Simple Logistics Channel

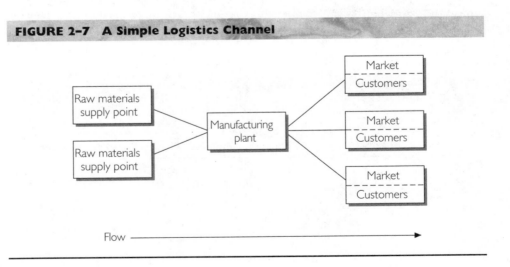

FIGURE 2-8   A Multi-Echelon Logistics Channel

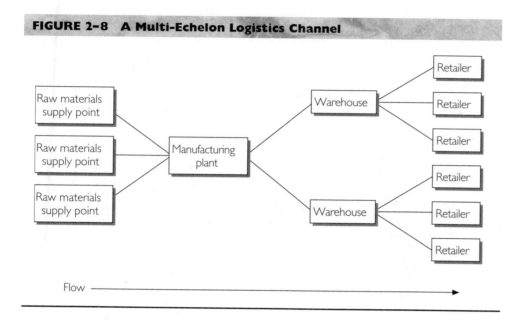

this instance, the control is more difficult because of the additional storage and transportation.

Figure 2–9 illustrates a complex, comprehensive channel. In this instance, the task of achieving an effective logistical flow in the channel is far more formidable. This figure very realistically portrays the situation confronting many large organizations operating in the United States.

Some instances involving production of a basic good like steel, aluminum, or chemicals may further complicate the situation because companies may be a part of more than one channel. For example, the steel may be sold to auto manufacturers, container manufacturers, or file cabinet producers. Duplication of storage facilities, small-shipment transportation, conflict over mode choices, and other problems may contribute to inefficiency in the channel. Communications problems may also exist.

In attempting to overcome these problems, companies employ different strategies. For example, some organizations integrate vertically in order to control the product over several stages in the logistics channel. Some strong companies dominate the channel to achieve efficiency. In any case, we can appreciate the complicating factors of the complex channel. The various approaches to logistics should provide additional insights into relevant logistics activities. A discussion of systems analysis in logistics may further aid your understanding of logistics.

LOGISTICS AND SYSTEMS ANALYSIS

An earlier section pointed out that improvements in analysis and methodologies have facilitated the development of logistics. One such improvement was systems analysis, or the systems concept. A convenient starting point for this section is a brief discussion of the basic nature of systems analysis.

FIGURE 2–9   A Complex Logistics Channel

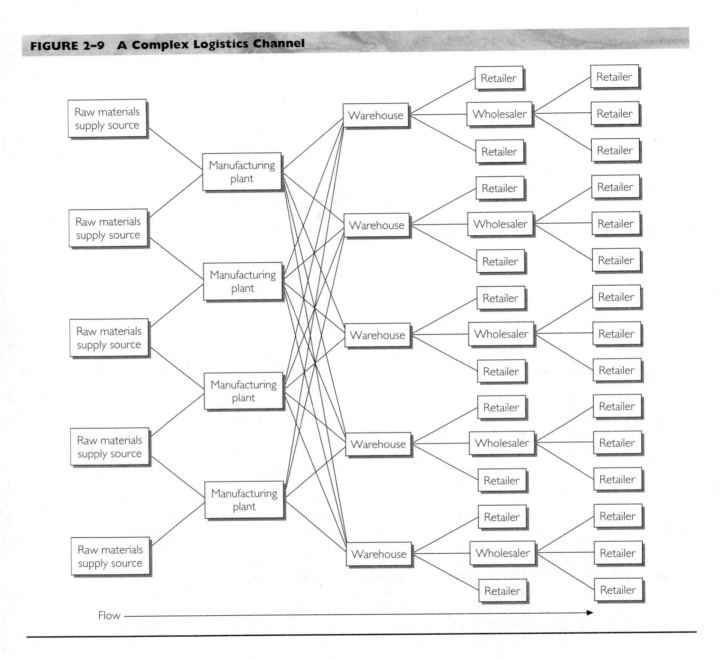

**concept of a
system**

Essentially, a system is a set of interacting elements, variables, parts, or objects that are functionally related to one another and that form a coherent group. The systems concept is something to which most people have been exposed at an early educational stage; for example, in science your instructor probably taught you about the solar system and how relationships among the planets, the sun, and the moon resulted in day and night, weather, and so forth. Later, in learning about the human body in biology, you viewed the parts of the body, such as the heart and the blood vessels, and their relationships as another system.

Perhaps in a power mechanics class, you learned about the internal combustion engine as a system. You probably learned that engine parts, such as the pistons, could have been larger in size and more efficient, but that their very efficiency may have overloaded other parts of the engine, causing it to break down. So the pistons had to be designed in harmony with other parts of the engine. In other words, the overall performance of the engine was more important than the performance of one part.

Cost Perspective

The preceding engine analogy provides insight into business system characteristics. If we measure efficiency by cost, an individual part of the system not operating at its lowest cost may contribute to the system's overall efficiency. For example, in a logistics context, perhaps water transportation is the cheapest alternative available to some company. If the company optimizes transportation alone, then water movement would be the best approach. However, moving freight by water may require increased inventory holdings, with associated increases in warehousing space and other costs. These additional costs may be greater than the amount saved by using water transportation. In other words, the transportation decision has to be coordinated with related areas such as inventory, warehousing, and perhaps packaging, to optimize the overall system or subsystem, not just transportation. The general tenet of the systems concept is that we do not focus on individual variables but on how they interact as a whole. The objective is to operate the whole system effectively, not just the individual parts.

optimization

Level of Optimality

Another aspect of the systems concept is that *levels of optimality* exist in the firm. We just stated that a firm should not optimize transportation at the expense of related logistics areas such as warehousing and packaging. At the same time, logistics is only one subsystem in the firm, and therefore the firm should not optimize it at another area's expense. For example, the logistics manager may want to give five-day delivery service to certain customers in order to eliminate some warehouses and inventory. But this may conflict with marketing, since the firm's competitors give three-day delivery service in the same sales area. Clearly, the firm must work out some compromise after analyzing the situation. Logistics may have to accept the three-day service as a working constraint imposed because of competition, and may have to design the best system within this constraint. Some individual or group at the organization's senior executive level has to examine the trade-offs between marketing and logistics in terms of the total organization's efficiency or profit.

functional relationships

In addition to marketing, the firm has to consider production, finance, and other areas (see Figure 2–10). In other words, the overall firm is a system that should be optimized. The firm may have to suboptimize internal subsystems to achieve the best overall position. Generally, this means that logistics may work within constraints such as set delivery times, minimum production run orders, and financial limits on warehouse improvements and construction. Such constraints, occasionally somewhat arbitrary, should be flexible within reason. Ideally, logistics managers should make decisions such as delivery times on a more individual or

constraints

FIGURE 2-10 Levels of Optimality in Economic Environments

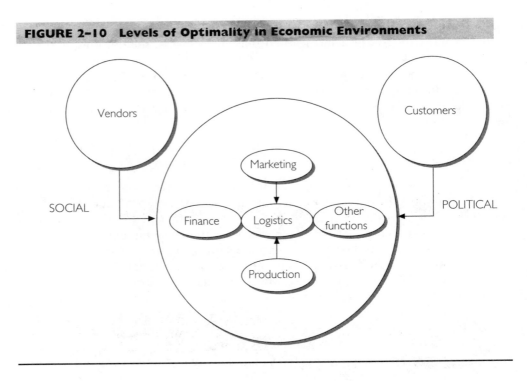

short-run basis, but organizations are sometimes too complex to make this possible from an operational standpoint. A dynamic simulation model would help to solve some of these problems and to allow more flexibility. We will say more about this point in the chapters covering management of logistics systems.

We should make one other point about optimality levels. Firms producing intermediate goods such as steel or having a multiple-product line very often operate in several supply chains.[15] Therefore, one might consider supply chain optimization or the external effects of a firm's decisions as a higher optimality level. For example, a container or pallet designed for shipping a firm's product in a manner consistent with the firm's overall needs may not be compatible with the ordering and receiving needs of customers. Therefore, in the final analysis, such an improvement may harm the supply chain's overall efficiency. The increased focus upon supply chains discussed in Chapter 1 will necessitate optimization at this higher level. It will be challenging, but the payoff potential is high.

TECHNIQUES OF LOGISTICS SYSTEM ANALYSIS

In this section, we will consider total cost analysis techniques for logistics systems. We will examine only the more basic methods; more sophisticated techniques of total cost analysis are discussed in a later section. The basic approaches examined here unite some of the concepts discussed thus far and provide a background for the material discussed in the book's next section.

TABLE 2–7 Static Analysis of C & B Chemical Company (50,000 Pounds of Output)

Plant logistics costs*	System 1	System 2
Packaging	$ 500	$ 0
Storage and handling	150	50
Inventory carrying	50	25
Administrative	75	25
Fixed cost	4,200	2,400
Transportation costs*		
To market warehouse	0	150
To customer	800	100
Warehouse costs*		
Packaging	0	500
Storage and handling	0	150
Inventory carrying	0	75
Administrative	0	75
Fixed cost	0	2,400
Total cost*	$5,775	$5,950

*In thousands of dollars.

Short-Run/Static Analysis

One general approach to total cost analysis for business logistics is known as short-run analysis. In a short-run analysis, we would look at a short-run situation and develop costs associated with the various logistics cost centers described previously. We would develop such cost information for each alternative system considered. We would then select the system with the lowest overall cost, as long as it was consistent with constraints the firm imposed on the logistics area. Some authors refer to this short-run analysis as static analysis.[16] Essentially, they are saying that this method analyzes costs associated with a logistics system's various components at one point in time or at one output level.

Example. For an example of static analysis, see Table 2–7. In this instance, a firm is presently using an all-rail route from the plant and the associated plant warehouse to the customers. At the plant warehouse, the chemicals are bagged and then shipped by rail to the customer. A proposed second system would use a market-oriented warehouse. The goods would be shipped from the plant to the market warehouse and then packaged and sent to the customer. Instead of shipping all goods by rail, the firm would ship them by barge to the warehouse, taking advantage of low bulk rates. Then, after bagging, the chemicals would move by rail from the warehouse for shipment to the customer.

In this example, the trade-off is lower transportation costs versus some increases in storage and warehousing. If the analysis is strictly static (at this level of output), the proposed system is more expensive than the present one. So, unless analysis

[Handwritten margin notes: "20 M.C. Essays 2 questions"; "$X = \dfrac{f.c._1 - f.c._2}{vc_1 - vc_2}$"; "X = output level (Total Cost) Pt. of difference; total cost = fixed cost + total variable cost"]

FIGURE 2–11 Dynamic Analysis

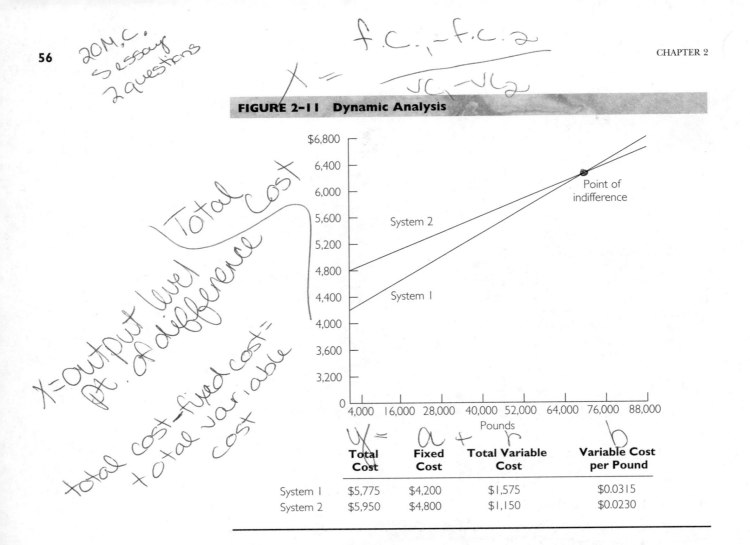

[Handwritten note under graph: "$y = a + b$"]

	Total Cost	Fixed Cost	Total Variable Cost	Variable Cost per Pound
System 1	$5,775	$4,200	$1,575	$0.0315
System 2	$5,950	$4,800	$1,150	$0.0230

provided additional information more favorable to the proposed system, the firm would continue with its present system.

However, we have two reasons to select the proposed system. First, we have no information about customer service requirements. The new market-oriented warehouse might provide better customer service, therefore increasing sales and profit and offsetting some of the higher cost of System 2.

Second, if we use a longer-run perspective (dynamic analysis) to look at the example (Figure 2–11), we find that although System 1 gives a lower cost at an output of 50,000 pounds, at approximately 70,500 pounds, System 2 becomes less expensive than System 1. Therefore, a company experiencing rapid sales growth may want to plan the shift to System 2 now. The start-up time for the new warehouse may necessitate the immediate planning.

Another reason why a firm might switch to System 2, even though it is presently experiencing lower costs with another system, is that the firm expects the second system to result in lower costs in the future. Since setting up a new system usually takes time, the firm may initiate the change in the near future. If this firm is growing relatively rapidly, it may achieve an output of 70,500 pounds in a fairly short time.

Long-Run/Dynamic Analysis

The second way to project the optimum system is to mathematically calculate the point of equality between the systems. In the example used here, System 1 and System 2 are equal at about 70,500 pounds of output. If we use a graph to determine the equality point, complete accuracy is difficult. For a mathematical solution, we simply need to start with the equation for a straight line ($y = a + bx$). In this particular case, a would be the fixed costs and b would be the variable cost per unit. The x would be the output level. If we want to solve for the point at which the two systems are equal, we can set the two equations up as equal and plug in the cost information appropriate to solve these equations. As is demonstrated here, at approximately 70,500 pounds the two systems are equal, and we see a point of indifference between the two systems:

System 1
Total cost = fixed cost + variable cost/unit × number of units
$$y = 4,200_1 + 0.0315x$$

System 2
$$y = 4,800 + 0.0230x$$

Trade-off point
$$4,800_1 + 0.0230x = 4,200_1 + 0.0315x$$
$$600_1 = 0.0085x$$
$$x = 70,588 \text{ pounds}$$

A particular firm may consider more than two logistics systems at one time. Many examples show a firm considering three or sometimes four systems. We can use the same basic methodology for plotting and mathematically solving for the points of indifference regardless of how many systems we analyze. Further, in a particular situation involving two systems, the cost functions may not necessarily intersect. Hence, one function will be lower than the other over the entire output range. When a firm considers three or more systems, two of them may intersect while the other occurs at a higher level in the quadrant. If we have three intersecting systems. two relevant intersection points or two relevant points of indifference usually occur. A third intersection would occur at a point above some other cost function and would not be relevant.

LOGISTICS IN THE FIRM: FACTORS AFFECTING THE COST AND IMPORTANCE OF LOGISTICS

This section deals with specific factors relating to the cost and importance of logistics. Emphasizing some of the competitive, product, and spatial relationships of logistics can help to explain the strategic role of a firm's logistics functions.

Competitive Relationships

Frequently, people's interpretation of competition is narrow in that they think only of price competition. While the price issue is certainly important, in many markets and circumstances customer service is a very important form of competition. For example, if a company can reliably provide its customers with its products in a relatively short time period, then its customers can often minimize inventory cost. A company should consider minimizing buyer inventory costs to be just as important as keeping product prices low, since minimizing such costs will contribute to more profit or in turn enable the seller to be more competitive. Therefore, customer service is of great importance to the logistics area.

length of order cycle

Order Cycle.   That order cycle length directly affects inventory requirement is a well-accepted principle of logistics management; stated another way, the shorter the cycle, the less inventory is required. Figure 2–12 shows this relationship. We will discuss order cycles in greater detail in the chapter dealing with order processing and information systems. For now, we can define order cycle as the time it takes for a customer to receive an order once he or she has decided to place it. It includes elements such as order transmittal time, order preparation time, and transportation time.

Figure 2–12 shows that longer order cycles require higher inventories. Therefore, if a firm can improve customer service by shortening customer order cycles, its customers should be able to operate with less inventory. It follows, then, that such a cost reduction could be as important as a price reduction.

nature of product

Substitutability.   Substitutability very often affects the importance of customer service. In other words, if a product is similar to other products, consumers may be willing to substitute a competitive product if a stockout occurs. Therefore, customer service is more important for highly substitutable products than for products that customers may be willing to wait for or back order. This is one reason firms spend so much advertising money making customers conscious of their brands. They want consumers to ask for their brands, and, if their brands are temporarily not available, they would like consumers to wait until they are.

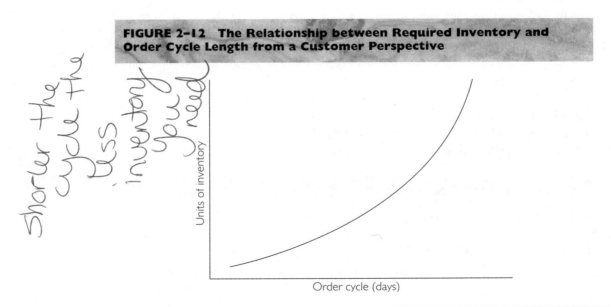

FIGURE 2–12   The Relationship between Required Inventory and Order Cycle Length from a Customer Perspective

Product substitutability varies greatly. Usually, the more substitutable a product, the higher the customer service level required. As far as a logistics manager is concerned, a firm wishing to reduce its lost sales cost, which is a measure of customer service and substitutability, can either spend more on inventory or spend more on transportation.

Inventory Effect. Figure 2–13 shows that by increasing inventory costs (either by increasing the inventory level or by increasing reorder points), firms can usually reduce the cost of lost sales. In other words, an inverse relationship exists between the cost of lost sales and inventory cost. However, firms are generally willing to increase the inventory cost only until total costs start to go up. They are typically willing to spend increasing amounts on inventory to decrease lost sales cost by larger amounts—in other words, up to the point at which the marginal savings from reducing lost sales cost equal the marginal cost of carrying added inventory. **relationship to lost sales**

Transportation Effect. A similar relationship exists with transportation, as we can see in Figure 2–14. Companies can usually trade off increased transportation costs against decreased lost sales costs. For transportation, this additional expenditure involves buying a better service—for example, switching from water to rail, or rail to motor, or motor to air. The higher transportation cost also could result from shipping more frequently in smaller quantities at higher rates. So, as indicated in Figure 2–14, firms can reduce the cost of lost sales by spending more on transportation service to improve customer service. Once again, most firms willingly do this only up to the point where the marginal savings in lost sales cost equal the marginal increment associated with the increased transportation cost. **relationship to transportation**

FIGURE 2–13 The General Relationship of the Cost of Lost Sales to Inventory Cost

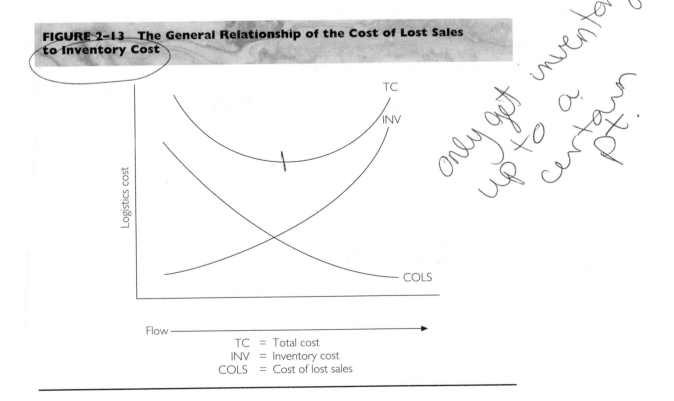

TC = Total cost
INV = Inventory cost
COLS = Cost of lost sales

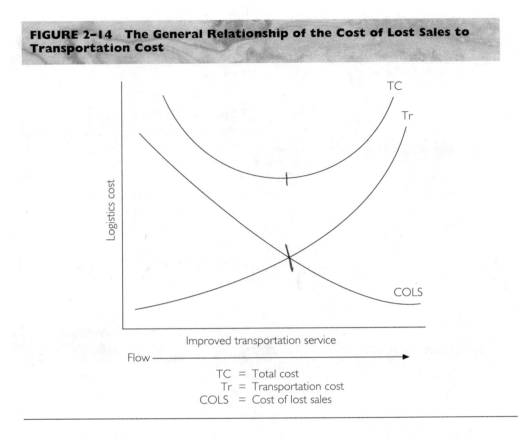

FIGURE 2–14 The General Relationship of the Cost of Lost Sales to Transportation Cost

TC = Total cost
Tr = Transportation cost
COLS = Cost of lost sales

Although showing inventory cost and transportation cost separately is convenient here, companies often spend more for inventory and for transportation almost simultaneously to reduce the cost of lost sales. In fact, improved transportation will usually result in lower inventory cost.* In other words, the situation is much more interactive and coordinated than is indicated here.

Product Relationships

A number of product-related factors affect the cost and importance of logistics. Among the more significant of these are the following: dollar value, density, susceptibility to damage, and need for special handling.

Dollar Value. A number of product aspects will have a direct bearing on logistics cost. First, the product's dollar value will typically affect warehousing costs, inventory costs, transportation costs, packaging costs, and even materials handling costs. As Figure 2–15 indicates, as the product's dollar value increases, the cost in each indicated area will also rise. The actual slope and level of the cost functions will vary from product to product.

---

*The lower inventory costs stem from smaller carrying capacity and faster transit times.

FIGURE 2–15 The General Relationship of Product Dollar Value to Various Logistics Costs

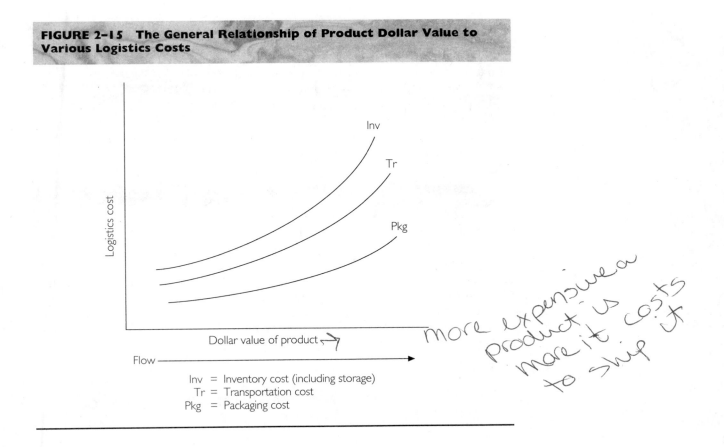

Inv = Inventory cost (including storage)
Tr = Transportation cost
Pkg = Packaging cost

more expensive a product is more it costs to ship it

impact on rates

Transportation rates reflect the risk associated with the movement of goods. There is often more chance for damage with higher-value goods; damage to such goods will cost the transportation company more to reimburse. Transportation companies also tend to charge higher rates for higher-value products because their customers can typically afford to pay a higher rate for such products. A relationship exists between the product value and the rate amount in transportation rate structures.

impact on warehousing

Warehousing and inventory costs will also go up as the dollar value of products increases. Higher value means more capital in inventory, with higher total capital costs. In addition, the risk factor for storing higher-value products will increase the possible cost of obsolescence and depreciation. Also, since the physical facilities required to store higher-value products are more sophisticated, warehousing costs will increase with increased dollar value.

impact on packaging

Packaging cost will also usually increase, because the firm uses protective packaging to minimize damage. A company spends more effort in packaging a product to protect it against damage or loss if it has higher value. Finally, materials handling equipment used to meet the needs of higher-value products is very often more sophisticated. Firms are usually willing to use more capital-intensive and expensive equipment to speed higher-value goods through the warehouse and to minimize the chance of damage.

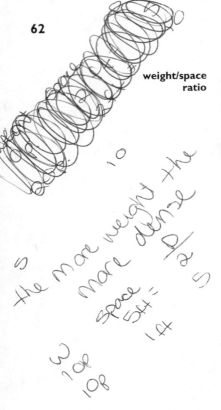

weight/space
ratio

Density.   Another factor that affects logistics cost is density, which refers to the weight/space ratio. An item that is lightweight compared to the space it occupies—for example, household furniture—has low density. The Gillette packaging situation described previously is another good example. Density affects transportation and warehousing costs, as Figure 2–16 shows. As we move from low density to high density, warehousing cost and transportation costs tend to fall.

In establishing their rates, transportation companies consider how much weight they can fit into their vehicles, since they quote their rates in terms of dollars and cents per hundred pounds. Therefore, on high-density items they can afford to give a lower rate per hundred pounds because they can fit more weight into a car. Density also affects warehousing costs. The higher the density, the more weight can fit in an area of warehouse space—hence, the more efficient the use of warehousing space. So both warehousing cost and transportation cost tend to be influenced in the same way by density.

Susceptibility to Damage.   The third product factor affecting logistics cost is susceptibility to damage (see Figure 2–17). The greater the risk of damage, the higher the transportation and warehousing costs. Transportation companies expecting greater product damage will charge higher rates, and warehousing cost will go up either because of damage or because of measures taken to reduce the risk of damage.

FIGURE 2–16   The General Relationship of Product Weight Density to Logistics Costs

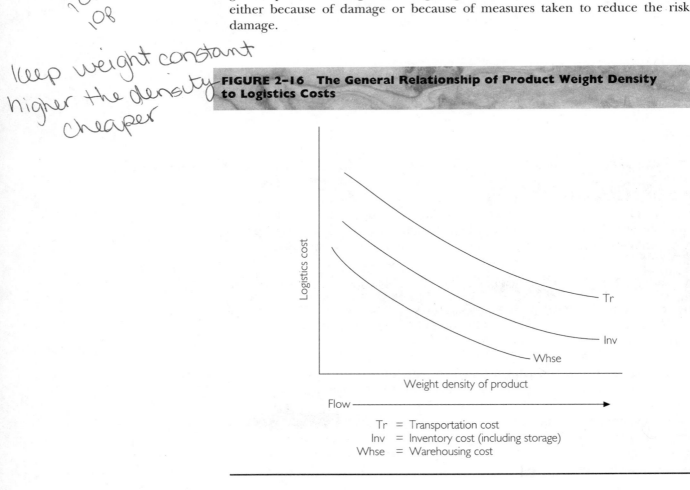

Tr = Transportation cost
Inv = Inventory cost (including storage)
Whse = Warehousing cost

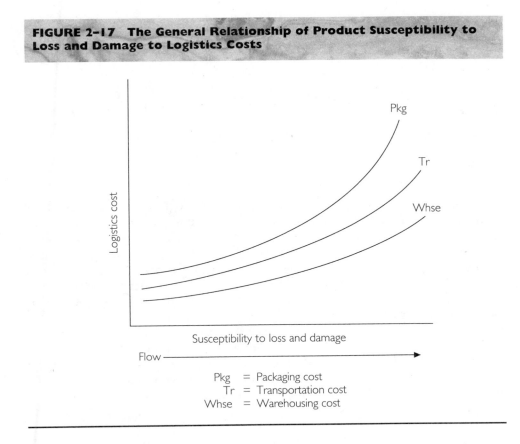

FIGURE 2-17   The General Relationship of Product Susceptibility to Loss and Damage to Logistics Costs

Pkg   = Packaging cost
Tr   = Transportation cost
Whse = Warehousing cost

Special Handling Requirements.   A fourth factor, related to damage susceptibility but somewhat distinct, is special handling requirements for products. Some products may require specially sized transportation units, refrigeration, heating, or stopping in transit. Special handling requirements, whether for transportation or for warehousing, will generally increase logistics cost.

Spatial Relationships

A final topic that is extremely significant to logistics is spatial relationships, the location of fixed points in the logistics system with respect to market and supply points. Spatial relationships are very important to transportation costs, since these costs tend to increase with distance. Consider the following example, which Figure 2–18 illustrates.

Example.   The firm located at B has a $1.50 production cost advantage over firm A, since firm B produces at $7.00 per unit as opposed to $8.50 per unit for firm A. However, firm B pays $1.35 for inbound raw materials ($0.60 + $0.75) and $3.50 for outbound movement to the market, for a total of $4.85 in per unit transportation charges. Firm A pays $0.90 for inbound raw materials and $1.15 for outbound movement, for a total of $2.05 in transportation charges. Firm A's $2.80 transportation cost advantage offsets the $1.50 production cost disadvantage. Firm

FIGURE 2-18   Logistics and Spatial Relations

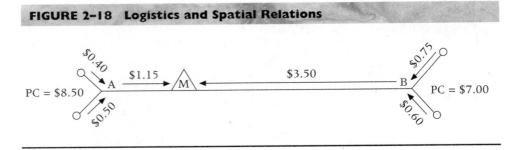

B may wish to look at alternative strategies for its logistics system in order to compete more effectively at M. For example, firm B may base its $3.50/unit transportation cost for shipping to the market on less-than-truckload rates (low-volume movements). The firm may consider using a warehouse at M and shipping in higher-volume rail carload lots at lower transportation costs.

distance factor   The distance factor or spatial relationships may affect logistics costs in ways other than transportation costs. For example, a firm located far from one or more of its markets may need to use a market-oriented warehouse to make customer deliveries in a satisfactory time period. Therefore, distance can add to warehousing and inventory carrying costs. It may also increase order processing costs.

Distance or spatial relationships are of such importance to logistics cost that logistics responsibilities include site location. We will consider location, or site analysis, in some detail at a later point in the text.

SUMMARY

- Logistics has developed as a major area of interest in business since World War II, but there is still much potential to improve logistics systems in companies.
- There are several good definitions of business logistics, including the Seven Rs definition and the Council of Logistics Management definition, which provide a good overview of logistical activities.
- On a macro basis, logistics costs as a percentage of gross domestic product have decreased, which has been beneficial to the economy.
- Improved logistics practices and management have led to the lower relative cost of logistics in the economy.
- Logistics adds place and time value to products and enhances the form and possession value added by manufacturing and marketing.
- Logistics has an important relationship to manufacturing, marketing, finance, and other areas of companies.
- Logistics managers are responsible for a number of important activities, including transportation, inventory, warehousing, materials handling, industrial packaging, customer service, forecasting, and others.
- Logistics systems can be viewed or approached in several different ways for analysis purposes, including materials management versus physical distribution, cost centers, nodes versus links, and channels. All four approaches are viable for different purposes.

- Logistics systems are frequently analyzed from a systems approach, which emphasizes total cost and trade-offs when changes are proposed. Either short-run or a long-run perspective can be used.
- The cost of logistics systems can be affected by a number of major factors, including competition in the market, the spatial relationship of nodes, and product characteristics.

STUDY QUESTIONS

1. Compare and contrast the Seven Rs definition of logistics with the definition provided by the Council of Logistics Management.

2. On a macroeconomic basis, the ratio of inventory to sales has declined over the last 15 years. Is this good or bad? Why? What factors have contributed to this trend?

3. Logistics costs as a percentage of GDP have been decreasing in recent years. What factors have contributed to this relative decline? What does the future hold for logistics costs?

4. Discuss the ways in which logistics contributes to economic value.

5. Manufacturing companies have traditionally used long production runs as a means to gain a cost advantage in the marketplace. What is the impact of these long production runs upon logistics? The more current approach to manufacturing is to have shorter production runs and more flexible setups. What impact does this approach have upon logistics?

6. Physical distribution has a special relationship to marketing. Why is this relationship so special? What is the nature of the overall relationship between logistics and marketing?

7. Logistics comprises a relatively large number of managerial activities. Discuss five of these activities and indicate why they are important to logistics systems.

8. Why would a company want to analyze its logistics system in terms of materials management versus physical distribution?

9. Compare and contrast the static analysis of logistics systems with dynamic analysis.

10. What product characteristics affect logistics costs? Discuss the effect of these characteristics upon logistics costs.

NOTES

1. Peter F. Drucker, "The Economy's Dark Continent," *Fortune* (April 1962): 103.
2. B. J. LaLonde and J. M. Masters, "The 1992 Ohio State University Survey of Career Patterns in Logistics," *Council of Logistics Management Annual Conference Proceedings* (Oak Brook, IL: Council of Logistics Management, 1992): 120–30.
3. D. J. Bowersox et al., *Logistical Excellence* (Burlington, VT: Digital Press, 1992): 8–12.
4. *Purchasing* (November 1994): 66.

5. M. C. Cooper et al., *Strategic Planning for Logistics* (Oak Brook, IL: Council of Logistics Management, 1992): 21–24.

6. Council of Logistics Management, "What's It All About," (Oak Brook, IL, 1992).

7. C. John Langley, Jr., "Evolution of the Logistics Concept," *Journal of Business Logistics* 7, no. 2: 2–4.

8. R. D. Shapiro and J. L. Heskett, *Logistics Strategy* (St. Paul, MN: West Publishing, 1985): 6.

9. Bowersox, *Logistical Excellence*, 28–30.

10. Tim Loar, "Patterns of Inventory Management and Policy: A Study of Four Industries," *Journal of Business Logistics*, vol. 13, no. 2 (1992): 69–95.

11. C. John Langley, Jr., "Adverse Impacts of the Washington Beltway on Residential Property Values," *Land Economics* 52, no. 1 (February 1976): 54–65; and Hays B. Gamble, Owen H. Sauerlender, and C. John Langley, Jr., "Adverse and Beneficial Effects of Highways Reflected by Property Values," *Transportation Research Record Number 508* (Washington, DC: Transportation Research Board, December 1974): 37–48.

12. E. Jerome McCarthy and William E. Perrault, Jr., *Basic Marketing: A Managerial Approach* 9th ed. (Homewood, IL: Richard D. Irwin, 1987): 46–52.

13. Philip Kotler, *Marketing Management: Analysis, Planning, and Control*, 5th ed. (Englewood Cliffs, NJ: Prentice-Hall, 1984): 463–64.

14. Roy Dale Voorhees and Merrill Kim Sharp, "Principles of Logistics Revisited," *Transportation Journal* (Fall 1978), 69–84.

15. J. L. Heskett, Robert M. Ivie, and Nicholas A. Glaskowsky, Jr., *Business Logistics: Management of Physical Supply and Distribution* (New York: Ronald Press, 1973): 26.

16. Heskett, *Business Logistics*, 454–69.

Case 2-1

TREXLER FURNITURE MANUFACTURING COMPANY

Trexler is a small manufacturer of upholstered furniture located in northeastern Pennsylvania. Although founded by J. Austin Trexler in the early 1990s, ownership has passed to Frank Ryan, who had been an executive at a local division of a larger furniture manufacturer. Although annual sales are $2.1 million, the firm has incurred annual losses or turned only minimal profits over the past five years. The product line consists of five major styles, all variants of colonial and traditional designs. Trexler, which has a reputation for quality, commands a relatively high price. Sofas, chairs, and recliners typify Trexler's furniture sizes; however, some small-volume specialty products are also in the line.

Trexler's market lies primarily within a 250-mile radius of the plant, and the firm has 200 active retailer accounts who place orders either for their own showroom floor stock or as customer orders based on floor samples and selections from fabric samples. A typical customer will order two pieces, such as two chairs or a sofa and a chair, but orders for either single or three or more pieces occasionally occur.

A single-plant operation, Trexler employs forty-eight people in trades such as woodworking, sewing, and upholstery. The operation produces nearly custom fur-

---

ADAPTED FROM: Richard R. Young, "Trexler Furniture Manufacturing Co. (A)," (University Park, PA: Penn State University, 1990). Reprinted with permission.

niture in a job-shop-type environment, given the company's relatively low volume and the permutations possible with three sizes, five styles, and approximately 100 different upholstery fabrics. The company ships finished product each day by uncrated furniture carrier.

The Management Meeting

"These setups are killing us," complained Scott Allen at the monthly meeting. "We change tooling several times a day, if not for style, then for size—sofas are different from chairs, which are different from recliners." Scott, the production manager, has been with the firm for many years, having been hired by Mr. Trexler himself.

"We're just a small operation though. What do you expect?" replied Frank Ryan, president, CEO, sole stockholder, and sometime salesman. "Maybe you've got a suggestion?"

"As a matter of fact, I do!" Scott exclaimed. "We could run sofas for one week, then chairs for three or four days, letting recliners fill out the second week, depending on what the current orders look like."

"Sounds okay to me, but what about the various styles?" quizzed Frank.

"We'd run more or less one day for each of the five styles. At the end of two weeks we'd begin the size/style cycle all over again," Scott replied.

Frank turned around and gazed out the window, collecting his thoughts. "That's still a lot of changes, but I suppose a style or a size change is still better than a style and a size change. Any idea what your suggestion could save us?"

"A single change only takes 72 percent of a double. We'd make thirteen in ten working days, compared to as many as three per day currently," interjected Lou Sciota. Although he is a foreman in the woodworking shop, Lou, with his long-term familiarity with the antiquated equipment, also serves as the plant engineer. He added, "Scott is right on this one. We'll produce more with the same labor costs, but with slightly less material due to improved scrap factors from the fewer changeovers."

"All right, guys, you've sold me," said Frank. "Have at it. I admit I've been on everyone's case to improve productivity, and you seem to have been listening."

End of the Quarter

Carol Muzzi, bookkeeper, plant accountant, and inside salesperson, put her spreadsheet down on the desk in front of Frank. "The good news," she explained, "is that our per-seat costs"—units of production are recorded as seats for costing purposes: sofas = 3, chairs = 1—"have been declining. The bad news: inventories are increasing and cash is at an all-time low." Dismayed, she added, "We're going to need a loan against the line of credit just to make payroll this Friday."

Frank looked at the numbers. "Unfortunately, you're right," he said. "What's happening here? If we don't get to the bottom of this and quick, I'll have to get our line of credit extended, and the bank won't be an easy sell. I need some answers right now!"

Case Question

1. Write a report that provides the answers Frank needs. What factors are causing Trexler's inventories to increase while keeping the company's profits at a minimum?

CHAPTER 3

THE INBOUND LOGISTICS SYSTEM

LEARNING OBJECTIVES

After reading this chapter, you should be able to do the following:

- Understand the role and nature of inbound logistics in a supply chain context.

- Explain the different types of inbound systems in a supply chain.

- Discuss the major materials management activities.

- Understand the procurement process.

- Identify the four steps necessary for effective procurement.

- Explain the criteria for evaluating vendors.

- Understand the major inventory techniques associated with materials management.

LOGISTICS PROFILE

THE ROBBINS COMPANY

The global competitive race does not go only to the fastest. "Reliability is the most important dimension of just-in-time service," declares Kevin O'Laughlin, a logistics consultant and partner at Price Waterhouse in Boston. Greater reliability in ocean transport has made it possible for Robbins Co., the Kent, Washington, maker of tunnel-boring machines, to expand from one U.S. plant to four plants worldwide in the past five years and to boost its global market share. Without just-in-time, the system "would not have been cost-effective," says traffic coordinator Russell Blood.

Robbins's basic problem was that its parts were too big and costly to ship by air, and until recently ocean transport was unreliable. The company needs to make reliable deliveries to Europe once or twice weekly from its Washington State plant via transcontinental train to the East Coast of the United States and on to Europe. Because of poor coordination among truck, train, and ocean carriers, containers often failed to reach ports on time. A missed loading could delay a shipment by weeks if an ocean carrier held up an entire voyage to wait for a late container.

Today many ocean transport routes, especially the trans-Atlantic lanes, run like clockwork, with a very high rate of on-time delivery. Even if there are problems, electronic data interchange (EDI) or even a fax keeps shippers like Robbins fully informed so they can make adjustments.

When Robbins started supplying its first European plant, in Great Britain, a few years ago, poor coordination between Robbins managers resulted in frequently missed truck, train, and vessel handoffs. On-time delivery to Europe was only a poor 50 percent, and product arrived up to three weeks late. Now, improved forward planning and coordination have boosted on-time delivery to 92 percent, with most cargo arriving no more than a day off schedule.

Before these changes were made, competing with European rivals for local business was almost impossible. Now the U.S. plant and other suppliers provide low-cost, high-tech parts to Robbins's European plants, enabling them to compete. Robbins has cut global inventories by half and tripled the share of lower-priced goods it sources globally to 30 percent. That figure is expected to rise to more than 50 percent in the next few years.

Not all goes perfectly for Robbins. Despite the creation of a single European market, Robbins and others often find customs to be an onerous impediment. Moving a finished machine from England to Austria recently forced Mr. Blood to head off delivery delays by flying to England for a week to resolve conflicting export procedures demanded by three different British customs officials. Fortunately, close communication with Robbins's London plant by fax helped Mr. Blood foresee the problem before it held up delivery. It's this kind of ability to anticipate problems that keeps global just-in-time going.

ADAPTED FROM: Gregory Miles, "Virtual Logistics," *International Business* (November 1994): 37–40.

Chapter 1 provided an overview of the logistics supply chain and indicated that today's environment requires management of the flow and storage of materials (raw materials, semifinished goods, and finished products) from vendor sources through to the ultimate customer. One convenient way to view the supply chain for a single company is to divide its logistics system into inbound logistics (materials management and procurement) and outbound logistics (customer service and channels of distribution).

The focus of this chapter is upon the inbound side of logistics systems, including procurement or purchasing and the related materials management activities. It is important to note that the inbound and outbound logistics systems share common activities or processes, since both involve decisions related to transportation, warehousing, materials handling, inventory management and control, and

common activities

packaging, as well as some other activities. Each of these common areas will be covered in some detail in subsequent chapters of this book. The purpose of this chapter is to provide an overview of the materials management and procurement activities of an inbound logistics system and to discuss more fully those activities that are especially important on the inbound side, such as procurement and inventory management.

INBOUND LOGISTICS ALONG THE SUPPLY CHAIN

A dimension of the inbound system that deserves consideration at the outset is the differences that exist among the inbound systems of different companies. These differences have important implications for the design and management of logistics supply chains.

mining firm → As you move along a supply chain made up of a series of individual companies (see Figure 3–1), you will see important differences in the inbound systems of the companies. The start of a supply chain could very well be a mining operation involving the extraction of coal or some ore commodity. In this instance, the inbound logistics system is essentially a part of the extractive or production process. Therefore, inbound logistics would be very difficult to separate out for analysis from the mining operation except to the extent that the extractive company purchases supplies for use in the mining process that must be stored and transported prior to the extractive process. An important point here is that extractive companies would be most concerned about their outbound system, which would be involved in delivering appropriate quantities of their commodity at the right time and place to the next firm in the supply chain. The inbound system of the extractive company would probably not receive as much separate attention as would the inbound system at the next firm in the supply chain.

steel firm As we move along this hypothetical supply chain, the next company could be a steel manufacturer. The coal would be an important raw material for this firm, and it would probably transform the coal to coking coal in its coke plant. However, it could also buy coking coal from an intermediary company that buys coal and specializes in producing coking coal. (Obviously, if the latter were true, we would have another company in our supply chain.)

FIGURE 3–1   A Food System Supply Chain

| Coal mine | Steel mill | Container plant | Food processor | Store |

In addition to the coking coal, the steel company would utilize several raw materials from a variety of vendor sources to produce the steel. These materials would have to be procured in appropriate quantities, transported, stored, and their arrivals coordinated via the production planning process in advance of the manufacturing process for producing the steel. Therefore, the steel company would be very much aware of its inbound logistics system and the need to coordinate inbound logistics activities.

The steel company would have some interesting contrasts between its inbound and outbound systems. On the inbound side, the nature of the raw materials, coking coal, iron ore, and so on, are such that they can be shipped in bulk in railcars and barges and stored outside in piles. On the other hand, the finished steel would need more sophisticated transportation, warehouses, inventory control, materials handling, and so on. Therefore, the inbound and outbound logistics systems could have some unique network design requirements.

Once the steel is produced, it would be ready to move along the supply chain **container firm** to the next firm, which could be another manufacturer such as an auto or a container manufacturer. Assuming that the supply chain we are concerned about will ultimately result in food products in a store, the next point would be the container company that produces cans of various sizes for the food processors. It is important to note that the steel company would usually be a part of several supply chains. That is, the steel company may also be selling to auto manufacturers, office supply producers, and other types of manufacturers.

After the can manufacturer, the next step in our supply chain would be the **food firm** food manufacturing plant, where processed food would be added to the cans of various sizes. Food processing companies frequently add labels later, since the same can of peas, for example, could be sold under as many as eight to ten different company labels. By storing the cans as "brights" and adding the labels when orders are received, the level of inventory can be reduced because of the reduction of uncertainty. That is, it is much easier to forecast the total demand for a certain size of canned peas than it is to forecast the demand for each company's labeled cans of peas, since individual market shares change.

Once an order for the peas has been received from a retailer, the labels can **retail store** be added and the peas shipped to the retailer's warehouse or store. When the peas finally end up in the store for sale, we have reached the last point in our supply chain, although you could argue that the cycle is not complete until the can of peas end up in a consumer's home. In fact, in today's environment, that can may be recycled after the peas are consumed and the materials may start back through part of the supply chain again—a reverse logistics system. (A section on reverse logistics systems is included in Chapter 15.)

This rather lengthy discussion of the supply chain illustrates a number of interesting aspects of inbound logistics. It shows that what is inbound for one company is frequently outbound for another company. Also, as we move along the supply chain, we are continually adding value, and the logistics costs will usually also increase because of the higher-value products. In addition, companies may be part of several supply chains.

Another dimension of our discussion of inbound logistics systems that is im- **complexity** portant is the difference in complexity that exists among companies. For example, an automobile manufacturer typically has about 13,000 individual parts in the inbound system in order to assemble or manufacture an automobile. The inbound system for the steel plant mentioned previously is relatively simple compared to that of the auto manufacturer. The steel company has a limited number of raw materials that are shipped in bulk and are stored outside. Some aspects of inbound logistics systems for steel production are challenging, but not nearly as challenging as the inbound system for automobile production.

As was indicated previously, the focus of this chapter is the inbound systems for logistics. We will examine each of the major activities that are a part of inbound systems. The discussion will be limited on some of these activities, such as transportation and warehousing, since these topics will receive extensive discussion in later chapters.

MATERIALS MANAGEMENT

integration   Effective supply chain management requires careful coordination of the inbound system of logistics, which is frequently referred to as materials management, and the outbound system, which is usually called physical distribution. While the focus in this chapter is upon the inbound system, the integration of the inbound and outbound systems is extremely important to the efficient and effective management of the logistics supply chain. Information flow is often the key ingredient to the coordination of inbound and outbound logistics systems. Since information regarding product demand flows down the supply chain from the marketplace or customer, and materials flow up the supply chain, the possibility exists that decisions related to the flow of materials will not be coordinated with the customer information flowing down. When there is a lack of integration, inefficiencies occur, especially with respect to inventory accumulation and/or lack of appropriate customer service levels. In today's complex environment, information needs to flow quickly in both directions for effective coordination.

definition   Materials management can be described as the planning and control of the flow of materials that are a part of the inbound logistics system. Materials management usually includes the following activities: procurement, warehousing, production planning, inbound transportation, receiving, materials quality control, inventory management and control, and salvage and scrap disposal.

Procurement*

importance   Effective procurement of goods and services contributes to the competitive advantage of an organization. The procurement process links members in the supply chain and assures the quality of suppliers in that chain. The quality of the materials and services that are input affects finished product quality and hence customer satisfaction and revenue. Input costs are a large part of total costs in many industries. With the importance of procurement as a determinant of revenues, costs, and supply chain relationships, it is easy to understand why it has recently been receiving more attention from both practitioners and academics.

definition   Procurement can be a complex process that is difficult at times to define, understand, and manage. However, to manage the process, it must be understood;

---

*This section is adapted from R. A. Novack and Stephen W. Simco, "The Industrial Procurement Process," *Journal of Business Logistics* 12, no. 1 (1991): 145–65.

to understand the process, it must be defined. Depending on the circumstances, procurement can be defined, in a narrow sense, as the act of buying goods and services for a firm or, in a broader perspective, as the process of obtaining goods and services for the firm. The procurement process is, however, more than just the culmination of an activity; it is the successful completion of a series of activities that often cut across organizational boundaries. To formalize the definition, then, procurement consists of all those activities necessary to acquire goods and services consistent with user requirements.

Porter, in his value chain, identified the strategic importance of procurement, since it includes such activities as qualifying new suppliers, procuring different types of inputs, and monitoring supplier performance.[1] As such, procurement serves as a critical link between members of the supply chain.

The activities described below for the procurement process apply to the purchase of both goods and services in industrial markets. These activities often cut across both functional boundaries (intrafirm) and organizational boundaries (interfirm) and cannot be effectively completed without input from all parties involved in the transaction. The successful completion of these activities maximizes value for both the buying and selling organizations, thereby maximizing value for the supply chain.

1. *Identify or reevaluate needs.* A procurement transaction is usually initiated in response to either a new or an existing need of a user (by an individual or department within the buyer's firm). In some instances, existing needs must be reevaluated because they change. In either case, once the need is identified, the procurement process can begin. The need can be identified by any of a variety of functional areas in the firm or even by someone outside the firm, for example, by customers.

2. *Define and evaluate user requirements.* Once the need has been determined, its requirements must be represented by some type of measurable criteria. The criteria may be relatively simple—for example, criteria for copy machine paper could be 8½ by 11-inch white paper of a certain bond weight—or they may be very complex if the company is buying a highly technical product. Using these criteria, the procurement professional can communicate the user's needs to potential suppliers.

3. *Decide whether to make or buy.* Before outside suppliers are solicited, the buying firm must decide whether it will make or buy the product or service to satisfy the user's needs. Even with a "make" decision, however, the buying firm will usually have to purchase some types of inputs from outside suppliers. This step has become much more important today, when more companies are outsourcing in order to focus upon their "core" activities.

4. *Identify the type of purchase.* The type of purchase necessary to satisfy the user's needs will determine the amount of time needed for the procurement process and the complexity of the process. The three types of purchases, from least amount of time and complexity to most amount of time and complexity, are (1) a straight rebuy or routine purchase, (2) a modified rebuy, which requires a change to an existing supplier or input, and (3) a new buy, which results from a new user need. In a straight rebuy or modified rebuy, several of the activities discussed in the remainder of this section can be eliminated; for example, there is no need to identify all possible suppliers.

5. *Conduct a market analysis.* A source of supply can operate in a purely competitive market (many suppliers), an oligopolistic market (a few large suppliers), or a monopolistic market (one supplier). Knowing the type of market will help the procurement professional determine the number of suppliers in the market, where the power/dependence balance lies, and which method of buying might be most effective—negotiations, competitive bidding, and so on. The information about market type is not always apparent, and some research may be necessary, using standard library sources such as *Moody's* or information from a trade association.

6. *Identify all possible suppliers.* This activity involves the identification of all possible suppliers that might be able to satisfy the user's needs. It is important at this stage to include possible suppliers that the buying firm has not used previously. Again, identifying all possible suppliers, especially with today's global environment, can be a challenge and may require some research. If the company is small, it may rely upon more common sources of such information, such as the telephone company's yellow pages directory.

7. *Prescreen all possible sources.* When defining and evaluating user requirements (as described in the second activity above), it is important to differentiate between demands and desires. Demands for a product or service are those characteristics that are critical to the user; desires are those that are not as critical and are therefore negotiable. Prescreening reduces the pool of possible suppliers to those that can satisfy the user's demands. In some instances, prescreening can be a relatively simple task. For example, in the case of the copy paper, the supplier will have it on hand regularly or will not have it available dependably. With parts for a computer, the situation may require a series of tests by internal engineering staff.

8. *Evaluate the remaining supplier base.* With the possible pool of suppliers reduced to those that can meet the user's demands, it is now possible to determine which supplier or suppliers can best meet the user's negotiable requirements, or desires. This activity may be accomplished through the use of competitive bidding if the procurement item or items are fairly simple or standard and there is a sufficient number of potential vendors. If these conditions do not exist, more elaborate evaluation may be necessary, using engineering tests or simulated end use situations, for example, to test seat belts for cars.

9. *Choose a supplier.* The choice of supplier also determines the relationship that will exist between the buying and supplying firms and how the "mechanics" of this relationship will be structured and implemented. This activity also determines how the relationships with the nonselected suppliers will be maintained. The actual choice will be based upon criteria to be discussed subsequently, such as quality, reliability, total required price, and so on.

10. *Receive delivery of the product or service.* This activity occurs with the first attempt by the supplier or suppliers to satisfy the user's needs. The completion of this activity also begins the generation of performance data to be used for the next activity.

11. *Make a postpurchase performance evaluation.* Once the service has been performed or the product delivered, the supplier's performance must be evaluated to determine whether it has truly satisfied the user's needs. This also

is the "control" activity. If supplier performance did not satisfy the user's needs, the causes for this variance must be determined and the proper corrective actions implemented.

All of the activities identified in this section are subject to influences beyond the control of the procurement professional. These influences can determine how effectively each activity is performed. They include intraorganizational and interorganizational factors and external factors such as governmental influences. For example, a change in marketing needs or manufacturing process may require repeating all or some of the activities identified above before the first iteration is completed. Financial failure of a potential vendor will also cause problems and necessitate repeated activities.

Managing the Procurement Process. Managing the procurement process can be difficult for a multitude of reasons, ranging from inflexible organizational structures to inflexible organizational cultures. However, most firms should find the process relatively easy. What must be remembered when dealing with these activities is that all firms are different and will have different requirements for the procurement process. A four-step approach can be used and adapted to a firm's particular needs. Based on the previous discussion of the procurement process activities, the following steps can be used to maximize effectiveness.

1. *Determine the type of purchase.* In the procurement process, identifying the type of purchase (the fourth purchase activity) will many times dictate the complexity of the entire process. For example, a straight rebuy situation will mean that all of the procurement activities were completed previously (when the purchase was a new buy or modified rebuy), and the only activities necessary would probably be the fourth, ninth, tenth, and eleventh. A modified rebuy may also not require all of the activities, but a new buy would normally require performing all of the activities discussed earlier.

2. *Determine the necessary levels of investment.* The procurement process requires two major types of investments by the firm: time and information. Time is expended by the individuals involved in making the purchase; the more complex and important the purchase, the more time must be spent on it, especially if it is a new buy. Information can be both internal and external to the firm. Internal information is gathered concerning user requirements and the implications that the purchase will have for the firm. External information concerning the input to be purchased may be gathered from supply chain members, from potential suppliers, and others. The more complex and important the purchase, the more information is needed for the procurement process to be effective. By determining the type of purchase (which is also a function of the user's needs), the procurement professional can determine the levels of investment necessary in the procurement process. Problems can occur when not enough or too much investment is made to satisfy a particular user's needs.

   Determining the level of investment needed in time and information to adequately meet a user's requirements is a firm-specific process. Once the level of investment is decided, the procurement process can take place.

3. *Perform the procurement process.* This is a relatively easy step to describe but can be a complex step to perform, depending on the situation. It includes

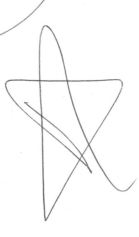

performing those activities necessary to effectively make a purchase and satisfy the user's requirements. This step also allows the procurement professional to collect data on the time and information actually used in making a specific purchase. The ability to measure the actual investment and how well a user's needs were satisfied is important to the final step in managing the procurement process.

4. *Evaluate the effectiveness of the procurement process.* This is a control step that asks two questions: (1) Were the user's needs satisfied? and (2) Was the investment necessary? Remember, the goal is to invest only enough time and information to exactly satisfy the user's needs. If the procurement process was not effective, the cause could be traced to not enough investment, not performing the proper activities, or mistakes made in performing one or more of the activities. In any case, when the procurement process is not effective, the manager must determine why and take corrective actions to make sure that future purchases will be effective. If the purchase satisfied the user's needs at the proper level of investment, the procurement process was effective and can serve as a reference for future purchases.

Thus, although the procurement process is complex, it can be managed effectively as long as the manager develops some systematic approach for implementing it. A key factor in achieving efficiency and effectiveness in this area is the development of successful supplier (vendor) relationships. In fact, many professional procurement/materials managers agree that today's global marketplace requires developing strong supplier relationships in order to create and sustain a competitive advantage. Companies such as NCR and Motorola go so far as to refer to suppliers (vendors) as partners and/or stakeholders in their company. When vendors are "partners," companies tend to rely more upon them to provide input into product design, engineering assistance, quality control, and so on.

The buyer-supplier relationship is so important that it deserves special discussion. (Note that in our previous discussion of procurement activities, supplier relations were involved in at least five of the activities.) The next section provides additional discussion of supplier relationships.

vendor partners   ***Supplier/Vendor Evaluation and Relationships.***   Many successful companies have recognized the key role that procurement plays in supply chain management, and that supplier/vendor relationships are a vital part of successful procurement strategies. "Good vendors do not grow on trees" is an adage that is often quoted by procurement professionals. This is especially true when companies reduce the total number of their suppliers, frequently in conjunction with total quality management (TQM) programs or just-in-time (JIT) production and inventory systems.

The strategy to utilize a smaller number of suppliers/vendors frequently means an alliance or partnership with suppliers/vendors because of the need to assure an adequate supply of quality materials over time at an optimum total acquired cost. The partnership/alliance concept encompasses more than just the procurement process, since partnerships are being developed today throughout the supply chain by companies. For example, partnerships are also evolving with transportation companies, contract logistics companies (third-party providers), and channels of distribution. Consequently, the partnership concept will be explained in some detail in Chapter 15, "Leading Edge Logistics Strategies."

At this stage suffice it to say that procurement professionals today recognize that quality management necessitates quality materials and parts. That is, the final product is only as good as the parts that are used in the process. Also, we need to recognize that the customer satisfaction process begins with procurement.

Another dimension of the supplier relationship is that procurement contributes to the competitive advantage of the company, whether the advantage be one of low cost, differentiation, or a niche orientation (using Porter's generic strategies).[2] Therefore, the procurement management program has to be consistent with the overall competitive advantage that a company is seeking to attain in the marketplace. For example, we would expect that Honda or Toyota would approach procurement differently than would Mercedes Benz or Lexus.

Even with a partnership or strategic alliance with a vendor, certain key criteria need to be considered in any procurement situation. The typical but key vendor/ supplier selection criteria are discussed in the section that follows.

Vendor Selection Criteria. The most important factor in vendor selection is usually   **quality**
quality. As was indicated earlier, quality often refers to the specifications that a user desires in an item (technical specifications, chemical or physical properties, or design, for example). The procurement professional compares the actual quality of a vendor's product with the specifications the user desires. In actuality, quality includes additional factors such as life of the product, ease of repair, maintenance requirements, ease of use, and dependability. In today's TQM environment, not only are quality standards higher, but the supplier may also have to assume the major responsibility for quality.

Reliability comprises delivery and performance history, the second- and third-   **reliability**
ranked factors for most procurement professionals. To prevent production line shutdowns resulting from longer-than-expected lead times, the buyer requires consistent, on-time deliveries. Also, the performance life of the procured product directly affects the quality of the final product, the manufacturer's warranty claims, and repeat sales. Finally, in cases of material malfunction, the buying firm considers the vendor's warranty and claim procedure a reliability measure. Reliability is often considered a part of a total quality management program. It should also be noted that the growing reliance upon foreign vendors presents some special challenges to the achievement of reliability because of the distances involved.

The third major vendor selection criterion, capability, considers the potential   **capability**
vendor's production facilities and capacity, technical capability, management and organizational capabilities, and operating controls. These factors indicate the vendor's ability to provide a needed quality and quantity of material in a timely manner. The evaluation includes not only the vendor's physical capability to provide the material the user needs, but also the vendor's capability to do so consistently over an extended time period. The buying firm may answer this long-run supply concern by considering the vendor's labor relations record. A record of vendor-labor unrest resulting in strikes may indicate that the vendor is unable to provide the material quantity the user desires over a long time period. A firm that buys from this vendor will incur increased inventory costs for storing material in preparation for likely disruptions in the vendor's business due to labor strife. Again, sourcing from global suppliers makes this assessment more challenging.

Financial considerations constitute the fourth major vendor selection criterion.   **financial**
In addition to price, the buying firm considers the vendor's financial position.

Financially unstable vendors pose possible disruptions in a long-run continued supply of material. By declaring bankruptcy, a vendor that supplies materials critical to a final product could stop a buyer's production. This criterion has become especially important in purchasing transportation service from truckload motor carriers, among which there has been a relatively high level of bankruptcies. With the trend toward companies utilizing a smaller number of carriers, the financial failure of such a supplier is a major problem and source of disruption in a supply chain.

desirable qualities   The remaining vendor selection factors may be grouped into a miscellaneous category of desirable, but not always necessary, criteria. Although the buyer might find the vendor's attitude difficult to quantify, attitude does affect the vendor selection decision. A negative attitude, for example, may eliminate a vendor for a buyer's consideration. The impression or image that the vendor projects has a similar effect on vendor selection. The importance of training aids and packaging will depend on the material the buyer is purchasing. For example, packaging is important to buyers of easily damaged material, such as glass, but not important to buyers purchasing a commodity that is not easily damaged, such as coal. Training aids would be significant to a firm selecting vendors to supply technical machinery such as computers and robots, but not to a firm seeking office supplies. Likewise, a buyer would consider the availability of repair service more important when buying technical machinery.

vendor location   Another vendor selection factor is geographical location. This question addresses the issue of whether to buy from local or distant vendors. Transportation cost is one obvious aspect of this issue. Other factors, such as the ability to fill rush orders, meet delivery dates, provide shorter delivery times, and utilize greater vendor-buyer cooperation, favor the use of local suppliers. However, distant vendors may provide lower prices, greater technical ability, greater supply reliability, and higher quality. This is again a choice faced more frequently in today's global environment.

factor importance   The relative importance of the vendor selection factors will depend upon the material the buyer is purchasing. When a buyer purchases a computer, for example, technical capability and training aids may be more important than price, delivery, and warranties. Conversely, a buyer of office supplies would probably emphasize price and delivery more than the other factors.

All of the criteria just discussed are important or can be important in certain procurement situations. However, the one criterion that generates the most discussion and/or frustration for procurement specialists is price or cost. Therefore, some extended discussion of this criterion is necessary.

The Special Case of Procurement Price*

We will begin by identifying the four generic sources of prices in procurement situations. This is somewhat basic but important to understand. The discussion of price becomes more complex when one adds an analysis of total acquired cost or value in the procurement process from a supply chain perspective. Total acquired cost and value will be discussed after our description of price sources.

---

*This section is adapted from J. L. Cavinato, "A Total Cost/Value Model for Supply Chain Competitiveness," *Journal of Business Logistics* 13, no. 2 (1992): 285–99.

Sources of Price.   Purchasing managers utilize four basic procedures to determine potential vendors' prices: commodity markets, price lists, price quotations, and negotiations. Commodity markets exist for basic raw materials such as grain, oil, sugar, and natural resources including coal and lumber. In these markets, the forces of supply and demand determine the price that all potential vendors will charge. Reductions in the supply of these materials or increases in demand usually result in increased prices; the converse is true for increases in supply or decreases in demand. **commodity markets**

Price lists are published prices that are generally used with standardized products such as gasoline or office supplies. The vendor's catalog describes the items available and lists their prices. Depending on the status, buyers may receive a purchaser discount from the list price. For example, a vendor may give a 10 percent discount to small-volume buyers (less than $1,000 per month) and a 35 percent discount to large-volume buyers (more than $10,000 per month). **price list**

Purchasers use the price quotation method for both standard and specialty items. It is particularly useful in promoting competition among suppliers. The process begins with the buyer sending potential vendors requests for quotes (RFQ). An RFQ contains all the necessary information regarding the specifications the purchaser requires and the manner in which potential suppliers are to present their offers. In turn, the vendors examine the cost they will incur in producing the material, considering the quantity the purchaser will order, the purchase's duration, and other factors that will affect the vendor's profitability. Finally, the purchaser compares the vendor's quoted price and offer specifications with those of other vendors. **price quotations**

The fourth procedure, negotiation, is useful when the other methods do not apply or have failed. Negotiation is particularly effective when the buyer is interested in a strategic alliance or long-term relationship. The negotiation process can be time-consuming, but the potential benefits can be significant in terms of price and quality. Negotiation is becoming more widely used by logistics managers buying goods and transport services. **negotiation**

The objective of the procurement process is to purchase goods and services at the "best" price, which may not be the lowest price per unit at the vendor source. This is particularly true from a global supply chain perspective. In all four settings described above, the base price needs to be evaluated in a total acquired cost context.

A generalized spectrum of expanding procurement approaches to the supply chain concept is presented in Figure 3–2. At the first level, the firm evaluates procurement and logistics functions simply on the basis of lowest price or lowest cost, without strong regard to the total costs to the firm. In this context, it is difficult to attain a total cost savings unless a manager or group becomes directly responsible for the two or more interfacing functions that might offer a total cost savings. As a company attempts to move from the lowest base or unit price to taking a supply chain perspective to create highest value, the procurement function becomes more strategic in nature.

For customer satisfaction, all costs and factors that affect costs and create value should be captured in the total acquired cost. As Figure 3–2 indicates, a hierarchy of costs and other factors build upward from raw materials through manufacturing, to distribution, to final marketing and selection and use by the ultimate customer in order to determine total acquired cost and the highest total value. The

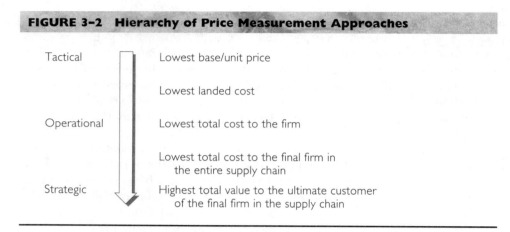

FIGURE 3-2   Hierarchy of Price Measurement Approaches

following discussion starts with the base cost and delineates the additional direct and indirect costs that need to be considered:

Traditional basic input costs. This is the primary price of the product or materials as paid by the firm. It is the traditional price buyers seek through bidding, negotiating, or in requests for quotes. It is easily measured, and it has long been the hallmark against which buyer performance is measured. But in a supply chain setting it is only one factor for the firm to evaluate and consider in the acquisition process.

Direct transaction costs. These are the costs of detecting, transmitting the need for, and processing the material flow in order to acquire the goods. It includes the process of detecting inventory need, requisitioning, preparing and transmitting the order documentation to the supplier, receiving the acknowledgment, handling shipping documents, and receiving information about input to inventory. This area was made more efficient during the 1980s with the advent of internal electronic mail systems that automated the purchasing requisition and order transmission process. Users inside the firm use electronic means to transmit their needs to purchasing. EDI is an extension of this process outbound to the supplier.

The use of blanket or systems contracting can also reduce transaction costs. These include direct ordering by users to suppliers, single consolidated billing, and user inspection and checking. Direct transaction costs are overhead types of costs that are not easily visible, but they represent time and effort that is not available for more productive value-added activities. Suppliers and interfacing carriers that reduce the need for these activities represent value to the buying firm.

Supply relational costs. These are the costs of creating and maintaining a relationship with a supplier. They include travel, supplier education, and the establishment of planning and operational links between purchasing and the supplier's order entry operation, as well as other links, including ones to traffic, engineering, research, and product development in both firms. In traditional purchasing settings, this includes the process of evaluating and certifying a supplier for quality and preferred supplier programs.

Landed costs. The inbound transportation flow includes two key cost elements: the actual transportation cost and the sales/F.O.B. terms. There are four different transportation options with inbound movements, supplier-selected for-hire carrier or private carrier and buyer-selected for-hire carrier or private carrier.

The sales terms define which firm owns the goods during transportation as well as invoice payment requirements. Transportation terms pertain to the carrier in the move between the supplier and buyer firm. There are nearly a dozen possible transportation terms that include different carrier payment and loss and damage claim options. Each one presents different relative costs to each party in the linkage, and for supply chain purposes the one that can perform the task or own the goods at the lowest overall cost has an advantage that can contribute to the overall chain. Both sales and transportation terms must be considered, and there are different direct costs, responsibilities, and indirect implicit costs of cash flow that are affected by each one of them.

Quality costs/factors. Quality pertains to the conformance of goods to a desired specification. It includes the cost of conformance, nonconformance, appraisal, and ultimate use costs. The required quality specification is often balanced against what the supplier can easily provide nearly 100 percent of the time. Often a product specification that is extremely tight requires extra costs but results in higher quality, which may reduce total cost.

Operations/logistics costs. This group includes four key areas:
- Receiving and make-ready costs are the costs of those flow activities occurring between the inbound transportation delivery of a good and its availability for use by production or other processes. These include the cost of unpacking, inspecting, counting, sorting, grading, removing and disposing of packaging materials (strapping, banding, stretch-shrink wrapping, pallets, etc.) and moving the good to the use point. A streamlined system such as direct forklift delivery to a production line is an example of an efficient receiving/make-ready process. Some leading edge carriers provide information links to the firm that include inspection checks, sequencing of the loads, and final count checks so that receiving processes can be reduced or eliminated.
- Lot size costs directly affect space requirements, handling flow, unit price, and related cash flows. These are a major cost of inventories.
- Production costs can be affected by suppliers of even seemingly similar goods. Extruded plastic for high-quality towel rods is an example. The plastic is an extruded tube that must be inflated with air and slipped over a metal or wooden rod. Original raw material quality, differing production processes, and in-transit humidity can cause two suppliers' goods to affect the production line significantly. One might allow assembly of 200 units per hour, while another might split or not form properly, wasting 10 percent of the sleeves and requiring the production line to operate at a slower speed. Thus, each one has a different cost of production operation.
- Logistics costs are also important in both upstream and downstream settings. These are cost factors that are affected by product size, weight, cube, and shape and their resulting impact upon transportation, handling, storage, and damage costs. Purchased goods and packaging materials have a direct bearing upon these subsequent process costs.

All firms in the supply chain add cost, and hopefully, value to a product as it moves through the supply chain. Value is added by reducing total acquired cost or by enhancing the function of the product. Each firm in the supply chain can contribute to or detract from these factors. The key is to focus downstream in the supply chain, but it is also important to note the key role that the procurement process can play at each point along the supply chain by being aware of a product's total acquired cost. Ideally, the focus should be upon the total value at the end of the supply chain. Therefore, the analysis should also include indirect financial costs (payment terms), tactical input costs (vendor capabilities), and strategic business factors (factors that cause customers to buy the product).

Other Materials Management Activities

As was indicated at the outset of this discussion, price can be a complex factor, since other aspects have to be considered as they relate to the base price. Thus far, the discussion of materials management functions has focused solely upon procurement. We will now turn to the additional materials management activities.

Warehousing. The *warehousing* function concerns the physical holding of raw materials until a firm uses them. Chapter 7 discusses general warehousing functions and decision areas. Although storing the raw materials a manufacturer will use in the production process is basically the same as storing finished products, raw materials storage and finished goods storage differ notably in terms of the type of facility each requires, the value of the stored items, and product perishability.

facilities required   Basic raw materials such as coal, sand, or limestone normally require an open-air warehouse facility; that is, a firm would merely dump the basic raw materials on the ground. Thus, the facility cost for storing basic raw materials is lower than the facility cost for storing other materials—finished goods, components, and other semifinished products, for example—that require an elaborate enclosed structure.

The value of raw materials is usually lower than that of finished goods, since the manufacturer enhances the value of the finished material, or processed raw material, during the manufacturing process. Last, basic raw materials usually suffer less damage and loss than finished goods because raw materials have lower value and need no protection from the elements.

Chapter 7 will discuss the warehousing function and the ways in which its activities and decisions affect logistics systems.

Production Planning and Control. In a manufacturing environment, *production planning and control* involves coordinating product supply with product demand. As Figure 3–3 shows, the starting point of the production planning and control process is the demand for the finished product the company produces and sells. This demand is the process's independent variable, since the seller cannot control customer demand.

The manufacturer must forecast, or estimate, customer demand. This sales forecast should indicate the sales amount the manufacturer expects for each item and the time period the sales projection covers. After establishing this independent customer demand, the manufacturer can provide the finished product supply either from available inventory or by producing the product.

FIGURE 3-3 Overview of Production Planning and Control

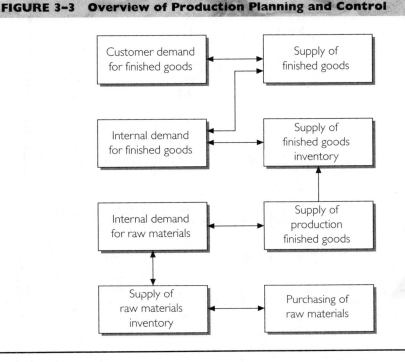

Thus, external demand establishes an internal demand for a finished product; and the manufacturer fills this demand from the existing stocks or from new production.

When demand requires production, the production scheduling manager uses the sales forecast to develop a production schedule. A production planner's main concerns include the following:

- Number of units of a specified product to be produced
- Time intervals over which production will occur
- Availability of materials and machines to produce the number of units required within the specified time frame

Production control results as the production manager specifies time intervals and develops order schedules for raw materials to supply the production schedule.

For example, suppose that sales forecasts estimate that a firm will sell 10,000 units of product A and 30,000 units of product B in March. The firm makes both products on the same machine, which produces 10,000 units per week. The production planner first determines how much, if any, production the firm requires to satisfy customer demand and to maintain target inventory levels. In this example, low inventory levels require the firm to produce all 40,000 units. Additionally, a special promotion has depleted product A's inventory quickly, giving product A scheduling priority. However, vendor labor strikes have made the material for product A unavailable until week 2. As a result, the production planner first schedules one week of product B, followed by one week of product A and then two weeks of product B. Obviously, this is a simple example.

Traffic. The *traffic* function manages the inbound transportation of materials. Transportation originates with the materials vendor, and the movement's destination is the buyer's plant. The inbound traffic activity supports the firm's supply effort in that the inbound transportation bridges the spatial and temporal gap existing between the buyer and the vendor, or seller.

The management of inbound traffic requires transportation knowledge and expertise similar to that necessary to handle the movement of finished goods outbound from the plant. The traffic manager must decide about the transportation mode, the routes, the rates, claims handling, carrier services, cost analysis, and regulations. Chapters 9 and 10 discuss these factors in detail.

vendor control In some situations, the vendor controls inbound transportation. F.O.B. delivered terms of sale characterize such cases. When the buyer relinquishes the traffic function to the vendor, the buyer assumes that the vendor will ship the materials as cost-efficiently as possible. However, such an assumption is not always true. The buyer should periodically analyze the cost-effectiveness of the vendor's transportation decision.

modal choice For basic raw materials, the traffic activity may involve rail or water transportation, the modes companies most commonly utilize to ship large volumes of low-value, high-density products, such as coal or sand. With the advent of rail deregulation, many of these shipments are moving into plants under contract rates with the railroads. The contracts usually specify providing a specific rate and service in return for a guarantee that the shipper will tender the carrier a guaranteed amount of freight.

rush shipments Finally, inbound traffic is normally under less pressure to provide "rush" shipments than is outbound traffic. The demand for raw materials is much more stable and predictable than the demand for finished goods, since economies of production dictate long production runs, which give way to fixed production schedules. However, inbound traffic must occasionally handle a rush shipment—if a plant receives damaged raw materials, for example. Also, with increased use of JIT, inbound transportation requires much stricter schedules. Occasionally, when a problem develops, inbound traffic must expedite (rush) a shipment.

inspection *Receiving.* The *receiving* process involves the actual physical receipt of the purchased material from the carrier. The receiving clerk, who must ensure that the goods a firm receives were those ordered and shipped, compares the materials indicated on the buyer's purchase order and the vendor's packing slip with the material the buyer has actually received. If discrepancies exist, the receiving department notifies the purchasing department, the material's users, and the accounts payable department.

damage claims Another critical inspection during the receiving process involves examining the received material for any physical damage. As will be discussed in Chapter 9, claims against the carrier for damage are easier to make if the receiving clerk notes on the bill of lading that the buyer received the shipment in damaged condition. When such a notation appears on the bill of lading, the carrier is presumed guilty of damaging the material. Any legal action places the burden on the carrier to prove that the carrier was not guilty of damaging the freight. Not noting damage on the bill of lading does not preclude the payment of a damage claim, but it puts an additional burden on the receiver (or owner) of the material to prove that the shipment was damaged when the carrier delivered it. Inbound traffic departments and receiving departments usually coordinate freight claims handling activities.

Quality Control. The *quality control* function, like the receiving function, attempts to ensure that the items a firm receives are those the firm ordered. However, the quality control function is directly concerned with defining the product's quality in terms of dimensions, design specifications, chemical or physical properties, reliability, ease of maintenance, ease of use, brand, market grade, and industry standard. The quality control area's specific concern is whether or not the product received meets the quality standards the buyer and seller set forth in the purchase agreement.

quality standards

The quality of the materials a manufacturer procures directly affects the quality of the finished product, and consequently affects the sale of the finished product. If a firm sells a defective product, the product's buyer will become dissatisfied and may refuse to purchase the firm's product in the future. In addition, a manufacturer who uses inferior materials in production may be legally liable for a hazardous or unreliable product. Thus, quality control function responsibilities cover the spectrum from market to legal concerns.

quality implications

Normally, inspecting each item that a buyer purchases is neither possible nor desirable. Quality inspectors usually examine a limited sample of the items purchased. For example, a quality inspector wanting to determine whether the life of a given vendor's light bulbs met longevity specifications would test a sample of the vendor's light bulbs. The quality control department would statistically examine the results and, on the basis of the tested sample, would decide to accept or reject the order received. The increased emphasis on quality in recent years has required vendors to develop their own statistical quality control programs. Today, many buyers insist upon total or 100 percent quality.

sample

Salvage and Scrap Disposal. The final activity in the materials management function involves disposing of *salvage, scrap,* excess, and obsolete materials. Although primarily concerned with buying, the materials management department has assumed this selling responsibility, since most marketing or sales departments must concentrate on selling the firm's finished products.

value of scrap

Scrap and salvage material that is useful to others has a certain value, and the disposal of these items provides income for the firm. The recent recycling trend has provided a ready market for many scrap and salvage items. For example, companies are using used oils and other scrap items such as olive pits and corncobs as fuel sources. And, as recent years of double-digit inflation have sent new equipment prices beyond the ability of many potential buyers to pay, more companies are buying or salvaging used equipment.

Certain scrap materials cannot be sold but must be disposed of in a safe and prescribed manner. One such commodity group is hazardous wastes—materials that are ignitable, corrosive, reactive (volatile), or toxic. Disposing of these hazardous materials is quite costly, and the generator of such materials is under specific legal liability to dispose of them properly.

disposal

The materials management function, as we indicated, occurs on the inbound side of the logistics pipeline. Customer service and distribution activity channels are on the pipeline's outbound side. But a firm must tightly coordinate both inbound and outbound logistics in today's highly competitive marketplace.

ON THE LINE

JIT II Comes of Age

Picture this. You're a purchasing manager for ACME Manufacturing. It's Monday morning, and for the first time in your 20-year purchasing career you arrive at the office knowing that:

- You won't receive an angry call from manufacturing about a quality reject on parts you bought.
- You won't get a panic call from a production planner wondering if you could possibly get your hands on 15,000 extra parts by tomorrow because ACME's biggest customer just revised its order.
- You won't get a call from your supplier informing you that parts you're expecting on Tuesday hit a transportation snag and won't arrive until Thursday.
- You won't need to call your supplier looking for parts that should have arrived on Friday.
- You won't receive an announcement from your supplier about how market conditions are such that your price will rise 10 percent and you're going on allocation.
- You won't receive a specification from design engineering for the next innovation in fasteners.

Instead of spending your day troubleshooting or otherwise occupied with non-value-added or negative-value activities, you will develop sources to support new products, analyze and improve materials management processes, and build market expertise that will benefit your company in future negotiations with suppliers.

You have time to dedicate to these value-added supply management activities because—a few years back—you took a big risk which turns out not to have been a very big risk at all. Instead of hiring buyers to support your department's increasing workload, you decided to empower supplier partners within your operation. In essence, you asked your long-term supply allies to dedicate experienced professionals to manage planning, transaction processing, and troubleshooting tasks associated with their supply programs. Where appropriate, these supplier employees operate on your floor space; in other cases, they use electronic links to manage these tasks from the supplier's site.

Now, if ACME's plant encounters a parts quality reject, it calls the supplier's on-site person. If your biggest customer revises its order unexpectedly, the supplier's dedicated employee may arrange an emergency production run at his or her plant. You don't fret or expedite late shipments, because your supplier is so in tune with your requirements that it no longer makes mistakes; in fact, your supplier compensates for anomalies in your materials planning system. And you won't encounter a spec for a specialty fastener (where standard will suffice) because your supplier's employee is available when ACME design engineers need answers.

If it sounds implausible, think again. Some of the nation's most innovative companies have been doing this for years. BOSE Corporation—a maker of premium audio products headquartered in Framingham, Massachusetts—began empowering suppliers back in 1986. BOSE director of purchasing and logistics Lance Dixon dubbed the practice JIT II because he saw it as a logical extension of the disciplines critical to an agile manufacturing environment (JIT, partnering, concurrent engineering). Today, BOSE has nine JIT II relationships with suppliers of plastics, metals, printing, computers and software, office products, and an array of transportation services.

SOURCE: Reprinted with permission of *Purchasing* (October 20, 1994): 41–42. Copyright © by Cahners Publishing Company.

A good example of the importance of and potential for integrating the supply chain is the Greencastle, Pennsylvania, facility of Corning Glass's Consumer Products Division. The giant Greencastle facility (warehouse, packaging center, and distribution center all in one) functions as a hub receiving about 300 million pounds of products each year and shipping about fifty million packaged sales units to its customers.

Having traditionally focused on the pipeline's customer service side, Corning Glass has in recent years recognized the importance of controlling materials management. As a part of a newly adopted JIT strategy, Corning has been reducing the number of its vendors/suppliers. The result has been an increase in inventory turns (velocity), as well as cost reductions and better quality. Customer service time has not suffered a bit; in fact, it has improved because of Corning's increased packaging line flexibility.

THE SPECIAL CASE OF INVENTORY

The management of inventory levels in the supply chain has often been the underlying rationale or "rallying cry" for the focus upon supply chain management. The interest in reducing inventory levels along the supply chain is indicative of the importance of inventory as a cost of doing business. In many companies, inventory is the first or second largest asset. As you will see in Chapters 5 and 6, inventory is an investment similar to a piece of equipment. Significant costs are associated with holding inventory.

Companies, therefore, can reduce their costs of doing business and improve their return on investment or assets (ROI/ROA) in many cases by decreasing inventory levels. It should be noted, however, that the investment in inventory can add value by reducing costs in other areas, such as manufacturing and transportation, or enhance sales through better customer service. Therefore, a balanced view is necessary when making inventory decisions, one that recognizes both the cost implications and potential benefits of maintaining inventory in the supply chain.

While inventory has been and will be referred to directly and indirectly in this text and will be the principal subject of two chapters, some extended discussion is necessary in this chapter. Materials management (inbound logistics) plays a major role in driving inventory levels up or down in a supply chain. It is generally recognized that final customer demand should be the magnet that pulls inventory through the pipeline, but production planners, schedulers, and purchasing agents sometimes operate somewhat independently of the outbound logistics system, as was indicated previously in this chapter. When a noncoordinated approach is taken, inventory levels can easily increase without improving customer service or lowering costs in another area.

In this section, we will examine several approaches to inventory control that have special relevance to materials management: just-in-time (JIT) systems and materials requirements planning (MRP) systems. Some reference will also be made to distribution resource planning (DRP) because of its relationship to MRP. Further discussion of DRP will be provided in Chapter 4, which covers outbound systems.

The Just-In-Time Approach

Perhaps the most widely discussed, innovative approach to inventory management is the *just-in-time*, or JIT, approach. In today's business environment people often refer to a JIT manufacturing process, JIT inventories, or a JIT delivery system. The commonsense phrase "just-in-time" suggests that inventories should be available when a firm needs them—not any earlier, nor any later. This section emphasizes additional factors that characterize a true just-in-time system.

Definition and Components of JIT Systems. Generally, just-in-time systems are designed to manage lead times and to eliminate waste. Ideally, product should arrive exactly when a firm needs it, with no tolerance for late or early deliveries. Many JIT systems place a high priority on short, consistent lead times. This may help to explain the recent popularity of "quick response" systems for inventory decision making.

Kanban

The just-in-time concept is an Americanized version of the Kanban system, which the Toyota Motor Company developed in Japan. *Kanban* refers to the informative signboards attached to carts delivering small amounts of needed components and other materials to locations within Japanese plants. Each signboard precisely details the necessary replenishment quantities and the exact time when the resupply activity must take place.

JIT operations

Production cards (*kan* cards) establish and authorize the amount of product to be manufactured or produced; requisition cards (*ban* cards) authorize the withdrawal of needed materials from the feeding or supply operation. Given a knowledge of daily output volumes, these activities can be accomplished manually, without the need for computer assistance. Finally, an *Andon* system, or light system, is used as a means to notify plant personnel of existing problems—a yellow light for a small problem, and a red light for a major problem. Either light can be seen by personnel throughout the plant. In this way, workers are advised of the possibility of an interruption to the production/manufacturing process, if the problem warrants such action.[3]

fundamental concepts

Experience indicates that effectively implementing the JIT concept can dramatically reduce parts and materials inventories, work in process, and finished product. In addition, the Kanban and just-in-time concepts rely heavily on the quality of the manufactured product and components, and also on a capable and precise logistics system to manage materials and physical distribution.

Four major elements underpin the just-in-time concept: zero inventories; short lead times; small, frequent replenishment quantities; and high quality, or zero defects. JIT, a modern approach to distribution, production, inventory, and scheduling management, is an operating concept based on delivering materials in exact amounts and at the precise times that companies need them—thus minimizing inventory costs. JIT can improve quality and minimize waste, and can completely change the way a firm performs its logistics activities. JIT, as practiced by the Japanese, is more comprehensive than an inventory management system. It includes a comprehensive culture of quality, vendor partnerships, and employee teams.

similarity to two-bin system

The JIT system operates in a manner very similar to the two-bin or reorder point system. The system uses one bin to fill demand for a part; when that bin is empty (the stimulus to replenish the part), the second bin supplies the part. Toyota has been very successful with this system because of its master production schedule, which aims to schedule every product, every day, in a sequence that intermixes all parts. Producing these products in small quantities through short production runs also creates a relatively continuous demand for supplies and component parts. In theory, the ideal lot size or order size for a JIT-based system is one unit. Obviously, this encourages firms to reduce or eliminate setup costs and incremental ordering costs.

reducing lead times

By adhering to extremely small lot sizes and very short lead times, the just-in-time approach can dramatically reduce lead times. For example, when manufacturing forklift trucks, Toyota experienced a cumulative material lead time of one month, top to bottom, including final assembly, subassembly, fabrication, and purchasing. American manufacturers of forklift trucks cited lead times ranging from six to nine months.[4]

In actuality, most individuals who have never studied inventory control systems do have exposure to JIT in their place of residence. The public water company and the electric company provide their "product" on a demand-responsive, just-in-time basis that does not require us to hold inventory. Meters monitor what we use, and we are charged accordingly. On the other hand, if we use bottled water or bottled gas, we may not be able to get them on a JIT basis.

JIT versus Traditional Approaches to Inventory Management. Table 3–1 highlights key ways in which the JIT philosophy differs from traditional inventory management in U.S. firms. This section discusses the critical differences.

First, JIT attempts to eliminate excess inventories for both the buyer and the seller. Some people feel that the JIT concept simply forces the seller to carry inventory that the buyer previously held. However, successful JIT applications will significantly reduce inventory for both parties.

reduce inventories

Second, JIT systems typically involve short production runs and require production and manufacturing activities to change frequently from one product to the next. Historically, U.S. manufacturing operations have benefited from the economies associated with lengthy production runs. Controlling and minimizing the cost of frequent changeovers is critical to a JIT program's success.

shorter production runs

Third, JIT minimizes waiting lines by delivering materials and components when and where firms need them. U.S. automobile manufacturers using the JIT approach, for example, typically have replenishment inventory delivered exactly where the manufacturer needs parts for finished product.

minimize waiting lines

Fourth, the JIT concept uses short, consistent lead times to satisfy the need for more inventory in a timely manner. This is why suppliers tend to concentrate their facilities within a radius near manufacturing facilities planning to use the JIT approach. For example, once the Saturn Corporation, a wholly owned subsidiary of

short, consistent lead times

TABLE 3-1 Traditional versus JIT Attitudes and Behaviors

Factor	Traditional	JIT
1. Inventory	Asset	Liability
Safety stock	Yes	No
2. Production runs	Long	Short
Setup times	Amortize	Minimize
Lot sizes	EOQ	1-for-1
3. Queues	Eliminate	Necessary
4. Lead times	Tolerate	Shorter
5. Quality inspection	Important parts	100% process
6. Suppliers/customers	Adversaries	Partners
Supply sources	Multiple	Single
Employees	Instruct	Involve

ADAPTED FROM: William M. Boyst, Jr. III, "JIT American Style." Proceedings of the *1988 Conference of the American Production & Inventory Control Society* (APICS, 1988): 468.

General Motors Corporation, decided to locate its plant in central Tennessee, many potential suppliers planned to locate new facilities in the surrounding area.

quality

Fifth, JIT-based systems rely on high-quality incoming products and components and on exceptionally high-quality inbound logistics operations. The fact that JIT systems synchronize manufacturing and assembly with timely, predictable receipt of inbound materials reinforces this need.

win-win relationships

Sixth, the JIT concept requires a strong, mutual commitment between the buyer and seller, one that emphasizes quality and seeks win-win decisions for both parties. JIT success requires a concern for minimizing inventory throughout the distribution channel (or the supply channel); JIT will not succeed if firms only push inventory back to another channel member.

inventory savings

Examples of JIT Successes.   Implementing the JIT concept has resulted in notable successes in the United States.[5] One such success occurred at Apple Computer's Macintosh plant in Fremont, California, where the company's goal of achieving twenty-five annual inventory turnovers translated into a reduction in float from ten weeks to two weeks, and a payback for the $20 million plant in just eighteen months. During the mid-1980s, General Motors Corporation credited JIT for the fact that its total raw material, work in process, and finished goods inventory increased by only 6 percent over two years, while production levels increased by 100 percent.

rail example

Other examples include a thirty-two minitrain that Conrail operates between a parts facility in Kalamazoo, Michigan, and a General Motors Oldsmobile plant in Lansing, Michigan.[6] The operation involves no railcar switching, and Conrail has successfully met its customers' pickup and delivery times.

motor carriers

Innovative motor carriers have designed supply systems that effectively fulfill JIT requirements. For example, Ryder Distribution Resources provides all inbound logistical support for direct materials moving into Saturn Corporation's plant in Spring Hill, Tennessee.[7] Similarly, Averitt Express, a Tennessee-based provider of high-quality regional and interregional freight transportation services, designed and operates a system for Saturn to ensure that indirect materials moving into the same plant meet JIT-based priorities.

Based on the availability of high-quality, dependable transportation services that can fit a JIT-based production system's precise demands, various automobile manufacturers have justified eliminating several previously significant freight consolidation systems. The functions of these centers have been replaced by the delivery of needed parts precisely when and where manufacturers need them.[8]

Figure 3–4 shows how a firm can use a transportation strategy known as the orderly pickup concept to meet JIT-based manufacturing needs. The diagram shows how a firm may use time-sequenced motor carrier pickup from suppliers in conjunction with rail-motor intermodal service to meet JIT requirements.

Some mention should also be made of the fact that not all JIT systems have been successfully implemented, nor can JIT be used in every situation. Successful implementation of JIT requires an integrated, coordinated effort among several functions in a company and members of the supply chain.

Summary and Evaluation of JIT.   The just-in-time concept can enable logistics managers to reduce unit cost and to enhance customer service. A close examination of JIT-based approaches shows that they resemble the more basic reactive systems

FIGURE 3–4 The Orderly Pickup Concept

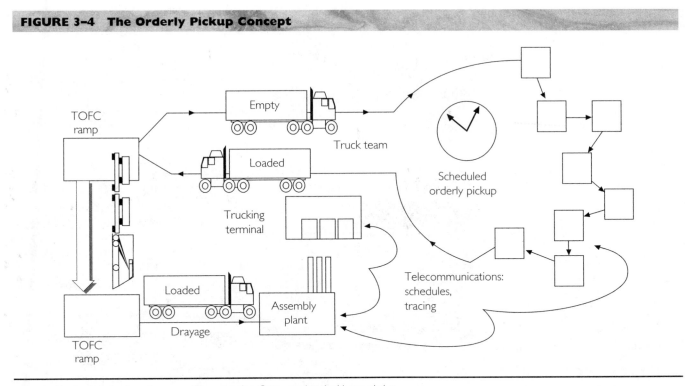

SOURCE: Charles B. Lounsbury, Leaseway Transportation Corp., reprinted with permission.

such as the economic order quantity (EOQ) and fixed order quantity approaches, since JIT is demand responsive.

comparison with traditional approaches

The principal difference between JIT and the more traditional approaches is the JIT commitment to short, consistent lead times and to minimizing or eliminating inventories. In effect, it saves money on downstream inventories by placing greater reliance on improved responsiveness and flexibility. Ideally, the use of JIT helps to synchronize the system so thoroughly that its functioning doesn't depend on inventories strategically located at points throughout the logistics system.

interface with manufacturing

Successful JIT applications also place a high priority on efficient and dependable production and manufacturing processes. Since JIT systems require the delivery of parts and subassemblies when and where the need arises, they rely heavily on the accuracy of the forecasting process used to anticipate finished product demand. In addition, timely JIT system operation demands effective and dependable communications and information systems, as well as high-quality consistent transportation services.

Business firms gaining additional experience with JIT-based approaches to manufacturing and logistics are sure to increasingly accept this concept. In fact, some companies, as indicated in the On the Line feature in this chapter, are expanding the JIT concept and referring to it as JIT II. The BOSE Corporation has been the prime proponent of this expanded role for vendors.

Materials Requirements Planning

Another inventory and scheduling approach that has received much recent attention is *materials requirements planning,* or MRP. Originally popularized by Joseph Orlicky, MRP deals specifically with supplying materials and component parts whose demand depends upon the demand for a specific end product. MRP's underlying concepts have existed for many years, but only recently have computers and information systems permitted firms to benefit fully from MRP and to implement such an approach.

Definition and Operation of MRP Systems. A materials requirements planning (MRP) system consists of a set of logically related procedures, decision rules, and records designed to translate a master production schedule into time-phased net inventory requirements, and the planned coverage of such requirements for each component item needed to implement this schedule. An MRP system replans net requirements and coverage as a result of changes in either the master production schedule, demand, inventory status, or product composition. MRP systems meet their objective by computing net requirements for each inventory item, time-phasing them, and determining their proper coverage.[9]

The goals of an MRP system are to (1) ensure the availability of materials, components, and products for planned production and for customer delivery; (2) maintain the lowest possible inventory level; and (3) plan manufacturing activities, delivery schedules, and purchasing activities. In so doing, the MRP system considers current and planned quantities of parts and inventory products, as well as the time used for planning.

MRP begins by determining how much end product customers desire, and when they need it. Then MRP "explodes" the timing and need for components based upon the scheduled end product need. Figure 3–5 shows how an MRP system operates by using these key elements:

- *Master production schedule.* Based on actual customer orders as well as demand forecasts, the master production schedule, or MPS, drives the entire MRP system. The MPS details exactly what end products a company must manufacture or assemble, and when the customers need them. In other words, the MPS will provide a detailed schedule of the various SKUs and when they must be produced.
- *Bill of materials file.* Just as a recipe specifies the ingredients needed to bake a cake, the bill of materials file specifies the exact amount of raw materials, components, and subassemblies needed to manufacture or assemble the end product. Besides identifying gross requirements as needed quantities, the bill of materials file tells when the individual inputs must be available. This file also identifies how the various inputs to one another relate and shows their relative importance to producing the end product. Therefore, if several components with different lead times need to be combined as a subunit, the BMF will indicate this relationship.
- *Inventory status file.* This file maintains inventory records so that the company may subtract the amount on hand from the gross requirements, thus identifying the net requirements at any time. The inventory status file also contains important information on such things as safety stock needs for certain items and lead times. The ISF plays a critical role in support of maintaining the MPS and helping to minimize inventory.

computing net requirements

goals of MRP system

exploding demand for component parts

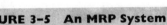
FIGURE 3-5   An MRP System

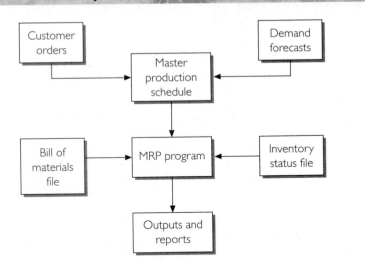

- *MRP program.* Based on the end product need specified in the master production schedule and on information from the bill of materials file, the MRP program first explodes the end product demand into gross requirements for individual parts and other materials. Then the program calculates net requirements based on inventory status file information and places orders for the inputs necessary to the production/assembly process. The orders respond to needs for specific quantities of materials and to the timing of those needs. The example in the next section clarifies these MRP program activities.
- *Outputs and reports.* After a firm completes the MRP program, several basic outputs and reports will help managers involved in logistics, manufacturing, and assembly. Included are records and information related to the following: (1) quantities the company should order and when, (2) any need to expedite or reschedule arrival dates or needed product quantities, (3) canceled need for product, and (4) MRP system status. Those reports are key to controlling the MRP system and in complex environments are reviewed every day to make appropriate modifications and provide information.

Example of an MRP System.   To understand the MRP approach more fully, consider a company that assembles egg timers. Assume that according to the master production schedule, the company desires to assemble a single, finished egg timer for delivery to a customer at the end of eight weeks. The MRP application would proceed as follows.

Figure 3–6 shows the bill of materials for assembling a single egg timer. The gross requirements for one finished product include two ends, one bulb, three supports, and 1 gram of sand. Figure 3–6 also shows that the company must add the gram of sand to the bulb before assembling the finished egg timer.

Table 3–2 displays the inventory status file for the egg timer example and calculates the net requirements as the difference between gross requirements and

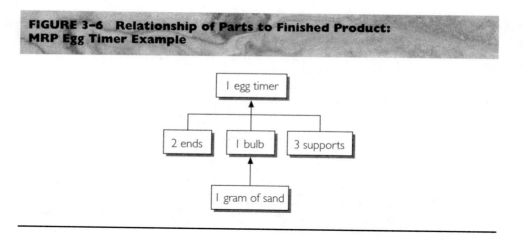

FIGURE 3-6 Relationship of Parts to Finished Product: MRP Egg Timer Example

the amount of inventory on hand. The table notes the lead time for each component. For example, the lead time needed to procure supports and bulbs is one week, whereas sand needs four weeks and ends require five. Once all components are available, the time needed to assemble the finished egg timer is one week.

Finally, Figure 3–7 is the master schedule for all activities relating to ordering and receiving components and assembling the finished egg timer. Because the company must have the single egg timer assembled and ready for customer delivery at the end of eight weeks, appropriate parts quantities must be available in the seventh week. The upper portion of Figure 3–7 shows this requirement.

Working backward from the need for parts in the seventh week, the lower portions of Figure 3–7 identify strategies for ordering and receiving component inventories. For example, for two ends requiring a lead time of five weeks, the company must place an order in the second week. For the one additional support requiring a lead time of a single week, the company should release an order during the sixth week. Finally, the company must order the bulb in the sixth week for delivery in the seventh, and order the sand in the second week for delivery in the sixth.

This example illustrates how the MRP-based approach relates to inventory scheduling and inventory control. In effect, the MRP program itself would perform the calculations involved in Figure 3–7. Once the program develops the master schedule, reports present this information in a format suitable for manager use. The company would place orders for needed parts in quantities and at times described.

TABLE 3-2 Inventory Status File: MRP Egg Timer Example

Product	Gross Requirements	Inventory on Hand	Net Requirements	Lead Time (in weeks)
Egg timers	1	0	1	1
Ends	2	0	2	5
Supports	3	2	1	1
Bulbs	1	0	1	1
Sand	1	0	1	4

FIGURE 3-7 Master Schedule: MRP Egg Timer Example

EGG TIMERS (LT=1)	1	2	3	4	5	6	7	8
Quantity needed								1
Production schedule							1	

ENDS (LT=5)	1	2	3	4	5	6	7	8
Gross requirements							2	
Inventory on hand	0	0	0	0	0	0	0	
Scheduled receipts							2	
Planned order releases		2						

SUPPORTS (LT=1)	1	2	3	4	5	6	7	8
Gross requirements							3	
Inventory on hand	2	2	2	2	2	2	2	
Scheduled receipts							1	
Planned order releases						1		

BULBS (LT=1)	1	2	3	4	5	6	7	8
Gross requirements							1	
Inventory on hand	0	0	0	0	0	0	0	
Scheduled receipts							1	
Planned order releases						1		

SAND (LT=4)	1	2	3	4	5	6	7	8
Gross requirements						1		
Inventory on hand	0	0	0	0	0	0		
Scheduled receipts						1		
Planned order releases		1						

In actual practice, MRP is exceptionally suitable for planning and controlling the ordering and receipt of large numbers of parts and products that may interact during assembly or manufacture. With the exception of very simple problems such as the egg timer example, computerization is virtually a prerequisite to using MRP-based applications. Only through the processing speed and manipulative capabilities of modern computer systems can a firm perform MRP's inner workings cost-effectively.

Summary and Evaluation of MRP Systems.   Having established the master production schedule, the MRP program develops a time-phased approach to inventory scheduling and inventory receipt. Because it generates a list of required materials in order to assemble or manufacture a specified number of finished products, MRP represents a "push" approach. Correspondingly, this encourages purchase order and production order development. Typically, MRP applies primarily when the demand for parts and materials depends upon the demand for some specific end product. MRP can deal with systemwide material supplies.

responsiveness   Since actual demand is key to the establishment of production schedules, MRP systems can react quickly to changing demand for finished products. Although some JIT proponents feel that a "pull" approach is inherently more responsive than a "push" approach such as MRP, the reverse is sometimes true. MRP systems can also help firms to achieve other typical JIT objectives, such as those pertaining to lead time management and elimination of waste. In short, MRP can achieve objectives more commonly associated with the JIT-based approaches, while at times decisions made through the pull concept do not reflect the future events for which the JIT policies are intended.

strengths   The principal advantages of most MRP-based systems include the following:

- They try to maintain reasonable safety stock levels, and to minimize or eliminate inventories whenever possible.
- They can identify process problems and potential supply chain disruptions long before they occur and take necessary corrective action.
- Production schedules are based on actual demand as well as on forecasts of end product needs.
- They coordinate materials ordering across points in a firm's logistics system.
- They are most suitable for batch or intermittent production or assembly processes.

limitations   Shortcomings of MRP-based approaches include the following:

- Their application is computer intensive, and making changes is sometimes difficult once the system is in operation.
- Both ordering and transportation costs may rise as a firm reduces inventory levels and possibly moves toward a more coordinated system of ordering product in smaller amounts to arrive when the firm needs it.
- They are not usually as sensitive to short-term fluctuations in demand as are order point approaches (although they are not as inventory intensive, either).
- They frequently become quite complex and sometimes do not work exactly as intended.[10]

advanced approaches   ***A Note Concerning MRPII Systems.***   In recent years, *manufacturing resource planning*, or MRPII, a far more comprehensive set of tools than MRP alone, has become

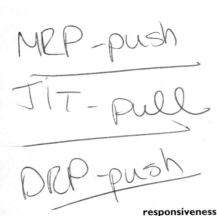

available. Although MRP is a key step in MRPII, MRPII allows a firm to integrate financial planning and operations/logistics.

MRPII serves as an excellent planning tool, and it helps describe the likely results of implementing strategies in areas such as logistics, manufacturing, marketing, and finance. Thus, it helps a firm to conduct "what if?" analyses and to determine appropriate product movement and storage strategies at and between points in the firm's logistics system.

MRPII is a technique used to plan and manage all of the organization's resources and reaches far beyond inventory or even production control, to all planning functions of an organization.[11] It is a holistic planning technique, one that can draw together all of the corporate functional areas into an integrated whole. The ultimate benefits of MRPII include improved customer service through fewer shortages and stockouts, better delivery performance, and responsiveness to changes in demand. Successfully implementing MRPII should also help to reduce inventory costs and the frequency of production line stoppages, and create more planning flexibility.[12]

Newer, more responsive approaches are developing rapidly. The integration of MRPII and JIT (known as MRPIII), for example, is a potentially-valuable development to logistics manufacturing and the whole firm.

Distribution Resource Planning

Fundamentally, *distribution resource planning (DRP)* applies MRP principles and techniques to the flow and storage of finished products destined for the marketplace. Thus, where MRP sets a master production schedule and then "explodes" into gross and net requirements, DRP begins with customer demand, classified as independent demand, and works backward toward establishing a realistic and economically justifiable systemwide plan for ordering the necessary finished products. Using the best available forecasts of finished product demand, DRP develops a time-phased plan for distributing product from plants and warehouses to points where it is available to customers. In practice, DRP allocates available inventory to meet marketplace demands; thus, it is a push approach.

DRP is far more responsive than MRP to real marketplace needs in terms of product availability and receipt timing. The most noticeable difference between MRP and DRP is that DRP can adjust and readjust its ordering patterns to accommodate dynamic, changing inventory needs. The DRP approach also responds better to systemwide inventory needs, as opposed to just those specific to a single facility. Chapter 4 discusses DRP in more detail.

similarity to MRP

DRP can handle increased demand better then MRP

customer inventories

SUMMARY

- The supply chain can be viewed as inbound logistics and outbound logistics; the focus of this chapter is on the inbound system. Effective supply chain management requires the careful coordination of inbound and outbound systems.
- Inbound logistics systems can vary in terms of importance, scope, cost, and complexity, depending on where the company is located in the supply chain, the nature of the product, and the market situation in which the product is sold.

- The procurement area plays a major role in materials management, and procurement is an important link in the supply chain.
- The procurement process can be broken down into a set of activities that include identifying a need, defining and evaluating user requirements, deciding whether to make or buy, identifying the type of purchase, performing a market analysis, identifying potential suppliers, prescreening possible vendors, evaluating remaining suppliers, choosing a vendor, receiving delivery of the product or service, and making a postpurchase evaluation.
- The procurement process activities can be more effectively managed by following a four-step process: (1) determine type of purchase; (2) determine necessary level of investment; (3) perform the procurement process; (4) evaluate the effectiveness of the procurement process.
- In selecting vendors, a number of criteria should be utilized, including quality, reliability, capability, financial viability, and other factors, such as location.
- There are four basic sources of price: commodity markets, price lists, price quotation, and price negotiation.
- The purchase price is a matter of great importance, but it is much more complex than just the base unit price, since it requires the analysis of added value along the supply chain to deliver the highest total value to the ultimate customer.
- In addition to procurement costs, materials management includes warehousing, production planning and control, traffic, receiving, quality control, and salvage and scrap disposal.
- Materials management also includes inventory management, which includes the use of techniques such as JIT, MRP, and DRP.

STUDY QUESTIONS

1. Inbound logistics systems can vary in scope and complexity among different companies. Explain the differences that can exist between inbound logistics systems. What is the source of the differences?

2. The procurement process can be described in terms of a set of activities that should be used in the purchase of goods and services. Briefly discuss these activities.

3. Maximizing the effectiveness of the procurement process is a major goal of an organization. What steps can be taken to help ensure that the process is maximized?

4. A key part of the procurement process is the selection of vendors. What criteria are commonly used in this selection process? Which criteria should be given the highest priority? Why?

5. What are the major sources of prices in the purchase of goods? Under what circumstances would these sources be utilized?

6. What are the components of total acquired cost? Is it realistic to expect companies to consider all of these components?

7. What role does warehousing play in materials management systems? Can the importance of warehousing vary among companies?

8. "JIT is more than an inventory control system." What is meant by that statement? Do you agree with the statement?

9. Discuss the advantages and disadvantages of MRP.

10. What is the role of quality management in materials management systems?

NOTES

1. Michael E. Porter, *Competitive Advantage* (New York: Free Press, 1985): 11–16.
2. Porter, *Competitive Advantage*, 33–34.
3. Walter E. Goddard, "Kanban or MRPII—Which Is Best for You?" *Modern Materials Handling* (5 November, 1982): 42.
4. Goddard, "Kanban or MRPII—Which Is Best for You?" 45–46.
5. "How Just-in-Time Inventories Combat Foreign Competition," *Business Week* Special Report, (14 May 1984): 176E.
6. Joan M. Feldman, "Transportation Changes—Just-in-Time," *Handling and Shipping Management* (September 1984): 47.
7. Details concerning Ryder's involvement with Saturn Corporation may be found in Ray A. Mundy, Judy A. Ford, Paul E. Forney, and Jerry Lineback, "Innovations in Carrier Sourcing: Transportation Partnership," *1989 Council of Logistics Management Annual Conference Proceedings* (Oakbrook, IL: CLM, 1989): 109–14.
8. For additional ideas, see Daniel Goldberg, "JIT's Next Step Moves Cargo and Data," *Transportation & Distribution* (December 1990): 26–29.
9. Joseph Orlicky, *Materials Requirements Planning* (New York: McGraw-Hill, 1975): 22.
10. Denis J. Davis, "Transportation and Inventory Management: Bridging the Gap," *Distribution* (June 1985): 11.
11. John Gatorna and Abby Day, "Strategic Issues in Logistics," *International Journal of Physical Distribution and Materials Management* 16: (1986): 29.
12. For additional information regarding MRPII, see Oliver W. Wright, "MRPII," *Modern Materials Handling* (12 September 1980): 28.

Case 3-1

CENTRAL SYSTEMS CORPORATION

Company Background

Central Systems Corporation is the world's largest manufacturer of telephone switching equipment. Central has divisions in Pittsburgh (central office products), Minneapolis (small business products), and Atlanta (consumer products and the manufacture of all company-owned tooling). It also has a satellite factory in Glasgow, Scotland, and a printed circuit plant outside of Frankfurt, Germany, as well as sales offices in Sunbury, UK; Hamburg, Germany; and Singapore. Central supplies all types of telephone equipment, including large PBX switchers, small business equipment, and home units. The company estimates that it enjoys a 35 percent share of the market.

Distribution

Despite its worldwide market, Central has only two distribution points for its products: warehouses at Pittsburgh and Sunbury, UK. Because of the increasingly competitive nature of the market, Central management has recently made a commitment to provide superior customer service.

This commitment has two main points: (1) customer orders received by 3:00 P.M. will be shipped by 5:00 P.M., and (2) next-day delivery will be provided if the customer requests it. Significant investment in information systems and distribution center configurations have been made to support these commitments.

Sales in the United States, however, have been declining, with customers in western states complaining about the high cost of next-day delivery. Contributing to the problem is the fact that Central's competitors have western distribution centers. To overcome the problem, Central undertook a study and learned that of all possible locations, Denver should be its logical choice.

Originally scheduled for May 1994, the center's opening was advanced to mid-February by Central's extremely dynamic and results-oriented president, Bill Grabowski. To assure that this new schedule will be met, he has assigned a task force to the project consisting of the department heads of human resources, customer service, purchasing, information systems, and national warehousing. Although a building in Denver has been leased, employees still need to be hired and trained, materials handling and computer equipment procured, communications lines installed, and stock transfers initiated. Most important, the new location has to be aggressively promoted among the customers.

Purchasing

Residing in Pittsburgh, Central's purchasing department consists of a director, five purchasing agents, three buying assistants, and clerical support. Purchasing functions at the other locations ultimately report to Pittsburgh.

As company policy, Central attempts to achieve at least fifteen inventory turns per year while offering a product line of more than 700 items. This requires extensive cooperation between production and purchasing for assembly components, as well as coordination with the OEM suppliers. A rolling twelve-month forecast is maintained, with the schedule for next month being firm, the second month somewhat flexible, the third yet more flexible, and thereafter totally flexible.

Mid-February is now only two months away, and, as a result of being involved in the Denver Task Force, the purchasing director realizes the potential impact that the project will have on the rest of the company.

Case Questions

The following is a list of questions that the director feels are necessary to answer as soon as possible:

1. How can the task force best integrate its efforts so that a smooth opening occurs?
2. How should shipments from the OEM suppliers be coordinated to the three warehouses?
3. Which items and in what quantities need to be stocked at each of the warehouses?

SOURCE: Prepared by Michael Patton, C.P.M. under the direction of Dr. Richard Young.

Case 3-2

LEOLA MILLING COMPANY

Jennifer Roberts, distribution manager for Leola Milling, has become increasingly aware that the company has a major problem as it continues to try to reduce inventories while maintaining the levels of service its customers have come to expect.

Company and Product

Founded in 1887, Leola Milling has provided high-quality bakery flours to commercial bakeries as well as to the consumer market. While commercial customers tend to have consistent buying patterns as well as brand loyalty, Leola finds that consumers have only minimal loyalty, but generally prefer known names over the store brands. Demand is highly seasonal, with the annual peak occurring just before Thanksgiving and slacking off dramatically during January and February. To offset this, both Leola and its major supermarket chain accounts run special deals and sales promotions at various points during the year.

Production planning, located at the Leola, Pennsylvania, headquarters has responsibility for controlling inventory levels at the plant warehouse at Buffalo as well as the three distribution centers (DCs) located in Washington, Pennsylvania; Columbus, Ohio; and Pittsfield, Massachusetts. Planning has routinely been based on past history. No forecasting is performed, at least not in a formal sense. DCs are replenished by rail from Buffalo, and lead times are typically seven days, with forty-eight to fifty-four pallets per car, depending on the type used. Should emergencies occur, eighteen pallets can be shipped by truck with a one-day transit time.

Recently Leola has experienced two major stockouts for its consumer-size of 5-pound sacks of bleached white flour. One of these was due to problems in milling operations, the other occurred when marketing initiated a "buy one, get one free" coupon promotion. Since these events, planning has become overly cautious and errs on the side of having excess inventories at the DCs. Additionally, two other events have affected DC throughput: (1) implementation of direct factory shipments for replenishing the five largest supermarket chains, and (2) a price increase making Leola flour more expensive than its national brand competitors such as Gold Medal.

Current Situation

Of the 1,660 pallets in the Pittsfield warehouse, Leola shows only 396 pallets for open orders. This has led the company to use outside storage, where there is another 480 pallets. Flour is easily damaged; hence Leola prefers to minimize handling. Overstocking at the DC alone costs $1.85 per pallet for outside storage, to which must be added $4.25 per pallet for extra handling and $225.00 per truckload for transportation. Similar scenarios are being played out at the other DCs as well.

Possible Solutions

Jennifer Roberts has been contemplating various approaches to solving the inventory issue. Clearly, product needs to be in place at the time a consumer is making a buying decision, but Leola cannot tolerate the overstocking situation and the stress it is putting on facilities and costs.

Her first thought is that a new information system is needed that not only provides timely and accurate information, but extensively shares it throughout the organization. Several questions immediately came to mind; however, she needs additional information before coming to any conclusions.

Case Questions

1. What role might the DCs play in developing useful forecasts?
2. Could a postponement strategy work for Leola? Commercial flour and consumer flour are the same product, differentiated only by packaging.
3. Organizationally, might inventory control be more effective if reporting occurred elsewhere within the firm?
4. There are several good distribution requirements planning software packages on the market. How might such an application benefit Leola?
5. To assure the future effectiveness of any approach, a cross-functional team should be considered. Who should be included in its membership? Why?

SOURCE: Prepared by Leslie Marple under the direction of Dr. Richard Young.

CHAPTER 4

THE OUTBOUND LOGISTICS SYSTEM

LEARNING OBJECTIVES

After reading this chapter, you should be able to do the following:

- Understand the important role of outbound logistics in the logistics supply chain.

- Explain the differences that exist among companies in terms of the scope, complexity, and significance of their outbound logistics systems.

- Understand major trends in outbound logistics strategies.

- Discuss the importance, contribution, and role of customer service in outbound logistics systems.

- Define customer service from different perspectives.

- Understand the basic elements of customer service that are important to logistics managers.

- Explain the standards of performance that are used to measure and evaluate customer service.

- Discuss how companies use customer service to achieve and sustain competitive advantage.

- Understand the nature and role of channels of distribution in outbound logistics systems and the relationships among channels of distribution.

- Discuss alternative channel systems.

- Explain the strategic impact of integrating channel systems.

LOGISTICS PROFILE

RICHFOOD

Richfood, a wholesaler based in Mechanicsville, VA, has embarked on an ambitious cross-docking program that is one of the first attempts to tie together the system—from supplier to store level. Three grocery suppliers and twelve stores will be involved.

The suppliers load multi-SKU orders by store on pallets and ship them to Richfood's distribution center. Richfood immediately shifts the pallets from its receiving dock over to its shipping dock and sends them on outbound trucks, along with warehouse-picked goods, to the stores. This quick response outbound logistics system reduces inventory levels and cost and provides a high level of customer service by keeping goods in stock.

By setting up pallets with multiple items, rather than just one product, the suppliers are taking cross-docking to a new level, observers say. Cross-docking is based upon the concept of moving goods through a warehouse in 24 hours or less and reduces outbound cycle time.

This is Richfood's first cross-docking experience with suppliers. However, the wholesaler, like many others, has been engaged in cross-docking with other wholesalers— in this case, McKesson and Fleming, which supply Richfood with health and beauty items and general merchandise. Orders of those products come into Richfood's distribution center and are immediately shipped out with other products to retailers.

One of the major challenges Richfood faces with the new system is to get retailers comfortable with a new method of distribution. Normally, when retailers need a product, they can be confident that it's sitting in Richfood's warehouse. With cross-docking, there is more apprehension on retailers' part as to whether logistics will flow properly.

Richfood is encouraging its retailers to use the cross-docking program to drive costs out of the system. With cross-docking the firm will be able to save significant amounts of labor in the distribution center. It won't be putting a (cross-docked) product in the distribution center and then selecting it. The cross-docked deliveries are determined by individual stores' computer-generated predictions of weekly case usage, based on scan data.

To make sure that product gets to the retailer on time, Richfood has set up an electronic data interchange (EDI) link with the three suppliers participating in this experiment. Suppliers can transmit advance shipping notices to tell Richfood what's being delivered for cross-docking. The wholesaler, in turn, can notify its retailers that they will be getting a pallet load made up of certain items on a particular day.

This receiving of advance shipping notices via EDI makes Richfood one of the most progressive users of EDI in the industry. Most grocery operators have used EDI for purchase orders or invoices, and a few have started to use it for promotional announcements.

By speeding up the distribution process, cross-docking puts new pressure on both manufacturers and distributors. Manufacturers participating in cross-docking need to commit to a tight time frame for replacing damaged or unshipped product—using expensive methods such as UPS if necessary. Distributors, for their part, need better-trained employees.

Making cross-docking a reality requires a number of significant changes. Like any new practice, cross-docking forces distributors to coordinate shipments from vendors that participate in cross-docking with shipments from those that don't.

More significantly, warehouses may have to be modified to feature more doors at the shipping dock to accommodate cross-docking. With additional doors, trailers can wait longer for inbound shipments bearing loads for cross-docking without tying up trucks that need to be used for regular loads. The magical intersection between receiving and outbound doesn't occur too often. The savings, however, justify such moves. The outbound systems of a growing number of companies are developing cross-docking facilities to improve product flow.

ADAPTED FROM: Michael Garry, "Cross-Docking: The Road to ECR," *Progressive Grocer* (August 1993): 107–11.

T he outbound logistics system usually receives more attention in the logistics literature than inbound logistics. In Chapter 2, it was noted that the initial development of interest in logistics after World War II focused upon physical distribution or outbound logistics. The underlying rationale was an explosion of costs due to increased inventory expenses associated with higher-valued products and product line proliferation, as well as increased transportation costs because of smaller shipments of the higher-valued products. The transportation cost increases were exacerbated by a regulatory environment that made it difficult to negotiate "win-win" situations and made it relatively easy for transportation companies to pass on their cost increases to shippers through the regulatory process.

early interest

Companies cannot afford to neglect their inbound logistics systems, as was noted in Chapter 3. Today's environment offers much opportunity to improve efficiency (lower costs) and increase effectiveness by managing the inbound system and coordinating it with the outbound system. But many companies still focus more upon outbound systems because of the costs involved and because managing the outbound system well makes it easier to achieve and sustain market share. Customers are usually "touched" most directly by outbound logistics systems, and hence the outbound system will be the source of the most complaints and/or compliments.

inbound systems important

Many of the logistics strategies discussed in this book have been developed in response to outbound logistics systems or as a means of strategically positioning companies to improve their competitive advantage in the marketplace. The cross-docking implemented by Richfood (see Logistics Profile) is a good example of a company changing its outbound system to improve market position. It is important to note, however, that outbound logistics systems cannot operate effectively in most instances without well-managed and coordinated inbound systems. In fact, the current emphasis upon reducing cycle times and developing pull inventory systems and flexible manufacturing makes it even more critical that the inbound and outbound systems be coordinated. It is almost impossible in today's environment to manage inbound and outbound systems in the same company as separate processes.

synergism of inbound and outbound

Consider the case of National Semiconductor of Santa Clara, California, one of the largest chipmakers, whose products end up in automobiles, computers, telecommunication equipment, and so on. In the early 1990s, the company began to closely examine and evaluate its logistics systems. It had to start by trying to determine what its then-current system was costing the company, because it really had no idea. National Semiconductor was producing silicon wafers at six fabrication plants (four in the United States and two in other countries) and then shipping the wafers to seven assembly plants (mostly in Southeast Asia). Finally, the products had to be delivered to some very large customers, such as IBM, Compaq, Ford, and Toshiba, at their factories, which were scattered around the world.[1]

National Semiconductor

National Semiconductor found that it had inventory sitting throughout its logistics supply chain, both inbound and outbound. It also found that 95 percent of the orders it received were delivered about 45 days after the order was placed, which was not especially customer responsive. Furthermore, the company found that the remaining 5 percent of orders often took up to 90 days to deliver. Customers were not sure which 5 percent would be late, so they frequently requested 90 days of inventory.[2]

45-day service

four-day service   National Semiconductor reengineered its logistics supply chain and made it much simpler. A key feature of the redesigned logistics network was the utilization of a centralized distribution facility in Southeast Asia, from which all orders would be filled and shipped airfreight, by Federal Express, to customer locations. Now the company can fill orders in four days. However, the new delivery and customer service level of its outbound system could not be achieved without a reengineered inbound system that is coordinated with the outbound system.[3]

lower cost, higher revenue   National Semiconductor's success in improving customer service by reducing order cycle time is interesting also because it was achieved with lower costs. Sales increased by $584 million over a two-year period, and logistics costs fell from 2.6 percent of sales revenue to 1.9 percent.[4] It is quite a success story, one that is being duplicated in other companies such as Sears, Compaq, Laura Ashley, and Saturn, to name a few.

Results such as those achieved by National Semiconductor are achievable, but not without a thorough understanding of the activities and processes indigenous to logistics supply chains. Chapter 3 stressed that inbound and outbound systems share some common activities, such as transportation, inventory, warehousing, and materials handling. However, like inbound systems, outbound systems have some activities that are unique or deserve special emphasis, such as customer service and channels of distribution. Before discussing these unique topics and some related ones, we should examine outbound systems along the supply chain, as we did with inbound systems.

OUTBOUND LOGISTICS ALONG THE SUPPLY CHAIN

Chapter 3 provided a discussion of inbound logistics systems among firms in a supply chain producing canned food for consumers. The examination of this supply chain noted that there were differences among the inbound systems along the supply chain. That same observation is also quite accurate for outbound systems.

food supply chain   Some interesting comparisons can be made using the same food product supply chain that was used in Chapter 3. The extraction company, as was indicated, would most likely focus upon outbound logistics, since the inbound system is essentially a part of the mining operation. At the other end of the supply chain, the retail store would focus upon the inbound logistics system, since the outbound logistics are essentially a part of store operations, and the customers, especially in a self-serve store, provide their own outbound logistics, including order filling, packing, materials handling, and delivery. While some retail outlets provide order filling and delivery—for example, catalog product companies such as Land's End or appliance stores—an increasing number of customers use self-service types of stores. IKEA (one of the largest home furnishing distributors in the world) operates its logistics system so that customers even assemble the furniture they buy. Club and warehouse stores also operate in an environment where the customers assume a larger role in operations and logistics. The important point is that retail stores are most concerned with only half of the logistics system, namely, inbound logistics.

steel company   The steel company has both inbound and outbound logistics systems that require coordination. However, as was noted previously, its outbound system would usually receive more attention because the finished steel is of higher value and requires more sophisticated logistics support in transportation, warehousing, and inventory control than do the inbound raw materials. On the other hand, if we were discussing a supply chain that focused upon autos, the inbound system of the car manufacturer would typically handle up to 13,000 parts and would be more complex than the outbound system that delivers the finished autos to the dealer for sale to customers. The outbound system of an airplane manufacturer such as Boeing would be even simpler than that of an auto manufacturer, but its inbound system, with 50,000-plus parts with varying lead times, would be almost mind-boggling.

From an outbound system perspective, the food processor in the Chapter 3 supply chain would have the most challenging outbound system because the canned peas would probably be only one of several thousand stock-keeping units (SKUs) that the food processor would handle. A food producer such as Pillsbury, General Foods, or General Mills would be dealing with a variety of "paths" (channels of distribution) to the ultimate consumer, including wholesalers, brokers, sales agents, and retail stores. Companies like this are a part of what has been called the package goods or grocery industry. Their logistics networks and systems are complex and complicated, with many opportunities to accumulate inventory and otherwise operate inefficiently. In fact, the potential to improve logistics in the supply chain of this industry is so great that it has initiated an industrywide effort known as efficient consumer response (ECR) that is aimed at taking inventory out of the total supply chain for all companies, with the goal of saving $30 billion per year.

food producer

The companies that are a part of the package goods or grocery manufacturer's industry are good examples of the importance of managing outbound logistics—$30 billion certainly gets your attention. But other companies have similar challenges and opportunities. Today's environment may be captured best by the following quote:

> May your trucks run full, your warehouses stay empty, and your supply chains come alive with the sound of cooperative suppliers and truly delighted customers.[5]

With that quote in mind, we will take up a discussion of customer service.

CUSTOMER SERVICE

No discussion of outbound logistics systems would be considered complete without the inclusion of customer service, since customer service is really the fuel that drives the logistics supply chain engine. Having the right product show up at the right time, in the right quantity, without damage or loss, to the right customer is an underlying principle of logistics systems that recognizes the importance of customer service.

Customer service has received widespread attention over the last ten or more years. Peters and Waterman, in their popular nonfiction best seller, *In Search of Excellence*,[6] lauded the importance of "getting close to your customers" as a means of achieving success in business. "Getting close to your customer" had several dimensions, but certainly one of the important aspects of this directive was having

getting close to customers

ON THE LINE

Channel Integration Is the New Way to Leverage Logistics for Higher Productivity

Kmart is doing it. So are Kodak and Lee Apparel. These three companies recently adopted a new approach to inventory management. They all began sharing information with suppliers or with retailers to coordinate the flow of product from warehouse to store floor.

This new inventory management concept goes by the name of "channel integration." The process depends upon retailers sharing information on sales at the store level with their suppliers (point-of-sale information). This exchange of information enables suppliers to manufacture in response to demand (pull system) for a product and ship only the product needed. Most importantly, it allows both supplier and retailer to carry minimum inventory in their warehouses.

Channel integration builds upon two other practices prevalent in today's distribution climate: quick response and continuous replenishment. With quick response, a supplier reacting to electronic orders from a retailer ships swiftly to meet demand. Under continuous replenishment, a supplier manages the retailer's inventory, supplying product on a continuous basis. Channel integration takes both of those practices a step further by providing a framework for retailer and supplier to work *together* to manage the inventory pipeline, i.e., a partnership.

Another company involved in channel integration is the Lee Apparel Co. based in Merriam, KS, which is part of the giant Reading, PA, based clothing maker, the VF Corp. Last summer, Lee began a replenishment program with nine retailers, supplying them with jeans and other merchandise within seven days based on point-of-sale data. In the case of four of those retailers, Lee automatically ships the jeans to maintain what it calls "a model stock." Basically, a model stock is the mix of products that Lee and the retailer determine they should keep in a store to maximize sales.

Point-of-sale data are transmitted electronically from the retailer to Lee on either a weekly or a daily basis. The retailer can easily convey the identity of a fast-selling product because each garment is bar coded. That is, every Lee garment shipped to a store comes with a Universal Product Code (UPC) bar code that's attached at the manufacturing plant. When that bar code is scanned at the checkout counter, the retailer's computer records the item's style, color, and size. "A registered sale is a consumer vote for a particular size and style."

But Lee uses the point-of-sale data for more than just determining what to ship. That information is also used to drive its production. Sales information allows Lee to adjust its flexible manufacturing operation, which is based on production of "core" items.

SOURCE: "Supply-Chain Management '90s Style," *Traffic Management* (May 1992): 57, 59. Reprinted with permission of *Traffic Management* magazine (May 1992). Copyright © by Cahners Publishing Company.

a logistics system that could be responsive to customer orders and understand their requirements.

market-driven quality The total quality management programs that were mentioned in Chapter 3 have a link to customer service. In fact, IBM uses the motto "Market-Driven Quality," which includes not only a quality product but also a "bundle" of quality-related services that support the product and sustain the relationship with the customer, with the end objective being complete customer satisfaction. Again, IBM sees logistics as having a very important role in the area of customer service and as being an area that can add value for customers by driving down their costs of doing business with IBM.

consumer awareness Another aspect of customer service that deserves mention in this introductory section is a point that was covered in Chapter 1, which noted the growing consumer awareness of the price/quality ratio and the special needs of today's consumers, who are time conscious and who demand flexibility. The 1980s and the 1990s have been a period of growing awareness of the special needs of consumers and the distribution network that serves them. Today's consumers are a different breed. They have high standards for quality, and brand loyalty is not necessarily something that they support. Essentially, they want products at the best price, with the best level of service, and at times convenient to their schedules. Successful companies have adopted customer service approaches that recognize the importance of speed, flexibility, customization, and reliability.

The Logistics/Marketing Interface

We must recognize that customer service is often the key link between logistics and marketing. If the logistics system, particularly outbound logistics, is not functioning properly and a customer does not receive a delivery as promised, the company could lose future sales. We need to remember that manufacturing can produce a good product at the right cost, and marketing can sell it. But if logistics does not deliver it when and where promised, the customer will be dissatisfied.

We could consider this description of the relationship between logistics and marketing a traditional view. Figure 4–1 depicts this traditional role of customer service at the interface between marketing and logistics. The relationship manifests itself in this perspective through the "place" dimension of the marketing mix, which is often used synonymously with channel of distribution decisions and the associated customer service levels provided. In this context, logistics plays a static role that is based upon minimizing the total cost of the various logistics activities within a given set of service levels, probably as dictated by marketing. **traditional view**

It is safe to say that this particular vision of logistics and its relationship to marketing is one that dominated logistics literature in the years preceding what might be termed the "supply chain revolution." From this traditional point of view, the usual trade-off was seen as being, "if we increase the level of customer service, then logistics costs will automatically increase."

However, as we saw earlier, National Semiconductor reengineered its system to increase customer service (shortening order lead times from 45 days to 4 days) and, in doing so, significantly reduced the relative cost of logistics. The type of change envisioned in the National Semiconductor case would probably not be possible using the traditional framework for analysis. This situation required a more dynamic, proactive approach that recognized the value-added role of logistics supply chains in creating and sustaining competitive advantage and providing win-win outcomes. **new vision**

Daryl White, the chief financial officer of Compaq Computer, suggests

> We've done most of what we have to do to be more competitive. We've changed the way we develop products, manufacture, market, and advertise. The one piece of the puzzle that we haven't addressed is logistics. It's the next source of competitive advantage, and the possibilities are astounding.[7]

This new perspective emphasizing value added is providing the basis for National Semiconductor and other companies, such as Sears, Procter & Gamble, Nabisco, and Hershey, to improve both efficiency and effectiveness. Becton Dickinson (BD), which was the subject of the Logistics Profile in Chapter 1, is a good example of a company that has recognized the proactive, value-adding role of customer service in the logistics supply chain. As was indicated previously, BD attempts to manage the supply chain on an integrated basis, with the intent of **service adds value**

FIGURE 4–1   The Traditional Logistics/Marketing Interface

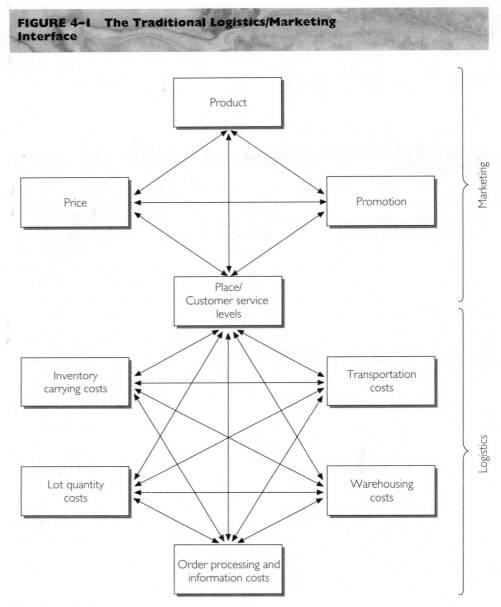

Marketing objective:
Allocate resources to the marketing mix to maximize the long-run profitability of the firm.

Logistics objective:
Minimize total costs, given the customer service objective, where:

Total costs = Transportation costs + warehousing costs + order processing and information costs + lot quantity costs + inventory carrying costs

ADAPTED FROM: Douglas M. Lambert, *The Development of an Inventory Costing Methodology: A Study of the Costs Associated with Holding Inventory* (Chicago: National Council of Physical Distribution Management, 1976): 7.

providing high levels of customer service and high-quality goods to satisfy customers throughout its supply chain. Essentially, the company envisions delivering the best product and services at the lowest total system cost. Becton Dickinson has even gone so far as to create a new operating division called Supply Chain Services.[8]

The implementation of the BD vision through its new operating division is illustrated in Figure 4–2. The figure emphasizes that BD will provide the same level of commitment to supply chain services that it provides to product development. That is, the company will continually enhance the service provided to its partners in the supply chain in an effort to create the highest level of value for the entire supply chain.

Figure 4–2 suggests a more dynamic interface between marketing and logistics **dynamic interface** that is much more appropriate, given today's emphasis upon the supply chain, than the static interface shown in Figure 4–1. This is not to say that cost is no longer important (note the reference to lowest cost in the discussion of BD above). What we are suggesting is that the integrated supply chain be maximized instead of only one segment of the chain, which might result in suboptimization of the rest of the chain.

Defining Customer Service

Anyone who has ever struggled to define customer service soon realized the difficulty of explaining this nebulous term. Thus, different people will understandably have different interpretations of just what customer service means.

We can think of customer service as something a firm provides to those who **levels of product** purchase its products or services. According to marketers, there are three levels of product: (1) the core benefit or service, which constitutes what the buyer is really buying; (2) the tangible product, or the physical product or service itself; and (3) the augmented product, which includes benefits that are secondary to, but an integral enhancement to, the tangible product the customer is purchasing. In this context, we can think of logistical customer service as a feature of the augmented product that adds value for the buyer.[9] Other examples of augmented product features include installation, warranties, and after-sale service.

Extending our thinking along these lines, a firm could achieve a competitive advantage by providing superior levels of logistical customer service. Thus, a potential benefit exists in viewing customer service as a "product" that may add significant value for a buyer.

This view of logistics as it relates to the augmented product is quite consistent with the Becton Dickinson perspective, and is one that in today's environment plays a major role in augmenting value along the supply chain. It may not be as exciting to some individuals, but the role is critical for success in the marketplace.

A fundamental point to recognize is that customer service is a concept whose **types of customer** importance reaches far beyond the logistics area. Customer service frequently af- **support/service** fects every area of the firm by attempting to ensure customer satisfaction through the provision of aid or service to the customer.

Examples of the various forms that customer service may take include the following:

- Revamping a billing procedure to accommodate a customer's request
- Providing financial and credit terms

- Guaranteeing delivery within specified time periods
- Providing prompt and congenial sales representatives
- Extending the option to sell on consignment
- Providing material to aid in a customer's sales presentation
- Installing the product
- Maintaining satisfactory repair parts inventories

FIGURE 4–2   Two Ways of Creating Supply Chain Value

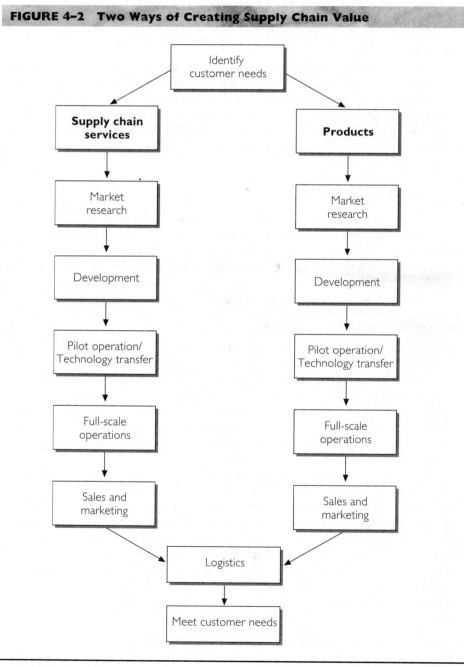

SOURCE: Becton Dickinson.

This section examines customer service within a logistics supply chain. However, customer service can, as the list above indicates, have many interpretations throughout the firm. The numerous nonlogistical aspects of customer service may add value for the customer, and a firm should include these aspects within its overall marketing effort.

While customer service has no single widely used definition, customer service is often viewed in three principal ways. We can think of them as three levels of customer service involvement or awareness.[10]

levels of involvement

- *Customer service as an activity.* This level treats customer service as a particular task that a firm must accomplish to satisfy the customer's needs. Order processing, billing and invoicing, product returns, and claims handling are all typical examples of this level of customer service. Customer service departments, which basically handle customer problems and complaints, also represent this level of customer service.

definition

- *Customer service as performance measures.* This level emphasizes customer service in terms of specific performance measures, such as the percentage of orders delivered on time and complete and the number of orders processed within acceptable time limits. Although this level enhances the first one, a firm must look beyond the performance measures themselves to ensure that its service efforts achieve actual customer satisfaction.
- *Customer service as a philosophy.* This level elevates customer service to a firm-wide commitment to providing customer satisfaction through superior customer service. This view of customer service is entirely consistent with many firms' contemporary emphasis on quality and quality management. Rather than narrowly viewing customer service as an activity or as a set of performance measures, this interpretation involves a dedication to customer service that pervades the entire firm and all of its activities.

The least important level of involvement for most companies would be viewing customer service as an activity. From this perspective, customer service activities in logistics are at the transactional level. For example, accepting product returns from customers in a retail store adds no value to product: it is merely a transaction to appease the customers. There would be little or no opportunity to add value through customer service.

The focus upon performance measures for customer service is very important because it provides a method of evaluating how well the logistics system is functioning. Over time, such measures provide benchmarks to gauge improvement, which is especially important when a firm is trying to implement a total quality management program. But this level of involvement is not sufficient.

The final level, customer service as a philosophy, broadens the role of customer service in the firm. However, this still may not be sufficient unless the value-added dimension is included as the goal of the corporate customer service philosophy. The definition of customer service that will be used in this text is as follows:

> Customer service is a process for providing competitive advantage and adding benefits to the supply chain in order to maximize the total value to the ultimate customer.

The customer service issue has many dimensions and is truly complex. A firm must fully control numerous customer service elements through effective business logistics management. Successfully implemented, high levels of logistics customer

complexity of customer service

service can easily become a strategic way for a company to differentiate itself from its competitors.

Elements of Customer Service

Customer service is an important basis for incurring logistics costs. Economic advantages generally accrue to the customer through better supplier service. As an example, a supplier can lower customer inventories by utilizing air rather than truck transportation. Lower inventory costs result from air transport's lower transit time, which will lower order cycle time, but the transportation costs will be higher than those for truck transportation. The supplier's logistics manager must balance the high service level the customer desires and the benefits the supplier may gain from possible increased sales against the cost of providing that service. The logistics manager must strike a balance among customer service levels, total logistics costs, and total benefits to the firm. However, as the National Semiconductor example illustrated, there are situations where cost can be lowered and service improved.

food industry example The food industry illustrates the importance of customer service factors and how they will probably change over time. Table 4–1 lists customer service factors that are important in the food industry. The first column is for 1995; the second column projects customer expectations for 2000. We can also be certain that the 1995 data represents a customer service level higher than that for 1990.

If the table provided data from another industry, the percentages would probably be different, but the upward direction of customer service standards would be the same. Companies both within and outside of the food industry implement such improvements in response to market pressures, and lower costs frequently accompany these improvements.

four main dimensions Customer service has multifunctional interest for a company, but from the point of view of the logistics function we can view customer service as having four traditional dimensions: time, dependability, communications, and convenience. This section explores the ways in which these elements affect the cost centers of both buyer and seller firms.

Time. The *time* factor is usually order cycle time, particularly from the perspective of the seller looking at customer service. On the other hand, the buyer usually refers to the time dimension as the lead time, or replenishment time. Regardless

TABLE 4–1 Customer Service Elements for the Food Industry

Element	1995	2000
Product availability	98%	99%
Order cycle time	9 days	7 days
Complete orders shipped	90%	94%
Accurate invoices provided	90% of invoices	93%
Damaged products	1%	0.5%

SOURCES: Grocery Manufacturers of America and A. T. Kearney, *Customer Service Data for Food Industry,* 1995, p. 5. Used with permission.

of the perspective or the terminology, several basic components or variables affect the time factor.

Successful logistics operations today have a high degree of control over most, if not all, of the basic elements of lead time, including order processing, order preparation, and order shipment. By effectively managing activities such as these, thus ensuring that order cycles will be of reasonable length and consistent duration, seller firms have improved the customer service levels that they provide to buyers. National Semiconductor Company, discussed previously, is a good example of a firm making a significant reduction in order cycle time. **control over lead time**

Order transmittal. Order transmittal consists of the time it takes an order to travel from customer to seller. Order transmittal time can vary from a few minutes by telephone to several days by mail. A seller moving from slow to fast order transmittal reduces lead time but may increase the cost of order transmittal.

The computer has revolutionized order transmittal. Computers linking buyers with sellers permit the buyer to log onto the seller's computer. Once online, the buyer can determine product availability and other information, such as the probable shipping date. The buyer then selects the items he or she desires and transfers the order electronically to the seller for processing. This technique, known as electronic data interchange (EDI), is increasingly being used by buyers and sellers. **use of computers**

The Bergen Brunswig Corporation, a drug and health care distributor, has adopted such an automated order-entry system. The company maintains that this system is largely responsible for increasing the company's income by 20 percent. Reduced lead time made possible through reductions in order transmittal time has resulted in improved customer service and increased sales income.[11]

Order processing. A seller requires time to process the customer's order and make it ready for shipment. This function usually involves checking the customer's credit, transferring information to sales records, transferring the order to the inventory area, and preparing shipping documents. Many of these functions can occur simultaneously through the effective use of electronic data processing equipment. Often, a seller's aggregate savings in operating costs will more than exceed the capital investment required to implement modern technology, particularly today when computer hardware and software have decreased significantly in cost.

Order preparation. Order preparation time involves "picking" the order (see Chapter 7) and packaging the item for shipment. Various types of materials handling systems affect order filling and preparation in different ways. These systems can vary from a simple manual system to one that is highly automated. Consequently, preparation time can vary considerably. The logistics manager has to consider the costs and benefits of the alternatives.

For example, one U.S.–based manufacturer of cans and containers purchased a microcomputer system to help control order picking, labor productivity, and excessive training time at its four warehouse locations. The company realized a considerable productivity gain in its order-picking area through more efficient order-picking procedures. The computer generates an order-picking **productivity gains** slip that is stamped with the time of issue. When the equipment operator completes the order selection and returns the order-picking slip, the time is stamped again, measuring the operator's performance as well as the order-picking time. Management easily detects inefficient, unproductive operation (or operators) and implements corrective action.[12]

transit times

Order shipment. Order shipment time extends from the moment the seller places the order upon the vehicle for movement until the buyer receives and unloads it. Measuring and controlling order shipment time may be difficult when a seller uses for-hire carriage. To reduce the for-hire carriage transit time, the seller must use a faster carrier (one with a shorter transit time) within the current mode or utilize a faster transport mode and incur higher transportation costs.

Chrysler Corporation's Service and Parts Operations division has established an integrated contract carriage system and a computerized parts locating and order system to produce prompt and dependable delivery service for small, less-than-truckload shipments. The system, called Mopar Dedicated Delivery System (DDS), provides next-day delivery to most of its dealers from the company's eighteen distribution centers located throughout the United States. Mopar makes over 80 percent of its deliveries at night through a passkey operation. The company drivers receive keys to the dealer's facility, where deliveries are made to secured areas. The night deliveries reduce the delays normally produced by daytime highway traffic and dealer congestion.[13]

Modifying all four of the elements that contribute to lead time may be too costly. The firm may therefore make modifications in one area and permit the others to operate at existing levels. For example, investing in automated materials handling equipment may be financially unwise for the firm. To compensate for its higher manual order processing time, the firm could switch from mail to telephone order transmittal and use motor transportation instead of rail. This would permit the firm to reduce lead time without increasing its capital investment in automated materials handling equipment.

Guaranteeing a given level of lead time is an important advancement in logistics management. We may see its impact in the efficiencies that accrue both to the customer (inventory costs) and to the seller's logistics system and market position. But the concept of time, by itself, means little without dependability.

Dependability. To some customers, *dependability* can be more important than lead time. The customer can minimize his or her inventory level if lead time is fixed. That is, a customer who knows with 100 percent assurance that lead time is ten days could adjust his or her inventory levels to correspond to the average demand (usage) during the ten days and would have no need for safety stock to guard against stockouts resulting from fluctuating lead times.

inventory level and stockout costs

Cycle time. Lead time dependability, then, directly affects the customer's inventory level and stockout costs. Providing a dependable lead time reduces some of the uncertainty a customer faces. A seller who can assure the customer of a given level of lead time, plus some tolerance, distinctly differentiates its product from that of its competitor. The seller that provides a dependable lead time permits the buyer to minimize the total cost of inventory, stockouts, order processing, and production scheduling.

FIGURE 4–3 Example of the Frequency Distribution of Lead Time

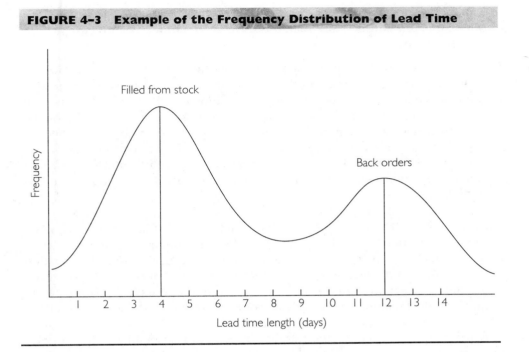

Figure 4–3 graphs a frequency distribution pertaining to lead time, measured in days. The graph is bimodal. It indicates that lead time tends to be in the vicinity of either four days or twelve days. The customer typically receives within four days orders that the seller can fill from stock. Orders that the seller cannot fill from available stock, and for which the customer must place a back order, typically result in a total order cycle time of approximately twelve days.

Dependability encompasses more than just lead time variability. More generally, dependability refers to delivering a customer's order with a regular, consistent lead time, in safe condition, and in harmony with the type and quality of items the customer ordered.

Safe delivery. An order's safe delivery is the ultimate goal of any logistics system. As was noted earlier, the logistics function is the culmination of the selling function. If goods arrive damaged or are lost, the customer cannot use the goods as he or she intended. A shipment containing damaged goods aggravates several customer cost centers—inventory, production, and marketing.

Receiving a damaged shipment deprives the customer of items for sale or production. This may increase stockout costs in the form of forgone profits or production. To guard against these costs, the customer must increase inventory levels. Thus, unsafe delivery causes the buyer to incur higher inventory carrying costs or to forgo profits or production. This situation would be unacceptable for a company interested in minimizing or eliminating inventories through some form of just-in-time program.

stockout costs

In addition to the preceding costs, an unsafe delivery may cause the customer to incur the cost of filing a claim with the carrier or returning the damaged item to the seller for repair or credit. (Depending upon the F.O.B. terms of sale and other sales agreement stipulations, the seller, not the buyer, may be

claims

responsible for these costs.) The seller will probably be aware of these two costs, since he or she will be more or less directly involved in any corrective actions that may be necessary.

lost sales or lost production

Correct orders. Finally, dependability embraces the correct filling of orders. A customer who has been anxiously awaiting the arrival of an urgently needed shipment may discover upon receiving the shipment that the seller made an error in filling the order. The customer who has not received what he or she requested may face potential lost sales or production. An improperly filled order forces the customer to reorder, if the customer is not angry enough to buy from another supplier. If a customer who is an intermediary in the marketing channel experiences a stockout, the stockout cost (lost sales) also directly affects the seller.

order information

Communications. The two logistics activities vital to order filling are the communication of customer order information to the order-filling area and the actual process of picking out of inventory the items ordered. In the order information stage, the use of EDI (electronic data interchange) can reduce errors in transferring order information from the order to the warehouse receipt. The seller should simplify product identification such as codes in order to reduce order picker errors.

EDI can not only reduce the number of errors in order filling but can also increase inventory velocity in the pipeline. Combining EDI with bar coding can improve a seller's service and lead to lower costs. In fact, EDI, along with bar coding, can help a seller to improve most logistics functions.

For example, Quill Corporation, the largest independent distributor of office products in the United States, uses a bar code scanning system to effectively control the shipment of more than 12,000 cartons a day.[14] Through catalogs, customers can order any of 7,500 SKUs. Data electronically transmitted from the bar codes helps with carrier routing, billing, inventory control, and a variety of other tasks. The system helped Quill to reduce transportation expenses by $1 million per year while improving customer service.

seller-customer channel

However, customer contact can be as important as accurate electronic data interchange. Communication with customers is vital to monitoring customer service levels relating to dependability. Customer communication is essential to the design of logistics service levels. The communication channel must be constantly open and readily accessible to all customers, for this is the seller's link to the major external constraints that customers impose upon logistics. Without customer contact, the logistics manager is unable to provide the most efficient and economical service; in other words, the logistics manager would be playing the ball game without fully knowing the rules.

two-way street

However, communication must be a two-way street. The seller must be able to transmit vital logistics service information to the customer. For example, the supplier would be well advised to inform the buyer of potential service level reductions so that the buyer can make necessary operational adjustments.

In addition, many customers request information on the logistics status of shipments. Questions concerning shipment date, the carrier, or the route, for example, are not uncommon. The customer, who needs this information to plan operations, expects the logistics manager to provide answers.

Convenience. *Convenience* is another way of saying that the logistics service level must be flexible. From the logistics operations standpoint, having one or a few standard service levels that applied to all customers would be ideal. But this assumes that all customers' logistics requirements are homogeneous. In reality, this is not the situation. For example, one customer may require the seller to palletize and ship all shipments by rail; another may require truck delivery only, with no palletization; still others may request special delivery times. Basically, logistics requirements differ with regard to packaging, the mode and carrier the customer requires, routing, and delivery times.

flexibility

Convenience recognizes customers' different requirements. A seller can usually group customer requirements by such factors as customer size, market area, and the product line the customer is purchasing. This grouping, or market segmentation, enables the logistics manager to recognize customer service requirements and to attempt to fulfill those demands as economically as possible.

different customer requirements

We can attribute the need for convenience in logistics service levels to the differing consequences the service levels have for different customers. More specifically, the cost of lost sales will differ among the customer groups. For example, a customer purchasing 30 percent of a firm's output loses more sales for the firm than a customer buying less than 0.01 percent of the firm's output does. Also, the degree of competitiveness in market areas will differ; highly competitive market areas will require a higher service level than less-competitive market areas will. The profitability of different product lines in a firm's market basket will limit the service level the firm can offer; that is, a firm may provide a lower service level for low-profit product lines.

customer profitability

However, the logistics manager must place the convenience factor in proper operational perspective. At the extreme, meeting the convenience needs of customers would mean providing a specific service level policy for each customer. Such a situation would set the stage for operational chaos; the plethora of service level policies would prevent the logistics manager from optimizing the logistics function. The need for flexibility in service level policies is warranted, but the logistics manager should restrict this flexibility to easily identifiable customer groups. He or she must examine the trade-off between the benefits (improved sales and profits or elimination of lost profits) and the costs associated with unique service levels in each specific situation.

Performance Measures for Customer Service

The four traditional dimensions of customer service from a logistics perspective—time, dependability, convenience, and communication—are essential considerations in developing a sound and effective customer service program. These dimensions of customer service also provide the underlying basis for establishing standards of performance for customer service in the logistics area.

Table 4–2 expands these four elements into a format that has been used by companies in developing customer service policy and performance measurement standards. The traditional performance measures that have been used are stated in the right-hand column. Typically, such measures were stated from the perspective of the seller, for example, orders shipped on time, orders shipped complete, product availability when an order was received, order preparation time, and so on.

TABLE 4-2 Elements and Measurement of Customer Service

Element	Brief Description	Typical Measurement Unit(s)
Product availability	The most common measure of customer service. Usually defined as percent in stock (target performance level) in some base unit (i.e., order, product, dollars).	% availability in base units.
Order cycle time	Elapsed time from order placement to order receipt. Usually measured in time units and variation from standard or target order cycle. Note: Frequently, product availability and order cycle time are combined into one standard. For example, "95 percent of orders delivered within 10 days."	Speed and consistency.
Distribution system flexibility	Ability of system to respond to special and/or unexpected needs of customer. Includes expedite and substitute capability.	Response time to special requests.
Distribution system information	Ability of firm's information system to respond in timely and accurate manner to customers' requests for information.	Speed, accuracy, and message detail of response.
Distribution system malfunction	Efficiency of procedures and time required to recover from distribution system malfunction (i.e., errors in billing, shipping, damage, claims).	Response and recovery time requirements.
Postsale product support	Efficiency in providing product support after delivery, including technical information, spare parts, or equipment modification, as appropriate.	Response time, quality of response.

SOURCE: Bernard J. LaLonde, "Customer Service," Chapter 11 in *The Distribution Handbook* (New York: The Free Press, 1985): 244.

The new supply chain environment for customer service has resulted in much more rigorous standards of performance. The performance measures are now stated from the point of view of the customer:

- Orders received on time
- Orders received complete
- Orders received damage free
- Orders filled accurately
- Orders billed accurately

If the seller is concerned only with customer service prior to shipping, as per traditional measures, the buyer may not be satisfied and the seller may not know it, because of problems occurring during the delivery process. Furthermore, the seller using traditional measures would have no basis upon which to evaluate the extent and magnitude of the problem. The current approach, focusing the measurement at the delivery level, not only provides the database to make an evaluation, but, also, and perhaps more importantly, provides an early warning of problems as they are developing. For example, if the standard for on-time delivery is 98 percent, and it slips during a given month to 95 percent, an investigation may show that a carrier is not following instructions or even that the buyer is at fault by not being ready to accept shipments.

The on-time delivery measure is even more demanding today because buyers often give appointment times for warehouse and/or store deliveries on the outbound side of logistics. As Chapter 3 indicated, the JIT programs of today's companies also necessitate narrow delivery time "windows" for vendors. Overall, making deliveries on time is much more difficult currently and will be even tougher in the future.

Another aspect of the supply chain environment is that the excellent companies are using multiple measures of customer service simultaneously. Using multiple measures makes it much more difficult to achieve high levels of customer service. For example, assume that a company was using only one of the following:

95 percent of orders delivered on time

93 percent of orders filled completely

97 percent of orders delivered damage free

Achieving one of these performance levels—for example, 95 percent of orders delivered on time—would be challenging but very possible by focusing upon the activities necessary to attain the required performance. But trying to achieve all three performance levels simultaneously for every order and to attain a "perfect order" level like 95 percent would be difficult. For example, even if a company hit each of the above standards individually, it might find its perfect order measure to be 72 percent or less because the misses would not occur at the same time for a single order. That is, an order might be on time and damage free, but it might not be complete because of a stockout. Consequently, it would not be a perfect order. Achieving a perfect order performance level of 95 percent with three or more measures being utilized simultaneously is indicative of the requirements of today's supply chain environment.

Implementing Customer Service Standards. This section highlights the keys for successfully developing and implementing customer service standards.
setting standards

The first point is to be wary of adopting easily achievable performance standards; such standards may be too low to be of practical value. While setting and adhering to a meaningful standard should help to differentiate your firm from the competition, setting standards at unrealistically low levels will not help to establish a competitive advantage.

Second, some current management philosophies—such as the Deming Method for Quality—are very critical of any acceptable quality level (AQL) set below 100 percent. This does not mean that a firm can achieve 100 percent performance at all times. The use of 100 percent represents an attitude more than a measurement. From a practical viewpoint, however, establishing an AQL that is less than 100 percent will generally limit, rather than encourage, superior performance.
levels of quality

Third, the firm should develop customer service policies and standards through customer consultation. After adopting these standards, the firm should formally
communication with customers

communicate them to customers. Certain firms prefer to keep silent about their customer service standards and to avoid letting their customers know their exact policies and performance targets. The best approach, however, is to communicate these policies and standards to customers very openly.

control of customer service
Fourth, the firm should develop procedures to measure, monitor, and control the customer service quality called for by the firm's performance measures and standards. Using techniques such as statistical process control (SPC), obtaining feedback, and taking corrective action are essential to success. When customer service standards are ineffective, the firm should not hesitate to amend or discontinue them as appropriate.

A Note on Inbound System Service Levels

Up to this point, we have been considering customer service levels from the outbound side of logistics. A brief digression into service levels for inbound logistics will reveal some similarity to those for outbound systems.

One hundred percent service is almost a necessity on the inbound side. As we noted previously, disruptions in the flow of goods to the consumer aggravate the consumer's costs. However, the consumer can often substitute products, and even if substitutes are unavailable, the cost of a stockout in forgone sales and profits may be quite small in comparison with the cost of a stockout on the inbound side.

Short lead times usually preclude the possibility for substituting raw materials. First, raw material suppliers are not as widely available as suppliers of finished goods. Second, a particular raw material's unique technical standards may prevent a firm from substituting even a highly similar material. In short, the lack of alternative raw material suppliers, coupled with the possible technical incompatibility of different suppliers' raw materials, greatly restrains a firm's ability to substitute raw materials during a stockout.

cost of physical supply stockout
Without this substitution possibility, a disruption in physical supply service may result in a plant closing, temporary layoffs, and high start-up costs when the raw material finally arrives. Temporarily closing a plant may mean paying labor for a partial day's wage (depending upon union contract terms), even though no production occurs during this time. If the temporary stockout is prolonged, the firm will furlough labor, increasing future unemployment compensation rates. In addition, once the stockout is alleviated, overtime production might be necessary to replace reduced finished goods inventory or to fill back orders for finished goods. If finished goods inventory is depleted, the firm will forgo profits as well. Last, the firm still incurs the plant's overhead costs throughout the nonproductive period.

In short, the cost of a stockout on the inbound side is very great. This extremely high cost greatly increases the "value" of a raw material facing a stockout; that is, the item assumes an emergency value much higher than the item's price. The emergency value of raw materials requires the logistics manager to utilize movement and storage functions that he or she would not normally use.

For example, consider a possible stockout of a door handle, valued at 50 cents per handle, at a plant manufacturing auto bodies. A stockout of the 50-cent handle would stop the auto body assembly line and incur corresponding costs for labor that reported for work but could not complete the shift. The company values this lost productivity at $160,000 per shift (assuming 1,000 employees at $20/hour for 8 hours). In addition, the company incurs plant overhead even though no production occurs, a cost of $200,000 per day (assumed cost). Thus, the auto body manufacturer in this example values the cost of the door handle stockout at $360,000 per day.

In addition, a raw material stockout may cause intracompany and intercompany effects. The chain reaction of shortages may affect other plants that depend upon the stopped auto body plant, possibly causing work stoppages. Thus, a raw material stockout at one plant may affect the operations of other manufacturing plants in the firm's system or the firm's customers.

To offset the door handle stockout, the auto body manufacturer would probably utilize air transportation. The door handle's airfreight cost may be ten times the handle's value ($5 per handle for airfreight, versus 50 cents for the handle itself). However, considering the potential stockout cost, the handle assumes an emergency value of $360,000 in this example, justifying the cost of airfreight.

For bulk raw materials such as coal, iron ore, and sand, providing uninterrupted supply service normally entails high inventory levels rather than premium transportation. The physical characteristics of bulk commodities permit the use of inexpensive warehousing facilities—an open-air facility is usually adequate—and preclude the use of airfreight. In addition, the bulk materials' value is relatively low, requiring a fairly low capital investment.

For example, we might find that an electric utility company utilizing coal stockpiles a 60- to 120-day coal supply. In this example, the potential costs of stockouts (the social and economic costs to all users of electricity) are astronomical. Also, the volume of coal the company uses in one day would make the use of premium transportation (air or even truck) a physical impossibility. Therefore, the potentially devastating cost of an electric supply stoppage justifies the capital investment associated with a ninety-day inventory of coal.

Overview of Customer Service

It would be difficult to summarize all the discussion and analysis related to customer service that have been presented here. In an attempt to capture in summary form some important points about customer service, we offer the following observations:

- If the basics of customer service are not in place, nothing else matters.
- Customers may define service differently.
- All customer accounts are not the same.
- Relationships are not one-dimensional.
- Partnerships and added value can "lock up" customers.

Figure 4–4 offers a more comprehensive view of the issues related to customer service. This list of questions can be used as a guide in developing a sound customer service policy and statement of appropriate standards of performance. The questions posed in Figure 4–4 can also be answered by a cross-functional team to develop a consensus in the area of customer service.

The next section focuses upon channels of distribution. The material that has been covered on the topic of customer service is very relevant and closely related to this discussion, since for many manufacturers the channels of distribution are actually their customers. Therefore, the development of customer service policy and standards relates directly to what manufacturers need to serve their "customers."

FIGURE 4-4 Customer Service Issues

- What do our customers feel about present levels of service?

- Do their perceptions match up with ours?

- How do our services compare to those of our competitors?

- Are we using appropriate standards and measurements to monitor our service performance?

- Is it possible to segment our customers according to the varying degrees of service they require?

- Can we produce the same levels of service we are presently providing in a more cost-effective manner?

- Can improved customer service be used as a strategic weapon to provide an important competitive advantage?

- In the minds of our customers, how important is service compared to other elements of the marketing mix, such as price, promotion, and products?

CHANNELS OF DISTRIBUTION

As was suggested at the beginning of this chapter, no discussion of outbound logistics would be complete without reference to channels of distribution. Technically, a channel of distribution is one or more companies or individuals who participate in the flow of goods and services from the producer to the final user or consumer.

Many companies use other companies or individuals to distribute some or all of their products to the final consumer. Consider the example of Nabisco Foods. When we stop at a grocery store to pick up a bag of Oreo cookies, a tube of Crest toothpaste, and a can of Planter's peanuts, we are buying a relatively small quantity of several companies' products. We do not want to visit three different stores to purchase these products, and Nabisco and other manufacturers do not want to operate their own stores in proximity to every possible buyer.

channel efficiency   So, for cost efficiencies and customer convenience, Nabisco Foods sells in large quantities to other companies who can get the product to a location convenient for the consumer more efficiently than Nabisco could; that is, these companies leverage costs through the volume of several product lines. This does not mean that Nabisco may not sell directly to some users or customers. Large restaurants, schools, military installations, large chains, and other organizations that purchase in large quantities may actually buy directly from Nabisco Foods.

Most customers, however, purchase Nabisco's Life Savers or Royal Pudding from another company, usually a retail store. In fact, the retail store may buy from

FIGURE 4–5   Examples of Channels of Distribution for the Food Products Manufacturing Industry

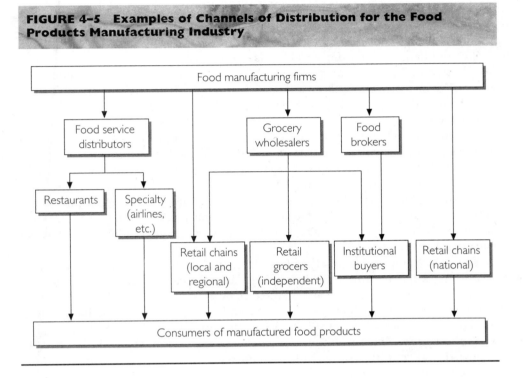

a wholesaler or broker, so several "layers" can separate Nabisco from Mrs. Novack in Mountaintop, Pennsylvania, when she purchases Nabisco's Ritz crackers.

As we pointed out previously, certain companies only sell directly to their ultimate customers. Boeing Aircraft Corporation is an example. However, many companies sell some part of their product line through distribution channels. Figure 4–5 presents an overview of the possible channel arrangements. Keep in mind that a company such as Nabisco may use several of the alternatives that Figure 4–5 depicts.

An important point here is that the channel company—Kmart, Wal-Mart or Toys "R" Us—is the manufacturer's real customer. Therefore, a manufacturer discussing customer service is usually talking about Thrift Drug Stores or some other retailer, not about an individual consumer.

The Growth and Importance of Channels of Distribution

A virtual revolution has been occurring in the ranks of the companies that make up the distribution industry, which we have referred to as channels of distribution. Nowhere has this been more apparent than at the retail level, with the dramatic growth in companies that are usually called mass merchandisers, such as Wal-Mart, Kmart, Sears, and Target; and the category retailers, for example, Toys "R" Us, Home Depot, and Staples.

Much has been written about the mass merchandisers and club stores and their impact upon many small and medium-size towns and cities where the small and medium-size retailers have been "squeezed" and some forced out of business. Main Street in some instances has been decimated. The more efficient, lower-priced mass merchandisers have a competitive advantage over the smaller retailers. Even the number of regional supermarkets has declined as the mass merchandisers have expanded into food and package goods.

We could argue about the social impact and merits of the changing face of the distribution industry and of small-town USA, but it would not be particularly relevant to our focus on outbound logistics systems. However, this trend toward larger, more efficient retailers has also had a major economic impact on logistics supply chains.

The mass merchandisers and other large retailers have changed the nature of logistics, leading to what some have called the Wal-Mart effect, by demanding customized or tailored logistics systems to meet their particular needs. Historically, the large manufacturers with successful brands, such as Procter & Gamble, General Foods, Nabisco, Hershey, and so on, exercised the most influence and power in the flow of goods to the ultimate consumers. They tended to emphasize product development and brand management with homogeneous (vanilla) logistics systems to all customers.

The "new retailers" revolted against this convention. They were not willing to accept the same treatment as JoPa's Deli and Grocery in Brooklyn. They demanded special service, such as scheduled deliveries, special pallet packs, advance shipment notice, cross-docking capability, and so on. They wanted high-quality, specialized logistics services with the lowest possible prices for the products they were purchasing. This revolution was similar to the consumer revolution that we discussed earlier, with its demand for high quality, lowest price, and maximum flexibility.

The 1980s and particularly the 1990s have been characterized by a rash of logistics-related strategies and tactics that have been developed largely in response to the customer and consumer revolution. Efficient consumer response (ECR), vendor managed inventories (VMI), continuous replenishment (CR), direct store delivery (DSD), everyday low pricing (EDLP), supply chain management (SCM), quick response (QR), and others are illustrative of the developments and changes that have occurred.

The successful retailers have based much of their efficiency upon good logistics systems. Wal-Mart is frequently lauded in logistics circles for its efficiencies in warehousing (cross-docking), transportation, materials handling, and other logistics processes. The new retailers understand the importance of good logistics and know that it gives them business power. Sears Merchandise Group has hired Gus Pagonis, the retired three-star general and logistics hero of the Persian Gulf War, who managed that 7,000-mile supply chain. He has been brought in to reengineer the logistics system at Sears and has already made major strides in this direction.

IKEA, the Swedish furnishings company, is another example of a super retailer who has expanded into a giant enterprise with efficient logistics and good business acumen. IKEA has grown from a small Swedish mail-order operation to the largest retailer of home furnishings in the world, with over 100 stores and revenues near $5 billion. Its logistics operation is the featured centerpiece of its global business system, with a network of fourteen warehouses that link to point-of-sales data in all the stores. The warehouses operate as logistical control points, consolidation centers, and transit hubs. They play a proactive part in the integration of supply and demand, decreasing the need to provide storage for production runs, anticipate retail demand, and eliminate storage.

It is fair to say that the large retailers, wholesalers, and other channel members are reshaping the logistics of supply chains in conjunction with manufacturers and third-party providers. Distributors are key members of many supply chains. Overall, the traditional role of channels of distribution is not an accurate reflection of their importance and scope of influence. They not only help with change, they create change.

The appendix to this chapter summarizes the major marketing aspects of channels of distribution.

A SPECIAL NOTE ON INVENTORY FOR OUTBOUND SYSTEMS

One definition that has been offered for logistics is that it is the management of inventory, whether in motion or at rest, for the purpose of satisfying customers. Nowhere is this description of logistics more appropriate than with outbound logistics, where inventory is the "glue" for the individual logistics system and even the supply chain and at the same time is the focus of constant scrutiny to reduce or eliminate it. This somewhat paradoxical role of inventory as both a problem and a solution can frequently make logistics managers paranoid as companies strive to increase market share and improve return on investment by lowering inventory cost.

The key to dealing with inventory is to recognize that it has to be managed from a systems perspective, in which the trade-offs are measured comprehensively and accurately. Decreasing or increasing inventory will affect not only direct inventory costs but also other areas of logistics such as warehousing, transportation, materials handling, customer service, and probably the manufacturing, marketing, and finance functions. Too frequently, the real costs of changes in inventory policy are not adequately measured; that is, firms use inappropriate measures or ignore certain costs. Chapters 5 and 6 provide a comprehensive analysis of the many dimensions of inventory to apprise the reader of the true cost of inventory. Two specific topics related to inventory will be covered in this chapter: the cost of inventory stockouts and DRP systems. Some additional, more general observations will also be offered.

The cost of stockouts is especially germane to our discussion of outbound logistics because it so directly affects customer service and the channels of distribution. We should have adequate measures to help us make good decisions.

EXPECTED COST OF STOCKOUTS

A principal benefit of inventory availability, and hence of customer service, is to reduce the incidence of stockouts. Once we develop a convenient way to calculate the cost of a stockout, we can use stockout probability information to determine the expected stockout cost. Last, we can analyze alternative customer service levels directly by comparing the expected cost of stockouts with the revenue-enhancing benefits of customer service.

This section examines stockout issues that relate more to finished goods inventories than to inventories of raw materials or component parts. Calculating stockout costs for finished goods is generally more formidable than calculating these costs for raw materials. We must, however, address issues relating to both of these inventory types. An earlier section of this chapter dealt specifically with inbound logistics supplies and stockout costs.

effects of stockouts

A *stockout* occurs when desired quantities of finished goods are not available when and where a customer needs them. When a seller is unable to satisfy demand with available inventory, one of four possible events may occur: (1) the customer waits until the product is available; (2) the customer back orders the product; (3) the seller loses a sale; or (4) the seller loses a customer. From the viewpoint of most companies, we have listed these four outcomes from best to worst in terms of desirability and cost impact. Theoretically, scenario 1 (customer waits) should cost nothing; this situation is more likely to occur where product substitutability is very low.

Back Order

nature of cost

A company having to back order an item that is out of stock will incur expenses for special order processing and transportation. The extra order processing traces the back order's movement, in addition to the normal processing for regular replenishments. The customer usually incurs extra transportation charges because a back order is typically a smaller shipment and often incurs higher rates. Also, the seller may need to ship the back ordered item a longer distance—for example, from a plant or warehouse in another region of the country. In addition, the seller may need to ship the back order by a faster and more expensive means of transportation. Therefore, we could estimate the back order cost by analyzing the additional order processing and additional transportation expense. If customers always back ordered out-of-stock items, the seller could use this analysis to estimate the cost of stockouts. The seller could then compare this cost with the cost of carrying excess inventory.

Lost Sales

direct loss

Most firms find that although some customers may back order, others will turn to alternative supply sources. In other words, most companies have competitors who produce substitute products; and when one source does not have an item available, the customer will order that item from another source. In such cases, the stockout has caused a lost sale. The seller's direct loss is the loss of profit on the item that was unavailable when the customer wanted it. Thus, a seller can determine direct loss by calculating profit on one item and multiplying it by the number the customer ordered. For example, if the order was for 100 units and the profit is $10 per unit, the loss is $1,000.

special explanation

We should make three additional points about lost sales. First, in addition to the lost profit, we might include an amount for the cost of the salesperson who made the initial sale. The sales effort was wasted and in that sense was an opportunity loss. Whether including such a cost is valid would depend upon whether the company uses salespeople in its marketing effort. Second, determining the amount of a lost sale may be difficult in some circumstances. For example, numerous companies customarily take orders by telephone. A customer may initially just inquire about an item's availability without specifying how much he or she desires. If an item is out of stock, the customer may never indicate a quantity, and the seller will not know the amount of the loss. Other problems may cause difficulties but are not insurmountable. For example, although developing a system for recording lost sales in telephone-order situations is often difficult, a seller can overcome this problem through sampling techniques. Third, estimating how a particular stockout will affect future sales within other product lines is difficult.

In the likely event that a firm will sustain lost sales with inventory stockouts, the firm will have to assign a cost along the lines we suggested earlier. Then the firm should analyze the number of stockouts it could expect with different inventory levels. An example of this technique is given later. The seller should then multiply the expected number of lost sales by the profit loss plus additional assigned cost, if any, and compare the cost with the cost of carrying safety stock. **calculation**

Lost Customer

The third possible event that can occur because of a stockout is the loss of a customer; that is, the customer permanently switches to another supplier. A supplier who loses a customer loses a future stream of income. Estimating the customer loss that stockouts can cause is difficult. Marketing researchers have attempted to analyze brand switching for some time. Such analysis often uses management science techniques along with more qualitative marketing research methods. This is usually the most difficult loss to estimate because of the need to estimate how many units the customer may have purchased in the future. **difficult nature**

Determining the Expected Cost of Stockouts

To make an informed decision as to how much inventory to carry, a firm must determine the expected cost it will incur if a stockout occurs. That is, how much money will the firm lose if a stockout occurs? **procedure**

The first step is to identify a stockout's potential consequences. These include a back order, a lost sale, and a lost customer. The second step is to calculate each result's expense or loss of profit and then to estimate the cost of a single stockout. For the purposes of this discussion, assume the following: 70 percent of all stockouts result in a back order and a back order requires extra handling costs of $6.00; 20 percent result in a lost sale for the item, and this loss equals $20.00 in lost profit margin; and 10 percent result in a lost customer, or a loss of $200.00.

Calculate the overall impact as follows:

$$
\begin{aligned}
70\% \text{ of } \$\ \ 6.00 &= \$\ \ 4.20 \\
20\% \text{ of } \$\ 20.00 &= \ \ \ \ 4.00 \\
10\% \text{ of } \$200.00 &= \ \underline{20.00}
\end{aligned}
$$

Total = estimated cost per stockout = $28.20

Since $28.20 is the average dollar amount the firm can save by averting a stockout, the firm should carry additional inventory to protect against stockouts only as long as carrying the additional inventory costs less than $28.20.

A firm can easily use this information when formally evaluating two or more logistics system alternatives. For each alternative, the firm would need to estimate the potential number of stockouts and to multiply those numbers by the estimated cost of a single stockout. This would represent a way to include stockout costs in the overall decision-making process.

DISTRIBUTION RESOURCE PLANNING (DRP)

Distribution resource planning (DRP) is a widely used and potentially powerful technique for outbound logistics systems to help determine the appropriate level of inventory. In actuality, the success stories involving DRP indicate that companies can improve customer service (decrease stockout situations), reduce the overall level of finished goods inventories, reduce transportation costs, and improve distribution center operations. With this potential, it is no wonder that manufacturers are interested in implementing DRP systems.

As was indicated in Chapter 3, DRP is usually used with an MRP (materials requirements planning) system, which attempts to manage and minimize inbound inventories, particularly where numerous items are needed, as is the case in the automobile industry. Items that need to be combined and used in the assembly of a finished product usually have varying lead times. Therefore, MRP is tied to the master production schedule, which indicates which items are to be produced each day and the sequence in which they will be produced. This schedule is then used as the basis to forecast the actual parts needed and when they will be needed. When the master production schedule is combined with the lead times necessary for each item, a schedule can be developed that indicates when each item has to be ordered. The quantity is determined by comparing inventory status with the total number of items needed to meet the production schedule.

MRP minimizes inventory to the extent that the master production schedule accurately reflects what is needed to satisfy customer demand in the marketplace. If the production schedule does not match demand, the company will have too much of some items and too little of others.

The underlying rationale for DRP is to more accurately forecast demand and to explode that information back for use in developing production schedules. In that way a company can minimize inbound inventory by using MRP in conjunction with production schedules. Outbound (finished goods) inventory is minimized through the use of DRP. Most DRP models are more comprehensive than stand-alone MRP models, and they also schedule transportation.

DRP develops a projection for each SKU and requires[15]

- Forecast of demand for each SKU
- Current inventory level of the SKU (balance on hand, BOH)
- Target safety stock
- Recommended replenishment quantity
- Lead time for replenishment

This information is used to develop replenishment requirements. One of the key elements of a successful DRP system is the development of a DRP table, which consists of a variety of elements including the SKU, forecast, BOH, scheduled receipt, planned order, and so on. Table 4–3 illustrates the DRP table for chicken noodle soup at the Columbus Distribution Center. The table shows only nine weeks, but a DRP table would typically show 52 weeks and would be a dynamic document that would undergo continual change as the data, especially demand, changed. Individual tables provide useful information, but combining tables can lead to increased advantage. For example, combining all of the individual SKU

TABLE 4–3   DRP Table for Chicken Noodle Soup

Columbus Distribution Center—Distribution Resource Planning									
	Jan.				**Feb.**				**March**
Week	**1**	**2**	**3**	**4**	**5**	**6**	**7**	**8**	**9**
CHICKEN NOODLE:	Current BOH = 4,314		Q = 3,800	SS = 1,956		LT = 1			
Forecast	974	974	974	974	989	1,002	1,002	1,002	1,061
Sched. receipt	0	0	3,800	0	0	0	3,800	0	0
BOH-ending	3,340	2,366	5,192	4,218	3,229	2,227	5,025	4,023	2,962
Planned order	0	3,800	0	0	0	3,800	0	0	3,800
Actual order									

Q = Quantity
SS = Safety stock
LT = Lead time

SOURCE: A. J. Stenger, "Distribution Resources Planning," Penn State University, class example.

tables of items shipped from one source can provide useful information about consolidation possibilities and when to expect orders to arrive at a warehouse. Essentially, the combining of tables helps to develop efficient production plans and shipping plans, as illustrated in Figure 4–6.

FIGURE 4–6   Combining DRP Tables

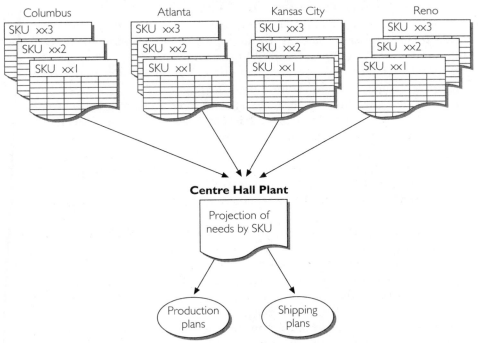

ADAPTED FROM: A. J. Stenger, "Distribution Resources Planning," *The Distribution Handbook* (New York: The Free Press, 1994).

DRP, particularly when combined with MRP, is a powerful tool that can lead to better customer service and lower total logistics and manufacturing costs.

Inventory control is a special challenge in today's supply chains, and efforts such as efficient consumer response (ECR) focus primarily upon reducing inventory levels in the supply chain to reduce costs. Tools such as MRP can help, but it is also necessary to assess the true costs of inventory, especially stockouts.

SUMMARY

- Outbound logistics systems have received the most attention in many companies, but even in today's customer service environment, outbound and inbound systems must be coordinated.
- Outbound systems, like inbound systems, vary in scope, importance, and complexity along the supply chain. A steel company's outbound system would be less complex than that of a food producer.
- Customer service is a major focus for most companies, and customer service cuts across functional lines. Logistics plays a key role in customer service, since it has the responsibility for assuring final delivery.
- Customer service is usually the key interface between logistics and marketing. Traditionally, this interface has been seen as part of the "place" dimension of the marketing mix, but that perspective is too narrow and static today. We need to view the interface between marketing and logistics as a part of the supply chain.
- Customer service is a part of the augmented product from the point of view of marketers, and this perspective is consistent with the concept of value added to the product as illustrated by Becton Dickinson.
- Customer service is frequently viewed in three principal ways—as an activity, as a performance measure, and as a philosophy. It is important to include the value-adding role of customer service in the supply chain.
- The four major elements of customer service from a logistics perspective are time, dependability, communication, and flexibility.
- The major determinants of order cycle time are transmittal time, processing time, preparation time, and delivery time. The emphasis today is on reducing order cycle time, which requires a detailed analysis of the components of cycle time.
- In order to be efficient and effective in providing and managing customer service, we have to provide performance standards and measure performance against these standards. Many measures have been used, and traditionally they have focused on the seller. Today, there is an emphasis upon measuring what happens at the buyer level.
- The standards of performance for customer service have continued to increase to higher levels and have become multidimensional.
- Service is also important on the inbound side of logistics and may require even higher standards of performance because of the threat of a plant shutdown.
- Channels of distribution play an important role in getting products to the ultimate consumer at the best cost and price.
- There has been a virtual revolution in the distributor industry with the growth of large retailers such as the mass merchandisers, sector retailers, price clubs, and deep discounters. These retailers have forced much change in the practice of logistics.

- Inventory also plays a special role in outbound logistics systems. It is important in today's environment, which emphasizes reduction of inventory, that the true costs be recognized and measured. Tools such as DRP allow the logistics manager to manage inventories more effectively.

STUDY QUESTIONS

1. Outbound logistics systems are said to have received more attention than inbound logistics systems. Why would this be true? What are the pitfalls of such an emphasis?

2. "Outbound logistics systems may vary from firm to firm along the same supply chain." Do you agree with this statement? Why or why not?

3. Customer service is frequently viewed as the primary interface between logistics and marketing. Discuss the nature of the interface and how that interface may be changing.

4. What is meant by the term "augmented product"? How does this concept relate to customer service and logistics?

5. Companies can have three levels of involvement with respect to customer service. Discuss and evaluate each of the three levels.

6. Discuss the nature and importance of the four logistics-related elements of customer service.

7. Order cycle time is an important component of customer service. Discuss the four major components of order cycle time.

8. Managing customer service requires measurement. Discuss the nature of the performance measures used in the customer service area.

9. What is the role of channels of distribution in the outbound logistics system? How has that role been changing in recent years?

10. Members of channels of distribution are looked upon by some manufacturers as partners. Why has this trend developed?

NOTES

1. Ronald Henkoff, "Delivering the Goods," *Fortune* (November 28, 1994): 64–78.
2. Henkoff, "Delivering the Goods."
3. Henkoff, "Delivering the Goods."
4. Henkoff, "Delivering the Goods."
5. Henkoff, "Delivering the Goods," 78.
6. T. J. Peters and R. H. Waterman, *In Search of Excellence* (New York: Harper & Row, 1982).
7. Henkoff, "Delivering the Goods," 64.
8. Becton Dickinson, *Annual Report* (1994).
9. Philip Kotler, *Marketing Management,* 5th ed. (Englewood Cliffs, NJ: Prentice-Hall, 1990): 225–26.

10. B. J. LaLonde, "Customer Service," Chapter 11 in *The Distribution Handbook* (New York: The Free Press, 1985): 243.

11. Fred Moody, "Examples of Excellence," *Canadian Transportation Journal* (May 1991): 17–19.

12. Moody, "Examples of Excellence."

13. Moody, "Examples of Excellence."

14. J. L. Cavinato, "How to Keep Customers Coming Back for More," *Distribution* (December 1989): 60.

15. A. J. Stenger, "Materials Resources Planning," *Distribution Handbook* (New York: The Free Press, 1994): 89–97.

Case 4-1

WALTON SEED COMPANY

"We have to do something about our customer service levels and our inventory turns," complained Lisa Williams, CEO for Walton Seed Company, to Jason Greaser, the new director of logistics. Jason immediately wanted to know the details of the problem, since he had just joined Walton Seed and had not had an opportunity to really delve into any of its problems. Lisa responded, "Let me give you some of the background and you can put that education to use that you received at Penn State." Jason smiled and said, "I am really interested in addressing some of the major problems and issues that Walton Seed has in the logistics area, so I can put my education and experience to good use. We had a similar problem at CBL Electronics, where I did my internship. While I realize that the products are different, there may be some common threads."

Background

Walton Seed Company was founded by Eric Walton in Toledo, Ohio, and subsequently moved to York, Pennsylvania. Traditionally, Walton's niche was as a high-quality seed company selling grass, flower, and vegetable seeds through a mail-order catalog. But it subsequently started to distribute through small, family-owned hardware and variety stores. As the business grew, the company expanded its distribution to several smaller wholesalers, who gave Walton additional market coverage in Ohio, Indiana, Illinois, and New York. Walton still continued its catalog business in the Middle Atlantic states and served retailers directly in Pennsylvania, Maryland, and New Jersey.

The seed business is such that sales are traditionally very heavy in the spring and early summer and drop off dramatically for the rest of the year. Catalog sales help to spread out demand a little by making sales promotions in the January/February mailing, when people start thinking "spring" to help get through the winter. But overall, sales are still very concentrated. Therefore, Walton pushes inventory out into its warehouse during the fall and winter to be ready for the big spring and summer sales spurt.

During the season, the company runs out of certain types of seeds and has an abundance of others. The wholesalers and retailers complain about the stockouts. Sometimes they will accept substitutions, but not often enough. The wholesalers and retailers do not provide in-season sales information and tend to buy large quantities prior to the start of the season.

Another matter worrying Lisa Williams is the decline in the number of independent hardware and variety stores, with the growth of Wal-Mart, Home Depot, Lowes, and others of similar size. Walton does not sell to those stores, directly or indirectly, because Walton has positioned itself at the higher end of the market with high-quality seeds.

Walton really wants to increase its late summer and fall sales of grass seeds and perennial flower seeds, to spread out demand and also to avoid stockouts, which result in lost sales and customers.

The Problem

"Well, Jason, there you have it in a nutshell," said Lisa. "It is an exasperating situation, and we need your help in solving these problems."

"Wow, you are right!" replied Jason, "There are really challenging issues; I won't be able to claim that you didn't give me anything significant to sink my teeth into. Do you have anything specific that you want me to start with, since this is such a comprehensive set of problems?"

Case Questions

Here are the questions Lisa wants Jason to answer:

1. How can we improve in-season sales forecasting and develop a logistics system that is more responsive to demand and sales?
2. What are some of the special logistical issues that we will need to consider if we attempt to sell to the mass merchandisers?
3. What standard(s) of performance should we use for measuring customer service?

Case 4–2

BEIERLEIN DISTRIBUTORS

Background

For more than 25 years, Beierlein Distributors of Galesburg, Illinois, has enjoyed a continued record of growth and profitability. Beierlein serves more than 500 stores in the Midwest and is a retailer-owned food distributor company. Beierlein's growth has been driven in part by forward buying of promotions by grocery manufacturers and other inflation-driven market gains.

The grocery manufacturers have, over the years, developed a pattern of having end-of-the-quarter sales promotions, which offer substantially reduced prices so that their sales can meet quarterly objectives or quotas. Beierlein, like other wholesalers, has taken advantage of the sales promotions to buy large quantities of those discounted products, which then give it ample inventory to provide to stores for 60 to 90 days in the future.

Now Beierlein is faced with a problem: The grocery manufacturers are promoting and implementing a new ECR approach that will essentially eliminate the end-of-the-quarter deals and the "margins" that the stores have depended upon for their profitability. Beierlein is also concerned about the stores' ability to compete over the longer run with the mass merchandisers and price clubs.

Current Situation

Jim Beierlein, president of the food cooperative wholesaling company, has decided that they really need a new vision that will transform Beierlein from a traditional type of wholesale/warehouse operation into a cost-efficient, consumer-oriented organization that develops partnerships with other members of the supply chain. To that end, "Big Jim" has decided to hire Nittany Logistics Associates (NLA), a well-established logistics consulting company, to help Beierlein Distributors attain the new vision that he has for the company.

Case Questions

These are the questions that Jim Beierlein wants the consultants to address:

1. What types of cost savings could we realize under the new ECR approach? What would the advantage be to Beierlein?
2. What steps could we take to provide lower inventory requirements for our stores?
3. Are there any new technologies that Beierlein could use to improve its logistics systems?

APPENDIX 4A

CHANNELS OF DISTRIBUTION

CHANNEL FUNCTIONS AND INTERMEDIARIES

A channel of distribution is one or more companies or individuals who participate in the flow of goods and services from the producer to the final user or consumer. This encompasses a variety of intermediary firms, including those that we can classify as wholesalers or retailers. Since most companies find that distribution channel decisions are critical to their overall success, this topic should be an educational priority for all corporate managers. In the logistics area, understanding and appreciating the area of channels is a prerequisite to effective strategy formulation, operations, and control.[1]

Managing distribution channels requires a firm to coordinate and integrate marketing and logistics activities in a manner consistent with overall corporate strategy. Two channels, the transactional channel and the logistical channel, are related. The transactional channel refers to the marketing related transactions associated with channels of distribution, e.g., billing, accounts receivable, etc. The logistical channel refers to the actual flow of goods through the channel (wholesalers, retailers, etc.) to the ultimate consumer.

Effective channel management necessitates a good grasp of the management alternatives and guiding principles applicable to each of these. We should also note the four basic functions of logistical channel members: sorting out, accumulating, allocating, and assorting. We can classify channel systems as either direct or indirect, and we can further subdivide indirect channels into traditional and vertical marketing systems (VMS). With the VMS, some degree of implicit or explicit relationship exists among the firms in the channel, and firms in the channel have considerable opportunity to coordinate their activities.

This appendix, which elaborates further on the topic of distribution channels, covers several areas that are important to logistics managers today. The first section covers channel systems in detail. It also describes industry-specific channels of distribution to show some of the available alternatives that companies use. The second section discusses channel issues in general. The third section directs attention to factors of specific interest to service sector channels. The fourth section examines the evaluation and measurement of channel effectiveness.

This appendix focuses upon institutions and processes that are of direct relevance to the transactional and logistical channels. For a channel to properly per-

FIGURE 4A-1   Alternative Channels of Distribution

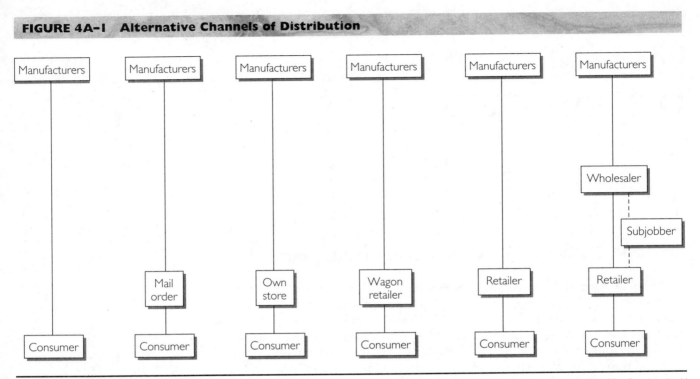

SOURCE: James F. Robeson and David T. Kollatt, "Channels of Distribution," *The Distribution Handbook* (New York: The Free Press, 1994): 226. Reprinted with the permission of The Free Press, an imprint of Simon & Schuster from *The Distribution Handbook*, James F. Robeson, Editor-in-Chief and Robert G. House, Associate Editor. Copyright © 1985 by The Free Press.

form its activities, however, it must include another important channel participant: a *facilitating* agency or institution. Examples include firms that provide transportation, warehousing, and distribution services; advertising agencies and marketing research firms; and firms that provide financial and insurance services.

CHANNEL SYSTEMS

example of a channel system

Figure 4A–1 presents some of the principal channels of distribution a manufacturing firm may consider to see that its products are ultimately available for purchase by consumers or industrial users. The diagram shows that a channel may consist of various levels, and it may have both *vertical* (e.g., manufacturer–wholesaler–retailer–end user) and *horizontal* (among firms at the same level) dimensions. A firm need adopt no single channel of distribution for its products. Typically, firms use a variety of channels to see that products are available for end users to purchase.

A Systems Approach to Channels

Channels are *systems* of organizations that work in a coordinated manner toward some common goal.[2] A channel must meet five criteria to qualify as a system:

FIGURE 4A-1   Alternative Channels of Distribution—Continued

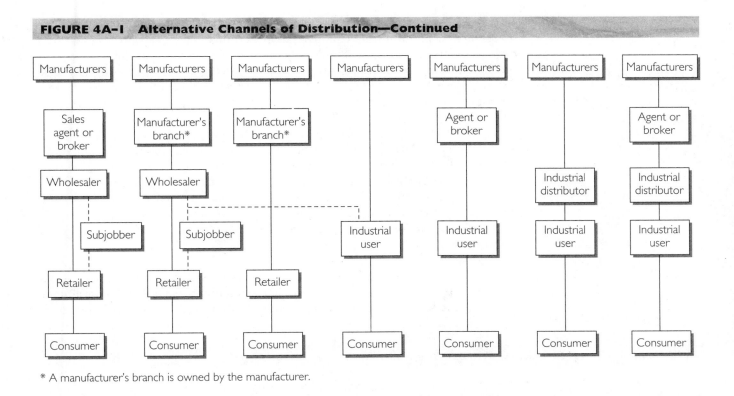

* A manufacturer's branch is owned by the manufacturer.

- There must be a set of cooperating institutions.
- There must be an objective that transcends individual objectives in the performance of channel activities.
- The channel must involve a sequence of activities; orders flow toward the supplier, products flow toward the market.
- The channel must include several different types of flows simultaneously.
- Channel performance must increase through central coordination of the individual decisions of each channel member.[3]

A channel system is a complex mechanism. To meet its objectives, a successful channel system places significant demands on its member entities and requires an exceptional degree of transactional as well as logistical coordination of activities among those various firms.

Major Types of Channel Intermediaries

Institutionally, channel intermediaries, or channel middlemen, may be participants in either the wholesale or retail trade. We will discuss both here, and briefly summarize the specific alternative forms available under each.

Wholesalers. The *1984 Industrial Outlook* describes three principal types of entities in the wholesale distribution industry: merchant wholesalers; manufacturer's sales branches and offices; and agents, brokers, and commission merchants.[4] Merchant wholesalers account for the largest share of sales, employment, and firms and establishments.

The wholesaler's role is broad and complex. This role includes selling goods to retailers or to industrial, commercial, institutional, farm, and professional business users. In addition to selling, wholesalers frequently perform some other functions, including maintaining inventories of goods; extending credit; physically assembling, sorting, and grading goods in lots; breaking up bulk lots for redistribution in smaller lots; and various types of promotion such as advertising and label design.[5]

Figure 4A–2 shows one way of illustrating the differences among various wholesale institutions. Merchant wholesalers or merchant intermediaries take title to the goods. In the case of agents and brokers, title is not transferred—their role principally involves identifying potential buyers and earning a commission. Manufacturers' branches and outlets represent manufacturer-owned establishments that exist to give the manufacturer direct access to the marketplace. These branches and outlets are a form of channel intermediary within a *direct* channel system, in contrast to an *indirect* channel system.

Retailers. The principal function that retail establishments serve is to make product available for consumers and industrial users to purchase. Retail establishments may take the form of traditional stores and places of business or may sell through

FIGURE 4A-2   Classification of Wholesaling Middlemen

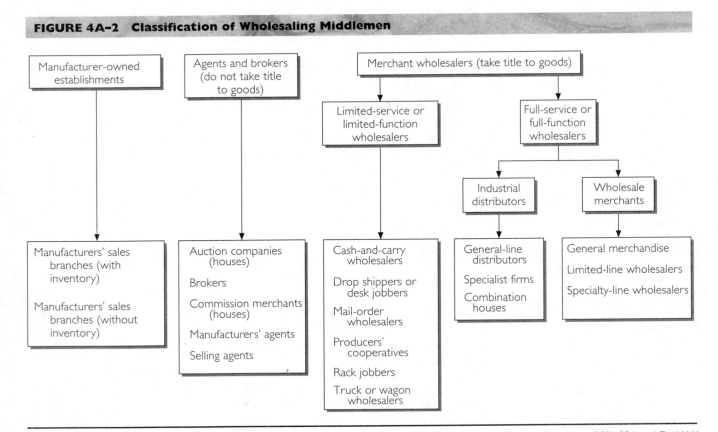

SOURCE: Ralph M. Gaedeke and Dennis H. Tootelian, *Marketing Principles and Applications* (St. Paul, MN: West Publishing Company, 1983): 256; and David W. Cravens and Robert B. Woodruff, *Marketing* (Reading, MA: Addison-Wesley Publishing Company, 1986): 396.

an innovative, nonstore approach, such as by telephone, mail order, computer, door-to-door, or vending machine.

Retail firms are important channel participants for many products. They can significantly affect the manufacturing firm's logistics function and the other activities of channel members. Given the trend among some of the large firms toward concentrating retail activity, other channel members have been pressured to absorb much of the responsibility for carrying inventory and ensuring that it is available for delivery to retail locations in a timely manner. Fortunately, many industries are developing effective vertical marketing systems, which can facilitate the streamlining of overall logistics and distribution activities within the channel.

Functional Shiftability

Figure 4A–3 compares how functional activities may be performed in a conventional (traditional) channel with how they may be performed in a vertical mar-

conventional versus VMS

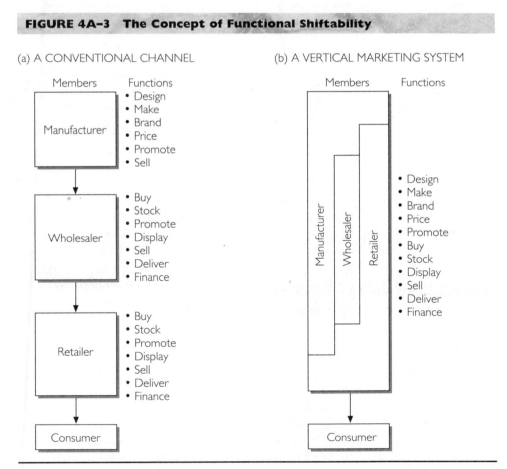

FIGURE 4A-3   The Concept of Functional Shiftability

(a) A CONVENTIONAL CHANNEL

(b) A VERTICAL MARKETING SYSTEM

SOURCE: This illustration is from David T. Kollatt, Roger D. Blackwell, and James F. Robeson, *Strategic Marketing* (New York: Holt, Rinehart & Winston, 1972): 289. Used with permission of Blackwell Associates.

FIGURE 4A–4   Example Channels of Distribution—Industrial Gas Manufacturing Industry

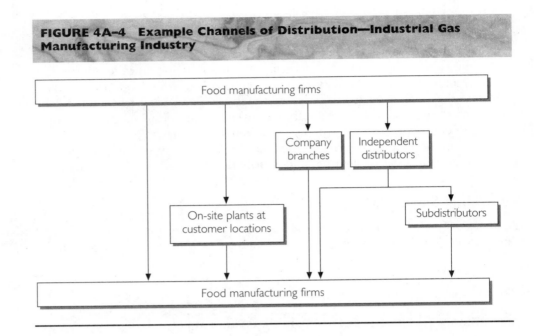

keting system. In a conventional channel, each participant performs a relatively standard set of activities, and these activities are likely to overlap. In contrast, in vertical marketing systems, activities or functions may be *shifted* among the manufacturer, wholesaler, and retailer in a manner most consistent with the overall interests of the channel itself.

Examples

Figure 4A–4 shows examples of channels of distribution that are applicable to the industrial gas manufacturing industries. See also Figure 4–5 in Chapter 4, which shows channels of distribution applicable to the food and manufacturing industries. These figures provide a valuable perspective on channel structure in relation to these specific industries.

CHANNEL ISSUES

Intensity of Distribution

desired intensity Aside from making a general decision regarding channels of distribution, firms must determine the distribution intensity they desire. This intensity falls into three generic categories: intensive, exclusive, and selective.

Intensive distribution involves seeing that product is available for purchase at as many wholesale and retail establishments as possible. The principal goal is to achieve widespread market coverage. This decision typically requires considering a wide range of channel alternatives, and involves making logistical and transactional arrangements with numerous firms and other entities throughout the various channels. Of the three categories, intensive distribution requires the greatest responsiveness from the logistics function of channel members.

Exclusive distribution occurs when a manufacturer severely limits the number of intermediaries involved in channel activities. This limitation usually applies to both wholesale and retail establishments. It typically provides those firms with exclusive rights to distribute the product over a particular geographical area or sales territory. The principal advantage to the manufacturing firm is the ability to exert considerable control over prices and ancillary services provided to purchasers of the product.

Selective distribution falls somewhere in between the other two. To a certain degree, it "narrows" the specific channel intermediaries authorized to handle a particular product. Firms choosing this alternative are interested in achieving a breadth of market coverage while retaining a degree of control over pricing and services.

Cooperation, Conflict, and Competition

Any study of distribution channels also studies the behavior among the firms constituting the channel. Perhaps most commonly discussed are topics relating to cooperation, conflict, and competition within and among distribution channels.[6]

Cooperation refers to a joint effort by channel members to achieve a goal or set of goals that are of mutual interest. For cooperation to exist, channel members must agree that they have mutual concerns, must work together toward achieving those common goals, and must collectively be able to create logistical and transactional channels that will enable the whole channel to be competitive in the marketplace.

cooperation

The success of vertical marketing systems requires cooperation among channel members. Through this form of distribution channel, manufacturers, wholesalers, and retailers have the greatest chance of working together toward accomplishing their common goals.

Conflict refers to a situation in which channel members may have competing objectives, and in which achieving optimal operation for the whole channel is difficult. Channel conflict may take the form of *horizontal* conflict, in which parallel members of a distribution channel are at odds over some issue. For example, conflict may arise between fast-food retailers of a specific brand who perceive that their sales territories overlap.

conflict

Of principal concern here, however, is *vertical* conflict, which may arise among members of the manufacturer–wholesaler–retailer distribution channel. For example, a wholesale intermediary may disagree with pricing, product availability, and other policies that the manufacturer establishes. In this instance, conflict will likely result. From a physical supply channel perspective, a manufacturer may place significant demands on the capabilities of vendors providing needed materials and supplies. If those demands do not acknowledge the overall needs of the channel and of the member firms, conflict is likely to result.

Often, one of the firms in a distribution channel emerges as the channel activity leader, becoming the *channel captain*. This phenomenon is critical to the success of many channel relationships, where one firm takes an aggressive role in seeing that the overall channel system functions as it should. The channel captain's ability to induce change is sometimes referred to as *power*, a topic that researchers have also treated in depth. Generally, researchers treat power in conjunction with the topic of *dependence,* or the extent to which channel members depend upon one another to achieve desired results.

competition Finally, *competition* is of significant interest. This includes competition between parallel members of distribution channels (e.g., automobile dealers selling the same brand within a given geographical area) and between various distribution channels (e.g., between food supermarkets and convenience stores). Both cases involve issues of concern from the perspective of both the transactional channel and the logistical channel.

The issues of cooperation, conflict, and competition within and between distribution channels are complex. The more we understand about these topics, the more likely we are to conceptualize and implement successful relationships in an overall channel system.

Legal Considerations

legal environment One environment in which firms make channel decisions is the legal environment. While the advice of qualified legal counsel has no substitute, logistics and marketing managers should at least understand the fundamental legal issues that may affect decision making regarding distribution channels.[7]

Laws. The first topic relates to the laws that can directly affect marketing channels. Of particular interest are the following: the Sherman Act (1890), the Clayton Act (1914), the Federal Trade Commission Act (1914), and the Robinson-Patman Act (1936).

- *The Sherman Act (1890).* The Sherman Act represents the fundamental antitrust legislation in the United States. It prohibits monopoly practices and conspiracies that restrain trade. In terms of specific effects on channels, the Sherman Act prohibits monopolistic conspiratorial practices from controlling distribution channels.
- *The Clayton Act (1914).* This law strengthened the Sherman Act by outlawing price discrimination and prohibiting other practices that tend to substantially lessen competition or create a monopoly. This act affects the channels area by specifically prohibiting practices such as tying arrangements (in which a seller requires that the purchaser either buy another product from the seller or agree not to use or purchase competitors' goods), and exclusive dealing (which would limit the supply sources available to purchasers). The Celler-Kefauver Act of 1950 broadened the impact of the Clayton Act to apply to acquisitions and mergers among firms that are vertically aligned in a distribution channel, in addition to horizontal mergers and acquisitions.
- *The Federal Trade Commission Act (1914).* This legislation established the Federal Trade Commission to enforce the provisions of the Clayton Act. In effect, this act forbade "unfair methods" of competition, including those identified in the Sherman Act and the Clayton Act, as well as other practices that may be injurious to competition.
- *The Robinson-Patman Act (1936).* This law prohibited price discrimination on goods of "like grade and quality," unless the seller could cost-justify the difference in prices. The Robinson-Patman Act also made it illegal for buyers

to set up "dummy" brokerage firms that would purchase goods at prices lower than those available to the purchaser itself. Before the passage of this act, larger firms often set up dummy firms to acquire products at prices lower than those sellers offered the firms' (smaller) competitors.

Practices. Another interesting topic regards practices that relate to the channel decision and that have legal implications. Because the list of possible practices is too broad to completely cover here, we will limit our discussion to dual distribution, exclusive dealing, full-line forcing, tying agreements, and vertical integration.

- *Dual distribution.* The many firms involved in this practice develop and maintain two or more distribution channels for their products. For example, a firm may distribute its products through a vertical marketing system as well as through traditional distribution channels. In such a case, interpretations of prevailing legislation principally protect the rights of the traditional channel's independent members.
- *Exclusive dealing.* Laws against exclusive dealing prohibit a seller from requiring the buyers to either deal exclusively in that seller's product brand or refrain from buying competitors' products for resale.
- *Full-line forcing.* This practice occurs when a seller requires a buyer to carry a full line of its products in order to sell any specific product line item available from that seller. This practice becomes illegal when it prevents other suppliers from securing business with firms that have had a full line forced upon them and therefore have no capacity to handle anyone else's products.
- *Tying agreements.* These agreements occur when a seller requires a buyer to purchase some other product as well, or when the buyer agrees not to buy a particular product from a competing firm. This illegal practice would tend to restrict the range of channel alternatives available for both marketing and logistics managers.
- *Vertical integration.* Firms today show a very evident trend toward developing vertical marketing systems, which involve integrating and coordinating the interests of entities vertically aligned in a distribution channel. Referring back to the Clayton Act of 1914 as amended by the Celler-Kefauver Act of 1950, it is clear that any such vertical arrangements must not substantially lessen competition or create a monopoly.

Since certain channel-related practices are illegal, managers who make distribution channel decisions need to understand the full range of relevant laws and legal issues.

CHANNELS IN THE SERVICE SECTOR

Given the recent growth of service industries in the United States, it is logical to examine the applicability of the channels to the industries such as health care, transportation, and food retailing. Each of these industries has well-defined procurement/physical supply needs, and discussing these in terms of the distribution channel decision is easy.

By using the university-level educational system as an example, we can examine how service industry firms *distribute* outputs and services. Universities distribute various educational programs through a number of channels. In addition to the full roster of day courses for degree students, many universities offer night and weekend courses for both degree students and those seeking continuing or executive-level education. Courses are sometimes taught at remote locations either physically or through the use of state-of-the-art video and telecommunications equipment, and various courses are available on magnetic media in a self-paced educational format. We could cite similar distribution examples for firms in other service industries.

EVALUATING THE PERFORMANCE OF CHANNEL MEMBERS AND CHANNEL SYSTEMS

measurement and evaluation

After making and implementing a decision regarding a channel of distribution, a firm should develop some ongoing means to evaluate channel system and channel member performance. In performing this evaluation, most manufacturers use some combination of the following channel member characteristics:

- Sales performance
- Inventory maintained
- Selling capabilities
- Attitudes
- Competition
- General growth prospects

Firms may use three approaches to apply these performance criteria. The first involves developing separate performance evaluations on one or more criteria, as Table 4A–1 indicates. The second is to informally combine multiple criteria, and the third is to formally combine multiple criteria.[8] Any of these approaches will provide information that will help a firm to evaluate the performance of individual channel members.

Figure 4A–5 provides a perspective on the overall topic of channel system performance. It suggests that the firm examine four specific areas: channel member

TABLE 4A–1 Channel Member Performance Evaluation Using Criteria Separately

Criterion	Frequently-Used Operational Performance Measures	Procedure for Combining Measures
1. Sales performance	1. Gross sales 2. Sales growth over time 3. Sales made/sales quota 4. Market share	No attempt made to combine the operational performance measures within or among the criteria categories
2. Inventory maintenance	1. Average inventory maintained 2. Inventory/sales 3. Inventory turnover	
3. Selling capabilities	1. Total number of salespeople 2. Salespeople assigned to manufacturer's product	

SOURCE: Bert Rosenbloom, *Marketing Channels* (Chicago, IL: The Dryden Press, 1987): 355.

FIGURE 4A-5 An Environmental Framework for Channel System Performance

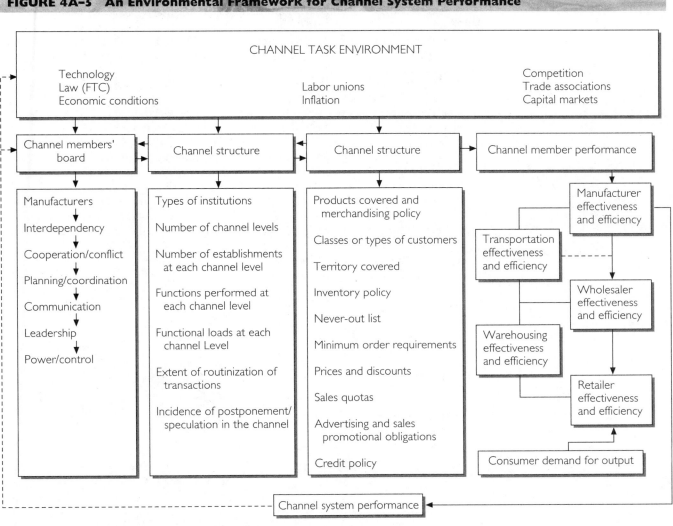

SOURCE: Adel I. El-Ansary, "Perspectives on Channel System Performance," in *Contemporary Issues in Marketing Channels* (Norman, OK: University of Oklahoma, 1979): 53.

behavior, channel structure, channel policies, and channel member performance. This figure goes beyond measuring individual channel members' contributions, and relates to the channel system as a whole.

By utilizing any of these measurement approaches, a firm will enhance the likelihood that the channel decision will produce results acceptable in terms of the company's intended goals.

NOTES

1. There are several excellent sources of information on the topic of distribution channels, including Bert Rosenbloom, *Marketing Channels,* 3d ed. (Chicago: Dryden Press, 1987);

Louis P. Bucklin, *Competition and Evolution in the Distributive Trades* (Englewood Cliffs, NJ: Prentice-Hall, 1972); Louis W. Stern and Adel I. El-Ansary, *Marketing Channels*, 2d ed. (Englewood Cliffs, NJ: Prentice-Hall, 1982); Bruce Mallen, *Principles of Marketing Channel Management* (Lexington, MA: Lexington Books, 1977); and Donald J. Bowersox, M. Bixby Cooper, Douglas M. Lambert, and Donald A. Taylor, *Management in Marketing Channels* (New York: McGraw-Hill, 1980).

2. See Philip B. Schary, *Logistics Decisions: Text and Cases* (Chicago: Dryden Press, 1984): 32.

3. Schary, *Logistics Decisions*, 32.

4. U.S. Department of Commerce, *1984 Industrial Outlook* (Washington, DC: U.S. Department of Commerce, Bureau of Industrial Economics, 1984): 47–1.

5. U.S. Department of Commerce, *1984 Industrial Outlook*, 47–1.

6. Additional information and direction regarding cooperation, conflict, and competition are available in sources such as those listed in note 1.

7. Portions of this section have been adapted from Rosenbloom, *Marketing Channels*, 89–99; David W. Cravens and Robert B. Woodruff, *Marketing* (Reading, MA: Addison-Wesley, 1986): 451–54; David M. Cravens, Gerald E. Hills, and Robert B. Woodruff, *Marketing Decision Making*, rev. ed. (Homewood, IL: Irwin, 1980), 513–33; and McCarthy and Perrault, *Basic Marketing*, 126–31.

8. Rosenbloom, *Marketing Channels*, 345.

SUGGESTED READINGS FOR PART I

Bonney, Joseph. "Supply Chain Management: Treat It Like a Product," *American Shipper* (February 1994): 39–42.

Canna, Elizabeth. "Harnessing the Giants: Asea Brown Boveri," *American Shipper* (May 1994): 48–52.

Cavinato, Joseph C. "A Total Cost/Value Model for Supply Chain Competitiveness," *Journal of Business Logistics* 13 no. 2 (1992): 285–302.

Cooke, James Aaron. "Supply Chain Management '90s Style," *Traffic Management* (May 1992): 57–59.

Cooper, Martha, C. "The 'How' of Supply Chain Management," *NAPM Insights* (March 1994): 30–32.

Cooper, Martha C., and Lisa M. Ellram. "Characteristics of Supply Chain Management and the Implications for Purchasing and Logistics Strategy," *International Journal of Logistics Management* 4 no. 2 (1993): 13–24.

Davis, Thomas. "Effective Supply Chain Management," *Sloan Management Review* 34, no. 4 (Summer 1993): 35–46.

Ellram, Lisa M. "The 'What' of Supply Chain Management," *NAPM Insights* (March 1994): 26–27.

Ellram, Lisa M., and Martha C. Cooper. "Supply Chain Management, Partnerships, and the Shipper—Third Party Relationships," *International Journal of Logistics Management* 1, no. 2 (1990): 1–10.

Fox, MaryLou; Thomas Kraska; and Kenneth Steele. "Optimizing Supply Chain Operations through Integrated Logistics Systems," *Annual Proceedings of the Council of Logistics Management* 1 (1988): 209–35.

Gahorna, John L.; Norman H. Chorn; and A. Day. "Pathways to Customers: Reducing Complexity in the Logistics Pipeline," *International Journal of Physical Distribution and Logistics Management* 21, no. 8 (1991): 5–11.

Gomes-Casseres, Benjamin. "Group versus Group: How Alliance Networks Compete," *Harvard Business Review* 72, no. 4 (July-August 1994): 62–74.

Greenblatt, Sherwin. "Continuous Improvement in Supply Chain Management," *Chief Executive* (June 1993): 40–43.

Henkoff, Ronald. "Delivering the Goods," *Fortune* 130, no. 11 (November 28, 1994): 64–78.

Hewitt, Frederick. "Supply Chain Integration: Myths and Realities," *Annual Proceedings of the Council of Logistics Management* 1 (1992): 334–41.

Houlihan, John B. "International Supply Chains: A New Approach," *Management Decision* 26, no. 3 (1988): 13–19.

Jones, Thomas C., and Daniel W. Riley. "Using Inventory for Competitive Advantage through Supply Chain Management," *International Journal of Physical Distribution and Materials Management* 15, no. 5 (1985): 16–26.

LaLonde, Bud; Kee-Hian Tan; and Mike Standing. "Forget Supply Chains, Think of Value Flows," *Transformation* (Summer 1994): 24–31.

Lee, Hau, and Corey Billington. "Managing Supply Chain Inventory: Pitfalls and Opportunities," *Sloan Management Review* 33, no. 3 (Spring 1992): 65–73.

Lester, Thomas. "Squeezing the Supply Chain," *Management Today* (March 1992): 68–70.

McCutcheon, David M.; Amitabh S. Raturi; and Jack R. Meredith. "The Customization-

SUPPLY CHAIN MANAGEMENT

Responsiveness Squeeze,'' *Sloan Management Review* 35, no. 2 (Winter 1994): 89–99.

Muller, E. J. "Key Links in the Supply Chain," *Distribution* 92, no. 10 (October 1993): 52–56.

Norman, Richard, and Rafael Ramirez. "From Value Chain to Value Constellation: Designing Interactive Strategy," *Harvard Business Review* 71, no. 4 (July-August 1993): 65–77.

O'Keefe, Peter. "How to Add Value," *Journal of the Institute of Logistics and Distribution Management* 1, no. 2 (September 1993): 2–4.

Sandelands, Eric. "Managing the Supply Chain," *International Journal of Physical Distribution and Logistics Management* 24, no. 3 (1994): 37–48.

Steven, Graham C. "Integrating the Supply Chain," *International Journal of Physical Distribution and Materials Management* 8, no. 8 (1989): 3–8.

Stewart, Thomas. "Welcome to the Revolution," *Fortune* 128, no. 15 (December 13, 1993): 66–80.

Towill, D. R.; M. Naim; and J. Wikner. "Industrial Dynamic Simulation Models in the Design of Supply Chains," *International Journal of Physical Distribution and Logistics Management* 22, no. 5 (1992): 3–13.

Turner, J. R. "Integrated Supply Chain Management: What's Wrong with This Picture?" *Industrial Engineering* 25, no. 12 (December 1993): 52–55.

DIMENSIONS OF LOGISTICS

Biciocchi, Steve. "Every Business Should Want Superior Distribution," *Industrial Engineering* 24, no. 9 (September 1992): 22–28.

Blackwell, Michael. "Building Strong Ties," *Distribution* 93, no. 6 (June 1994): 42–45.

Bradley, Peter. "Logistics Joins Link in Automotive Supply Chain," *Purchasing* 116, no. 4 (March 3, 1994): 57–58.

Braithwaite, Alan, and Leighton Morgans. "The Supply Chain Game," *Journal of the Institute of Logistics and Distribution Management* 12, no. 5 (June 1993): 10–14.

Chow, Garland; Trevor D. Heaver; and L. E. Henviksson. "Logistics Performance: Definition and Measurement," *International Journal of Physical Distribution and Logistics Management* 24, no. 1 (1994): 17–28.

Cooke, James Aaron. "Why Sears Turned Logistics Inside Out," *Traffic Management* 31, no. 5 (May 1992): 30–33.

Foster, Thomas A. "In Difficult Years, Logistics Shines," *Distribution* 91, no. 9 (July 1992): 6–10.

Fuller, J. B.; J. O'Connor; and R. Rawlinson. "Tailored Logistics: The Next Advantage," *Harvard Business Review* 71, no. 3 (May-June 1993): 87–98.

Goodson, George O. "Planning a Logistics Makeover," *Inbound Logistics* 12, no. 3 (March 1992): 29–32.

Gooley, Toby B. "How to Meet the Big 8 Logistics Challenges," *Traffic Management* 33, no. 11 (November 1994): 57–61.

Jackson, George C.; Jeffrey J. Stoltman; and Audrey Taylor. "Moving Beyond Trade-offs," *International Journal of Physical Distribution and Logistics Management* 24, no. 1 (1994): 4–10.

Koselka, Rita. "Distribution Revolution," *Forbes* (May 25, 1992): 54.

MacDonald, Mitchell E. "How Logistics Can Make the Cash Register Ring," *Traffic Management* 32, no. 6 (June 1993): 61–67.

McGinnis, Michael; Sylvia K. Boltic; and C. M. Kochunny. "Trends in Logistics Thought: An Empirical Study," *Journal of Business Logistics* 15, no. 2 (1994): 273–303.

New, Colin. "The Use of Throughput Efficiency as a Key Performance for the New Manufacturing Era," *International Journal of Logistics Management* 4, no. 2 (1993): 95–104.

Novack, R. A.; Lloyd M. Rinehart; and Michael V. Wells. "Rethinking Concept Foundations in Logistics Management," *Journal of Business Logistics* 13, no. 2 (1992): 233–268.

Powers, Richard F. "Career Paths," *American Shipper* 35, no. 11 (November 1993): 36–42.

Stevens, Larry. "Back from the Brink," *Inbound Logistics* 12, no. 9 (September 1992): 20–23.

Trunick, Perry A. "Logistics: An Agent for Change in the 1990s," *Transportation and Distribution* 34, no. 11 (November 1993): 36–41.

Vail, Bruce. "Logistics, Fifth Avenue Style," *American Shipper* 36, no. 8 (August 1994): 49–51.

Buxbaum, Peter A. "Doing Their Level Best," *Distribution* 93, no. 4 (April 1994): 42–49.

Birou, Laura M., and Stanley E. Fawcett. "Supplier Involvement in Integrated Product Development," *International Journal of Physical Distribution and Logistics Management* 24, no. 5 (1994): 4–14.

Cavinato, Joseph L. "Evolving Procurement Organizations: Logistics Implications," *Journal of Business Logistics* 13, no. 1 (1992): 27–46.

Daugherty, Patricia J.; Dale S. Rogers; and Michael S. Spencer. "Just-In-Time Functional Models: Empirical Test and Validation," *International Journal of Physical Distribution and Logistics Management* 24, no. 6 (1994): 20–26.

Dysart, Joe. "Bose Knows JIT II," *Inbound Logistics* 13, no. 2 (February 1993): 28–32.

Dysart, Joe. "On Site Medicine Man," *Inbound Logistics* 13, no. 8 (August 1993): 30–31.

Ellram, Lisa M. "Life Cycle Patterns in Industrial Buyer-Seller Partnerships," *International Journal of Physical Distribution and Materials Management* 21, no. 9 (1991): 12–21.

Ellram, Lisa M. "International Purchasing Alliances: An Empirical Study," *International Journal of Logistics Management* 3, no. 1 (1992): 37–45.

Ellram, Lisa M. "A Taxonomy of Total Cost of Ownership Models," *Journal of Business Logistics* 15, no. 1 (1994): 171–91.

Ellram, Lisa M., and Sue Perrett Siferd. "Purchasing: The Cornerstone of the Total Cost of Ownership Concept," *Journal of Business Logistics* 14, no. 1 (1993): 163–84.

Fawcett, Stanley E.; Laura Birou; and Barbara C. Taylor. "Supporting Global Operations through Logistics and Purchasing," *International Journal of Physical Distribution and Logistics Management* 23, no. 4 (1993): 3–11.

Forger, Gary. "Jeep Puts JIT into High Gear," *Modern Materials Handling* 48, no. 1 (January 1993): 42–45.

Gentry, Julie J. "Strategic Alliances in Purchasing Transportation is the Vital Link," *International Journal of Purchasing and Materials Management* (Summer 1993): 10–17.

Gerwin, Donald. "Manufacturing Flexibility: A Strategic Perspective," *Management Science* 30, no. 4 (April 1993): 395–410.

Handfield, Robert B. "Role of Inbound Logistics in Developing Time Based Competition," *International Journal of Purchasing and Materials Management* (Winter 1993): 2–10.

Havington, Lisa. "Purchasing and Logistics Get Their Acts Together," *Inbound Logistics* 12, no. 5 (May 1992): 20–25.

Lee, Huei, and Dee M. Wellan. "Vendor Survey Plan: A Selection Strategy for JIT/TQM Suppliers," *International Journal of Physical Distribution and Logistics Management* 23, no. 7 (1993): 39–45.

Leenders, Michael R.; Jean Nollet; and Lisa M. Ellram. "Adapting Purchasing to Supply Chain Management," *International Journal of Physical Distribution and Logistics Management* 24, no. 1 (1994): 40–42.

Mehanty, R. P., and S. G. Deshmulch. "Use of Analytical Hierarchic Process for Evaluating Sources of Supply," *International Journal of Physical Distribution and Logistics Management* 23, no. 3 (1993): 22–28.

Monczka, Robert M.; Robert J. Trent; and Thomas J. Callahan. "Supply Base Strategies to Maximize Supplier Performance," *International Journal of Physical Distribution and Logistics Management* 23, no. 4 (1993): 42–54.

Morgan, James P., and Sheila Cayer. "What It Takes to Make World Class Suppliers," *Purchasing* 113, no. 2 (August 13, 1992): 50–61.

O'Neal, Charles. "Concurrent Engineering with Early Supplier Involvement," *International*

THE INBOUND LOGISTICS SYSTEM

Journal of Purchasing and Materials Management (Spring 1993): 2–9.

Presutti, William D. "The Single Source Issue: U. S. and Japanese Sourcing Strategies," *International Journal of Purchasing and Materials Management* (Winter 1992): 2–9.

Ruriani, Deborah. "Inbound Logistics Comes of Age," *Inbound Logistics* 13, no. 2 (February 1993): 33–36.

Schlender, Brenton R. "How Toshiba Makes Alliances Work," *Fortune* 128, no. 8 (October 4, 1993): 116–120.

Schmenner, Roger W. "The Merit of Making Things Fast," *Sloan Management Review,* The Best of MITs 1992, 27–34.

Steiner, George, and Scott Yeomans. "Level Schedules for Mixed-Model, Just-In-Time Processes," *Management Science* 39, no. 6 (June 1993): 728–35.

Swenseth, Scott R., and Byung K. Park. "Jointly Determined Cycle Time Models for Manufacturers with Multiple Vendors," *Journal of Business Logistics* 14, no. 2 (1993): 127–43.

Tallon, William J. "The Impact of Inventory Centralization on Aggregate Safety Stock," *Journal of Business Logistics* 14, no. 1 (1993): 185–204.

Toll, Erich E. "Jaguar: Fastest Cat in the North Atlantic," *Inbound Logistics* 13, no. 1 (January 1993): 20–24.

Tucker, Marvin W., and David A. Davis. "Key Ingredients for Successful Implementation of Just-In-Time," *Business Horizons* 36, no. 3 (May-June 1993): 59–65.

Venkatesan, Ravi. "Strategic Sourcing: To Make or Not To Make," *Harvard Business Review* 70, no. 6 (November-December 1992): 98–107.

Wagner, William. "Changing Role and Relevance of Purchasing," *International Journal of Physical Distribution and Logistics Management* 23, no. 9 (1993): 12–20.

Weber, Charles A., and Lisa M. Ellram. "Supplier Selection Using Multi-Objective Programming," *International Journal of Physical Distribution and Logistics Management* 23, no. 2 (1993): 3–14.

Weiss, Julian M. "Beauty and the Beast," *Inbound Logistics* 13, no. 3 (March 1993): 20–24.

Witt, Clyde E. "Inventory Versus JIT: Ford's Solution," *Materials Handling* 48, no. 12 (November 1993): 42–45.

Witt, Clyde E. "New Plant Defines Motorola's Vision on CFM," *Materials Handling Engineering* (May 1992): 46–52.

OUTBOUND LOGISTICS

Abrahamsson, Mats. "Time Based Distribution," *International Journal of Logistics Management* 4, no. 2 (1993): 75–84.

"Actel's New Information System Turbo Charges Customer Support," *Customer Satisfaction* 6, no. 16 (August 1993): 1–6.

Aertsen, Freek. "Contracting Out the Physical Distribution Function," *International Journal of Physical Distribution and Logistics Management* 23, no. 1: 23–29.

Andel, Tom. "Expanding Demand for Cycle Time Reduction," *Transportation and Distribution* 35, no. 10 (October 1994): 95–102.

Andraski, Joseph C. "Foundations for Successful Continuous Replenishment Programs," *International Journal of Logistics Management* 5, no. 1 (1994): 1–8.

Aron, Laurie Joan. "Grocers Have Service in Store for Consumers," *Inbound Logistics* 13, no. 5 (May 1993): 16–21.

Aron, Laurie Joan. "Making Virtual Inventory a Reality," *Inbound Logistics* 14, no. 3 (March 1994): 44–47.

Artzt, Edwin L. "Customers Want Performance, Price and Value," *Transportation and Distribution* 34, no. 7 (July 1993): 32–34.

Barks, Joseph V. "Squeezing Out the Middleman," *Distribution* 93, no. 1 (January 1994): 30–34.

Bonney, Joseph. "Sales Terrific: Problems a Mess," *American Shipper* (April 1994): 64–66.

Bowman, Robert. "Balancing LTL Service," *Distribution* 91, no. 11 (November 1992): 60–72.

Buxbaum, Peter. "Cleaning Up the Mess," *Distribution* 93, no. 13 (December 1994): 40–42.

Cooke, James A. "Beyond Quality . . . Speed," *Traffic Management* 33, no. 6 (June 1994): 32–37.

Cooke, James A. "A Quick Response Success Story," *Traffic Management* (October 1992): 54–57.

Coutinho-Rodrigues, J. J.; J. C. N. Climaco; and J. R. Current. "A P.C.-Based Interactive Decision Support System for Two Objective Direct Delivery Problems," *Journal of Business Logistics* 15, no. 1 (1994); 305–22.

Fernie, John. "Quick Response: An International Perspective," *International Journal of Physical Distribution and Logistics Management* 24, no. 6 (1994): 38–46.

"Going from Process-Based to Customer-Focused," *Customer Satisfaction* 7, no. 10 (May 1994): 1–2.

Gooley, Toby B. "Partnerships Can Make the Customer-Service Difference," *Traffic Management* 33, no. 5 (May 1994): 40–45.

Higgenson, J. K., and J. H. Bookbinder. "Policy Recommendation for a Shipment Consolidation Program," *Journal of Business Logistics* 15, no. 1 (1994); 87–112.

Holcomb, Mary Collins. "Customer Service Measurement: A Methodology for Increasing Customer Value through Utilization of the Taguchi Strategy," *Journal of Business Logistics* 15, no. 1 (1994): 29–52.

"Hot Technologies for the 1990s," *Traffic Management* (August 1992): 31–42.

Innis, Daniel E., and Bernard J. LaLonde. "Customer Service: The Key to Customer Satisfaction, Customer Loyalty, and Market Share," *Journal of Business Logistics* 15, no. 1 (1994): 1–27.

Innis, Daniel E., and Bernard J. LaLonde. "Modeling the Effects of Customer Service Performance on Purchase Intentions in the Channel," *Journal of Marketing Theory and Practice* 2, no. 2 (Spring 1994): 45–60.

Keough, Jack. "Teamwork Saves Timken $3 Million in Inventory," *Industrial Distribution* 83, no. 3 (March 1994): 26–28.

Keough, Jack; George M. Fedor; and John Johnson. "Distribution's Emerging Role," *Industrial Distribution* 83, no. 5 (May 1994): 39–46.

LaLonde, Bernard J., and James M. Masters. "Emerging Logistics Strategies: Blueprints for the Next Century," *International Journal of Physical Distribution and Logistics Management* 24, no. 7 (1994): 35–47.

Muller, E. J. "Faster, Faster. I Need It Now," *Distribution* 93, no. 2 (February 1994): 30–36.

Novack, R. A.; L. M. Rinehart; and C. J. Langley Jr. "An Internal Assessment of Logistics Value," *Journal of Business Logistics* 15, no. 1 (1994): 113–52.

"Retail Distribution: Custom Handling That Goes with the Flow," *Modern Materials Handling* 40, no. 6 (May 1994): 30–33.

"Retail Distribution and Logistics," *Chain Store Age Executive*, Section Two (May 1993): 1–40.

Thomas, Jim. "The Right Place at the Right Time," *Distribution* 92, no. 12: 60–69.

Witt, Clyde E. "Quick Response: Custom Tailored by Palm Beach Company," *Materials Handling Engineering* (February 1993): 40–45.

PART II

LOGISTICS SUPPLY CHAIN PROCESSES

It is critical in managing the logistics supply chain to understand the basic processes that are part of both the inbound and outbound components of logistics systems. Part II provides an in-depth discussion and analysis of the basic processes that can add value and/or lower costs.

The first two chapters in this section examine a critical activity for all logistics systems, that is, inventory. Chapter 5 provides a broad perspective of inventory in the logistics supply chain. Chapter 6 examines approaches to inventory decisions and control. Chapter 6 also builds upon the information developed in Chapter 3 on inventory techniques used in inbound logistics systems.

Chapter 7 discusses warehousing in logistics supply chains. The basic nature of and rationale for warehousing are presented, as well as the major decisions that need to be made in the warehousing area for effective management and control. Chapter 8 examines the related topics of materials handling and packaging, which have a significant impact upon warehousing and inventory. Chapter 8 provides an overview of both materials handling and packaging and also examines the critical issues for both topics.

Chapters 9 and 10 cover transportation, which is frequently the largest single cost in a logistics system. Chapter 9 gives an overview of all the transportation alternatives available to a logistics manager, with an emphasis upon their advantages and disadvantages. Chapter 10 looks at the management of the transportation activity, with particular emphasis upon strategy and the operational aspects of transportation management.

Chapter 11 discusses order processing and information systems. In today's environment, information is a key ingredient for lowering costs and improving customer service. Information is the "glue" for the order cycle and other areas of logistics. Information will continue to be a major ingredient for success in the 21st century.

INVENTORY IN THE LOGISTICS SYSTEM

LEARNING OBJECTIVES

After reading this chapter, you should be able to do the following:

- Understand and appreciate the importance of inventory to the economy.

- Identify current shifts in inventory positioning and placement throughout the logistics channel.

- Discuss why companies carry physical supply inventories and physical distribution inventories, and know what functions or purposes are served by these inventories.

- Calculate inventory costs, including carrying cost, order/setup cost, and expected stockout cost.

- Classify inventory according to the ABC method of inventory analysis.

- Evaluate how effectively companies manage inventories.

AT&T's Process Redesign

Several years ago, American Telephone & Telegraph decided its inventories had gotten out of hand. So the company attacked the problem in the obvious way—by reducing overstock.

Alas, the excess inventory levels wouldn't stay down. They'd drop for a while, then inch back up. "People would go in and identify stuff that wasn't needed any more," said Donald R. "Bob" Smith, supervisor of the Operations Research Analysis Group at AT&T Bell Laboratories. "Once that effort was gone, the inventory would come back again." The problem, Smith said, was that inventory was reduced but processes for managing supplies weren't changed.

In the ensuing years, AT&T and other corporations have developed processes for getting control of inventory. AT&T has cut its inventory by $200 million, to $2.9 billion.

Competitive Edge

Smith and others indicated that managing the full inventory stream is increasingly being used to allow companies to gain a competitive edge.

Redesigning the processes by which inventory is managed can have a significant impact on a manufacturer's profitability, Smith pointed out. But it's a difficult business, involving numerous players—from suppliers and manufacturers to distributors and customers.

What processes can a manager use to reduce inventory using full-stream techniques?

First, you have to look at the various types of inventory and understand how they work. Smith divided them into five categories: pipeline, economies of scale, overstock, dead stock, and safety stock.

To get rid of pipeline inventory without shrinking business volume, a manager can reduce the time interval.

"If you have a transportation interval of a week, and a $50 million business volume, you're going to have $1 million worth of goods in the transportation network," Smith said. "Decrease that time interval and you optimize local inventory," he added.

Inventories based on economies of scale go up and down with customer demand. By narrowing market uncertainties, the number and variety of manufacturing setups can be decreased. Inventory batches are thus reduced.

Dead stock, or outdated inventory, can be reduced by shortening the lead time for production, delivery, and sales. That gives the product less time to become obsolete, and is especially important for high-tech electronic equipment, Smith said.

Modeling

The most important tool for reducing inventories, however, is a modeling technique used by AT&T called time-phased inventory management. It gives the manager the ability to predict the amount of safety stock needed by measuring uncertainties in supply and demand.

Smith put it this way: "Safety stock is really an interaction of uncertainties related over an interval. Interval reduction can reduce safety stock, because your uncertainty time is shortened."

The challenge for the decision maker, Smith said, is to measure uncertainties throughout the supply chain, then take that data and use inventory models to make predictions.

ADAPTED FROM: Ann Hagen, "AT&T's Approach to Inventory Control," *American Shipper* (April 1993): 42. Used with permission.

I nventory management and control is a key activity area within the business logistics process. To magnify the importance of this statement, one consulting firm has even referred to business logistics as "the management of inventory, at rest or in motion." Not unexpectedly, the effective and efficient management of inventory is critical to the satisfactory performance of the entire business logistics function.

This chapter focuses on general issues relating to the role of inventory in the logistics system. Following a discussion highlighting the role and significance of inventory, we will address inventory costs and approaches for classifying inventory. The chapter will conclude by discussing ways to evaluate the effectiveness of a company's approach to inventory management.

It is critical to understand that one of the very highest priorities today is to streamline and coordinate logistics processes and to find ways to improve customer service while reducing levels of inventory throughout the logistics pipeline. Traditional logistics systems were structured around the notion that ample amounts of inventory are essential to carry. Progressive approaches suggest that excess costs of carrying inventory need to be eliminated whenever possible. This emphasis on recognizing and coordinating logistics processes is consistent with the approach taken by AT&T as discussed in the Logistics Profile. While AT&T's experience showed that the redesigning of processes by which inventory is managed can have a significant impact on profitability, it was found that the task was quite complex and involved numerous players within the supply chain.

Chapter 6 will identify and describe inventory management approaches that have proven effective in today's business environment. Together, these two chapters will help you to understand how inventory relates to and is an element of the overall logistics process that can create value for the customer.

THE IMPORTANCE OF INVENTORY

Although this book's principal thrust is the management of business logistics within the firm, understanding the importance of inventory from a broad, macroeconomic perspective is useful. We will briefly discuss how inventory relates to the overall economy and then describe several specific ways in which inventory is critical to the individual firm.

Inventory in the Economy

Table 5–1 summarizes the U.S. Gross National Product (GNP) and the levels of manufacturing and trade inventories over the 1974 to 1994 time period, and calculates the ratio of inventories to GNP. Figure 5–1 shows the behavior of this calculated ratio over the twenty-one-year time period.

percentage of GNP

It is apparent from Figure 5–1 that inventory as a percentage of GNP has been declining in recent years, from approximately 17 to 20 percent in the 1970s to a current level in the range of 13 to 14 percent. This decline is largely due to four factors. First, firms have become more expert at managing inventory in general, and thus have succeeded in improving inventory "velocity," or the inventory turnover rate (to be discussed later in this chapter). Second, innovations and improvements in communications and information technology have helped companies to

TABLE 5-1 Percentage Ratio of Manufacturing and Trade Inventory to GNP

Year Ending	In Current Dollars		Ratio of Inventory to GNP
	GNP ($ trillion)	Inventory ($ billion)	
1974	1.43	286	20.00
1975	1.55	288	18.58
1976	1.72	319	18.55
1977	1.92	351	18.28
1978	2.16	397	18.38
1979	2.42	444	18.35
1980	2.63	483	18.37
1981	2.94	520	17.69
1982	3.07	520	16.94
1983	3.31	510	15.41
1984	3.78	546	14.44
1985	4.00	645	16.13
1986	4.24	657	15.50
1987	4.53	683	15.08
1988	4.87	735	15.09
1989	5.23	780	14.91
1990	5.46	820	15.02
1991	5.68	815	14.35
1992	5.96	832	13.96
1993	6.38	862	13.51
1994	6.73	893	13.27

DATA SOURCE: *Survey of Current Business: U.S. Statistical Abstract*, U.S. Department of Commerce; and Robert V. Delaney, reprinted with permission.

METHODOLOGY: Heskett, Ivie, and Glaskowsky, *Business Logistics*, 2d ed. (New York: Ronald Press, 1973): 19–21. Inventory investment reflects manufacturing, wholesale, and retail trade inventory as defined by the Bureau of Economic Analysis, U.S. Department of Commerce.

become more effective in terms of how they manage inventories. The availability of technologies such as EDI (electronic data interchange) have resulted in companies being able to do business on a daily basis with less inventory. Third, increased competitiveness in our transportation industries has resulted in greater opportunities for shippers to purchase high-quality as well as customized services, thus reducing to some extent the need to carry large inventories. Fourth, overall sensitivity to the incurring of excess and non-value-added cost has motivated many firms to identify ways to reduce and even eliminate unnecessary levels of inventory.

Inventory in the Firm

Experience shows that recent inventory trends have a relevant impact on inventory management at the level of the individual firm. This section discusses topics highlighting the importance of inventory within the firm.

Growth and Significance of Inventory Cost. Increased product line variety has resulted in greater levels of inventory for many firms. For example, if Procter &

product line proliferation

FIGURE 5-1 Percentage Ratio of Manufacturing and Trade Inventory to GNP (in current dollars)

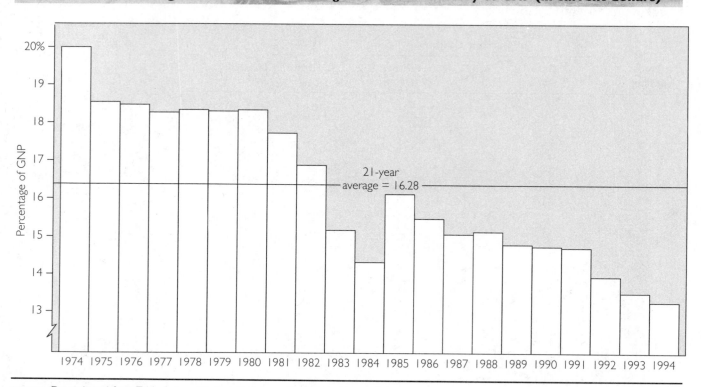

SOURCE: Data adapted from Table 5–1, and Robert V. Delaney. Reprinted with permission.

Gamble were to estimate future baby diaper sales at 500,000 boxes, it must also break down this figure by color (e.g., pink versus blue), package size, and absorbency before making final production and inventory decisions. Rather than carrying a basic inventory of 500,000 boxes plus an additional 40,000 to 50,000 boxes of safety stock, the company may need a total inventory (base plus safety stock) of 700,000 to 750,000 boxes to accommodate safety stock for each line item variety.

inventory carrying cost

To illustrate how increased inventory affects costs, consider a hardware discount store that carries $1 million in average inventory. As will be explained later in this chapter, firms generally calculate annual inventory carrying costs as a percentage of average inventory dollar value. Assuming that this percentage has been calculated at 20 percent, the annual cost of carrying the $1 million in inventory is $1 million × .20 = $200,000. If average inventory levels rise to $1.5 million, the annual carrying cost would increase from $200,000 to $300,000.

Assuming that this example company has an overall profit margin equal to 5 percent of sales, sales would have to increase by $2 million to offset an average inventory increase of $100,000 (i.e., $100,000 ÷ 5% = $2,000,000).

inventory as a percentage of assets

Inventory in Relation to Overall Asset Structure.   From another perspective, inventory investment often represents a significant percentage of a company's total assets. While this may vary from firm to firm, inventory investment may often equal or exceed 50 percent of a company's total asset base. Table 5–2 includes selected

TABLE 5-2   Selected Financial Data, 1992

Company	Current Sales ($ billion)	Total Assets ($ billion)	Average Inventory ($ billion)	Inventory as a Percentage of Total Assets
Manufacturing				
Ford Motor	$100.1	26.8	5.4	20.1%
General Electric	56.3	44.5	4.6	10.3%
Kraft General Foods	28.8	6.9	2.9	42.0%
Wholesalers and Retailers				
Bergen Brunswig	5.0	1.2	0.55	45.8%
Fleming Co.	12.9	1.4	0.96	68.6%
K-Mart	38.0	10.5	8.80	83.8%
The Limited	6.9	1.8	0.80	44.4%
Kroger	22.1	2.1	1.60	76.2%

SOURCE: 1992 corporate annual reports.

financial data for several prominent U.S.-based companies involved in manufacturing and/or wholesale/retail activity. As the table indicates, inventory as a percentage of total assets tends to be smaller for firms in the manufacturing sector, due to the generally greater expenditures for plant and equipment, thus expanding the company's overall asset base.

Current Trends toward Shifting Inventory in the Logistics Channel.   Although overall levels of inventory needed to support U.S. manufacturing and trade operations (i.e., inventories as a percentage of GNP) have declined in recent years, at times there has been a somewhat uneven impact on firms in the logistics channel. In response to cost pressures, for example, many retail and wholesale firms have aggressively reduced their levels of inventories and effectively shifted the burden to manufacturers and suppliers. While to some extent this is a logical strategy, the immediate effect is only to shift responsibility for maintaining inventories to "upstream" channel members, which does little to make the overall channel function more efficiently.

shifting and eliminating inventories

Since suppliers in such situations ultimately need to recoup the costs of carrying additional inventory, inevitably this expense will pass through to retail and wholesale customers as an added expense of doing business. A preferable solution, and one gaining in popularity today, is to identify an inventory strategy that effectively represents a win-win proposition for both buyers and sellers of product. As a result, there has been significant recent interest in the development of approaches to inventory management that purposely try to reduce overall levels of inventory in the logistical channel. Some of these, such as quick response and efficient consumer response (ECR), will be discussed in Chapter 6.

Overall, firms should be realistic as well as open-minded in terms of savings opportunities through inventory cost reduction. As we will discuss in this chapter and throughout the text, a company should seek innovative solutions that will reduce expense and improve service. They may not always be obvious, but these solutions may be very effective once identified.

RATIONALE FOR CARRYING INVENTORY

Although modern firms increasingly try to minimize or eliminate inventory whenever possible, understanding why businesses hold or accumulate inventory can be useful. After discussing materials inventories and physical distribution inventories, we will direct attention toward a general framework for viewing the functional types of inventories. This section concludes by summarizing the importance of inventory to functional areas of business other than business logistics.

logistics channel   Figure 5–2 indicates a number of points in the logistics channel at which accountable amounts of inventory may be found. In essence, inventories of raw

FIGURE 5-2 Potential Inventory Locations

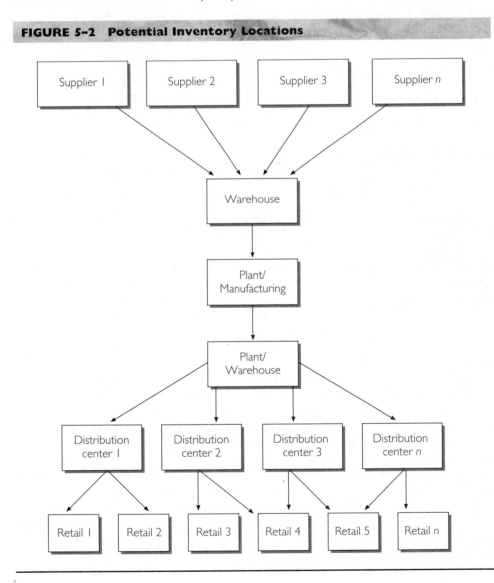

materials, components, semifinished product, and maintenance and repair items are typically found at supplier locations, materials warehouses, or in the plant or manufacturing facility. Correspondingly, inventories of finished or intermediate products may be found at locations such as plant or manufacturing facilities, plant warehouses, market-oriented distribution centers, and retail or point-of-use locations. Figure 5–2 serves as a reminder that there are numerous points in the logistics channel at which inventories may be found. Assuming that there is a significant commitment to satisfying the needs of the end customer, the task of reducing or eliminating inventories at key points in the overall process is truly challenging. It is this objective, however, that is central to the logistics strategies of many firms today.

Physical Supply Inventories

The first inventories we will consider are those that support a firm's processing, manufacturing, or assembly functions. Among the principal reasons for accumulating such inventories are the following: purchase economies, transportation savings, safety stock, speculative purchase, seasonal supply, and supply source maintenance.

Purchase Economies. One reason for accumulating physical supply inventory is that the company may be able to realize purchase economies. For example, firms may buy raw materials in large quantities because of available price discounts. Although the company will need to store what it does not immediately use, the increased inventory costs may be less than what the company saves by buying in large quantities. This is becoming important to firms involved in offshore sourcing activity, which may result in significant quantity discounts. In such cases, companies are trading off between a purchase price discount and storage costs. As long as the amount saved on the purchase price exceeds storage costs, these companies are willing to accumulate raw materials inventory.

discount versus storage cost

Although this logic makes sense, it is not unusual for companies to stockpile inventories of materials and component parts without regard to whether or not the true cost trade-offs justify doing so. Adherence to the strategy of carrying materials inventories to take advantage of purchase price discounts is a practice that needs to be supported by a conscientious and objective analysis of the full range of relevant costs.

Transportation Savings. A second reason for accumulating physical supply inventory may be transportation savings. Frequently, firms associate transport savings with the purchase economies discussed earlier. A firm purchasing large quantities can ship large quantities. Many firms ship raw materials in carload, truckload, or bargeload lots to decrease transportation costs. In some instances, firms make shipments in multiple carloads or even trainloads at even lower rates per hundredweight.

carload/truckload savings

The transportation cost usually represents a significant part of the final selling price of raw materials. Because volumes moved are large and transportation is so important, even a small reduction in the per-hundredweight rate can often be significant. At the same time, raw materials usually incur relatively low inventory and warehousing costs. For example, a firm can often dump a raw material such

impact on selling price

as coal on the ground without any storage shelter. Consequently, reducing transportation costs through increased volume movement often reduces total costs, since inventory and warehousing costs may not increase as much as the transport cost decreases. This situation will vary depending upon the item's value. Auto manufacturers may, for example, find raw material inventory costs to be too high to justify accumulating large supplies of such materials prior to their use.

production shutdown

Safety Stock. A third reason for physical supply inventory would be to prevent an emergency production shutdown. In other words, many firms hold a certain amount of inventory as buffer or safety stock in case of shipping delays or some problem in filling orders. Shutting down an assembly line because raw materials are out of stock may cost thousands of dollars per hour. The amount of raw materials held depends upon the probability of delayed delivery and upon the volume of raw materials the firm utilizes.

future uncertainties

Speculative Purchase. A fourth possible reason for physical supply inventory is for speculative purchases or hedging against future price increases, strikes, changing political policies, delayed deliveries, rising or falling interest rates, or currency fluctuations in world markets. Also, the future supply of raw materials to some firms may be uncertain. For example, a threat of a steel industry strike leads the automobile industry to accumulate steel in case the strike occurs. And Japanese consumer goods manufacturers may sometimes stockpile finished product inventories in the United States because they are concerned that the United States will institute tariffs, quotas, or other import barriers.

interruption in supply

Seasonal Supply. Seasonal supply availability is a fifth reason for accumulating physical supply inventory. Agricultural products such as wheat or other grains are good examples of items available only at certain times of the year. With such products, firms may need an accumulation of supply to meet demand throughout the year. In some cases, the means of transportation may affect seasonal availability. For example, iron ore moves across the Great Lakes or down the St. Lawrence River. Ice closing the waterways interrupts the supply of iron ore each winter. In this instance, the best choice for a steel company is to accumulate seasonal inventories of iron ore, even though increased carrying costs may be incurred. This additional cost is more than justified when compared with the additional transportation expense which would be realized if year-round shipments by another mode were desired. The net result also allows the steel company to balance its production on a year-round basis, thus lowering production expense as a per-unit basis.

supplier efficiencies

Maintenance of Supply Sources. A sixth reason for holding physical supply inventory is to maintain supply sources. Large manufacturing firms very often use small vendors or suppliers who manufacture subassemblies or semifinished goods for the large firm even when the firm can produce such items itself. They may use the vendor or supplier in much the same way a company uses a public warehouse; when they do not have enough productive capacity to meet their peak demands, they buy from the vendor or supplier.

One problem with this approach is that small vendors or suppliers may be "captive." In other words, their only customers may be one or two large manufacturers. If the large manufacturer chose not to buy from the small vendor during certain times of the year the small vendor could be completely cut off and possibly forced to close down and lay off its employees. When the large manufacturer again needs materials, the small vendor would have to try to hire its employees back again. This could cause costs to rise, or it could cause quality to drop if the vendor has to hire new employees. So the large manufacturer may choose to give the small vendor off-season business to keep it operating—at least at partial capacity. Such action would mean a certain amount of inventory accumulation, but this may be less expensive than changing vendors or getting a small vendor started up again. The trade-off in this instance is usually lower vendor prices and/or higher quality against the inventory holding cost.

Physical Distribution Inventories

The second inventory type consists principally of finished goods awaiting shipment to customers. Reasons for accumulating physical distribution inventories include transportation savings, production savings, seasonal demand, customer service, stable employment, and providing goods for resale.

Transportation Savings. One reason companies may accumulate inventories of finished or semifinished product is similar to a reason for accumulating raw materials: transportation economies. By shipping in carload or truckload quantities rather than less-than-carload (LCL) or less-than-truckload (LTL) quantities, a company may experience lower per-unit transportation rates. As long as the transportation cost savings exceed any expenses associated with warehousing the additional volumes of product, it will be advantageous to ship in the larger quantities. Also, shipments in large volumes may experience better service, such as faster transit times and more reliable and consistent service. These results will help to reduce other costs such as in-transit inventory carrying cost and potential costs of lost sales due to product unavailability at point of sale or use.

volume discounts

Firms frequently associate transportation economies involving physical distribution inventory with the use of market-oriented warehouses or distribution centers. Companies ship from their plants to strategically located market-oriented facilities in carload or truckload quantities. The company can then ship the items shorter distances to customers in LTL or small package quantities to minimize costs.

market-oriented warehouses

Traditionally, firms have associated lower rates and better service with larger shipments, but today many shippers can negotiate lower rates and higher service levels for smaller shipments as well. Transportation companies are generally willing to customize their rates and services to meet individual shippers' needs. Shippers should carefully identify their price and service needs and negotiate terms of sale with the transportation companies most capable of satisfying those needs.

Production Savings. A second justification for accumulating physical distribution inventories relates to the issue of production economies. Traditionally, it was felt by many people involved with manufacturing management that the best way to optimize production expense was to have long, uninterrupted production runs for selected items. As a result, it was not unusual for firms to find themselves with significant levels of finished product inventories, which would not be needed until

production runs

some future point in time. This strategy was justified by the theory that the expense of carrying higher levels of finished product inventories was exceeded by the aggregate production savings.

Current thinking, however, is that companies should be trying to develop ways to manufacture efficiently in smaller quantities, perhaps by reducing line change-over expense, lowering per-unit manufacturing costs, and so on. As a result, the idea that firms can justify carrying large finished goods inventories has been challenged, and thus many firms have found that the cost of carrying the excess inventories can exceed any production cost savings.

order versus stock   Another interesting situation is that of firms that produce to order rather than to stock. This commonly results in shorter production runs, and companies have learned to master the art and science of lowering the expense of frequent line changeovers. Production to order virtually eliminates the need to carry finished product inventories, and this benefit is often financially considerable. For example, the Ping brand of golf clubs, manufactured by Karsten Corporation, is produced to order, and a production backlog of several weeks is not at all uncommon.

Seasonal Demand.   A third reason for accumulating finished goods is that a company may have seasonal demand for its product. Having productive capacity to meet the peak seasonal demand may not be efficient, and the company would be better off producing more regularly throughout the year with a smaller plant. Such a strategy would require warehousing facilities to store finished goods during low-demand periods, so as to ensure a lower per-unit production expense. Once again, the firm would trade off inventory cost against lower production costs and perhaps decreased plant investment.

apparel industry   Significant changes have occurred in the apparel industry, for example, which is highly seasonal and which characteristically includes significant levels of inventory. By focusing on better demand forecasts, the availability and analysis of point-of-sale (POS) sales information, and very high-quality, time-sensitive transportation services, this industry has been able to remove large amounts of inventory from the logistics pipeline. As we will discuss in Chapter 6 concerning the quick-response strategy, the apparel industry has reduced overall inventory and logistics costs significantly and has also enhanced the levels of service experienced by its retail customers.

substitutability   *Customer Service.*   A fourth reason, very important from a marketing viewpoint, is that a firm may hold physical distribution inventory to improve customer service or to reduce the cost of lost sales. We previously discussed substitutability and its effect on sales and cost. Where substitutability is high, firms may locate finished goods inventories reasonably close to their customers to allow expedient deliveries. The trade-off is between the cost of lost sales and inventory carrying cost.

In keeping with recent enhancements to information technology and the ways in which companies are operating highly effective customer service centers from centralized locations, a recent trend has been to partition inventories into groups depending on the levels of customer service that are needed. While there has been some evidence of companies making sure that high-priority items are available at or near major market areas, the use of high-quality, express logistics services such as FedEx, UPS, and Airborne justify holding these items at central points for immediate, time-sensitive delivery when they are needed.

Stable Employment. A fifth reason for holding physical distribution inventory is to maintain stable employment. This is particularly important if the company does not want to lose skilled labor. The trade-off is against long-run labor cost and product quality. Although holding inventory to stabilize employment is not feasible for long periods, companies may find it expedient as a short-term tactic to produce cost efficiencies.

skilled labor

Goods for Resale. A sixth reason for holding finished goods inventory is to meet timely customer needs. A firm would be wise to have on-hand inventories sufficient to satisfy demand as it occurs. At the same time, however, the firm holding the inventories should work closely with its customers to avoid incurring extra expenses through unnecessarily high inventory levels.

customer service

Functional Types of Inventory

Thus far, this section has addressed reasons that may justify a firm in holding inventory as part of its materials management or physical distribution responsibility. Another way to view inventory is in the context of its seven principal functions. We will address these in the following discussion. As indicated in the Logistics Profile, AT&T also segmented its inventories into various types. Although they chose a smaller number of categories, AT&T recognized that there were key differences in terms of the functions served by different types of inventory.

The first functional type of inventory is *cycle stock,* the portion of a company's inventory that is depleted through normal sale or use and replenished through the routine ordering process. This inventory type also refers to the amounts of product the firm regularly consumes during normal business activity. As we will discuss in the next chapter, firms hold cycle stock to respond to demand or usage occurring under certainty of demand and lead time length.

cycle stock

The second type of inventory includes *goods in process,* because of the time necessary to manufacture goods, and *goods in transit.* Sometimes called *work in process,* or *WIP,* goods in process, or semifinished goods, are important in a manufacturing situation. Inventory in transit refers to inventory that a carrier is transporting to a buyer. Because the purchasing firm sometimes has an ownership interest in goods that are in transit, carrying this inventory holds relevant financial implications. In-transit inventory also may refer to inventory that the selling firm still owns while the goods are being transported to the customer. Appendix 6A addresses the topic of in-transit inventory in detail.

in-process stock

The third functional type of inventory is *safety stock,* or *buffer stock,* which protects against uncertainties in demand rate, lead time length, or both. Firms hold safety stock in addition to cycle stock for the purpose of protecting against such uncertainties and their consequences. Holding safety stock helps a firm to avoid the negative, customer-related consequences of being out of stock when demand increases unexpectedly.

safety stock

Estimating stockout cost is a prerequisite to determining the appropriate amount of safety stock. Having estimated stockout cost, a firm should carry additional safety stock only if doing so does not cost more in dollars than the stockout the firm is averting.

The fourth type of inventory is *seasonal stock,* which the firm accumulates and holds in advance of the season during which the firm will need it. Industries

seasonal stock

typically requiring significant seasonal stock include apparel, sporting goods, and automotive. In addition, firms may ship many Christmas toys manufactured overseas between January and June to the United States during the spring and summer months, and inventory the toys in the summer and early fall months before moving them to U.S. retail stores. Firms may also inventory products such as tomato juice before sale to accommodate seasonal growing and harvesting.

promotional stock

The fifth inventory type is *promotional stock,* held so that a firm's logistics system may respond quickly and effectively to a marketing promotion or price deal that a firm intending to pull a product through the distribution channel offers to customers. Firms frequently accumulate products such as televisions, VCRs, tires, and many tobacco products for such purposes. The success of many marketing promotions depends heavily on the capability of the firm's logistics system to infuse large amounts of product into the marketplace on relatively short notice.

speculative stock

The sixth type of inventory is *speculative stock.* Most commonly associated with materials needed by companies involved in manufacturing or assembly operations, this inventory protects against price increases or constrained availability. For example, U.S.-based firms stockpile component parts and subassemblies purchased from firms in areas such as Korea, Japan, and Singapore. This protects these U.S. firms against the uncertainties mentioned earlier and against others such as import quotas and tariffs. In addition, many food companies, such as Hershey Chocolate Company, Pillsbury, and Kraft General Foods, must actively participate in the world futures markets for ingredient commodities essential to their products.

dead stock

The seventh inventory type, *dead stock,* has no value for normal business purposes. A firm may ship dead stock to a company location where the product has real business value, sell or distribute it into overseas markets, or dispose of it in a manner that meets company and environmental standards. As indicated in the Logistics Profile, AT&T found that shortening lead time for production, delivery, and sales were keys to reducing dead stock. By giving the product (high-tech electronic equipment) less time to become obsolete, the company was able to reduce the quantities of stock that served no useful purpose.

More than 200 firms interested in deriving economic value from dead stock now belong to the Investment Recovery Association. This group explores effective ways for organizations to sell off or transfer used or surplus supplies, and results among its members have been impressive. For example, the income and/or savings from such programs may be ten to fifteen times the average cost of administering the programs.

Specific examples include Weyerhaeuser Co., whose fifteen-year-old investment recovery program has evolved into a full-fledged retailing operation. The stores offer used lumbering equipment and other gear, and even stock other companies' surplus goods. Mead Corporation markets surplus mill equipment to firms having similar needs. After trying to find uses for surplus items inside the company, Phillips Petroleum Co. opens its 66,000-square-foot warehouse (its "showroom") to the public one day every other month to sell off excess merchandise.

The Importance of Inventory in Other Functional Areas

functional interfaces

An earlier chapter explored how logistics interfaces with an organization's other functional areas, such as marketing and manufacturing. Nowhere is the interface usually more prominent than in the inventory area. As background for analyzing the importance of inventory in the logistics system, we should examine how logistics relates to other functional business areas on inventory matters.

- *Marketing* desires high customer service levels and well-replenished inventory stocks in order to assure product availability and to meet customer needs as quickly and completely as possible.
- *Manufacturing* typically desires long production runs and the lowest procurement costs as well as early production of seasonal items in order to minimize manufacturing costs and to avoid overtime payments.
- *Finance* desires low inventories in order to increase inventory turnover, reduce current assets, and receive high capital returns on assets.

The preceding statements clearly show why other functional areas are interested in inventory. Also, finance area objectives may obviously conflict with marketing and manufacturing objectives. A more subtle conflict sometimes arises between marketing and manufacturing, although high inventory levels interest both areas. The long production runs that manufacturing may desire could cause shortages of some products needed by marketing to satisfy customer demand. For example, manufacturing may want to continue a particular production run up to 5,000 units at a time when marketing needs another product currently in short supply.

Many companies can make a case for using a formal logistics organization to resolve these inventory objective conflicts. Inventory has an important impact on logistics, and in many logistics organizations, inventory is the pivotal activity. The logistics manager is in an excellent position to analyze inventory trade-offs not only with other logistics areas but also with the functional areas discussed here. In some instances, this can almost be an arbitrator's role.

arbitrator role of logistics

Proper inventory management and control affects customers, suppliers, and the organization's major functional departments. In spite of the many possible advantages to having inventory in a logistics system, the inventory holding costs are a major expense, and the logistics system should emphasize reducing inventory levels.

INVENTORY COSTS

Inventory costs are important for three major reasons. First, inventory costs represent a significant component of total logistics costs in many companies. Second, the inventory levels that a firm maintains at points in its logistics system will affect the level of service the firm can provide to its customers. Third, cost trade-off decisions in logistics frequently depend upon and ultimately affect inventory carrying costs.

importance of inventory costs

This section provides basic information concerning the costs that logistics management should consider when making inventory policy decisions. The major types include inventory carrying costs, order/setup costs, expected stockout costs, and in-transit inventory carrying costs.

Inventory Carrying Cost

In a landmark research project, Douglas M. Lambert cited four major components of inventory carrying cost: capital cost, storage space cost, inventory service cost, and inventory risk cost.[1] Each cost type has a unique nature, and the particular calculation for each includes different expenses or costs.

Capital Cost.   Sometimes called the *interest* or *opportunity* cost, this cost type focuses upon what having capital tied up in inventory costs a company (in contrast to using capital in some other financially productive way). Stated differently, "What is the implicit value of having capital tied up in inventory, instead of using it for some other worthwhile project?"

The capital cost is frequently the largest component of inventory carrying cost. A company usually expresses it as a percentage of the dollar value of the inventory the company holds. For example, a capital cost expressed as 20 percent of a product value of $100 equals a capital cost of $100 × 20%, or $20. Similarly, if the product value is $300, then the capital cost will be $60.

calculating capital cost

In practice, determining an acceptable number to use for capital cost is no small task. In fact, most firms find that determining capital cost may be more of an art than a science. One way of calculating capital cost for inventory decision making requires identifying the firm's *hurdle* rate, the minimum rate of return expected of new investments. In this way, the firm may make inventory decisions in much the same way as it decides to spend money for advertising, building new plants, or adding new computer equipment.

For example, assume that the average value of a company's inventory is $300,000. This inventory is a capital asset for the company, like a machine or any other capital investment. Therefore, if the company bases its capital cost on a 15-percent hurdle rate, then the capital cost is $45,000 ($300,000 × 15%) per year.

accurate inventory costing

The inventory valuation method is critical to accurately determining capital cost, and is subsequently critical to determining overall inventory carrying cost. According to Stock and Lambert, "the opportunity cost of capital should be applied only to the out-of-pocket investment in inventory. . . . This is the direct variable expense incurred up to the point at which inventory is held in storage."[2] Thus, the commonly accepted accounting practice of valuing inventory at fully allocated manufacturing cost is unacceptable in inventory decision making because raising or lowering inventory levels financially affects only the variable portion of inventory value, and not the fixed portion of allocated cost. Including inbound transportation costs in inventory value, however, is consistent with this advice, and firms should include such cost measurements whenever possible.

A final suggestion on the topic of capital cost is to strive for accurate, comprehensive calculations of relevant cost elements. Although it is sometimes tempting, the inclination to use industry averages or percentage figures found in textbooks (such as 25 percent) not only will be misleading, but may produce highly inaccurate results.

Storage Space Cost.   This category includes handling costs associated with moving products into and out of inventory, and storage costs such as rent, heating, and lighting. Such costs may vary considerably from one circumstance to the next. For example, firms can often unload raw materials directly from railcars and store them outside, whereas finished goods typically require safer handling and more sophisticated storage facilities.

fixed versus variable expenses

Storage space costs are relevant to the extent that they either increase or decrease as inventory levels rise or fall. Thus, firms should include variable rather than fixed expenses when estimating space costs as well as capital costs. Perhaps we can clarify the issue by contrasting public warehouse use with private warehouse use. When a firm uses public warehousing, virtually all handling and storage costs vary directly with the magnitude of stored inventory. As a result, these costs are all relevant to decisions regarding inventory. When a firm uses private warehousing, however, many storage space costs (such as depreciation on the building) are fixed and, as such, are not relevant to the inventory carrying cost.

Inventory Service Cost. Another component of inventory carrying cost includes insurance and taxes. Depending upon the product value and type, the risk of loss or damage may require high insurance premiums. Also, many states impose a tax on inventory value, sometimes on a monthly basis. High inventory levels resulting in high tax costs can be significant in determining specific locations where firms inventory product. Insurance and taxes may vary considerably from product to product, and firms must consider this when calculating inventory carrying costs.

insurance and taxes

Inventory Risk Cost. This final major component of inventory carrying cost reflects the very real possibility that inventory dollar value may decline for reasons largely beyond corporate control. For example, goods held in storage for some time may become obsolete and thus deteriorate in value. Also, fashion apparel may rapidly deteriorate in value once the selling season is actively underway or over. This phenomenon also occurs with fresh fruits and vegetables when quality deteriorates or the price falls. Manufactured products may face similar risks, although typically not to the same degree. An extreme example would be the case of very high-value products such as computers and peripherals, or semiconductors, which may experience relatively short product life cycles. In such instances, the cost of obsolescence or depreciation may be very significant.

risk and obsolescence

Any calculation of inventory risk costs should include the costs associated with obsolescence, damage, pilferage, theft, and other risks to inventoried product. The extent to which inventoried items are subject to such risks will affect the inventory value and thus the carrying cost.

Calculating the Cost of Carrying Inventory

Calculating inventory carrying cost for a particular item stored in inventory involves three steps. The first is to identify the value of the item stored in inventory. According to traditional accounting practices, the three most widely recognized approaches include valuing inventory on first-in/first-out (FIFO) basis, last-in/first-out (LIFO) basis, or average cost. The most relevant value measure for inventory decision making is the cost of goods sold or the variable manufactured cost of product currently coming into the firm's logistics facilities. Again, this is because raising or lowering inventory levels affects only the variable portion of inventory value, and not the fixed portion.

valuation of inventory

The second step is to measure each individual carrying cost component as a percentage of product value, and to add the component percentages together to measure inventory carrying cost. Thus, carrying cost is typically expressed as a percentage of product value. In computing storage space, inventory service, and inventory risk costs, it may be helpful to first calculate these costs in dollar terms and then to convert to percentage figures.

carrying cost percentages

TABLE 5-3 Example of Carrying Cost Components for Computer Hard Disks

Cost	Percentage of Product Value
Capital	12%
Storage space	2
Inventory service	3
Inventory risk	8
Total	25%

calculation of carrying cost

   The last step is to multiply overall carrying cost (as a percentage of product value) by the value of the product. This will measure the annual carrying cost for a particular amount of inventory.

Example. Suppose that a company manufactures hard disks for personal computers at a variable manufactured cost of $100 per unit. Table 5–3 lists the carrying cost components as a percentage of product value. The annual cost of carrying a single hard disk in inventory is calculated as follows:

   $100 × 25% = $25 per year

Nature of Carrying Cost

concept of average inventory

Items with basically similar carrying costs should use the same estimate of carrying cost per inventory dollar. However, items subject to rapid obsolescence or items that require servicing to prevent deterioration may require separate cost estimates. The estimate of carrying cost per inventory dollar expressed as a percentage of the inventory value carried during the year will reflect how carrying costs change with inventory value. Table 5–4 shows that as average inventory increases (i.e., as the inventory level increases), annual carrying cost increases, and vice versa. In

TABLE 5-4 Inventory and Carrying Cost Information for Computer Hard Disks

Order Period	Number of Orders per Year	Average Inventory* Units	Average Inventory* Value†	Total Annual Inventory Carrying Cost‡
1 week	52	50	$ 5,000	$ 1,250
2 weeks	26	100	10,000	2,500
4 weeks	13	200	20,000	5,000
13 weeks	4	650	65,000	16,250
26 weeks	2	1,300	130,000	32,500
52 weeks	1	2,600	260,000	65,000

*One week's inventory supply is 50 units.
†Value per unit is $100.
‡Percentage carrying cost is assumed to be 25%.

other words, carrying cost is variable and is directly proportional to the number of average inventory units or the average inventory value.

Order/Setup Cost

A second cost affecting total inventory cost is ordering cost or setup cost. Ordering cost refers to the expense of placing an order for additional inventory, and does not include the cost or expense of the product itself. Setup cost refers more specifically to the expense of changing or modifying a production or assembly process to facilitate product line changeovers, for example.

Order Cost.   The costs associated with ordering or acquiring inventory have both fixed and variable components. The fixed element may refer to the cost of the information system, facilities, and technology available to facilitate order placement activities. This fixed cost remains constant in relation to the number of orders placed.

There are also a number of costs that vary in relation to the number of orders that are placed for more inventory. Some of the types of activities that may be responsible for these costs include (1) reviewing inventory stock levels; (2) preparing and processing order requisitions or purchase orders; (3) preparing and processing receiving reports; (4) checking and inspecting stock prior to placement in inventory (although this activity should be minimized as part of a commitment to total quality management and "doing it right the first time"); and (5) preparing and processing payment. While the roles played by certain people and processes may seem trivial, they become very important when considering the total range of activities associated with placing and receiving orders.

activities affecting cost

Setup Cost.   Production setup costs may be more obvious than ordering or acquisition costs. Setup costs are expenses incurred each time a company modifies a production line to produce a different item for inventory. The fixed portion of setup cost might include use of the capital equipment needed to change over production facilities, while the variable expense might include the personnel costs incurred in the process of modifying or changing the production line.

production changeover

Nature of Cost.   Separating the fixed and variable portions of order/setup cost is essential. Just as calculations should emphasize the variable portion of inventory capital cost, calculations of order and setup costs should emphasize the variable portion of these expenses. As we will discuss in Chapter 6, this emphasis becomes central to developing meaningful inventory strategies.

When calculating yearly ordering costs, firms usually start with the cost or charge associated with each individual order or setup. Correspondingly, the yearly number of orders or setups affects the total order cost per year; this number is inversely related to individual order size or to the number of units manufactured (production run length) within a simple setup or changeover. Table 5–5 shows this general relationship.

general relationship

As we can see in Table 5–5, more frequent order placement results in customers placing a larger number of smaller orders per year. Since both small and large orders incur the variable expense of placing an order, total annual order cost will increase in direct relation to the number of orders placed per year. As long as

TABLE 5-5 Order Frequency and Order Cost for Computer Hard Disks

Order Frequency	Number of Orders per Year	Total Annual Order Cost*
1 week	52	$10,400
2 weeks	26	5,200
4 weeks	13	2,600
13 weeks	4	800
26 weeks	2	400
52 weeks	1	200

*Assuming a cost per prder of $200.

yearly sales and demand remain the same, total annual order or setup cost will relate directly to the number of order or setups per year, and will relate inversely to individual order size or individual production run length.

decreasing significance *Future Perspectives.* Although an accurate, comprehensive statement of inventory cost must include the portion related to order/setup activities, the magnitude of these costs is likely to decrease in the future. Considering the move to highly automated systems for order management and order processing, and the streamlining of inventory receiving practices, the variable cost of handling individual orders is certain to lessen significantly. In firms where "vendor-managed inventory" programs are underway, the concept of placing orders itself loses significance, and there the concept of order cost loses relevance. Similarly, as firms improve their ability to quickly and efficiently change over production processes, the variable expense associated with this task will decrease as well. While there may always be a measurable element of order/setup cost, this expense is likely to become less relevant in the future than it is today.

Carrying Cost versus Order Cost

trade-off perspective As shown in Table 5–6, order cost and carrying cost respond in opposite ways to changes in number of orders or size of individual orders. Total cost also responds to changing order size. Close examination indicates that order costs initially decrease more rapidly than carrying costs increase, which brings total costs down. In other words, a positive trade-off occurs, since the marginal savings in order costs exceed the marginal increment in inventory costs. However, at a certain point this relationship begins to change, and total costs start to increase. Here a negative trade-off occurs because the marginal order cost savings are less than the marginal carrying cost increase. We can view this set of relationships in cost curve terms as shown in Figure 5–3.

Expected Stockout Cost

Another cost critical to inventory decision making is stockout cost—the cost of not having product available when a customer demands or needs it. When an item is unavailable for sale, a customer may accept a backorder for future availability

TABLE 5-6 Summary of Inventory and Cost Information

Order Period	Number of Orders per Year	Average Inventory* (Units)	Total Annual Order Cost†	Change in Total Order Cost	Total Annual Inventory Carrying Cost‡	Change in Total Carrying Cost	Total Cost
I week	52	50	$10,400		$ 1,250		$11,650
				− 5,200		+ 1,250	
2 weeks	26	100	5,200		2,500		7,700
				− 2,600		+ 2,500	
4 weeks	13	200	2,600		5,000		7,600
				− 1,800		+11,250	
13 weeks	4	650	800		16,250		17,050
				− 400		+16,250	
26 weeks	2	1,300	400		32,500		32,900
				− 200		+32,500	
52 weeks	I	2,600	200		65,000		65,200

*Assume sales or usage at 100 units per week.
†Order cost is $200.
‡Value is $100 per unit and carrying cost is 25%.

of the needed product, or perhaps purchase (or substitute) a competitor's product, directly taking profit from the firm experiencing the stockout. If the firm permanently loses the customer to its competitor, the profit loss will be indirect but longer lasting. On the physical supply side, a stockout may result in no new materials or in semifinished goods or parts, meaning idle machine time or even shutting down an entire manufacturing facility.

FIGURE 5-3 Inventory Costs

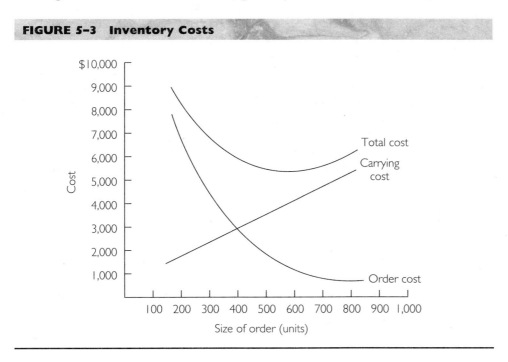

Safety Stock.   Most companies facing a stockout possibility will allow for safety, or buffer, stock to protect against uncertainties in demand or the lead time necessary for resupply. The inventory decision maker's difficulty is deciding how much safety stock to have on hand at any time. Having too much will mean excess inventory, whereas not having enough will mean stockouts and lost sales.

carrying cost   Developing information for deciding what level of safety stock to maintain is a difficult task. Measuring the carrying cost associated with different safety stock levels can be similar to measuring carrying cost in general. First determine a percentage carrying cost that includes capital cost, storage space cost, inventory service cost, and inventory risk cost. Then multiply this percentage figure by the dollar value per unit and the number of units involved.

We should make two points here. First, although the safety stock carrying cost is likely the same as the carrying cost for cycle stock, safety stocks are inherently riskier and implicitly more costly to carry than cycle stock. For simplicity, this text assumes that the same inventory carrying cost applies to both safety stock and cycle stock. Second, most decisions determining recommended safety stock levels involve probability analysis. The next chapter highlights this in a discussion of inventory decision making in the case of uncertainty.

stockout costs   *Cost of Lost Sales.*   Determining the carrying cost for safety stock inventory may be relatively straightforward. Determining the cost of not having an item available for sale, however, may be much more challenging. For a company dealing with raw materials or supplies for a production line, a stockout may mean wholly or partially shutting down operations. Such operations cutbacks are particularly critical for firms involved in just-in-time manufacturing or assembly operations, as discussed previously on the topic of materials management.

To best decide how much safety stock to carry, a manufacturing firm should thoroughly understand the cost consequences of shutting down its operation if needed input parts or materials were unavailable. The firm should first determine the hourly or daily production rates and then multiply these by the profit loss on the number of units not produced. For example, if a plant with an hourly production rate of 1,000 units and a per-unit profit of $100 shuts down for four hours, the loss would be $400,000. This figure may be somewhat conservative, however, since the firm may need to pay wages to workers despite a temporary shutdown. The firm may also need to consider the overhead costs often assigned or allocated to each production unit.

Calculating how the cost of lost sales for finished goods will affect a customer is usually more complex than calculating the cost for a raw materials stockout. As we discussed earlier, the three principal results of a finished goods stockout are backorders, lost sales, and lost customers, ranked from best to worst in desirability.

Inventory in Transit Carrying Cost

F.O.B. terms   Another possible inventory cost is that of carrying inventory in transit. This cost may be less apparent than the three discussed previously. However, under certain circumstances, it may represent a very significant expense. For example, a company selling its product F.O.B. ("free-on-board") destination is responsible for transporting the product to its customers, since title does not pass until the product reaches the customer's facility. Financially, the product, though still in the seller's inventory, will be contained in a transportation company vehicle or perhaps in the company's private truck.

Since this "moving" inventory is company-owned until delivered to the customer, the company should consider its delivery time part of its carrying cost. The faster delivery occurs, the sooner the transaction is completed and the company may receive payment for the shipment. Since faster delivery typically means higher-cost transportation, the company may want to analyze the trade-off between transportation cost and the cost of carrying inventory in transit. Appendix 6A specifically addresses this situation.

trade-offs

Determining Cost of In-Transit Inventories. An important question at this point is how to calculate the cost of carrying inventory in transit—that is, what variables should a firm consider? An earlier discussion in this chapter focused on four major components of inventory carrying cost: capital cost, storage space cost, inventory service cost, and inventory risk cost. While these categories are all valid, they apply differently to the cost of carrying inventory in transit.

comparison with warehouse inventory

First, the capital cost of carrying inventory in transit generally equals that of inventory in the warehouse. If the firm owns the inventory in transit, the capital cost will be relevant.

Second, storage space cost generally will not be relevant to inventory in transit, since the transportation service supplier typically includes equipment and necessary loading and handling within its overall price or rate.

Third, while taxes generally would not be relevant to inventory service costs, the need for insurance requires careful analysis. For example, liability provisions for using common carriers are fairly specific, and a firm using a common carrier may not need to consider additional insurance (with the exception of certain "umbrella" coverages, for example). Firms using private fleets or writing contracts with for-hire transportation suppliers may place greater value on making suitable arrangements for insurance.

Fourth, obsolescence or deterioration are lesser risks for inventory in transit, because the transportation service typically takes only a short time. Thus, this inventory cost is less relevant here than it is for inventory in the warehouse.

Generally, carrying inventory in transit typically costs less than carrying inventory in the warehouse. However, a firm seeking to determine actual cost differences most accurately should examine the details of each inventory matter in depth.

CLASSIFYING INVENTORY

Multiple product lines and inventory control require companies to focus upon more important inventory items and to utilize more sophisticated and effective approaches to inventory management. Inventory classification is usually a first step toward efficient inventory management. While we could have saved classification for the next chapter, which deals with the tools of inventory control, we will cover the topic now because it demonstrates an important aspect of most inventory decisions.

Cost Control Means Lower Inventories: The Case of Volvo GM Heavy Trucks

A clear message is sounding throughout the business community: "Measure and control costs." Complicating matters is the demand to maintain high service levels. These two goals have focused top management attention squarely on transportation and distribution.

In reevaluating capital deployment, corporate and financial officers are examining the size of their inventory investment. Controlling inventory levels can be a real key to controlling the size of this investment. Unfortunately, however, our financial systems sometimes encourage companies to build, rather than to reduce, inventories. This happens, for example, when companies focusing on savings in operating costs and expenses such as labor end up producing goods at a rate which inadvertently raises finished product inventories.

According to the industry marketing logistics manager for Digital Equipment Corporation, measuring inventory cost and service performance requires a systematic inventory management approach. This makes it easier to evaluate exactly the inventory carrying costs and production timing and to break down related costs such as transportation and warehousing.

As an example of a concerted commitment to effective inventory management, Volvo GM Heavy Trucks carefully examined its options when consolidating parts operations for White, General Motors, and the Volvo lines it handles. It improved parts receiving and parts storage, and reduced outbound freight using a single central parts distribution location. It also found that, since the location was near customers and suppliers, inbound freight costs were less.

Volvo GM calls its approach cost-effective logistics. Consolidating the three parts lines and opening a truck assembly plant uncovered some interesting facts. One was the realization that logistics costs were higher than direct labor costs. That was one reason for not heavily automating the assembly plant. Volvo GM chose to concentrate on materials and material control to manage costs. The company regularly picks up parts from its vendors, consolidates, and ships the parts in truckload quantities to its new Westerville, Ohio, parts distribution center (DC).

Their approach to cost-effective logistics also caused Volvo GM to look closely at plans to open a distribution center to serve another assembly plant. Creating a warehouse within a warehouse at the central parts redistribution center allowed Volvo GM to avoid a planned warehouse construction that would have cost $7 to $8 million. They also found that work-in-process inventories were $2 million lower than expected.

Volvo GM set inventory goals for its five parts levels based on the parts' value. A separate service level exists for what Volvo GM calls truck-off-road. Otherwise, Volvo picks dealer stock orders received through a dealer communications network once a week. Component value sets stocking levels and turns. Parts valued over $18,000 (A items) should turn 25 times per year; B items 18 times per year; C items 8; D items 3; and E items 1.5 times per year.

An important part of Volvo GM's cost-effective logistics approach is the interface established with carriers and consolidators. They make every effort to eliminate less-than-truckload freight by consolidating into truckload on a daily basis. Parts coded for a storage carousel or outbound carrier arrive at the DC from 2,000 vendors. The parts DC can also ship directly to the point of use within a Volvo GM assembly plant.

At the Volvo GM assembly plant in Orrville, Ohio, components not received directly at a point of use are received onto a conveyor and pass by a computer station for identification. Those materials are then stored in a warehouse area under the same roof as the assembly plant. The entire receiving and warehousing area is 5,000 square feet.

Business can achieve much in inventory management by coordinating efforts across functional boundaries. In the future, more "inventory in motion" will place emphasis on transportation to provide high service levels at reasonable cost.

ADAPTED FROM: Perry A. Trunick, "Cost Control Means Lower Inventories," *Transportation & Distribution* (April 1989): 16–17. Copyright © 1989, Penton Publishing Inc., Cleveland, OH.

ABC Analysis

ranking system   The need to rank inventory items in terms of importance was first recognized in 1951 by H. Ford Dicky of General Electric.[3] He suggested that GE classify items according to relative sales volume, cash flows, lead time, or stockout costs. He used what we now refer to as ABC analysis for his particular classification scheme. This system assigns items to three groups according to the relative impact or value of the items that make up the group. Those thought to have the greatest impact or value, for example, constituted the A group, while those items thought to have a lesser impact or value were contained in the B and C groups, respectively.[4]

Pareto's Law, or the "80-20 Rule."   Actually, ABC analysis is rooted in Pareto's law, which separates the "trivial many" from the "vital few."[5] In inventory terms, this suggests that a relatively small number of items or stock-keeping units (SKUs) may account for a considerable impact or value. A 19th-century Renaissance man, Vilfredo Pareto suggested that many situations were dominated by a relatively few vital elements, and that the relative characteristics of members of a population were not uniform.[6,7] His principle that a relatively small percentage of a population may account for a large percentage of the overall impact or value has been referred to as the "80-20 rule," which has been found to prevail in many situations.

80-20 rule

For example, marketing research might find that 20 percent of a firm's customers account for 80 percent of its sales; or a university might find that 20 percent of its courses generate 80 percent of its student credit hours. Or a study might find that 20 percent of a city's people account for 80 percent of its crime. Although the actual percentages may differ somewhat from example to example, some variation of the 80-20 rule usually applies.

examples

Inventory Illustration.   Figure 5–4 demonstrates ABC analysis as it applies to inventory management. The diagram indicates that only 20 percent of the items in the product line account for 80 percent of total sales. The items that make up this 20 percent are referred to as A items, due to the significant portion of sales for which they are responsible. The items in the B category account for approximately 50 percent of the items in the product line, yet make up only an additional 15 percent of total sales. Finally, the C items are represented by the remaining 30 percent of the items, which account only for approximately 5 percent of sales.

ABC inventories

In many ABC analyses, a common mistake is to think of the B and C items as being far less important than the A items, and subsequently to focus most or all of management's attention on the A items. For example, a decision might be made to assure very high in-stock levels for the A items and little or no availability for the B and C items. The fallacy here relates to the fact that all items in the A, B, and C categories are important to some extent, and that each set of items deserves its very own strategy to assure availability at an appropriate level of cost. This thinking has led some firms to differentiate inventory stocking policies by ABC category, making sure that the A items are available either immediately or through the use of express logistics services. The B and C items, while perhaps available at an upstream location in the logistics channel, could be available in a timely manner when needed.

relative importance

There are a number of additional reasons not to overlook the importance of the B and C items. Sometimes, the use of B and C items may be complementary to the use of A items, meaning that the availability of B and C items may be necessary for the sale of A items. Or in some instances the C items might be new products that are expected to be successful in the future. In other cases, the C

FIGURE 5–4 ABC Inventory Analysis

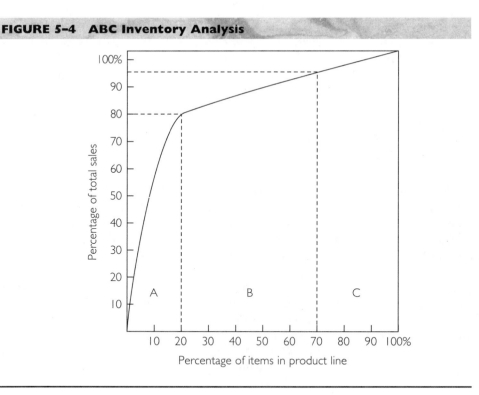

items may be highly profitable, despite the fact that they may account for only a small portion of sales.

steps in ABC
analysis

Performing an ABC Classification.   ABC classification is relatively simple. The first step is to select some criterion, such as sales revenue, for developing the ranking. The next step is to rank items in descending order of importance according to this criterion and to calculate actual and cumulative total sales revenue percentages for each item. This calculation should help to group the items into ABC categories.

Table 5–7 shows how to base an ABC inventory analysis on sales revenue generated per line item. The first column identifies the ten items in the Big Orange product line. The second and third columns show the annual sales and percentage of total annual sales represented by each item. The fourth and fifth columns show sales and items, respectively, as percentages of the total. From these columns emanate statements such as "20 percent of the items account for 80 percent of the sales." The last column places each item into ABC classification on the basis of annual item sales revenues.

This last step assigns the items into ABC groups. This step is the most difficult, and no simple technique is available. While the analysis is supported by data inputs that are presumably accurate, the ultimate decisions will require subjective judgment on the part of the decision maker. As one examines item rankings, significant natural "breaks" sometimes appear. But this is not always the case, and the

TABLE 5–7   ABC Analysis for Big Orange Products, Inc.

Item Code	Annual Sales ($)	Percentage of Annual Sales	Cumulative Percentages Sales	Items	Classification Category
64R	$ 6,800	68.0%	68.0%	10.0%	A
89Q	1,200	12.0	80.0	20.0	A
68J	500	5.0	85.0	30.0	B
37S	400	4.0	89.0	40.0	B
12G	200	2.0	91.0	50.0	B
35B	200	2.0	93.0	60.0	B
61P	200	2.0	95.0	70.0	B
94L	200	2.0	97.0	80.0	C
11T	150	1.5	98.5	90.0	C
20G	150	1.5	100.0	100.0	C
	$10,000	100.0%			

decision maker will have to consider other variables such as the item's importance and the cost of managing individual item types. Also, we should note that the data in the fourth and fifth columns of Table 5–7 are the basic data points from which Figure 5–4 was constructed. This should bring our understanding of ABC inventory analysis full circle.

Moving beyond the simple ABC analysis based on total sales by line item, William C. Copacino suggests that a modified ABC analysis be performed using gross profit dollars per line item and line item order frequency as potential segmenting variables. He suggests using multiple measures of impact or value and then developing a weighting scheme to stratify items into the ABC categories.[8] This approach broadens the focus beyond just sales volume considerations and places attention on often overlooked issues such as item profitability (which affects overall profitability) and order frequency (which affects customer service performance). Furthermore, this more comprehensive approach allows users to examine the suitability of different criteria, different weightings of the criteria, and ultimately the impact of alternative classification policies on issues of strategic importance—sales volume, profitability, customer service, and inventory investment.

further insight

EVALUATING THE EFFECTIVENESS OF A COMPANY'S APPROACH TO INVENTORY MANAGEMENT

A product buyer must be confident that suppliers and vendors have that product available when and where the buyer needs it. Similarly, a product seller's ability to manage inventory effectively should translate into a more satisfied customer base. Thus, both buyers and sellers should consider several questions when evaluating the effectiveness of a firm's inventory management approach.

The first question to raise is whether the company's customers are satisfied with existing levels of customer service. Insight into this issue can be gained by inquiring into matters such as customer loyalty, order cancellation experience, and stockouts, and evaluating the company's general relationships with all channel

customer satisfaction

partners. If there are areas where customer service levels need to improve, perhaps using more dependable transportation suppliers would help to enhance customer satisfaction.

backordering/ expediting
The second question is how frequently a need for backordering or expediting occurs. The more frequently these occur, the less effective an inventory system is presumed to be. The company's inventory management approach may not respond promptly to signals for reordering and resupplying inventory levels. Or the company may need an ABC inventory system or faster and more dependable transportation services to see that inventory is available when and where the customer needs it.

inventory turnover
A third question involves inventory turnover measures calculated for an entire product line and for individual products and product groupings. Buyers and sellers should question whether these measures are increasing or decreasing and how they vary among different stocking points in the firm's distribution system.

Inventory turnover, sometimes referred to as inventory velocity, is calculated by dividing annual sales in dollars by average inventory measured in dollars. Assuming that the inventory valuation bases are equivalent (e.g., both are valued in terms of retail price or cost of goods sold), the resulting figure measures how many times per year average inventory turns over.

For example, assume that a firm values its yearly product sales at $50,000, and calculates its average on-hand inventory to be $10,000. The number of inventory "turns" per year would be $50,000 ÷ $10,000, or five. The firm could say either that average inventory turns five times per year or that on the average, an inventory item stays on the shelf for one-fifth of a year—or 10.4 weeks.

Inventory turnover varies widely among firms in different industries and also among firms in similar industries. Inventory turnover typically ranges from five to ten turns for many manufacturing firms and from ten to twenty turns for wholesale and retail firms, through whose systems inventory moves rapidly. In either case, buyers and sellers must have specific details about a firm and its logistics system before estimating inventory turnover. (We should not view the percentages cited here as industry standards, but only as representing certain firms in the industries identified.)

While more inventory turns per year often implies more effective inventory management, customer service sometimes suffers if turnovers cause needed inventoried items to be unavailable. A firm interested in increasing its inventory turns while maintaining customer service levels should switch to faster and more reliable transportation services or improved order processing systems, which will justify lowering its safety stock investment and therefore its overall inventory levels. Examining inventory turnover by individual products or facilities may help to identify trouble spots in a firm's logistics system.

As Table 5–8 indicates, as inventory turnover increases, both average inventory and the cost of carrying the average inventory will show decreases. These same relationships are shown in Figure 5–5. Also, according to studies by Cass Information Services and the Ohio State University, it is expected that inventories at plant warehouses and company-field warehouses will experience increased turns in the years ahead. The projections, based on survey research, are indicated in Figure 5–6.

ratio of inventory to sales
A fourth question to raise is whether overall inventory as a percentage of sales rises or falls as a company's sales increase. Generally, given effective inventory

TABLE 5-8 The Relationship among Inventory Turnover, Average Inventory, and Inventory Carrying Costs

Inventory Turnover	Average Inventory	Inventory Carrying Cost*	Incremental Savings in Carrying Cost	Cumulative Savings in Carrying Cost
1	$20,000,000	$6,000,000	—	—
2	10,000,000	3,000,000	$3,000,000	$3,000,000
3	6,666,667	2,000,000	1,000,000	4,000,000
4	5,000,000	1,500,000	500,000	4,500,000
5	4,000,000	1,200,000	300,000	4,800,000
6	3,333,333	1,000,000	200,000	5,000,000
7	2,857,143	857,143	142,857	5,142,857
8	2,500,000	750,000	107,143	5,250,000
9	2,222,222	666,667	83,333	5,333,333
10	2,000,000	600,000	66,667	5,400,000

*Assume that inventory carrying cost equals 30%.

management, this figure should decline as sales increase. If a firm's inventories are rising at a rate equal to or faster than its sales, the firm may need to reconsider its overall inventory policies. Commonly, many firms experiencing a growing demand for their products will "overinventory" those products where customers are concentrated. A more suitable alternative might be to centralize supplies of such items and to depend upon capable transportation suppliers and enhanced order processing systems to provide timely product delivery to customers.

FIGURE 5-5 Saving Inventory Dollars by Increasing Inventory Turns

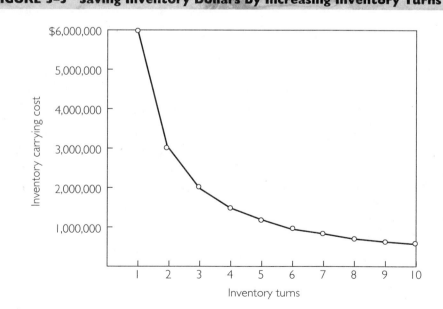

FIGURE 5-6 Past and Projected Inventory Turnover of Finished Goods

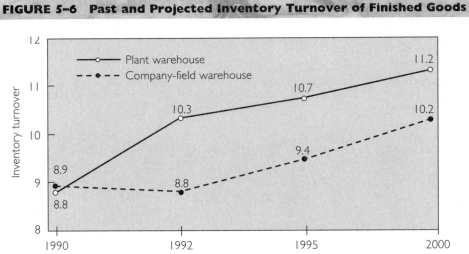

SOURCE: Cass Information Services and the Ohio State University, 1993. Used with permission of Dr. Bernard J. LaLonde.

SUMMARY

This chapter introduced some fundamental concepts relating to the role and importance of inventory in the logistics system. The following key points summarize these concepts for a meaningful discussion of how inventory decisions are made in today's business environment:

- Inventory as a percent of overall business activity continues to decline. Explanatory factors include: greater expertise in managing inventory; innovations in information and communications technology; greater competitiveness in markets for transportation services; and emphasis upon reducing cost through the elimination of non-value-added activities.
- As product lines proliferate and the number of SKU's increase, the cost of carrying inventory becomes a significant expense of doing business.
- Retail and wholesale firms place pressures on other supply chain participants to significantly reduce or eliminate unnecessary inventories, while at the same time ask for improvements in terms of logistical customer service.
- There are a number of principal reasons for carrying physical supply inventories, as well as physical distribution inventories. Principal "functional types" of inventory include: cycle stock; goods in process or goods in transit; safety stock; seasonal stock; promotional stock; speculative stock; and dead stock.
- Principal types of inventory cost are inventory carrying cost, order/setup cost, expected stockout cost, and in-transit inventory carrying cost.
- Inventory carrying cost is composed of capital cost, storage space cost, inventory service cost, and inventory risk cost. There are precise ways to calculate each of these costs.
- ABC analysis is a useful tool to improve the effectiveness of inventory management.
- There are a number of key questions and issues that may be raised in order to evaluate the effectiveness of a company's approach to inventory management.

STUDY QUESTIONS

1. What are the major trends relating to inventory in the U.S. economy? What factors help to explain recent declines in inventory as a percent of GNP?

2. Why is inventory important to the entire logistics channel? What priorities are in evidence today regarding the treatment of inventories throughout the logistics channel?

3. Select a company and discuss reasons for holding inventory in terms of materials management inventory and physical distribution inventory.

4. Identify the major functional inventory types. Discuss the basic difference between cycle stock and safety stock.

5. What are the major components of inventory carrying cost? How would you measure capital cost for making inventory policy decisions?

6. How can inventory carrying cost be calculated for a specific product? What suggestions would you offer for determining the measure of product value to be used in calculations of inventory carrying cost?

7. Explain the differences between inventory carrying costs and order costs.

8. Why is it generally more difficult to determine the cost of lost sales for finished goods than it is for raw materials inventories?

9. Discuss the cost of carrying inventory in transit.

10. You have been called in as a consultant to a large drugstore chain that has 24,000 inventory line items. Explain how inventory classification could help this company to better control its inventory.

11. What key questions would you raise when judging the effectiveness of a company's inventory management approach? If the calculated value of inventory as a percentage of sales appears to be rising, would this concern you? Explain.

12. How is inventory turnover calculated, and what is the nature of the relationship between inventory carrying cost and inventory turnover?

NOTES

1. Douglas M. Lambert, *The Development of an Inventory Costing Methodology: A Study of the Costs Associated with Holding Inventory* (Chicago: National Council of Physical Distribution Management, 1976).

2. Douglas M. Lambert and James R. Stock, *Strategic Logistics Management,* 3rd ed. (Homewood, IL: Irwin, 1993): 378–379.

3. Robert Goodell Brown, *Advanced Service Parts Inventory Control,* 2d ed. (Norwich, VT: Materials Management Systems, 1982): 155.

4. David P. Herron, "ABC Data Correlation," in *Business Logistics in American Industry,* ed. Karl Ruppenthal and Henry A. McKinnel, Jr. (Stanford, CA: Stanford University, 1968): 87–90.

5. Thomas E. Hendrick and Franklin G. Moore, *Production/Operations Management,* 9th ed. (Homewood, IL: Irwin, 1985): 173.

6. Lambert and Stock, *Strategic Logistics Management:* 426–429.

7. Jay U. Sterling, "Measuring the Performance of Logistics Operations," Chapter 10 in *The Logistics Handbook*, ed. James F. Robeson and William C. Copacino (New York: The Free Press, 1994): 226–230.
8. William C. Copacino, "Moving Beyond 'ABC' Analysis," *Traffic Management* (March 1994): 35–36.

Case 5-1

BELLWETHER CORPORATION

Eighty-Eight Enterprises, Inc., has just acquired the Bellwether Corporation. Eighty-Eight is a diversified manufacturer of sporting goods and casual furniture. It feels that Bellwether's high-quality line of tennis rackets and related products can help even out seasonal imbalances in Eighty-Eight's product line.

Martha Rodino, senior vice president of logistics at Eighty-Eight, has been asked to evaluate the effectiveness of Bellwether's logistics system, with particular emphasis on inventory management. She agrees that this task will provide her company with valuable insight as it considers merging the operations of the two companies.

As she begins her preliminary analysis of Bellwether, Rodino finds that the company produces a full line of tennis rackets, from all-aluminum models at the lower end to graphite-based composition models at the upper end. Each model is available in a number of sizes and colors, and the total number of SKU's is forty-eight. The company also sells related items such as towels, bags, and caps, which contribute an additional 120 SKU's. Rodino has been told that the tennis racket line accounts for approximately 60 percent of the company's gross revenues, but only 35 percent of its net income.

Bellwether inventories its products at three distribution centers located strategically throughout the United States, and sells them through tennis specialty shops, department stores, mass merchandisers, and catalogs. After touring the three distribution centers, Rodino feels that Bellwether's average inventory levels might be unnecessarily high.

Case Questions

1. What additional information should Rodino gather before finalizing her evaluation of Bellwether's inventory system?
2. What critical issues should Eighty-Eight address before deciding to merge its logistics operations with Bellwether's?

OK JEANS

At OK Jeans, inventory control blends the big and the small. This maker of children's apparel is enjoying some good times. Its nearly 15-percent annual growth rate has significantly increased traffic volumes between its corporate distribution center in Harrison, Arkansas, and its twelve manufacturing locations.

Largely responsible for smooth merchandise flow is a battery-powered microcomputer that a bar code wand and an FM radio receiver connect to the host mainframe. As a result, warehouse workers have a truly personal computer, and order pickers communicate with the computer without leaving their trucks.

Inventory handling at OK Jeans has improved measurably since the company installed this new equipment, largely because bar-coded labels replaced printed forms and other cumbersome paperwork. And by utilizing real-time inventory tracking, OK Jeans has eliminated its quarterly physical inventory counts, which used to shut down operations for two days. The computer also forces order pickers to follow the company's first-in/first-out selection process. By streamlining operations and reducing inventory reporting inaccuracies, computers are improving OK Jeans' growth rate.

Case Questions

1. What additional benefits do you feel OK Jeans probably derived from its investment in computer equipment?
2. What cost trade-offs are inherent in this situation? What factors would be important to a company considering greater computerization of its inventory procedures?
3. What other initiatives and priorities might OK Jeans examine when considering future growth?

ADAPTED FROM: Bruce Heydt, "Inventory Casebook: Oshkosh B'Gosh," *Distribution* (May 1987): 38–39. Reprinted by permission of Chilton's DISTRIBUTION Magazine, Radnor, PA.

CHAPTER 6

INVENTORY DECISION MAKING

LEARNING OBJECTIVES

After reading this chapter, you should be able to do the following:

- Understand the fundamental differences among approaches to managing inventory.

- Appreciate the rationale and logic behind the economic order quantity (EOQ) approach to inventory decision making, and be able to solve some problems of a relatively straightforward nature.

- Realize how variability in demand and order cycle length affects inventory decision making.

- Know how inventory will vary as the number of stocking points decreases or increases.

- Recognize the contemporary interest in and relevance of time-based approaches to inventory management.

- Understand the details and impact of the quick-response (QR) and efficient consumer response (ECR) approaches to inventory management and overall functioning of the supply chain.

- Make needed adjustments to the basic EOQ approach to respond to several special types of applications.

TEAM HANES

How would you like to be in a retail business where consumers' purchases tomorrow can be dramatically influenced by the outcome of tonight's Bulls versus Knicks showdown? Or where the NFL announcement of a new franchise in Charlotte can send demand soaring for Panthers sweatshirts both regionally and nationally? Or where a slumping star can cause thousands of unwanted T-shirts to be left behind? This type of demand volatility can create operational and logistical nightmares. The end result can include the very challenging task of managing the availability of thousands of stock-keeping units (SKUs), the result of multiple seasons, sports, graphics, styles, and sizes. And, by the way, your retail customer wants five inventory turns annually and expects five-day order turnaround, 95 percent order fill rates, and account-specific price tagging.

To respond to these customer needs, Team Hanes, part of Sara Lee Knit Products, launched its "vendor management program" for licensed sports apparel sold in mass retail markets. Team Hanes's solution was to work more closely with the retailer to manage the category. This included setting and actively monitoring store-level model stocks, placing weekly replenishment orders based on point-of-sale (POS) sell-through data, and shipping price-ticketed product directly to stores. By managing the entire supply chain from the retail floor back through production, Team Hanes would be able to compress cycle times, eliminate inventory holding points (such as retail distribution centers), and respond better to volatile consumer demand.

Team Hanes's former approach to supply chain management relied on at least three discrete inventory buffers to smooth the flow of goods through production and provide a reliable response to volatile consumer demand. This concept, however, was found to have three principal shortcomings: (1) at each step back in the supply chain from the retailer, volatility of demand increased and forecast accuracy decreased, the result being excessive overages of some items and excessive stockouts on other items at various points in the supply chain; (2) there was a failure to respond quickly to changes in demand at the retail level; and (3) similar inventory control approaches were used for all items, regardless of variability of demand.

To overcome these problems, Team Hanes adopted an operational infrastructure that meets demand more reliably and with less systemwide inventory than under the previous approach. The business system that was developed relies heavily on the use of store-level POS data in order to set model stock levels to meet projected demand, not the last few weeks of historical sales. The new approach also eliminates the need for retailers to hold inventories in their distribution centers and replenishes in-store model stocks directly from the Team Hanes Distribution Center. Production run sizes are optimized by item to balance economic order quantity (calculated based on item-specific volume characteristics) against forecast consumer demand over the near term. Raw materials inventories are held in the form of blank garments, which are sized based on the projected print schedule, ensuring a match between production plans and blank inventories.

This business system is designed to consistently and reliably deliver Team Hanes's unique value to retailers as the business grows. It allows Team Hanes to manage the end-to-end supply chain for licensed sports apparel, maximizing revenue and profitability for both the retailer and itself.

ADAPTED FROM: Jamie Bonomo, Bruce Onsager, and Robert Roche, "Building the Quick Response Infrastructure for Growth: A Case Example," *Logistics!* (Summer, 1994): 9–11. Used with permission.

Chapter 5 developed the rationale for inventory in a logistics system and addressed several fundamental aspects of inventory management. An important part of that chapter analyzed major cost categories that are relevant to the inventory decision: inventory carrying costs, order/setup costs, and expected stockout costs.

This chapter places the content of Chapter 5 in an operational context by describing in detail how inventory management decisions are made. In addition, it focuses attention on a number of newer, more progressive approaches to time-based, replenishment logistics. Coupled with the discussions in Chapters 3 and 4 relating to JIT, MRP, MRPII, and DRP, this chapter should help the student understand how companies make inventory decisions and how they develop overall strategies that rely on significant reductions of inventory in the logistics pipeline.

FUNDAMENTAL APPROACHES TO MANAGING INVENTORY

basic issues

Historically, managing inventory involved two fundamental questions: *how much* to reorder and *when* to reorder. By performing a few simple calculations, an inventory manager could easily determine acceptable solutions to these issues. Today, questions regarding *where* inventory should be held and *what* specific line items should be available at specific locations challenge the creativity and analytical capabilities of inventory decision makers.

managing inventories

Each question is still relevant, but managing inventory in today's business environment is challenging and usually involves selecting an overall strategy from a range of alternatives. At the same time that inventory decision making has become more complex, firms have placed more pressure on themselves to structure logistics systems to manage inventories more effectively and to lower cost and improve service as well. In practice, the difficulty of selecting an acceptable approach will depend on the circumstances under which the company operates and the extent to which certain simplifying assumptions can be made. Generally, the more complex the circumstances, the more sophisticated the inventory approach required.

balancing cost with service

Regardless of the approach selected, inventory decisions must consider issues relating to cost and to customer service requirements. Figure 6–1, which illustrates the general relationship between inventory and customer service levels, suggests that increasing investments in inventory may result in higher levels of customer service. While there is some validity to this relationship, a high priority today is on identifying logistics solutions that will result in higher levels of customer service along with reduced investments in inventories. Several factors make this an achievable objective: (1) more responsive order processing and order management systems; (2) enhanced ability to strategically manage logistics information; (3) more capable and reliable transportation resources; and (4) improvements in the ability to position inventories so that they will be available when and where they are needed. Thus, the higher priority today is on identifying the total logistics solutions that will lead to increases in overall customer service levels and reductions in total logistics cost. The discussion of Team Hanes in this chapter's Logistics Profile provides a good example of how one firm has been moving toward restructuring and modernizing its supply chain as a means of achieving such objectives.

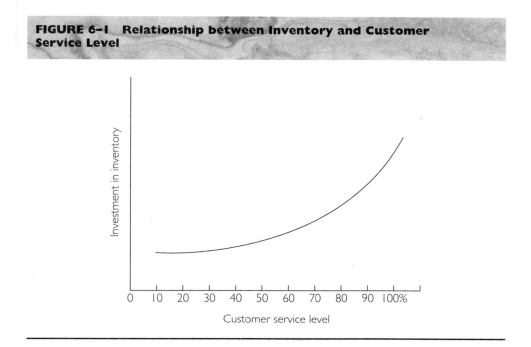

FIGURE 6–1 Relationship between Inventory and Customer Service Level

Investment in inventory (vertical axis)

Customer service level: 0 10 20 30 40 50 60 70 80 90 100% (horizontal axis)

Key Differences among Approaches to Managing Inventory

Given the various approaches to managing inventory that are available and used today, it is important to know the key ways in which they differ. These differences include dependent versus independent demand, pull versus push, and systemwide versus single-facility solutions to inventory management issues.

Dependent versus Independent Demand. This distinction is important to selecting an appropriate inventory management approach. According to Joseph Orlicky, "Demand for a given inventory item is termed 'independent' when such demand is unrelated to demand for other items—when it is not a function of demand for some other inventory item. . . . Conversely, demand is defined as 'dependent' when it is directly related, or derives from, the demand for another inventory item or product."[1] For example, the demand for finished automobiles is independent; the demand for tires is dependent on the desired quantity of finished automobiles. Orlicky suggests that this dependency may be *vertical* (such as when a product's assembly requires a component part) or *horizontal* (for example, when an instruction booklet must accompany a finished product).

    nature of demand

Thus, for many manufacturing processes, basic demand for most raw materials, component parts, and subassemblies *depends* upon demand for the finished product. In contrast, demand for many end-use items, which are typically warehoused and inventoried, is *independent* of the demand for any other higher-order manufactured item.

An important point to remember is that developing inventory policies for items exhibiting independent demand will require forecasting expected demand for these items. Alternatively, forecasting is less relevant for items having dependent demand, since the needed quantities of these items depend entirely upon the demand for the end product being manufactured or assembled. For items having dependent demand, needed quantity projections and receipts timing will rely wholly on the forecast needs for the end product.

Of the approaches to inventory management discussed in Chapters 3 and 4, JIT, MRP, and MRPII are generally associated with items having dependent demand. In such instances, the demand for individual parts and items typically depends on the demand for the finished end product. Alternatively, DRP generally involves the movement and positioning of items having independent demand. The economic order quantity (EOQ) approach to be discussed later in this chapter, applies most frequently to items having demand that may be characterized as independent.

Pull versus Push.[2]   Another important distinction between inventory management approaches is the issue of pull versus push. Sometimes called a "reactive" system, the pull approach relies on customer demand to "pull" product through a logistics system. In contrast, the "push," or proactive, approach uses inventory replenishment to anticipate future demand.

example   As an example, a fast-food system such as McDonald's basically runs on a pull system, while a catering service basically operates on a push system. McDonald's cooks hamburgers generally in response to current demand. In effect, individual purchases "trigger" more food item production. In contrast, the catering service tries to have a picture-perfect idea of what customers will need and when, and pushes food items to where customers need them, at the right time and in the right quantity.[3]

hybrid system   While this distinction may seem simple enough, the McDonald's pull system may be quite effective in a downtown location with a steady stream of customers but may suffer in a high-traffic, peak-demand location such as a major airport concourse. In this instance, a pull and push system hybrid would be appropriate.

A principal attribute of pull systems is that they can respond quickly to sudden or abrupt changes in demand. Alternatively, a push system meets systemwide inventory needs in accordance with some master plan in an orderly and disciplined way. In general, the pull system applies more to independent demand, and the push system to dependent demand. A deficiency of many pull systems is that product orders are typically triggered at individual stock-keeping locations; thus, the need for similar or identical items at parallel network facilities is uncoordinated. In contrast, push systems adapt better to the coincident needs of parallel logistics network facilities. Finally, pull systems sometimes involve only one-way communications between point of need and point of supply, while push systems tend to involve more two-way communications between point of need and point of supply.

environmental conditions   Bowersox, Closs, and Helferich,[4] summarizing ideal environmental conditions for each approach, suggest that the pull, or reactive, approach would be most suitable when either order cycle time or demand levels are uncertain, or when market-oriented warehouses or distribution centers have capacity limitations. The push, or planning-based, approach is most appropriate for highly profitable segments, dependent demand, scale economies, supply uncertainties, source capacity limitations, or seasonal supply buildups. In general, push systems are more prevalent among organizations having greater logistics sophistication.

Characteristically, JIT is a pull system, since firms place orders for more inventory only when the amount on hand reaches a certain level, thus pulling inventory through the system as needed. Having established the master production schedule, the MRP program develops a time-phased approach to inventory scheduling and inventory receipt. Because it generates a list of required materials in order to assemble or manufacture a specified number of finished products, the MRP and MRPII approaches are push based. Similar to these, but on the outbound or physical distribution side of logistics, DRP involves the allocation of available inventory to meet marketplace demands. Thus, it also is a push-based strategy.

The EOQ-based approach, to be discussed later in this chapter, is generally pull based, but contemporary applications include elements of a push strategy as well. While this permits the EOQ technique to be reactive when necessary, it also allows the preplanning of certain inventory decisions in a proactive, or push, manner. In fact, many EOQ-based systems in evidence today are hybrid approaches that include elements of pull- and push-based strategies.

Systemwide versus Single-Facility Solution.   A final inventory management issue is whether the selected approach represents a systemwide solution or whether it is specific to a single facility, such as an individual warehouse or distribution center. Each approach has advantages and disadvantages. The principal factors associated with the *systemwide* approach are the time and expense of developing a truly comprehensive solution to a network's inventory problems, and also the question of whether or not it will work, once developed and implemented. The *single-facility* approach is less expensive and more straightforward in development terms. Its inherent risk is that it may produce optimal single-facility results that may be suboptimal from a systemwide perspective.

Essentially, the JIT and EOQ-based approaches are more applicable to single-facility decision making. The MRP and DRP approaches can deal more effectively with issues relating to the systemwide positioning of inventories and related decisions.

Overall, those choosing an approach must carefully consider its comprehensiveness. The two extremes offer very different perspectives on the problem. Those choosing must gain an early understanding of the specific advantages and disadvantages of each approach, given any specific inventory problem. Such understanding will reveal important trade-offs and provide information sufficient for a rational choice between the available alternatives.

Principal Approaches and Techniques for Inventory Management

In many business situations, the variables affecting the decision regarding the approach to inventory management are almost overwhelming. Therefore, models developed to aid in the decision process are frequently abstract or represent a simplified reality. In other words, models generally make simplifying assumptions about the real world they attempt to represent.

The complexity and accuracy of a model relate to the assumptions the model makes. Typically, the more the model assumes, the easier the model is to work with and understand; however, simple model output is often less accurate. The model developer or user must decide upon the proper balance between simplicity and accuracy. The best advice is to seek out models that are as simple and direct as possible but that do not assume away too much reality.

The remainder of this chapter contains an in-depth treatment of several approaches and techniques that are in common use today by inventory managers.

Included are the fixed order quantity approach under conditions of certain and uncertain demand and lead time length (also known as the economic order quantity, or EOQ, approach) and the fixed order interval approach. Following a discussion of how inventory will be affected as the number of distribution centers changes, the chapter focuses on a number of contemporary, time-based approaches to replenishment logistics. Included are quick response (QR) and efficient consumer response (ECR). Although these approaches attempt to synchronize flows of product and information to be consistent with end-user or consumer needs, their implementation can be very comprehensive in terms of the overall supply chain. These discussions should complement the coverage in Chapter 3 of techniques such as JIT, MRP, and MRPII, which relate more directly to the physical supply side of logistics, and the treatment in Chapter 4 of DRP, which is oriented more toward the outbound movement of finished product and related information.

FIXED ORDER QUANTITY APPROACH (CONDITION OF CERTAINTY)

As its name implies, the *fixed order quantity* model involves ordering a fixed amount of product each time reordering takes place. The exact amount of product to be ordered depends upon the product's cost and demand characteristics and upon relevant inventory carrying and reordering costs.

EOQ approach   Firms using this approach generally need to develop a minimum stock level to determine when to reorder the fixed quantity. This is usually called the *reorder point*. When the number of items in inventory reaches the predetermined level, the fixed order quantity (also called the economic order quantity, or EOQ) is "automatically" ordered. In a sense, the predetermined ordering level triggers the next order.

triggering orders for inventory   Sometimes firms call the fixed order quantity approach a *two-bin* system. When the first bin is empty, the firm places an order. The stock amount in the second bin represents the inventory quantity the firm needs until the new order arrives. Both notions (trigger and bin) imply that a firm will reorder or produce stock when the amount on hand decreases to some predetermined level. Again, the amount ordered depends upon the product's cost and demand, along with inventory carrying and reordering costs. The stock ordering level (number of units) depends upon the time it takes to get the new order and upon the product demand or sales rate during that time—such as how many units the firm sells per day or per week.

reorder point   For example, if a new order takes two weeks to arrive and a firm sells ten units per day, the reorder point will be 140 units (14 days $\times$ 10 units/day).

Inventory Cycles

Figure 6–2 shows the fixed order quantity model. The figure shows three inventory cycles, or periods. Each cycle begins with 4,000 units, the fixed quantity ordered or produced, and reordering occurs when inventory on hand falls to a level of 1,500 units. Assuming that the demand or usage rate and the lead time length are constant and known in advance, the length of each cycle will be a constant five weeks. This is an example of the application of the fixed order quantity model in the case of certainty.

FIGURE 6–2 Fixed Order Quantity Model under the Condition of Certainty

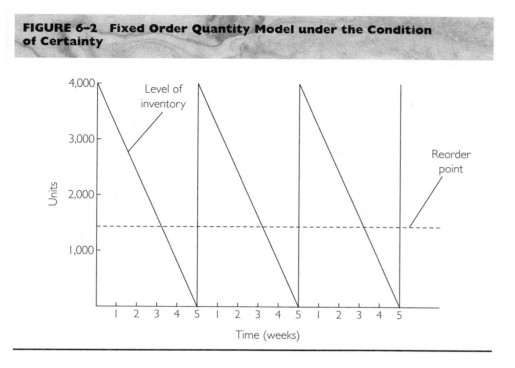

As we suggested earlier, establishing a reorder point provides a trigger or signal for reordering the fixed quantity. For example, most people have reorder points for personal purchases such as gasoline. On a trip, one may customarily stop to fill the tank when the gauge indicates one-eighth of a tank. Or, similarly, one may wait until a dashboard light indicates that the gas supply has reached some minimum point.

Business inventory situations base the reorder point upon lead time or replenishment time, the time it takes to replenish an order or manufacture the fixed quantity. The constant monitoring necessary to determine when inventory has reached the reorder point makes the fixed order quantity model somewhat expensive, although a computer can monitor inventory at little marginal cost per transaction. Generally, this approach can be sensitive to demand without carrying too much excess inventory.

sensitivity to demand changes

Simple EOQ Model

The following are the principal assumptions of the simple EOQ model:

assumptions

1. A continuous, constant, and known demand rate
2. A constant and known replenishment or lead time
3. The satisfaction of all demand
4. A constant price or cost that is independent of the order quantity or time (e.g., purchase price or transport cost)
5. No inventory in transit
6. One item of inventory or no interaction between items
7. Infinite planning horizon
8. No limit on capital availability

certainty   The first three assumptions are closely related and basically mean that conditions of certainty exist. Demand in each relevant time period (daily, weekly, or monthly) is known, and usage rate is linear over time. The firm uses or depletes inventory on hand at a constant rate and knows the time needed to replenish stock. In other words, lead time between order placement and order receipt is constant. This means that neither demand nor the time it takes to produce or receive replenishment stock will vary. As a result, the firm has no need to be concerned about stockouts and, consequently, stockout costs.

Some individuals feel that the assumptions of certainty make the basic model too simplistic—and, consequently, the output decisions too inaccurate. Although this charge is true in certain cases, several important reasons justify using the simple model. First, in some businesses demand variation is so small that making the model more complex is too costly for the extra accuracy achieved. Second, firms just beginning to develop inventory models frequently find the simple EOQ model convenient and necessary because of the limited data available to them. Some firms get caught up in sophisticated models with simple data, and the end results are probably no more accurate than they would have been if the firm had used the simple model. Third, simple EOQ model results are somewhat insensitive to changes in input variables. That is, such variables as demand, inventory carrying cost, and ordering cost can change without significantly affecting the calculated value of the economic order quantity.

The fourth assumption, regarding constant costs, essentially means that the firm offers no volume price discounts. It also means that the prices are relatively stable.

no in-transit inventory   The assumption that there is no inventory in transit means that the firm purchases goods on a delivered-price basis (purchase price includes delivery) and sells them F.O.B. shipping point (the buyer pays transportation charges). On the inbound side, this means that title to the goods does not pass until the buyer receives them. On the outbound side, title passes when the product leaves the plant or shipping point. Under these assumptions, the company has no responsibility for goods in transit; that is, the company pays no in-transit inventory carrying costs.

Capital availability, the eighth assumption, may be important, but this decision is sometimes made outside the logistics area. If capital constraints do exist, they may result in an upper limit on inventory lot size.

inventory and order costs   Given the assumptions listed above, the simple EOQ model considers only two basic types of cost: inventory carrying cost and order or setup cost. The simple model analyzes trade-offs between these two costs. If the model focused only on inventory carrying cost, which varies directly with increases in lot size, the order quantity would be as small as possible (see Figure 6–3). If the model considered only order cost or setup cost, large orders would decrease total order costs (see Figure 6–4). The lot size decision attempts to minimize total cost—that is, carrying cost plus setup or order cost—by reaching a compromise between these two costs (see Figure 6–5).

Mathematical Formulation. We can develop the EOQ model in standard mathematical form, using the following variables:

R = annual rate of demand or requirement for period (units)
Q = quantity ordered or lot size (units)
A = cost of placing an order or setup cost ($ per order)

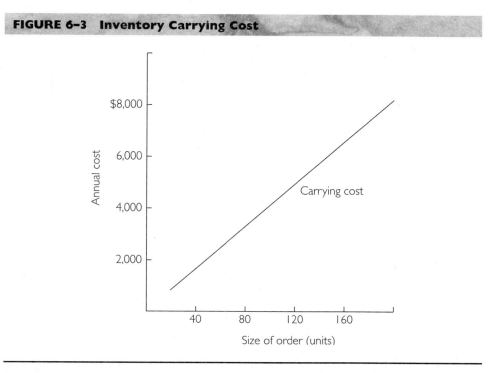

FIGURE 6-3 Inventory Carrying Cost

Carrying cost

Annual cost

$8,000

6,000

4,000

2,000

40   80   120   160

Size of order (units)

V = value or cost of one unit of inventory ($ per unit)
W = carrying cost per dollar value of inventory per year
       (% of product value)
$S = VW$ = storage cost per unit per year* ($ per unit per year)
t = time (days)
TAC = total annual cost ($ per year)

Given the previous assumptions, we can express the total annual cost in either of the following forms:

$$\text{TAC} = \frac{1}{2} \, QVW + A\frac{R}{Q}$$

or

$$\text{TAC} = \frac{1}{2} \, QS + A\frac{R}{Q}$$

The first term on the right-hand side of the equation refers to inventory carrying cost; it states that these costs equal the average number of units in the economic order quantity during the order cycle ($\frac{1}{2}Q$) multiplied by the value per unit (V) multiplied by the carrying cost (W). In Figure 6–6, called the sawtooth model, the equation's logic becomes more apparent. The vertical line labeled Q represents the amount ordered or produced at a given time and the

inventory carrying cost

---

*When we substitute VW for S, storage cost becomes a function of price paid per unit bought—namely, volume.

FIGURE 6-4 Order or Setup Cost

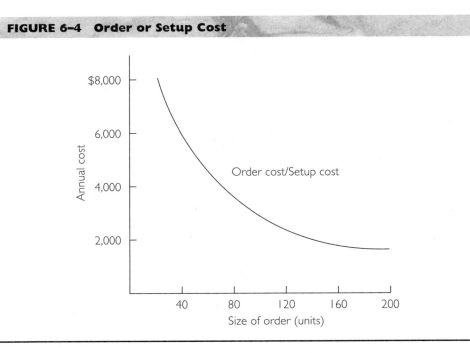

amount on hand at the beginning of each order cycle. During the order cycle (t), a firm depletes the amount of product on hand at the rate represented by the slanted line. Demand is known and constant, and the firm uses inventory at a uniform rate over the period. The average number of units on hand during this period affects the inventory carrying cost. The average number on hand, given the constant demand rate, is simply one-half of the initial amount (Q). The broken horizontal line in Figure 6–6 represents average inventory. The logic is very simple. Assuming that Q is 100 and that daily demand is 10 units, 100 units would last 10

FIGURE 6-5 Inventory Costs

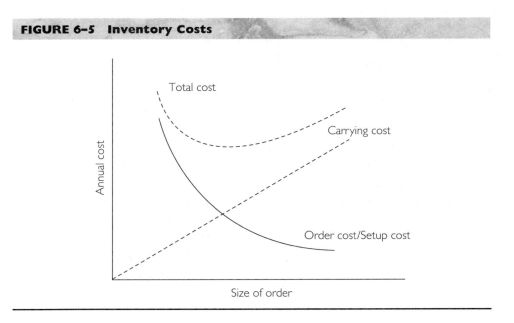

FIGURE 6-6 Sawtooth Model

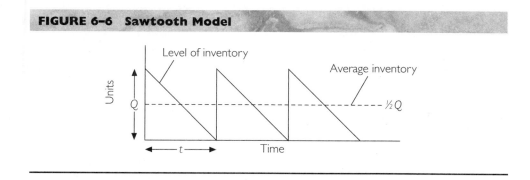

days (*t*). At the period's halfway point, the end of the fifth day, 50 units would still be left, which is one-half of *Q* (¹/₂ × 100).

Determining the average number of units is not enough, as the equation indicates. Knowing the value per unit, which depends upon the product, is still necessary. Knowing the percentage carrying cost, which depends upon the product and the firm's warehousing operations, is also necessary. The larger the *Q* amount, the higher the inventory carrying cost will be. We described this general relationship earlier: increasing carrying cost accompanies larger inventory lots or orders. As the present context shows, larger inventory order quantities will last longer, therefore increasing carrying costs. Given constant demand, average inventory will increase as the economic order quantity increases [see Figures 6–7(a) and 6–7(b)]. **order size and inventory**

The second term in the equation refers to order cost or setup cost. Again, we assume order cost to be constant per order or setup. Therefore, if *Q* increases, the number of orders per year will be smaller, since annual demand is constant. It follows, then, that larger order quantities will lower annual order costs. **order cost**

Although we have explained the general nature of carrying cost and order cost, we must still determine *Q*, the economic order quantity. As we indicated previously, this involves trading off inventory carrying cost and order cost. We can determine *Q* by differentiating the TAC function with respect to *Q*, as follows:

$$\text{TAC} = \frac{1}{2} QVW + A\frac{R}{Q}$$

$$\frac{d(\text{TAC})}{dQ} = \frac{VW}{2} - \frac{AR}{Q^2}$$

Setting $d(\text{TAC})/dQ$ equal to zero and solving for *Q* gives

$$Q^2 = \frac{2RA}{VW}$$

or

$$Q = \sqrt{\frac{2RA}{VW}}$$

or

$$Q = \sqrt{\frac{2RA}{S}}$$

FIGURE 6-7   Sawtooth Models

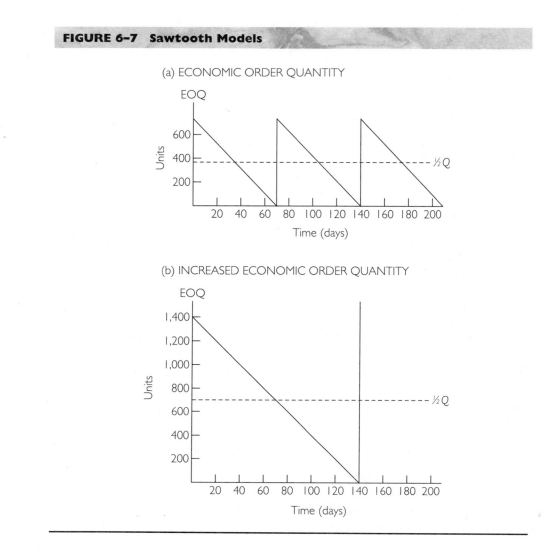

(a) ECONOMIC ORDER QUANTITY

(b) INCREASED ECONOMIC ORDER QUANTITY

example   The following assumptions illustrate how the formula works in actual practice:

V = $100 per unit
W = 25%
S = $25 per unit per year
A = $200 per order
R = 3,600 units

To solve for Q, the example proceeds as follows:

$$Q = \sqrt{\frac{2RA}{VW}} \qquad\qquad Q = \sqrt{\frac{2RA}{S}}$$

$$= \sqrt{\frac{(2)(3,600)(\$200)}{(\$100)(25\%)}} \qquad\qquad = \sqrt{\frac{(2)(3,600)(200)}{\$25}}$$

$$= 240 \text{ units} \qquad\qquad = 240 \text{ units}$$

TABLE 6-1 Total Costs for Various EOQ Amounts

Q	Order Costs AR/Q	Carrying Cost ½ QVW	Total Cost
100	$7,200	$1,250	$8,450
140	5,143	1,750	6,893
180	4,000	2,250	6,250
220	3,273	2,750	6,023
240	3,000	3,000	6,000
260	2,769	3,250	6,019
300	2,400	3,750	6,150
340	2,118	4,250	6,368
400	1,800	5,000	6,800
500	1,440	6,250	7,690

Analysis. Table 6–1 and Figure 6–8 show the preceding solution's trade-offs and logic. The illustrations show how inventory carrying cost and total cost vary as *Q* ranges from a low of 100 units to a high of 500 units.

As the table shows, the lower values for *Q* incur high order costs, as expected, but carrying costs are low. As *Q* increases to 240, ordering costs decrease because the number of orders per year decreases, but carrying costs increase because of the higher average inventories. Beyond 240 units, the incremental increase in carrying costs exceeds the incremental decrease in order costs, so total costs increase.

quantity/cost relationships

By defining the optimum *Q* in total cost terms, the information in Table 6–1 shows that a *Q* of 240 is optimal. Figure 6–8 also demonstrates this. Note, however, that the TAC curve between EOQ values of 180—200 and 300—320 is quite shal-

FIGURE 6-8 Graphical Representation of the EOQ Example

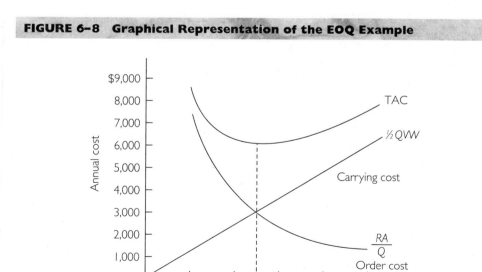

low. This means that the inventory manager can alter the EOQ considerably without significantly affecting TAC.

Reorder Point

A previous discussion indicated that knowing when to order was as necessary as knowing how much to order. The *when,* generally called a reorder point, depends on inventory level—that is, some number of units. Under the assumptions of certainty, a firm needs only enough inventory to last during the replenishment time or lead time. Therefore, given a known lead time, multiplying lead time length by daily demand determines the reorder point.

Replenishment time consists of several components: order transmittal, order processing, order preparation, and delivery. The time involved depends on factors such as the means of transmitting the order from buyer to seller, whether the vendor must produce the item being ordered or can fill it from available stock, and the transportation mode used. We will discuss the many variables affecting lead time later in this chapter.

example calculation   Using the previous example, assume that order transmittal takes one day; order processing and preparation, two days; and delivery, five days. This results in a total of eight days for replenishment time or lead time. Given that demand is ten units per day ($3,600 \div 360$), the reorder point will be 80 units (8 days $\times$ 10 units per day).

A Note Concerning the Min-Max Approach

One widely used adaptation of the fixed order quantity approach is the *min-max* inventory management approach. With the traditional approach, inventory will implicitly deplete in small increments, allowing a firm to initiate a replenishment order exactly when inventory reaches the reorder point.

demand patterns   The min-max approach applies when demand may be larger and when the amount on hand may fall below the reorder point before the firm initiates a replenishment order. In this case, the min-max approach increments the amount ordered by the difference between the reorder point and the amount on hand. In effect, this technique identifies the *minimum* amount that a firm should order so that inventory on hand will reach a predetermined *maximum* level when the firm receives the order. While the min-max system is very similar to the EOQ approach, individual order amounts will tend to vary.

According to Ronald H. Ballou, the min-max approach is most appropriate when demand is *lumpy,* or *erratic.* This type of demand is frequently, but not exclusively, limited to slow-moving items. Also, the lumpy demand characteristic may actually occur in up to 50 percent of the SKUs for many firms.[5]

Summary and Evaluation of the Fixed Order Quantity Approach

Traditionally, the EOQ-based approach has been a cornerstone of effective inventory management. While not always the fastest way to respond to customer demand, the fixed order quantity approach has been a useful and widely used technique.

Recently, however, many companies have become more sophisticated in their use of EOQ-based approaches, adapting them to include a push as well as a pull orientation. As a result, many EOQ-based systems effectively blend both push and pull concepts. As we indicated earlier, push, or proactive, inventory management approaches are far more prevalent in firms having greater logistics sophistication.

recent emphasis on push systems

One principal shortcoming of the EOQ-based approach is that it suits inventory decision making at a single facility more than it suits decision making at multiple locations in a logistics network. Also, the EOQ approach sometimes encounters problems when parallel points in the same logistics system experience peak demands simultaneously. This happens, for example, when many consumers simultaneously stock up on groceries before a major snowstorm. The EOQ system alone, reacting only to demand levels as they occur, would respond too slowly to replenish needed inventory.

shortcomings

We stated at the outset that the simple EOQ approach, though somewhat unrealistic because of the number of assumptions it requires, is still useful because it illustrates the logic of inventory models in general. Actually, firms can adjust the simple model to handle more complex situations. More than 200 variations now assist inventory-related decision making in various areas. Appendix 6A covers applications of the EOQ approach in four special instances: (1) when a firm must consider the cost of inventory in transit; (2) when volume transportation rates are available; (3) when a firm uses private carriage; and (4) when a firm utilizes in-excess rates.

relaxing assumptions

Typically, firms associate EOQ-based approaches with independent, rather than dependent, demand. The overall approach explicitly involves carrying calculated average inventory amounts; the trade-offs among inventory, order/setup, and expected stockout costs justify carrying these amounts. As we refine our ability to design flexible and responsive logistics systems and to significantly reduce marginal ordering and setup expenses, the value of this trade-off based approach will diminish. Therefore, we will focus attention away from approaches such as EOQ and toward other techniques for managing inventory.

independent demand

FIXED ORDER QUANTITY APPROACH (CONDITION OF UNCERTAINTY)

Under the assumptions used until now, the reorder point was based on the amount of stock remaining in the warehouse. We assumed that the usage or sales rate was uniform and constant. After selling the last unit of a particular EOQ amount, a firm received another order or batch, thus incurring no stockout costs (lost sales). Although assuming such conditions of certainty may be useful, these conditions do not represent the usual operating situation for most organizations.

certainty

Most companies would not find conditions of certainty normal, for a variety of reasons. First, customers usually purchase products somewhat sporadically. The usage rates of many items vary depending on weather, social needs, psychological needs, and a whole host of other factors. As a result, sales of most items vary day by day, week by week, or season by season.

demand variations

In addition, several factors can affect lead time or replenishment time. For example, transit times can and do change, particularly for distances over 500 miles, despite carrier efforts. In fact, for a firm deciding what transportation mode or

transit time variations

agency to use or choosing a particular transportation company within a particular mode, the reliability of expected carrier transit times is an important factor.

order processing time variations

Another factor that can cause variations in lead time or replenishment time is order processing and transmittal. Mailed orders can cause delays. Clerks can overlook a particular order or develop undesirable backlogs. Problems in this area have led firms to develop and enhance computer systems for order processing and associated activities.

For a firm producing or manufacturing an item to order, production schedules can vary for a number of reasons. Other factors that could have an effect on lead time or replenishment time have been discussed throughout the preceding chapters.

damage

In addition to varying demand rates and replenishment times, the logistics manager can experience problems with merchandise lost in transit or damaged, in which case the firm would have to reorder the goods. Even though the carrier would usually be liable, the damage could cause a short-run stockout situation, resulting in lost sales. Figure 6–9 shows the fixed order quantity model under conditions of uncertainty.

probability distributions

Sometimes the inventory situation may seem hopeless. Fortunately, this is not the case. Statisticians refer to these variables as *stochastic,* or random, variables. Experience with a particular company and associated study will enable the manager to develop probability distributions for these variables and to apply expected-value analysis to determine the optimum reorder point.

safety stock

The manager may choose several approaches to solving the problem. An essential factor in any approach is the level of safety stock, or buffer stock, a firm requires to cover variations. Logistics managers must analyze requirements very carefully so as not to maintain too much safety stock, because it incurs excess

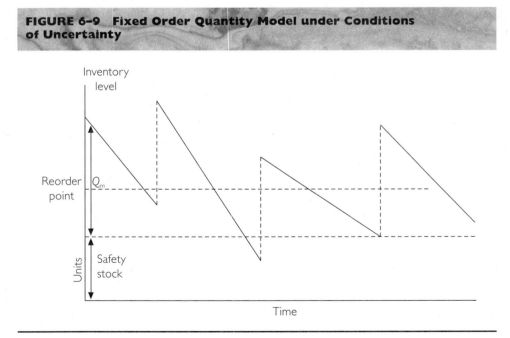

FIGURE 6–9 Fixed Order Quantity Model under Conditions of Uncertainty

inventory cost. On the other hand, a company without enough safety stock will experience a stockout, with consequent loss of sales.

Reorder Point—A Special Note

As we noted previously, the reorder point under the basic model is the inventory level sufficient to satisfy demand until the order arrives. Calculating the reorder point is straightforward, since demand or usage is constant, as is lead time. Therefore, a firm can multiply daily demand or usage by lead time in days and place an order for the determined quantity when inventory reaches the reorder point. Under uncertainty, the firm must reformulate the reorder point to allow for safety stock. In effect, the reorder point becomes the average daily demand during lead time plus the safety stock, as Figure 6–9 depicts. The following discussion clarifies this recalculation.

reorder point with safety stock

Uncertainty of Demand

Dealing first with only one factor that may cause uncertainty is easiest. The best and most common factor to examine is the sales rate or usage rate. As we focus on this variable, the following assumptions about the EOQ model still apply:

1. A constant and known replenishment or lead time
2. A constant price or cost that is independent of order quantity or time (e.g., purchase price or transport cost)
3. No inventory in transit
4. One item of inventory or no interaction between items
5. Infinite planning horizon
6. No limit on capital availability

In discussing uncertainty in sales, logistics managers emphasize balancing the cost of carrying safety stock against the cost of a stockout (lost sales).

balancing cost

In a fixed quantity model with an established reorder level, introducing uncertainty into the analysis initially affects the inventory level needed to cover sales during lead time. Recall that in the previous example, conditions of certainty resulted in an EOQ amount of 240 units and a reorder point of 100 units. In other words, the inventory period began with 240 units on hand, and reordering occurred when inventory reached a level of 100 units.

The fact that sales may vary—and that the time elapsing between a level of 240 units and 100 units may also vary—is not critical to the inventory problem when conditions of uncertainty exist. Determining whether 100 units is the best amount to have on hand at the start of the lead time or replenishment cycle *is* critical. Thus, raising the reorder level accounts for safety stock. However, raising it too high will leave too much stock on hand when the next order arrives. Setting it too low will cause a stockout.

Using the previous problem, assume that the hypothetical firm's demand during lead time ranges from 100 units to 160 units, with an average of 130 units. Furthermore, assume that demand has a discrete distribution varying in ten-unit blocks and that the firm has established probabilities for these demand levels (see Table 6–2).

example

TABLE 6-2 Probability Distribution of Demand during Lead Time

Demand	Probability
100 units	0.01
110	0.06
120	0.24
130	0.38
140	0.24
150	0.06
160	0.01

In effect, the firm must consider seven different reorder points, each corresponding to a possible demand level listed in Table 6–2. Using these reorder points, we can develop the matrix that appears in Table 6–3.

While Table 6–3 shows many of the possible situations confronting the hypothetical firm, it does not use information from the probability distribution of demand. Using the probability distribution of demand would permit the firm with seven possible reorder points to determine the expected units "short" or "in excess" at each point during lead time.

Assume that the firm experiences a stockout cost (k) of $10 per unit whenever a customer demands a unit that is not in stock. The profit lost on the immediate sale and future sales is an opportunity cost.

We calculate inventory carrying cost associated with safety stock in the same way as we calculated carrying cost for the simple EOQ model. We still assume the value per unit of inventory to be $100, and the percentage annual inventory carrying cost is 25 percent. Remember that the percentage figure is for the annual cost of inventory in the warehouse. Therefore, the $25 we derive by multiplying 25 percent by $100 is the annual cost per unit of inventory in the warehouse. The $25 contrasts with the $10 stockout cost, which is a unit cost per cycle or order period. Therefore, as Table 6–4 shows, multiplying $10 by the number of cycles or orders per year puts this cost on an annual basis.

Table 6–4 develops expected units short or in excess by multiplying the number of units short or in excess by the probabilities associated with each demand level.

TABLE 6-3 Possible Units of Inventory Short or In Excess during Lead Time with Various Reorder Points

Actual Demand	Reorder Points						
	100	110	120	130	140	150	160
100	0	10	20	30	40	50	60
110	−10	0	10	20	30	40	50
120	−20	−10	0	10	20	30	40
130	−30	−20	−10	0	10	20	30
140	−40	−30	−20	−10	0	10	20
150	−50	−40	−30	−20	−10	0	10
160	−60	−50	−40	−30	−20	−10	0

TABLE 6-4 Expected Number of Units Short or In Excess

Actual Demand	Probabilities	Reorder Points							
		100	110	120	130	140	150	160	
100	0.01	**0.0**	0.1	0.2	0.3	0.4	0.5	0.6	
110	0.06	−0.6	**0.0**	0.6	1.2	1.8	2.4	3.0	
120	0.24	−4.8	−2.4	**0.0**	2.4	4.8	7.2	9.6	
130	0.38	−11.4	−7.6	−3.8	**0.0**	3.8	7.6	11.4	
140	0.24	−9.6	−7.2	−4.8	−2.4	**0.0**	2.4	4.8	
150	0.06	−3.0	−2.4	−1.8	−1.2	−0.6	**0.0**	0.6	
160	0.01	−0.6	−0.5	−0.4	−0.3	−0.2	−0.1	**0.0**	

Calculation of Lowest-Cost Reorder Point

	100	110	120	130	140	150	160	
1. Expected excess per cycle (of values above diagonal line)	0.0	0.1	0.8	3.9	10.8	20.1	30.0	(e)
2. Expected carrying cost per year	0	$ 2.50	$ 20.00	$ 97.50	$270	$502.50	$750	(VW)
3. Expected shorts per cycle (of values below diagonal line)	30.0	20.1	10.8	3.9	0.8	0.1	0.0	(g)
4. Expected stockout cost per cycle	$ 300	$ 201	$ 108	$ 39	$ 8	$ 1	$ 0	(gk) = G
5. Expected stockout costs per year	$4,500	$3,015	$1,620	$585	$120	$ 15	$ 0	$\left(G\dfrac{R}{Q}\right)$
6. Expected total cost per year (2 + 5)	$4,500	$3,017.50	$1,640	$682.50	$390	$517.50	$750	

We can add the numbers below (shorts) and above (excesses) the horizontal line, as the lower portion of Table 6–4 shows, to find the number of units the firm expects to be short or in excess at each of the seven possible reorder points. The variables for this calculation are as follows:

e = expected excess in units

g = expected shorts in units

k = stockout cost in dollars per unit stocked out

$G = gk$ = expected stockout cost per cycle

$G\dfrac{R}{Q}$ = expected stockout cost per year

eVW = expected carrying cost per year for excess inventory

After performing the calculations indicated in Table 6–4, we may determine the total cost for each of the seven reorder levels. In this instance, the lowest total cost corresponds to the reorder point of 140 units. Although this number does not guarantee an excess or shortage in any particular period, overall it gives the lowest expected total cost per year: $390.

Note that the number of orders per year used in step 5 of Table 6–4 came from the preceding problem with conditions of certainty. That number was the only information available at that point. Now we can expand the total cost model to include the safety stock cost and stockout cost. The expanded formula would appear as follows:

$$\text{TAC} = \frac{1}{2}QVW + A\frac{R}{Q} + (eVW) + \left(G\frac{R}{Q}\right)$$

Solving for the lowest cost gives

$$\frac{d(\text{TAC})}{dQ} = \left[\frac{1}{2}VW\right] - \left[\frac{R(A + G)}{Q^2}\right]$$

Setting this equal to zero and solving for Q gives

$$Q = \sqrt{\frac{2R(A + G)}{VW}}$$

Using the expanded model and the computed reorder point of 140 units, we can determine a new value for Q as follows:

$$Q = \sqrt{\frac{2 \cdot 3,600 \cdot (200 + 8)}{100 \cdot 25\%}}$$

$$= 242 \text{ (approximately)}$$

Note that Q is now 242 units with conditions of uncertainty. Technically this would change the expected stockout cost for the various reorder points in Table 6–4. However, the change is small enough to ignore in this instance. In other cases, recalculations may be necessary. The optimum solution to the problem with conditions of uncertainty is a fixed order quantity (EOQ) of 242 units, and the firm will reorder this amount when inventory reaches a level of 140 units (the calculated reorder point).

Finally, the situation requires a recalculation of total annual cost:

$$\text{TAC} = \frac{1}{2}QVW + A\frac{R}{Q} + eVW + G\frac{R}{Q}$$

$$= \left(\frac{1}{2} \cdot 242 \cdot \$100 \cdot 25\%\right) + \left(200 \cdot \frac{3,600}{242}\right) + (10.8 \cdot \$100 \cdot 25\%) + \left(8 \cdot \frac{3,600}{242}\right)$$

$$= \$3,025 + \$2,975 + \$270 + \$119$$

$$= \$6,389$$

The $6,389 figure indicates what happens to total cost when we introduce conditions of uncertainty with respect to sales into the model. Introducing other factors, such as the lead time variable, would increase costs even more.

Uncertainty of Demand and Lead Time Length

This section considers the possibility that both demand and lead time may vary. It builds upon the preceding section in attempting to make this inventory approach more realistic. As expected, however, determining how much safety stock to carry will be noticeably more complex now than when only demand varied.

demand during lead time   As in the previous section, the critical issue is just how much product customers will demand during the lead time. If demand and lead time are constant and known in advance, calculating the reorder point (as we did in the section covering case of certainty) would be easy. Now that both demand and lead time may vary,

FIGURE 6-10 Normal Distribution

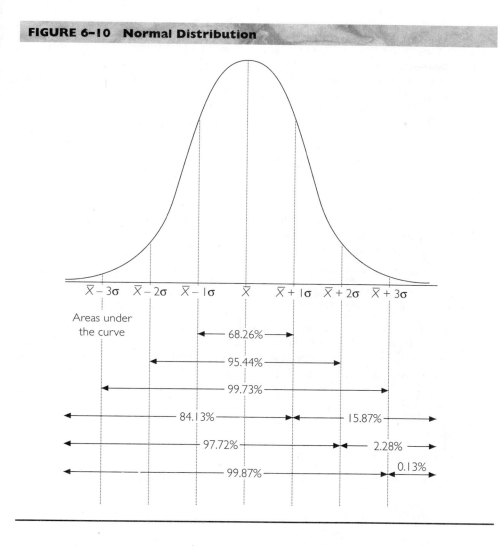

the first step is to study the likely distribution of demand during the lead time. Specifically, we must accurately estimate the mean and standard deviation of demand during lead time.

Figure 6–10 illustrates three key properties of a normal distribution. The normal distribution is symmetrical, and its mean (average) equals its mode (highest point). Approximately 68.26 percent of the area under the normal curve lies within one standard deviation (1σ) from the mean, 95.44 percent within two standard deviations (2σ), and 99.73 percent within three standard deviations (3σ). Figure 6–10 also shows the areas under the curve that lie to the left and right of one, two, and three standard deviations from the mean.

After calculating values for the mean and standard deviation of demand during lead time, we can describe the stockout probability for each particular reorder point. For example, imagine that Figure 6–10 represents demand distribution during lead time. Setting the reorder point equal to $\overline{X} + 1\sigma$ will result in an 84.13 percent probability that lead time demand will not exceed the inventory amount available. Increasing the reorder point to $\overline{X} + 2\sigma$ raises the probability of not incurring a stockout to 97.72 percent; reordering at $\overline{X} + 3\sigma$ raises this probability

normal distribution

to 99.87 percent. Note that in the case of uncertainty, increasing the reorder point has the same effect as increasing the safety stock commitment. A firm must ultimately find some means to justify carrying this additional inventory.

calculations   We may calculate the mean and standard deviations for lead time demand using the following formulas:[6]

$$\overline{X} = \overline{R}(\overline{X}_{LT})$$

and

$$\sigma = \sqrt{\overline{X}_{LT}(\sigma_R)^2 + \overline{R}^2(\sigma_{LT})^2}$$

where

$$\begin{aligned}
\overline{X} &= \text{mean (average) demand during lead time} \\
\sigma &= \text{standard deviation of demand during lead time} \\
\overline{X}_{LT} &= \text{mean (average) lead time length} \\
\sigma_{LT} &= \text{standard deviation of lead time length} \\
\overline{R} &= \text{mean (average) daily demand} \\
\sigma_R &= \text{standard deviation of daily demand}
\end{aligned}$$

example   For example, if the mean and standard deviations of daily demand are twenty and four units, respectively, and if the mean and standard deviations of lead time length are eight and two days, respectively, we calculate the mean and standard deviations of demand during lead time as follows:

$$\begin{aligned}
\overline{X} &= \overline{R}(\overline{X}_{LT}) \\
&= 20(8) \\
&= 160
\end{aligned}$$

$$\begin{aligned}
\sigma &= \sqrt{\overline{X}_{LT}(\sigma_R)^2 + \overline{R}^2(\sigma_{LT})^2} \\
&= \sqrt{8(4)^2 + 20^2(2)^2} \\
&= \sqrt{1,728} \\
&= 41.57, \text{ or } 42
\end{aligned}$$

Using the procedure suggested earlier, setting the reorder point at $\overline{X} + 1\sigma$, or 202 units, reveals an 84.13 percent probability that demand during the lead time will not exceed the inventory available. Stated differently, the probability of a stockout is only $100\% - 84.13\%$, or 15.87%, when we set the reorder point at one standard deviation from the mean. Table 6–5 shows these figures and the

TABLE 6–5   Reorder Point Alternatives and Stockout Probabilities

Reorder Point	Probability of No Stockout Occurring	Probability of a Stockout Situation
$\overline{X} + 1\sigma = 202$	84.13%	15.87%
$\overline{X} + 2\sigma = 244$	97.72%	2.28%
$\overline{X} + 3\sigma = 286$	99.87%	0.13%

ones computed for setting the reorder point at two and three standard deviations from the mean. A firm should thoroughly compare the financial and customer service benefits of avoiding stockouts with the cost of carrying additional safety stock before choosing a reorder point.

FIXED ORDER INTERVAL APPROACH

The second form of the basic approach is the *fixed order interval* approach to inventory management, also called the *fixed period* or *fixed review period* approach. In essence, this technique involves ordering inventory at fixed or regular intervals, and generally the amount ordered depends on how much is in stock and available at the time of review. Firms customarily count inventory near the interval's end and base orders on the amount on hand at the time.

In comparison with the basic EOQ approach, the fixed interval model does not require close surveillance of inventory levels; thus, monitoring is less expensive. A firm can order low-valued items infrequently and in large quantities, checking only infrequently to determine exactly how much is on hand at any particular time.

lower cost of monitoring inventory

In other instances, delivery schedules or salespeople's visits necessitate this approach. This happens frequently in retail food stores, where deliveries may be daily for some items, weekly or biweekly for others, and monthly for still others. The store can determine a desired inventory level in advance and order enough each time to bring the number of units up that level.

If demand and lead time are constant and known in advance, then a firm using the fixed order interval approach will periodically reorder exactly the same amount of inventory. If either demand or lead time varies, however, the amount ordered each time will vary, becoming a result of demand as well as lead time length. For example, as Figure 6–11 indicates, a company starting each period with 4,000 units and selling 2,500 units before its next order will have to reorder 2,500 units plus

FIGURE 6–11 Fixed Order Interval Model (with Safety Stock)

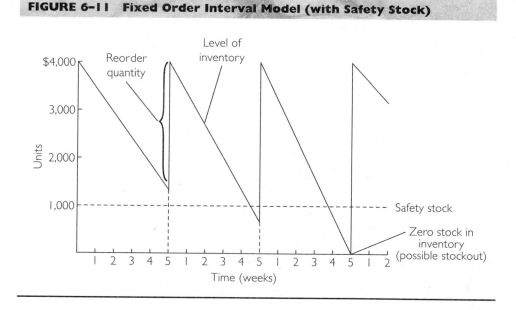

the units it anticipates selling during the lead time to bring inventory up to the desired beginning level of 4,000 units. Figure 6–11 shows an instance in which the amount ordered differs from one five-week period to the next.

Like the fixed order quantity approach to inventory management, the fixed order interval approach typically combines elements of both the pull and push philosophies. This shows again how firms, in an effort to anticipate demand rather than simply reacting to it, are developing systems that incorporate the push philosophy.

INVENTORY AT MULTIPLE LOCATIONS—THE SQUARE ROOT LAW

In their aggressive efforts to take cost out of logistics networks, firms are searching for new ways to reduce levels of inventory without adversely affecting customer service. A currently popular approach is to consolidate inventories into fewer stocking locations in order to reduce aggregate inventories and their associated costs. Correspondingly, this strategy requires the involvement of capable transportation and information resources to see that customer service is held at existing levels and is even improved whenever possible.

underlying principle   The square root law (SRL) helps determine the extent to which inventories may be reduced through such a strategy. Assuming that total customer demand remains the same, the SRL estimates the extent to which aggregate inventory needs will change as a firm increases or reduces the number of stocking locations. In general, the greater the number of stocking locations, the greater the amount of inventory needed to maintain customer service levels. Conversely, as inventories are consolidated into fewer stocking locations, aggregate inventory levels will decrease. The extent to which these changes will occur is understood through application of the square root law.[7]

calculation   The square root law states that total safety stock inventories in a future number of facilities can be approximated by multiplying the total amount of inventory at existing facilities by the square root of the number of future facilities divided by the number of existing facilities:

$$X_2 = (X_1) \ (\sqrt{n_2/n_1})$$

where

n_1 = number of existing facilities

n_2 = number of future facilities

X_1 = total inventory in existing facilities

X_2 = total inventory in future facilities

example   To illustrate, consider a company that presently distributes 40,000 units of product to its customers from a total of eight facilities located throughout the United States. Current distribution centers are located in Boston, Chicago, San Francisco, Los Angeles, Dallas, Orlando, Charlotte, and Baltimore. The company is evaluating an opportunity to consolidate its operations into two facilities, one in Memphis, Tennessee, and the other in Reno/Sparks, Nevada. Using the square root law, the total amount of inventory in the two future facilities is computed as follows:

n_1 = 8 existing facilities

n_2 = 2 future facilities

X_1 = 40,000 total units of product in the 8 existing facilities

Thus,

X_2 = total units of product in the 2 future facilities

= (40,000) $(\sqrt{2/8})$

= (40,000) (0.5)

= 20,000 units

Based on the results of this analysis, the two future facilities would carry a total inventory of 20,000 units. If the company designed them to be of equal size, and if market demand was equal for the geographic areas, each of these distribution centers would carry one-half of this total, or 10,000 units. Conversely, if for some reason the company considered increasing the number of distribution centers from 8 to, say, 32, total inventory needs would double from 40,000 to 80,000 units. (Use the formula to check this for yourself.)

Based on data from an actual company, Table 6–6 shows the total average units of inventory implied by specific numbers of distribution centers in the system. For example, as stocking locations increase from 1 to 25, the total average number of units in inventory increases from 3,885 units to 19,425 units. This is consistent with application of the SRL. Table 6–6 also shows the percentage change in inventories as the number of distribution centers in the system increases.

Although the square root law is simply stated, the model is based on several **assumptions** reasonable assumptions: (1) inventory transfers between stocking locations at the same level are not common practice; (2) lead times do not vary, and thus inventory centralization is not affected by inbound supply uncertainty; (3) customer service level, as measured by inventory availability, is constant regardless of the number of stocking locations; and (4) demand at each location is normally distributed.[8] In addition, it has been shown that the potential for aggregate inventory reduction through consolidation of facilities will be greater when the correlation of sales

TABLE 6–6   Example Impacts of Square Root Law on Logistics Inventories

Number of Warehouses (n)	$\sqrt{n}$	Total Average Inventory (units)	Percent Change
1	1.0000	3,885	—
2	1.4142	5,494	141%
3	1.7321	6,729	173%
4	2.0000	7,770	200%
5	2.2361	8,687	224%
10	3.1623	12,285	316%
15	3.8730	15,047	387%
20	4.4721	17,374	447%
23	4.7958	18,632	480%
25	5.0000	19,425	500%

between stocking locations is small to negative and when there is less sales variability at each of the stocking locations.[9]

SUMMARY AND EVALUATION OF TRADITIONAL APPROACHES TO INVENTORY MANAGEMENT

relationship to ABC analysis   Some authors have argued that there are really four basic forms of the inventory model: fixed quantity/fixed interval, fixed quantity/irregular interval, irregular quantity/fixed interval, and irregular quantity/irregular interval. In a firm knowing demand and lead time length with certainty, either the basic EOQ or the fixed order interval approach will be the best choice (and would produce the same answer). If either demand or lead time varies, however, approach selection must consider the potential consequences of a stockout. In instances involving A items, a fixed quantity/irregular interval approach may be the best. The irregular quantity/fixed interval approach might be the best when C items are involved. Only under very restrictive circumstances could a firm justify using the irregular quantity/irregular interval approach to inventory management.

importance of trade-offs   The fixed order quantity (EOQ) and fixed order interval approaches have proven to be effective inventory management tools when demand and lead time are relatively stable, as well as when significant variability and uncertainty exist. Most importantly, studying these approaches requires us to gain familiarity with the inherent logistics trade-offs critical to inventory policy decision making.

new concepts   As was suggested earlier, firms in today's business environment that are expanding beyond the basic order quantity and order interval approaches have had considerable success with newer concepts such JIT, MRP, MRPII, and DRP, which were discussed in Chapters 3 and 4. Also, there is currently significant interest in the application of a number of contemporary approaches to replenishment logistics, including quick response and efficient consumer response. The remainder of this chapter is devoted to a discussion of these approaches. Throughout each of these discussions, the need to have a knowledge and understanding of applicable logistics trade-offs will be reinforced.

number of DCs   The issue of inventory at multiple locations in a logistics network raises some interesting questions concerning the most appropriate number of distribution centers, their location, the SKUs to be carried at each, and their overall strategic positioning. There is a growing priority on understanding the economics of facility location and inventory positioning, as firms search for lower-cost yet service-sensitive logistics alternatives. Beyond the content of this chapter, the coverage of logistics network design and facility location in Chapter 12 should provide a useful perspective.

TIME-BASED APPROACHES TO REPLENISHMENT LOGISTICS

impacts on supply chain   In recent years, major changes have been occurring in the ways in which firms manage supply chain logistics activities. In short, significant effort has been directed toward streamlining the functioning of the supply chain, with the joint objectives of reducing cost and improving responsiveness to the consumer or end-user customer. This strategy may be referred to as *replenishment logistics,* because it reflects a basic shift in logistics strategy from a supply-side push orientation to a demand-side pull orientation.

As was discussed in Chapter 3, the just-in-time (JIT) approach has been widely accepted as an effective strategy for managing the movement of parts, materials, semifinished product, and related information from points of supply to further manufacturing or assembly processes. This chapter will introduce and discuss two strategies that focus more specifically on the outbound-to-customer realm of logistics and that have a broader orientation to the total supply chain. These are quick response (QR) and efficient consumer response (ECR). A major difference is that the outbound-to-customer side of most businesses has less stability than the inbound activity, which relates more to production schedules and so on. While the development of QR and ECR has been most prevalent in the textile/apparel and grocery industries, respectively, the conceptual bases for these approaches extend to other industries as well.

QR and ECR

Overall Directions for Time-Based Approaches[10]

Companies have recognized that time-based logistics strategies can enhance supply chain efficiency and effectiveness and can also help to differentiate capabilities from those of the competition. The principal drivers of such change include reducing the length and variability of the order cycle; order fulfillment at the time and place desired by the consumer or end-user customer; improved ability to manage and control information, both within the firm and in conjunction with supply chain partners; and reducing inventories yet improving responsiveness to customer needs throughout the supply chain. As a result, firms have enjoyed reduced cost and improved service, which have translated into higher levels of customer satisfaction, greater market share, and increased profitability.

drivers of change

In recent years, a number of major retailing organizations have taken leadership roles in the move toward time-based replenishment. Companies such as Wal-Mart, K-Mart, and Target Stores have worked closely with suppliers to develop responsive supply chain approaches that function at lower cost and produce higher levels of logistical customer service. While these firms obviously have their own interests to protect, they view the overall responsibility as extending throughout all stages of the logistics supply chain. The modernization of the Team Hanes supply chain, described in the Logistics Profile at the beginning of this chapter, is also an excellent example of the overall movement toward replenishment logistics.

major retailers

Figure 6–12 identifies four practices that are generally associated with the concept of replenishment logistics. Each is discussed briefly here:

Continuous-Replenishment (CRP) Inventory Systems. The objective of CRP systems is to develop order fulfillment and delivery systems that will eliminate stockout situations yet significantly reduce pipeline, or supply chain, inventories. To accomplish these objectives, it is necessary to have continuously updated point-of-sale (POS) data to drive inventory requirements forecasts, replenishment orders, and product flows from supplier to warehouse to retail store. CRP inventory systems synchronize the timing of product receipt with consumer or end user demand.

FIGURE 6-12   Four Directions for Replenishment Logistics

Direction	Objective	Key Programs
Continuous-replenishment (CRP) inventory systems	Bring supply more in line with the rhythm of demand	Automated systems that enable distributors to stock and reorder goods based on actual consumer sales (i.e., point-of-sale transactions)
Flow-through distribution systems	Take every bit of wasted space, handling activities, time, and therefore costs out of the process	New methods that increase the speed of product flow by reducing inventory and relying on timely, coordinated, and dependable transportation and material handling
Pipeline logistics organizations	Institutionalize key product flow processes, cultivate "total pipeline view," and coordinate operations	New roles and responsibilities that remove barriers to communication, rationalize accountability, encourage coordination, and provide incentives for aggressive management of the logistics pipeline
Pipeline performance measures	Establish objective tools for improving management control of processes and motivating appropriate decision making ("You can't manage what you can't measure")	Precise criteria, accurate decision rules, and consistent procedures that support management objectives and take into account total pipeline performance

SOURCE: Mercer Management Consulting, *New Ways to Take Costs Out of the Retail Food Pipeline* (Atlanta, GA: Coca-Cola Retailing Research Council, 1994): 7. Used with permission.

emphasis on flow   *Flow-Through Distribution Systems.*   This practice stresses the need for timeliness and consistency of logistics processes, with the objective of emphasizing the flow and distribution of inventory, rather than storage of inventory at strategically located positions in the supply chain. Techniques such as cross-docking, store-ready packaging, warehouse automation, improved receiving capabilities, and the use of third-party logistics providers can assist in moving to flow-through distribution systems.

focus on customer   *Pipeline Logistics Organizations.*   Of interest here is the need to develop organizational structures, incentives, and relationships that can integrate and focus management of the total replenishment logistics process. In addition to furthering the prevalence of supply chain partnerships and so on, the overriding emphasis is on the ability of all supply chain participants to focus on the needs of the consumer or end-user customer.

Pipeline Performance Measures.   Implied here is the need for precise criteria, accurate decision rules, and consistent procedures to guide supply chain activity in

ON THE LINE

Continuous Replenishment Process Helps Mills Better Manage Inventories

Controlling inventory levels is becoming increasingly important as pulp and paper companies seek ways to improve their global competitive position. With government regulatory pressures on industry, as well as stockholder pressure to show short-term profits, companies must be innovative in finding ways to generate profits without increasing costs. Reducing inventories is an excellent way to achieve this goal while releasing cash for other profit-generating projects.

Carrying lower inventories has risks as well. Companies that learn how to provide continuous improvement in customer service while managing inventory costs will have a competitive advantage. Therefore, inventory management must be the effort, with continuous replenishment the process, and reliable operations and reduced inventories the result. The confidence built up over time with a successful inventory management system will lead to lower inventories much more comfortably and productively than would forced cost reductions.

In August 1990, Procter & Gamble Paper Products Co.'s tissue/towel plants carried $7.7 million worth of one of its wood pulps on site and en route from its supplier in Grande Prairie, Alberta, Canada, where there was another $6.5 million invested in the same pulp. P&G was also paying for local storage, handling, and freight, as well as demurrage on this pulp. This costly procedure and large inventory protected against a perception that P&G had an unreliable supplier and inconsistent rail service. But through a new partnership with the pulp supplier and the carriers, P&G began to manage its inventory with a continuous-replenishment process.

By June 1992, P&G and Grande Prairie were carrying $10.6 million of this pulp for a 26 percent inventory reduction, while increasing its usage by 15 percent. Cash no longer tied up in inventory equaled $3.6 million, and the carrying costs that were eliminated generated an annual savings of $775,000. Although a traditional strategy of many firms has been to establish ad-ditional distribution centers in an effort to improve customer service, P&G's information-based continuous-replenishment process validated its usefulness by eliminating excess inventory, helping to reduce waste and lower the supplier's cost. A key ingredient of success was the very excellent partnership relationships that developed among P&G, Grand Prairie, and the transportation suppliers who were involved.

To take full advantage of inventory management and get maximum cost improvement, inventories must be controlled from start to finish. In addition to the distribution system, production cycles on both ends of the supply chain are major influences on the inventory at both ends. The process manager needs to understand the variability of the distribution network and the production cycles on both ends of the supply chain. Those variables inserted into a statistical model will generate realistic inventory targets.

The continuous-replenishment process is a tool used to manage the flow of products to a customer in order to maintain those statistically based inventory levels. Most companies will find that they have been carrying far more safety stock than a statistical analysis would indicate is needed, but that comfort level will be hard to break until they gain confidence with the new supply system.

Inventory, which is expensive, has been more available than information, which is less expensive. As we move deeper into the "Information Age," we will begin to take advantage of the computer (sophistication, yet simplification) to provide data to people throughout the supply chain. Timely, accurate data generates information that allows for better business decisions, which lead to managing time rather than cost. Reliable supply systems made possible by continuous-replenishment processes will be a prerequisite to the next generation of business management.

ADAPTED FROM: Doug Warner, "Process of Continuous Replenishment Helps Mills Better Manage Inventories," *Pulp & Paper* (October, 1993): 75–78. Used with permission.

a direction that will help to achieve overall objectives. This will require a reorientation for most firms from an emphasis on measurement of internal performance to a total supply chain perspective. In essence, this involves performance measures that can help to optimize the functioning of the entire supply chain, rather than suboptimizing portions of it.

Principal Strategic Approaches

Although there are numerous initiatives and approaches that are consistent with the objectives of replenishment logistics identified above, perhaps the two best known are quick response (QR) and efficient consumer response (ECR).

Quick Response (QR)

textile/apparel industry The popularity of quick response (QR) began in 1986 when Roger Milliken of Milliken & Company challenged the textile and apparel industry to identify new strategies that could be adopted by domestic manufacturers and retailers to respond to changing environments.[11] Specifically, firms in the textile and apparel industry were faced with a number of very real challenges to their domestic market positioning: (1) offshore competition, which enjoyed a lower cost base; (2) mergers and acquisitions, which had become very common in the early and mid-1980s; (3) recent successes of warehouse clubs and discount mass merchandisers; (4) the proliferation of shopping centers; and (5) continued adversarial relationships between many manufacturing and retailing firms.

competitive pressures In response to these threats, firms in the textile and apparel industry formed the Voluntary Inter-Industry Communications Standards Committee (VICS) to explore ways to improve competitive positioning. This organization of manufacturers and retailers of textiles and apparel products was formed to accomplish several objectives: (1) select the most appropriate bar coding technology; (2) determine information standards and protocols to facilitate the flow and functioning of an integrated information system (for example, bar codes, EDI, purchase orders, advance shipment notifications, and so on); and (3) set priorities for the training and education of industry professionals to diffuse knowledge of the standards and of quick response.[12]

definitions While there are numerous definitions of quick response, the director of quick response at Milliken & Company refers to QR as "Marketing 101 . . . that is, getting the right product at the right place, at the right time, and at the right price."[13] A report from the Textile Institute suggests that QR is "an operational philosophy and a set of procedures aimed at maximizing the profitability of the product pipeline."[14] In essence, quick response is a "method of maximizing the efficiency of the supply chain by reducing inventory investment. Just as JIT works to reduce inventory investment for manufacturers by scheduling the delivery of products to assembly lines, QR does approximately the same thing for manufacturers, wholesalers, and retailers."[15]

quick response partnership *Functioning of QR.* In actuality, quick response is a very effective, relatively new approach to synchronizing product and information flows in a logistics network. In terms of its operation, the QR program is a partnership in which the "vendor commits to meet specific service performance criteria such as cycle time, service levels and fill rates, EDI communications, and possible vendor managed inventory (VMI) with a stated turns goal. The retailer commits to provide accurate, timely

FIGURE 6-13 Basic Elements of Quick Response (QR)

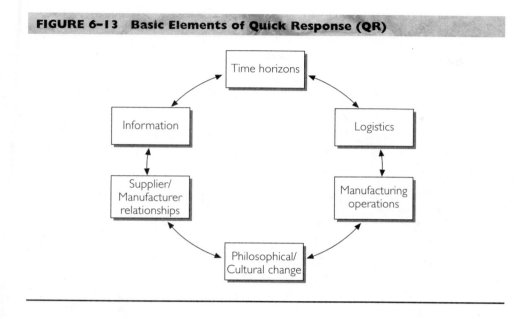

demand information and to feature the manufacturer's products among those of only a few preferred vendors. The performance criteria applied to suppliers are significantly higher and more precise than any previously seen in the American marketplace. The most aggressive retailers are now requiring up to 26 turns in their warehouses, 100 percent fill rates, and 7-day maximum cycle time from order placement to delivery." [16]

Structure of QR.   Figure 6–13 indicates the basic elements of quick response. These elements incorporate the following specific capabilities:

- Shorter, compressed time horizons
- Real-time information available by SKU
- Seamless, integrated logistics networks that depend on rapid incoming transportation, strategic cross-docking operations, and effective store receipt and distribution systems
- Partnership relationships between manufacturers and retailers, including sharing of processes and information
- Redesign of manufacturing operations and processes to reduce lot sizes and changeover times, enhance flexibility and responsiveness, and coordinate master production schedules with forecasts and actual customer orders
- Commitment to total quality management, process improvement, and "service response logistics"

Examples of QR Successes.   As was indicated above, the U.S. textile and apparel industry was the first to embrace the quick response process. Figure 6–14 depicts the structure of this industry in the United States. As the figure indicates, the overall supply chain includes suppliers of fiber, fabric, and apparel products, as well as retail firms and the consumers themselves. Figure 6–14 provides informa-

major progress

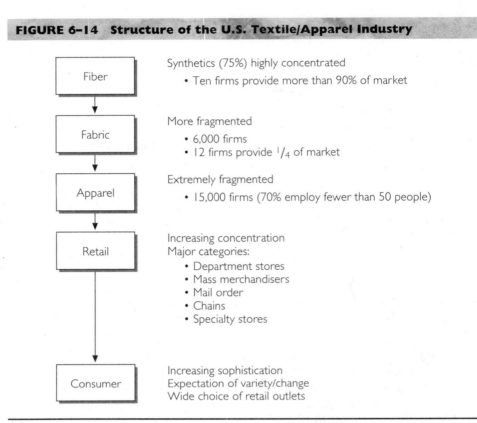

FIGURE 6-14 Structure of the U.S. Textile/Apparel Industry

Fiber
Synthetics (75%) highly concentrated
- Ten firms provide more than 90% of market

Fabric
More fragmented
- 6,000 firms
- 12 firms provide $1/4$ of market

Apparel
Extremely fragmented
- 15,000 firms (70% employ fewer than 50 people)

Retail
Increasing concentration
Major categories:
- Department stores
- Mass merchandisers
- Mail order
- Chains
- Specialty stores

Consumer
Increasing sophistication
Expectation of variety/change
Wide choice of retail outlets

SOURCE: Janice H. Hammond, "Coordination in Textile and Apparel Channels: A Case for 'Virtual' Integration," working paper, Harvard University, 1991. Used with permission.

tion concerning the characteristics of some of these intermediaries in the supply chain. Included are fiber manufacturers such as DuPont and Hoechst Celanese, fabric manufacturers such as Milliken & Company and Burlington Industries, and apparel manufacturers such as Levi Strauss and Haggar Apparel Company.

Table 6–7 provides a startling look at the estimated revenue losses due to forced markdowns, stockouts, and inventory carrying cost in the textile/apparel pipeline

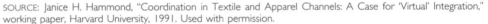

TABLE 6-7 Revenue Losses in the Apparel Pipeline (Percent of Retail Sales)

	Fiber and Textile	Apparel	Retail	Total
Forced markdowns	0.6%	4.0%	10.0%	14.6%
Stockouts	0.1	0.4	3.5	4.0
Inventory @ 15% carrying cost	1.0	2.5	2.9	6.4
Total	1.7%	6.9%	16.4%	25.0%

SOURCE: N. Alan Hunter, *Quick Response in Apparel Manufacturing: A Survey of Revenue Losses in the Apparel Pipeline (The American Scene)* (Manchester, U.K.: The Textile Institute, 1990): 31. Used with permission.

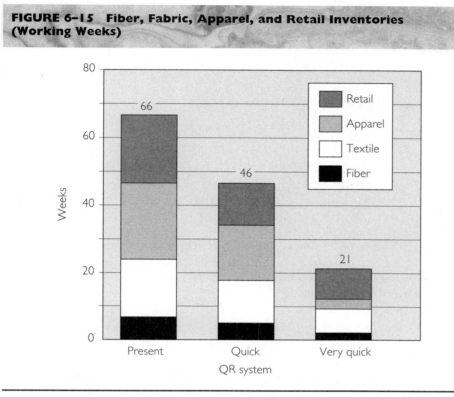

FIGURE 6–15 Fiber, Fabric, Apparel, and Retail Inventories (Working Weeks)

SOURCE: N. Alan Hunter, *Quick Response in Apparel Manufacturing: A Survey of the Fiber, Fabric, Apparel and Retail Inventories (The American Scene)* (Manchester, U.K.: The Textile Institute, 1990). Used with permission.

prior to implementation of QR. The bottom line is that as much as 25 percent of retail sales revenues may have been "wasted." This information is consistent with a statement made by Mr. Joseph Haggar, president of Haggar Apparel Co., that "department stores are out of stock 20 percent of the time—an estimated $25 billion worth of lost business. Quick response (QR) should enable companies to cut stockouts by at least 50 percent. That means an increase of more than $12 billion in retail business."[17]

Figure 6–15 summarizes the magnitude of the fiber, fabric, apparel, and retail **results** inventories that existed prior to implementation of QR and the levels that were expected following the initial implementation, as well as longer-term results. For example, the information in Figure 6–15 suggests that the textile/apparel industry traditionally had a total of 66 weeks of fiber, fabric, apparel, and retail inventories. This figure was expected to decrease to 46 weeks upon implementation of QR, and ultimately to 21 weeks over the longer term.

Documented successes of quick response include the following:

- *Benetton*, multinational retailer of fashion apparel, instituted QR linkages among its manufacturing, warehousing, and sales operations and its retail customers. Results included shipment of complete orders in four weeks, including manufacturing. The system is highly dependent on bar coding, EDI links between retailers and Benetton, a highly automated distribution center, and computer-integrated manufacturing (CIM).[18]

FIGURE 6-16   Quick Response Impact on Sales

Assume:	8,000 basic styles of shoes, 30 SKUs per style
	Average retail price $12 per SKU
	80 stores in system, operating 12 months per year
	Current average 10% of all SKUs were out of stock

Then:	8,000	Basic styles of shoes
	×10%	Percent out of stock
	800	Out-of-stock styles
	×30	SKUs per style
	24,000	Out-of-stock SKUs
	×12	Average retail price
	288,000	Potential increase in sales in one month, one store
	×80	Stores
	×12	Months
	$276,480,000	Annual potential sales increase for the corporation

ADAPTED FROM: "Quick Response Technologies," *Chain Store Executive* (March 1991): 6B. Copyright © Lebhar Friedman, Inc., 425 Park Ave., New York, NY 10022. Used with permission.

- *Haggar Apparel Company,* in its "H.O.T." (Haggar Order Transmission) program, reduced order processing time from two weeks to one day, boosted retailers' sales by an average of 27 percent, increased turns and reduced stockouts, and reduced customer turnaround to four days.[19]
- *Dillard's Department Stores* experienced increased inventory turns from 4.1 to 8.9 and sales that were 42 percent ahead of projection as a result of QR. Dillard's move to product scanning at all locations, as well as to EDI communications, resulted in fewer stockouts and minimization of "forced" markdowns.[20]

Figure 6–16 provides a series of calculations that show how annual potential sales may increase for a corporation as a result of a move to QR that produces greater accuracy of demand forecasts and improved in-stock percentages.

Benefits of QR.   Overall, the move to QR can have a significant impact on both retailers and manufacturers. Specifically, the move to faster order placement and shorter lead times will help to reduce cycle stock. Correspondingly, rapid reaction to demand patterns, coupled with more reliable lead times, will lead to reduced need for safety stock. Fast response to sales trends will produce lower markdowns and higher sales. Finally, higher sales and lower markdowns will result in greater profitability and reduced total channel costs.

differing trade channels   According to Cleveland Consulting Associates, different trade channels will have divergent views concerning how to implement the quick-response approach. Even within an existing channel, individual customers will have unique needs based on their own operating conditions and merchandising approach. Table 6–8 suggests some of the areas of priority for quick response that may differ among food, drug, mass merchant, and toy/hobby chains.

TABLE 6-8 Replenishment Needs of Different Industry Channels

Food	Drug	Mass Merchant	Toy/Hobby Chains
One-for-one replacement of sales	Product-dependent replenishment requirements	Replenish to an inventory level	Replenish to sales and promotion forecast
Ship to DCs and direct store delivery	Ship to DCs	Ship to stores or DCs based on economics	Ship bulk products to stores, conveyables to DCs
Next-day service	Weekly service	Weekly or bimonthly service	Seasonally different shipment timing

SOURCE: Cleveland Consulting Associates, "Responsiveness by Design," *CCA White Paper* (Cleveland, OH: Cleveland Consulting Associates, 1991). Used with permission.

Efficient Consumer Response

A second prominent time-based approach to replenishment logistics is efficient consumer response, or ECR. Defined in a major report by several grocery industry organizations, ECR can be thought of as a "strategy in which distributors and suppliers are working closely together to bring better value to the grocery customer. By jointly focusing on the efficiency of the total grocery supply system, rather than the efficiency of individual components, they are reducing total system costs, inventories, and physical assets while improving the consumer's choice of high-quality, fresh grocery products."[21] The report estimated the total potential savings in the U.S. grocery industry supply chain to be in excess of $30 billion.[22]

The report continues by stating that "the ultimate goal of ECR is a responsive, consumer-driven system in which distributors and suppliers work together as business allies to maximize consumer satisfaction and minimize cost. Accurate information and high-quality products flow through a paperless system between manufacturing and check-out counter with minimum degradation or interruption within and between trading partners."[23] This ECR concept is illustrated in Figure 6–17. Additional detail is provided in Figure 6–18, which illustrates several steps that are critical to the ECR process.

goal of ECR

FIGURE 6-17 Vision of the ECR System

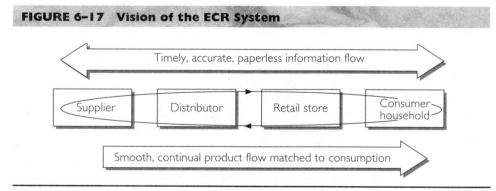

SOURCE: Kurt Salmon Associates, Inc., *Efficient Consumer Response: Enhancing Consumer Value in the Grocery Industry* (Washington, DC: Food Marketing Institute, 1993): 1. Used with permission.

FIGURE 6-18   Anatomy of Efficient Consumer Response

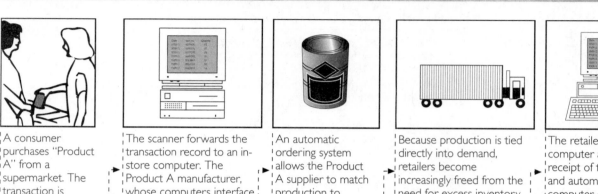

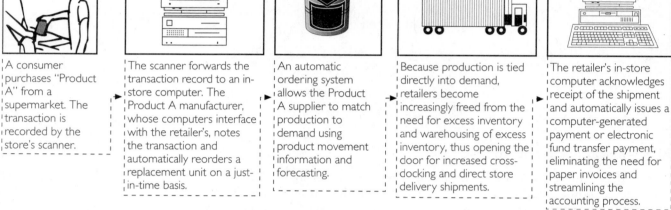

| A consumer purchases "Product A" from a supermarket. The transaction is recorded by the store's scanner. | The scanner forwards the transaction record to an in-store computer. The Product A manufacturer, whose computers interface with the retailer's, notes the transaction and automatically reorders a replacement unit on a just-in-time basis. | An automatic ordering system allows the Product A supplier to match production to demand using product movement information and forecasting. | Because production is tied directly into demand, retailers become increasingly freed from the need for excess inventory and warehousing of excess inventory, thus opening the door for increased cross-docking and direct store delivery shipments. | The retailer's in-store computer acknowledges receipt of the shipment and automatically issues a computer-generated payment or electronic fund transfer payment, eliminating the need for paper invoices and streamlining the accounting process. |

ADAPTED FROM: Gene Hoffman, "ECR: Investment in the Future," *Grocery Marketing* (June 1993): 30. Original illustrations were by Bonnie James. Used with permission.

Although the emphasis to date has been on the development and implementation of ECR in the grocery industry, the underlying strategy is applicable to a wide variety of industries and product types. Even in the case of business-to-business market structures, where there may be no end user who represents the "consumer," the underlying principles of ECR are highly applicable. Of significant interest today are the tasks of validating the ECR concept as a strategy for supply chain integration and of identifying key prerequisites to successful implementation.

The ECR Process.   According to a report by CSC Consulting, ECR represents an attempt to reengineer the logistics system across company lines, enabled in large measure by information technology that collects, arranges, and distributes key data. By working together, manufacturers and retailers are able to cut costs and maximize profits better than they could by struggling against one another. According to CSC Consulting, a key to the success of ECR is to focus on the distribution "process," rather than on the traditional functional areas of business such as accounting, marketing, or manufacturing.[24]

ECR implementation priorities

Figure 6–19 identifies several key elements of business strategy for both manufacturing and retail firms and lists seven basic capabilities that must be integrated in a comprehensive implementation of ECR. The first four of these—integrated EDI, continuous replenishment, computer-assisted ordering, and flow-through distribution—have been discussed previously in the context of overall directions for time-based approaches to replenishment logistics. The use of activity-based costing (ABC) helps firms to assess the cost/value relationships of various tasks that are performed in the logistics process, and to either eliminate or redesign inefficient

FIGURE 6–19   Efficient Consumer Response: Broad Operating Capabilities Tailored to Each Unique Partner

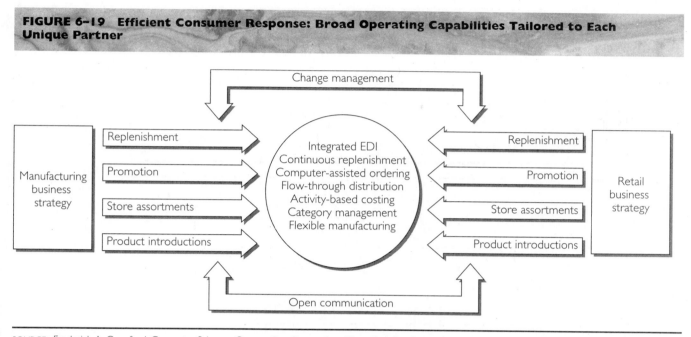

processes. Category management has been recognized as a key way for both manufacturers and retailers to optimize the design, introduction, promotion, stocking, and resupply of a given product category both to better utilize store shelf footage and to maximize profitability. Finally, while most ECR initiatives do not focus specifically on manufacturing flexibility, it is generally agreed that the ultimate success of an overall ECR strategy depends on the ability of a company to match production to actual demand.

Anticipated Results.   Figure 6–20 provides a comparison of average throughput time for a dry grocery chain before and after ECR implementation. Overall, the illustration suggests a reduction in total throughput time from 104 to 61 days following the channelwide implementation of ECR. Looking in greater detail at the sources of these savings, a significant portion is due to reductions in inventories at the distributor warehouse position from 40 days to 12 days. Lesser, yet still significant savings are projected to occur at the supplier warehouse and the retail store levels.

Figure 6–21 shows the results of an analysis of the cost structure of a dry grocery supply chain before and after ECR implementation. As indicated, total cost would be expected to decrease by approximately 10.8 percent, with all categories of expense indicating at least a moderate decrease. Among the types of costs expected to experience significant decreases are store operations, logistics, selling/buying, and marketing.

According to Richard Sherman, the overall reductions in inventory and total channel cost are due largely to the fact that ECR "allows an entire channel to act like a single firm." [25] His experience suggests that the fundamental change is a move toward time-phased replenishment and away from event-driven replenish-

results

channel impacts

FIGURE 6–20 Average Throughput Time of Dry Grocery Chain Before and After ECR Implementation

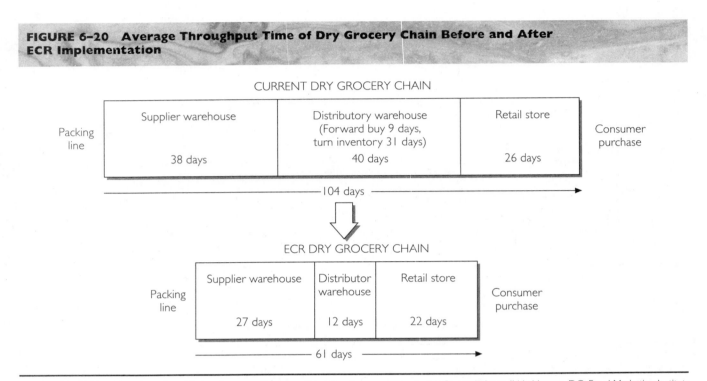

SOURCE: Kurt Salmon Associates, Inc., *Efficient Consumer Response: Enhancing Consumer Value in the Grocery Industry* (Washington, DC: Food Marketing Institute, 1993): 28. Used with permission.

ment. Rather than having a firm begin its replenishment process when it receives an order from the next firm downstream in the channel, the move to ECR involves the free flow of consumer or end-user POS data to participating firms throughout the supply chain. As a result, channel members can time-phase their replenishment instead of merely reacting to an order. The resulting sharing of POS sales and inventory information throughout the supply chain facilitates improved scheduling, consolidation, unitization, and deployment.

"acceleration principle"   Sherman also highlights details concerning the very relevant "acceleration principle." Suggested by Forrester in 1958, this principle states that a 10 percent change in demand at the point of sale results in a 40 percent fluctuation in demand upstream in the channel. While the increased fluctuation is caused by amplification of variability due to time delays, the problem occurs because channel participants react to unanticipated change when it reaches their position in the channel, without an awareness of the point in time that the change actually occurred.[26]

Overall Impact of ECR. Figure 6–22 summarizes the principal differences between the traditional approach to supply chain management and the ECR approach. Traditionally, the consumer goods supply chain has been defined by a buy, make, move, sell paradigm. Beginning with the acquisition of materials by manufacturers, product was forced through the pipeline for ultimate purchase by consumers or end-user customers. The ECR-based approach involves a reversal of this process to one that focuses on the sell, move, make, and buy processes, in that order. All

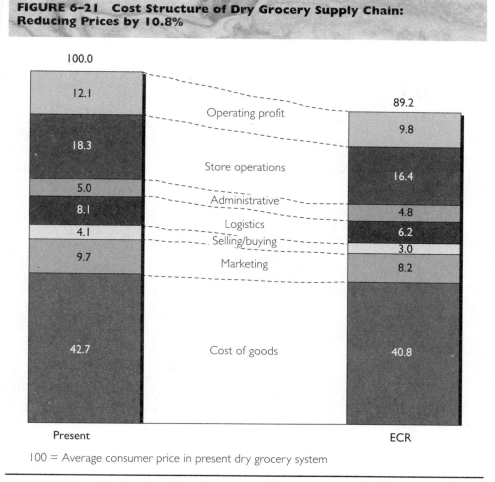

FIGURE 6-21 Cost Structure of Dry Grocery Supply Chain: Reducing Prices by 10.8%

100.0

Present

ECR

100 = Average consumer price in present dry grocery system

SOURCE: Kurt Salmon Associates, Inc., *Efficient Consumer Response: Enhancing Consumer Value in the Grocery Industry* (Washington, DC: Food Marketing Institute, 1993): 30. Used with permission.

activity is triggered by an actual sale to a consumer or an actual order generated by a customer. This transaction sets in motion the other steps in the ECR, or supply chain, process.

Key Issues

Before leaving the topic of time-based approaches to replenishment logistics, it is useful to identify several key issues that will have a significant impact on the successful implementation of concepts such as QR and ECR.

significant factors

Appropriate Use of Available Tools.   Included here are inventory management tools and demand-based forecasting models to pull product through the supply chain to when and where it is needed. Also of importance will be financial and nonfinancial measurement systems to document progress and performance. Included

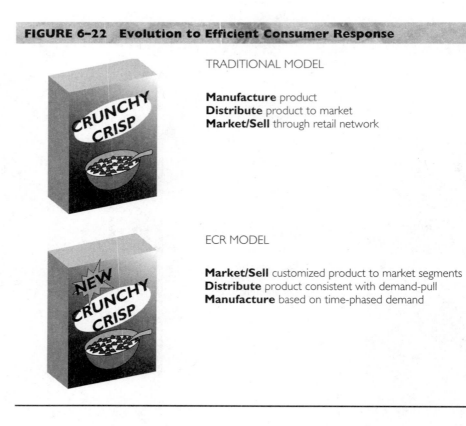

FIGURE 6–22   Evolution to Efficient Consumer Response

TRADITIONAL MODEL

Manufacture product
Distribute product to market
Market/Sell through retail network

ECR MODEL

Market/Sell customized product to market segments
Distribute product consistent with demand-pull
Manufacture based on time-phased demand

among the latter are systems relating to customer satisfaction, cycle times, productivity, and reliability.

Availability of Point-of-Sale (POS) Transaction Data.   As was suggested earlier, the availability of real-time POS data is essential to the functioning of an effective time-based replenishment system. To be useful, this data must be shared in a timely manner with supply chain participants, including partners that may be several stages upstream from the point of demand or end use.

Use of Inventory Segmentation.   As was recommended in the discussion of ABC analysis in Chapter 5, it is important to consider the segmenting of inventory based on some combination of factors such as value, velocity, variability of demand, and so on. This facilitates the development of highly customized supply chain strategies based on the customers' needs.

Strategic Use of Cross-Docking.   The move to replenishment logistics relies extensively on the use of cross-docking rather than the more traditional "move-store, move-store" paradigm. If the ultimate destination of a product coming into a distribution center can be specified, then the flow of product can be virtually uninterrupted as it moves through the facility.

Forward-Thinking Logistics and Corporate Leadership. Perhaps the most important and essential ingredient to the success of replenishment logistics is enlightened and enthusiastic logistics and corporate leadership. The willingness to consider new approaches and technologies and to "think outside the box" are absolutely necessary in order to move forward with new priorities such as QR and ECR.

SUMMARY

- Traditionally, key inventory decisions involve how much to reorder, when to reorder, and where inventory should be held or positioned to be of maximum value.
- Key differences among approaches to managing inventory are dependent versus independent demand, pull versus push, and systemwide versus single-facility solutions.
- The fixed order interval, or EOQ-based, approach to inventory management illustrates the concept of trade-offs. Implementation of the EOQ approach focuses attention on how much and when to reorder.
- The management of inventory becomes significantly more complex when demand and/or lead times begin to vary.
- The fixed order interval approach is another traditional approach to inventory management.
- The "square root law" is very helpful for determining the changes in systemwide inventories that will accompany either reductions or increases in the number of stocking points.
- Recent attention has turned to time-based approaches to inventory replenishment. Major directions that have been identified are continuous-replenishment (CRP) systems, flow-through distribution systems, pipeline logistics organizations, and pipeline performance measures.
- Two of the principal strategic approaches to replenishment logistics are quick response (QR) and efficient consumer response (ECR).

STUDY QUESTIONS

1. In what major, fundamental ways may inventory management approaches differ? What is the key distinction between the push and pull approaches?

2. Explain the importance of the assumptions used in the simple EOQ model.

3. What basic trade-off does the simple EOQ approach to managing inventory consider? How do we calculate average inventory when using this methodology?

4. What does *uncertainty* mean in the context of inventory management?

5. What significance does the reorder point have in the basic EOQ model? How does this differ when using the EOQ under the condition of uncertainty, in contrast to using it under the condition of certainty?

6. Compare the advantages and limitations of the fixed order quantity and the fixed order interval approaches to inventory management.

7. Perkalater Carriers employs a large fleet of trucks. To keep fleet operations running smoothly, it must order 540 tires annually at a cost of $200 per tire. The company orders the tires by telegram from the Midland Tire Company. Each order costs $48. Perkalater stores the tires in a central warehouse in Pittsburgh, Pennsylvania, which is the company's headquarters. The estimated carrying cost for holding the tire inventory is 25%.

   a. Assuming 360 days per year, what is the firm's optimum EOQ for tires?

   b. What is the total annual ordering and storage cost if Perkalater purchases the tires in EOQ-size lots?

   c. If the total lead time for the tires is six days, what is the reorder point?

8. A retail department store manager would like to determine an appropriate EOQ-based inventory policy for an item that is stocked and available for sale. The retailer estimates that demand for the item will be 2,000 units per year. The cost per order is $80, the item value is $40, and inventory carrying cost is 20 percent. The retailer is open for business 250 days per year. The lead time necessary to receive additional supplies of the item is ten working days.

   a. Using the fixed order quantity approach, what is the EOQ for this item?

   b. What is the total annual ordering and inventory carrying cost if the store procures this item in EOQ-size lots?

   c. What is the reorder point?

9. Using the information from question 8, assume that demand varies somewhat. The following table shows a probability distribution of demand during the lead time:

Demand	Probability
60	0.1
70	0.2
80	0.4
90	0.2
100	0.1

   a. Assuming that stockouts cost $5 per occurrence, what reorder point value will minimize the sum of the expected stockout costs and the cost of carrying safety stock?

   b. Calculate the revised EOQ.

   c. What revised total annual inventory cost do the new reorder point and EOQ suggest? Include all relevant costs in your calculations.

10. In general terms, explain the square root rule.

11. What is meant by "replenishment logistics"? What do we mean when we say that it is a "time-based" approach to logistics strategy?

12. What are the principal drivers of change toward replenishment logistics? What major practices are commonly associated with the concept of replenishment logistics?

13. How does quick response (QR) work? In what way(s) are EDI and VMI important to the quick-response process?

14. What benefits have firms experienced as a result of the implementation of QR?

15. What is efficient consumer response (ECR), and how does it differ from traditional approaches?

16. What basic capabilities are essential to integrate into a comprehensive implementation of ECR?

17. How does the acceleration principle relate to inventory in the supply chain? In what way does ECR help to reduce the effect of this phenomenon?

18. In what important ways does ECR represent a move from the traditional to the more progressive functioning of the supply chain?

NOTES

1. Joseph Orlicky, *Materials Requirements Planning* (New York: McGraw-Hill, 1975): 22.

2. Portions of the following discussion have been adapted from David J. Closs, "An Adaptive Inventory System as a Tool for Strategic Inventory Management," *Proceedings of the 1981 Annual Meeting of the National Council of Physical Distribution Management* (Chicago, IL: National Council of Physical Distribution Management, 1981): 659–79. Also, see John W. Hummel and Alan J. Stenger, "An Evaluation of Proactive vs. Reactive Replenishment Systems," *International Journal of Physical Distribution and Materials Management* 18, no. 4: 3–13.

3. This analogy has been drawn from Uday Karmarkar, "Getting Control of Just-In-Time," *Harvard Business Review* (September–October 1989): 122–31.

4. Donald J. Bowersox, David J. Closs, and Omar K. Helferich, *Logistical Management*, 3rd ed. (New York: Macmillan, 1986): 227.

5. Ronald H. Ballou, *Business Logistics Management*, 3rd ed. (Englewood Cliffs, NJ: Prentice-Hall, 1992): 438–39.

6. Use of these formulas requires that demand and lead time length be independent, meaning *unrelated* in a statistical sense. If they are not independent, then the formula must be modified slightly to produce the statistical precision and accuracy desired. Note that we have simplified the discussion in this section. A recommended source for further study is Robert G. Brown, *Smoothing, Forecasting and Prediction of Discrete Time Series* (Englewood Cliffs, NJ: Prentice-Hall, 1962): 366–67.

7. See D. H. Maister, "Centralization of Inventories and the 'Square Root Law'," *International Journal of Physical Distribution and Materials Management* 6, no. 3 (1976): 124–34; Walter Zinn, Michael Levy, and Donald J. Bowersox, "Measuring the Effect of Inventory Centralization/Decentralization on Aggregate Safety Stock: The 'Square Root Law' Revisited," *Journal of Business Logistics* 10, no. 1 (1989): 1–14; and David Ronen, "Inventory Centralization/Decentralization–The 'Square Root Law' Revisited Again," *Journal of Business Logistics* 11, no. 2 (1990): 129–42.

8. Zinn, Levy, and Bowersox, "Measuring the Effect of Inventory Centralization/Decentralization on Aggregate Safety Stock," 2.

9. Zinn, Levy, and Bowersox, "Measuring the Effect of Inventory Centralization/Decentralization on Aggregate Safety Stock," 14.

10. Portions of the following discussion are based on information contained in *New Ways to Take Costs Out of the Retail Food Pipeline*, a study conducted for the Coca-Cola Retailing Research Council by Mercer Management Consulting (Atlanta, GA, 1994): 7–11.

11. Portions of this discussion are included in Judy Schmitz, "Quick Response Review," prepared at Michigan State University, July 21, 1992.

12. See Judy Schmitz, "Quick Response Review," and Kenneth B. Ackerman, "Quick Response—Its Meaning for Warehouse Managers," *Ackerman Warehousing Forum* 8, no. 3 (February, 1993): 1–3.

13. Andersen Consulting, "Quick Response: Is it Right for Your Company?" *Logistics Perspectives,* Issue 4 (Fall, 1991): 2.

14. N. Alan Hunter, *Quick Response in Apparel Manufacturing: A Survey of the American Scene* (Manchester, U.K.: The Textile Institute, 1990).

15. Kenneth B. Ackerman, "Quick Response."

16. Herbert W. Davis and Company, *Davis Database* 18, no. 3 (June, 1993): 1–4.

17. E. J. Muller, "Quick Response Picks Up Pace," *Distribution* (June 1990): 38–42.

18. C. John Langley, Jr., and Robert J. Quinn, "Quick Response and Its Benefits," presentation to IBM Consumer Goods Customer Executive Council, 1992.

19. William P. Hakanson, "Quick Response Programs Impacting Warehousing and Inventory Control," *Production & Inventory Management Review with APICS News* 8, no. 8 (August 1988): 42.

20. Langley and Quinn, "Quick Response and Its Benefits."

21. Kurt Salmon Associates, Inc., *Efficient Consumer Response: Enhancing Consumer Value in the Grocery Industry* (Washington, DC: Food Marketing Institute, 1993): 1.

22. Kurt Salmon Associates, *Efficient Consumer Response,* 3.

23. Kurt Salmon Associates, *Efficient Consumer Response,* 1.

24. CSC Consulting, *Perspectives: Reengineering Consumer Goods Businesses* (Waltham, MA: CSC Consulting, 1994): 13–15.

25. Richard J. Sherman, "ECR: Another Acronym? . . . Or a Real Opportunity for the Warehousing Industry," presentation at the 1995 Annual Conference of the Warehousing Education and Research Council. See also Richard J. Sherman, "ECR Vision to Reality: Creating Innovative Strategies to Astonish Customers," *1994 Council of Logistics Management Annual Conference Proceedings* (Oak Brook, IL: CLM, 1994): 137–55.

26. Sherman, "ECR: Another Acronym?"

Case 6-1

TRUMP RAILCAR CORPORATION

Trump Railcar Corporation is one of the premier builders of railroad cars. As a matter of fact, Trump's covered-hopper grain cars are the envy of the business, and the transportation equipment that Trump manufactures is the finest available anywhere. In an attempt to modernize its procurement and ordering practices, Trump's vice president of logistics, Craig Janney, is incorporating trade-off analysis into his next purchase of journal bearings.

Before his analysis, Janney had been purchasing high-quality journal bearings on a monthly basis. Usage rates were fairly consistent for this needed part, and so Trump's policy was to order sixty cases every month. Each case contains eight individual bearings; each bearing weighs 32.5 pounds and costs $40. Current freight bill information shows that the transportation cost for each sixty-case shipment is $814. According to Tommy Trump, the company's chief financial officer, the best figure for inventory carrying cost is 12 percent per year.

As an alternative, Janney is considering ordering only once every three months, at which time he would obtain 180 cases of bearings. This idea seems interesting, particularly because Janney projects the inbound transportation expense to be $1,300 for each 180-case shipment, rather than $814 for each 60-case monthly shipment.

Case Questions

1. How would you evaluate the apparent trade-off between inventory carrying cost and transportation cost? Which alternative would you prefer, and why? Be sure to support your conclusions with appropriate analysis.
2. Overall, what do you think of Trump's approach to this inventory decision? What approaches do you feel might be more effective than trade-off analysis? What are their advantages and disadvantages?

Case 6-2

AUTOEUROPE LTD.

The vice president of logistics at AutoEurope is perplexed. To support the repair parts operation for the Swiss manufacturer of luxury automobiles, AutoEurope operates 24 distribution centers across Europe. Recently, AutoEurope's logistics group has come under pressure to reduce cost and also to improve service. Current shipments to retailer customers are mostly by rail and truck, and customer surveys report the length of the average order cycle to be two weeks, or ten business days. There is some dissatisfaction with this level of service, as well as with the growing frequency of "out-of-stock" situations. Thus, some customers seem to be moving toward the use of "generic" repair parts.

AutoEurope's repair parts inventories consist of 60,000 SKUs, and activity levels average approximately 25,000 line items per day. The average value of inventory in the twenty-four DCs is approximately 230 million Swiss francs, or US$200 million, and DC inventory turns over four times per year. The total transportation expense from the twenty-four DCs to individual retailers is estimated at US$30 million per year. AutoEurope is concerned about its overall levels of investment in inventory, and has learned from the company's chief financial officer that the current cost of carrying inventory is thought to be 30 percent.

Case Questions

1. What savings might be expected if AutoEurope were to reduce its number of distribution centers from twenty-four to six? What issues would you raise regarding the feasibility of actually capturing this level of savings?
2. Rather than reducing the number of points from which the repair parts are shipped, AutoEurope is considering the use of Express Logistics, a service that would reduce transit time significantly, thus reducing average order cycle time to one week, or five business days. Given the high quality of Express Logistics services, AutoEurope also feels that overall inventory investment in the 24 DCs could be reduced by 25 percent. However, the use of Express Logistics would add an expense of US$10 million to the yearly transportation bill, and there is some concern that the improved service would be too expensive to afford. What do you think?
3. What other suggestions would you have for AutoEurope in terms of improving the cost and service aspects of its parts distribution business? What additional information would be critical for AutoEurope's vice president of logistics to have before making any decisions regarding this matter?

SPECIAL APPLICATIONS OF THE EOQ APPROACH

ADJUSTING THE SIMPLE EOQ MODEL FOR MODAL CHOICE DECISIONS— THE COST OF INVENTORY IN TRANSIT

Chapter 1 mentioned the trade-off possibilities between inventory costs and transportation decisions regarding choice of mode. Implied in this discussion was the idea that longer transit times resulted in higher inventory costs. This is because in-transit inventory carrying costs will be incurred by the firms having ownership of the goods while they are being transported. In effect, the carrying costs of inventory in transit will be similar to the carrying costs of inventory in the warehouse. There are differences between inventory in transit and inventory in the warehouse, but basically the company is responsible for inventory in both instances. There is always some cost attached to having inventory, whether it is sitting in a warehouse or plant or moving to another point. Therefore, if modes of transportation have different transit times and different rates (prices) with other variables being equal, the trade-off between transportation rates and the inventory cost associated with the transit times should be examined. The transportation rates are usually easy to obtain. However, to calculate the cost of carrying inventory in transit, it will be necessary to modify the basic or simple EOQ model.

transit times   Recall that the simple EOQ model essentially considered only the trade-off between order or setup costs and the carrying cost associated with holding inventory in a warehouse. To consider how different transit times affect transportation and its cost, the company must relax one basic assumption of the EOQ model and adapt the model accordingly.

F.O.B. assumption   One assumption of the simple EOQ model was that inventory incurred no cost in transit, because the company either purchased inventory on a delivered-price basis or sold it F.O.B. plant. If conditions change so that the company makes purchases F.O.B. origin or sells products on a delivered-price basis, then it will be necessary to consider the cost of carrying inventory in transit. Figure 6A–1 depicts a modified sawtooth inventory model; the lower half shows the inventory in transit.

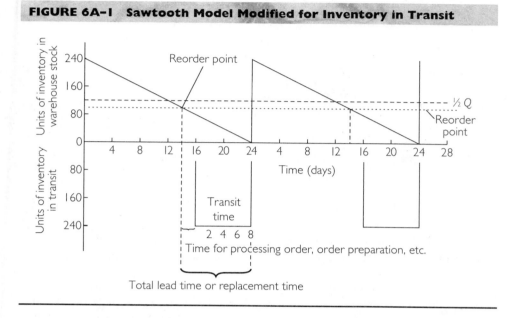

FIGURE 6A-1   Sawtooth Model Modified for Inventory in Transit

The Sawtooth Model Adjusted

Comparing the lower half of Figure 6A–1 with the upper half, which depicts inventory in the warehouse, we can see two differences relevant for calculating the appropriate costs. First, inventory is usually in transit for only part of the cycle. Typically, the number of inventory shipping days would be less than the number of days that inventory from the preceding EOQ replenishment would be in the warehouse. Second, inventory in transit is not used up or sold; warehouse inventory may be used up or sold.

part of cycle period

Since inventory in transit has these two distinctive characteristics, the cost of carrying inventory in transit will differ from that of storing inventory in the warehouse. We can calculate this cost in several ways. If a daily inventory-in-transit carrying cost were available, we could multiply it by the number of days in transit. We could calculate this daily cost by multiplying the inventory-in-transit value by a daily opportunity cost. After multiplying this cost by the number of transit days, we could multiply it by the number of orders per year or cycles per year. This would give an annual cost of inventory in transit. In effect, this resembles the procedure we followed when calculating the cost of inventory in the warehouse.

cost development

Consider the following:

Y = cost of carrying inventory in transit
V = value/unit of inventory
t = order cycle time
t_m = inventory transit time
M = average number of units of inventory in transit

We calculate the value of M as follows:

$\dfrac{t_m}{t}$ = percentage of time inventory is in transit per cycle period

Therefore,

$$M = \frac{t_m}{t} Q$$

We could rewrite this as follows:

$$t(\text{days in cycle}) = \frac{360 \ (\text{days in year})}{R/Q \ (\text{cycles per year})}$$

$$t = 360 \frac{Q}{R}$$

$$M = \frac{(t_m Q)}{360} \frac{R}{Q}$$

$$M = \frac{t_m}{360} R$$

The two approaches to calculating M give the same result, given the preceding assumptions. The second equation for M, however, is frequently more useful, since the variables are given in the problem.

Now that we have developed a way of calculating the average number of units in transit, all that remains is to multiply this figure by the value per unit and the percentage annual carrying cost of inventory in transit. The result will be a dollar cost for inventory in transit that compares to the dollar cost of inventory in the warehouse:

$$\frac{t_m}{t} QVY$$

We could write the new total inventory cost equation in either of the following forms:

$$\text{TAC} = \frac{1}{2} QVW + A\frac{R}{Q} + \frac{t_m}{t} QVY$$

or

$$\text{TAC} = \frac{1}{2} QVW + A\frac{R}{Q} + \frac{t_m}{360} RVY*$$

Example of Modal Selection

We can measure the trade-off between transit times and transportation cost using the total cost formula developed in the preceding section. First review the infor-

---

*Differentiating this equation and solving for Q with the expanded total cost formula results in the same equation as the previous one, since the last term added is not a function of Q; that is,

$$Q = \sqrt{\frac{2RA}{VW}}$$

mation provided in the example in Chapter 6 to demonstrate the simple EOQ model:

$R = $ 3,600 units (annual demand)
$A = $ \$200 (cost of one order or setup)
$W = $ 25% (cost of carrying inventory in warehouse)
$V = $ \$100 (value per unit)
$Q = $ 240 units (this would remain the same)

Now consider that a hypothetical company is choosing between two transportation modes (rail or motor) and that the following information is available:

Rail: 8 days in transit time
$3 per hundred pounds
Motor: 6 days transit time
$4 per hundred pounds

Next assume that the company will ship the same amount, 240 units, regardless of mode. If each unit weighs 100 pounds, this represents 24,000 pounds, or 240 hundredweight (cwt). The cost of carrying inventory in transit (Y) is 10 percent. Given the preceding variables, we may examine the two alternatives using the formula developed previously.

The first step is to look at the product's total inventory cost if the company decides to ship by rail:

$$\text{Total inventory cost (rail)} = \left(\frac{1}{2} \cdot 240 \cdot \$100 \cdot 25\%\right) + \left(\$200 \cdot \frac{3,600}{240}\right) + \left(\frac{8}{24} \cdot 240 \cdot \$100 \cdot 10\%\right)$$
$$= \$3,000 + \$3,000 + \$800$$
$$= \$6,800$$

If we add the transportation cost to the inventory cost, the total cost would be

$$\text{Total cost (rail)} = \$6,800 + \left(\$3 + 240 \cdot \frac{3,600}{240}\right)$$
$$= \$6,800 + \$10,800$$
$$= \$17,600$$

The next step is to determine the total inventory cost if the company ships the items by motor:

$$\text{Total inventory cost (motor)} = \left(\frac{1}{2} \cdot 240 \cdot \$100 \cdot 25\%\right) + \left(\$200 \cdot \frac{3,600}{240}\right) + \left(\frac{6}{24} \cdot 240 \cdot \$100 \cdot 10\%\right)$$
$$= \$3,000 + \$3,000 + \$600$$
$$= \$6,600$$

Once again we should add the transportation cost to the inventory costs:

$$\text{Total cost (motor)} = \$6,600 + \left(\$4 \cdot 240 \cdot \frac{3,600}{240}\right)$$
$$= \$6,600 + 14,400$$
$$= \$21,000 \text{ by motor}$$

Given these calculations, the rail alternative would be less costly and thus pref-   **trade-offs**
erable. Before leaving this section, we should examine the trade-offs more closely.

As you can see, the rail alternative has a higher inventory cost because of the slower transit time, but the transportation cost savings offset this. The net effect is an overall savings by rail.

Finally, we should note that the procedure suggested in this section is based on conditions of certainty. If transit times varied, we would need to establish probabilities and approach the solution in a more sophisticated manner.

ADJUSTING THE SIMPLE EOQ MODEL FOR VOLUME TRANSPORTATION RATES

lower rate for larger volume

The basic EOQ model discussed previously did not consider the possible reductions in transportation rates per hundredweight associated with larger-volume shipments. For example, the hypothetical company in the previous illustration decided that 240 units was the appropriate quantity to order or produce. If we assume again that each unit weighed 100 pounds, this would imply a shipment of 24,000 pounds. If the rate on a shipment of 24,000 pounds (240 cwt) was $3 per hundred pounds (cwt) and the rate for a 40,000-pound shipment was $2 per cwt, knowing whether to ship 400 units (40,000 pounds) instead of the customary 240 units would be worthwhile.

total cost equation

Shippers transporting a specified minimum quantity (weight) or more commonly publish volume rates on carload (rail) and truckload (motor carrier)* quantities. Therefore, in inventory situations, the decision maker responsible for transporting goods should consider how the lower-volume rate affects total cost. In other words, in addition to considering storage (holding) cost and order or setup cost, the decision maker should consider how lower transportation costs affect total cost.

Cost Relationships

Sometimes the economic order quantity suggested by the basic model may be less than the quantity necessary for a volume rate. We can adjust the model to consider the following cost relationships associated with shipping a volume larger than the one determined by the basic EOQ approach.

- *Increased inventory carrying cost for inventory in the warehouse.* The larger quantity required for the volume rate means a larger average inventory ($\frac{1}{2}Q$) and consequently an increased inventory carrying cost.
- *Decreased order or setup costs.* The larger quantity will reduce the number of orders placed and the ordinary costs of order placement and/or order setup.
- *Decreased transportation costs.* The larger quantity will reduce the cost per hundredweight of transporting the goods, consequently lowering transportation costs.
- *Decreased in-transit inventory carrying cost.* Carload (CL) and truckload (TL) shipments usually have shorter transit times than less-than-carload (LCL) or less-than-truckload (LTL) shipments, and the faster time generally means a lower cost for inventory in transit.

---

*Motor carriers often publish different LTL rates and TL rates on quantities of 500, 2000, and 5000 pounds.

Figure 6A–2 represents the cost relationships and considers possible transportation rate discounts (volume rates versus less-than-volume rates). The total cost function "breaks," or is discontinuous, at the quantity that permits a company to use the volume rate. Therefore, we cannot use the cost function for the transportation rate discount or discounts in the original EOQ formulation. Rather, we must use sensitivity analysis, or a sensitivity test, to determine whether total annual costs are lower if the company purchases a quantity larger than the basic EOQ amount. Note that although Figure 6A–2 indicates that using the volume rate will lower total cost, this does not necessarily have to be the case. For example, if the inventory dollar value was very high, then the increased storage (holding) costs could more than offset reductions in order and transport cost.

Mathematical Formulation

Although there are several ways to analyze opportunities for using volume transportation rates, a useful method is to calculate and compare the total annual costs of the EOQ-based approach with those of the volume-rate-based approach. The following symbols will be useful in this analysis:

$$\text{TAC} = \text{inventory carrying cost} + \text{order cost} + \text{transportation cost} + \text{in-transit inventory carrying cost}$$
$$\text{TAC}_b = \text{total annual cost at basic EOQ}$$

FIGURE 6A–2   EOQ Costs Considering Volume Transportation Rate

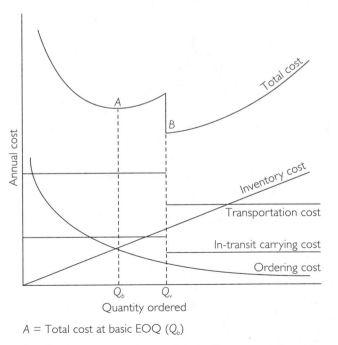

A = Total cost at basic EOQ (Q_b)

B = Total cost at quantity associated with transportation volume rate

TAC_v = total annual cost at volume rate quantity
Q_b = basic EOQ
Q_v = volume rate quantity
t_m = time in transit for less-than-volume shipment
t_n = time in transit for volume shipment
H = less-than-volume rate (high rate)
L = volume rate (low rate)

We calculate each total annual cost as follows:

$$\text{TAC}_b = \frac{1}{2}Q_bVW + A\frac{R}{Q_b} + HQ_b\frac{R}{Q_b} + \frac{t_m}{t}Q_bVY$$

$$\text{TAC}_v = \frac{1}{2}Q_vVW + A\frac{R}{Q_v} + LQ_v\frac{R}{Q_v} + \frac{t_n}{t}Q_vVY$$

Noting that $HQ_b\dfrac{R}{Q_b}$ can be written simply as HR and that $LQ_b\dfrac{R}{Q_b}$ can be written simply as LR, we can reduce these equations to the following:

$$\text{TAC}_b = \frac{1}{2}Q_bVW + A\frac{R}{Q_b} + HR + \frac{t_m}{t}Q_bVY$$

$$\text{TAC}_v = \frac{1}{2}Q_vVW + A\frac{R}{Q_v} + LR + \frac{t_n}{t}Q_vVY$$

Transportation Rate Discount Example

An example that builds upon the previous problem will illustrate in this section how transportation rate discounts produce possible annual cost savings.

For this new example, assume the following variables:

H = \$3.00/cwt (assume each unit weighs 100 pounds)
L = \$2.00/cwt with a minimum of 40,000 pounds (with each unit weighing 100 pounds, this would be 400 units, or 400 cwt)
t_n = 6 days (time in transit for volume movement)
Y = 10% (carrying cost of inventory while in transit)
Q_v = 400 units
t_v = 40 days (length of a single inventory cycle for Q_v = 400 units)

From the previous problem, we know that

R = 3,600 units (3,600 cwt) (annual sales)
A = \$200 (cost of placing an order or cost of setup)
V = \$100/cwt/unit (value per unit)
W = 25%
Q_b = 240 units (240 cwt, or 240,000 pounds)
t_m = 8 days (time in transit for LTL movement)
t = 24 days (length of a single inventory cycle or period)

Solving for TAC_b and TAC_v:

$$\text{TAC}_b = \left[\frac{1}{2} \cdot 240 \cdot \$100 \cdot 25\%\right] + \left[\$200 \cdot \frac{3{,}600}{240}\right]$$

$$+ [\$3 \cdot \$3{,}600] + \left[\frac{8}{24} \cdot 240 \cdot \$100 \cdot 10\%\right]$$

$$= \$17{,}600$$

$$\text{TAC}_v = \left[\frac{1}{2} \cdot 400 \cdot \$100 \cdot 25\%\right] + \left[\$200 \cdot \frac{3{,}600}{500}\right]$$

$$+ [\$2 \cdot \$3{,}600] + \left[\frac{6}{40} \cdot 400 \cdot \$100 \cdot 10\%\right]$$

$$= \$14{,}240$$

Since TAC_b exceeds TAC_v by \$3,360, the most economical solution is to purchase the larger quantity, 400 cwt. Reductions in ordering, transportation, and in-transit inventory carrying costs offset the increased cost of holding the larger quantity.

We may modify this analysis to consider potential volume discounts for purchasing in larger quantities. The same procedure of calculating and comparing total annual costs under the various alternatives applies, providing we make minor modifications to the equations.

ADJUSTING THE SIMPLE EOQ MODEL FOR PRIVATE CARRIAGE

Many companies that use their own truck fleet or that lease trucks for private use assess a fixed charge per mile or per trip, no matter how much the company ships at any one time. In other words, since operating costs such as driver expense and fuel do not vary significantly with weight, and since fixed costs do not change with weight, many companies charge a flat amount per trip rather than differentiate on a weight basis. Therefore, since additional weight costs nothing extra, it is logical to ask what quantity the company should ship.

The basic EOQ model can handle this analysis, since the fixed trip charge is comparable to the order cost or setup cost. Therefore, the decision maker must trade off the prospect of a smaller number of larger shipments against the increased cost of carrying larger average inventory amounts.

fixed cost per trip

If T_c represents the trip charge, we can write the formula as follows:

$$\text{TAC} = \frac{1}{2}QVW + \frac{R}{Q}A + \frac{R}{Q}T_c$$

We can derive the basic model as

$$\text{EOQ} = \sqrt{\frac{2R(A + T_c)}{VW}}$$

From the previous example, we can add a charge of $100 per trip:

$$\text{EOQ} = \sqrt{\frac{2 \cdot \$3,600 \cdot (\$200 + \$100)}{\$100 \cdot 25\%}}$$

$$= \sqrt{\frac{\$2,160,000}{\$25}}$$

$$= \sqrt{86,400}$$

$$= 293.94$$

The EOQ size has been increased to 293.94 units because of additional fixed charges associated with private trucking costs.

ADJUSTING THE SIMPLE EOQ MODEL FOR THE ESTABLISHMENT AND APPLICATION OF IN-EXCESS RATES*

We can adjust the basic inventory analysis framework discussed in Chapter 6 to utilize an in-excess rate. Through in-excess rates, carriers encourage heavier shipper loadings. The carrier offers a lower rate for weight shipped in excess of a specified minimum weight. A logistics manager must decide whether the company should use the in-excess rate and, if so, the amount the company should include in each shipment.

Consider the following example: The CBL Railroad has just published a new in-excess rate on items that the XYZ Company ships quite often. CBL's present rate is $4/cwt with a 40,000-pound minimum (400 cwt). The in-excess rate just published is $3/cwt on shipment weight in excess of 40,000 pounds up to 80,000 pounds. The XYZ logistics manager presently ships in 400-cwt lots. The manager wants to know whether XYZ should use the in-excess rate, and, if so, what quantity the company should ship per shipment.

XYZ supplied the following data:

$R = $ 3,200,000 pounds (32,000 cwt) (annual shipments)
$V = $ \$200 (value of item per cwt)
$W = $ 25% of value (inventory carrying cost/unit value/year)

Each item weighs 100 pounds.

XYZ should use the in-excess rate as long as the annual transportation cost savings offset the added cost of holding a larger inventory associated with heavier shipments. That is, realizing the transportation cost savings of the in-excess rate will increase XYZ's inventory carrying cost. The optimum shipment size occurs

*This section is adapted from James L. Heskett, Robert M. Ivie, and Nicholas A. Glaskowsky, *Business Logistics* (New York: Ronald Press, 1964): 516–20.

when annual net savings are maximal, that is, when annual transport savings minus the annual added inventory carrying cost are the greatest.

In developing the savings and cost functions, we will use the following symbols:

S_r = savings per cwt between present rate and new in-excess rate

Q = optimum shipment quantity in cwt

Q_m = old minimum shipment quantity in cwt

The annual net savings equals the annual transport savings minus the annual added inventory carrying cost, or $N_s = S_y - C_y$.

The annual transport savings equals the number of shipments per year times the savings per shipment, or

$$S_y = \frac{R}{Q} S_r(Q - Q_m)$$

where R/Q is the number of shipments per year, $Q - Q_m$ is the amount of shipment weight the company will ship at the lower in-excess rate, and $S_r(Q - Q_m)$ is the transportation savings per shipment. Rewriting the equation for S_y results in the following:

$$S_y = RS_r\left(1 - \frac{Q_m}{Q}\right)$$

The annual added inventory carrying cost, C_y, equals the added inventory carrying costs of the consignor (shipper or seller) and the consignee (receiver or buyer). The calculations must consider the consignee's added inventory, since the seller must pass these savings on as a price discount to encourage the buyer to purchase in larger quantities, or the seller will incur this cost if the shipment goes to the seller's warehouse or distribution center, for example.

We calculate the added average inventory—the difference between the average inventories with the larger shipment quantity and the smaller (present) shipment quantity—as follows:

$$\text{Consignor's added inventory} = \frac{1}{2}Q - \frac{1}{2}Q_m$$

$$\text{Consignee's added inventory} = \frac{1}{2}Q - \frac{1}{2}Q_m$$

$$\text{Total added inventory} = 2\left(\frac{1}{2}Q - \frac{1}{2}Q_m\right) = Q - Q_m$$

$C_y = WV(Q - Q_m)$, where $V(Q - Q_m)$ equals the value of added inventory and W equals the inventory carrying cost per dollar value. Table 6A–1 and Figure 6A–3 show the savings and cost relationships developed here.

The function that maximizes annual net savings is

$$N_s = S_y - C_y = RS_r\left(1 - \frac{Q_m}{Q}\right) - WV(Q - Q_m)$$

TABLE 6A-1 Annual Savings, Annual Cost, and Net Savings by Various Quantities Using Incentive Rates

Q	S_y	C_y	N_s
400	0	0	0
410	781	500	281
420	1,524	1,000	524
430	2,233	1,500	733
440	2,909	2,000	909
450	3,556	2,500	1,056
460	4,174	3,000	1,174
470	4,766	3,500	1,266
480	5,333	4,000	1,333
490	5,878	4,500	1,378
500	6,400	5,000	1,400
505	6,654	5,250	1,404
510	6,902	5,500	1,402
520	7,385	6,000	1,385
530	7,849	6,500	1,349
540	8,296	7,000	1,296
550	8,727	7,500	1,227
560	9,143	8,000	1,143
570	9,544	8,500	1,044
580	9,931	9,000	931
590	10,305	9,500	805
600	10,667	10,000	667
610	11,017	10,500	517
620	11,355	11,000	355

Taking the first derivative, setting it equal to zero, and solving for Q results in the following:

$$\frac{d(N_s)}{dQ} = RS_r \frac{Q_m}{Q^2} - WV = 0$$

$$WV = \frac{RS_r Q_m}{Q^2}$$

$$Q^2 = \frac{RS_r Q_m}{WV}$$

$$Q = \sqrt{\frac{RS_r Q_m}{WV}}$$

Now, taking the data from the problem posed in this example, we find the solution as follows:

$$Q = \sqrt{\frac{(32,000)\,(\$1.00)\,(400)}{(0.25)\,(\$200)}} = \sqrt{256,000} = 506 \text{ cwt}$$

The conclusion is that the XYZ Company should use the in-excess rate and should ship 50,600 pounds in each shipment.

FIGURE 6A-3   Net Savings Function for Incentive Rate

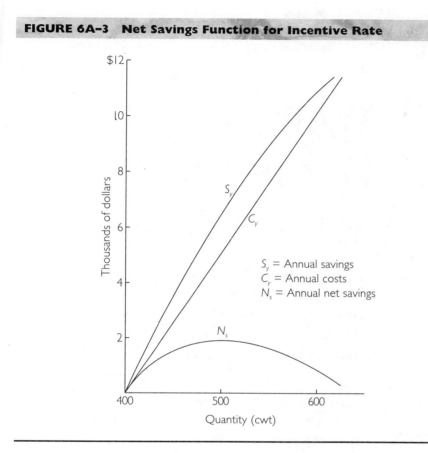

S_y = Annual savings
C_y = Annual costs
N_s = Annual net savings

SUMMARY

The four adjustments to the basic EOQ approach discussed in this appendix all relate to decisions important to the logistics manager—modal choice, volume rates, private trucking, and in-excess rates. We could include other adjustments, but these four should be sufficient in most cases. While all of the adjustments discussed here assume a condition of certainty, other adjustments may require modifying the model for conditions of uncertainty.

CHAPTER 7

WAREHOUSING DECISIONS

LEARNING OBJECTIVES

After reading this chapter, you should be able to do the following:

- Discuss the strategic role warehousing plays in the logistics system.

- Explain the basic rationale for warehousing in light of transportation consolidation, product mixing, service, contingency protection, and smoothing.

- Develop an analytical framework for basic warehousing decisions.

- Distinguish between the different warehouse activities requiring space in the warehouse design.

- Discuss the major principles of warehouse layout design.

- Compare the use of private versus public warehousing.

- Explain public warehousing services, regulations, and pricing.

- Discuss the rationale for using contract warehousing as opposed to public or private warehousing.

- Describe the decision-making approach used to determine the number of warehouses in the logistics system.

LOGISTICS PROFILE

BOEING COMMERCIAL AIRPLANE GROUP

The Boeing Commercial Airline Group, located in Renton, Washington, is the world's largest manufacturer of commercial jet airplanes. The company has two warehouses, located in Renton and Everett, Washington, that receive parts and supplies for nearby manufacturing plants. From these two warehouses, parts are shuttled to the plants daily to supply the assembly lines.

These two warehouses are using state-of-the-art computerized voice-recognition systems to improve warehouse labor efficiency and inventory accuracy.

About two years prior to installing voice-recognition systems, Boeing asked its suppliers to place bar codes on all inbound parts shipments. This would enable Boeing to scan the parts at the receiving dock and electronically enter the information into the inventory control system. This process was developed to reduce inventory errors due to manual data entry and to improve productivity and efficiency.

However, not all suppliers complied with the request, and Boeing searched for an automated backup system to replace the labor-intensive data operator process for creating bar codes for these shipments.

The automated system selected by Boeing is the Talkman, a voice-recognition system developed by VoCollect, Inc. The Talkman is a voice data-collection terminal and software that can be programmed to recognize more than 1,000 words. The system is speaker dependent, which means that the terminal must be trained to recognize an individual operator's voice. Each operator creates a voice template for every word used during discussions with the computer.

The voice-recognition system enables the operator at the receiving area to speak into a head-mounted microphone that is connected by radio frequency to the computer. As the boxes are placed onto the conveyors for inspection, the operator speaks the pertinent information about the part into the microphone. The computer then reads back the data, providing a double-check when the inbound material is stored.

The voice-recognition system has improved labor efficiency at the warehouse by eliminating the data entry clerks. In addition, the receiving clerk enters the data directly into the computer and is able to verify the data while the box is still in the receiving area. Having the information entered directly at the source has improved the accuracy of the data and the receiving operation. With more accurate data, inventory accuracy has improved.

In the future, voice-recognition technology will be used not only for incoming parts inspection but also for directing the picking and packing operations, particularly in companies with multilingual workforces.

SOURCE: James Aaron Cooke, "Can We Talk?" *Traffic Management* (December 1994): 36–39. Used with permission.

Warehousing in the 1990s has a different focus than in the recent past. Traditionally, warehousing served the strategic role of long-term storage for raw materials and finished goods. Manufacturers produced for inventory and sold out of inventory stored in the warehouse. Warehouses had to support inventory levels of 60 to 90 days' supply. Most facilities had a nominal activity level.

With the arrival of just-in-time, partnership, and logistics supply chain philosophies in the 1980s and 1990s, the warehouse has taken on a strategic role of attaining the logistics goals of shorter cycle times, lower inventories, lower costs, and better customer service. The warehouse of today is not a long-term storage facility; the activity level in the facility is fast paced. Attention is given to the speed with which a product moves through the facility. In many companies the product is in the warehouse for just a few days or even a few hours.

To meet customer demands for shorter cycle times and lower prices, logistics managers are examining the warehouse process for productivity and cost improvements. Warehouses are being redesigned and automated to achieve order processing and cost goals and are being relocated to achieve overall supply chain customer service goals.

THE NATURE AND IMPORTANCE OF WAREHOUSING

We often define warehousing as the storage of goods. Broadly interpreted, this definition includes a wide spectrum of facilities and locations that provide warehousing, including the storage of iron ore in open fields, the storage of finished goods in the production facility, and the storage of raw materials, industrial goods, and finished goods while they are in transport. It also includes highly specialized storage facilities such as bean and grain elevators, tobacco warehouses, potato cellars, and refrigeration facilities. Every product manufactured, grown, or caught is warehoused at least once during its life cycle (from creation to consumption). Given this fact, we can easily understand why warehousing is of national economic importance. In 1993, warehousing costs in the United States totaled $61 billion dollars, as Table 7–1 indicates. The United States spent a total of $670 billion dollars on logistics, which equaled 10.5 percent of the nation's entire gross domestic product (GDP). Warehousing cost amounted to 0.96% of GDP.

creating time utility

In a macroeconomic sense, warehousing performs a very necessary function. It creates time utility for raw materials, industrial goods, and finished products. The proximity of market-oriented warehousing to the customer allows a firm to serve the customer with shorter lead times. More important, warehousing increases the utility of goods by broadening their time availability to prospective customers. In other words, by using warehouses, companies can make goods available *when* and *where* customers demand them. This warehousing function continues to be increasingly important as companies and industries use customer service as a dynamic, value-adding competitive tool.

THE ROLE OF THE WAREHOUSE IN THE LOGISTICS SYSTEM: A BASIC CONCEPTUAL RATIONALE

The warehouse is a point in the logistics system where a firm stores or holds raw materials, semifinished goods, or finished goods for varying periods of time. Holding goods in a warehouse stops or interrupts the flow of goods, adding cost to the product or products. Some firms have viewed warehousing cost very negatively; in short, they sought to avoid it if at all possible. This view is changing due to the realization that warehousing can add more value than cost to a product. Other firms, particularly distributors or wholesalers, went to the opposite extreme and

TABLE 7–1 Components of 1994 Logistics Cost

		$ Billions
Inventory Carrying Costs		
Interest		53
Taxes, obsolescence, depreciation		161
Warehousing		63
	Subtotal	277
Transportation Costs		
Motor Carriers		
Public and for hire		96
Private and for own account		109
Local freight services		128
	Subtotal	333
Other Carriers		
Railroads		33
Water carriers		22
Oil pipelines		10
Air carriers		17
Forwarders		5
	Subtotal	87
Shipper Related Costs		5
Distribution Administration		28
	Total Logistics Cost	$730

SOURCE: Cass Information Systems, in Jim Thomas, "Down But Not Out," *Distribution* (July 1995): 6.

warehoused as many items as possible. Neither end of the spectrum is usually correct. Firms should hold or store items only if possible trade-offs exist in other areas.

The warehouse serves several value-adding roles in a logistics system: transportation consolidation, product mixing, service, contingency protection, and smoothing. As Figure 7–1 demonstrates, companies will sometimes face less-than-truckload (LTL) and less-than-carload (LCL) shipments of raw materials and finished goods. Shipping goods long distances at LTL or LCL rates is more costly than shipping at full truckload or carload rates. By moving the LTL and LCL amounts relatively short distances to or from a warehouse, warehousing can allow a firm to *consolidate* smaller shipments into a large shipment (a carload or truckload), with significant transportation savings. For the inbound logistics system, the warehouse would consolidate different suppliers' LTL or LCL shipments and ship a volume shipment (TL or CL) to the firm's plant. For the outbound logistics system, the warehouse would receive a consolidated volume shipment from various plants and ship LTL or LCL shipments to different markets.

transportation consolidation

A second warehousing function may be customer order *product mixing*. Companies frequently turn out a product line that contains thousands of "different" products, if we consider color, size, shape, and other variations. When placing orders, customers will often want a product line mixture—for example, five dozen four-cup coffee pots, six dozen ten-cup coffee pots with blue trim and ten dozen with red trim, and three dozen blue salad bowl sets. Because companies often

product mixing

FIGURE 7–1 **Transportation Consolidation**

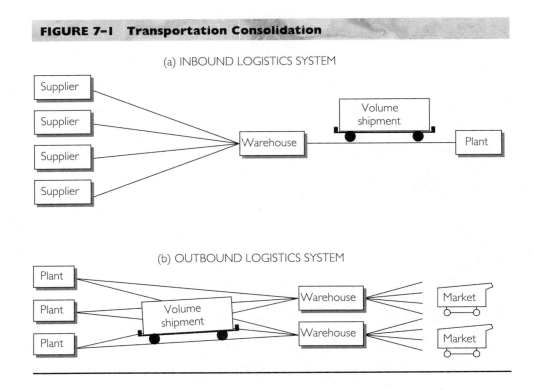

(a) INBOUND LOGISTICS SYSTEM

Supplier
Supplier
Supplier
Supplier
Warehouse
Volume shipment
Plant

(b) OUTBOUND LOGISTICS SYSTEM

Plant
Plant
Plant
Volume shipment
Warehouse
Warehouse
Market
Market

produce items at different plants, a company that did not warehouse goods would have to fill orders from several locations, causing differing arrival times and opportunity for mix-ups. Therefore, a product mixing warehouse for a multiple-product line leads to efficient order filling (see Figure 7–2). By developing new mixing warehouses near dense urban areas, firms can make pickups and deliveries in smaller vehicles and schedule these activities at more optimum times to avoid congestion.

In addition to product mixing for customer orders, companies using raw materials or semifinished goods (e.g., auto manufacturers) commonly move carloads of items mixed from a physical supply warehouse to a plant (see Figure 7–2). This strategy not only reduces transportation costs from consolidation, but also allows the company to avoid using the plant as a warehouse. This strategy will become increasingly popular as increased fuel expenses raise transport costs. For firms using sophisticated strategies such as MRP (materials requirements planning) or JIT (just-in-time) systems, supply warehouse use is essential.

cross-docking   Cross-docking is an operation that facilitates the product mixing function. In a cross-docking operation, products from different suppliers arrive in truckload lots, but instead of being placed into storage for later picking, they are moved across the warehouse area to waiting trucks for movement to particular customers. For example, Menlo Logistics operates a cross-docking operation for Office Max, an office supply retailer. The incoming materials are picked from the delivering truck or from temporary storage locations to fill a specific store order and moved across the dock to a truck destined for the store. The whole process is completed in a matter of hours. Excess product and small items are stored temporarily to await

FIGURE 7–2   Supply and Product Mixing

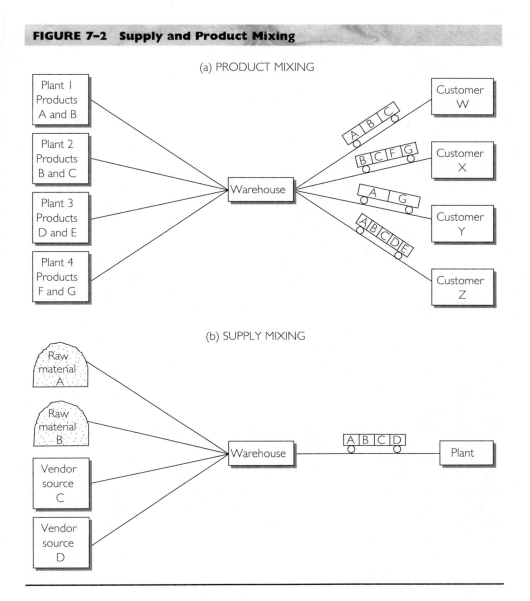

scheduled store deliveries and to permit sorting of inbound loads of mixed products.

A third warehouse function is to provide *service*. The importance of customer service is obvious. Having goods available in a warehouse when a customer places an order, particularly if the warehouse is in reasonable proximity to the customer, will usually lead to customer satisfaction and enhance future sales. Service may also be a factor for physical supply warehouses. However, production schedules, which a firm makes in advance, are easier to service than customers: while customer demand is often uncertain, physical supply stockout costs sometimes seem infinite.

service

FIGURE 7-3 Basic Warehousing Decisions

Ownership: Private versus public
Design and layout
Centralized versus decentralized
Number
Location
Size
Items stocked
Employee safety

contingencies A fourth warehousing function is *protection against contingencies* such as transportation delays, vendor stockouts, or strikes. A potential trucker's strike will generally cause buyers to stock larger inventories than usual, for example. This particular function is very important for physical supply warehouses in that a delay in the delivery of raw materials can delay the production of finished goods. However, contingencies also occur with physical distribution warehouses—for example, goods damaged in transit can affect inventory levels and order filling.

smoothing A fifth warehousing function is to *smooth* operations or decouple successive stages in the manufacturing process. Seasonal demand and the need for a production run long enough to ensure reasonable cost and quality are examples of smoothing—that is, preventing operations under overtime conditions at low production levels. In effect, this balancing strategy allows a company to reduce its manufacturing capacity investment.

As we can see, warehousing functions can make important contributions to logistics systems and company operations. However, we must also view warehousing in a trade-off context; that is, warehousing's contribution to profit must be greater than its cost.

BASIC WAREHOUSING DECISIONS

private versus public warehousing A number of important decisions or choices, including ownership, number, size, location, and stocking, relate to warehousing management. (See Figure 7–3.) The first item we will consider is *ownership*. In arranging warehousing space, an organization has two basic alternatives: *private* ownership of facilities or use of *public* warehouses.* To choose between the two or to combine them is a major ware-

*A third alternative is *leased* warehousing. Generally this means leasing a complete facility at a fixed fee per year. The basic nature of this arrangement closely resembles private warehousing, so we will treat them synonymously in this discussion.

housing decision. Many firms combine public and private warehousing because of varying regional market conditions and other factors, such as seasonality.

A firm has to approach the ownership decision in a trade-off framework. Certain operations lend themselves to private warehousing, whereas others lend themselves best to public facilities where a firm rents space or contracts on a shorter-term basis according to need. We will examine each alternative's cost variations, favorable use conditions, and advantages in a later section.

Related to the private warehousing decision are decisions concerning warehouse design and layout. A firm deciding to use a private warehouse must make a number of decisions about how to utilize the facility most effectively, which we will discuss later in the text.

Another important warehousing decision is whether the firm will use a *centralized* approach or a *decentralized* approach in providing warehousing facilities. This decision essentially concerns how many warehouses the firm should provide. In some instances, the decision will be relatively simple because of the firm's size. That is, small and medium-size firms with a regional market area often will need only one warehouse. Usually, only large firms with national or international market areas need to examine the question in detail.

centralized versus decentralized warehousing

As with the private versus public warehousing decision, a firm has to use a trade-off framework in analyzing the need for warehouses in various areas. A particular firm's demand and supply conditions will make one alternative more attractive than others. For example, a firm manufacturing or distributing a highly competitive and substitutable product on a national basis may need to use decentralized warehousing to give rapid service in its market area.

A firm has to closely coordinate the decision about *number* of warehouses with its decision about transportation alternatives. For example, airfreight makes possible rapid national market coverage from one or two strategically located warehouses. Although the cost of airfreight is relatively high, a company can nevertheless trade it off against savings in warehousing and inventory costs. As the next section explains, a number of transportation alternatives make the decision about warehouse numbers a real challenge, particularly when we consider this decision in conjunction with the public versus private warehouse alternative.

Very closely related to the decisions regarding warehouse number and a centralized or decentralized approach are two other warehousing decisions: warehouse *size* and warehouse *location*. If a company is using public warehousing, the size question is less important; such a company can usually expand or contract space according to its needs at different times. Similarly, the location decision becomes less important when a company uses public warehousing. Although the firm has to decide where to use public warehousing, the exact location is fixed, and the firm can change its decision if necessary.

warehouse size and location

As with other logistics decisions, a firm must examine location in a trade-off perspective. The firm must achieve a desired level of customer service at the least possible total logistics cost. By analyzing the warehouse's intended function, a firm can determine general locations, such as high-service facilities near markets, raw materials mixing close to production, or a combination of other factors. The choice of an exact location must rely on factors such as transportation, the market, and local characteristics. These decisions, once implemented, may be very costly to change, especially in private warehousing; therefore, proper consideration of all factors is essential.

layout   Size and location questions are of paramount importance to firms using private warehousing and, in particular, to firms that have to provide national or international market coverage. In addition to making the five warehouse decisions we cited earlier, firms have to decide how to lay out the warehouse's interior. In other words, the firm has to make decisions about aisle space, shelving, equipment, and all the other physical dimensions of the interior warehouse. Another decision is how to arrange stock most efficiently in the warehouse.

items stocked   Still other warehousing decisions involve what items the firm should stock and how much stock the firm should assign to various warehouses, but these questions are relevant only if the firm has multiple warehouse locations. A firm having a number of locations must decide whether all warehouses will carry the entire product line, whether each warehouse will specialize to some extent, or whether the warehouses will combine specialization and general stocking. Some aspects of this decision, particularly when a firm knows the location of warehouses, size, and demand, make a convenient linear programming decision.

employee safety   Other concerns, such as employee risks due to the monotonous and dangerous work in many traditional warehouses as well as to handling of hazardous materials and sanitation, will also influence efficiency improvement decisions. Efficiency also involves the interaction with materials handling equipment, as we will discuss later in the text.

Warehousing decisions are important and require close attention. Improving efficiency and productivity will be a major management focus in warehousing operations. Properly utilizing space through carefully planned inventory management and distribution operations will be more important in the future than building additional facilities. Moreover, warehouse decisions interact very closely with other areas of the logistics system. We will explore some of these decisions in detail in this chapter. Before addressing these questions, we will discuss the warehouse and its basic functions in the logistics system.

BASIC WAREHOUSE OPERATIONS

movement   The basic warehouse operations are *movement* and *storage*. Storage is probably the most obvious warehouse operation, whereas movement may seem incongruous. However, movement is a very vital aspect of warehousing, and we can divide this aspect into four somewhat distinct operations: (1) receiving goods into the warehouse from the transport network; (2) transferring goods into a particular location in the warehouse; (3) selecting particular combinations of goods for customer orders or raw materials for production; and (4) loading goods for shipping to the customer or to the production line. All four involve short-distance movement.

The movement function characterizes a distribution and cross-docking warehouse for finished goods. Goods brought to distribution and cross-docking warehouses "move" through the warehouse rapidly; that is, there is rapid inventory turnover. The reason for rapid stock turnover is the high cost of holding finished goods inventory for long time periods. Finished goods have high value, need more sophisticated storage facilities, and have greater risks for damage, loss, and obsolescence, all contributing to higher inventory costs. So moving goods quickly and efficiently through the distribution warehouse is almost mandatory.

storage   The other very important warehousing function is more obvious—the storage or holding of goods. In cross-docking warehouses, the storage or holding function is very temporary or short-term. In fact, some items will "turn" in twenty-four to forty-eight hours. Firms often associate holding goods for longer time periods (over ninety days) with raw materials or semifinished goods, because they have a lower value, involve less risk, require less-sophisticated storage facilities, and may involve quantity purchase discounts.

Note, however, that warehouses may hold even finished goods for time periods longer than the preceding comments suggest. In some instances, the longer time is for final processing. For example, a winemaker or distiller may have to store certain alcoholic beverages, which may be considered finished after processing, for conditioning or aging purposes.

In addition, for firms facing very erratic demand for their goods, accurately forecasting inventory requirements is quite difficult. If substitutability is an associated problem, then the firm may need to carry relatively large inventories to preclude stockouts. Although such an approach is costly, it is sometimes necessary. Such a problem occurs in fashion goods; here, firms pass on the higher inventory cost in the form of higher prices.

One common reason for holding finished goods longer than ninety days is that **seasonal demand** seasonality of demand enters the picture, and the distribution channels for distributing the goods to the ultimate consumer may be relatively long. For example, manufacturers of Christmas cards, paper, and accessories will start to accumulate inventory for the Christmas season in late June or July and will often complete the production of such items by November. The products will start moving out to wholesalers and other intermediaries in early September or even in late August. But the manufacturers will retain some stock until mid-November or possibly later to satisfy stockouts by shipping quickly and directly to retailers.

Other companies are in very similar situations; although they may not need to store items as long as Christmas-item manufacturers do, they nevertheless hold finished goods for longer than 30 days, very often for 90 to 120 days. Firms may store seasonal goods for relatively longer periods as a trade-off against increased production costs. In other words, by lengthening production runs and eliminating overtime, a firm can usually trade off reduced production costs against increased storage costs.

All warehouses provide both movement and storage. One function is usually more accentuated, depending upon the warehouse's orientation in the system. The facility's layout affects a warehouse's basic or emphasized operations. While there is no magic formula that states exactly what layout design a firm should use, there are certain basic aspects that we consider here.

WAREHOUSE LAYOUT AND DESIGN

To understand warehouse layout and design, some background information on a typical warehouse's basic space requirements is necessary. (See Figure 7–4.) This discussion of space requirements relates quite closely to the discussion of basic warehouse operations. Before looking specifically at the types of space a firm needs, we will comment briefly about determining how much space a firm requires.

The first step in determining warehouse space requirements is to develop a demand forecast for a company's products. This means preparing an estimate in units for a relevant sales period (usually thirty days) by product category. Then

FIGURE 7–4   Warehouse Space Requirements

the company will need to determine each item's order quantity, usually including some allowance for safety stock. The next step is to convert the units into cubic footage requirements, which may need to include pallets and which usually include an allowance of 10 to 15 percent for growth over the relevant period. At this point, the company has an estimate of basic storage space requirements. To this the company must add space needs for aisles and other needs such as lavatories and meeting rooms. Warehouses commonly devote one-third of their total space to nonstorage functions. Many companies make these space decisions through computer simulation. The computer can consider a vast number of variables and can help predict future requirements; good software packages are available.

transportation interface   One additional warehouse space requirement provides an interface with the transportation part of the logistics system—*receiving and shipping*. While this can be one area, efficiency usually requires two separate areas. In considering these space needs, a firm must choose whether to use the dock area outside the building or to unload goods out of the vehicle directly into the warehouse. The firm will have to allow for turnaround space and possibly for equipment and pallet storage. Also important are areas for staging goods before transportation and for unitizing consolidated shipments. In addition, this area may need space for checking, counting, and inspecting. The volume and frequency of the throughput will be critical in determining receiving and shipping space needs.

order-picking space   Another space requirement in physical distribution warehouses is for *order picking* and *assembly*. The amount of space these functions need will depend upon order volume and the product's nature, along with the materials handling equipment. This area's layout is critical to efficient operations and customer service. We will discuss this aspect later in an analysis of layout requirements.

storage space   A third type of space is the actual *storage* space. In a warehouse, a firm must use the full volume of the cubic storage space as efficiently as possible. A firm can derive the amount of storage space from the analysis we described earlier in this section, and it will be the largest single area in the warehouse. As with the order picking area, a firm will have to consider storage area layout in detail. We will cover this topic in a subsequent section.

Finally, a firm must consider three additional types of space. First, many physical distribution warehouses have space for *recouping*—that is, an area to salvage undamaged parts of damaged cartons. Second, administrative and clerical staff generally require *office space*. Finally, rest rooms, an employee cafeteria, utilities, and locker rooms require *miscellaneous* space. The amount of space these last three categories require will depend upon a number of variables. For example, the average amount of damaged merchandise and the feasibility of repacking undamaged merchandise will determine recouping space needs. The space requirement for a cafeteria and locker rooms will depend on the number of employees.

Layout and Design Principles

While the discussion thus far has delineated a typical warehouse's various space needs, we need to consider layout in more detail. We will first consider some general layout design principles (see Figure 7–5) and then examine layout in the context of the space categories discussed previously.

The most commonly accepted warehouse design and layout principles are as follows: First, use a one-story facility wherever possible, since it usually provides more usable space per investment dollar and usually is less expensive to construct. Second, use straight-line or direct flow of goods into and out of the warehouse, as Figure 7–6 illustrates, to avoid backtracking and inefficiency.

A third principle is to use efficient materials handling equipment and operations. The next chapter explores materials handling fundamentals. Among other benefits, materials handling equipment improves efficiency in operations.

A fourth principle is to use an effective storage plan in the warehouse. In other words, the firm must place goods in the warehouse in such a way as to maximize warehouse operations and avoid inefficiencies. Stated simply, we are trying to util-

FIGURE 7–5 Principles of Warehouse Layout Design

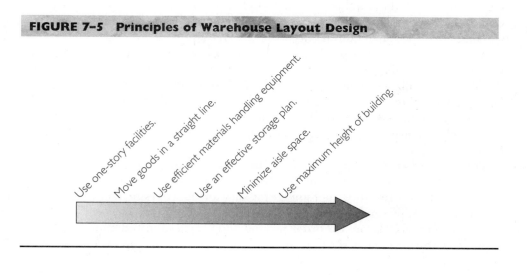

FIGURE 7–6   Basic Warehouse Configuration

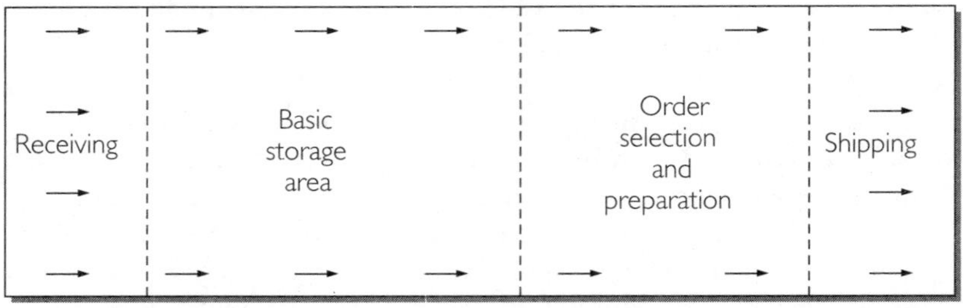

ize existing space as completely and effectively as possible while providing both adequate accessibility and protection for the goods we are storing.

A fifth principle of good layout is to minimize aisle space within the constraints that the size, type, and turning radius of materials handling equipment impose. We must also consider the products and the constraints they impose.

A sixth principle is to make maximum use of the building's height—that is, to utilize the building's cubic capacity effectively. As the next chapter points out, this usually requires integration with materials handling. Though vehicles capable of maneuvering in small aisles and stacking higher-than-conventional materials can be very expensive, such equipment offers potentially large overall systems savings because using height costs only one-fifth the cost of building the same cubic footage horizontally. What's more, a high-rise building (40 to 50 feet high) attains almost the same cubic footage as a building 25 feet high, with less than half of the floor space, thus cutting land costs.

With these general principles in mind, we can focus upon the design requirements of some of the warehouse's basic space areas. With regard to the shipping and receiving areas, a firm will have to consider whether to place stock temporarily in these areas and whether to store equipment here. The turning requirements of materials handling equipment will also influence needs in this area. The firm must also analyze the number of bays, as well as their size and shape. The type of carrier the firm utilizes, product characteristics, and materials handling equipment will influence the bay requirements.

In regard to the order-picking and preparation area, we must keep in mind that, in a physical distribution warehouse, nearly constant movement characterizes this section. Utilizing cubic space effectively is difficult because of the need to keep items within order pickers' reaching distance. While utilizing materials handling equipment can overcome this problem to some extent, a firm will never completely resolve the problem, because constant movement requires more open space.

layout for order picking and preparation

There are three basic ways to lay out the order-picking and preparation area. One is to use the general area approach, which basically mixes the order-picking and preparation area with the storage area, with appropriate racks and order preparation equipment (see Figure 7–7).

The second basic layout for order picking and preparation is the modified area approach, which provides separate storage and order preparation areas (see Fig-

FIGURE 7–7   General Area Configuration for Order Picking

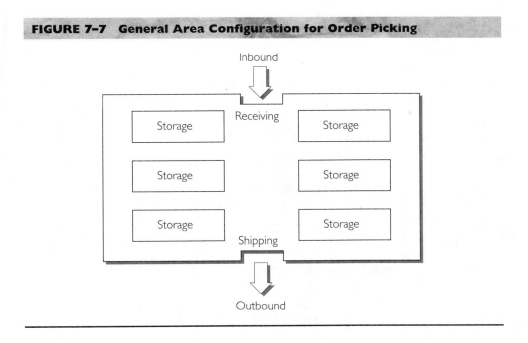

ure 7–8). To allow better access, the order-picking bays are usually smaller than the storage bays. The firm will stock the order-picking bays on a regular basis and will usually make provision for partial and full boxes. Separating order picking from storage reduces picking time and distance but also reduces the facility's flexibility. The third basic layout for order picking and preparation is the reserve/active

FIGURE 7–8   Modified Area Configuration

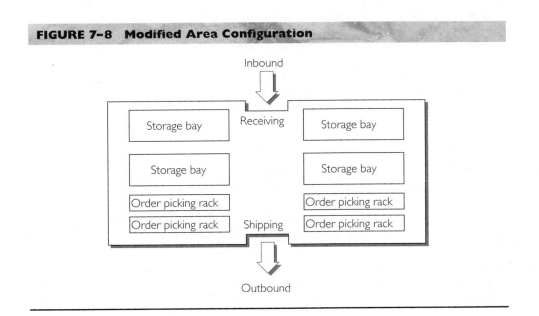

FIGURE 7–9   Reserve/Active Area Approach

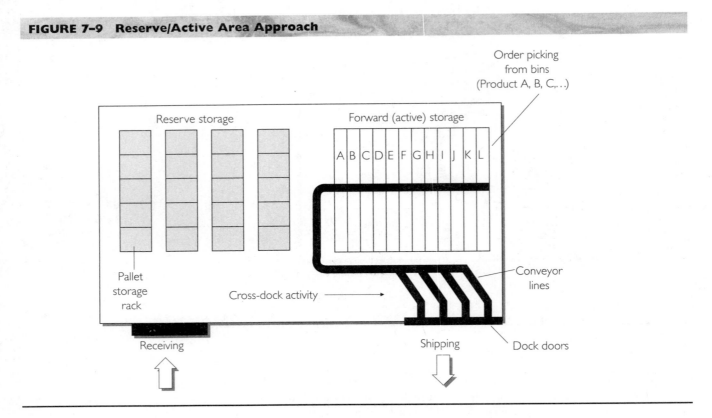

area approach (see Figure 7–9). This approach, which is more complex than the modified area approach, subdivides the storage area into two more areas: (1) reserve storage and (2) active or forward storage. The reserve storage area would be located next to the inbound receiving area. The active or forward storage area would be located next to the order-picking and preparation area. When the inventory in the active storage location falls to a certain level, warehouse personnel replenish the inventory with items from the reserve storage area. With the reserve/active system, the active storage area racks usually flow directly into the order-picking areas.

Layout and Design Objectives

cubic capacity utilization   As stated previously, an underlying principle of layout design in the warehouse's storage area is to fully use the cubic capacity. One storage area design feature that lends itself to this objective is the use of larger storage bays having more limited access. The turnover or throughput level will affect the storage bays' actual size. For example, when turnover is very low, as in physical supply warehouses, the bays can be wide and deep, with limited access, and the aisles can be narrow. Increased turnover necessitates better access, and, consequently, smaller bays and wider aisles. The customer service requirements of the physical distribution warehouse necessitate quick access.

Warehouse layout's protection and efficiency objectives provide a good framework for determining the use of warehouse space. Looking first at the protection aspect, we can develop some general guidelines. First, warehouse space utilization should separate hazardous materials such as explosives, flammable items, and oxidizing items from other items so as to eliminate the possibility of damage. Second, the firm should safeguard products requiring special security against pilferage. Third, the warehouse should properly accommodate items requiring physical control such as refrigeration or heat. Fourth, warehouse personnel should avoid stacking or storing light or fragile items near other items that could cause them damage.

protection

The government has recently increased regulation of the movement and storage of hazardous materials, including radioactive materials, explosives, and many other items. This is particularly important since any product can be hazardous in certain situations or under certain conditions.

The efficiency aspect has two dimensions. One is the effective *utilization of space* in the warehouse, which means utilizing the facility's height and minimizing aisle space. The second efficiency dimension is the *placement of stock* in the warehouse so as to minimize labor costs or handling costs.

efficiency

A firm usually achieves efficiency by analyzing three variables. First is an item's activity level. The firm should store faster-moving items in the most accessible areas. This could mean a location near a shipping area or simply a shelf position that is neither too high nor too low. Second, size can affect efficiency. The firm may store large and bulky items near the shipping area to minimize handling time. Third, if the load size is large compared with the order size, storing the commodity close to the shipping area will minimize handling costs.[1]

Though mechanized systems are not the solution for every warehouse, these systems frequently offer great potential to improve distribution efficiency. Careful planning should consider all the risks of investing in automation. These risks include obsolescence due to rapid technological change, market fluctuations, and return on the large investment. The planning stages of mechanization also call for an operations analysis. Mechanization generally works best when items are regularly shaped and easily handled, when order selection is the middle range of activity, and when product moves in high volumes with few fluctuations. The next chapter looks into the various types of mechanized equipment available.

mechanization

A company should not make warehousing decisions once and then take them for granted; rather, the company should monitor productivity regularly during warehouse operations. While monitoring methods vary widely, the company should set goals and standards for costs and order-handling efficiency and then measure actual performance in an attempt to optimize the warehouse's productivity. By improving productivity, a company can improve its resource use; increase cash flow, profits, and return on investments; and provide its customers with better service.

productivity

To begin a productivity program, a company should divide warehouse operations into functional areas and measure each area's productivity, utilization, and performance, focusing on improvements in labor, equipment, and facilities and making comparisons with standards if they exist. Repeating measurements can show relative trends. There is no single measure of warehouse productivity, but the method the company chooses must have the following attributes: validity, coverage, comparability, completeness, usefulness, compatibility, and cost-effectiveness.

resources   The resources a warehouse uses when measuring productivity are labor, facilities, equipment, energy, and financial investment. In a company-owned warehouse, the functions the company measures are receiving, putaway, storage, replenishment, order selection, checking, packing and marking, staging and order consolidation, shipping, and clerical and administration.

improvements   Four methods for improving warehouse productivity are recommended.[2] First, reduce distances traveled through the warehouse by examining the planning of facility stock location, data handling, and materials handling. Second, increase the size of the units the facility handles, possibly by working with marketing to encourage larger customer orders. Third, seek round-trip use for warehouse equipment. Finally, improve cubic utilization by increasing the storage space. The firm may also improve productivity by improving the lighting, clearing blocked aisles, changing task orientations, and efficiently handling information.

Firms could also view productivity from a customer service perspective. Such measurements could include the percentage of orders the company filled correctly, lost records, or stockouts. Regardless of the criteria, the company should utilize this information as feedback to correct any problems in materials storage and movement.

computers   Many firms are using warehouse computers to solve problems and make decisions. Functions for which a firm can effectively use computers include sales and cost analysis, calculation of order cycle time, inventory control, traffic management, and layout planning. A firm's customer service program can also use them to inform customers and internal managers of order progress, damage situations, and transportation. Terminals located at various distribution stages can quickly provide order status information (see Figure 7–10). Companies can also retain operational control through computer links with a public or contract warehouse.

Using a voice-recognition system, Boeing's warehouse efficiency and receiving accuracy were improved. (See the Logistics Profile at the beginning of this chapter.) Receiving clerks speak to the computer to enter and verify inbound product information. The system has enabled Boeing to eliminate data entry clerks and improve inventory accuracy.

THE OWNERSHIP DECISION

Earlier in this chapter we stated that one important warehousing decision is whether to use private or public warehousing. In other words, should the company purchase or build its own warehouse or warehouses, or should it rent public warehouse space on an as-needed basis? Both approaches have advantages and disadvantages.

In 1992 companies stored approximately 70 percent of finished goods inventory in private warehouses, 20 percent in public warehouses, and 8 percent in transportation vehicles (in transit). By the year 2000, private warehousing will decrease to 63 percent, and public and in-transit storage will increase to 22 percent and 13 percent, respectively.[3]

variable cost   Figure 7–11 shows a general cost comparison between a public warehouse and a private warehouse. As we can see, the public warehouse is all variable cost. As the volume of throughput in the warehouse increases, the company has to rent

FIGURE 7-10 The Computerized Warehouse

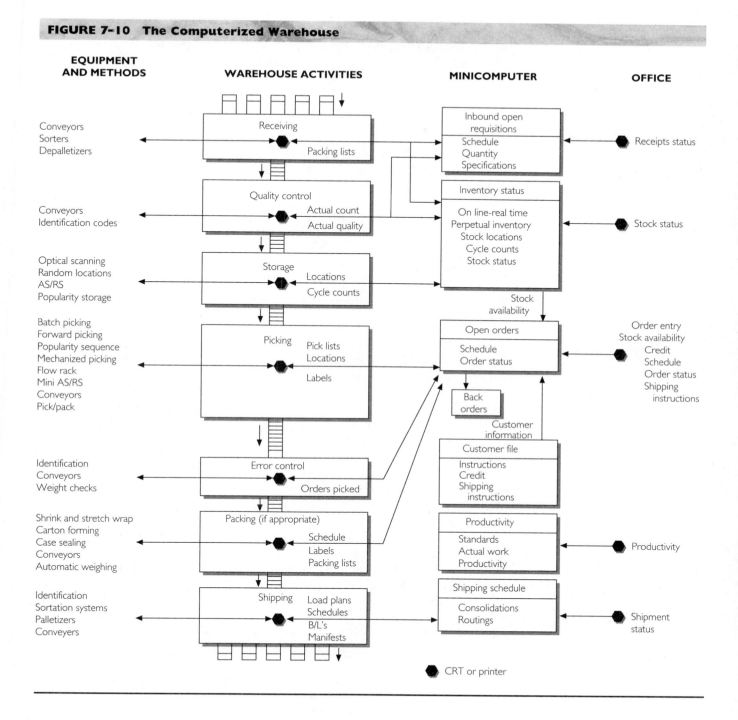

more space. This space is available at a specific charge per square foot or per cubic foot. Thus, the cost will rise proportionately to the amount that the company stores in the warehouse. The cost function is linear in this instance. As the next

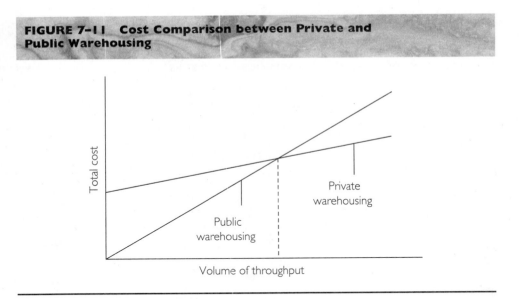

FIGURE 7–11   Cost Comparison between Private and Public Warehousing

section explains, obtaining lower rates for larger volumes in a public warehouse may be possible, but the curve will taper off at the upper end. The general relationship will remain the same.

fixed cost The private warehouse, on the other hand, has a fixed cost element, which we can attribute to elements such as property taxes and depreciation, in its cost structure. The variable portion of the warehouse operating cost would usually increase more slowly than the cost of the public warehouse because of the profit and the cost of marketing the public facility. Consequently, at some point the two cost functions will meet, or be equal. Generally, at lower output volumes, the public warehouse is the best alternative. As volume increases, companies are able to use private facilities more efficiently; that is, they can spread the fixed costs over the large output volumes.

This is a somewhat simplistic view of the situation confronting many firms, particularly large multiple-product-line companies that may be involved with anywhere from 5 to 100 warehouses. However, for two reasons, such a simplistic perspective may be fairly realistic even for more complex situations. First, companies often add warehouses one at a time, and, because of different market and cost circumstances, the choice in each new instance could be between private and public. Second, even when a company is adding more than one warehouse, the locational circumstances are often quite different and require the company to analyze each warehouse in terms of the ownership question.

At this point it would be appropriate to investigate some characteristics of firms and their products that result in their using private or public warehousing. Table 7–2 summarizes these characteristics or factors.

throughput volume Because of fixed costs, the private warehouse situation requires a relatively high throughput volume to make the warehouse economical. Since the fixed costs occur irrespective of use, the company must have a volume sufficient to "spread out" the fixed cost so that the private warehouse's average cost (fixed plus variable) is lower than the public facility's. This analysis implies two assumptions. One

TABLE 7-2 Firm Characteristics Affecting the Ownership Decision

Firm Characteristics	Private	Public
Throughput volume	High	Low
Demand variability	Stable	Fluctuating
Market density	High	Low
Special physical control	Yes	No
Customer service required	High	Low
Security requirements	High	Low
Multiple use needed	Yes	No

assumption, as Figure 7–11 indicates, is that the variable cost per unit (the slope of the function) for the private warehouse is less than the variable cost per unit for the public warehouse. Otherwise the private warehouse would never be less expensive. The other assumption is that the usage rate or throughput is stable throughout most of the year. If this is not true, then the company will have problems with the size decision and will be unable to utilize its space efficiently.

Stability of demand is often a critical factor in private warehousing, as it is in private trucking. Many products have seasonal sales. However, many large firms and some smaller firms have multiple-product lines, and this helps to stabilize the warehouse throughput to build the volume necessary for an economical private warehouse. Examples would be companies like General Foods or General Mills. When coffee sales drop off in the summer, they sell more tea for iced-tea drinkers.

stable demand

Another factor conducive to private warehousing is a dense market area relatively close to the warehouse or numerous vendors relatively close to a physical supply warehouse. As a previous section indicated, rates for small shipments (LTL or LCL) are relatively high per mile. Therefore, paying the relatively high small-shipment rates quickly uses up the savings that usually accrue by shipping in bulk (CL or TL) to a warehouse. Consequently, in low-population-density areas, firms often find using several public warehouses in different locales more economical than "putting together" enough volume for a private warehouse and having to serve a rather broad geographical area.

dense market area

An additional reason why a private warehouse might benefit a firm more is for control purposes. This can encompass physical control for such things as security or refrigeration and service control for customers and plants. Certain raw materials and finished goods are highly susceptible to theft or to loss of value from damage or spoilage. Although public warehouses are usually reputable firms and must exercise care in storing goods, the chances of loss may be higher than with private warehouses. Even if the public warehousing company pays for losses, the loss of customer goodwill or production efficiencies may be too great. In some regions, public warehousing firms will not store particular products because of their hazardous nature or for some other reason. If a firm manufacturing such products decides that storage in that region is important, the only option will be to use a private facility. Customer service competition is another control factor favoring private warehousing. Although this rationale can lead to too much private warehousing, it nevertheless has become an increasingly important justification for private warehousing. This is particularly true with more sophisticated computer-based information systems that coordinate inventory control and order processing.

control

Quality Quest—Error Reduction

The penalty for a misshipment going to a JIT assembly line was sufficiently severe that one distribution warehouse made a commitment to try to eliminate errors through corrective measures and training.

The company uses a technique known as variation reduction, which involves not only tracking errors but also eliminating their cause. This approach forces managers to go beyond the usual practice of merely putting a band-aid on the problem.

Pareto analysis helped to identify the most frequent handling errors; mistakes in outbound loading topped the list. Getting at the causes has helped the company learn a lot about its processes and its operations.

When the number of wrong putaway locations spiked recently, for example, management traced the problem to the application of duplicate labels on incoming materials. Digging deeper, they identified a miscommunication between the shipper and the warehouse.

Because errors can often result from occasional carelessness, part of the company's training strategy involves constant reinforcement. "If you don't make quality an important issue, why should you expect your workers to care about it?" says one company manager.

Another key aspect of the program is its focus on successes, not just failures. A worker who makes no mistakes in a particular month receives special recognition. Top people also achieve team leader status in the organization. Management reasons that by moving such outstanding performers to positions of influence and authority, the entire company benefits.

SOURCE: "One Firm's Strategy for Error Reduction," *Modern Materials Handling* (mid-May 1994): 28. Copyright © 1994 by Cahners Publishing, Division of Reed Elsevier Inc. Reprinted with permission.

Competition through customer service is an increasingly viable force that will justify varying strategies.

multiple use   One final justification for private warehousing may be combining this facility's use with the firm's other regional needs. For example, sales representatives and customer service representatives can have offices in the same building, with a lower total cost than having offices in two local facilities. The firm would have to combine this consideration with other cost justifications.

Companies currently using or contemplating using private warehousing find that the preceding characteristics interact to justify their use of private warehousing. Because they have volume, stability, dense markets, and the need to exercise control, firms with multiple-product lines often find private warehousing particularly economical for physical distribution. And because they usually have multiple plant operations, they also find private warehousing most economical for physical supply.

At this point, we might ask if public warehousing is ever economical. The answer is yes. In fact, if we reflect on the characteristics that made private warehousing economical, we can find many firms for whom public warehousing is most economical. A firm wishing to use public warehousing should know the various services such warehousing offers, as well as such things as regulation and pricing practices. Before covering these topics, the next two sections examine the importance of public warehousing.

PUBLIC WAREHOUSING

The previous section mentioned the growth of private warehousing in conjunction with customer service competition. This does not mean that public warehousing has declined or even maintained the status quo. Instead, public warehousing has grown and prospered, and has been a very dynamic and changing industry. In particular, public warehousing for general merchandise, which most companies would use most frequently, has grown rapidly. The largest users of public warehousing are retail chain stores, because of their product volume and their use of warehousing with other functions, such as purchasing and transportation to various outlets.[4]

A company with no large inventory accumulations or a very seasonal need for warehousing space could not utilize a private warehouse consistently and efficiently. A company shipping in small quantities for long distances (to dispersed customers or plants) would also usually find a public warehouse more economical, as would a firm entering a new market area where the sales level and stability are uncertain. Such conditions will usually necessitate using a public warehouse until the firm effectively penetrates the market. If the market venture is successful and experience shows the necessary volume and stability, then the firm can institute private warehousing.

Rationale for Public Warehousing

The first and most significant reason for using public warehousing is financial; it requires no or limited capital investment by the company. The company must accomplish any capital investment only after careful planning. Even though interest rates have dropped, they remain highly volatile; this will have a considerable effect on a project's return on investment. When a company builds, it establishes a long-term financial commitment. Therefore, the firm incurs capital payback risks through continued profitable use or sale of the facility. This assumes that the firm has adequately forecast and located consumer demand and concentration, and that technological breakthroughs in construction, transportation, or warehouse systems will not make the facility obsolete. For automated warehouses, the consideration of facility obsolescence becomes even more acute. A firm having made inaccurate predictions might have to sell or lease a warehouse to continue capital payback. By using public warehousing, companies can avoid the capital investment and financial risks of owning their own warehouses.

limited capital investment

A second advantage of public warehousing is flexibility. A firm can rent space for thirty-day periods, enabling the firm to react quickly to movements in demand or changes in the quality of transportation services. Exploring new markets requires location flexibility. Public warehousing enables a firm to immediately launch in, expand in, or pull out of new, untried markets without lingering distribution costs.

flexibility

Public Warehousing Services

Public warehouse personnel can perform such tasks as testing, assembly, price marking, and lot number marking. In addition, they offer packaging, order picking, stretch wrapping, order fulfillment, and EDI transmissions. Contract warehousing, a public warehousing subgroup, provides these highly specialized services only to major or special accounts. Contract warehousing can offer a feasible alternative to private warehousing. Public warehousing can provide, at the right price, almost all of the services that are available in private warehousing.

In addition, a public warehouse or a public warehouse manager at a private facility can offer two traditional public warehousing services: a bonding service and field warehousing. In both instances, the public warehouse manager is responsible for goods, issues a receipt for them, and cannot release the goods unless the requester meets certain conditions.

bonded warehousing In bonded warehousing, the user is usually interested in delaying the payment of taxes or tariffs, or even avoiding their payment altogether. Because taxes are relatively high on certain items such as cigarettes and liquor, the seller, who is liable for the taxes, may want to postpone paying them until the goods are immediately ready for sale. The same may be true of imported items that a seller needs to hold in inventory before sale. If a public warehouse holds the items in bonded custody, the seller does not have to pay the tax or duty until the warehouse releases the items.

In special cases, items may be imported and later exported without entering the "stream of commerce." In such instances, if a warehouse holds the items in bond, the seller may avoid the tariff altogether. The alternative would be to apply for a rebate after exporting the goods. Using free trade zones or free port areas accomplishes essentially the same thing. Sellers can import goods to these points and pay no tariff if they later reexport them.

field warehouse A field warehouse situation occurs when a firm requests a receipt for goods stored in a public warehouse or under a public warehouse manager's supervision in a private warehouse. The firm usually plans to use the warehouse manager's receipt as collateral for a loan. The receipt is a negotiable instrument whereby title to the goods is transferable. This service is attractive to individuals or companies that have accumulated inventory and that need working capital. While most attractive to small and medium-size companies, it is a potentially valuable service for all companies.

All in all, public warehousing today offers many valuable services, from the traditional storage function to complete inventory management and associated customer services. A dynamic dimension of the logistics industry, public warehousing offers the logistics manager many possible alternatives. An additional public warehousing area is legal control, which we will consider in the next section.

Public Warehousing Regulation

In spite of public warehousing's for-hire or public nature, the government has exercised very little control over this industry's affairs. This is in sharp contrast to the transportation industry's for-hire segment, particularly the common carrier. There are probably a number of reasons for the difference in regulatory control, but the underlying cause is that the warehousing industry has never caused public clamor for regulation by discriminating against its users, as was the case in the 19th-century rail industry.

liability Several regulatory acts have affected public warehousing. The most comprehensive and important was the *Uniform Warehouse Receipts Act of 1912.* This act did several things. First, it defined the warehouse manager's legal responsibility. The public warehouse operator is liable only for exercising *reasonable* care. So if the public warehouse manager refused to pay for damages he or she felt were basically beyond his or her control, the user would have the *burden of proof* to attempt to show that the warehouse manager was liable.

Once again, this contrasts sharply with the common carrier situation, wherein the carrier bears the burden of proof when damage occurs and has only several allowable excuses from liability. This does not mean that the public warehouse assumes no responsibility for damage or loss—that is, liability. Rather, the situation is one of relative degrees of liability, and the comparison simply shows the transportation industry's special case.

In addition to establishing the public warehouse manager's legal responsibility, the Uniform Warehouse Receipts Act defined the types of receipts that the public warehouse manager can issue for items stored. The act recognized two basic types of receipts—negotiable and nonnegotiable. As we indicated previously, if the receipt is negotiable, then the title to the goods the public warehouse manager holds is transferable. So, in effect, the "holder" of the receipt owns the goods; in other words, the holder can sign over the receipt like a check.

receipts

The act also set forth certain receipt information requirements. Required information included the warehouse location, the receipt's issuance date, the warehousing service rate, a description of the goods, signatures of the parties, and the instrument type. These requirements primarily protect the public warehousing user and anyone taking advantage of the receipt's negotiable aspects.

While public warehouse regulation and service is important, the logistics manager is also very much interested in public warehousing rates or charges, which is the topic of the next section.

Public Warehousing Rates

The public warehouse sells service in terms of a facility with fixed dimensions. The warehouse usually sells the service on a space basis per time period—for example, dollars per square foot per time period. Although the warehouse company in a sense has a less complicated pricing structure than a transportation company does, the logistics manager should understand the basic factors affecting rates, keeping in mind that rates are negotiable.

Value. As we indicated previously, a public warehouse has a certain legally defined liability for goods stored. The risk increases with higher-valued goods, and rates generally reflect the higher risk of higher-valued goods.

The logistics manager may be able to reduce his or her rate by using protective packaging to decrease the chance of damage, and also by marking packages to specify care in handling and perhaps in position. If the public warehouse believes that these efforts diminish risk, the rates will be reduced.

Fragility. Warehouse rates must consider commodities' general susceptibility to damage because of the risk to the warehouse company. The logistics manager may reduce the risk of damage by using protective packaging, and consequently reduce the warehouse rates. Once again, the trade-off is between the warehouse rate reduction and the increased packaging cost.

Damage to Other Goods. In a public warehouse setting, incompatible stored goods always run the risk of damaging each other. In a sense, this is a two-way risk. Your product may damage another, or your product may be particularly susceptible to damage from some other product. Chemicals and food are obvious examples, but other more subtle ones exist. For example, automobile tires may have an adverse effect on certain products, even causing color change in some instances. Using proper packaging may reduce the risk, but once again the logistics manager should view this in a trade-off context.

Volume and Regularity.   While the cost of using a public warehouse is generally variable, the warehouse company itself will experience fixed costs. Therefore, use volume and regularity will influence the rates, since the company can "spread" its fixed costs; that is, volume and regularity will help achieve efficiencies in terms of lower per-unit costs. Many public warehouse users, who may use public warehouses to handle peak seasonal demands on their own facilities, may be unable to offer regular use. In other cases, a logistics manager may be able, by proper planning, to use the public warehouse systematically, consequently reducing the warehouse rates.

Weight Density.   Warehouses generally set rates in terms of space, usually square footage. However, warehouses will sometimes base charges on weight density. In other words, like transportation carriers, warehouses will assess charges on a hundredweight basis. Therefore, the warehouse manager will have to assess higher charges for light and bulky items. Even users whose charges the warehouse does not assess in this fashion should be concerned about weight density because it affects their ability to use the space they rent efficiently. For example, lightweight assembled items will use up a lot of space per unit of weight. Perhaps the seller could store the same number of items in a smaller space if the items were packaged unassembled.

Services.   Public warehousing is a comprehensive and sophisticated industry today, willing and able to offer a variety of services beyond the general storage function. Such services have associated charges—and the more service, usually the higher the charge. However, having the public warehouse provide the services may be less costly, particularly in low-sales-density areas, than providing them privately.

   As the preceding discussions show, logistics managers can influence the rates they pay for public warehouses. While these rate-influencing opportunities require analysis to prove their economic justification, the logistics manager should explore the options nevertheless.

CONTRACT WAREHOUSING

A growing public warehousing trend is the use of contract or third-party warehousing. It is estimated that contract warehouses will hold 5.7 percent of the finished goods by 2000, up from 4.4 percent in 1992.[5] Contract warehousing is a customized version of public warehousing in which an external company provides a combination of logistics services that the firm itself has traditionally provided. The contract warehousing company specializes in providing efficient, economical, and accurate distribution services.

   The logistics manager must differentiate contract warehousing from general public warehousing. Firms desiring "above average" quality and service should use contract warehousing. These warehouses are designed to adhere to higher standards and specialized handling needs for products such as pharmaceuticals, electronics, and high-value manufactured goods. On the other hand, firms desiring average product handling service levels should use public warehousing. In essence, contract warehousing is a partnership between the manufacturer and the warehousing firm. Because of these partnerships, contract warehousing companies service a smaller client base than traditional public warehousing companies do. The contract warehouse provides space, labor, and equipment tailored to handle a client's specific product needs.

The contract warehousing company makes a market basket of customized logistics services available to a limited number of warehouse users. Examples of these services include storage, break-bulk, consolidation, order assortment, spot stocking, in-transit mixing, inventory control, transportation arrangement, logistics information systems, and any additional logistics support services a user requires. Rather than providing only storage, the contract warehousing firm provides the logistics services package the user requires to support a firm's logistics channel.

customized services

Even though contract warehousing and distribution has grown substantially, the concept is still in its infancy in terms of overall understanding and use. In the past, companies needing to cut costs turned to the manufacturing operations. Companies contracted out component or subassembly production or outsourced overseas where labor costs were lower. Presently, companies are turning to logistics operations for potential cost reductions. By using contract warehousing services, a company can also outsource its logistics operations. By contracting out their secondary business functions, firms can concentrate on manufacturing and marketing.

Contract warehousing has many strategic, financial, and operational advantages over private or traditional public warehousing. The main advantage is cost reduction. We will elaborate on this in the next section. Other important advantages are as follows.

Compensate for Seasonality in Products.   A contract distributor can handle the peaks and troughs typical in seasonal industries more effectively than a private distributor can. For example, a contract distributor may have several contracts with companies having peak sales in the winter and virtually no sales in the summer. To offset this cycle, the distributor also contracts with companies having peak sales in the summer and virtually no sales in the winter. This alternating pattern of peak sales allows the contract distributor to utilize its equipment and capacity more effectively throughout the year than could a private warehouse handling one-season products.

Increase Geographical Coverage.   Contract distribution can increase a company's geographical market coverage through a network of facilities. A company could have warehouse locations in different regions without investing in numerous private facilities. Ideally, a contract warehouse firm would have strategically located facilities and services, enabling the customer to deal with one warehousing management and one set of warehousing logistics service standards in different warehousing locations.

The reason for the decline in private warehousing is due, in part, to the rising use of contract warehousing. Many companies are reducing their private warehouses down to only a few centralized facilities and contracting out regional market coverage to a contract warehousing firm. With this private and contract warehousing network, a company can remain in direct control of the centralized facilities, while using the contract warehouses to lower direct labor costs and increase geographical market coverage.

Gain Flexibility in Testing New Markets.   Contract logistics flexibility can enhance customer service. Firms promoting existing products or introducing new ones can use short-term contract distribution services to test market demand for the products. When a company wants to enter a new market area, building a new distribution facility could take years. However, by using a contract distribution network, the company could immediately use an existing facility to service customers in the new area.

Gain Management Expertise and Dedicated Resources.   Contracting out is a unique opportunity to hand a company's logistics function over to a team of managers who are distribution experts. These experts can provide innovative distribution ideas and cost-reducing product-handling procedures. For some contracts, the contract distributor will dedicate space, workers, and materials handling equipment exclusively to the client's products. In this way, the contract warehouse is like several different private warehouses under one roof.

Permit Off-Balance-Sheet Financing.   Hiring a contract distributor to perform distribution operations can increase a company's return on investment (ROI), allowing the company to invest only in those assets that support its primary business. Physical distribution assets for a private warehouse yield the lowest ROI of all corporate assets, tie up corporate funds, and sometimes are not fully utilized. In addition, these assets represent an opportunity cost to invest funds elsewhere. Contracting out the distribution services takes these assets off the balance sheet, increasing a company's ROI. Even though these assets are on the contractor's balance sheet, they are dedicated to the company's logistics needs.

Reduce Transportation Costs.   Because they handle a high volume of products from different client accounts, contract warehouses offer significant freight savings by consolidating freight into full truckloads (TL).

Along with its advantages, contract warehousing has some disadvantages. The major one is losing control of the logistics function. Losing direct control of operations is one of a company's greatest fears when considering the use of contract distribution services. With contract warehousing, the company exerts less control over personnel, hiring practices, policies, and procedures. On the same line, companies with high-value products such as pharmaceuticals must be very cautious to reduce employee theft as much as possible. Hiring an outside company to handle products is more risky than using a private facility.

Other obstacles to the use of contract warehousing include contract costs possibly exceeding private costs and remaining unjustified, management and union acceptance problems, lack of product volume, incompatibility with company needs, and insufficient understanding of contract warehousing and its value. Table 7–3 shows the results of a survey on reasons for and against outsourcing a company's logistics functions.

TABLE 7–3   Reasons For and Against Outsourcing Logistics Functions

Reasons for Outsourcing

Cost reduction	60%
Lower labor costs	49%
Flexibility	31%
Better information systems	30%
Improved delivery/service	23%

Obstacles to Outsourcing

Loss of control	18%
Not cost justified	11%
Management/union acceptance	6%
Lack of volume	6%
Inflexible/incompatible	5%
Don't understand/recognize value	4%

SOURCE: Arthur D. Little, "Survey on Third-Party Logistics," *Traffic Management* (October 1988): 6.

Contract versus Private Warehousing

The overriding question a company must ask when comparing an internal private warehouse with an external contract warehouse is, Can the contract warehouse provide higher service performance for the same or less money than our private warehouse? If the answer is yes, the contract warehouse should be the optimum choice. If the answer is no, then the company must evaluate the trade-offs between the better service's higher costs. A company can quantitatively measure a contract warehouse's service performance level by measuring the number of cases the warehouse ships per hour, attainment of a standard fill rate percentage, and percentage of on-time deliveries.

The answer to the above question is more often yes because contract distributors whose management focuses on maximizing warehouse efficiency can run their operations more cheaply than privately operated ones. In addition, contract warehouse wage rates and benefits are lower than those in a manufacturer's privately owned warehouse. When companies combine these reasons, the cost of contract warehousing may be up to 37 percent less expensive than that of private warehousing. Table 7–4 shows the percentage breakdown of private warehousing costs for 1995.

Privately owned warehouses tend to operate as cost centers, while contract distributors operate their facilities as profit centers. The private warehouse option might seem favorable in that this cost structure has no added profit built in. However, the contract distributor has to make a profit in order to run its operations. This profit orientation motivates the contract distributor to operate as efficiently as possible. User fees reimburse the distributor for operating costs and provide a profit margin. In contrast, a company's product sales pay *only* for a private warehouse's operating costs.

TABLE 7–4   Private Warehousing Costs Projected for 1995

Category	
Warehouse labor	39.5%
Direct storage	23.2%
Handling equipment	10.3%
Utilities	5.3%
Administration	11.6%
General administration	10.2%

SOURCE: B. LaLonde and R. Delaney, *Trends in Warehousing Costs, Management, and Strategy* (Oak Brook, IL: Warehousing Education and Research Council, 1993): 6.

Cost Comparisons

A company choosing between private warehousing and contract warehousing must compare each option's operating costs. In order for this comparison to be as accurate as possible, the company must make a complete and comparable cost analysis for both warehousing options. For example, an analysis that excludes the private warehouse's cost of depreciation would underestimate the true operating costs and bias the analysis. All warehouse types (public, private, and contract) generally incur the same cost elements. The differences are due to variations in the accounting methods a company uses to calculate each cost element.

Performing a cost comparison analysis is complex. We can further divide two main warehouse expenditures, direct handling and direct storage, to illustrate this complexity. Direct handling expenses refer to all costs a company incurs when moving products into, through, and out of the warehouse (variable expenses). Direct handling activities include unloading inbound/loading outbound vehicles, palletizing/sorting goods, placing goods in storage, and filling orders. Direct storage expenses occur regardless of product volume (fixed expenses). Table 7–5 shows a complete breakdown of these expenditures, along with examples of each.

In addition to determining the least costly warehousing option, the interested company should visit a contract warehouse to observe the facility, operations, equipment, personnel, and management.

The Contract

Before using third-party services, the user or company purchasing an outside distribution company's services negotiates a contract with the contract facility operator. A legal agreement between the two parties, the contract specifically states the following information: the time period the contract covers, the operator's service fee, the specific services upon which the parties have agreed, terms and conditions, responsibilities, performance measurements. and default clauses. The user must provide large amounts of "sensitive" information, such as lists of customers, vendors, and sales, to enable the third party to function effectively within the parameters the contract establishes. Companies use state-of-the-art information transfer technology to achieve third-party warehousing efficiencies in accurately filling specific customer orders.

TABLE 7-5   Breakdown of Direct Storage Expenses

I. DIRECT HANDLING EXPENSE
   A. Warehouse Labor
      1. Direct payments to employees (wages, bonuses)
      2. Compensated fringe benefits (pension, insurance)
      3. Compensated time off (holidays, sick pay)
      4. Statutory payroll taxes (worker's compensation)
      5. Purchased labor (temporary labor)
      6. Fees and compensated time (training)
   B. Handling Equipment
      1. Lite trucks and attachments (fuel, parts maintenance)
      2. Special-purpose handling equipment (shrink-wrap equipment, conveyors)
   C. Other Handling Expenses
      1. Pallets (to load/store products)
      2. Supplies (small tools, tape, printed forms)
      3. Detention/demurrage (transportation carrier charges for unloading delays)
      4. Recouping warehouse damage
      5. Trash hauling (recycling)

II. DIRECT STORAGE EXPENSE
   A. Facility
      1. Rent or depreciation and interest
      2. Real estate taxes
      3. Insurance
      4. Exterior maintenance (the building itself)
   B. Grounds (areas surrounding facility)
   C. Storage Equipment (racks, shelving)
   D. Facility Modification (to accommodate a change in product line/operations)
   E. Utilities (heat, electricity)
   F. Interior Maintenance (painting, repairs)
   G. Security (alarm systems, guard service)

SOURCE: DCW-USA, Inc., *How To Determine Total Warehousing Costs* (1990): 24.

A primary contract element is space. A company can contract space through a lease, flexible space rental, or a sublease agreement. With a lease agreement, the user leases the facility for a certain time period, usually one year. The fee includes fixed costs such as lighting, heat, and property maintenance, while the user provides labor. A flexible space rental agreement occurs when the warehouse charges the user only for the space or actual square footage the company uses. Warehouses charge user costs on a per unit basis: costs per pallet, per hundredweight (cwt), or per cubic foot, for example. In a sublease agreement, the contract facility provides both the management and labor for the user. In all three agreements, the user may promise to conduct a minimum monetary or volume amount of business with the contract warehouse during the contract's life.

Other factors that a company should consider when assessing needed services and cost allocations include materials handling equipment and clerical or office services. The type and amount of materials handling equipment a company will use depends upon the inbound and outbound transportation mode, unit size (item, case, pallet), and product variety of the stock-keeping units (SKUs). Clerical or office services refers to processing documents such as bills of lading, purchase orders, and inventory records. The contract should state which party is responsible for these functions.

Liability

When drawing up a contract, a company and a warehouse must include the liability issue. With respect to public warehousing, the Uniform Commercial Code (UCC) states that the warehouse operator is liable for any damage, loss, or injury to the goods his or her failure to exercise reasonable care might cause. Unless the warehouse and its client agree otherwise, the warehouse operator is not liable for unavoidable damages. If unavoidable damages occur, the company owning the goods assumes the liability. However, in a contract arrangement, the warehouse operator can choose to assume the risk for unavoidable damages. To compensate for this added responsibility, the warehouse operator will charge the user a higher contract rate.

Transportation Companies

By diversifying their regular operations, transportation companies have begun to provide third-party logistics services. Most large national motor carriers now offer warehousing services such as packaging and light assembly. The Contract Distribution Division of Federal Express has taken third-party logistics one step further by providing services such as freight audits, order entry system operation, inventory management, and picking and packing of goods. This type of system is replacing some manufacturers' in-house logistics departments at a lower operating cost.

A company finalizes its decision to utilize a third-party distributor by comparing the total cost with the third party to the total cost without this service. The logistics manager must weigh the third party's advantages against its disadvantages. The third-party system's total cost will be the determining factor.

THE NUMBER OF WAREHOUSES

One of the logistics manager's most important tasks is to decide how many warehouses to have in the system. As was the case when examining private versus public warehousing, evaluating the general cost trade-offs in such decisions would probably be best.

increasing the number of warehouses

Figure 7–12 depicts how increasing the number of warehouses in a logistics system affects important physical distribution costs. As the number of warehouses increases, transportation cost and the cost of lost sales decline, whereas inventory cost and warehousing cost increase.

Consolidating shipments into carload or truckload lots with lower rates per hundredweight decreases transportation costs. On the outbound side, increasing the number of warehouses brings the warehouses closer to the customer and market area, reducing both transportation distance and costs.

Warehousing costs increase because the total amount of space always increases with a larger number of warehouses. For example, a firm with only one warehouse that has 200,000 square feet would not be able to operate at the same sales level with two facilities having 100,000 square feet each. Maintenance, offices, lavatories, lunchrooms, and other facilities need a certain, almost fixed amount of space. Also, aisles use up a higher proportion of space in smaller warehouses.

FIGURE 7-12 Logistics Cost Related to the Number of Warehouses

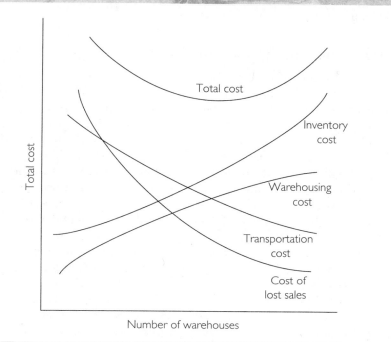

In addition, since a company increasing its number of warehouses carries more total inventory, inventory cost increases. The larger amounts of inventory require more total space. More inventory is necessary because the difficulty of predicting demand may force a company with two or more warehouses to maintain overly high levels of a product line's slower-moving items at each facility. Moreover, as companies increase their number of warehouses, growing product lines will likely require more total space, even at the same sales volumes.

As Figure 7–12 indicates, as the number of warehouses increases, total cost will generally decline. However, total costs begin to rise as increasing inventory and warehousing costs offset decreasing transportation costs and the cost of lost sales. Of course, the total cost curve and the range of warehouses it reflects will be different for each company.

Companies often increase their number of warehouses to improve customer service, to reduce transportation costs, and to provide storage for increased product volumes. Surprisingly, decreasing a system's number of warehouses is becoming the preferred way to met the same needs. Warehouse building and operating costs are great. In contrast, by reducing the number of warehouses, a company can eliminate those unproductive facilities that incur wasteful costs. Combining the utilization of fewer warehouses with a reliable transportation system can improve customer service and lower transportation costs through consolidation opportunities. With fewer warehouses and greater volumes of products to move, a company must increase throughput rates or inventory turns. By increasing its number of inventory turns, a company will lower its inventory carrying costs.

decreasing the number of warehouses

The next section explores factors that affect the number of warehouses. Keep in mind that a company has to consider a total cost framework when deciding on its number of warehouse facilities.

Factors Affecting the Number of Warehouses

customer service

One factor affecting the number of warehouses is the need for customer service. The need for rapid customer service in local market areas usually correlates strongly with the degree of product substitutability. If competitors are giving a market area rapid service, a company with inferior customer service lead times will lose sales volume. The company may waste sales promotion and advertising efforts if customers are unable to purchase the product when they want it.

Another closely related factor is inadequate transportation. In other words, if a company needs rapid customer service (low lead times), fast transport service is a possible alternative. If adequate transportation service is unavailable, the company may add another warehouse. Logistics managers who feel that transportation service is deteriorating often investigate warehouses as an alternative.

small-quantity buyers

An additional factor favoring decentralized warehousing is small-quantity buyers. The cost of shipping many LCL and LTL shipments from a centralized warehouse to customers would be much higher than that of shipping CL or TL to decentralized warehouses and then shipping LCL or LTL to customers in the local market. As we indicated previously, retailers and wholesalers, increasingly conscious of the cost of maintaining inventory, often wish to buy smaller quantities more frequently. If they desire the same approximate lead time, then a company may need to warehouse goods in a closer location. This suggests the distribution channel's importance to warehousing requirements. If small retailers and wholesalers are a part of the channel, then the company can expect small orders and a possible need for more warehouses.

A final factor favoring decentralized warehousing would be instances when customers allow insufficient lead times before being stocked out. Also, if demand is erratic, decentralized warehousing will help a company to prevent stockouts.

SUMMARY

- Warehousing plays a strategic role in attaining overall logistics cost and service goals.
- The basic rationale for warehousing includes transportation consolidation, product mixing, service, contingency protection, and smoothing.
- The basic warehousing decisions involve ownership, design and layout, centralization versus decentralization, number, location, size, items stocked, and employee safety.
- Movement and storage are the primary warehouse operations.
- The design and layout of a warehouse must allow space for receiving, shipping, order picking, order assembly, storage, offices, and miscellaneous activities.
- The major principles of warehouse layout design are: use one-story facilities, move goods in a straight line, use efficient materials handling equipment, use an effective storage plan, minimize aisle space, and use the maximum height of the building.

- The decision to use private or public warehousing examines total cost and is affected by throughput volume, demand variability, market density, special physical control requirements, customer service needs, security, and multiple-use needs.
- Public warehousing is a variable component in the logistics system and provides a wide array of services.
- Public warehousing is regulated as to rates, liability, and receipts.
- Contract warehousing, or logistics outsourcing, provides customized services under contract with a storer of goods. The major reason for using contract warehousing is cost reduction, and the major obstacle is loss of control.
- The greater the number of warehouses in a logistics system, the lower the transportation and lost sales cost, but the higher the warehousing and inventory cost.

STUDY QUESTIONS

1. During the 1990s, many companies are focusing upon the logistics pipeline to meet their customers' needs for shorter lead times or response times. How can warehousing help companies to achieve quicker response times?

2. Some managers argue that warehousing can aid companies in providing value-added service for their customers. What is your view of this statement?

3. Inventory models and macro presentations of logistics costs generally consider warehousing to be a component of inventory carrying costs. Some individuals feel that this approach understates the importance of warehousing. What do you think?

4. The CBL Products Company, a toy manufacturer, has recently hired you as a consultant to investigate their logistics system, with particular emphasis upon warehousing. Your first assignment is to prepare a concise report that outlines the major reasons for warehousing, with a particular focus upon CBL.

5. Public warehousing use is increasing among many large manufacturers in the 1990s. Why would a company like Procter & Gamble, which produces a wide variety of consumer products such as Crest toothpaste, Ivory and Tide soaps, Pringle's snack chips, and Prell shampoo, move toward public warehousing?

6. Movement and storage are the two basic functions that warehouses provide. The warehouse type, however, influences which of these two functions a company would emphasize in a particular warehouse. Why is this generally true?

7. Delsey Foods Company's vice president of logistics is evaluating the order picking area's layout in their new Cincinnati, Ohio, warehouse. She has asked you as director of warehousing to provide her with an overview of the alternative layout patterns, to recommend one of the three, and to justify your recommendation.

8. Efficient warehouse design is receiving more attention in many companies. Discuss the dimensions of efficiency and why it is receiving so much emphasis.

9. How is the trend toward JIT inventory control systems likely to affect the number of warehouses companies operate? Why?

10. What is contract warehousing? How does it differ from public warehousing? Why are so many companies moving toward contract warehousing?

NOTES

1. General Service Administration, *Warehouse Operations* (Washington, DC: Government Printing Office, 1964): 2.
2. Kenneth B. Ackerman, *Warehousing* (Washington, DC: Traffic Service Corporation, 1977): 162–165.
3. Bernard J. LaLonde and Robert V. Delaney, *Trends in Warehousing Costs, Management, and Strategy* (Oak Brook, IL: Warehousing Education and Research Council, 1993): 4.
4. *Public Warehouse Study* (Washington, DC: McKinsey, 1970).
5. LaLonde and Delaney, p. 4.
6. Michael G. Lepihuska, "What Is Contract Warehousing?" *Distribution Center Management* 25, no. 1 (January 1990): 2.

Case 7-1

VANITY PRODUCTS

John Vance, president of Vanity Products, is reading the latest financial results reported in the company newsletter. Every time he reads this year's financials, he recalls the company's early days and the struggle to get retailers to stock his new line of bathroom vanities, mirrors, and light fixtures. Today, the company is straining to produce enough product to meet retailer demand.

Vanity Products (VP) manufactures a variety of bathroom accessories, including vanities (medicine chests), mirrors, lighting fixtures, and shelving. The products are made of rust- and chip-resistant molded plastic and come in a variety of modern designs and colors. The plastic construction permits VP to produce a high-quality bathroom accessory at an affordable price.

In the middle 1980s, John focused the company's marketing attention on the large home center chain stores: Home Depot, Wal-Mart, Sears, and so on. Today, more than 80 percent of VP's sales are to these retail chains, and they account for 95 percent of its growth. Without these chain store customers, VP would still be a small, struggling manufacturer.

John's pleasant memories quickly fade to the realities of dealing with these large chain retailers. In the past two years, VP has been required to install EDI software that permits the buyers to assess VP's inventory data file to determine availability, to place orders, and to verify shipment status. The latest demand from one of the chains, which is a precursor of what the others will want, is for VP to reduce cycle time by shipping orders directly to the stores.

Currently, VP receives an order that is a consolidation of store orders to be served from a chain distribution warehouse. The order is sent in truckload quantity to the distribution warehouse, where the individual store order is broken out and sent to the store. Now, each store will be ordering separately, and VP is to deliver the order within five working days.

When John approached Tom White, manager of logistics, with the latest demand, Tom was not very comforting. He indicated that freight costs would certainly increase because VP would be shipping less-than-truckload quantities at higher freight rates. This higher freight cost could be offset with freight consolidation software that combines store shipments into truckload quantities for peddle runs. John liked the idea of keeping freight costs down, because VP would have great difficulty increasing prices because of competition.

However, the freight consolidation strategy would increase the shipment holding time prior to dispatch, thereby making it difficult for VP to meet the requirement that orders be delivered in five working days. Since cycle time reduction is the primary objective of the chain store's demand, any process adding to the delivery time would not be acceptable.

Tom is working on an idea to establish a series of distribution warehouses in the market areas where the chain stores are located. Tom's vision includes truckload shipments from the plants to the distribution centers, and cross-docking of products from incoming trucks to trucks delivering orders to specific stores. In addition, each distribution warehouse would maintain a minimal level of inventory to meet emergency orders placed by local stores.

John is skeptical of Tom's distribution warehouse idea because he feels it would increase capital costs, inventory levels, and transportation costs. He is not even certain it would meet the delivery time requirements.

Case Questions

1. Analyze the logistics service and cost constraints imposed on VP by the chain store's latest demand.
2. What is your opinion of Tom White's proposal for establishing a series of distribution warehouses?
3. What ownership and management structures would you recommend for the distribution warehouses?
4. Develop a process map depicting the information and product flows in Tom's proposal.

CHAPTER 8

MATERIALS HANDLING AND PACKAGING

LEARNING OBJECTIVES

After reading this chapter, you should be able to do the following:

- Discuss the effect of materials handling and packaging on logistics.

- Describe the four dimensions and the objectives of materials handling.

- Discuss the different types of materials handling equipment and the criteria used to select this equipment.

- Explain the cross-functional role of packaging in a company.

- Discuss the role of packaging in the logistics system.

- Describe the various types of packaging materials available and their relative advantages and disadvantages.

- Explain the rationale for using bar codes to identify packages.

- Discuss containerization as a packaging concept for intermodal shipments.

HOME DEPOT REQUIRES SUPPLIERS TO USE SLIPSHEETS

Beginning January 1, 1995, Home Depot's 5,000 suppliers are shipping compatible products on slipsheets, not pallets. The slipsheet is a thin piece of plastic that acts as a platform, like the pallet, to provide stability and ease of handling for a unitized load.

The wood pallet is the traditional method of shipping unitized loads in the United States. In fact, the wood pallet has been in use for approximately 50 years. Home Depot feels the time for slipsheets is now because the regulatory environment of the 1990s makes disposal of wood pallets costly and imposes criminal penalties for improper disposal of wood pallets. Also, advances in equipment technology make the use of slipsheets a viable alternative.

The switch to slipsheets was a drastic change imposed on Home Depot's suppliers. Suppliers did not have the necessary equipment to move slipsheet loads nor to stretch-wrap the loads. So why put its vendors through this traumatic operational and financial change?

The primary reason for requiring vendors to use slipsheets is the financial and environmental costs associated with pallets. The cost of a new pallet, which the vendor incorporates into the price charged Home Depot, ranges from $4.50 for a lightweight pallet to $10.00 for a heavy-duty hardwood pallet. This compares to a slipsheet cost of $0.86 for plastic and $0.56 for corrugated board. One vendor estimated that slipsheets will save $218,000 with plastic and $236,000 with corrugated slipsheets for its 60,000 SKU annual shipments.

The cost to dispose of a pallet in a landfill is about $2.50 to $4.00, depending on the landfill rates in the area. Some municipalities are placing a surcharge on pallets going to the landfill. Plastic and corrugated slipsheets are recyclable, and plastic slipsheets make four to five trips before being recycled.

To overcome these disposal costs and environmental constraints, Home Depot experimented with one-way pallet rental, pallet return programs, and mulching of the pallets, with the mulch being sold at its stores. After analyzing these alternatives with slipsheets, Home Depot concluded that the benefits of slipsheets outweighed those of the others.

Vendor resistance was the primary obstacle to Home Depot's slipsheet conversion. Vendors, including trucking companies, were reluctant to use slipsheets because they lacked experience with the technology and they lacked the equipment required to move slipsheet loads. The capital expenditures were not overwhelming: a push/pull adapter for a forklift is $5,000, and a stretch wrap machine is $15,000. Some motor carriers not equipped with the necessary equipment would break down slipsheet loads and load the individual boxes as top freight or filler freight to utilize the entire cube of the trailer.

Following successful trials by more than 200 vendors, the initial resistance to slipsheets dissipated. Vendors found that the slipsheets reduced product damage because the forklift operator must take greater care with slipsheets. Another advantage is that loading and unloading time was reduced by $2^1/_2$ hours compared to nonunitized loads.

The Home Depot stores posed another obstacle. Store employees were unaccustomed to using the push/pull attachments on the standard forklifts, and the attachments made maneuvering in the tight areas of the storerooms difficult. Working with forklift manufacturers, Home Depot developed a more user-friendly slipsheet-compatible forklift. Now the store employees embrace the slipsheet.

The decision to switch from pallets to slipsheets was a relatively easy one—the economics and environmental issues supported slipsheets. The implementation problems were operational difficulties and vendor reluctance to change. Home Depot used its market power to gain vendor acceptance and then worked with the vendors and with its own employees to solve the operational problems.

So far, the slipsheet program is a success.

SOURCE: Tom Andel, "You Must Use Slipsheets," *Transportation & Distribution* (December 1994): 69–76. Reprinted with permission of *Transportation & Distribution*, December 1994. Copyright © 1994 Penton Publishing, Inc.

The logistics system can be described as a pathway where products flow from supplier to end user. Typically, products move from the vendor through a number of intermediate facilities to the end user. This movement function is most often performed by a transportation company over long distances.

However, there is considerable product movement within a facility. This intra-facility movement, known as materials handling, is as critical to the overall efficiency of the logistics system as the intercity or intercountry movement by a transportation company. The movement of products from transport vehicles into storage and vice versa affects overall order cycle time, customer service levels, and logistics costs.

The efficiency of the materials handling process is, in part, a function of packaging. The size of and protection afforded by the package affect the type of material handling equipment used and the level of product damage incurred. The package has an impact on the stacking height of the product in the warehouse and thereby on the utilization and cost of the warehouse.

For example, a company manufacturing tailpipes and mufflers faces two different materials handling requirements. Because of their rectangular shape, the mufflers can be packed on a standard pallet that is easily handled with a forklift. The tailpipe, conversely, is not a standard shape, cannot be palletized, and requires manual handling. The materials handling system for mufflers is automated, whereas it is manual for tailpipes, and the cost of handling one unit of each product will differ.

The ability of the materials handling and warehousing system to respond to customer service policy needs plays a key role in the logistics system's overall success. In this chapter we will focus on the purposes, objectives, and underlying principles of materials handling and packaging decisions as they relate to the achievement of effective levels of customer service.

MATERIALS HANDLING

definition
Materials handling is very important to any warehouse's efficient operation, both in terms of transferring goods in and out and in moving goods to various locations in the warehouse. The term *materials handling* is somewhat difficult to define. Some people picture elaborate equipment designed to move goods in a warehouse, such as forklift trucks or conveyor equipment. Others visualize the actual manual handling of the goods. In fact, elaborate mechanical equipment, manual labor, or a combination can perform materials handling. We can think most conveniently of materials handling as *efficient short-distance movement that usually takes place within the confines of a building such as a plant or a warehouse and between a building and a transportation agency.*

In a modern logistics system, specially designed equipment most often performs this short-distance movement; hence, thinking of materials handling from an equipment perspective is not unusual. However, manual movement is also materials handling. The key factor is efficiency, whether the movement is mechanical, manual, or both. Most systems are a combination.

movement
Materials handling has four dimensions: movement, time, quantity, and space. The movement aspect of materials handling involves the conveyance of goods (raw

materials, semifinished goods, and finished goods) into and out of storage facilities as well as within such facilities. Efficient materials handling, then, means efficient movement of goods to, from, and within the storage facility.

The time dimension of materials handling is concerned with readying goods **time** for production or for customer order filling. The longer it takes to get raw materials to production, the greater the chance of work stoppage, higher inventories, and increased storage space. Likewise, the longer it takes to move finished goods to the shipping area, the longer the order cycle time and the lower the customer service.

The quantity issue addresses the varying usage and delivery rate of raw materials **quantity** and finished goods, respectively. Materials handling systems are designed to assure that the correct quantity of product is moved to meet the needs of production and customers.

Materials handling equipment consumes space in the warehouse and plant. **space** This space in a facility is fixed, and the materials handling system must utilize this space effectively. Forklifts adapted with extensions can reach 25 to 30 feet, thereby increasing the capacity utilization of the warehouse.

The materials handling area does not usually belong exclusively to the logistics manager. In a manufacturing firm, materials handling activities can occur in several additional areas, but they are most frequently the bailiwick of the production or manufacturing manager. Here we also find short-distance movements occurring in conjunction with the manufacturing process. This short-distance movement may also be manual or mechanical.

However, this text will discuss materials handling from the logistics manager's **coordination** perspective. Most often, the logistics manager's materials handling responsibility occurs in and around warehouses or plants' warehousing sections. Materials handling may require some coordination with individuals, such as the production manager, at least in the purchase of equipment and perhaps maintenance. Manufacturing and logistics may also need to interchange equipment. In designing or purchasing materials handling systems, a firm must look not only at the technology available but also at the entire organization's long-range plans.

Objectives of Materials Handling

The general objectives of materials handling, listed in Figure 8–1, apply to areas besides logistics and have varying importance for the logistics manager.

One basic materials handling objective is to increase the warehouse facility's **increase effective** usable capacity. A warehouse has fixed interior length, width, and height—that is, **capacity** cubic capacity. Utilizing as much of this space as possible will minimize the warehouse's operating cost.

The use of warehouse space usually has two aspects. One is the ability to use the building's height as much as possible. Many warehousing facilities waste much space by not storing goods as high as possible. Figure 8–2 illustrates the importance of a warehouse's vertical space. Horizontal warehouse space is usually the most obvious and easiest to fill. But the vertical dimension is also a cost factor, and a warehouse operation must utilize this space effectively in order to be efficient. The vertical dimension is, therefore, the biggest challenge. Warehouse managers must focus on cubic space, not just on floor space. Later, this chapter describes devices to effectively utilize vertical space in a warehouse.

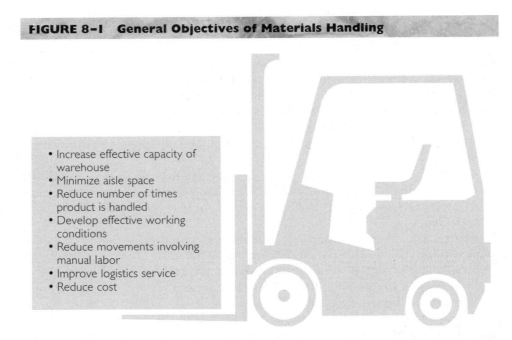

FIGURE 8-1   General Objectives of Materials Handling

- Increase effective capacity of warehouse
- Minimize aisle space
- Reduce number of times product is handled
- Develop effective working conditions
- Reduce movements involving manual labor
- Improve logistics service
- Reduce cost

In order to save space and to reduce travel time in their Mahwah distribution center, Jaguar combined the active order-picking area with reserve storage. The active picking actually takes place at the two lower levels, with reserve storage above. This enables Jaguar to utilize overhead or cube space and to store inventory up to 22 feet high in an area where cubic space is often difficult to use. Materials handling equipment and storage aids enable Jaguar to use this otherwise unusable space.[1]

A second aspect of space utilization is to minimize aisle space while avoiding aisles narrow enough to impede movement in the warehouse facility. The type of materials handling equipment a company uses will affect aisle width. Forklift trucks, for example, very often require turning space, and they may necessitate much wider aisles than required by other types of materials handling equipment. Figure 8–3 illustrates the necessity of aisle space in a storage facility. The illustration, which shows items moving out of a railcar into the warehouse, is an example of the warehouse's interface role. From the transportation equipment (railcar or tractor-trailer), the items move to a storage area. The equipment performing this short-distance movement needs adequate turning and maneuvering space. The figure also shows the need to separate items in the storage area, for access purposes.

improve operating efficiency   Another materials handling objective is to reduce the number of times a company handles goods. As we noted in our discussion of warehousing, a company usually moves products into a warehouse and places them in a storage area, then moves them to an order selection area to be "picked" and made up into orders, and finally moves the products again to ready them for shipment to customers. This process necessitates several unavoidable movements. In some warehouses, however, a company may move goods several times in each area. The company must avoid this additional handling if a warehouse is to operate efficiently. There-

FIGURE 8-2 Utilization of a Warehouse's Cubic Capacity

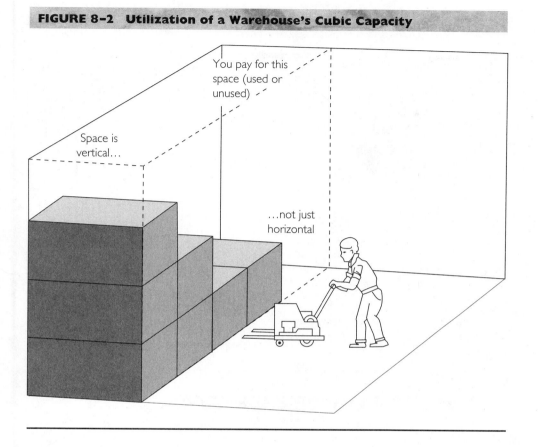

You pay for this space (used or unused)

Space is vertical…

…not just horizontal

fore, the design of any materials handling system and its associated activities should minimize movements to, within, and from a warehouse.

At times, extra movement is unavoidable. Because of overcrowding, any firm may have to temporarily store and then move products. However, an efficiently designed materials handling system should minimize the number of movements and allow products to flow through the warehouse rapidly and efficiently.

The key to minimizing movements is control. Merck Pharmaceuticals has an integrated control handling system that uses a four-unit load-automated guided vehicle (AGV) to deliver and retrieve stock to and from a ten-aisle area in the storage section. In one warehouse move, the system stores stock and retrieves material orders, thus saving movement and time.[2]

Figure 8–4 illustrates the need to sort and check items as they come into the warehouse in order to assign them an appropriate location and to avoid unnecessary rehandling. The figure shows this process to be manual, which is still fairly common in small and medium-size companies. A company could highly automate this whole process by using bar coding techniques (discussed later in this chapter). Whether the process is manual or automated, a company has to eliminate unnecessary handling by planning an efficient materials handling system.

The objective of effective working conditions has a number of significant dimensions in the logistics area, including safety. All materials handling systems, whether in connection with logistics or manufacturing, should minimize danger to nearby workers while enhancing productivity.

develop effective working conditions

FIGURE 8–3 Efficient Use of Aisle Space

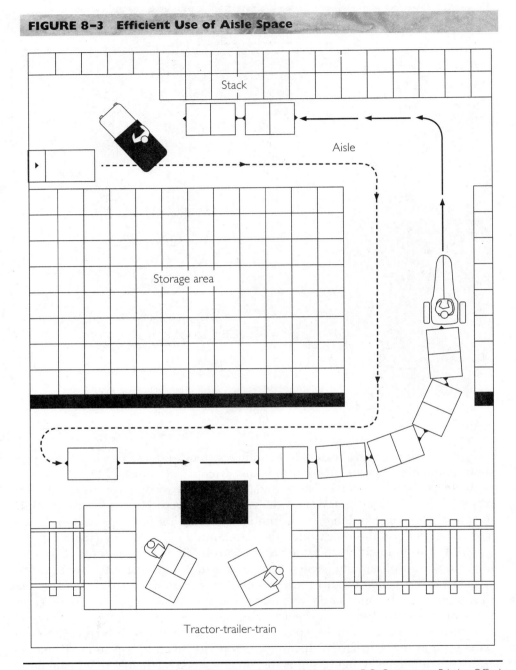

SOURCE: General Services Administration, *Warehouse Operations* (Washington, DC: Government Printing Office).

As we stated previously, materials handling usually combines automation and manual labor. Most manual effort usually occurs in the order-picking area. Therefore, a company has to create an environment that motivates people to get the job done.

reduce heavy labor

Another part of this objective is to eliminate as much as possible short-distance warehouse movements, which are monotonous and involve heavy manual labor.

FIGURE 8-4 Efficient Warehouse Operations

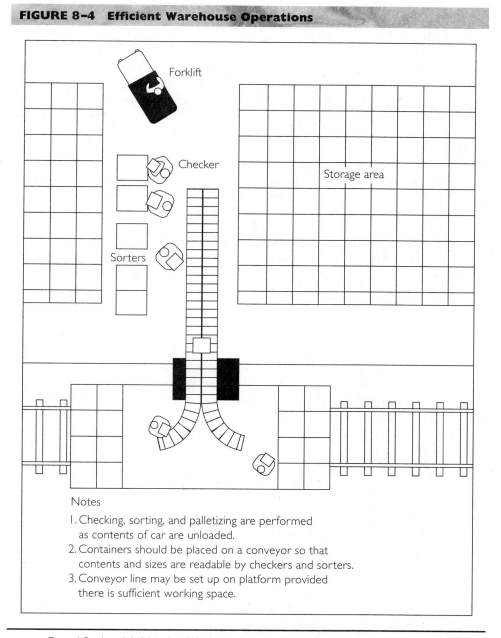

Forklift

Checker

Storage area

Sorters

Notes

1. Checking, sorting, and palletizing are performed as contents of car are unloaded.
2. Containers should be placed on a conveyor so that contents and sizes are readable by checkers and sorters.
3. Conveyor line may be set up on platform provided there is sufficient working space.

SOURCE: General Services Administration, *Warehouse Operations* (Washington, DC: Government Printing Office).

While completely eliminating all routine movements or boring warehouse work is difficult, the materials handling system should perform as much of this work as possible.

Taken to its logical conclusion, this objective suggests that companies should automate warehouses as much as possible. For a variety of reasons, including cost efficiencies, firms have attempted to eliminate warehouse labor personnel. Firms may encounter difficulty in minimizing or eliminating order selection personnel in physical distribution warehouses because some companies often receive orders for a small number of a stock-keeping unit (SKU). Consider, for example, Hallmark cards, where the typical order requires only one to three boxes of a certain card. Companies will usually handpick orders requiring small numbers of a large variety of items. This is also true of Kinney Shoes, where each shoe length and width is an SKU. In contrast, some companies receive orders for individual SKU pallet loads; these companies find automation quite feasible. Robots are a potential alternative to handpicking small numbers of items from different SKUs.

improve logistics service

Materials handling improves efficiency by making the logistics system respond quickly and effectively to plant and customer requirements. Materials handling plays a key role in getting goods to customers on time and in the proper quantities. By efficiently moving goods into the warehouse, locating stock, accurately filling orders, and rapidly preparing orders for shipment to customers, materials handling is very important to outbound logistics. In inbound logistics terms, materials handling serves company plants in much the same way.

The service objective receives much attention from the logistics manager. He or she must constantly ensure that the materials handling system will respond quickly and efficiently to customers' orders and to a production schedule's requirements. Some companies spend a lot of time and effort trying to reduce transportation time by twelve or twenty-four hours. At the same time, their materials handling systems may be adding several days to the time elapsing after a customer places an order. Customer service improvements that may be possible through improvement in materials handling are easy to overlook.

Many firms recognize the need for flexible materials handling within their customer service program. Firms need to integrate materials handling requirements not only with the company's departmental needs, but also with customers' needs.

A good example of a company that emphasizes the logistics service objective is Lincoln Electric, a manufacturer of welding equipment and supplies and electric motors. Lincoln Electric has six distribution centers that carry a full line of the company's products. It has established a targeted order fill rate of 98 percent and an order filling time of 24 hours or less for 98 percent of the orders. To accomplish this, Lincoln Electric uses a computer system to monitor demand and schedule replacement orders for the distribution centers. All products and stocking locations are bar coded, enabling warehouse personnel to use handheld scanners to enter product stock locations for later use by the computer to delineate an order pick list.[3]

reduced cost

Effective materials handling can contribute to a cost minimization program by increasing productivity (by providing more and faster throughput). Also, utilizing space more efficiently and misplacing items less frequently will lead to decreased cost.

Moen Incorporated, a plumbing manufacturer, modified its marketing channel to sell directly to retailers as well as through wholesalers and distributors. To provide the value-added services demanded by this new marketing channel, Moen redesigned its logistics system. It automated the materials handling process, in particular the order-picking system. The prior system was a manual process whereby an order picker would fill one order at a time from a piece of paper. The new computerized system tells the order picker to pick a number of units of one item to fill multiple orders. This reduces the number of steps the person makes and has increased the number of orders picked per day by 100 percent. This increased productivity translates into a 30 percent reduction in labor costs.[4]

All of these objectives are important and interrelated. In the 1990s, materials handling helps companies to minimize warehouse investment and to achieve higher inventory turns.

Guidelines and Principles for Materials Handling

Materials handling requires detailed analysis that can incorporate sophisticated mathematical techniques or modeling. This dimension of materials handling involves complex concepts that are beyond the scope of this textbook. In practice, the logistics manager can ask experts to provide detailed analysis. Therefore, logistics managers do not have to provide such analysis themselves.

However, in order to effectively plan and control materials handling, the logistics manager should recognize some guidelines and principles. Table 8–1 lists twenty of the most commonly accepted principles of efficient materials handling. Asterisks denote principles that deserve special emphasis.

The distances materials are moved in a warehouse should be as short as possible. This will minimize labor and equipment costs. A company should give the popularity principle some consideration, storing high-volume items at the shortest distance from the shipping area. And once items are in motion they should stay in motion as long as possible. Stopping and starting are expensive for labor and equipment. Also, routes of materials should be on the same level as much as possible given a particular building configuration. Moving items up and down contributes to higher labor and equipment costs. In addition, a company should minimize the number of times and the length of time it handles an item.

Companies should use mechanical and automated equipment for materials whenever travel routes, volume, and cost trade-offs justify this investment. In other words, mechanization and automation are not a panacea for low cost and efficiency. Some very effective materials handling systems utilize a fairly high ratio of labor to equipment. For example, at its Camp Hill, Pennsylvania, facility Kinney Shoe Company operates a very cost-efficient system with what would appear to be a high labor input.

Materials handling equipment should be as standard as possible and as flexible as possible to lower cost; the equipment should use gravity as much as possible and should minimize the ratio of deadweight to payload.

Dock Equipment

The proliferation of products on the market today makes materials handling selection a very dynamic process. We will now discuss the various equipment categories companies could use in designing a materials handling system. Our objective is to appreciate how and when a company might use such equipment in a logistics system. Keep in mind, however, that because of many new technological advances, logistics managers need much information when making a decision in this area.

TABLE 8-1   Principles of Materials Handling

  1. *Planning Principle.* Plan all materials handling and storage activities to obtain maximum overall operating efficiency.

  2. *Systems Principle.* Integrate as many handling activities as is practical into a coordinated operations system covering vendor, receiving, storage, production, inspection, packaging, warehousing, shipping, transportation, and customer.

* 3. *Materials Flow Principle.* Provide an operation sequence and equipment layout that optimize materials flow.

* 4. *Simplification Principle.* Simplify handling by reducing, eliminating, or combining unnecessary movements and/or equipment.

* 5. *Gravity Principle.* Utilize gravity to move material wherever practical.

* 6. *Space Utilization Principle.* Make optimum use of the building cube.

  7. *Unit Size Principle.* Increase the quantity, size, or weight of unit loads or their flow rates.

  8. *Mechanization Principle.* Mechanize handling operations.

  9. *Automation Principle.* Provide automation that includes production, handling, and storage functions.

*10. *Equipment Selection Principle.* In selecting handling equipment, consider all aspects of the material handled—the movement and the method to be used.

*11. *Standardization Principle.* Standardize handling methods, as well as types and sizes of handling equipment.

*12. *Adaptability Principle.* Use methods and equipment that adapt to the widest variety of tasks and applications, except where special-purpose equipment is justified.

 13. *Deadweight Principle.* Reduce ratio of mobile handling equipment deadweight to load carried.

 14. *Utilization Principle.* Plan for optimum utilization of handling equipment and labor.

 15. *Maintenance Principle.* Plan for preventive maintenance and scheduled repairs of all handling equipment.

 16. *Obsolescence Principle.* Replace obsolete handling methods and equipment when more efficient methods or equipment will improve operations.

 17. *Control Principle.* Use materials handling activities to improve control of production, inventory, and order handling.

 18. *Capacity Principle.* Use handling equipment to improve production capacity.

 19. *Performance Principle.* Determine handling performance effectiveness in terms of expense per unit handled.

 20. *Safety Principle.* Provide suitable methods and equipment for safe handling.

*Principles that deserve particular emphasis.

ADAPTED FROM: College-Industry Committee on Materials Handling, Materials Handling Institute, Pittsburgh, PA, 1990.

Materials handling begins at the loading dock when a truck containing the goods arrives and needs to be unloaded. The faster the warehouse unloads the goods, the greater its throughput capability. Due to the constant activity, both the receiving and shipping dock activities need to be efficient. In order to load or unload the goods safely and quickly, the warehouse should utilize the necessary dock equipment. The following section describes important dock equipment such as forklifts, dock bumpers, dock levelers, dock seals, trailer restraint systems, and pallets.

Forklifts.   One type of dock equipment common to many materials handling systems is the forklift truck (see Figure 8–5), a very versatile piece of equipment that a company can provide at a very reasonable cost. Able to perform several useful materials handling tasks, the forklift is individually powered and is available with various lift arrangements. Warehouses usually use forklifts in conjunction with pallets.

The forklift truck operates very efficiently, and companies can use it in a variety of ways. Its major disadvantage is that it requires an operator, who may very often be idle when the forklift is not in use. But, all things considered, it is probably the most popular and most common type of materials handling equipment in existence. Even the smallest firm with the simplest materials handling system can often afford a forklift truck. Its biggest advantage is its versatility in moving goods from one warehouse section to another or in transferring goods into and out of transportation equipment.

In selecting forklift trucks, a company should consider normal equipment variations such as lifting capacity, lifting height, power source (gasoline, battery, or propane gas), the aisle space the forklift needs, and speed. Manufacturers today

FIGURE 8–5   Forklift Truck

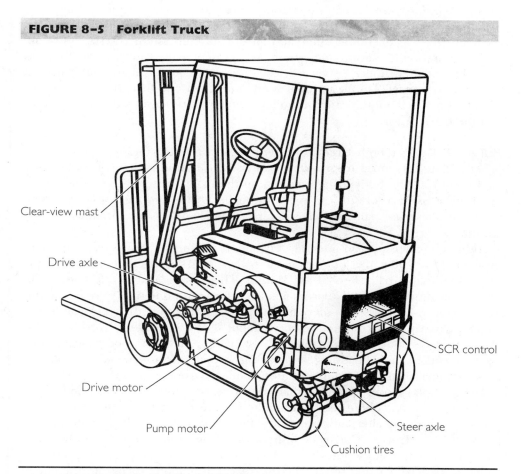

SOURCE: *Modern Materials Handling* (March 1989): 69.

offer a wide selection of forklift trucks, including trucks that handle slipsheets instead of pallets, electric trucks, narrow-aisle high-stacking trucks, compact forklifts, and trucks with greater lifting capacity. Computer-controlled lift trucks, designed for use with or without a driver, are also becoming popular for use in the dark, in extreme temperatures, or with hazardous materials.

Dock Bumpers.   Dock bumpers are molded rubber pieces that protect the building from the impact of a docking trailer backing into it and from a trailer shifting in weight during loading or unloading.

Dock Levelers.   Dock levelers level out the angle between the dock and the trailer by providing a ramp that enables the forklift to drive into the trailer safely. The greater the ramp angle, the greater the chance of an accident.

Dock Seals.   A dock seal is a cushioned frame around the dock door opening that connects the trailer to the dock. Its purpose is to create a seal blocking any outside weather, smoke, and fumes from entering the warehouse.

Trailer Restraint Systems.   Vehicle restraints prevent the trailer from drifting away from the dock during loading or unloading. Since this drifting causes many dock accidents, the Occupational Safety and Health Administration (OSHA) must approve a warehouse's restraining system. While a company can use wheel chocks or wedge molded rubber under a truck's tires, these methods are ineffective on ice, snow, or gravel. The best system is an automated one that uses a lighting or sound system to communicate the trailer's safety status between the dock worker and the truck driver.

Pallets.   Pallets are both basic and essential to materials handling operations. A pallet's main function is to provide a base to hold individual items together (see Figure 8–6). Once the items are stacked on the pallet, materials handling equipment, most often a forklift, can move the pallet to the proper storage location. Companies also use pallets when shipping products from the warehouse to the customer.

   Although pallets play an integral distribution role, their use has one important problem. Most companies do not recycle pallets, even though they can; and many used or unusable pallets go to the landfill. This issue is of growing concern to both environmentalists and logistics managers who must find ways of reducing this waste. Table 8–2 shows the alternative pallet materials and their environmental effects. Wood pallets continue to serve about 85 to 90 percent of pallet users' needs. Wood is both biodegradable and recyclable. Shredded wood pallets can be used for mulch, animal bedding, and packaging material; however, the market for these products is still limited. In addition, damaged wooden pallets are easy to fix.

   For example, grocery products manufacturers, the largest users of wooden pallets, currently repair about sixty-eight million pallets each year. Pressed wood fiber pallets, a recyclable alternative to wood pallets, are nail-free, which helps protect products from damage. Corrugated fiberboard pallets reduce weight in the trailer and provide better shock absorbency than wood, and companies can sell the used pallets as recyclable paper scrap. The pharmaceutical, food processing, and chemical industries use plastic and metal pallets because these pallets are easy to clean

FIGURE 8-6   Pallet Types

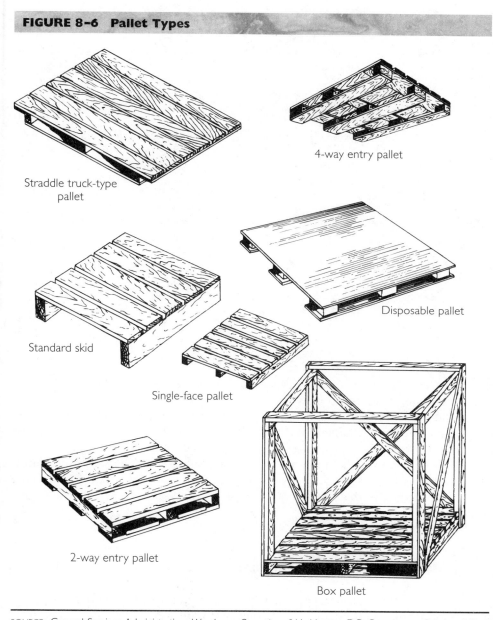

Straddle truck-type pallet

4-way entry pallet

Standard skid

Disposable pallet

Single-face pallet

2-way entry pallet

Box pallet

SOURCE: General Services Administration, *Warehouse Operations* (Washington, DC: Government Printing Office).

and keep sanitary. Recycled plastic pallets become products such as orange highway construction barriers or compact discs. All pallet materials have recycling potential. By recycling pallets, the warehouse will receive salvage value from recycling firms instead of paying disposal costs.

As was indicated in the logistics profile at the beginning of this chapter, Home Depot has switched from using pallets to plastic slipsheets. The plastic slipsheet eliminates the problem of pallet disposal and return, thereby lowering disposal costs. At the same time, Home Depot is experiencing a reduction in the amount of product damage. The plastic slipsheet is being reused four to five times, with

TABLE 8-2   Pallet Type Comparison

Material	Durability*	Repairable?	Environmental Impact	Typical Application
Wood	Medium	Yes	Material is biodegradable and recyclable	Grocery; automotive; durable goods; hardware
Pressed wood fiber	Medium	Yes	Material is recyclable and can be burned without leaving fuel residues	Printing; metal stampings; plumbing fixtures; building materials
Corrugated fiberboard	Low	No	Material is biodegradable and recyclable	One-way shipping applications in grocery; lightweight paper products; industrial parts
Plastic	High	No	Material is recyclable	Captive or closed-loop systems; FDA, USDA applications; automotive
Metal	High	No	Material is recyclable	Captive or closed-loop systems; FDA, USDA applications; military

*We define durability as a pallet's expected number of trips.
SOURCE: *Modern Materials Handling* (April 1990): 53.

the final trip being to a plastic recycler who turns the spent slipsheet into a new one for another four to five trips.

Another method used extensively in the grocery industry is pallet rental. The leading pallet rental company is Chep USA. Under the Chep plan, a grocery manufacturer rents the pallet for a one-way trip to the wholesaler or retailer. When the product is removed from the pallet, the wholesaler or retailer sends the empty pallet to one of Chep's regional depots. The average cost of a typical Chep pallet trip is $2.50 to $4.50; that compares to $8.00 to $10.00 for a new pallet used for a one-way trip.[5]

Other Materials Handling Equipment

Conveyors.   Conveyors, a very popular form of materials handling equipment, play an important role in advancing productivity and improving bottom-line operating results, particularly in the mechanized distribution center or warehouse. These systems decrease handling costs, increase productivity of workers and equipment, and provide an interface with management information systems.

roller versus belt conveyor

There are two basic types of conveyors (see Figure 8–7). The first, a *roller conveyor,* basically uses the gravity principle. The conveyor is inclined, and goods move down the conveyor by force of their own weight, typically at a slow pace depending on the conveyor's incline. The other type is the *wheel conveyor,* or *belt* or *towline conveyor,* which requires power equipment. Such conveyors move goods either on a level or up inclines to a warehouse section. Companies will use a roller conveyor wherever possible to minimize their operating costs.

FIGURE 8-7 Materials Handling Equipment

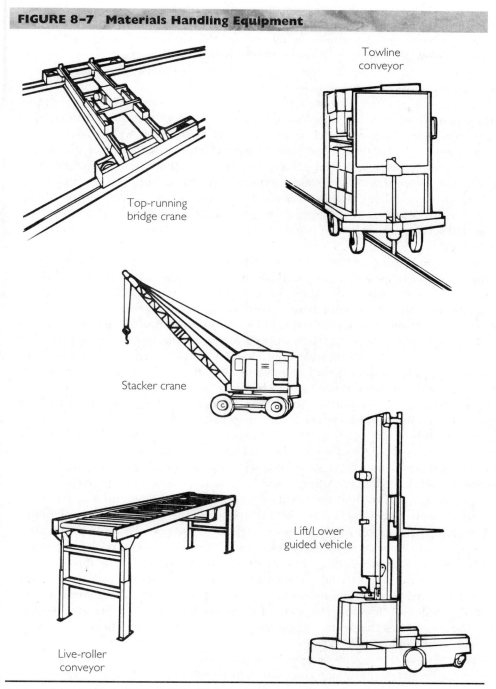

Towline conveyor

Top-running bridge crane

Stacker crane

Live-roller conveyor

Lift/Lower guided vehicle

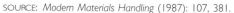

SOURCE: *Modern Materials Handling* (1987): 107, 381.

Many companies consider conveyors advantageous because they can be highly automatic and, therefore, can eliminate handling costs. They also may save space since they can use narrow aisles and can operate on multiple levels in the same area. Conveyor systems often have low operating costs.

advantages   Conveyors equipped with scanners and other automatic devices enable companies to move goods very efficiently and quickly from one warehouse area to another. Scanners can keep inventory records by recording packages moving on conveyors, and can track storage locations. Finally, scanners enable managers to use computers to rapidly locate goods.

A modern conveyor system is very expensive and requires a large capital investment. It is also fixed in location; that is, it lacks versatility. Designing a conveyor system requires much time and effort, particularly with reference to a company's future needs. If conditions change, changing the conveyor system may be necessary, often at a very high cost. Organizations that invest in complex conveyor systems are usually large and successful manufacturing firms. Using conveyors to automate a large distribution warehouse, for example, generally requires a significant investment of funds in a very complex and sophisticated conveyor system. However, companies can install some very simple conveyors at a very reasonable cost.

capital-intensive   In analyzing the possibility of using warehouse conveyor systems, an organization must decide whether its materials handling approach should be capital-intensive or labor-intensive. Many large companies with sophisticated logistics requirements find capital-intensive systems such as elaborate conveyors to be extremely worthwhile because of reduced labor costs and possible improvements in distribution time. However, such approaches are not necessarily right for all companies. More labor-intensive approaches may be much more appropriate. Comparing labor-intensive and capital-intensive materials handling methods is analogous to comparing private and public warehousing. In other words, conveyor systems have a very important fixed cost segment, and a company must have throughput volume sufficient to defray or spread the fixed costs.

One disadvantage of conveyors is the possibility of equipment malfunction, which could cause logistics system delays. However, conveyor users can minimize operational problems. To avoid exceeding the equipment's capacity and causing breakdowns, the company using conveyors must consider the dimensions and weight of each unit the conveyors will carry. The company must consider the load's center of gravity when loads travel on inclined or declined conveyors, are handled in start-stop operations, or are transferred while in motion. To avoid problems, a company must operate a conveyor at the rate for which the company intended it. This rate may vary, depending on unit sizes; and these sizes will be mixed.

Conveyors can handle loads of almost any size, shape, weight, or fragility. However, users must determine, before they purchase equipment, the items a specific conveyor will handle and its expected functions—sortation, for example. Following the guidelines this section suggests will contribute to an effective conveyor system.

Trends show that conveyor usefulness will continue to increase as automation technologies develop. Already conveyors can be valuable tools in data generation and product monitoring systems, and their use in computerized inventory control is quite common.

Cranes.   Companies can utilize a variety of cranes in warehouses (see Figure 8–7). The two basic types are *bridge cranes* and *stacker* or *wagon cranes*. Bridges cranes are more common in physical supply warehouses or where companies have to move, store, and load heavy industrial goods such as steel coils or generators.

ON THE LINE

Why Units of Twelve?

Have you ever wondered why items are packed in quantities of twelve? Or in factors of twelve, such as six or three? The typical answers are "We've always shipped in quantities of twelve," or "It is the industry standard."

Some people have postulated that the roots of the twelve per package rule are biblical because throughout the Bible reference is made to twelve. Others claim that at one time humans had six fingers on each hand, thereby permitting a person to count to twelve on his or her hands. The notion of a six-digit hand also gives credence to the six-pack.

Another theory for the magical twelve is grounded in the U.S. linear measurement system. A foot contains 12 inches, a yard has 36 inches (3 × 12), and a mile has 63,360 inches (5,280 × 12). Thus, it is natural for us to pack products in lots of twelve.

However, there are no federal regulations nor mystical industry standards that require the piece count per package to be twelve. Neither the U.S. Constitution nor any industry trade association has mandated twelve as the piece count per package. It just happened.

The question that management must ask is, Does twelve per package make economic sense? Consumers have told many sellers that they do not want to buy twelve items at one time. For example, chewing gum is sold five sticks per pack, 9-volt radio batteries are packaged in quantities of two, and lawnmower spark plugs are sold one per package.

So, why do companies continue to place twelve items in a package? Does it make economic sense? Why not five, seven, thirteen, or anything other than twelve? These are the haunting packaging questions for the 21st century.

Stacker cranes have become increasingly popular in physical distribution warehouses because they can function with narrow aisles, effectively utilizing a warehouse's cube capacity. This equipment is also very adaptable to automation. Fully automated stacker cranes on the market today can put stock into and take it out of storage areas without an operator. The computer equipment such systems utilize can select the best storage placement and recall this placement later. Stacker cranes are commonly used in conjunction with elaborate shelving systems.

Though not usually as expensive as conveyor systems, cranes are also capital-intensive equipment. Handling very heavy items may require bridge cranes; a company should justify stacker cranes on a cost basis. The advantage of bridge cranes is the ability to lift heavy items quickly and efficiently. The advantages of stacker cranes are the effective use of space and the possibility for automation.

Automatic Guided Vehicle (AGV) Systems. AGVs are machines that connect receiving, storing, manufacturing, and shipping. Firms can track these vehicles, either roaming freely or on a fixed path, with computers that make traffic control decisions. Essentially, automated guided vehicles (AGVs) travel around the warehouse or manufacturing plant carrying various items to a particular programmed destination. Since these AGVs do not require a driver, labor costs are reduced.

The double-pallet jack, another vehicle that does not require a driver, can transport two pallet loads between warehouse areas. As with AGVs, a computer can guide the double-pallet jack to its destination along a floor-wired guide.

Also available is a variety of other, more specialized equipment, including draglines that pull carts in a continuous circle in a warehouse, elevators, hoists, and monorails.

Order Picking and Storage Equipment

One of the main functions of a physical distribution warehouse is order picking, the process of identifying, selecting, retrieving, and accumulating the proper items for customer orders. Although order picking by nature is labor-intensive, an effectively designed order-picking and storage system can enhance the speed, accuracy, and cost-effectiveness of the order-picking process. Most storage systems primarily try to use warehouse space effectively. Because the cost of labor, equipment, and space for order picking equals about 65 percent of total warehouse operating costs, any improvement that reduces these costs is greatly important. This section covers two main equipment types: picker-to-part and part-to-picker. Picker-to-part systems include bin shelving, modular storage drawers, flow racks, mobile storage systems, and order-picking vehicles. Part-to-picker systems include carousels and miniload automated storage and retrieval systems (AS/RS). Figure 8–8 illustrates these systems.

Picker-to-Part Systems.   In picker-to-part systems, the order picker must travel to the pick location within the aisle.

- *Bin shelving.* Bin shelving is the oldest and most basic storage system available for storing small parts. The main advantages of bin shelving are the low initial cost and the ability to divide units into various compartments. However, the system underutilizes cubic space by not using a bin's full size and by requiring shelf height to be within a person's reach.
- *Modular storage drawers.* Modular storage drawers are cabinets that are divided into drawers and further subdivided into compartments. Their main advantage is their ability to hold a large number of SKUs. Their main drawback is height: the drawers cannot be more than approximately 5 feet high because the order picker must look into them when picking an order.
- *Flow racks.* Flow racks store items in cartons having a uniform size and shape. The cartons, which warehouse personnel replenish from the rack's back end, flow on rollers, by gravity, to the rack's front or aisle end for order picking. A main advantage to this system is that the back-to-front item movement ensures first-in/first-out (FIFO) inventory turnover. Flow racks can also hold full pallets of items.
- *Mobile storage systems.* Mobile storage systems need only one order-picking aisle because a motorized system can slide the racks, shelves, or modular drawers to the left or right. The order picker can slide the racks apart to expose the aisle in which he or she needs to pick an order. Slower picking speed due to the shift time offsets the advantage of high storage density.
- *Order-picking vehicles.* Order-picking trucks and person-abroad storage and retrieval (S/R) vehicles increase order-picking rates and maximize cubic space utilization. The order picker rides or drives the vehicle horizontally or vertically to the pick location. Some of these vehicles move automatically, allowing the order picker to perform another task while traveling.

Part-to-Picker Systems.   In part-to-picker systems, the pick location travels through an automated machine to the picker. These systems have a higher initial cost than picker-to-part systems, but utilizing automated storage and retrieval equipment speeds up order-picking operations, improves inventory control, and increases prof-

FIGURE 8–8 Order-Picking Equipment

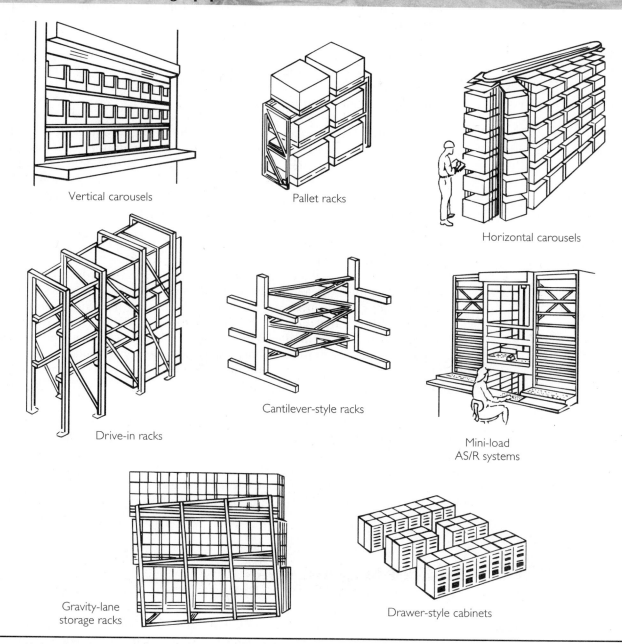

Vertical carousels

Pallet racks

Horizontal carousels

Drive-in racks

Cantilever-style racks

Mini-load
AS/R systems

Gravity-lane
storage racks

Drawer-style cabinets

SOURCE: *Modern Materials Handling*, 1992 Casebook Reference Issue (September 1991): 97.

its. Part-to-picker systems minimize travel time. By comparison, in static shelving systems, workers spend up to 70 percent of their time traveling.

- *Carousels.* Carousels are shelves or bins linked together through a mechanical device that stores and rotates items for order picking. The two main types of carousels are horizontal and vertical.

Horizontal carousels are a linked series of bins that rotate around a vertical axis. A computer locates a needed part and rotates the carousel until the part location stops in front of the order picker's fixed position. Automated systems attempt to minimize wait times and maximize order-picking times. For this reason, an order picker usually works two carousels. In this way, the picker can pick from one carousel while waiting for the other carousel to rotate to a needed item. Industries that use horizontal carousels include aviation, electronic, paper, and pharmaceutical.

Vertical carousels differ from horizontal ones in two ways: the bins are enclosed for cleanliness and security, and the carousel rotates around a horizontal axis. The vertical carousel operates on a continuous lift principle, rotating the necessary items to the order picker's work station. This vertical storage approach cuts floor space use by 60 percent and increases picking productivity by up to 300 percent over racks and shelving of equal capacity. Some industries that use vertical carousels include electronic, automotive, aerospace, and computer.

- *Miniload automated storage and retrieval systems (AS/RS).* The most technically advanced order-picking system is the miniload AS/RS, which efficiently uses storage space and achieves the highest accuracy rate in order picking. The AS/RS machine travels both horizontally and vertically to storage locations in an aisle, carrying item storage containers to and from an order-picking station at the end of the aisle. At the order-picking station, the order picker programs the correct item-picking sequence. The AS/RS machine retrieves the next container in the sequence while the order picker obtains items from the present container. The miniload AS/RS utilizes vertical space and requires few aisles, but this system is very expensive.

Mezzanines.   Mezzanines are a double-layered storage system that utilizes a second level of bin shelving, modular storage cabinets, flow racks, or carousels above the first storage level. Instead of using up square footage space, the mezzanine adds a second level to utilize the warehouse's cubic capacity more efficiently. A steel grating usually divides the two levels, which workers access by stairs. The mezzanine is not part of the building's actual construction, so its location is flexible (see Figure 8–9).

TYPES OF MATERIALS HANDLING EQUIPMENT—A DESIGN PERSPECTIVE

flexible path   Companies often divide materials handling equipment into three design categories. The first category is *flexible-path equipment,* which includes manual hand trucks, all forklift trucks, and some other picking equipment. Its design advantages are versatility and flexibility. However, it is customarily more labor-intensive.

continuous-flow   The second category is *continuous-flow fixed-path equipment,* which includes con-
fixed path   veyors and draglines. These are usually very efficient and highly automated. However, the investment is high; often specializing in certain products, they usually have limited versatility; and they have limited flexibility. For a company with volume flow and uniform product size, this approach has many cost advantages.

FIGURE 8–9   Mezzanines

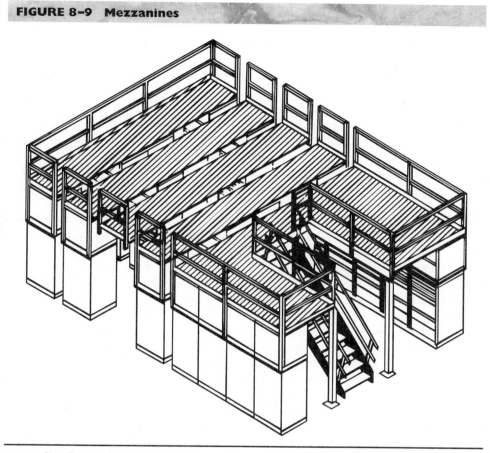

SOURCE: *Plant Engineering* (8 March 1980): 81.

A third type is *intermittent-flow fixed-path equipment*. Including cranes, monorails, and stacker crane equipment, this category combines the efficiency of continuous-flow equipment with the ability to stop unneeded equipment.

intermittent-flow fixed path

By recognizing the need for equipment able to efficiently move goods within, into, and out of the warehouse, manufacturing firms and equipment manufacturers have revolutionized the whole materials handling area. The number of equipment types available today could overwhelm a materials handling system designer. But these equipment choices also represent an important challenge because of their potential for improving a logistics system.

An interesting question is whether logistics managers should be actual experts in the design of materials handling equipment. This is very unlikely. Usually, the logistics manager depends on the advice of the organization's engineering staff or various equipment managers. However, logistics managers should know about their own systems and their particular needs. This enables logistics managers to establish general parameters for a materials handling system and provides a framework for choosing the best system for a particular company or firm. In the next section, we will discuss some of the logistics manager's criteria for selecting equipment.

EQUIPMENT SELECTION FACTORS

Several factors affect the type of materials handling equipment a company should use. These factors offer the logistics manager guidelines for analyzing company requirements. He or she must approach this analysis in trade-off terms, measuring benefits against costs.

physical attributes of product and packaging

United States firms produce a vast array of products. Even individual companies sometimes produce numerous different products. A materials handling system that moves books in or around a warehouse is quite distinct from one that stores automobile tires or chain saws. Therefore, the physical attributes of the product or product group handled, affects the type of materials handling equipment used.

For example, item weight will influence a system's design. Large pieces of equipment that a firm must store in a warehouse may negate the use of something like a conveyor system and may require overhead bridge cranes. If a product is small and lightweight, usually a firm can use any of several categories of materials handling equipment. The product and its weight, size, packaging, value, handling ability, and susceptibility to damage all influence the type of equipment a company uses. Therefore, the logistics manager should first consider the product and its dimensions when deciding which equipment options are available and most appropriate for a firm's materials handling system. Because of his or her transportation and inventory experience, the logistics manager will know the company's product or products and the factors that will affect materials handling equipment use.

Since the 1970s, the government has become increasingly interested in the movement of hazardous materials, including radioactive materials and other chemicals. A materials handling setting must take this into account. For example, certain raw materials with unique handling characteristics require loose, rather than packaged, movements. Lately, companies have debated the use of slurry systems versus dry bulk systems to move bulk products.

characteristics of physical facility

A warehouse facility's physical characteristics also influence the use of materials handling equipment. Very often we visualize a large, well-lit, one-story facility with very few obstacles, which will be conducive to the use of conveyors, forklift trucks, shelves, or any type of materials handling equipment discussed here. Sometimes, however, this type of facility is not possible. A company may have to use a mobile storage facility where conveyors, for example, would not be feasible. Or it may be using an old warehouse that has low ceilings, negating the use of shelving or containers, or one with floors that are unable to support a heavy-duty forklift truck. Firms do not always have the option of using the best type of facility, and the facility itself will affect the type of equipment a firm can use.

If the company is designing a brand-new warehousing facility, then all the equipment options described here are probably available. If it is dealing with an existing facility, particularly if it is old, then the company faces some constraints on the type of equipment it can use.

time requirements

Time is a logistics system factor in various ways, and it does affect materials handling. Because customers expect to receive orders in a reasonable time period, time is critical in a market or distribution warehouse where a firm stores its valuable finished goods. These companies will select materials handling equipment that enables them to move goods into, around, and out of the warehouse as fast as possible.

Rapid movement characterizes the distribution or transit warehouse, and we often find the most sophisticated and largest variety of materials handling equipment in these facilities. These warehouses, usually automated, will utilize elaborate and sophisticated conveyor systems, automatic storage placers, and all of the materials handling equipment we have discussed here.

On the other hand, if we are talking about a storage warehouse or one that a firm uses primarily in conjunction with the manufacturing facility to store semi-finished goods and perhaps basic materials, then time is not usually as critical. The equipment would be more basic, and automating such a facility might be unnecessary.

Because of trade-off possibilities, a firm for whom time is critical may be much more willing to invest large amounts of money in sophisticated materials handling equipment. Investing more in a materials handling system enables the firm to increase sales or have savings in other areas.

These factors will provide the logistics manager a basic framework for analyzing his or her particular needs and the materials handling equipment options available to his or her company. After this analysis, the manager can look at what the most likely equipment manufacturers can offer in each category. The logistics manager can also get additional engineering information from the company's own staff, which will help further in designing the system that will best meet the company's particular needs. Although the final selection of a system and its equipment will require a lot of detail, knowing the equipment available and the factors the selection involves provides the basis for developing an efficient system for any organization.

Sources of Information

In evaluating materials handling equipment alternatives, a number of sources provide help and insight.

Computers can estimate storage/retrieval requirements. One recently developed program estimates net cube requirements, storage location requirements, and activity and storage/retrieval configuration, and runs a sensitivity analysis. Often, switching to an expensive system is unnecessary. Rather, a firm should try to reduce picking time by increasing the accuracy of storage and inventory information and by optimizing the goods placement for manual retrieval.

Many large companies and some small ones have staff engineers who can help the logistics manager analyze the situation. These individuals can provide detailed guidance once the logistics manager has completed an initial analysis.

Equipment manufacturers maintain a staff of engineers who can provide their company cost data on possible alternatives. Equipment has become so specialized today that this may be the best way to get detailed cost information.

Another possibility is to use consultants to analyze need and select the best equipment. Although such organizations are sometimes expensive, they often provide a very reasonable analysis based upon the costs of using alternative resources.

In addition to these, companies can use sources such as trade associations and self-study. While both of these usually provide only simplified data, they often provide a convenient starting place.

PACKAGING

Other individuals, in addition to the logistics manager, may be concerned about a product's packaging. Like materials handling, packaging connotes different things to different people. Since packaging involves a number of organizational areas, these areas will need to coordinate their packaging concerns. Packaging may contribute nothing to a product's value, but its influence on distribution costs is considerable.

marketing

Packaging is of interest to the marketing area. It may be a way of selling a product or at least of providing product information to the customer.

production

Packaging also concerns production managers, since they are often responsible for placing goods into the package and since a package's size, shape, and type will very often affect labor efficiency. Production managers may look at a package from a perspective somewhat different from that of the marketing manager or even the logistics manager.

legal

Packaging may also concern the organization's legal section, particularly today. Companies must provide information about what a package contains. Thus, some coordination may be necessary between logistics and a company's legal staff.

warehousing

But packaging is especially important to the logistics manager. The size, shape, and type of packaging will influence materials handling and will affect warehouse operations. Also, from a logistics manager's point of view, packaging is quite important for effective damage protection, not only in the warehouse but during transportation.

transportation

Package size may affect a company's ability to use pallets or shelving or different types of materials handling equipment. Many companies design packages that are too wide or too high for efficient use of either a transportation agency or a warehouse. So coordinating the size of packaging with warehousing and with transportation is quite important. Also, damaged goods are likely to lower future sales, so packaging must prevent goods from arriving in a damaged condition. Poor packaging can also contribute to higher handling costs. In short, packaging interacts with the logistics system in a number of different and important ways. The following section discusses more explicitly the role of packaging in logistics.

The Role of Packaging

identify product and provide information

A very important packaging function is to provide information about the product the package contains. Looking at this from the perspective of a marketing manager who is trying to sell a product in competition with other products on a supermarket shelf might be easiest. The package should provide information that would make the product more appealing to the customer. The package must also provide handling information. For example, if the package is easily damaged, or if it should be set in only one position, the package should say so.

Information provision is also important to logistics people. Goods stored in a warehouse must bear the proper identification so that warehouse personnel can locate them easily and correctly. When designing a package, firms may spend a lot of time and effort making sure that it provides information to warehouse personnel. Companies can use color codes for placing goods in a warehouse. The company should note the weight on the package in order to inform people lifting the package or to determine what can rest on top of it.

Techniques for providing information include color coding, universal product codes, heat transfers, computer-readable tables, symbols, and number codes. A firm's technique or combination of techniques will depend on the organization's particular circumstances.

A major packaging concern is the ease of handling in conjunction with materials handling and transportation. Large packages, for example, may be desirable from a production perspective, but the contents' size and weight might cause problems for materials handling equipment or for transfer into and out of transportation equipment. So any packaging design should try to maximize handling ease in the warehouse and during transportation. Handling ease is also quite important to the production manager, who places the goods in the package.

improve efficiency in handling and distributing packages

The important considerations of package design fall into three areas. The first is the package's physical dimensions. The design must consider space utilization in terms of the warehouse, transport vehicle, and pallets. The product's physical dimension must also take into account the company's materials handling equipment. The second consideration is the package's strength. The package designer must analyze the package's height, handling, and the type of equipment that will handle the package. The final consideration is package shape.

With customer service playing an ever-increasing role in logistics planning, companies need to integrate their packages with customers' materials handling equipment. A special package that can interface with a company's innovative equipment may move products inexpensively through its system; however, a customer's incompatible equipment will impair their ability to receive and store those goods. In this situation, customer service value may be lost.

customer interface

A logistics manager's major concern is protecting the goods in the package. In the warehouse, for example, where moving goods could drop from a conveyor or be hit with a forklift truck, the package must provide the product adequate protection. Protection is also important when a transportation agency handles the product. Some agencies minimize packaging requirements for products with low damage susceptibility. So the type of transportation agency used will affect the packaging needed to protect the product from damage. Protection can also mean protecting products from contamination resulting from contact with other goods, water damage, temperature changes, pilferage, and shocks in handling and transport. Sometimes packaging must support the weight of products stacked above it, or provide even weight distribution within the package to facilitate manual and automatic materials handling.

protect product

Changes in federal and state regulations have also affected packaging's protection aspect, especially in food and drug product areas, where companies must design packaging to reduce consumer anxieties about tampering.

What Is Packaging?

We generally discuss two types of packaging: *consumer packaging,* or *interior packaging;* and *industrial,* or *exterior packaging.* The marketing manager is usually most concerned about the former because consumer or interior packaging provides information important in selling the product, in motivating the customer to buy the product, or in giving the product maximum visibility when it competes with others on the retail shelf. Marketing personnel often refer to consumer packaging, which has to appeal to the customer, as a silent salesperson.

On the other hand, industrial or exterior packaging is of primary concern to the logistics manager. This packaging protects goods that a company will move and store in the warehouse and also permits the company the effective use of transportation vehicle space. It also has to provide information and handling ease, as our discussion of the role of packaging indicated.

Although talking about packaging as a dichotomy is convenient, and quite often we can divide packaging in this way, the two areas do overlap. We cannot design the interior (consumer) package without considering the exterior or industrial package. Spending a lot of time and effort trying to minimize damage through an exterior package makes no sense if a company does not provide interior protection. Therefore, marketing and logistics have to coordinate packaging's consumer and industrial dimensions. These areas must also interact with production area people, since they typically join the two packaging types.

Packaging Materials

Many different exterior packaging materials are available to the logistics manager. In fact, as in materials handling, a packaging materials revolution has occurred in the last decade. At one time the use of harder materials, such as wood or metal containers, was widespread. But these added considerable shipping weight, which increased transport costs since transportation companies bill customers for total weight, including packaging.

softer materials   In recent years, companies have tended to use softer packaging materials. Corrugated materials have become popular, particularly with respect to package exterior. However, the plastic materials companies use to cushion the product inside the box have possibly done the most to revolutionize packaging. These materials enable manufacturers to highly automate the packaging area and to maximize protection while minimizing costs. In addition, plastic provides the lowest weight-to-protection shipping ratio.

Cushioning materials protect the product from shock, vibration, and surface damage during handling. Cushioning materials include shrink-wrap, air bubble cushioning, cellulose wadding, corrugated paper, and plastics. We can divide the plastics into expanded polystyrene, polyurethane, foam-in-place, and polyethylene. Table 8–3 shows a comparison of the various cushioning materials.

plastic   Companies often use shrink-wrap for consumer package goods, either alone or in conjunction with containers and slipsheets. It provides protection and stability, helps to reduce pilferage, and deters product tampering while items are in a warehouse. Shrink-wrap allows companies to stop using corrugated paper boxes. Warehouse personnel place the interior package directly on a pallet and shrink-wrap it. This also displays the item prominently for identification and helps to reduce overall logistics costs. In large warehouse-type retail operations, stores receive pallet loads directly and remove the shrink-wrap, making the product immediately accessible to the consumer. Since removing items from a box and placing them on a shelf is unnecessary, the retailer also saves money.

Air bubble cushioning is made of plastic sheets that contain air pockets. Cellulose wadding is composed of tissue paper layers. By forming upright columns in a box, corrugated inserts help prevent a product from getting crushed. Expanded polystyrene (EPS), the most popular cushioning material, is also recyclable. The loose-fill EPS commonly appears as foam peanuts or shells. Polyurethane (PU),

TABLE 8-3 Comparison of Cushioning Materials

Material	Material Cost	Static Loading	Resiliency	Typical Applications
Air bubble	Low	Light to medium	Good	Void fill Wrapping Keyboards Plastic and metal parts Service centers
Cellulose wadding	Low	Light to medium	Fair	Surface protection Furniture Plastic parts
Corrugated	Low	Light to heavy	Fair	Blocking and bracing Rugged parts
Expanded polystyrene: Loose fill	Low	Light to medium	Fair	Void fill Books Plastic and metal parts
Molded	Low	Light to medium	Fair	Appliances Computers Electronic hardware
Polyurethane	High	Light to medium	Excellent	Computers Electronics Medical instruments
Foam-in-place	Medium	Medium to heavy	Good	Electronics Service centers Spare parts
Polyethylene	High	Medium to heavy	Excellent	Disk drives Fragile electronics Printers

SOURCE: "Playing the Protective Packaging Game," *Modern Materials Handling* (April 1989): 65.

the softest foam, provides cushioning for lightweight products. Foam-in-place polyurethane is a mixture of two chemicals that produce a foam that expands and molds to a product's exact shape. Polyethylene (PE) provides lightweight cushioning for heavy products.

These materials are inexpensive and highly protective. In addition, their light weight helps to minimize transportation costs. If a packaging revolution has occurred, we can probably attribute it to the development of these materials.

When selecting packaging materials, companies today must consider environmental protection. Consumer advocates as well as government regulations have affected distribution planning. Examples include Food and Drug Administration restrictions on food product packaging. And, with recent consumer panics over pharmaceutical product tampering, the government has implemented stricter packaging materials requirements.

environment

Another concern is the waste that containers and packaging produce. By the year 2000, the United States will produce more than 220 million tons of solid waste anually.[6] Figure 8–10 shows that in 2000, 38.1 percent of the municipal solid

waste

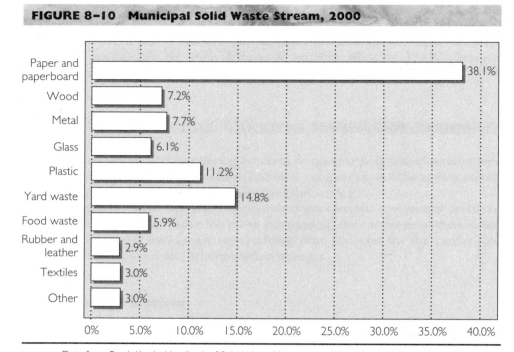

FIGURE 8–10 Municipal Solid Waste Stream, 2000

Paper and paperboard	38.1%
Wood	7.2%
Metal	7.7%
Glass	6.1%
Plastic	11.2%
Yard waste	14.8%
Food waste	5.9%
Rubber and leather	2.9%
Textiles	3.0%
Other	3.0%

SOURCE: Data from Frank Kreth, *Handbook of Solid Waste Management* (New York: McGraw-Hill, 1994): 3–5.

waste stream will be paper and paperboard, which are essentially packaging materials. In addition, other packaging materials such as glass (6.1 percent), wood (7.2 percent), metal (7.7 percent), and plastic (11.2 percent) will add considerably to the waste stream. Granted, not all of these materials are packaging, but a considerable portion is.

recycling One way to reduce this waste is to reduce the overall packaging a company uses. Another way is to recycle packaging materials. State and local governments have proposed and implemented much legislation to enforce business and community recycling. For example, under Rhode Island's Solid Waste Management Act, businesses must remove 70 percent of all recyclable materials, including corrugated paper, aluminum, wood, and glass, from their waste stream.[7]

Package Selection

Packaging has two logistics concerns: the physical dimensions (size and shape) and the type of material. These factors establish guidelines for the logistics manager.

physical dimensions One factor that affects a package's physical dimensions is the product's characteristics—things such as size, shape, and weight. Shoes, which are relatively uniform in size and shape, are much different from glassware, which can vary considerably. Also important are logistics system characteristics: the transportation mode, the number of handlings, materials handling equipment, and storage length. Finally, the logistics-marketing interface will have an impact. Coordination and compromise between these two areas will influence the package's size and shape.

A product's physical dimension will affect a company's packaging material choices. Firms handle small consumer products like glassware differently than computers or auto tires. The transportation mode will also affect the materials a company uses. Airlines and motor carriers require much less packaging than do rail or water carriers. With the advent of deregulation, the common carriers have allowed shippers to experiment with new packaging techniques. Packaging still influences carrier rates, which will be higher for less-protective packaging or for packages that are less dense. Contract and private carriage allow shippers to package goods as they like without rate penalties. Storage time is another factor affecting the material type. Usually, the longer the storage period, the better the packaging that must be used. Finally, the production requirements influence materials selection.

materials

Unitizing or palletizing is the process of accumulating and stacking individual cases or other containers to form a single, larger unit. This process saves handling and transportation costs, better utilizes space, reduces damages and loading and unloading time, and improves customer service. However, the firm unitizing/deunitizing costs and requires expensive specialized handling equipment.

unitizing or palletizing

PACKAGING DESIGN CONSIDERATIONS

In developing an appropriate interior and exterior packaging design, we must recognize that a product's package is usually in five basic locations over the product's lifetime. This is particularly true for consumer nondurables or so-called package goods. The five locations are the plant, the warehouse, the transportation unit, the retail outlet, and the home or place of use.

In each instance, we must answer appropriate questions about the packaging. For example, in the home, a consumer may destroy the package immediately or may use it to provide storage until the item is gone. Powdered laundry soap is one product that is stored in its package. Another question is whether the package is returnable and reusable. And we may want to know where the consumer is likely to store the package. The longer the package's potential life cycle and the more hostile the storage area, the more durable and sturdy the package will have to be.

In all the other locations, we must answer similar questions. The responses will provide marketing and logistics with valuable package design input.

We may also examine packaging design from the perspective of various logistics areas and of other major areas like marketing and manufacturing. From the logistics side, we should consider packaging design questions in terms of warehousing, transportation, materials handling, and procurement. For warehousing, we would want to study factors such as stacking requirements and cube problems. For transportation, we would want to know things such as the mode or modes, the equipment type, and the geographic areas. For materials handling, we will need to know the equipment type, if any, and the need to unitize. Designing the appropriate package requires some very important inputs.

BAR CODING

A discussion of packaging would be incomplete without a discussion of bar coding. Lineal bar code symbols that an optical scanner can read are having a major impact upon distribution logistics. Although the use of bar code technology caught on in the 1970s and took a huge leap in the 1980s, only 10 percent of companies had complete bar code implementation in 1994.[8]

A bar code is a series of parallel black and white bars, both of varying widths, whose sequence represents letters or numbers. This sequence is a code that scanners can translate into important information such as a shipment's origin, the product type, the place of manufacture, and the product's price. Bar code systems are simple to use, accurate, and quick; and they can store large amounts of information.

Different industries use different bar code standards. A bar code standard states the language the code uses, the print quality companies expect on the label, the type of information the label contains, and the information format. Over thirty major U.S. industries have developed written standards for bar coding in manufacturing and warehouse operations.[9] For example, different standards include the Automotive Industry Action Group (AIAG) standards and the Universal Product Code that the grocery industry uses. With one bar code language standard, suppliers and vendors in a particular industry can easily read each other's package labels.

scanners   Bar code scanners fall into two main categories: automatic and handheld. Automatic scanners are in a fixed position and scan packages as they go by on a conveyor belt. In contrast, a worker can carry the portable handheld scanner or wand throughout the warehouse. In order to read bar codes, these optical scanners emit light beams and translate the reflections bouncing off the black and white bars into electrical signals. These electrical signals, which the scanner records as binary digits of 1s and 0s, form the code.

Most of us encounter bar coding in large retail outlets like supermarkets, where clerks now scan individual package bar codes at the cash register. Supermarkets have almost eliminated the practice of labeling every item with a price tag. More important, the bar code contributes to much more effective retail inventory control. The scanner and cash register, along with a backup computer system, enable the retail outlet to closely monitor sales and, therefore, inventory levels. The instantaneous transmission of information has allowed companies greater central control and inventory reduction in many retail locations.

Bar coding had its initial logistics impact when companies used it on cartons and monitored or scanned the codes as the cartons flowed into a warehouse. Bar coding at the warehouse improves data collection accuracy, reduces receiving operations time and data collection labor, and helps to integrate data collection with other areas, leading to better database and inventory controls. Companies can assign items more quickly into the warehouse, and warehouse personnel can select and prepare orders much more rapidly.

CONTAINERIZATION

Containers are essentially big boxes into which firms place small loads. Once commodities are loaded into a container, the individual items are not handled again until final delivery. The container permits economical and efficient transfer of unitized loads among different modes of transportation.

Containers come in a variety of sizes, generally in lengths of 10, 20, and 40 feet for international shipments. The cargo container is usually weatherproof, permitting storage outside or transport in open-top railcars or on a ship's deck. The container's construction is rugged enough for movement by mechanical means such as forklifts or cranes and for interchange between or among modes.

The container has gained wide acceptance in the international movement of manufactured goods. Railroads and motor carriers have joined forces to provide through movement of containers from the interior of the United States to foreign countries. Special double stack railcars are used to transport two containers per car. The use of double-stack trains has greatly increased the economic viability of containerized shipments.

On the domestic front, a number of long-haul trucking companies, J. B. Hunt and Schneider National, for example, began using domestic containers for long-distance (greater than 800 miles) moves. The trucking companies bring a domestic container to the shipper's dock for loading, then transport the container to the railroad for a long-haul, intercity move. At the destination, the trucking company delivers the container to the consignee.

Very simply, containers are attractive to users because of reduced cost. Containerization reduces transportation cost, handling cost, loss and damage, inventory cost, paperwork, and packaging cost.

SUMMARY

- Materials handling and packaging affect a company's transportation and warehousing activities.
- Materials handling is the short-distance movement of goods that takes place within the confines of a building such as a plant or warehouse and between a building and a transportation vehicle.
- Materials handling has four dimensions: movement, time, quantity, and space.
- The objectives of materials handling are to increase the effective capacity of facilities, improve operating efficiency, develop effective working conditions, improve logistics service, and reduce cost.
- The forklift and the pallet are the two major types of dock materials handling equipment. Other types of equipment are more capital-intensive and include conveyors, cranes, automatic guided vehicle systems, and a variety of order-picking and storage systems.
- Materials handling equipment falls into three design categories: flexible path, continuous-flow fixed path, and intermittent-flow fixed path.
- The selection of materials handling equipment involves considering the physical attributes of the product and packaging, the characteristics of the physical facilities, and time requirements.
- Packaging affects marketing, production, warehousing, and transportation.
- The logistics concern with packaging involves product identification, ease of handling, efficient use of storage facilities and transportation vehicles, the environment, and product protection.
- New packaging materials offer greater protection with lesser weight.
- Bar coding is an electronic method of identifying the package and its contents, and it enhances the efficiency of product storage and retrieval.
- Containers are big boxes that permit unitizing of loads and offer lower logistics costs for intermodal shipments, both domestic and international.

NOTES

1. Karen Auguston, "How Jaguar Ships Orders on Time, Every Time," *Modern Materials Handling* (February 1991): 74–75.
2. *Modern Materials Handling* (January 1991): 69.
3. John J. Hach, "Less Warehousing, Better Distribution," *Transportation & Distribution* (March 1995): 108–115.
4. Toby B. Gooley, "Moen Catches the Retail Wave," *Traffic Management* (October 1994): 40–45.
5. Tom Andel, "Pallet Providers Dealing from New Deck," *Transportation & Distribution* (August 1994): 65–70.
6. Frank Kreth, *Handbook of Solid Waste Management* (New York: McGraw Hill, 1994): 3–5.
7. "Packaging in the 90s—The Environmental Impact," *Modern Materials Handling* (June 1990): 54.
8. *Logistics Management and Technology* (Chicago: KPMG Peat Marwick, 1994): 7.
9. Gary Forger, "Bar Code Label Standards," *Modern Materials Handling* (November 1990): 43.

STUDY QUESTIONS

1. We frequently define materials handling as short-distance movement. What exactly does that mean? Where does this short-distance movement take place? Why are logistics managers concerned about materials handling?
2. One objective of materials handling is to increase effective capacity, that is, to improve space utilization. How does materials handling help to achieve this? How do materials handling systems differ with respect to this objective?
3. Review Table 8–1, Principles of Materials Handling. How would you prioritize and/or classify these principles if your firm asked you to make a presentation to a group of non-logistics managers to help them understand materials handling?
4. Forklift trucks are generally considered the most popular form of materials handling equipment. Why are they so popular? Analyze forklift trucks in terms of their ability to help companies achieve materials handling objectives.
5. One major area in a physical distribution center is order picking. Compare and contrast this area's two major system types.
6. Materials handling equipment selection needs to consider three major factors. Select three different products and discuss those three factors in terms of the three products.
7. What functional areas in a company are interested in packaging? What is the nature of their respective interests? What types of disagreements may arise because of these varying interests?
8. How has bar coding affected packaging and materials handling?
9. What are the current trends in packaging? Which of these trends will have the biggest impact upon logistics in the later part of this decade? Why?
10. Packaging has a direct relationship to logistics cost and service. Please explain, using examples.

Case 8-1

LIGHT FIXTURES, INC.

Light Fixtures, Inc. (LF) manufactures lighting fixtures at five plants throughout the United States. LF produces more than 700 different fixtures that are designed for the remodeling sector of the residential and commercial remodeling industry. During the 1990s LF experienced double-digit annual sales growth because of the trend in remodeling older homes, apartments, and offices.

LF sells its lighting fixtures through 150 lighting distributors who service local hardware and lighting fixture stores. Of the 150 distributors, approximately 20 account for more than 70 percent of LF's annual sales. The large distributors buy truckload quantities of different SKUs, whereas the smaller distributors buy in less-than-truckload quantities. The typical truckload shipment contains 22 pallets.

At a recent sales associates' meeting, John Ronald and Val Walen, sales associates for the two largest LF distributors, voiced the distributors' desires for LF to develop a pallet return program. These two distributors were experiencing increased pressure from the hardware and lighting fixture stores to pick up used pallets. Since the stores did not have an outlet for used pallets and did not want to incur the high disposal cost being charged by local landfills, they wanted the distributors to pick up used pallets.

Because other sales associates had expressed similar requests from their distributors, the issue was directed to Frank Dean, logistics manager. Initially, Frank felt that a pallet return program was a frivolous request by sales associates who were trying to win points with the distributors. But in the past week, Frank has received phone calls from the distribution managers at three of the largest distributors. He is now convinced that some type of pallet return program has to be developed.

Following some preliminary research, Frank discovers that the company uses 57 different types of pallets. The pallets vary by size and durability (heavy, medium, and light duty). Each of the five plants uses different pallet types.

Returning empty pallets in quantities of less than a full truckload is uneconomical because the freight cost will be greater than the price of a new pallet ($8.00). A standard 48-foot trailer can hold about 400 empty pallets. The average distance from distributor to plant is 600 miles, and the average truckload rate is $1.30 per mile. The cost to handle the pallet at the plant is $0.50 per pallet.

Since 22 pallets of finished products make a full truckload, it will take about 20 truckloads of finished product to generate a full truckload of empty pallets. The average distributor buys five truckloads per month and it will take four months to accumulate a full truckload quantity. The distributors will store the empty pallets either in their warehouse or outside. The distributors have asked for a $2.00 per pallet credit to cover their handling and storage costs.

Case Questions

1. Examine the cost components in the supply chain for the return of empty pallets.
2. Analyze the economics of returning used pallets.
3. What other costs and operating issues need to be considered?
4. What is your recommendation for a pallet return policy?

CHAPTER 9

THE TRANSPORTATION SYSTEM

LEARNING OBJECTIVES

After reading this chapter, you should be able to do the following:

- Explain the economic role transportation plays in the economy.

- Discuss the economic and service characteristics of the basic modes.

- Describe the carrier selection process.

- Discuss the economic effect of rates, transit time, reliability, capability, accessibility, and security in the carrier selection decision.

- Compare the advantages and disadvantages of using common, contract, exempt, and private carriers—the four legal classes of carriers.

- Discuss the economic and service characteristics of intermodal transportation and explain the dominance of rail-truck (piggyback) intermodal service.

- Discuss the economic rationale of using containerization.

- Discuss the economic and service characteristics of indirect and special carriers.

LOGISTICS PROFILE

CONSOLIDATED FREIGHTWAYS, INC.

Consolidated Freightways is one of a growing number of transportation companies that is providing multimodal transportation services to meet the integrated logistics needs of today's shippers.

Through a dozen subsidiaries Consolidated Freightways provides various trucking, intermodal, contract logistics, air cargo, and customs brokerage services. Within some of the service areas a shipper has the choice of more than one provider.

Consolidated Freightways is probably best known for its trucking operations. There are five trucking subsidiaries: CF Motor Freight, Canadian Freightways, Con-Way Western Express, Con-Way Central Express, and Con-Way Southern Express.

CF Motor Freight provides intermediate and long-haul trucking of less-than-truckload (LTL) freight. It operates a network of more than 500 terminals serving all 50 states as well as Mexico, Puerto Rico, the Caribbean, and Latin and Central America. Canadian Freightways provides long-haul and regional LTL and TL services in Canada and international (U.S.–Canada) service via gateways with CF Motor Freight. The three Con-Way carriers supply next-day and second-day regional trucking service in the U.S.

Another Con-Way company, Con-Way Transportation Services, offers door-to-door intermodal movement of full truckload shipments via rail piggyback. It also provides international shipping services.

International shipping support services are available from Milne & Craighead Customs Brokers. General customs brokerage, shipment clearance, documentation, and import/export consulting services are offered by this subsidiary.

Air cargo services are available from Emery Worldwide. Emery is a global airfreight company that operates dedicated aircraft and a ground fleet for door-to-door airfreight service. Emery Customs Brokers provides customs brokerage, shipment clearance, and documentation services for international shipments.

Finally, contract logistics services are available from Menlo Logistics. Menlo provides logistics management services, including carrier management, dedicated fleet and warehouse operations, just-in-time (JIT) inbound material delivery programs, customer order processing, and freight bill payment and auditing.

Consolidated Freightways and many other trucking, rail, and air carriers are becoming one-stop transportation (logistics) centers. They offer not only a variety of basic modal services but also intermodal and logistics services. As today's logistics managers integrate the logistics supply chain, the one-stop transportation center is the carrier of the future.

ADAPTED FROM: Consolidated Freightways, Inc., 1994 Annual Report to Shareholders.

The transportation system is the physical link connecting a company's customers, raw material suppliers, plants, warehouses, and channel members—the fixed points in a logistics supply chain. The fixed points in the logistics system are where some activity temporarily halts the flow of goods in the logistics pipeline. The transportation companies utilized to connect these facilities affect not only the transportation costs but the operating costs at these facilities.

This chapter is concerned with the transportation system in the logistics system. We will focus on the fundamental relationship between transportation and the logistics supply chain, the carrier selection decision, and the characteristics of alternative transportation providers.

THE ROLE OF
TRANSPORTATION IN LOGISTICS

bridge over buyer-seller gap

Conceptually, a company's logistics supply chain is a series of fixed points where the goods come to rest and transportation links. The transportation link permits goods to flow between the various fixed points and bridges the buyer-seller gap. The transportation carrier a company utilizes to perform the link service is a decisive factor in determining the efficiency of operating the supply chain facility and partially determines the company's competitive edge and product demand in a given market area.

value added

Knowledge of the transportation system is fundamental to the efficient and economical operation of a company's logistics function. Transportation is the physical thread connecting the company's geographically dispersed operations. More specifically, transportation adds value to the company by creating time and place utility; the value added is the physical movement of goods to the place desired and at the time desired.

For a firm to function without the aid of transportation is virtually inconceivable in today's global economy. Most companies are geographically divorced from their supply sources, thereby making them dependent upon transportation to connect the supply source to the consumption point. Labor specialization, mass production, and production economies normally do not coincide with the area where demand for the good exists. Thus, transportation is necessary to bridge this buyer-seller spatial gap.

global impact

As supply chains become increasingly longer in our global economy, the transportation function is connecting buyers and sellers that may be tens of thousands of miles apart. This increased spatial gap results in greater transportation costs. In addition, operations within this international marketplace require more transportation time, which necessitates higher inventories and resulting higher storage costs. Therefore, the greater the buyer-seller gap, the greater the transportation and storage costs.

importance in economy

The total dollars spent in the U.S. to move freight reveal the importance of transportation in the economy. In 1993, the U.S. spent an estimated $397.4 billion to move freight, or 6.26 percent of the GNP.[1] This total expenditure included shipper costs of $4.0 billion for loading and unloading freight cars and for operating and controlling the transportation function.

importance in company

As an example of transportation's relative importance in a company, a study of 1994 physical distribution (outbound only) costs revealed that total distribution costs represented 7.7 percent of sales and that the outbound transportation cost amounted to 3.09 percent of sales, or 39.0 percent of total distribution costs. Warehousing cost was 2.12 percent of sales; customer service and order processing accounted for 0.47 percent of sales; administration was 0.35 percent of sales; and, inventory carrying cost was 1.93 percent of sales.[2] Outbound transportation was clearly the largest component of total physical distribution costs.

To say that transportation is logistics implies that transportation operates independently of other logistics functions. Nothing could be further from the truth, because transportation directly affects a facility's operation. The quality of the transportation service provided bears directly upon inventory costs and stockout costs at a facility as well as upon the cost of operating the facility.

cost-service trade-off

For example, if a company switches from rail to air transportation to move raw materials from a vendor to the plant, the air carrier's increased speed, or lower transit time, permits the company to hold lower inventories to meet demand during transit time and to use less warehousing space and less-stringent product packaging. But the company realizes these advantages at the expense of higher transportation costs. Thus, a firm cannot make the transportation decision in a vacuum; applying the total cost or systems approach requires a company to consider how the transport decision will affect other elements of the logistics system.

THE TRANSPORT SELECTION DECISION

As was indicated above, the transportation expenditures companies incur involve significant dollar amounts; and the carrier's service quality affects other logistics operating costs and the demand for the company's product. The company controls these expenditures and service levels through the transportation decision.

This section will focus on the process of selecting a carrier and factors relevant to that decision. The carrier selection decision process provides the framework for the discussion of the different types of transportation providers that follows this section.

The Transportation–Supply Chain Relationship

The carrier selection decision is a specialized purchasing process whereby a firm purchases the services of a carrier to provide the necessary link among logistics facilities. The carrier selected directly affects the operation of the logistics facility and other logistics system functions.

The carrier selection decision, then, entails more than merely evaluating the prices of different transportation methods. It must also consider the other costs associated with how the transport method's service affects the facility operation. The transit time different methods incur will affect the inventory level; that is, the longer the transit time, the greater the inventory level the company requires to protect against stockouts until the next shipment arrives. The transport method's dependability and the degree of safe delivery also affect the inventory levels held at a facility, the utilization of materials handling equipment and labor, and the time and cost of communicating with the carrier to determine shipment status or to seek reparations for goods damaged in transit.

scope of transport selection decision

A company's knowledge of carrier prices and pricing practices can simplify the carrier selection decision. Measuring and evaluating the logistical implication of the carrier cost determinant is much easier than measuring carrier service performances; logistics personnel know carrier rates and can easily compute an alternative's direct transportation cost. However, basing transport method selection upon lowest transport costs does not guarantee the least-cost decision for the whole logistics supply chain.

The Carrier Selection Decision

As we have noted, the carrier selection decision is a specialized purchasing process. As with any procurement decision, vendor price (carrier rate) is not the only selection criterion the firm considers. True, the carrier rate is an important factor

specialized purchasing process

in the decision, but the firm must consider the quality of the service and how this service affects facility operating costs.

modal choice   Carrier selection is a twofold process, as Figure 9–1 indicates. First, the firm selects a transportation mode. The choices include the basic modes of rail, water, truck, air, and pipeline. In addition, intermodal transportation, which uses two or more modes to provide service over a given traffic lane, is available. The most common forms of intermodal transportation include rail-truck (piggyback), truck-air, and rail-water.

specific carrier   The second step in the decision is to select a specific carrier from within the
choice chosen mode or intermodal form. The specific carrier selection requires the firm to choose the legal carrier type: common, contract, exempt, or private. The number of alternative carriers is much greater in the specific carrier selection phase than in the modal phase. For example, while the basic modal choice is limited to five alternatives, the number of regulated motor carriers from which a firm may choose is approximately 55,000.

repetitive   Generally, a firm considers the carrier selection decision a repetitive purchase
decision decision. That is, a company deciding to use motor carriers does not review this decision every time it selects a carrier to provide link service. The decision to use trucks remains in effect until the firm makes a major review of overall transportation costs and/or makes a major change in its logistics system. This repetitive decision characteristic also applies to the specific carrier decision. The firm uses the selected carrier repeatedly until the carrier's service level or rate becomes unacceptable.

The modal selection phase has received a great deal of attention. This usually involves evaluating the rates and service levels of alternative modes and intermodal forms. The firm selects the mode or intermodal form that occasions the lowest total logistics costs and then applies this analysis to the specific carriers within the selected mode (or intermodal). Given today's deregulated transportation environment, carrier rates and service performance do vary among carriers within the same mode.

FIGURE 9–1   The Carrier Selection Decision

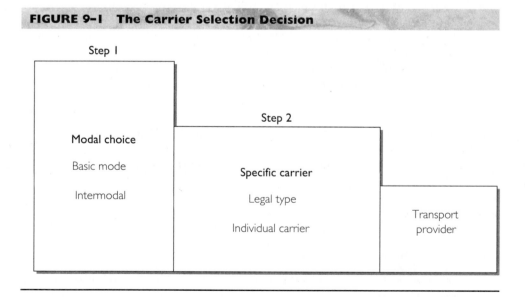

Most carriers in a given mode have the technical characteristics to provide the same level of service, but these service levels can and do vary greatly from one carrier to another. Also, since the cost structures are essentially the same for carriers in a given mode, the rates of alternative carriers in that mode are quite similar for a given movement. But, given the market and operating conditions different carriers face, the rates carriers within a given mode charge may vary somewhat. Thus, allowing for slight rate disparities, the transport rate is not the most important criterion in selecting a specific carrier; but the rate is important in modal selection. Carrier service performance, then, becomes the relevant determinant for selecting a specific carrier from one mode.

service

Carrier Selection Determinants

What, then, are the criteria firms use to evaluate the alternative modes and carriers? According to the carrier selection literature, the salient selection determinants are carrier costs and service performance. The relevant service performance determinants are transit time, reliability, capability, accessibility, and security. We will now discuss how carrier cost and service determinants interact in the firm's logistics function.

Transportation cost was the predominant carrier selection determinant in early carrier selection works. The transportation cost includes the rates, minimum weights, loading and unloading facilities, packaging and blocking, damage in transit, and special services available from a carrier—for example, stopping in transit.

transportation cost

Transportation cost analysis is oriented toward evaluating alternative modes, since the rates, minimum weights, loading and unloading facilities, packaging, and blocking will vary from one mode to another. However, the importance of transportation costs has receded somewhat with the advent of the business logistics concept, which now focuses attention upon the cost trade-offs existing between the service a carrier provides and facility operation costs. Even so, the transportation cost disparities prevalent in today's deregulated environment remain an important criterion in the carrier selection decision.

Transit time is the total time that elapses from the time the consignor makes the goods available for dispatch until the carrier delivers same to the consignee. This includes the time required for pickup and delivery, for terminal handling, and for movement between origin and destination terminals. *Reliability* refers to the consistency of the transit time a carrier (the link supplier) provides.

transit time and reliability

Transit time and reliability affect inventory and stockout costs (which take the form of lost sales or forgone productivity). Shorter transit times result in lower inventories, while more dependability causes lower inventory levels or stockout costs. With a given level of lead time, a firm can minimize inventories and consequently inventory carrying costs. But if the transit time is not consistent, the firm must increase inventories above the level that a consistent transit time would require. More specifically, a facility now must hold larger amounts of inventory as a safety factor against stockouts that could arise from inconsistent service.

inventory and stockout costs

The marketing implications of reliable transit time are product differentiation and a competitive advantage in the marketplace. Thus, if your firm can provide a customer with a shorter and more dependable transit time than your competitor, the customer can reduce inventory or stockout costs and your firm can increase sales. Sales are quite sensitive to consistent service, and the logistics manager must

product differentiation

concentrate on carrier transit time and reliability to differentiate a firm's product in the marketplace.

capability and accessibility

Capability and accessibility determine whether a particular carrier can physically perform the transport service desired. *Capability* refers to the carrier's ability to provide the equipment and facilities that the movement of a particular commodity requires. Equipment that can provide controlled temperatures or humidity and special handling facilities are examples of capability factors. *Accessibility* considers the carrier's ability to provide service over the route in question. Accessibility refers to a carrier's physical access to facilities. The geographic limits of a carrier's route network (rail lines or waterways) and the operating scope that regulatory agencies authorize constrain a carrier's accessibility. A carrier's inability to meet the desired capability and availability service requirements can eliminate the carrier from consideration in the carrier selection decision.

security

Security concerns the arrival of goods in the same condition they were in when tendered to the carrier. Although the common carrier is held liable for all loss and damage, with limited exceptions, the firm does incur costs when the carrier loses goods or delivers them in a damaged condition. Unsafe service results in opportunity costs of forgone profits or productivity because the goods are not available for sale or use. To guard against these opportunity costs, a firm will increase inventory levels, with resulting increased inventory costs. The continued use of an unsafe carrier will adversely affect customer satisfaction and, consequently, sales.

A firm using a common carrier holds the carrier liable for damage to the lading. To recover the damage value, the shipping firm must file a claim with the carrier. This entails a claim preparation and documentation cost, as well as legal fees if the firm has the claim settled through the courts. Therefore, frequent damage to the commodities also aggravates the cost associated with claim settlement.

The Pragmatics of Carrier Selection

transit time reliability

Figure 9–2 gives the relative importance of the carrier selection determinants for firms selecting motor carriers in today's deregulated environment. The most important criterion is the quality of the service the carrier provides, that is, transit time reliability. The impact of reliable transit time and total transit time (importance rank 3) on inventory and stockout costs and customer service is of paramount importance today.

carrier rates

limited carriers

Transportation deregulation has provided transportation users with increased opportunity to negotiate both rates and services with carriers. This greater reliance on the marketplace has increased interest in the rate the carrier charges. Shippers are generally utilizing fewer carriers in order to become more important to the carrier and thereby to increase their negotiating power with the carrier.

financial stability

Transportation rates, the carrier's willingness to negotiate rate changes, and the carrier's financial stability reflect the negotiating strategy inherent in the deregulated environment. Today's shippers utilize their economic buying power in the marketplace to realize lower transportation rates from carriers. But this highly competitive motor carrier industry has experienced over 10,000 bankruptcies since 1980. The heightened possibility of bankruptcy increases the service disruption risk; and the magnitude of this risk increases as firms implement a reduced carrier strategy.

FIGURE 9-2 Importance Ranking of Carrier Selection Determinants

Determinant	Rank
Transit time reliability or consistency	1
Door-to-door transportation rates or costs	2
Total door-to-door transit time	3
Willingness of carrier to negotiate rate changes	4
Financial stability of the carrier	5
Equipment availability	6
Frequency of service	7
Pickup and delivery service	8
Freight loss and damage	9
Shipment expediting	10
Quality of operating personnel	11
Shipment tracing	12
Willingness of carrier to negotiate service changes	13
Scheduling flexibility	14
Line-haul services	15
Claims processing	16
Quality of carrier salesmanship	17
Special equipment	18

SOURCE: Edward J. Bardi, Prabir Bagchi, and T. S. Raghunathan, "Motor Carrier Selection in a Deregulated Environment," *Transportation Journal* 29, no. 1 (Fall 1989): 4–11.

Shippers give capability and accessibility average importance, as the factors ranked from 6 to 15 show. The security criterion of freight loss and damage ranks ninth in importance, and the claims processing factor ranks sixteenth.

sales rep

Less important selection determinants are the quality of carrier salesmanship and special equipment. Shippers making the carrier selection decision give little importance to the quality of the carrier sales representative. Special equipment is not an important selection determinant for shippers who require standard equipment, but for those requiring special equipment the carrier who has it is the only one the shipper will use.

special equipment

THE BASIC MODES
OF TRANSPORTATION

The basic modes of transportation available to the logistics manager are rail, motor, water, pipeline, and air. Each mode has different economic and technical structures, and each can provide different qualities of link service. This section examines how each mode's structure relates to the cost and quality of link service possible with the basic modes—the basis for the modal selection analysis.

Distribution of ton-miles (an output measurement combining weight and distance, or tonnage multiplied by miles transported) among the modes shows each mode's relative importance. Table 9–1 shows this distribution. These data suggest that the relative importance of rail transport has lessened and that the importance of motor and pipeline transport has increased substantially. Air transport has continued to advance in property movement. On the surface, these data suggest that

TABLE 9-1 Distribution of Inventory Freight by Modes (For-Hire and Private) (Billions of Ton-Miles)

	Rail		Motor		Pipeline		Water		Air	
	Amt	%	Amt	%	Amt	%	Amt	%	Amt	%
1940	379	61.3	62	10.0	59	9.5	118	19.1	0.02	0.00
1960	579	44.1	285	21.8	229	17.4	220	16.7	0.89	0.07
1970	771	39.7	412	21.3	431	22.3	219	16.5	3.3	0.17
1980	932	37.5	555	22.3	588	23.6	407	16.4	4.8	0.20
1990	1,100	37.9	735	25.3	584	20.2	475	16.4	10.4	0.40
1993	1,183	38.1	871	28.0	572	18.4	467	15.0	11.6	0.37

SOURCE: *Transportation in America*, 12th ed. (Lansdowne, VA: Eno Transportation Foundation, Inc., 1994): 7.

shipping firms increasingly use "premium" transportation—motor and air—to provide a desired level of customer service by trading off higher transportation costs (motor and air, as compared with rail and water) for lower facility costs. In 1993, motor carriers received 78.5 percent of the U.S. freight expenditures; rail, 7.9 percent; air, 4.0 percent; water, 5.3 percent; and oil pipeline, 2.2 percent.[3]

Railroads

capability　All for-hire railroads in the United States are classified as common carriers* and are thus subjected to the legal service obligations we will discuss later. Since the Interstate Commerce Commission imposes no legal restraints or operating authority regulations regarding the commodities railroads may transport, railroads have a distinct advantage in availability and in the ability to provide service to "all" shippers. This is not to imply that railroads can transport any product anywhere, for the accessibility of rail transportation does have limitations. But with respect to the ability to transport a wide variety of goods, the railroads have a distinct advantage over other common carriers in the different modes. Railroads are not restricted as to the cargo type they may transport; rather, all railroads are legally, as well as physically, capable of transporting all commodities tendered for transportation.

limited number of carriers　The railroad industry consists of a small number of large firms. There are about 500 railroads, of which a dozen have revenues exceeding $50 million per year, with the remainder having less than $50 million in revenues. This rather limited number of carriers may suggest limited rail service availability, but the railroads are required to provide through service, which makes rail service available to points beyond a particular carrier's geographic limits.

market structure　This mode's economic structure partly accounts for the limited number of rail carriers. Railroads, which fall within that infamous group of business undertakings labeled as "natural monopolies," require a large investment in terminals, equipment, and trackage to begin operation, and the accompanying huge capacity allows the railroads to be a decreasing-cost industry. As output (ton-miles) increases, the average per-unit production cost decreases. Thus, having fewer railroads in

---

*Several years ago, the ICC exempted from economic regulation railroad movement of fresh fruits and vegetables, piggyback freight, and boxcar traffic.

TABLE 9–2 Average Revenue per Ton-Mile (in Cents)

Year	Rail*	Motor*	Water†	Oil Pipeline	Air
1975	2.04	11.60	0.518	0.368	28.22
1980	2.85	18.00	0.770	0.999	46.31
1984	3.09	22.16	0.818	1.272	50.20
1988	2.72	23.17	0.754	1.364	43.63
1993	2.52	24.30	0.735	1.526	45.41

*Class 1 rail and motor carrier.
†Barge lines.
SOURCE: "Transportation in America," 12th ed. (Lansdowne, VA: Eno Transportation Foundation, Inc., 1994), 9.

operation in a given area and permitting those few firms to realize inherent large-scale output economies is economical and beneficial to society.

Through mergers, seven railroads—Burlington Northern; ConRail; CSX Transportation; Norfolk Southern; Atchison, Topeka & Santa Fe; Southern Pacific; and Union Pacific—have evolved as the dominant (84 percent of the 1993 industry revenue) carriers in the industry. Many of these carriers have acquired nonrail transportation companies such as trucking and water carriers, permitting one organization to provide multimodal transportation service to shippers.

Railroads are primarily long-distance, large-volume movers of low-value, high-density goods. The reason for these long-distance, large-volume rail movements is ingrained in the mode's economic and technical characteristics. The railroad's decreasing cost structure suggests that large-volume, long-distance movements lower the average production cost by increasing output (ton-miles) and thereby spreading the fixed costs over a greater output base.

long distance and large volume

A major advantage of using railroad transportation is the long-distance movement of commodities in large quantities at relatively low rates. Products of forests, mines, and agriculture are the major commodities railroads transport. For these low-value, high-density products, transportation costs account for a substantial portion of their selling price. Railroads tend to serve the inbound portion of the logistics supply chain. As Table 9–2 shows, rail transportation has one of the lowest revenue per ton-mile of all modes, and it has the lowest revenue per ton-mile of the modes capable of transporting general commodities domestically—rail, motor, and air.

Low accessibility is one primary disadvantage of rail transport. Accessibility refers to the carrier's ability to provide service to and from the facilities in a particular situation. The rail carrier cannot deviate from the route that the rail trackage follows. If a shipper or consignee is not adjacent to the rail right-of-way, rail transport is not easily accessible. To use rail service, a shipper or consignee not adjacent to the track must utilize another transport mode—namely, truck—to gain access to the rail service. Thus, rail service may not be advantageous in logistics situations such as the ultimate delivery of consumer goods to retail outlets.*

low accessibility

---

*Railroads are using *piggyback* (trailer-on-flatcar) service to overcome inaccessibility. A rail flatcar moves a motor truck trailer between origin and destination terminals, but a truck transports the trailer over the highways to the consignor and consignee. We will discuss piggyback service in greater detail in a later section of this chapter.

long transit times   Rather long transport time is another disadvantage of rail transport. The problem occurs in the classification yard, where the carrier *consolidates* boxcars, or marshalls them into train units. This huge physical task, which requires consolidating boxcars going in a similar direction and breaking out cars that have reached their destination or that the carrier must transfer to another train unit, adds to the overall slow speed of rail transport.

reliability and safety   Railroads favorably provide other service qualities important to the logistics manager—reliability and safety. Weather conditions disrupt rail service less than they disrupt the service of other modes; such conditions cause only minor fluctuations in rail transit time reliability. Rail safety incurs greater costs. Moving goods by rail requires considerable packaging and resultant packaging costs. This stems from the car classification operation, in which the carrier couples cars at impacts ranging from 1 to 10 miles per hour, and from the rather rough ride that steel wheels running on steel rails provide. But these service qualities differ among particular carriers, and the logistics manager must research such qualities carefully.

Today's railroad industry is changing considerably in response to the economy, deregulation, and the logistics approach of business. The traditional markets of low-value, high-density, high-volume products (grain, steel, coal, etc.) are stagnant or declining. Deregulation has increased the competitive pressures for railroads to lower rates, and the railroads have responded through the contract ratemaking provisions of the Staggers Act of 1980. Finally, the railroads are experiencing pressures from logistics managers to improve service (lower transit times) and to integrate with other modes (primarily trucking).

During the past ten years the railroads have made considerable improvements in productivity. They have abandoned unused tracks, sold off unprofitable lines (regional railroads), reduced the work force, and modified labor work rules. Increased computer use is enabling the industry to improve train movement efficiency, saving fuel and labor costs.

Railroad mergers are another possible strategy for improving productivity. Larger companies offer the opportunity for economies of scale and lower rates to the shipping public. Serious merger talks have taken place among the top twelve major railroads, and there is speculation that the top twelve could become the top six by the end of the century.

intermodal   New market penetration is another railroad strategy that has improved profitability. The major new market being entered is intermodal freight. During the last few years intermodal traffic has increased dramatically, with expectations of double-digit increases in the latter part of the 1990s. Railroads have developed the stack train that hauls two containers on one specially designed flatcar. This service is used primarily by international shippers who integrate water carriage to and from foreign countries with rail domestically to form an integrated transportation process.

In response to shipper demand for lower cost and faster service for long-distance shipments, motor carriers and railroads have formed partnerships. Two notable trucking partners are J. B. Hunt and Schneider National, who have announced plans to add 40,000 domestic containers to their fleets.

IMC   Additionally, railroad intermodal traffic is growing because of a new type of transportation company, the intermodal marketing company, or IMC. The IMC is an intermediary who solicits intermodal traffic from shippers and gives it to the railroad to transport. The IMC initially started as a marketing effort to seek freight to fill empty containers moving back to the West Coast and on to Pacific Rim countries. Now the IMCs have contracted with railroads to ship a given number of containers per train over specific traffic lanes.

Motor Carriers

The motor carrier is very much a part of any firm's logistics supply chain; almost every logistics operation utilizes the motor truck, from the smallest pickup truck to the largest tractor-semitrailer combination, in some capacity. The United States' sophisticated highway network permits the motor carrier to reach all points of the country. Therefore, the motor carrier can provide transportation service to virtually all shippers. Table 9–1 points out that motor carriers have made great inroads into the number of ton-miles that carriers transport in the United States. Figure 9–3 offers an overview of the motor carrier industry.

Unlike the railroads, the regulated for-hire portion of the motor carrier industry consists of both common and contract carriers. Exempt for-hire carriers and private carriers are also available. Approximately 40 percent of the intercity ton-miles of truck-transported freight moves through regulated carriers—common and contract. Exempt and private carriers transport the remaining 60 percent.

types of legal carriers

The exempt carrier primarily transports agricultural, fish, and horticultural products—the exempt commodities to which the next section refers. While private carriers transport a variety of products, private truck transportation most commonly moves high-value, high-rated traffic and commodities requiring "personalized" service such as driver-salesperson operations.

FIGURE 9–3   Overview of Interstate Motor Carrier Industry

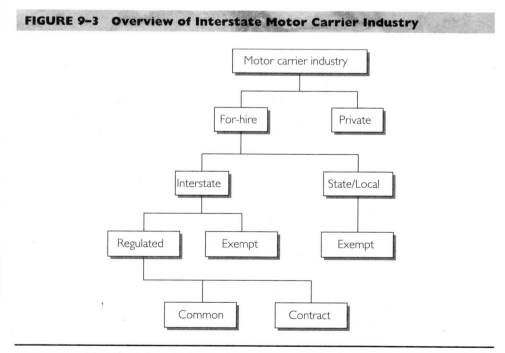

ADAPTED FROM: John J. Coyle, Edward J. Bardi, and Robert A. Novack, *Transportation*, 4th ed. (St. Paul, MN: West Publishing Co., 1994), 136.

large number of small carriers

The regulated motor carriers consist of a large number of relatively small firms. In 1994, there were approximately 55,000 regulated motor carriers. Of this total, only 2 percent had annual revenues greater than $5 million; approximately 95 percent had annual revenues less than $1 million.

This large number of carriers is due in part to the low capital that entering the trucking business requires. High variable cost and low fixed cost characterize the cost structure. The motor carrier does not require extensive terminal and equipment investment and does not invest in its own highway. The government builds and maintains the highway, and the carrier pays for highway use through fees such as use taxes and licensing charges. These variable expenses contribute to the high-variable-cost structure.

availability and operating authority

The large number of motor carriers suggests a high availability. For example, many more motor carriers than railroads are available in an area. However, the operating authorities granted particular carriers have limited motor carrier availability somewhat. These operating grants limit the type of commodity a carrier may transport and the area within which the carrier may provide service. A common motor carrier of property may have operating authority to transport only general commodities, household goods, heavy machinery, liquid petroleum products, building materials, or explosives, for example. Regulation precludes it from transporting any other commodity unless the Interstate Commerce Commission gives specific authorization. The carrier's authorized service area may be a broad regional area, particular states, or particular cities; and the authorization may restrict the carrier's service provision over regular routes or irregular routes. A carrier's ICC-defined ability to transport given commodities between particular points, rather than the number of carriers serving an area, determines regulated motor carriers' availability.

high accessibility

The controls regulating the commodities transported and the areas served directly affect the accessibility of particular carriers. But the major advantage of motor transport over other modes is its inherent ability to provide service to any location. Truck transportation need not provide service only to customers located adjacent to a track, waterway, or airport. For the logistics manager, the motor carrier is the most accessible transportation mode existing to serve domestic markets today.

transit time

Motor carrier operations do not involve coupling trailers together to form long "train" units, because each cargo unit (trailer) has its own power unit and can be operated independently. Thus, on truckload movements, the shipment goes directly from the shipper to the consignee, bypassing any terminal area and consolidation time. Such technical and operational characteristics enable the motor carrier to provide transit times lower than those for rail and water, but higher than that for air.

reliability

Weather conditions and highway traffic can disrupt motor service and thus affect transit time reliability. These factors affect the dependability of all motor carriers. A specific carrier's reliability relates to the operating efficiency the carrier achieves for a given link; this reliability may vary among the given carrier's links.

manufactured goods

While some motor carriers transport low-value products, such as coal and grain, and move products over long distances, motor carriers primarily transport manufactured commodities over relatively short distances. Characterized by high value, manufactured commodities include textile and leather products, rubber and plastic products, fabricated metal products, communication products and parts, and photographic equipment.

The physical and legal constraints on carrying capacity make motor transport somewhat amenable to small shipments. This directly affects inventory levels and the shipment quantity necessary for gaining a lower truckload (volume discount) rate. Because of the smaller shipment size coupled with lower transit times, the logistics manager can reduce inventory carrying costs while maintaining or improving customer service levels. **small shipment size**

Generalizing the other relevant service attribute, safety, is difficult for motor carriers. The packaging required for motor carrier movements is less stringent than that required for rail or water; pneumatic tires and improved suspension systems make the motor carrier ride quite smooth. Again, the degree of safety for a given link depends upon the actual operations of individual carriers. **safety**

The logistics manager must consider the relatively high cost of using a motor carrier. As Table 9–2 points out, the average truck revenue per ton-mile is approximately nine times that of rail and thirty-three times that by water. This again suggests that commodities shippers move by truck must be of value high enough to sustain the transportation costs, or that trade-offs in inventory, packaging, warehousing, or customer service costs must warrant the use of this higher-cost mode. **high cost**

Since the passage of the Motor Carrier Act of 1980, competition in the for-hire motor carrier industry has increased tremendously. The easing of regulatory entry controls has permitted thousands of new carriers to enter the industry and to compete for existing freight. To gain a market share, the new carriers, as well as the existing carriers, offer lower rates and improved service. Rate discounts are the norm today; some carriers offer shippers discounts as high as 50 to 60 percent. Lower fuel and labor costs help many carriers to sustain these large rate discounts.

The competitive environment has been a mixed blessing to shippers. On the positive side, lower motor carrier rates have enabled shippers to reduce transportation costs and improve profitability. On the negative side, the downward pressure on rates has contributed to approximately 10,000 carrier bankruptcies since 1980. These have caused logistics disruptions ranging from minor delivery delays for freight caught in the bankrupt carrier's system to temporary halting of a firm's transportation function until the firm can find a carrier to replace a key link provider.

Many trucking companies have established nonunion subsidiaries to combat low profitability. As seen in the Logistics Profile section at the beginning of this chapter, the ConWay carriers, which are nonunion trucking subsidiaries of Consolidated Freightways, Inc., have made substantial growth and are a major supplier of trucking service today. Finally, most large trucking companies have created logistics outsourcing companies. These logistics outsourcing firms provide multiple logistics services for clients, as evidenced in the Logistics Profile section.

Water Carriers

Water transportation, a major factor in U.S. development, remains an important factor in today's economy. In the early stages of U.S. development, water transportation provided the only connection between the United States and Europe, the market area for U.S. agricultural production and the source of manufactured goods. Thus, many larger industrial cities in both the United States and Europe are located along major water transport routes.

Domestic. Domestic commodity movements take place along the Atlantic, Gulf, and Pacific coasts, as well as inland along internal navigable waterways such as the

FIGURE 9–4 Overview of the Domestic Water Carrier Industry

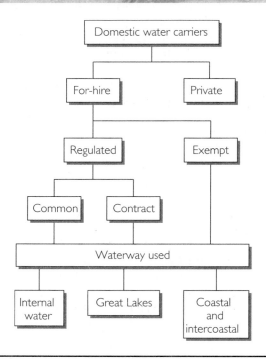

SOURCE: John J. Coyle, Edward J. Bardi, and Robert A. Novack, *Transportation*, 4th ed. (St. Paul, MN: West Publishing Co., 1994), 217.

Mississippi, Ohio, and Missouri Rivers and the Great Lakes. As Figure 9–4 indicates, water carriers are classified as internal water carriers, Great Lakes carriers, and coastal and intercoastal carriers. Internal water carriers operate on the internal navigable waterways. Great Lakes carriers operate on the Great Lakes and provide service to shippers along the northern border of the United States. Coastal carriers operate between points on the same coast, whereas intercoastal carriers operate between points on the Atlantic and the Pacific via the Panama Canal.

legal carrier types   All four legal classifications of carriers exist in water transportation. Regulated for-hire common and contract carriers transport approximately 5 percent of the intercity ton-miles for water-transported freight, and exempt and private carriers transport the remaining 95 percent.

cost structure   Rather low capital entry restraint and operations exempt from federal economic regulation account partly for a large portion of the unregulated domestic traffic transported by water. To begin operation, a water carrier requires no investment for the right-of-way—nature provides the "highway" and public expenditures maintain the facility. The water carrier requires only the entry capital necessary for equipment. Thus, the investment does not preclude private water transport as it does private rail transport. Exemption exists for the transportation of bulk commodities or bulk oil products, and these are the major commodities shippers transport by water.

service characteristics   Water carriers are primarily long-distance movers of low-value, high-density cargoes that mechanical devices easily load and unload. Mineral, agricultural, and forest products are the major commodities transported. Carriers move these products in large quantities: one barge can transport about 1,500 tons.

The principal advantage of using water transport is its low cost. Table 9–2 shows that the average revenue per ton-mile for water carriage is lower than that for rail, motor, and air. Thus, water transport is most advantageous for commodities with a low value-to-weight relationship, or for commodities in which the transportation cost is a significant portion of the selling price.

In return for this low rate, the shipper receives a slow movement method. Water transport possibly provides the highest transit time of all modes. Weather conditions affect internal and Great Lakes operations—ice and low water levels disrupt service. In addition, water transport has greatly restrained accessibility. Only shippers adjacent to the waterway can use water transport directly. In other situations, water carriage use requires a prior or subsequent land transport movement. Thus, the major disadvantages of water transport are long transit times and low accessibility.

long transit time

low accessibility

International. As was indicated previously, transport by ship is by far the most widely used international shipment method. In 1986, ocean carriage accounted for approximately 60 percent of worldwide freight movements. Companies ship almost any conceivable cargo type by sea, but most ocean cargo consists of low weight-to-value commodities such as petroleum, minerals, and dry bulk items.

Types of Ships. The most common type of ocean vessel in use today is the *general cargo ship*. These ships, usually engaged to transport shipload cargoes on a contract basis, have large cargo holds and are equipped to handle a large variety of cargo. Many of these ships also have what is called a *tween deck*, a deck between the main deck and the main holds in which the carrier commonly stows palletized cargo. Some carriers equip cargo ships with large side doors, which allow easy access for forklifts loading pallets. Most carriers equip cargo ships with derricks, which allow them to load and discharge cargo at ports that lack up-to-date cargo handling equipment. This feature is very important for ships transporting goods to less-developed portions of the world.

general cargo ships

Bulk carriers carry cargoes with low value-to-weight ratios, such as ores, grain, coal, and scrap metal. Very large openings on these ships' holds allow easy loading and unloading. Watertight walls dividing the holds allow a ship to carry more than one commodity at a time.

bulk carriers

Tankers carry the largest amount of cargo by tonnage. These ships range in size from World War II–era tankers of 18,000 tons to VLCCs (very large crude carriers), some of which top 500,000 tons. Tankers are constructed in much the same way as bulk carriers, but with smaller deck openings. Considering the oil spill problem, the use of double-hulled tankers has become preferable to more conventional single-hulled tankers. Another, less common type of tanker ship, referred to as an LNG ship, carries liquified natural gas. The largest of these vessels can carry enough natural gas to heat New York City for a winter week.

tankers

Container ships are becoming increasingly more important in today's market. These ships are specially designed to carry standardized containers, which are commonly rated in TEUs (twenty-foot equivalent units) or FEUs (forty-foot equivalent units). Some of the larger container ships today carry upwards of 5,000 TEUs on board a single vessel. Also, container ships can carry a wide variety of cargo,

container ships

including many products that require special handling, temperature control, and so on.

The containers are preloaded at their origin and then placed aboard ship, allowing lower port loading and unloading costs. Containers allow direct access to inland points through intermodal arrangements, but require specially designed heavy-lift derricks for loading and unloading. Many smaller ports cannot afford the investment required to handle this type of cargo.

RO-RO

Roll-on-roll-off (RO-RO) vessels are another type of ship proving its value in international trade. RO-ROs are basically large ferry ships. The carrier drives the cargo directly onto the ship using built-in ramps and drives or tows it off at its destination. Toyota currently operates several RO-RO ships to carry automobiles from Japan to the United States and Europe. Each ship can transport 2,000 or more cars at a time. On the return trip, the vessels carry grain or coal for use in Japan.

RO-ROs allow carriers to use standard highway trailers to transport cargo. This can be an advantage in less-developed areas where ports lack container handling facilities. RO-ROs can also carry oversized cargoes such as large earth-moving equipment or cranes, which carriers can drive directly onto the ship.

Combination RO-RO/container ships are also becoming common. The rear of these ships have built-in ramps. They also have movable decks and inner partitions. The carrier can change the ship configuration so that it may carry various combinations of containers and RO-RO cargo.

OBO

Oil-bulk-ore (OBO) *vessels* are multipurpose bulk carriers that are able to carry both liquid and dry bulk products. The development of these vessels allowed the shipowner to carry cargoes on most legs of a voyage, whereas previously the vessel may have had to transit in ballast (empty) due to the trade patterns of the products shipped.

barges

Oceangoing barge vessels are prominent in the U.S.-to-Puerto Rico trade and in the Hawaiian interisland trade. In practice, these vessels are towed by an oceangoing tug, as opposed to being pushed like barges on the inland waterways. Compared to the RO-RO vessels, the oceangoing barge is very inexpensive. Currently, the largest of these barges measures 730 feet long and 100 feet wide and has a capacity of 512 trailers on three decks.

Air Carriers

Passenger movement is the air carrier's principal business; passenger revenue accounts for the majority of air carrier business. In the movement of freight, air transport is somewhat nascent, accounting or less than 1 percent of the total intercity ton-miles of freight.

The air carrier industry is highly concentrated in a limited number of carriers. The major carriers earn nearly 90 percent of the industry's revenue; the revenue these carriers generate is primarily from passenger transport.

The type of designations used for air carriers differ somewhat from those used for rail and motor. For-hire air carriers are classified as follows:

- *Certificated:* carrier holding a certificate to operate large aircraft
- *Noncertificated:* carrier that does not hold a certificate to operate because it operates aircraft with a maximum payload of 18,000 pounds and sixty seats
- *All-cargo:* carrier that transports cargo only

ON THE LINE

The Iron Highway

The Iron Highway is a piggyback train designed to compete with trucks for trips as short as 300 miles. Intermodal carriers historically have been unable to compete with trucks on transits of less than 700 to 800 miles. On short distances, the time and cost of terminal transfer has been too big of a handicap for intermodal to overcome.

The Iron Highway uses a 1,200-foot continuous platform that can accommodate any trailer size and can be loaded and unloaded at sites outside the rail intermodal yard. The continuous platforms are segmented at 28-foot intervals, providing a deck for rapid roll-on-roll-off loading without an elaborate terminal.

The technology is designed to run with a self-powered control cab at each end. This will free the Iron Highway from dependence on conventional locomotives and will improve transit times.

CSX Intermodal and CP Rail (Canadian) will test the Iron Highway over two traffic lanes: Chicago to Detroit and Toronto to Montreal. The goal is to have a network of Iron Highways stretching from Chicago to Montreal. Eventually, 35 to 40 Iron Highway units will operate on the route, providing departures as frequent as those offered by trucks.

SOURCE: Adapted with permission from Joseph Bonney, "CSXI, CP To Test Iron Highway," *American Shipper* (November 1994): 81.

- *International:* certificated carrier that operates between the United States and a foreign country
- *Air taxi:* noncertificated carrier that will fly anywhere on demand with a maximum payload of 18,000 pounds and sixty passengers
- *Commuter:* noncertificated carrier that operates with a published timetable
- *Major:* carrier with annual revenues greater than $1 billion
- *National:* carrier with annual revenues between $75 million and $1 billion
- *Large regional:* carrier with annual revenues between $10 million and $75 million
- *Medium regional:* carrier with annual revenues less than $10 million

The logistics manager may use any of the preceding air carrier classes to transport freight.

The air carrier cost structure consists of high variable costs in proportion to fixed costs, somewhat akin to the motor carrier cost structure. Like motor and water carriers, air carriers do not invest in a highway (airway). The government builds terminals, and carriers pay variable lease payments and landing fees for their use. The equipment cost, though quite high, is still a small part of the total cost.

cost characteristics

Major commercial air carrier freight movement started as a passenger business by-product. Excess capacity existed in the plane's "belly," offering potential room for freight movement. As cargo demand grew, the carriers began to seriously consider this business arena. Now the scheduled carriers have dedicated equipment specifically to freight movement and operate freight service to meet freight shippers' ever-growing needs. The all-cargo lines have always concentrated upon cargo transportation.

The major advantage of using air transportation is speed. Air transport affords a distinct advantage in low transit time over long distances. Thus, air transport is

low transit time

necessary for moving emergency shipments or shipments that are highly perishable in terms of both spoilage and lost sales or productivity.

high cost   Cost is the major disadvantage of using air transportation, and it precludes many shippers from utilizing this mode. The average revenue per ton-mile for air carriers is approximately 18 times that of rail and 2 times that of motor transport (see Table 9–2). Commodities with a high value-to-weight relationship can sustain this high transport cost because transportation is a smaller portion of the commodity's selling price than is inventory holding cost. In this shipping situation, the logistics manager can reduce inventory levels and inventory costs and can rely upon air transport speed to meet demand.

limited accessibility   Air transport accessibility is somewhat limited. Most firms using air carriers must rely upon land carriers to transport freight to and from the airport. The most common and feasible mode is the motor carrier; firms utilize both local for-hire and private motor carriage to overcome air carrier inaccessibility.

reliability   Air transport reliability is also somewhat of a disadvantage. Weather conditions interrupt air service. These conditions result in increased transit time and adjusted higher inventory levels. But the advent of instrument flying and the adoption of these devices at a greater number of airports is minimizing this service interruption.

international   Air transport has become a very viable alternative to water (ocean) transport for international shipments. The reduced air transit time, reduced delays and port handling costs, and reduced packaging costs enable exporters and importers to reduce overall logistics costs and improve customer service. Again, the logistics manager must trade off the high air transport rate against other logistics cost reductions in order to justify using this method.

Pipelines

The pipeline industry refers to oil pipelines, not natural gas pipelines. However, the Federal Energy Regulatory Commission, which regulates approximately 130 oil pipelines, also regulates natural gas pipelines just as it regulates any other public utility.

limited capability   Pipeline transportation is not suitable for general commodity transportation; rather, its use is restricted to the movement of liquid petroleum products. Some firms have attempted to move commodities such as coal in a slurry form, but moving such commodities by pipeline has not been a viable alternative to other modes—namely, water and rail.

limited accessibility   Pipeline accessibility is limited. Only shippers adjacent to the pipeline can use this mode directly. Shippers not located adjacent to the pipeline require another, more accessible mode such as water, rail, or truck to transport products to or away from the pipeline. The speed is quite slow, typically less than 10 miles per hour, resulting in long transit times; however, weather conditions do not disrupt pipeline service.

cost characteristics   The pipeline cost structure is one of high fixed costs and low variable costs, quite similar to that existing for the railroads. The investment in the line, terminals, and pumping stations contributes most to this cost structure.

low cost   Low cost, as compared with other modes, is the major advantage to using oil pipelines. However, the inability to transport solids limits its usefulness in the logistics system of a firm manufacturing durable goods.

Performance Rating of Modes

The logistics manager bases the transportation mode decision upon cost and service characteristics. Table 9–3 summarizes each mode's relative advantages and disadvantages. Note that the ratings in this table are generalizations; the exact relationship among specific carriers of different modes may vary.

LEGAL CLASSIFICATIONS OF CARRIERS

Transportation firms engaged in interstate transportation of property are classified into four categories: common, contract, exempt, and private. The first three are for-hire carriers; the last is not. The firm wishing to move its goods in its own vehicles provides private transportation, and the firm does not make private carrier service available to other shippers of regulated goods.

Common Carrier

The *common carrier* is a for-hire carrier that serves the general public at reasonable charges and without discrimination. Economically the common carrier is the most highly regulated of all the legal carrier types. The economic regulation imposed upon these carriers acts to protect the shipping public and to ensure sufficient transport service within normal limits. Using a common carrier in the logistics system requires the logistics manager to know how those regulations affect the type and quality of common carrier transport.

    The essence of this regulation is located in the legal service requirements under which the common carrier operates: to serve, to deliver, not to discriminate, and to charge reasonable rates. These service requirements contain the underlying principle of public protection, for the common carrier is a business enterprise affecting the public interest. To guarantee the transportation service the economy requires, the federal government has imposed regulatory controls on common carriers. The government does not impose these legal service requirements upon the other types of carriers.

definition

service requirements

TABLE 9–3 Performance Rating of Modes by Selection Determinant

Selection Determinants	Modes				
	Railroad	Motor	Water	Air	Pipeline
Cost	3	4	2	5	1
Transit time	3	2	4	1	—
Reliability	2	1	4	3	—
Capability	1	2	4	3	5
Accessibility	2	1	4	3	—
Security	3	2	4	1	—

1 = Best, lowest; 5 = Worst, highest.

serve the public   To meet its public service requirement, the common carrier must transport all commodities offered to it. The common carrier cannot refuse to carry a particular commodity or to serve a particular point within the carrier's scope of operation. The logistics manager's supply of transportation services seems assured, since the common carrier cannot refuse to transport the firm's commodities, even if the movement is not profitable for the carrier. However, this service requirement has two qualifications: one, the carrier must provide service up to the limits of its physical capacity, where the plant level necessary to meet normal carrier demand determines capacity; and two, the common carrier must serve shippers within the carrier's shipping public.

defined by ICC or DOT operating authority   The Interstate Commerce Commission regulates entry into the common carrier transportation sector for rail, motor, and water transport, and the Department of Transportation (DOT) regulates air transport entry. A firm seeking common carrier authority must show it is fit, willing, and able to provide service. For railroads, the test also includes public need and convenience.

liability for damage   The delivery requirement refers to the common carrier's liability for the goods in its care. The common carrier must deliver goods in the same condition they were in when the carrier received them at the shipment's origin. More specifically, the common carrier is liable for all goods lost, damaged, or delayed while in its care. This absolute level of liability has limited exceptions: acts of God, acts of public enemy, acts of public authority, acts of the shipper, and defects inherent in the goods. The logistics manager, then, can transfer the risk of cargo damage, or the bearing of this risk, to the carrier when using a common carrier.

no discrimination   The shipping public finds additional protection in the requirement that the common carrier not discriminate among shippers, commodities, or places. *Discrimination* is when a carrier charges different rates or provides different service levels for essentially similar movements of similar goods. There are, however, permissible forms of discrimination. For example, common carriers may favor larger-volume shippers by charging lower rates for volume movements and higher rates for less-than-volume movements. Cost difference justifies quoting different rates for volume and less-than-volume movements.

charge reasonable rates   Finally, the duty to charge reasonable rates constrains the carrier from charging excessively high or low rates. This requirement has two protective dimensions: it protects the shipping public from rates that are too high, and it protects the carrier from charging rates that are too low. The second protective dimension ultimately protects the public by ensuring continued transportation service.

In summary, we might consider the common carrier the backbone of the transportation industry. The common carrier makes itself available to the public, without providing special treatment to any one party, and operates under rate, liability, and service regulations. Most logistics systems use the common carrier extensively.

Contract Carrier

definition   The *contract carrier* is a for-hire carrier that does not serve the general public, but rather serves one or a limited number of shippers with whom it is under specific contract. The contract carrier also operates under economic regulations, but has no legal service obligations imposed upon it. The contract contains terms pertaining to the carrier's rates, liability, and type of service and equipment. Usually, a contract carrier's rates are lower than those of common carriers. The government controls entry into this transportation sector but does not require the contract carrier to prove public convenience and necessity.

The contract carrier provides a specialized type of service to the shipper. Because the carrier does not serve the general public, it can tailor its services to meet specific shippers' needs by utilizing special equipment and arranging special pick-ups and deliveries. In general, the logistics manager may assume that contract carriage is essentially similar to private transportation, at least in service level terms.

tailored service

Use of the contract carrier has greatly increased in the 1990s. Logistics managers are using contract carriage to assure service levels and rates. Contract carriage enables the shipper to protect against unilateral decisions by common carriers to change rates and rules.

Exempt Carrier

The *exempt carrier* is a for-hire carrier exempt from economic regulation regarding rates and services. The laws of the marketplace determine the rates, services, and supply of such carriers. The only controls over entry into this transport industry sector are capital requirements, which do not seriously restrict some modes.

definition

An exempt carrier gains this status by the commodity it hauls or by the nature of its operation. For example, a motor carrier is an exempt carrier when transporting agricultural products, newspapers, livestock, and fish; and a rail carrier is exempt when hauling fresh fruit. Carriers whose operation type provides exemption include motor carriers whose operations are primarily local; water carriers that transport bulk commodities such as coal, ore, grain, or liquid; air carriers that haul cargo; and rail carriers that transport piggyback shipments.

service

The limited number of exempt carriers—that is, the limited number of situations in which carrier exemption is possible—restricts the availability of such service. But for moving commodities such as agricultural products, where exempt carriage is possible, firms make significant use of these carriers. The primary reason for using an exempt carrier is lower transport rates. For the movement of industrial commodities, the exempt carrier does not provide viable link service.

Private Carrier

A *private carrier* is essentially a firm's own transportation. The private carrier is not for-hire and not subject to federal economic regulations. More specifically, private carriage involves any person who transports in interstate or foreign commerce property of which such person is the owner, lessee, or bailee, when such transportation is for the purpose of sale, lease, rent, or bailment, or in furtherance of any commercial enterprise. A private carrier's crucial legal distinction is that transportation must not be the controlling firm's primary business; stated differently, the carrier owner's primary business must be some commercial endeavor other than transportation. Private motor carriers may charge 100%-owned subsidiaries an intercorporate hauling fee.

definition

primary business

The most prevalent private transportation type is by motor vehicle; private carrier is nearly synonymous with private motor carrier. The relative ease of meeting motor transport capital entry requirements and the high degree of accessibility by motor vehicle have made this mode most advantageous to shippers wishing to provide their own transportation. We should point out that private transportation by water primarily moves bulk raw materials. To a much lesser extent, private rail carriers move bulk products short distances within a plant, between plants, or from plants to rail sidings. Firms use private aircraft extensively to move company personnel and, to a lesser degree, to move emergency property shipments.

rationale   The basic reasons for a firm to enter into private transportation are cost and service. When for-hire carrier rates increase, many firms find private transport a means of controlling transportation costs. Basically, a firm can reduce private transportation costs by conducting the private carrier operation as efficiently as a for-hire operation. If this same efficiency is possible, private transport theoretically should cost less, since the firm pays no for-hire carrier profit. However, one major operational problem, the empty backhaul,* may actually elevate profit.

advantages   By using private transportation, a firm gains greater control and flexibility in responding to buyer and plant demands. This increased control and flexibility may result in lower inventory levels, greater customer satisfaction, and greater efficiency at the loading and unloading docks. The firm can also use private equipment as an advertising medium.

disadvantages   Private transportation does have some disadvantages. The main ones are large capital requirements and problems in labor and management. The capital the firm invests in the transport fleet has alternative uses in other firm operations, and this capital must provide a return that at least equals other investment opportunities. The labor problems arise from the firm's dealing with a new labor union. Administrative problems may arise when the firm utilizes existing managers to manage a private transport operation. Finally, the current deregulated environment has produced substantially lower for-hire carrier rates, occasionally making private transportation more costly.

INTERMODAL TRANSPORTATION

definition   *Intermodal transport* services refers to the use of two or more carriers of different modes in the through movement of a shipment. Carriers offer such services to the public by publishing a rate from origin to destination for one carrier of each available mode. In other situations, the logistics manager, through routing, uses different modes to get a product to its final destination.

rationale   The logistics manager often must utilize different transport modes to service a given link. While intermodal services are necessary for numerous reasons, the basic reasons are the various modes' service characteristics and costs. For example, the limited accessibility of air transport requires coordination with a land carrier to make the pickups and deliveries. Similar inaccessibility applies to rail, water, and pipeline, but not to motor, which has a definite advantage here. By manipulating the modes, a logistics manager can overcome a given mode's service disadvantages and retain the mode's basic advantage, usually low cost. This is the primary motivation for combining rail and water to move coal or grain: the rail segment improves water transport's accessibility, and the water portion permits savings by providing low-cost service for the long-distance portion of the move.

---

*The *empty backhaul* refers to a vehicle going from origin to destination loaded, and returning empty.

Intermodal services maximize the primary advantages inherent in the combined modes and minimize their disadvantages. The combined services will have both the good and the bad aspects of the utilized modes. For example, the coordination of rail and water will have a lower total cost than an all-rail movement, but a higher cost than all-water. Likewise, the combined system's transit time will be lower than that of an all-water movement but higher than that of all-rail. The decision to use combined modes must consider the effect on total logistics costs.

Various types of intermodal service exist, as Figure 9–5 shows. The most prevalent forms have been truck-rail, truck-water, and truck-air. However, rail-water, pipeline-water, and pipeline-truck also occur.

We can attribute extensive motor carrier use in intermodal service to the extremely high accessibility motor transport allows. Birdyback, fishyback, and piggyback services are examples of coordination in which a carrier physically transfers the motor carrier trailer, with the cargo intact, in another mode. Birdyback combines the accessibility of motor with the speed of the airline; fishyback couples motor accessibility with the low cost of water carriage; and piggyback adds the truck's accessibility to the low cost of rail service. In each case, the combined service suffers the disadvantages of one of the modes involved; for example, birdyback has the disadvantage of air transport's high cost.

The ultimate intermodal service is the transportation company, which provides all modal services. That is, it makes rail, motor, water, air, and pipeline transportation services available to the public. The advantages of such a transportation company lie in its ability to utilize the most efficient and economical modal services to meet shipper needs. A number of companies offer different modal services. CSX Corporation operates a railroad, water carrier, and trucking company. Consolidated Freightways offers through its subsidiaries trucking, air, and intermodal services.

One substantial stumbling block to intermodal service is that carriers are reluctant to participate. The ICC can require rail and water carriers to cooperate, but the commission does not hold the same power over other modal pairs. The carriers coordinate willingly, even eagerly, to move a product that any one carrier could not transport in its entirety. But when one carrier can transport the commodity the entire distance over its own lines, the carrier is hesitant to coordinate with other carriers.

types

transportation company

limitations

FIGURE 9-5 Types of Intermodal Services

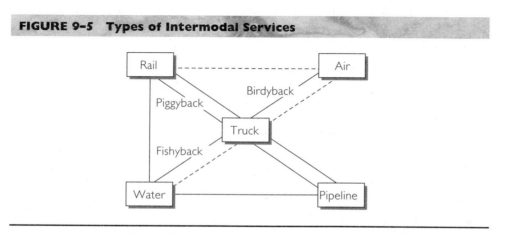

Another problem with intermodal services is the transfer of freight from one mode to another. This creates time delays and adds to transportation costs. Some forms of coordination eliminate this problem by transferring a motor carrier trailer to another transport mode. The motor carrier trailer's transferability is a special coordination form termed *containerization,* the trailer being a container.

Containerization

Simply stated, a container is a large rectangular box into which a firm places commodities to be shipped. After initial loading, the commodities themselves are not rehandled until they are unloaded at their final destination. Throughout the movement, the carrier handles the container, not the commodities; the shipper can transfer the container from one mode to another, eliminating the need to handle the commodities each time. Reducing commodity handling reduces handling costs, damage costs, theft and pilferage, and the time required to complete the modal transfer.

Containerization changes materials handling from a labor-intensive to a capital-intensive operation. Handling containerized freight requires less labor because the container is too large and too heavy for manual movement. Many firms that modify their materials handling systems to include cranes, forklift trucks, and other equipment capable of handling the large, heavy containers have found containerization to be a desirable avenue for increasing productivity and controlling materials handling costs, especially in periods of continually increasing labor costs.

Containerization has gained notable acceptance in international distribution. The service reduces the time and cost associated with shipment handling at ports and curtails damage and theft. Some firms containerizing shipments to foreign markets have reduced costs by from 10 to 20 percent and have increased the service level they provide to these markets.

land bridge   As was discussed earlier, a unique type of intermodal service using the container is the *land bridge,* which utilizes rail transportation to link prior and subsequent container moves by water transportation. For example, containers destined for Europe from the Far East move to the West Coast of the United States by water transportation. The containers move by rail to the East Coast, where a carrier loads them onto an oceangoing vessel for the final transportation to Europe. The rail movement provides the intermodal bridge between the two water moves and permits an overall transit time shorter than that of an all-water shipment.

Piggyback

Piggyback, or trailer-on-flatcar (TOFC), is a specialized form of containerization in which rail and motor transport coordinate. In piggyback, the carrier places the motor carrier trailer on a rail flatcar, which moves the trailer by rail for long distances. A motor carrier then moves the trailer for short-distance pickups and deliveries. This service combines the long-haul, low-cost advantage of rail with the accessibility of motor.

Recently deregulated, piggyback service mostly moves under contract. Generally, five basic piggyback plans are available. The groups able to utilize each plan are restricted as follows:

- Plan I: All motor carrier
- Plan II: All rail

- Plan III: Shipper provides trailer
- Plan IV: Shipper provides trailer and rail flatcar
- Plan V: Joint railroad and motor carrier

The vast majority of piggyback shipments move under Plan II. Since Plans III and IV require an investment in or lease of equipment, shippers do not use these plans to any great extent. Motor carriers use Plan I to reduce load pattern imbalances. Plan V generates very little volume since it requires the joint efforts of a railroad carrier and a motor carrier. If the shipment does not require this coordination, it will occur only when both parties benefit.

International Shipments

Almost every international shipment travels on more than one mode from its origin to its destination. Recent efforts have attempted to reduce shipping times and costs by increasing the various modes' compatibility and by trying new mode combinations.

In the early 1950s, Sea-Land's introduction of containers that trucks as well as ships could carry began the current revolution in shipping. Containers now come in several sizes and supply the major portion of break-bulk overseas shipping.

Containerized shipments have several advantages. Reduced loading times allow carriers to utilize their equipment more efficiently. Shippers benefit from shorter transit times and the reduced risk of pilferage and damage during loading and unloading. Savings may also result from reductions in required packing materials and insurance.

advantages

Containers also have several disadvantages. Not every port is equipped to handle containers, limiting the number of shipping routes available. Finding cargo for the container's backhaul may be difficult. Additionally, the carriers at the origin and destination are not always able to take advantage of the speed available in loading and unloading containers, decreasing the mode's efficiency.

disadvantages

Maritime bridges are prime examples of the savings available by combining modes. Using *double-stack* trains, which stack containers two high on railway flatcars, allows the railroads to operate their equipment more efficiently and to pass these savings on in the form of special intermodal rates, reducing overall shipping costs.

A very recent innovation is the *air/sea combination,* where carriers combine ocean and air transport to move a shipment. This method is most commonly used to ship high value-to-weight items from the Far East to Europe by way of the West Coast of the United States.

Shipping air/sea has two advantages. One, the cost of the combined modes is less than that of an all-air movement. Two, it is much faster than any of the available all-surface modes. Modern container ships can make the Pacific crossing from Japan to Seattle in ten days. When we combine this with the air leg from Seattle to Europe, total transit time will range from ten to fourteen days. This is approximately one-third of the all-ocean transit time and one-half of the land bridge time. The in-transit inventory savings will outweigh the increased cost of the premium modes.

Carriers also commonly use *roll-on-roll-off* in international trade. RO-RO is very similar to container shipping, except that the carrier uses standard truck trailers instead of containers, towing them onto the vessel at the port of origin and off at the destination. RO-RO, which transports automobiles and large mobile equipment such as tractors, has proven extremely useful for shipments to less-developed areas of the world where modern port facilities are unavailable. While RO-RO's advantages are basically the same as those of container shipping, RO-RO does not require special loading equipment.

INDIRECT AND SPECIAL CARRIERS

Another category of carriers offers specialized or intermediary transportation service. In some cases, these carriers have line-haul equipment; in others, they merely provide pickup and delivery and consolidate the service.

Moving shipments of less than 500 pounds creates serious operational problems for the major modes. To make the move economical, the carrier must consolidate the small shipments into larger ones, adding time and cost for the carrier and increasing transit times and transportation charges.

Small-Package Carriers

A number of transportation companies—namely, bus, express, and package carriers—have concentrated upon small freight movements. Bus lines move small packages in their vehicles' luggage compartments. These carriers have cargo capacity only in the space passenger luggage does not require, and therefore they do not require large shipments to make this service profitable. Coupled with frequent schedules, the bus lines offer a viable alternative to the logistics manager who must distribute many small package shipments.

United Parcel Service (UPS)

A common carrier motor firm, United Parcel Service (UPS), has made great strides in the efficient movement of small shipments. (Other carriers of this type include Roadway Package System and Pony Express Courier.) UPS, an innovator in terminal handling and in pickup and delivery scheduling, can transport small shipments profitably while providing better service and lower transit time than other major modes. Regulations limit the type of package a shipper can transport by UPS; at present, these restrictions are (1) a maximum weight of 150 pounds per package and (2) a maximum length and girth of 130 inches.

hub

Other express companies offer air transportation. Federal Express, the largest air express package delivery firm, utilizes a fleet of aircraft and ground vehicles to provide next-day delivery of small packages and envelopes throughout the United States and internationally. Its operation, like that of most air express companies, centers around a *hub* package distribution center. Typically, Federal Express picks up packages in the late afternoon, delivers them to the local airport, and flies them to the Memphis hub airport, where they arrive in the late evening hours. Federal Express then sorts the packages according to destination and reloads them onto aircraft scheduled for predawn arrival at the destination airport, where the service loads the packages onto ground vehicles for morning delivery to the consignee.

The major advantage of using air express companies is speed—the speed required to get needed parts, equipment, documents, sales literature, and specimens to their destinations the next day. But the high cost of such service generally prohibits the nonemergency shipment of low-value, high-density commodities.

Freight Forwarders

The domestic surface freight forwarder collects small shipments from shippers, consolidates these shipments into large loads, and presents the consolidated shipments to railroads or motor carriers for intercity movement. At destination, the freight forwarder breaks the load down into individual shipments and delivers them to the correct consignee. The domestic freight forwarder realizes its revenue from the difference between the high less-than-volume rate the shipper pays and the lower volume rate the for-hire carrier charges the freight forwarder. The main advantage of using a freight forwarder is lower transit time for small shipments.

consolidator

Shippers Associations

An indirect form of transportation known as the shippers association moves small shipments for shipper members. The shippers association consolidates shipments, presents the larger loads to for-hire carriers, and pays a lower rate for the larger-volume movement. The association passes on the lower-volume rate to its members.

Brokers

The freight *broker* is a person or firm that acts as an intermediary between the shipper and carrier. The broker acts as the carrier's sales agent and as the shippers' traffic manager. That is, the broker represents a number of carriers that need loads to move in given directions. With this knowledge of carrier capacity, the broker contacts the shippers and solicits freight to meet the carriers' needs. The broker typically charges the shipper the carrier's published rate, deducts 7 to 10 percent, and then remits the net amount to the carrier.

intermediary

There are two types of brokers: licensed and unlicensed. The *licensed* broker is licensed by the ICC and may arrange freight transportation with ICC-regulated carriers. The licensed broker operates under ICC-administered regulations, including entry control. An *unlicensed* broker, who does not require ICC licensing, may arrange freight transportation for exempt transportation such as local distribution, agricultural commodities, and piggyback. Many private fleet managers utilize broker services, seeking exempt commodity movement to eliminate the empty backhaul.

types

Since 1980, the number and use of brokers have dramatically increased. The Motor Carrier Act of 1980 reduced the entry requirements for brokers and motor carriers. The broker provides new, small trucking companies a marketing channel with a sales force capable of generating shipments from local shippers. At the same time, the broker offers the shippers access to these new, generally lower-cost carriers. In addition, brokers may offer consolidation services that afford the shipper additional savings.

A logistics manager selecting a broker should consider the broker's authority, liability, and billing. First, the manager should review the ICC broker license to make certain the broker is in fact licensed and subject to ICC regulations. Second, since the broker is not legally liable for damage a common carrier causes while transporting goods, the logistics manager must determine whether the broker will assist in filing claims with the carrier and whether the carrier the broker uses can

selection criteria

pay damage claims. Finally, the manager should determine if the broker's fees are included in or are in addition to the carrier's rate.

Intermodal Marketing Companies

The intermodal marketing company (IMC) is an intermediary that solicits freight for movement by intermodal rail. At the outset, the IMC acted as a sales representative for the railroad or steamship company seeking to fill empty containers moving back to origin. Today the IMC is more representative of the shipper's interests and seeks to improve intermodal service to meet shipper needs.

The largest IMCs include The Hub Group, Mark VII Transportation, APL Distribution Services, Alliance Shippers, Inc., GST Corporation, and Con-Way Intermodal. These companies had revenues exceeding $2.25 billion in 1994 and represent a major component of the intermodal transportation system.

advantages   The prime advantages of using an IMC are cost savings, consolidation, and improved transit time. The IMC normally consolidates enough freight to fill two piggyback trailers (the number of trailers loaded onto one flatcar), thereby reducing the time the carrier holds the freight before moving it. Some IMCs have contracted with railroads to provide 60 to 80 piggyback trailers per week. The IMCs then solicit freight with lower rates and a delivery guarantee, making piggyback more advantageous.

disadvantages   A disadvantage of using an IMC is liability for freight charges. The shipper normally pays the freight charge to the IMC. Should the IMC fail to pay the carrier, the shipper may be liable for paying the charges to the carrier. Another disadvantage is liability for damage. The IMC is not a carrier and is not legally liable for damage claims. Some IMCs provide claim liability protection, but the shipper should investigate the IMC before use.

international intermediaries   In addition to the indirect and special carriers discussed in this section, there are several types of intermediaries that are more closely related to the international shipping industry. Chapter 13 contains a description of the nature and importance of the foreign freight forwarder, non-vessel-owning common carriers, export management companies, export trading companies, customs house brokers, and ports.

SUMMARY

Typically, transportation represents the major cost component of the logistics supply chain. Transportation provides the bridge between the producer and the consumer, and the quality of the transportation service enables a firm to differentiate its product in the marketplace.

- The transportation system available to the logistics manager consists of the basic modes, intermodal, and indirect and special carriers.
- The carrier selection is twofold: selection of the mode and selection of the specific carrier.
- Factors determining carrier selection include transportation rate, transit time, reliability, capability, accessibility, and security.
- Railroads offer low cost for long hauls of large volumes, but they have accessibility limitations and long transit time.
- Motor carriers are very accessible and move products in small quantities with

low, consistent transit times. However, their costs are higher than the other modes, except air.

- Water transportation is relatively low cost and is desirable for moving large volumes over long distances. The prime disadvantage is long transit times and service disruptions caused by weather.
- Air carriers have very low transit times, but very high rates.
- Pipelines offer very low rates for the movement of liquids but are not a viable option for manufactured goods.
- There are four legal classes of carriers: common, contract, exempt, and private.
- Intermodal transportation is the combination of two or more basic modes to provide through movement. The dominant form is rail-truck, or piggyback.
- Containerization is the shipping of freight in a large box, or container, that is subsequently transferred from one carrier to another. It reduces freight handling and damage while improving transit time.
- The transportation system includes a number of indirect and special carriers, such as small package carriers, freight forwarders, shippers associations, brokers, and intermodal marketing companies.

STUDY QUESTIONS

1. When purchasing transportation services, the carrier with the lowest rate is usually not the carrier offering the lowest total cost. Explain.

2. What are the major advantages and disadvantages of each of the basic modes?

3. Normally, a firm delivers a low-cost part to its assembly plant via railroad. But when the plant is facing a stockout, the firm sends the part via airplane. What cost justification can the firm give for using air?

4. Why would a company use a common carrier when contract and exempt carriers offer lower rates?

5. Under what conditions is intermodal transportation advantageous?

6. Water transportation dominates international shipment. Explain.

7. What role does the container play in domestic and international shipments?

8. Under what circumstances would a firm utilize indirect or special carrier services?

9. Describe the economic rationale supporting one-stop transportation companies.

10. What transportation mode would a shipper likely use to transport basic raw materials? heavy manufactured goods? lightweight consumer goods? electronic products? Why?

NOTES

1. Eno Transportation Foundation, Inc., *Transportation in America*, 12th edition (Lansdowne, VA: Eno Foundation for Transportation, 1994), 5.

2. *Physical Distribution Cost and Service 1994* (Englewood Cliffs, NJ: Herbert W. Davis and Company, 1994), 3.

3. Eno Foundation for Transportation, *Transportation in America*, 5.

Case 9-1

NATIONAL APPLIANCE, INC.

Bob Reard, director of corporate transportation for National Appliance, Inc., has just hung up the phone after a lengthy discussion with Susan Jameson, vice president of logistics. National Appliance has just acquired an appliance distributor located in Paris, and the logistics department has two months to develop an operating process to support this European distributor with National Appliance products. The shipments to Paris will begin in approximately five months, and Mr. Reard is to prepare a transportation operating plan for these shipments.

National Appliance is a medium-size U.S. manufacturer of refrigerators and electric ranges. During the past fifteen years, National Appliance has increased its share of the refrigerator and electric range market from less than 2 percent to 20 percent. Part of the reason for this tremendous growth is that National Appliance offers high-quality products at low prices. In addition, National Appliance has vertically integrated both its supply and marketing channels. National believes that quality products result from actually owning and managing key component vendors and that quality marketing and sales efforts result from directly managing distributors and retail appliance outlets.

It surprised Mr. Reard to learn that National Appliance had purchased control of a European appliance distributor. There had been many rumors about expansion into the European market, but Mr. Reard had felt that National Appliance would merely develop a contractual relationship with a distributor in Europe, not purchase a distributor.

Purchasing the Paris distributor is the first major international business venture for National Appliance in its thirty-five-year history. During the late 1980s, the company had unsuccessfully attempted to market refrigerators in both Canada and Mexico; Mr. Reard had personally managed the truck shipments to both countries. Consequently, Mr. Reard and his staff have very limited international experience. They do, however, possess considerable expertise in domestic transportation, having successfully controlled both transportation costs and service during the company's rapid growth in the past fifteen years.

Given the emphasis on quality products and service, top management has mandated consistent, low lead times. National Appliance delivers domestic distributor orders in less than five days from the order date; the company allows no exceptions to this service policy. Truck transportation, including a private fleet, is the primary mode the company uses for both inbound and outbound shipments. Spare parts are normally shipped by ground express, but the company uses air express when the distributor or dealer needs a special part immediately. Ms. Jameson has established a logistics quality control program that measures carrier performance and has used Mr. Reard's managerial skills to assure acceptable performance from National Appliance carriers.

Having had little experience in international transportation, Mr. Reard feels a bit out of his element in developing an international transportation plan. Ms. Jameson has assured him that transportation is transportation and that the only difference between international and domestic transportation is distance.

Distance is going to be a major factor, since National Appliance has plants located in Memphis, Minneapolis, and Omaha. This long distance from the European market will contribute to two basic problems: high transport costs and long lead times. Moving the products from the plants to the Atlantic or Gulf ports will require some form of ground transportation. Ocean carrier shipment will be long, and Mr. Reard will have to arrange to move the product from the French entry port to Paris. Mr. Reard is sure that he can hire an international transportation manager, but he will have to pay a high salary.

With the logistics planning meeting set for the next morning at 8:00 A.M., Mr. Reard prepares the following transportation plan for Ms. Jameson:

1. Finished product from all three plants will be shipped by truck to New York/ New Jersey ports.
2. Water transportation will be used from New York/New Jersey to LeHavre, France.
3. Trucks will transport the products from LeHavre to the Paris distributor.
4. From Paris, the distributor will arrange transportation to the ultimate customer.
5. An international transportation manager will be hired.

Mr. Reard estimates that the total transit time required for this move will be approximately four weeks.

Case Questions

1. Assess the strengths and weaknesses of Mr. Reard's international transportation plan.
2. Develop an alternative international plan to present to Ms. Jameson, and provide justification sufficient to support its adoption.

Case 9–2

DOUBLE D TRUCKING

Double D Trucking was started by Douglas Dean in 1981 and has grown from a one-truck operation to a 550-tractor-trailer fleet serving shippers in a five-state region in the upper Midwest. Double D serves the automotive industry by providing inbound transportation to the assembly plants. It has a strategic alliance relationship with the Big Three auto makers and is the exclusive trucking company for a number of the auto suppliers.

From its inception Double D has been an innovator in the trucking industry. Douglas Dean is widely known for his willingness to adopt new equipment technology, computer systems, and management techniques. This cutting edge strategy has resulted in customer loyalty and employee allegiance. Double D promotes itself as a trucking company that has never lost a customer and never lost a day to labor disputes.

As Douglas Dean was preparing for a strategic planning meeting with top executives, he was mulling over recent trends in the trucking industry as well as the logistics field. Dean knew Double D was a profitable regional trucking company and registered high in customer satisfaction surveys. He also knew that to retain this enviable position he must continue to be innovative and provide the services customers need.

During the past two years, Double D has witnessed increased competition. Long-haul trucking has come under severe competitive pressure from rail piggyback, and the long-haul truckers see regional trucking as a profitable marketplace. Expediting carriers, trucking companies that provide rush deliveries, have made significant inroads into the automotive industry, where just-in-time management systems mandate minimal raw material inventories, guaranteed deliveries, and vendor penalties for late deliveries that result in production line stoppage.

The most perplexing trend to Dean is the growing vertical integration of trucking companies into other logistics services. A number of regional trucking companies have started warehousing divisions to provide sorting, kitting (putting pieces together to make up a kit), and cross-docking (moving freight across a dock to a waiting truck). Other carriers are adding third-party logistics divisions to manage a shipper/receiver's transportation and storage activities. Finally, a few trucking companies have started air carrier divisions, freight forwarding services, and logistics information services.

Dean also recognizes that this vertical integration of trucking companies is a result of customer demands. As manufacturers move to an integrated logistics supply chain approach, they are demanding that transportation suppliers provide other logistics services. In addition, shippers are reducing the number of vendors, including transportation suppliers, being used and asking the few vendors to provide a wider range of products and value-added services.

After considerable thought, Dean decides that the only viable, long-term strategy for Double D is to become a full-service logistics provider. Being only a trucking company will greatly impair the growth and profit potentials of Double D. The only question remaining for Dean is, what other logistics services are appropriate for Double D?

Case Questions

1. Assess the conclusion reached by Douglas Dean regarding the nature of today's trucking industry.
2. Do you agree that the logical strategic thrust for Double D is to vertically integrate and provide other logistics services? Why or why not?
3. Describe the analytical process you would use to evaluate alternative logistics services being added to Double D's market offering.
4. Describe the value-added services you would recommend that the strategic planning team consider for Double D.

CHAPTER 10

TRANSPORTATION MANAGEMENT

LEARNING OBJECTIVES

After reading this chapter, you should be able to do the following:

- Define proactive transportation management.

- Discuss the five transportation management strategies: reducing the number of carriers, negotiating with carriers, contracting with carriers, consolidating shipments, and monitoring service quality.

- Explain the rationale for economic regulation of transportation.

- Discuss the economic deregulation steps implemented by the federal government.

- Distinguish among the transportation documents: bill of lading, freight bill, and freight claims.

- Compare the domestic terms of sale with international Incoterms.

- Explain cost of service and value of service ratemaking and the effect of shipment weight and distance on freight rates.

- Discuss terminal and line-haul services offered by carriers.

LOGISTICS PROFILE

MICROAGE COMPUTER CENTERS, INC.

MicroAge Computer Centers, Inc. is a distributor of computer hardware systems and accessories. During the past five years annual revenues have increased an average of more than 40 percent and the current freight bill is $20 million.

Initially, the company served its 1,300 owner-managed locations in the United States from one distribution center located in Tempe, Arizona. Many of the East Coast shipments were shipped by air express to keep transit times low and remain competitive. Air express transit times were good, but the cost was too high.

MicroAge opened a second distribution center in Cincinnati to serve customers east of the Mississippi River and switched to motor carriers. The savings in freight expense offset the cost of the new Cincinnati distribution center.

The selection of the carriers to serve the distribution center was accomplished by a bid process. The company sent a letter to 300 less-than-truckload (LTL) carriers, inviting them to bid on the freight business. In the letter MicroAge requested the following services and rates:

- Consistent transit times range from one to three days
- A discount off a FAK class 77½ LTL rates
- A released value of $5.00 per pound
- A minimum charge of $30 per shipment
- An unloading allowance of $1.75 on inbound shipments
- Waivers of all accessorial charges
- An incentive rate providing discounts based on the carrier's monthly net revenue

MicroAge met with the 47 carriers who responded to the initial bid letter. In the meeting, the carriers were given a list of thirty service items that it wanted in the final contract. In addition, the carriers received two months of data on MicroAge shipments (pieces, weight, zip code, city, state) to help the carriers understand the operation and to determine costs and prices.

To evaluate potential carriers, the company rated carrier performance on a scale of 10 to 0. For example, on-time percentages from 97 percent to 100 percent received a 10; on-time percentages below 89% received a 0. Each performance rating was weighted by its total importance (see the table). The weighted performance ratings became the carrier's report card, which was used to reduce the number of potential carriers for the final negotiation phase.

MicroAge Carrier Performance Weights

On-time percentage	8%	Cut-off times	5%
Equipment availability	8%	Break-bulk usage	5%
Direct service points	8%	Hub locations	5%
Full state coverage	8%	EDI capability	5%
Discount percentage	8%	Bar code tracing	4%
FAK freight class	7%	Quality/safety program	3%
Claims ratio	6%	Operating ratio	3%
Claims payment	6%	Safety rating	2%
Cargo insurance	6%	Position for two-day service	2%

After three-hour negotiating sessions with the finalists, MicroAge selected ten motor carriers to serve over 90 percent of its customers east of the Mississippi River. Thus far, the bid process has resulted in a reduction in claims and freight cost of about 10 percent and an increase in on-time performance.

SOURCE: Jim Thomas, "Pump Up the Volume," *Distribution* (November 1994): 40–44. Used with permission of Distribution Magazine, November 1994.

Transportation costs, which represent approximately 40 to 50 percent of total logistics costs and 4 to 10 percent of the product selling price for many companies, may represent logistics management's major concern. Transportation decisions directly affect the total logistics costs, costs in other functional areas of the firm, and costs within other logistics channel members. This chapter focuses on the daily transportation management activities in today's deregulated transportation environment, concentrating specifically on transportation regulation, carrier pricing, services, and documentation. We will first direct our attention toward transportation management philosophy.

MANAGEMENT PHILOSOPHY

The passage of the transportation deregulation acts in 1977 and 1980 drastically changed the business climate within which the transportation manager operates. Before them, the climate emphasized the ability to operate effectively within regulation confines. Good transportation managers were those who worked within the system to ensure that competitors were not getting better rates or services, that is, who sought to achieve regulatory parity among transportation users.

seeking parity

The bureaucratic red tape of transportation regulation placed a stranglehold on management initiative. Pre-deregulation-era managers commonly defined transportation activities that prohibited regulations so as to achieve regulatory parity and to prevent other shippers from achieving favorable rates and services from a carrier. Innovative transportation management was difficult to develop because of regulatory constraints. By necessity, transportation managers armed themselves with a list of "thou shalt nots" that would squelch any and all suggestions company managers put forth.

Since 1980, the transportation environment has changed. The regulations shackling management decisions are gone. A transportation manager can no longer utilize the regulatory constraints to prevent a competitor from gaining a competitive advantage when a carrier offers the competitor better rates and services. In fact, contracting and the publication of individual carrier tariffs prevent the transportation manager from knowing what rates and services a carrier is providing to competitors.

With the regulatory safety net gone, the transportation manager must rely on traditional management techniques, using a proactive approach to identify and solve transportation problems and to provide the company with a competitive advantage in the marketplace.

proactive approach

A proactive management approach seeks to identify transportation problems and to postulate solutions that benefit the whole company. Without a regulatory rule book, transportation management is free to concentrate on innovative solutions to today's logistics and transportation challenges. Only managers' abilities and creativity and normal business law constraints limit the benefits of this proactive business strategy.

For example, suppose that a firm's sales decline in a particular market results from longer and less dependable lead times than those provided by the competition in that market. If the firm makes a modal switch from rail to truck, the increased cost of truck service would force the firm to increase prices or to incur a loss, neither of which is acceptable. Negotiating with carriers, establishing carrier contracts with prescribed service levels, and modifying loading procedures are alternatives that the transportation manager may explore to improve services and sales while maintaining acceptable costs.

negative versus positive approach
Today, the transportation manager actively participates in solving company problems. Companies no longer look upon transportation as a necessary evil; rather, transportation contains fundamental solutions to problems that plague a company's functional areas. Thus, today's transportation manager must understand other functional areas as well as the entire company, so as to seek logistics strategies that support other departmental and corporate strategies.

Reducing the Number of Carriers

market power
By reducing the number of carriers it uses, a shipping firm increases the freight volume and freight revenue that it gives to a carrier, thereby increasing its ability to have the carrier provide the rates and services the shipper needs. As the shipper concentrates its freight business in a limited number of carriers, the shipper becomes more important to each carrier; and each carrier, in becoming more dependent on the shipper's business, is more willing to negotiate with the shipper.

Being one of the carrier's largest customers gives the shipper significant negotiating power: the fear of losing the shipper's business motivates the carrier to comply with the shipper's demands for better rates and service levels. In essence, the shipper who is one of the carrier's A customers (part of the 20 percent of the carrier's customers who provide 80 percent of the carrier's sales revenue) possesses market power with the carrier.

For example, by using only 10 LTL carriers for all shipments east of the Mississippi River, MicroAge Computer Centers reduced freight costs by 10 percent and improved on-time delivery. (See the Logistics Profile at the beginning of this chapter.) Detroit Diesel reduced its carrier base from 131 carriers to fourteen, all under contract. The high level of service provided by these fourteen carriers facilitated a $30 million inventory reduction.[1] Texas Instruments currently uses 527 carriers, forwarders, customs brokers, and other service providers in 40 countries. In the near future the company plans to reduce its transport providers to approximately fifty, a 90 percent reduction.[2]

strategic alliance
This concentration of freight in a limited number of carriers not only increases market power, but also permits a company to develop a strategic alliance with the carriers it uses. In a strategic alliance, the shipper and the carrier, recognizing their mutual dependency, strive to be efficient so that both can survive and prosper. In addition to reducing transportation costs, the improved working relations within the strategic alliance reduce other logistics costs such as information processing, inventory, and warehousing.

Reducing the number of carriers a firm uses may also increase the possibility of providing a carrier with balanced loads of raw materials inbound and finished goods outbound. By reducing excess capacity, a balanced load pattern enables the carrier to reduce its costs and to offer lower rates. In addition, providing the carrier with balanced loads may increase the carrier's service level.

risks
A negative risk associated with concentrating business in a limited number of carriers is the firm's increased dependency on the carrier it uses. A shipper who uses only ten carriers is much more vulnerable to shipment disruptions and re-

sulting customer service declines than is a shipper who uses 100 carriers. With the 100-carrier strategy, losing one carrier requires the shipper to reallocate only 1 percent of its freight volume among the remaining ninety-nine carriers, which should pose no problem to carrier capacity and customer service levels. In the ten-carrier scenario, however, losing one carrier requires the shipper to secure shipping capacity equivalent to 10 percent of the shipper's volume, which the remaining nine carriers may not have the capacity to handle. This will force the shipper to use carriers unfamiliar with the shipper's freight, shipping procedures, and customer service requirements; will normally disrupt operating systems and customer service levels; and, possibly, will lead to higher transportation costs, since crisis stage allows the shipper little market power to negotiate favorable rates.

Single sourcing is the ultimate concentration of market power. By using one carrier, the shipper realizes the maximum market power for the freight dollars spent. Corporate-wide single sourcing poses a substantial risk of complete disruption of transportation operations if the carrier fails. However, single sourcing occurs at one facility or for one product (inbound or outbound).

Negotiating with Carriers

Today, carrier negotiation is the norm, and, in some situations, a daily function. The transportation manager must possess negotiating skills sufficient to secure the desired service level at the least cost. Successful carrier negotiation has enabled many companies either to remain competitive in the market or to increase competitive advantage through improved carrier service levels.

Market forces and regulatory constraints determine the negotiable factors between the carrier and the shipper. Generally, the negotiated factors revolve around the rates and services the carriers provide. The remaining economic regulations, the ICC (see the following section), and antitrust scrutiny imposed upon the truck and rail common carriers govern the negotiated rates and services; air carrier negotiations are subject to antitrust scrutiny only.

The marketplace determines the negotiable factors, assuming that these factors violate no regulatory constraints. The shippers' operational needs, customer demands, and company objectives determine the areas where negotiations will begin. (See the Logistics Profile for the service and rate requests made by MicroAge.) The shipper brings these needs to the carrier, who decides (negotiates) whether these needs are realistic. More than likely the carrier will respond with a counter-proposal that offers something less than what the shipper requested.

At other times the carrier will initiate negotiations. The carrier, who may have a specific need to eliminate an empty backhaul, specify pickup times, or increase tonnage, entices a shipper to respond, usually by offering a concession, such as a reduced rate. The shipper will analyze the carrier proposal and either accept or reject the offer or request a greater concession.

Throughout this negotiation, the market power each party enjoys influences the outcome. The shipper possesses market power in terms of the transportation business available in a given time period and can increase this market power by limiting the number of carriers it uses. The carrier possesses market power in terms of the carrier's importance to the shipper—that is, the availability of equal or better-quality service substitutes.

market power

Contracting with Carriers

The Motor Carrier Act of 1980 and the Staggers Act of 1980 increased shippers' ability to enter into contracts with carriers. Contracting enables the shipper to eliminate the uncertainties in rates and services that common carriers provide. Through the contract terms, the shipper can specify the rate and level of service that the carrier will provide and can dictate noncompliance penalties, thereby fixing service levels during the contract period.

specialized services   Contracting permits shippers that desire specialized services to purchase a unique or tailored service level that may not legally be available from the common carrier. The common carrier must provide service to all shippers without discrimination or preferential treatment. Recognizing the shipping public's need for specialized contract transportation, as opposed to a basic service level, Congress established the contract motor carrier classification in the Motor Carrier Act of 1935.

The Negotiated Rates Act of 1993 (NRA) defines what constitutes a legal contract of carriage with a motor carrier. A bona fide motor carrier contract must

- Be in writing and signed by both parties
- Contain the rates to be charged
- Cover a series of shipments (not just one)
- Meet the distinct needs of the shipper or dedicate equipment to the exclusive use of the shipper

Rail transportation has widely adopted contracting. A railroad negotiation normally establishes a contract rather than the rate discount common to motor carrier negotiations. Rail contracts normally specify a rate, the type of equipment the carrier will provide, and the service level the shippers expect (a fifteen-day maximum transit time on shipments from Chicago to Seattle, for example). The contract also dictates a minimum or guaranteed quantity that the shipper will tender to the carrier during the contract life.

JIT   Companies implementing the just-in-time (JIT) system use contracting to ensure safe, consistent, and fast service. The JIT system emphasizes low inventory levels and a reliance upon transportation to deliver goods as customers and logistics nodes need them. Transportation delays decrease production, increase inventory costs, and disrupt operations, which defeats JIT's objectives. Contracting with all transportation modes ensures the required transportation service level.

Consolidating Shipments

The freight volume a shipper tenders to a carrier directly relates to the freight rate the carrier charges. By consolidating shipments, the transportation manager can reap the benefits of the lower rates carriers charge for larger shipment volumes. That is, the manager may increase the weight of the shipment the shipper tenders to the carrier to the level that will enable the carrier to use TL (truckload) or CL (carload) rates. In addition, the motor carrier tariffs provide rate discounts at multiple weight levels such as 1,000 pounds, 2,000 pounds, and 5,000 pounds, thus encouraging shippers to consolidate small shipments into larger ones.

shipment size and rates   As a general rule, carriers charge lower rates for shipping larger quantities. Carrier cost per weight unit transported (pound, hundredweight, or ton) decreases as the shipment weight increases. For example, the carrier pickup cost does not vary with shipment size. The per-pound carrier pickup cost for a 2,000-pound shipment is 50 percent of that for a 1,000-pound shipment. (If the pickup cost is $50, the pickup cost per pound is $0.05 for the 1,000-pound shipment and $0.025 for the 2,000-pound shipment.) TL rates requiring 25,000- to 30,000-pound shipments may be 30 to 60 percent lower than LTL rates.

A shipper may utilize freight consolidation to support a competitive price marketing strategy. By consolidating shipments, the transportation manager realizes a lower carrier rate; and the shipper can translate this lower transportation cost per unit into a lower price for buyers purchasing the larger quantity. Thus, shippers can coordinate the quantity discounts they offer buyers with the rate reductions possible with consolidated shipment sizes.

quantity discounts

Monitoring Service Quality

Transportation service quality can differentiate a company's product, thereby providing the company with a competitive market advantage. An ability to get the product to the customer on a consistent, timely, and undamaged basis reduces the buyer's inventory and stockout costs. Thus, product differentiation through the transportation service a company provides is a significant nonprice marketing strategy.

product differentiation

However, a trade-off exists between transportation service quality and cost. The transportation manager must compare the quality of service required by buyers of the finished product against the level the shipper currently provides. If the buyers require three-day transit time and the shipper provides two-day transit time, the transportation manager is providing a better and more costly service level than the buyers demand. The transportation manager might correct the service level by negotiating a lower rate with the carrier in return for a longer transit time (three-day delivery instead of two-day delivery) or utilizing a slower but lower-cost mode of transportation.

service/cost trade-off

A fundamental element for implementing service quality monitoring is information. The transportation manager must have information regarding the customer service demands and the service level that current carriers provide. Without this information, the transportation manager cannot make a rational transportation service/cost decision that meets the shipper's established logistics and corporate goals.

Normal transportation documentation—the bill of lading, freight bill, customer shipping document, and so on—does not contain transportation service data. These source documents do not indicate the number of days the shipment is in transit, the transit time consistency, or the frequency and extent of shipment damage. The transportation manager must obtain these data directly from the shipment's receiver.

The bill of lading, freight bill, and customer shipping document indicate the date the shipper dispatched the shipment to the carrier, but not the date the consignee received it. To obtain the delivery date, the transportation manager could attach a return postcard to the shipment asking the consignee to indicate the reception date. Another method, which is more costly but more effective, is to conduct a phone survey. Some transportation managers have asked the sales force to request delivery service information from customers during sales calls.

transit time

Figure 10–1 is an example of a carrier evaluation report that bases its evaluation criteria upon the carrier selection factors we discussed in chapter 9. The figure assigns each criterion a weight indicating the criterion's importance to the company and gives the carrier's performance in each service and financial area a numerical rating. The criterion rating multiplied by the criterion importance gives a weighted rating; the sum of the weighted ratings provides an evaluation score for each carrier.

Using a carrier evaluation system like the one Figure 10–1 depicts provides the transportation manager with information that is vital to the achievement of the transportation, logistics, and corporate customer service strategies and goals.

FEDERAL REGULATION*

Federal regulation of transportation has been with us since the Act to Regulate Commerce passed in 1887. The years immediately preceding the enactment of this law were full of turmoil, for both shippers and carriers. Inland transportation was basically by railroad, and the carriers charged high rates when possible and discriminated against small shippers. Control over the transportation industry was important to U.S. economic growth and to assure a stable transportation service supply compatible with the needs of an expanding society.

public interest
We find the basis for federal economic regulation of transportation in transportation's significance to the overall economy of the United States. Transportation enables business to accomplish the very foundation of economic activity—the exchange of commodities from areas of oversupply to areas of undersupply. The transportation activity benefits all citizens; thus, we could argue that the government should provide transportation, just as it provides public interest functions such as the court system and national defense.

Traditionally, however, private enterprise has provided freight transportation. Through the dollars shippers spend, the marketplace identifies the resources that transportation companies commit to various transportation services and considers this resource allocation to be more efficient than that a governmental, political allocation could produce. Since the free enterprise marketplace has imperfections that may allow monopolies to develop, government control of transportation attempts to allocate resources in the public's interest by maintaining and enforcing the competitive market structure.

Overview of Federal Regulation

Before passage of federal economic regulation, several midwestern states had passed granger laws regulating transportation in their respective states. These laws attempted to correct the railroads' monopolistic price and service practices after the Civil War. However, in 1886, the Supreme Court held that a state could not regulate interstate traffic. This decision created an interstate transportation reg-

---

*For a thorough discussion of transportation regulation, see John J. Coyle, Edward J. Bardi, and Robert A. Novack, *Transportation*, 4th ed. (St. Paul, MN: West Publishing, 1994), Chapters 3 and 4.

FIGURE 10-1   Carrier Evaluation Report

Carrier: _____   Time period: _____

Criteria Import	Evaluation Criteria	Carrier Rating	Weighted Rating	Comments
	Meets pick-up schedules			
	Meets delivery			
	Transit time			
	Overall			
	Consistency			
	Claims			
	Frequency			
	Timely settlement			
	Equipment			
	Availablilty			
	Condition			
	Driver			
	Customer acceptance			
	Courtesy			
	Attitude			
	Scope of operations			
	Operating authority			
	Computer			
	EDI			
	Electronic billing			
	Billing			
	Errors			
	Timeliness			
	Tracing capabilities			
	Problem solving			
	Innovativeness			
	Management			
	Attitude			
	Trustworthiness			
	Financial			
	Operating ratio			
	Cash flow			
	Profitability			
	Rates			
	Accessorial charges			
	Handles rush shipments			
	Total weighted rating			

Evaluator: _____   Date: _____

ulation vacuum, which the federal government corrected in 1887 by passing the Act to Regulate Commerce.

legal service duties
The following legal service duties of common carriers best describe the public interest aspect of federal regulation: to serve, to not discriminate, and to charge reasonable rates (see Chapter 9). These common carrier legal service duties reflect the original and subsequent transportation acts. Government regulations essentially attempt to ensure that common carriers provide transportation service to all shippers without discrimination, and that they charge reasonable rates.

ICC
Congress established the Interstate Commerce Commission (ICC) as an independent regulatory agency to administer the transportation laws. To accomplish its administration charge, the ICC exercises legislative, judicial, and executive powers. For example, enforcement of statutes is an executive function, adjudicating the reasonableness of rates is a judicial function, and establishing rules is a legislative function. The ICC is limited by regulatory authority and is subject to review by the courts.

initial period
The 1887 act required carriers (railroads) to charge reasonable rates and to publish rates in tariffs that they were to make available to the public and file with the ICC. The act precluded personal discrimination and undue preference or prejudice (charging one person more or less than another for similar transportation service). The act also prohibited long- and short-haul discrimination, or charging less for a longer haul than a shorter one when the longer haul includes the shorter one, and made pooling agreements illegal when carriers shared traffic or revenues.

From 1887 to 1920, amendments made to the original act increased the ICC's control and enforcement power. This period of negative regulation restricted the carriers from providing rates and services that were not in the public's best interest. The Elkins Act of 1903 strengthened the laws governing personal discrimination by providing criminal penalties for carriers and shippers who failed to follow the published tariff rate (filed rate doctrine) and who offered and accepted rebates.

In 1906, the Hepburn Act gave the ICC the power to prescribe maximum rates and to control joint and through rates. The Hepburn Act contained the commodities clause, which prevented the railroads from hauling their own commodities and which brought pipelines under ICC jurisdiction. The Mann-Elkins Act of 1910 gave the ICC the power to suspend proposed rates, and in 1912 the Panama Canal Act made it illegal for a railroad to own common water carriers with which the railroad competed, unless the ICC approved.

After 1920, regulatory policy became more carrier promotional. This change emanated from the financial chaos the railroads experienced because of severe intermodal competition and the emerging motor carriers' intermodal competition. The new regulations attempted to promote the carriers' viability.

promotional
The Transportation Act of 1920 allowed the ICC to establish minimum rates. At this point, reasonable rates became compensatory to the carrier. The Emergency Transportation Act of 1933 permitted cooperative actions (e.g., joint facility use) among railroads to achieve economies of operations, and gave the ICC power over railroad mergers. By giving the ICC the authority to establish the minimum rate level, Congress indirectly attempted to protect the public by somewhat assuring a stable supply of transportation.

From 1935 to 1942, transportation regulation expanded to other modes, imposing regulation that was basically the same as that under which the railroads operated. The Motor Carrier Act of 1935 brought for-hire motor carriers and brokers under ICC control; the act controlled motor carrier entry by requiring new carriers to secure a certificate of public convenience and necessity. The Civil Aeronautics Act of 1938 established economic regulations over air carriers and created the Civil Aeronautics Board (CAB) as an independent regulatory agency to administer the regulations. In 1940, regulation similar to that for motor carriers brought domestic water carriers under ICC control. Finally, Congress passed economic regulation for domestic freight forwarders in 1942. **other modes**

Today, the ICC administers the federal economic regulations for railroads, motor carriers, and domestic water carriers. Domestic surface freight forwarders were deregulated in 1986. The Federal Maritime Commission administers ocean shipping regulations, and the CAB administered federal economic controls for air carriers until air carrier deregulation abolished the CAB in 1985 and transferred the remaining minimal economic regulations to the Department of Transportation. The Federal Energy Regulatory Commission administers pipeline economic regulations. **regulatory agencies**

Beginning in 1976, a number of transportation laws reduced the regulation imposed on transportation. Under these deregulation laws, transportation was to rely more on marketplace control over rates and services. We will discuss these deregulation amendments in the following section.

Deregulation

In 1977, Congress completely deregulated air cargo transportation. Air cargo carriers are no longer subject to convenience and entry controls, and air cargo rates are regulation free. **air carriers**

The Motor Carrier Act of 1980 "reregulated" rate controls over trucking; the act provided greater ratemaking freedom and encouraged rate competition among the carriers. Since 1984, motor carriers have not been permitted to collectively (through the rate bureau process) vote on or discuss single-line rate proposals. However, the carriers may discuss or vote on general rate increases or decreases. **trucking**

The Motor Carrier Act of 1980 allowed the carriers greater freedom to set rates in response to demand by establishing the *zone of flexibility*, which permits the carrier to raise or lower a rate by 15 percent per year without ICC intervention; the ICC presumes the rate to be reasonable if it is within the zone of flexibility. Furthermore, the act allowed a carrier and shipper to negotiate a reduced rate in return for a limited liability on the property the carrier transported.

However, a 1990 Supreme Court decision, Maislin v. Primary Steel, generated considerable confusion regarding the extent of deregulation for marketplace-determined common carrier rates. In the Maislin case, the Supreme Court held that the common carrier negotiated rate was legal only if it was published in a tariff and the tariff filed with the ICC. This filed rate doctrine is contained in the Elkins Act of 1903. From this decision stemmed numerous undercharge claims from bankrupt common motor carriers. The undercharge is based on the difference between the lower negotiated rate that the shipper paid and the higher rate filed with the ICC. In 1993 shippers faced a total undercharge bill estimated to be $32 billion.

The Negotiated Rates Act of 1993 (NRA) is directed toward providing a partial solution to the undercharge problem. The NRA gives shippers the option of settling undercharges on truckload shipments (greater than 10,000 pounds) for 15 percent of the claim amount. For less-than-truckload shipments (less than 10,000 pounds) the settlement option is 20 percent of the undercharge claim. It also exempted small businesses, charitable organizations, and scrap recyclers from undercharge claims from nonoperating common carriers.

However, the NRA did not solve the root problem of undercharges. The filed rate doctrine remains law. The 1994 Trucking Industry Regulatory Reform Act (TIRR) eliminated the filing requirement for common carriers using individually determined rates (as opposed to bureau-determined rates), but the TIRR did not eliminate the filed rate doctrine. The rationale used is that without filed rates the filed rate doctrine has no basis and there can be no undercharges from negotiated rates.*

The TIRR does not eliminate all undercharges, only those resulting from negotiated rates not being filed with the ICC. Undercharges resulting from billing errors are still possible.

The Federal Aviation Administration Reauthorization Act of 1994 eliminated intrastate economic regulation of motor carriers. Effective January 1, 1995, states are prohibited from requiring operating authority or regulating trucking rates, routes, and services. This means that any trucking company may haul freight between two points within the same state without obtaining operating authority or publishing rate, route, or service tariffs with the state. Intrastate freight rates should decrease with this act.

railroads In 1976, the Railroad Revitalization and Regulatory Reform Act, which established a zone of reasonableness, initially introduced railroad rate deregulation. The *zone of reasonableness* permitted a railroad to raise or lower rates by 7 percent from the rate level in effect at the beginning of the year. The act also allowed the ICC to grant exemptions from commodity traffic regulations when public interest did not require those regulations. This exemption has eliminated rate controls over the movement of piggyback traffic and fruit shipments, for example.

Finally, the Staggers Act of 1980 permitted rail carriers greater rate freedom by limiting ICC maximum rail rate jurisdiction to rates where railroads exercise market dominance, defined as rates that exceed 180 percent of variable costs. The zone of rate flexibility permits rail rate increases of 4 percent per year. The act limits collective ratemaking to carriers who can practicably participate in the joint movement. Railroads may establish contract rates for a specific shipper. Rail rate increases take effect in twenty days, and rate reductions take effect in ten days.

In summary, rate deregulation has been complete for air cargo and certain rail traffic types—piggyback, for example. For trucks and railroads, deregulation has increased ratemaking flexibility and rate competition among the regulated carriers.

---

*For additional information on the NRA and TIRR, see Edward J. Bardi, ''Recent Trucking Laws Trigger Major Changes,'' *Metal Center News* 34, no. 13 (December 1994): 32–35.

ON THE LINE

ICC Puts End to Candy Cane Dispute

The ICC, in its first public action since President Bill Clinton signed legislation into law rendering tariffs null and void (the Transportation Industry Regulatory Reform Act of 1994), ruled that candy cane commodity class ratings were reasonable.

The ruling brings to an end a shipper-carrier dispute that appeared to play a pivotal role in triggering enactment of legislation terminating most motor carrier tariff-filing requirements. The issue before the ICC was whether the commodity classification on candy canes should be the same as that for candy. The carriers contended that a higher rating, and thus higher rates, were necessary to reflect the light weight (low density) of candy cane shipments. The shippers argued that the higher classification rating was unreasonable and that candy canes should be classified as candy, which has a lower class rating.

In its decision the ICC rejected shipper challenges on the grounds that their weight data were faulty. The carriers, through the National Motor Freight Traffic Committee, weighed and measured more than 400 candy cane shipments and proved that the density of candy canes is lower than that of other candy. The decision noted in a footnote that the carriers had spent 20 years trying to get the candy cane classification increased.

Apparently not wishing to be portrayed as the grinches who stole Christmas, truckers were voluntarily hauling candy canes at the lower candy rating. Or was this gesture the economic reality of the marketplace and the need for business?

ADAPTED WITH PERMISSION FROM: "ICC Puts End to Candy Cane Dispute," *Traffic World* (September 5, 1994): 14.

DOCUMENTATION—DOMESTIC

Domestic transportation utilizes a number of different documents to govern, direct, control, and provide information about a shipment. This section focuses on the bill of lading, freight bill, claims, and F.O.B. terms of sale—the documentation that is most prevalent in interstate transportation.

Bill of Lading

The *bill of lading* is probably the single most important transportation document. It originates the shipment, provides all the information the carrier needs to accomplish the move, stipulates the transportation contract terms, acts as a receipt for the goods the shipper tenders to the carrier, and, in some cases, shows certificate of title to the goods. Figure 10–2 shows a typical bill of lading.

contract receipt

All interstate shipments by common carriers begin with the issuance of a properly completed bill of lading. The information on the bill specifies the name and address of the consignor and consignee, as well as routing instructions for the carrier. The bill also describes the commodities in the shipment, the number of items in each commodity description, and the commodity's class or rate. Many shippers provide their own bills of lading (short form), which show the shipper's preprinted name and describe the commodities the company most commonly ships. This reduces the time required to fill out the bill, thereby eliminating delays at the shipper's loading facilities.

Straight Bill of Lading. The *straight bill of lading* is a nonnegotiable instrument, which means that endorsement of the straight bill cannot transfer title to the

nonnegotiable

FIGURE 10-2 Bill of Lading

THIS MEMORANDUM is an acknowledgment that a Bill of Lading has been issued and is not the Original Bill of Lading, nor a copy or duplicate, covering the property named herein, and is intended solely for filing or records.

Received subject to the classifications, lawfully filed tariffs, and contracts in effect on the date of the receipt by the carrier of the property described in the Original Bill of Lading the property described below, in apparent good order, except as noted (contents and condition of contents of packages unknown), marked, consigned, and destined as indicated below, which said carrier being understood throughout this contract as meaning any person or corporation in possession of the property under the contract) agrees to carry to its usual place of delivery at said destination, if on its route, otherwise, to deliver to another carrier on the route to said destination. It is mutually agreed as to each carrier of all or any of said property over all or any portion of said route to destination, and as to each party at any time interested in all or any of said property, that every service to be performed hereunder shall be subject to all the terms and conditions of the Uniform Domestic Straight Bill of Lading set forth (1) in Uniform Freight Classification in effect on the date hereof, if this is a rail or a rail-water shipment, or (2) in the applicable motor carrier classification or tariff if this is a motor carrier shipment.

Shipper hereby certifies that he is familiar with all the terms and conditions of the said bill of lading, including those on the back thereof, set forth in the classification or tariff which governs the transportation of this shipment, and the said terms and conditions are hereby agreed to by the shipper and accepted for himself and his assigns.

*If the shipment moves between two ports by a carrier by water, the law requires that the bill of lading shall state whether it is "carrier's or shipper's weight." NOTE: Where the rate is dependent on value shippers are required to state specifically in writing the agreed or declared value of the property. The agreed or declared value of the property is hereby specifically stated by the shipper to be not exceeding_____ Per_____

BILL OF LADING NO.   950980R2

FROM **ANDERSONS INDUSTRIAL PROD DIVISION**
MAUMEE, OHIO

Subject to Section 7 of conditions of applicable bill of lading, if this shipment is to be delivered to the consignee without recourse on the consignor. The consignor shall sign the following statement.
The carrier shall not make delivery of this shipment without payment of freight and all other lawful charges.

_____THE ANDERSONS_____
(Signature of consignor)

If charges are to be prepaid, write or stamp here, "TO BE PREPAID"

TO BE PREPAID

SHIP TO EMPIRE BEARING & TRANS
165 BROAD AVENUE

FAIRVIEW   NO   07022

CUSTOMER NUMBER	CUSTOMER P.O. NO.	ORDER NO.	ORDER DATE	SHIP DATE	SHIP VIA
2132701	1619	950980	02/27/95	03/01/95	YELLOW FREIGHT TRUCK

WAREHOUSE	PALLETS	PRODUCT CODE	DESCRIPTION	UNIT WGT.	NO. OF UNITS	WEIGHT
1	1	SK191	LG. O.P. SK (95GAL)NON-AGRSV.	18.00	1	18
2	1	DP41	5 DRIP PANS W/40 PILLOWS O.O.	25.00	1	25
3	2	RP12	REPAIR PUTTY 12/CS	5.00	2	10
4	10	S100	18" X 18" H.WGT. PADS (100)	19.00	10	190
5	20	SW46	46"SLIKWIK SOC ABSORBENT 40/CS	63.00	20	1260
6						
7						
8						
9						
10						
11						
12						
13						
14						
15						
16						
17						
18						
19						
20						
21						

UNITS	TYPE	HM	DESCRIPTION AND NMFC ITEM	WEIGHT
20	CS		BOOMS, PADS, SWEEPS OR FORMS, DENS 10-12# PCF, ITEM 149265S7, CL 92.5	1260
12	CS		BOOMS, PADS, SWEEPS OR FORMS, DENS 6-8# PCF, ITEM 149265S5, CL 125	200
2	EA		BOOMS, PADS, SWEEPS OR FORMS, DENS 6-8# PCF, ITEM 149265S5, CL 125	143

34 ← TOTAL UNITS   CUST PHONE: 201 945 7850

THIS IS TO CERTIFY THAT THE ABOVE-NAMED MATERIALS ARE PROPERLY CLASSIFIED, DESCRIBED, PACKAGED, MARKED AND LABELED AND ARE IN PROPER CONDITION FOR TRANSPORTATION ACCORDING TO THE APPLICABLE REGULATIONS OF THE DEPARTMENT OF TRANSPORTATION.

SIGNATURE: TITLE:

X

	WEIGHT
PRODUCT WEIGHT	1603
CONTAINER WEIGHT	0
PALLET WEIGHT	110
TOTAL WEIGHT	1713

*SEND PREPAID FREIGHT BILL WITH BILL OF LADING TO:
TRAFFIC DEPARTMENT
P.O. BOX 119
MAUMEE, OHIO 43537

EXTRA PALLT WGT_____
ADJUSTED WEIGHT_____

LOAD NO.   95 09 80   TOT DELVY   1   STOP NO.   1   TOT PALLETS_____ & LOOSE PIECES_____

SHIPPER PER	X	CUSTOMER PER	X	NOTE IF SHIPMENT IS OVER, SHORT, OR DAMAGED		CARRIER PER	X
					DATE		

PERMANENT POST OFFICE ADDESS- BOX 119, MAUMEE, OH 43537

SOURCE: Courtesy of The Andersons Management Corporation. Used with permission.

goods the straight bill names. For firms using the straight bill of lading, the terms of sale upon which the buyer and seller agreed, the buyer and seller generally dictate where title to the goods passes. The carrier does not require presentation of the straight bill's original copy to effect delivery; the carrier must simply deliver the goods to the person or firm the straight bill of lading names as consignee.

Order Bill of Lading. The *order bill of lading* is a negotiable instrument showing certificate of title to the goods it names. Using the order bill of lading enables the consignor to retain security interest in the goods.* That is, the consignee must pay the goods' invoice value to obtain the original copy of the order bill of lading that must be presented to the carrier for delivery.

negotiable

Contract Terms. The bill of lading contains the *terms of contract* for movement by common carrier. The contract is between the shipper and the common carrier for the movement of the freight that the bill of lading identifies to the consignee that the bill identifies. The bill of lading contract contains nine sections. Section 1, delineating the extent of the carrier's liability, is a primary contract term.

The major terms of the common carrier's contract of carriage as found in the bill of lading sections are as follows:

exceptions to liability

1. *Common carrier liability.* The carrier is held liable for all loss, damage, or delay to the goods except for the following:

    Act of God—loss resulting from any unavoidable natural catastrophe. If the carrier had sufficient opportunity to avoid the catastrophe, the carrier is liable and cannot use this exception.

    Act of public enemy—loss resulting from armed aggression against the United States.

    Act of shipper—loss resulting from shipper's improper loading, packaging, or concealment of goods being shipped.

    Act of public authority—loss resulting from public agencies taking or destroying goods by due process of law.

    Inherent nature of the goods—the normal or expected loss of the products (e.g., evaporation).

2. *Reasonable dispatch.* The shipper holds the carrier liable for the actual loss or damage that results from an unreasonable delay in transit. No specific rule exists for determining reasonable time. The shipper examines the shipment's specifics to see if the delay was unreasonable under given circumstances.

3. *Cooperage and baling.* The owner pays such costs. The carrier may compress cotton or cotton linters and may commingle bulk grain shipments destined to a public elevator with other grain.

4. *Freight not accepted.* The carrier may store at the owner's cost any property the consignee does not remove within the free time. After notifying the consignor, the carrier may sell at public auction property the consignee refuses.

---

*When using a straight bill of lading, the shipper can retain security interest in the goods by using the C.O.D. (cash on delivery) service carriers offer. With a C.O.D. shipment, the carrier collects the invoice price of the shipment before delivering the shipment to the consignee.

5. *Articles of extraordinary value.* The carrier is not obligated to carry documents or articles of extraordinary value unless the classification or tariff specifically rates such items. This is one area where a common carrier can refuse to provide service.

6. *Explosives.* The shipper shall give the carrier full written disclosure when shipping dangerous articles. If there is no disclosure, the shipper is held liable for any damage such goods cause.

7. *No recourse.* The carrier has no legal recourse back to the shipper for additional charges after making delivery. If the shipper signs the no recourse clause and the carrier delivers the shipment, the carrier has recourse only to the consignee for additional freight charges for the shipment.

8. *Substitute bill of lading.* When a bill of lading is an exchange or substitute for another, the subsequent bill of lading shall encompass the prior bill's statements regarding shipment value, election of common law liability, and consignor's signature.

9. *Water carriage.* If water transportation is involved, the water carrier is liable for negligence in loading, and is responsible for making the vessel seaworthy and for outfitting and manning the vessel.

10. *Alterations.* The carrier's agent must note any changes, additions, or erasures to make such alterations enforceable.

delay   In essence, this brief discussion of the bill of lading contract terms describes the contract of carriage with a common carrier. The various rules and regulations the carrier's tariffs contain and those the ICC issues provide the finer detail in the contract. These contract terms are subject to regulatory scrutiny for compliance with common carrier duties and other transportation regulations.

Freight Bill

definition   The *freight bill* is the carrier's invoice for the charges the carrier incurs in moving a given shipment. ICC regulations stipulate the credit terms that common carriers may offer the shipper or consignee. The regulation of credit terms precludes discrimination; for example, it prevents the carrier from discriminating against a particular shipper by extending that shipper credit times shorter than those it grants others. Shippers must comply with the credit payment periods.

credit terms   The ICC permits railroads and motor common carriers to extend credit terms of fifteen to thirty days as published in their tariffs; that is, the shipper must pay freight charges within fifteen to thirty days of receiving the freight bill. Carriers may allow discounts for prompt payment and may add service charges for late payment. The carrier may require prepayment of the charges if, in the carrier's opinion, the commodity's value is less than the freight charges.

prepaid or collect   Freight bills may be either prepaid or collect. The prepaid or collect basis determines when the carrier will present the freight bill, not necessarily whether the shipper will pay the charges in advance or after the movement's completion. On a *prepaid* shipment, the carrier presents the freight bill on the effective day of shipment. On a *collect* shipment, the carrier presents the freight bill on the effective day of delivery. In both cases, the shipper must pay the bills within the maximum days of credit from presentation; but on the collect basis, the carrier extends the payment due date by the length of the transit time.

Traffic personnel may perform freight bill auditing internally. Internal auditing requires personnel with extensive carrier tariff and rate expertise. For companies lacking in-house expertise, external auditors, who usually receive a percentage of the overcharge claims paid, are available. The shipper must file overcharge claims with the carrier within three years of the shipment delivery date.

auditing

Claims

The *freight claim* is a document (with no prescribed format) that the shipper files with the carrier to recoup monetary losses resulting from loss, damage, or delay to the shipment or to recover overcharge payments. As we noted earlier, the common carrier is liable, with limited exception, for all loss, damage, or delay.

The shipper must file in writing freight claims with the carrier (originating, delivering, or on whose line damage occurred) within nine months of delivery, or, in the case of loss, within nine months of reasonable delivery. The carrier must acknowledge in writing the receipt of the claim within thirty days and must inform the claimant within 120 days after receipt whether the carrier will pay or refuse the claim. If the carrier does not dispose of the claim within 120 days, the carrier must notify the claimant of the reasons for failure to settle the claim at the end of each succeeding 60 days. If the carrier disallows the claim, the filing party has two years from the time of disallowance to bring legal action through the courts against the carrier.

time limits

Damage may be either visible or concealed. Visible damage, usually discovered at delivery, is damage that the consignee detects before opening the package. Concealed damage is not detected until the consignee opens the package. A problem arises with determining whether concealed damage occurred while the goods were in the carrier's possession or in the consignee's possession. Many carriers stipulate that the shipper must file concealed damage claims within fifteen days of delivery. This does not overrule the nine-month limitation, but the carrier will look more favorably upon the claim if the shipper files it within the stated policy period.

To support a claim, the claimant must submit the original bill of lading, the original paid freight bill, and some indication of the commodity's value (an invoice or price catalog, for example). If the consignee notes on the bill of lading that the goods were damaged when the carrier tendered them for delivery and the carrier indicated no such damage when picking up the shipment, the claimant has a prima facie case against the carrier. The original paid freight bill determines the amount the carrier will reimburse the claimant, since the courts have concluded that the carrier is liable for the commodity's market value at destination less any unpaid freight charges.

supporting document

The following principle establishes the damage claim's value: The claim shall restore the claimant to a condition as good as that in which the claimant would have been had the carrier safely delivered the goods. To determine this value, the claimant utilizes the original invoice, price catalog, and other factors to show the commodity's market value at destination. For commodities that do not have a ready market value, such as one-of-a kind items, the claimant may use cost accounting records to determine value.

A *released value* is an exception to the full value liability obligation. At the time of shipment the shipper may elect to release the value of the shipment to something less than its full value. This election reduces the carrier's liability in case of damage to the amount stipulated by the shipper. In return the shipper usually receives a lower freight rate.

Another exception to the full value liability is the automatic released-value rules that some carriers place in their rules tariffs. The automatic released value states that the value of the product is automatically reduced (released) to that stipulated in the tariff unless the shipper states otherwise on the bill of lading at the time of shipment.

F.O.B. Terms of Sale

The *F.O.B. terms of sale* determine the logistics responsibility that the buyer and seller will incur. Originally, F.O.B. referred to the seller's making the product free of transportation charges to the ship, or "free on board." More specifically, the F.O.B. terms of sale delineate (1) who is to incur transportation charges, (2) who is to control movement of the shipment, and (3) where the title passes to the buyer.

The F.O.B. term specifies the point to which the seller incurs transportation charges and responsibility and relinquishes title to the buyer. For example, *F.O.B. delivered* indicates that the seller incurs all transportation charges and responsibility to the buyer's destination and that title passes to the buyer at delivery. *F.O.B. origin* means the opposite: the buyer incurs all transportation charges and responsibility, and title passes to the buyer at the shipment's origin.

The terms a firm utilizes to sell its products or to purchase its raw material directly affect the magnitude of the transportation function. A firm that purchases raw materials F.O.B. origin and sells its finished product F.O.B. delivered would require extensive transportation management. In such a situation, the firm controls carrier selection and warehousing and also incurs transportation charges for all commodity movements. The firm can pass this responsibility on to the buyer or supplier by altering the terms of sale, thereby lessening its transportation management requirements.

The F.O.B. term also defines the party responsible for filing a damage claim. The party that possesses title to the goods must file the claim. If damage occurs after the shipment reaches the named point, the buyer would be responsible for filing the claim. Conversely, if damage occurs before the shipment reaches the named point, the seller would file the claim.

DOCUMENTATION—INTERNATIONAL

Export documentation is far more complicated than the documentation that domestic shipments require. Since the transaction involves different nations, political as well as economic considerations affect the documentation required. Specific documentation requirements vary widely from country to country. It is necessary to complete each document accurately, for a mistake may delay the shipment's delivery.

For discussion purposes, we will group the various documents into two categories: sales and transportation. Much of the information the documents require is similar, but each document serves a different purpose.

Sales Documents

The *sales contract* is the initial document in any international business transaction, and export sales contracts exhibit little uniformity. To reduce time and cost, the export sales contract should completely and clearly describe the commodities, price, payment terms, transportation arrangements, insurance requirements, the carriers, and any special arrangements the agreement may require.

sales contract

After negotiating the sales contract, the parties involved must determine the method of payment. The *letter of credit,* the most common payment method, provides a high degree of protection. Other forms of payment include cash, consignment, and open account. The letter of credit is a bank's assurance that the buyer will make payment as long as the seller meets the sales terms (export sales contract terms) to which the parties have agreed. When the seller complies with the sales conditions that the letter of credit states and presents a draft drawn in compliance with the letter of credit, the buyer makes payment to the exporter.

letter of credit

A letter of credit is drawn up and used in the following manner:

1. The buyer and seller make a contract for the sale of goods.
2. The buyer arranges for its bank to issue the seller a letter of credit in the sale amount.
3. The buyer's bank places the amount in the seller's bank.
4. The seller prepares a draft against the deposit and attaches the draft to the following documents:
    —Clean, negotiable bill of lading
    —Certificate of insurance
    —Seller's invoice
    —Letter of credit
5. The seller endorses the order bill of lading to the bank and receives the money.
6. The seller's bank endorses the bill of lading to the buyer's bank.
7. The buyer's bank endorses the bill of lading to the buyer.
8. The buyer takes the bill of lading to the carrier and picks up the shipment.

Terms of Sale

The international terms of sale are known as Incoterms. Unlike domestic terms of sale, where the buyers and sellers primarily use F.O.B. origin and F.O.B. destination terms, there are 13 different Incoterms. Developed by the International Chamber of Commerce, these Incoterms are internationally accepted rules defining trade terms.

The Incoterms define responsibilities of both the buyer and the seller in any international contract of sale. For exporting, the terms delineate buyer or seller responsibility for:

- Export packing cost
- Inland transportation (to the port of export)
- Export clearance
- Vessel or plane loading
- Main transportation cost
- Cargo insurance
- Customs duties
- Risk of loss or damage in transit

departure contract

E Terms. The E terms consist of one Incoterm, *Ex Works* (EXW). This is a departure contract that means the buyer has total responsibility for the shipment. The seller's responsibility is to make the shipment available at its facility. The buyer agrees to take possession of the shipment at the point of origin and to bear all of the cost and risk of transporting the goods to the destination. (See Table 10–1 for additional responsibilities of the E terms.)

F Terms. The three F terms obligate the seller to incur the cost of delivering the shipment cleared for export to the carrier designated by the buyer. The buyer selects and incurs the cost of main transportation, insurance, and customs clearance. *FCA,* Free Carrier, can be used with any mode of transportation. Risk of damage is transferred to the buyer when the seller delivers the goods to the carrier named by the buyer.

  FAS, Free Alongside Ship, is used for water transportation shipments only. Risk of damage is transferred to the buyer when the goods are delivered alongside the ship. The buyer must pay the cost of "lifting" the cargo or container on board the vessel. *F.O.B.,* Free on Board, is used only for water transportation shipments. The risk of damage is transferred to the buyer when the shipment crosses the ship's rail (when the goods are actually loaded on the vessel). The seller pays the lifting charge. (See Table 10–1 for additional responsibilities of the F terms.)

shipment contract

C Terms. The four C terms are shipment contracts that obligate the seller to obtain and pay for the main carriage and/or cargo insurance. *CFR,* Cost and Freight, and *CPT,* Carriage Paid To, are similar in that both obligate the seller to select and pay for the main carriage (ocean or air to the foreign country). *CFR* is used only for shipments by water transportation, while *CPT* is used for any mode. In both terms the seller incurs all costs to the port of destination. Risk of damage passes to the buyer when the goods pass the ship's rail (CFR) or when delivered to the main carrier (CPT).

  CIF, or Cost, Insurance, Freight, and *CIP,* Carriage and Insurance Paid To, require the seller to pay for both main carriage and cargo insurance. The risk of

TABLE 10–1 Summary of Incoterms Cost Obligations

Cost or Activity	EXW	FCA	FAS	FOB	CFR	CIF	CPT	CIP	DAF	DES	DEQ	DDU	DDP
Export packing	B	S	S	S	S	S	S	S	S	S	S	S	S
Export clearance	B	S	B	S	S	S	S	S	S	S	S	S	S
Inland transport (domestic)	B	S	S	S	S	S	S	S	S	S	S	S	S
Vessel/plane loading	B	B	B	S	S	S	S	S	S	S	S	S	S
Main transport	B	B	B	B	S	S	S	S	S	S	S	S	S
Cargo insurance	B	B	B	B	B	S	B	S	S	S	S	S	S
Customs duties	B	B	B	B	B	B	B	B	B	B	S	B	S
Inland transport (foreign)	B	B	B	B	B	B	B	B	B	B	B	B	S
Mode applicability	X	X	W	W	W	W	X	X	X	W	W	X	X

B= buyer; S = seller; W = water carrier; X = air, motor, rail, intermodal.

damage is the same as that for CFR and CPT. (See Table 10–1 for additional responsibilities of the C terms.)

D Terms.   The D terms obligate the seller to incur all costs related to delivery of **arrival contract** the shipment to the foreign destination. There are five D terms; two apply to water transportation only, and three apply to any mode used. All five D terms require the seller to incur all costs and the risk of damage up to the destination port.

DAF, Delivered at Frontier, means that the seller is responsible for transportation and incurs risk of damage to the named point at the place of delivery at the frontier of the destination country. For example, DAF Laredo, Texas, indicates that the seller is responsible for making the goods available at Laredo, Texas. The buyer is responsible for customs duties and clearance into Mexico. DAF can be used with all modes.

DES, Delivered Ex Ship, and *DEQ,* Delivered Ex Quay (wharf), are used with shipments by water transportation. Both terms require the seller to select and pay for the main carriage. Under DES the risk of damage is transferred when the goods are made available to the buyer on board the ship, uncleared for import at the port of destination. The buyer is responsible for customs clearance. With DEQ, risk of damage is transferred to the buyer when the goods, cleared for import, are unloaded onto the quay (wharf) at the named port of destination.

DDU, Delivered Duty Unpaid, and *DDP,* Delivered Duty Paid, are available for all modes. DDU requires the seller to incur all costs, except import duties, to the named place in the country of importation. Risk of damage passes to the buyer when the goods are made available, duties unpaid, at the named place. (DDU is similar to DES.) DDP imposes the same obligations on the seller as DDU plus the additional responsibility of clearing the goods for import and paying the customs duties. (DDP is similar to DEQ.) (See Table 10–1 for additional responsibilities of the D terms.)

Transportation Documents

After the buyer and seller reach an agreement as to sales and credit terms, the **export declaration** exporter files with exit port customs an *export declaration* (see Figure 10–3), which provides the Department of Commerce with information concerning the export shipment's nature and value. The required information usually includes a description of the commodity, the shipping weight, a list of the marks and numbers on the containers, the number and dates of any required export license, the place and country of destination, and the parties to the transaction.

A company requires an *export license* in order to export goods from the United **export license** States. These licenses fall into one of two categories. The *general license* allows the export of most goods without any special requirements. The commodities this license covers are general in nature and have no strategic value to the United States. On the other hand, certain items whose export the government wishes to control require a *validation export license.* Commodities requiring this type of license include military hardware, certain high-tech items such as microprocessors and supercomputers, and other goods for which control is in the national interest.

The *commercial invoice,* which the seller uses to determine the commodity's value **invoices** less freight and other charges is basically the seller's invoice for the commodities sold. The letter of credit and companies or agencies often require this invoice to

FIGURE 10-3 Shipper's Export Declaration

U.S. DEPARTMENT OF COMMERCE - BUREAU OF THE CENSUS - INTERNATIONAL TRADE ADMINISTRATION

FORM **7525-V** (1-1-88)   **SHIPPER'S EXPORT DECLARATION**   OMB No. 0607-0018

1a. EXPORTER (Name and address including ZIP code)

ZIP CODE   **2.** DATE OF EXPORTATION   **3.** BILL OF LADING/AIR WAYBILL NO.

b. EXPORTER'S EIN (IRS) NO.   **c.** PARTIES TO TRANSACTION
☐ Related   ☐ Non-related

4a. ULTIMATE CONSIGNEE

b. INTERMEDIATE CONSIGNEE

5. FORWARDING AGENT

6. POINT (STATE) OF ORIGIN OR FTZ NO.   **7.** COUNTRY OF ULTIMATE DESTINATION

8. LOADING PIER (Vessel only)   **9.** MODE OF TRANSPORT (Specify)

10. EXPORTING CARRIER   **11.** PORT OF EXPORT

12. PORT OF UNLOADING (Vessel and air only) **13.** CONTAINERIZED (Vessel only)
☐ Yes   ☐ No

14. SCHEDULE B DESCRIPTION OF COMMODITIES,
15. MARKS NOS., AND KINDS OF PACKAGES.   } (Use columns 17—19)

D/F (16)	SCHEDULE B NUMBER (17)	CHECK DIGIT	QUANTITY — SCHEDULE B UNIT(S) (18)	SHIPPING WEIGHT (Kilos) (19)	VALUE (U.S. dollars, omit cents) (Selling price or cost if not sold) (20)

21. VALIDATED LICENSE NO./GENERAL LICENSE SYMBOL   **22.** ECCN (When required)

23. Duly authorized officer or employee   The exporter authorizes the forwarder named above to act as forwarding agent for export control and customs purposes.

24. I certify that all statements made and all information contained herein are true and correct and that I have read and understand the instructions for preparation of this document, set forth in the "**Correct Way to Fill Out the Shipper's Export Declaration.**" I understand that civil and criminal penalties, including forfeiture and sale, may be imposed for making false or fraudulent statements herein, failing to provide the requested information or for violation of U.S. laws on exportation (13 U.S.C. Sec. 305; 22 U.S.C. Sec. 401; 18 U.S.C. Sec. 1001; 50 U.S.C. App. 2410).

Signature

Title

Date

Confidential - For use solely for official purposes authorized by the Secretary of Commerce (13 U.S.C. 301 (g).

Export shipments are subject to inspection by U.S. Customs Service and/or Office of Export Enforcement.

25. AUTHENTICATION (When required)

The "**Correct Way to Fill Out the Shipper's Export Declaration**" is available from the Bureau of the Census, Washington, D.C. 20233.

determine the correct value for insurance purposes and for assessing import duties. Some countries have special requirements (language, information requested, etc.) for the commercial invoice. Many countries also require a special form called a *consular invoice* for any incoming shipments. The consular invoice, which allows the country to collect import statistics, is usually written in the importing nation's language.

When a seller makes a shipment in a sealed container, a *carnet* is often issued. **carnet** A carnet indicates that the shipment has been sealed at its origin and will not be opened until it reaches its final destination. The container may then pass in transit through intermediate customs points without inspection. Carnets are very useful for intermodal shipments and for containers crossing several national boundaries between origin and destination. Much of the overland shipping in Europe travels under carnet.

A destination country that has made a treaty agreement to give favorable import duty treatment to certain U.S. goods often requires a *certificate of origin*, which certifies that the goods' origin is the United States. This prevents a shipper from applying the favorable import duty to foreign goods that the shipper merely reshipped from the United States.

The initiating document for any international shipment is the bill of lading **bill of lading** (B/L). One bill of lading, the *export bill of lading*, could govern the domestic portion of the move (from plant to port of exit), the intercountry portion (by ocean or air), and the foreign portion (from port of entry to final destination in a foreign country). In practice, most shipments move under a combination of domestic and ocean (or air) bills of lading.

The *ocean bill of lading* is similar to the domestic bill of lading we discussed earlier. The ocean bill of lading serves as the contract of carriage between the carrier and the shipper. It sets down the terms of shipment and designates the origin and destination ports. It also supplies shipment information, such as the quantity and weight, the freight charges, and any special handling requirements. The ocean bill of lading is hardly uniform. The carrier is able to add conditions to the bill of lading as long as the additions are not contrary to law.

As we discussed earlier, *order bills of lading* also provide evidence of ownership. Sellers can use these negotiable documents to transfer title of the goods.

The carrier issues a *clean bill of lading* when the cargo arrives aboard ship in good condition. If the goods show evidence of damage, the carrier will note this on the bill of lading and will not issue a clean B/L. After processing all the bills of lading, the carrier prepares a *ship's manifest*, which summarizes the cargo aboard the ship, listed by port of loading and destination.

The primary bill of lading contract terms concern the ocean carrier's liability. **liability** The Carriage of Goods by Sea Act of 1936 states that the ocean carrier is required to use due diligence to make its vessel seaworthy and is held liable for losses resulting from negligence. The shipper is liable for loss resulting from perils of the sea, acts of God, acts of public enemies, inherent defects of the cargo, or shipper negligence. Thus, the liability of the ocean carrier is less than that imposed upon a domestic carrier.

The terms of sale may also require a *certificate of insurance*. This certificate will state that the buyer or seller has obtained insurance adequate to cover any losses resulting during transit.

After the carrier has delivered the goods at the dock, the steamship agent issues **dock receipt** a *dock receipt* indicating that the domestic carrier has delivered the shipment to

airway bill

the steamship company. This document can be used to show compliance with a letter of credit's payment requirements and to support damage claims.

Another increasingly important document is the *universal airway bill,* a standardized document that air carriers use on all international air shipments. By reducing required paperwork to one document, the carrier reduces processing costs. Having a standardized document also helps to speed shipments through customs.

Improving Documentation

International transportation can become a paperwork jungle. A single shipment typically generates as many as forty-six different documents with 360 copies requiring forty-six working hours to process. Extreme cases may require as many as 158 documents with 690 copies.[3] Documentation costs may be as high as 10 percent of the value of foreign trade.

Several groups are trying to reduce the amount of documentation international transportation requires. The National Council on International Trade Documentation (NCITD) has developed a system to relay information electronically and to ultimately transit documents to a shipment's destination so that the buyer may inspect them before the goods arrive. This reduces the time required for customs processing. And, by developing export-import document format standards, both NCITD and the United Nations Conference on Multimodal Transport are working to simplify the form of the documentation.

EDI

Electronic data interchange (EDI) is also entering common use. Various nations and organizations are standardizing documentation and electronic requirements to create an international system for transmitting export-import information. Simplified documentation and electronic interconnecting will dramatically reduce information processing and transmission time, leading to savings and providing an incentive to increase international trade.[4]

CARDIS

The U.S. Customs Service has developed a system utilizing many of these innovations to clear shipments at several large U.S. ports. The Customs Service developed this system, called the *Cargo Data Interchange System* (CARDIS), using NCITD guidelines. It provides the following basic functions:

- *Shipment file maintenance* that contains all the data needed to move a shipment under one bill of lading
- *Electronic links* between all the parties involved in the shipment
- *Documentation* that produces documents needed to complete a specific shipment
- *Tracing* to provide a shipment's status until it reaches its destination and to supply provisions for updating the files
- A *statistical and summary report* that the system generates from the database
- *Government and company interfaces* to exchange data about shipments[5]

Using CARDIS will provide several advantages to American companies. First, the quicker data exchange will reduce cargo warehousing and handling costs by allowing earlier review of the customs documents. Second, automation and the reduced number of documents will greatly reduce clerical costs. Third, faster transmittal times will help to shorten shipment times, allowing quicker clearance of letters of credit. This will give a company savings on in-transit inventory costs.

Finally, an international classification system, the *Harmonized Commodity Description and Coding System,* has been developed to identify specific products with an internationally accepted identification number. The Harmonized Code permits consistent classification for transportation elements such as documentation and duties.

Harmonized Code

BASES FOR RATES

As we saw previously, the carriers, not the regulatory agency, establish the rates they charge. This section directs attention toward the bases carriers use or the factors they consider in determining rates. The following factors usually affect the rate: (1) the cost and value of service, which affect the different rates the carrier establishes for different commodities; (2) distance; and (3) the volume or weight of the shipment.

Cost of Service

Basing rates upon the *cost of service* considers the supply side of pricing. The cost of supplying the service establishes the floor for a rate; that is, the supply cost permits the carrier's viability by providing the rate's lower limit (see Figure 10–4).

A continual problem of what cost basis to use has plagued this area. Carriers have used fully allocated (average total) costs, as well as average variable costs and out-of-pocket (marginal) costs. In essence, this problem sets up subfloors to the lower rate limit: the carrier will base the higher limit upon fully allocated costs and will base the lower limit upon out-of-pocket costs. The ICC use of these bases has varied and depends upon the particular circumstances surrounding the case in question.

cost concepts

FIGURE 10–4 Limits on Rates

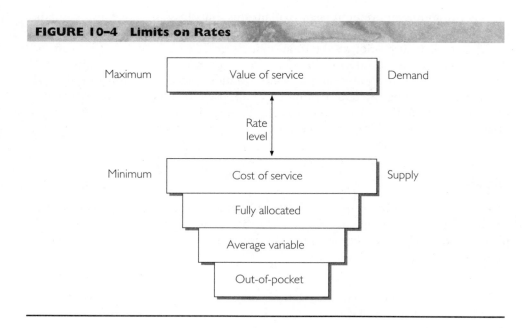

FIGURE 10-5   Example of Value of Service Pricing

Maximum rate = $0.50

A ———————————————————————————— B

A's production cost = $2.00   B's production cost = $2.50

---

common costs
• joint costs

Common and joint costs also increase the problem of using service cost as a basis for rates. The carrier incurs common and joint costs when producing multiple units of output; the carrier cannot directly allocate such costs to a particular production unit. (*Joint cost* is a particular type of common cost in which the costs a carrier incurs in producing one unit unavoidably produce another product. For example, moving a commodity from A to B unavoidably produces the movement capacity and cost from B to A—the backhaul.) The procedure the carrier uses to assign these costs determines the cost basis, permitting latitude for cost variations and, consequently, for rate variations.

Value of Service

Value of service pricing considers the demand side of pricing. We may define value of service pricing as "charging what the traffic will bear." This basis considers the transported product's ability to withstand transportation costs. For example, in Figure 10–5, the highest rate a carrier can charge to move producer A's product to point B is fifty cents per unit. If the carrier assesses a higher rate, producer A's product will not be competitive in the B market area. Thus, value of service pricing places the upper limit upon the rate.

rationale

Generally, rates vary by transported product. The cost difference associated with various commodity movements may explain this, but this difference also contains the value of service pricing concept. For higher-value commodities, transportation charges are a small portion of the total selling price. From Table 10–2, we can see that the transportation rate for diamonds, for a given distance and weight, is 100 times greater than that for coal; but transportation charges amount to only 0.01 percent of the selling price for diamonds, as opposed to 25 percent for coal. Thus, high-value commodities can sustain higher transportation charges; and carriers price the transport services accordingly—a specific application of demand pricing.*

Distance

Rates usually vary with respect to *distance;* that is, the greater the distance the commodity moves, the greater the cost to the carrier and the greater the transportation rate. However, certain rates do not relate to distance. One example of these is a *blanket rate.*

---

*We could argue that for high-valued goods the carrier bears a higher cost because of the increased liability risk in case of damage.

TABLE 10-2   Transportation Rates and Commodity Value

	Coal	Diamonds
Production value per ton*	$30.00	$10,000,000.00
Transportation charge per ton*	10.00	1,000.00
Total selling price	$40.00	$10,001,000.00
Transportation cost as a percentage of selling price	25%	0.01%

*Assumed.

A blanket rate does not increase as distance increases; the rate remains the same for all points in the blanket area the carrier designates. The postage stamp rate is one example of a blanket rate. No matter what distance you ship a letter, your cost as shipper (sender) is the same. In transportation, carriers have employed blanket rates for a city's commercial zone,** a given state, region, or a number of states, for example. In each case, the rate into (out of) the blanket area will be the same no matter where the destination (origin) is located in the blanket area.

blanket rate

Most transportation rates do increase as distance increases, but the increase is not directly proportional to distance. This relationship of rates to distance is known as the tapering rate principle. As Figure 10–6 shows, the rate increases as distance increases, but not linearly. The rate structure tapers because carriers spread terminal costs (cargo handling, clerical, and billing) over a greater mileage base. These terminal costs do not vary with distance; as the shipment's movement distance increases, the terminal cost per mile decreases. The intercept point in Figure 10–6 corresponds to the terminal costs.

tapering rate

Weight of Shipment

Carriers quote freight rates in cents per hundredweight (actual weight in pounds divided by 100 = hundredweight, or cwt) and determine the total transportation charge by the total weight of the shipment in cwt, and the appropriate rate per cwt. The rate per cwt relates to the shipped volume: carriers charge a lower rate for volume shipments and a higher rate for less-than-volume quantities. In essence, carriers offer a quantity discount for shipping large volumes (buying service in a large quantity).

Railroads term these quantity discounts carload (CL) and less-than-carload (LCL); motor carriers call them truckload (TL) and less-than-truckload (LTL). The CL and TL rates represent the lower, volume rates; and the LCL and LTL rates denote the higher, less-than-volume rates.

quantity discount

One noteworthy exception to the rate-volume relationship is the any-quantity (AQ) rate, which bears no relationship to volume shipped. The rate per cwt remains constant regardless of the volume a firm tenders to the carrier for shipment; that is, no quantity discount is available.

**We define the commercial zone as the city proper plus surrounding points, determined by population, and the rates to the city apply to the surrounding points within this limit.

FIGURE 10–6 Example of the Tapering Rate Principle

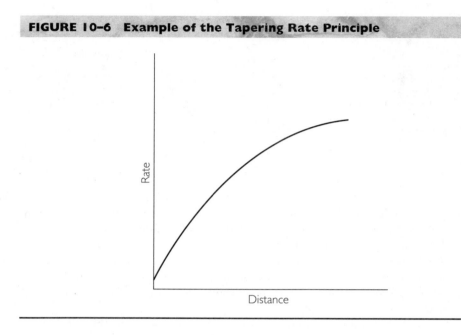

The pragmatics of carrier pricing are presented in Appendix 10A, following this chapter.

TRANSPORTATION SERVICES

The preceding material does not entirely delineate the nature of the transportation service. Carriers may seem merely to provide commodity movement service between two facilities; in reality, the carrier provides terminal and line-haul services as well as basic transport service. For some services, but not all, the carrier charges no additional fee. The transportation manager must recognize and take advantage of these "extra" services.

Terminal Services

Although carrier terminal operations fall outside the logistics manager's direct control, exploring the nature of this operation provides the logistics manager with some knowledge of the constraints that carrier terminals impose upon the provision of transportation service.

Terminal Functions. Essentially, the carrier's terminal performs five basic functions: concentration, dispersion, shipment service, vehicle service, and interchange.[6] Performing these functions requires time, and therefore affects the total transit time a carrier provides.

consolidation   *Concentration* is the consolidation of many less-than-volume shipments into one large shipment that the carrier can transport economically. Thus, if a shipper tenders a 2,000-pound shipment, the carrier will combine this shipment with other small shipments before dispatching it on toward destination. *Dispersion* is just the opposite; when a consolidated shipment arrives at the destination terminal, the carrier must break down the many shipments in the vehicle (break-bulk) for dispatch to the individual consignees.

break-bulk

Through *shipment service,* the carrier provides freight handling services for consolidation and dispersion and performs the clerical, billing, routing, and other functions for the shipment. *Vehicle service* essentially maintains a sufficient vehicle supply. The carrier must constantly review vehicle distribution among terminals to ensure a supply sufficient to provide the transport service the shipping public and regulatory requirements demand. Finally, *interchange* provides freight-exchange facilities for carriers coordinating to provide through service.

In addition to the preceding functions, the carrier's terminal provides pickup and delivery service. Pickup and delivery involve picking up movement-ready freight at the shipper's plant or making ultimate shipment delivery at the consignee's plant. Carriers may or may not charge for this service; the shipper must consult the carrier's rules and accessorial tariffs.

Loading and Unloading. The concentration function embraces the carrier's obligation to load and unload small shipments. For TL- and CL-size shipments, the shipper is required to load the vehicle and the consignee is required to unload it; but, if a firm wishes, the carrier will perform these services at an added cost. The shipper must consult the carrier's rules to determine loading (or unloading) requirements.

The carrier grants the shipper or consignee a specified amount of free time to load or unload a vehicle and assesses charges for holding the vehicle beyond the free time; these are known as *demurrage* (rail) and *detention* (motor) charges. For railroads, the free time for loading or unloading a boxcar is twenty-four to forty-eight hours, Saturdays, Sundays, and holidays excluded. The demurrage charge per railcar per day held varies by carrier.

demurrage and detention

The motor carrier industry has no standard detention rules and charges. Consequently, a shipper must consult each carrier's rules tariff to determine free time and detention charges. As a general rule, detention charges for holding the power unit and driver beyond the free time are higher than for holding the trailer only.

Shipment Monitoring. As we noted earlier, carriers quote transportation rates in terms of cents per cwt. Thus, the carrier needs the shipment's exact weight determined so that the carrier realizes the appropriate revenue and the shipper pays the correct charges. The carriers maintain weighing devices that the regulatory commissions control. A shipper may request a carrier to reweigh a vehicle and its contents if the shipper feels the original weight is in error. For some commodities, the carrier and shipper use an agreed weight per package, case, carton, or other container. If an agreed weight is in effect, the number of shipped packages times the agreed weight determines the total shipment weight.

weighing

In many situations, the transportation manager must know where a shipment is or when it will arrive at its destination. Such information eliminates customer ill will and stockouts and improves the utilization of materials handling equipment and labor. Carriers provide this monitoring function, known as tracing and expediting. *Tracing* is tracking a shipment's movement to determine its location in the transportation pipeline. *Expediting,* which utilizes the same procedure as tracing, has the objective of getting the shipment to its destination quicker than normal. Some motor carriers use satellites to monitor a vehicle's exact location.

tracing expediting

Line-Haul Services

Carriers also provide line-haul services that permit the logistics manager to effect changes in the original shipping order and to realize savings in transportation costs. The line-haul services are reconsignment and diversion, pool car (or truck) service, stopping in transit, and transit privilege.

Reconsignment and Diversion. Carriers use reconsignment and diversion interchangeably to mean a change in the shipment's destination and/or consignee with the shipper paying the through rate from origin to final destination. There is, however, a technical difference between the two. Reconsignment permits the shipper to change the destination and/or consignee after the shipment has reached its original destination but before the carrier has delivered it to the original consignee. Diversion enables the shipper to effect the same changes while the shipment is en route and before it reaches the original destination.

benefit   Shippers use reconsignment and diversion extensively in the movement of perishable products (fruits, etc.) and for movement in which the original consignee refuses the shipment or cancels the order. Shippers may start perishable products in movement before they have a buyer, using the time in transit to obtain a buyer. Having found a buyer, the shipper issues a reconsignment or diversion order with the buyer named as consignee. Or, when an original buyer decides not to accept an order, the shipper can utilize a reconsignment or diversion order to change the shipment's destination to a new buyer location or to have the shipment stopped and returned to the seller's location. These services permit the shipper to amend the original contract (bill of lading) with the carrier and to realize the benefits of the lower through rate (the tapering rate principle) from origin to new destination.

Pooling. Pool car or pool truck service permits the shipper to combine many LCL or LTL shipments into one CL or TL shipment and to send it to one destination and one consignee. The lower CL or TL rate applies to the combined shipments and thus effects savings for the shipper. Since the service requires one destination and one consignee, the shipper usually sends the shipment to a warehouse or drayage firm,* which breaks down or disperses the consolidated shipment into individual shipments and delivers them to the appropriate consignees. The warehouse manager or drayage firm assesses a fee for this service. For inbound movements, the opposite is possible: the warehouse manager can combine small shipments from a firm's suppliers and present them to a carrier, who delivers them to the firm's plant under a lower high-volume rate.

Stopping in Transit. Another service, stopping in transit (also known as drop shipping), allows the shipper to complete loading or to partially unload freight, and to pay on the highest weight in the vehicle at any time the lower TL or CL rate between the most distant destination and the origin. The shipper assesses a stop-off charge for each intermediate stop, but not for the final destination.

---

*A *drayage firm* is a motor carrier specializing in providing pickup and delivery service.

FIGURE 10–7 Example of Stopping-in-Transit Service

Toledo —————————— Chicago —————————— Milwaukee

50,000 lb.   25,000 lb.   25,000 lb.
(Total shipment)

Rates per cwt

	LTL	TL	Minimum Weight
Toledo to Chicago	$3.70	$2.50	50,000 lb.
Toledo to Milwaukee	$4.00	$2.75	50,000 lb.

Stop-off charge = $35.00 per stop-off

Figure 10–7 shows an example of stopping-in-transit service. The shipper at Toledo has two customers, located at Chicago and Milwaukee, that have purchased 25,000 pounds each. The shipper has two shipping options for these two shipments: (1) as two LTL shipments and (2) as one stopping-in-transit shipment. The cost of each is as follows:

1. Two LTL shipments:

Toledo to Chicago   = 250 cwt @ $3.70 = $ 925.00
Toledo to Milwaukee = 250 cwt @ $4.00 =   1,000.00
                                        Total cost = $1,925.00

2. Stopping-in-transit shipment:

500 cwt @ $2.75   = $1,375.00
Stop-off charge   =   35.00
              Total cost = $1,410.00

Use of the stopping-in-transit service saves $515.00.

Transit Privilege.   The final line-haul service is the transit privilege, which permits the shipper to stop the shipment in transit and to perform some function that physically changes the product's characteristics. With this privilege, carriers charge the lower through rate (from origin to final destination), rather than the higher combination of rates from origin to transit point and from transit point to final destination. Carriers have established the transit privilege for grain milling, steel fabrication, lumber processing, and storage of various commodities for aging.

SUMMARY

Transportation management encompasses the day-to-day functions of the transportation process. Considerable knowledge is required of transportation pricing, services, and regulation, both domestic and international, to manage the transportation process and to operate the logistics system efficiently.

- Transportation management embraces a proactive philosophy to identify and solve transportation problems.

- To increase negotiating power and facilitate partnerships, shippers are using a limited number of carriers.
- Carrier negotiating and contracting are a natural outgrowth of carrier deregulation. Both activities result in lower freight costs and improved services.
- Shipment consolidation is a strategy that combines smaller shipments into a larger shipment to realize lower freight rates inherent in carrier pricing.
- Economic regulation of transportation placed controls over carrier entry, prices, and services. Today, economic deregulation of transportation emphasizes the marketplace, not government, as the mechanism for control.
- Carrier performance quality is measured with a carrier evaluation technique that uses a rating scale to rate carrier performance.
- Domestic documentation includes the bill of lading, freight bill, and freight claim. The bill of lading is the contract of carriage and a receipt for the goods tendered to the carrier. The freight bill is the carrier's invoice, and the freight claim is a shipper request for reimbursement for freight loss and damage.
- Common carriers are liable for all loss and damage, with limited exceptions.
- International documentation consists of financial, customs, and transportation documents.
- For domestic trade there are basically two terms of sale, whereas for international trade there are thirteen.
- Transportation rates are based on either cost of service or value of service. Cost of service reflects the carrier's cost, while value of service considers how much the shipper is willing to pay.
- Freight rates vary with distance and weight. Rates increase with distance and weight shipped.
- In addition to basic movement service, carriers offer terminal and line-haul services. Terminal services include the terminal functions, loading and unloading, and shipment monitoring. Reconsignment and diversion, pooling, stopping in transit, and transit privilege are line-haul services.

STUDY QUESTIONS

1. Describe the transportation management philosophy existing today, pointing out the major strategies firms use.

2. Discuss the concept of market power and show how it relates to carrier negotiation and carrier contracting.

3. How would a transportation manager monitor the quality of service provided by the carriers used?

4. What is the basis of economic regulation of transportation? Explain the rationale for economic deregulation of transportation.

5. Discuss the benefits and costs of economic deregulation.

6. Describe the function of the following documents: bill of lading, freight bill, freight claim, certificate of origin, letter of credit, carnet, dock receipt, and airway bill.

7. Discuss the cost implications to the buyer of the thirteen Incoterms.

8. What is the economic implication of cost of service, value of service, shipment weight, and shipment distance in carrier pricing?

9. Discuss the economic and operation impact of a carrier's terminal services upon the shipper and carrier rates.

10. Describe the circumstances under which a company would utilize the line-haul services of reconsignment and diversion, pooling, stopping in transit, and transit privilege.

NOTES

1. Jim Thomas, "How To Rev Up a Partnership," *Distribution* (October 1994): 36–40.
2. Richard Knee, "Texas Instruments Pares Vendor List," *American Shipper* (November 1994): 58.
3. Philip Schary, *Logistics Decisions* (New York: Dryden Press, 1984): 397.
4. Paul S. Bender, "The International Dimension of Physical Distribution Management," in *The Distribution Handbook*, ed. James F. Robeson (New York: The Free Press, 1985): 796.
5. Bender, "The International Dimension of Physical Distribution Management," 809–10.
6. Roy J. Sampson and Martin T. Farris, *Domestic Transportation*, 4th ed. (Boston: Houghton Mifflin, 1979): 124.

Case 10-1

SPECIALTY METALS COMPANY

During the past two months, Thomas Train, vice president of transportation for Specialty Metals Company, a metals servicing company with operations in ten midwestern states, has been soliciting bids for the movement of tool steel, a specialty steel used for manufacturing tools and related products. Tom's goal is to reduce the shipping cost of this high-value steel. The supplier is located in Weirton, West Virginia, 350 miles from Specialty's Toledo, Ohio, service center. Steel Haulers, Inc., a regional contract motor carrier, currently moves the tool steel under contract. Steel Haulers' current rates are incremental: $2.80/cwt for shipments weighing less than 150 cwt, $2.60/cwt for shipments between 150 and 250 cwt, $2.40/cwt for shipments between 250 and 400 cwt, and $2.25/cwt for shipment weights in excess of 400 cwt up to a maximum of 450 cwt. The carrier submitted a rate of $2.25/cwt for weights in excess of 400 cwt two hours before the submission deadline for the carrier proposals.

For various equipment, financial, and/or management reasons, Tom has eliminated all but two carrier proposals. One of the two remaining carrier proposals is from Flatbed, Inc., a contract motor carrier that has an excellent reputation for providing specialized steel hauling service. Flatbed submitted a rate of $2.60/cwt with a minimum weight of 100 cwt; the carrier gives no discounts for larger shipments. The second carrier under consideration is the Middlewest Railroad, which submitted a piggyback rate of $2.45/cwt with a minimum of 200 cwt; the rate is for Plan 2, door-to-door piggyback service with a maximum shipment weight of

400 cwt per load. Both motor carriers will provide one-day transit time, while the piggyback transit time is three days.

The final proposal Tom is considering is a private trucking proposal submitted by the transportation department. The estimated total operating cost for the private fleet (including overhead and depreciation) is $50,000 per year; the investment the vehicles require is $85,000. This annual operating cost equates to $2.50/cwt with a minimum of 400 cwt per shipment and fifty shipments per year. The private truck proposal recognizes Specialty's inability to provide a load for the backhaul from Toledo to Weirton. But, given today's deregulated environment, the proposal assumes the private fleet will be able to solicit return loads from other Toledo shippers 30 percent of the time and generate $15,000 in annual backhaul revenue.

Specialty has a contract with the steel mill to purchase two million pounds of tool steel per year. Last year, tool steel shipments averaged 250 cwt per order. Tool steel has a purchase value of $250/cwt. Unloading costs would be the same under each proposal. The chief financial officer estimates Specialty's annual inventory carrying cost per dollar of average inventory stored to be 20 percent (15 percent for the cost of money and 5 percent for the cost of insurance, taxes, and handling); he estimates the cost to place an order to be $75. The inventory-in-transit cost is 15 percent per year.

Case Question

1. Tom indicated that he would decide on the bid proposals today. Given the facts of the different proposals, what would you advise Tom to do?

Case 10-2

DeReg Freight Line

Mr. John F. Klizer, president of DeReg Freight Line (DFL), was reviewing the final 1994 financial performance data for DFL. All financial criteria had improved substantially from 1993. In fact, since founding the company in 1990, DFL had set a company financial record each year.

DFL is a specialty motor carrier, having found a niche in providing expedited delivery service to the automotive industry. Klizer saw a need for expedited, time-definite service by the automotive manufacturers, who were implementing just-in-time systems. The auto manufacturers needed quick, reliable service to prevent assembly line closings resulting from parts shortages.

The ease of entry and flexibility of contracting meant that DFL was able to gain operating authority as a contract carrier to provide service to the auto manufacturers from automotive suppliers throughout the 48 contiguous states. Using innovative pricing with guaranteed delivery times, Klizer provided a value-added service that was well accepted by the auto industry. DFL has never missed a scheduled delivery time, and as a result of this high-quality service it has been very profitable.

By the end of 1994, the federal government had eliminated the need for common carriers to file tariffs containing individual rates with the Interstate Commerce Commission. This law did not appear to offer any great advantage to DFL because it is a contract carrier.

However, the intrastate deregulation appeared to Klizer to have great potential. Currently, DFL holds only interstate operating authority and consequently restricts its services to interstate moves. With intrastate deregulation DFL could haul parts from a supplier within the same state as the assembly plant. DFL would not need state operating authority as a common or contract carrier.

Intrastate shipments would be a new market for DFL. Early indications were quite positive from two of the auto assembly plants located in Tennessee. The transportation manager at these two plants called on January 1 to have DFL transport intrastate shipments. However, the rates requested by these shippers were approximately 25 percent lower than comparable interstate shipments.

Klizer recognizes the need to expand into new markets in order to continue the excellent growth record the company has experienced from its inception. He also is aware of the auto manufacturer's strategy of reducing the number of vendors used and to have those vendors provide multiple services (e.g., interstate and intrastate trucking service). Lastly, he is concerned that the apparent lower prices for intrastate shipments could transfer into the interstate market as well, causing overall lowering of profitability.

Case Questions

1. How would you assess the potential of the intrastate expedited trucking market?
2. What additional data would you want to have before advising Mr. Klizer?
3. Should DFL enter the intrastate trucking market?

THE PRAGMATICS OF CARRIER PRICING

One of the most difficult and confusing responsibilities of a logistics manager is determining the prices of various transportation services available for a logistics system's use. Determining how much it will cost to move a barrel of pickles from Toledo, Ohio, to New York City is not always easy.

To appreciate the problem, consider the nature of a transportation service. It would be simple if carriers sold all transportation service on the basis of ton-miles; that is, if we had to pay X dollars to move one ton of a product one mile. But carriers do not sell transportation services in ton-miles; rather, carriers sell transportation services for moving a specific commodity (pickles) between two specific points (Toledo and New York City). This fact gives us a glimpse of the enormous magnitude of the transportation pricing problem. There are more than 33,000 important shipping and receiving points in the United States. Theoretically, the number of different possible routes would be all the permutations of the 33,000 points. The result is in the trillions of trillions. In addition, we must consider the thousands and thousands of different commodities and products that firms might ship over any of these routes. On top of that, we must consider the different modes and different companies within each mode. We may also need to consider each commodity's specific supply-and-demand situation over each route.

Class Rates

Since quoting trillions and trillions of rates is impossible, the transportation industry has taken two major steps toward simplification.

shipping points   The first step was to consolidate the 33,000 shipping points into groups by dividing the nation into geographic squares. The most important shipping point (based on tonnage) in each square serves as the *rate base point* for all other shipping points in the square, reducing the potential number of distance variations for ratemaking purposes. The carriers determined the distances from each base point to every other base point and filed them with the ICC for publication in the National Rate Basis Tariff. The distance between any two base points is called the *rate basis number*. This first simplifying step reduced the number of possible origins and destinations for pricing purposes.

The second step deals with the thousands and thousands of different items that firms might ship between any two base points. The railroads have established a national scale of rates, placed on file with the ICC, which gives a rate in dollars per hundredweight (cwt) for each rate basis number. (Motor carriers have individual rate scales.) These rate scales are the basis for a simplified product classification system.

Classification simply means grouping together products with similar transportation characteristics so that one rating can be applied to the whole group. The four primary classification characteristics are density, stowability, ease or difficulty of handling goods, and liability. High-demand and high-value items might be placed in class 100, which means that carriers will charge them 100 percent of the *first class rate*. Low-value items, such as coal, might be placed in class 50, which means carriers will charge them 50 percent of the first class rate. This percentage number is a *class rating*, the group into which carriers place a commodity for ratemaking purposes.

Now the number of possible pricing situations is small enough to allow the formation of a transportation pricing system. We determine the price of moving a particular item between two particular points as follows: First, look up the rate basis point for the origin and for the destination. Then determine the rate basis number between the two base points. Next, determine the classification rating (class rating) for the particular product to be shipped. Then find the rate in the class rate tariff that corresponds to the appropriate rate basis number and class rating. Finally, multiply this rate, which is in cents per cwt, by the total shipment weight in cwt to determine the cost to move that specific product between those two points.

The word *tariff* commonly means almost any publication that a carrier or a tariff publishing agency produces that concerns itself with the pricing or service the carrier performs. All the information a shipper needs to determine the cost of a move is in one or more tariffs.

Now look at an example of the mechanics involved in determining the class rate charges for a motor carrier shipment. A firm wishes to ship 4,000 pounds of putty in steel-lined drums with metal covers from Reading, Pennsylvania, to Washington, D.C.

1. The rate basis number in Table 10A–1 is 98 (at the intersection of Reading, Pennsylvania, and Washington, D.C., in the vertical and horizontal portions of the tariff, respectively).
2. The class ratings and minimum weight, found in the classification for putty in steel-lined drums with metal covers (see Table 10A–2), are LTL = 55, TL = 35, and minimum weight = 36,000 lb. For interstate shipments we use the LTL rating of 55.
3. The table of class rates gives the applicable rate (see Table 10A–3); the intersection of the horizontal line of rate basis number 98 (the 92 to 99 group) and the vertical line of class 55 determine this rate. Since the 4,000-pound shipment falls between weight groups 2,000 and 5,000, we must compute the charges under both weight groups to determine the lowest cost. The appropriate rates are $2.33/cwt for 2,000 pounds and $1.77/cwt for 5,000 pounds.
4. We find the transportation charge by multiplying the rate per cwt by the number of cwt in the shipment, or

Margin notes: rate basis number

classification procedure

tariff

example

TABLE 10A-1 Table of Rate Basis Numbers

| | From Rate Groups (all cities in Pennsylvania) | | | | | | | |
	Allentown	Altoona	Bellefonte	Reading	Scranton	State College	Williamsport	York
To Rate Groups	**Apply Rate Basis Numbers**							
Baltimore ....MD	84	73	86	62	64	92	76	98
Barnesville ....MD	103	94	122	96	95	132	102	117
Newark ....NJ	98	90	96	101	92	113	84	76
Newark ....NY	61	76	60	76	76	76	60	77
New York ....NY	96	92	92	101	96	111	87	73
Washington ....DC	109	96	111	98	90	118	103	122
Wilmington ....DE	98	66	98	84	66	107	83	101

SOURCE: MAC Tariff 2-M.

$$4{,}000 \text{ lb} = \frac{4{,}000}{100} = 40 \text{ cwt}$$

The firm could ship the 40 cwt under the 2,000-pound rate of $2.33 or under the 5,000-pound rate of $1.77 as follows:

40 cwt @ $2.33 = $93.20
50 cwt @ $1.77 = $88.50

In this case, the shipper would elect the 4,000-pound shipment as a 5,000-pound shipment—in essence, shipping 1,000 pounds of phantom weight—and pay $88.50 rather than $93.20.

weight break We can compare the cost of shipping at a volume higher than actual weight to realize a lower rate and lower shipping cost with the cost of shipping at the actual

TABLE 10A-2 National Motor Freight Classification

Item	Articles	Classes LTL	TL	MW
149500	PAINT GROUP, Articles consist of Paints, Paint Material or Putty, as described in items subject to this grouping, see Note, item 149502.			
149502	NOTE—Commodities listed under this generic heading when tendered for shipment in Package 2452 are to be classified under the same provisions that apply when tendered to the carrier in boxes.			
149520	Aluminum, or Bronze Powders or Filters, in barrels, boxes or Package 2258	60	40	30
149580	Blue, ultramarine, forms or shapes, in barrels or boxes or in double bags	70	40	30
149590	Blue, ultramarine, lumps or powdered, see item 600000 for classes dependent upon agreed or released value:			
Sub 1	In containers in barrels or boxes	70	40	30
Sub 2	In bulk in double bags, double-wall paper bags, barrels or boxes	55	35	36
150110	Putty, in containers in barrels, boxes or crates or in bulk in barrels, steel putty drums, kits, pails or tubs, or steel-lined drums or tubs with metal or wooden covers	55	35	36

SOURCE: National Motor Freight Classification 100-P.

TABLE 10A–3 Class Tariff

Rate Basis No.	Weight Group	100	85	70	60	Classes 55	50	45	40	35
						Rates in Cents per 100 Pounds				
60 to 67	500 LTL	408	358	312	273	256	239			
	1,000 LTL	361	314	268	236	223	207			
	2,000 LTL	297	255	216	189	175	161			
	5,000 LTL	216	184	151	130	119	108			
	Truckload	169	144	120	103	95	89	82	73	64
76 to 83	500 LTL	470	410	355	311	291	270			
	1,000 LTL	421	365	310	273	256	238			
	2,000 LTL	356	304	256	223	208	191			
	5,000 LTL	271	230	190	163	149	136			
	Truckload	223	191	158	135	125	116	107	97	84
	TL 30,000	221	189	156	133	123	114	101	90	80
84 to 91	500 LTL	496	432	374	325	304	282			
	1,000 LTL	449	388	330	288	271	251			
	2,000 LTL	385	329	278	241	223	205			
	5,000 LTL	304	258	213	182	167	152			
	Truckload	263	223	187	159	147	136	125	*113	98
	TL 30,000	261	221	185	157	145	134	118	105	93
92 to 99	500 LTL	514	448	386	336	314	291			
	1,000 LTL	467	404	342	299	281	260			
	2,000 LTL	403	345	290	252	233	214			
	5,000 LTL	322	274	225	193	177	161			
	Truckload	285	242	201	171	158	147	136	122	106
	TL 30,000	283	240	199	169	156	145	129	114	101
100 to 109	500 LTL	566	492	423	367	343	317			
	1,000 LTL	519	448	379	330	310	286			
	2,000 LTL	455	389	327	283	262	240			
	5,000 LTL	374	318	262	224	206	187			
	Truckload	342	290	240	206	188	170	165	149	130
	TL 30,000	342	290	240	206	188	170	156	139	121
110 to 125	500 LTL	598	519	444	387	361	334			
	1,000 LTL	549	474	399	349	326	302			
	2,000 LTL	484	413	345	299	278	255			
	5,000 LTL	399	339	279	239	219	200			
	Truckload	365	310	254	219	200	185	177	159	138
	TL 30,000	365	310	254	219	200	185	168	152	131

Application of weight groups: 500 LTL: Applies on LTL or AQ shipments weighing 500 pounds or more but less than 1,000 pounds. 1,000 LTL: Applies on LTL or AQ shipments weighing 1,000 pounds or more but less than 2,000 pounds. 2,000 LTL: Applies on LTL or AQ shipments weighing 2,000 pounds or more but less than 5,000 pounds. 5,000 LTL: Applies on LTL or AQ shipments weighing 5,000 pounds or more. Truckload: Subject to minimum weights in NMFC (Note A). TL 30,000: Applies on truckload shipments where actual or billed weight is 30,000 pounds or more (Note A).

Note A: Where the charge under the rates for TL 30,000 pounds is lower than the charge under the rates for TL shipments subject to minimum weights of less than 30,000 pounds.

weight by determining the *weight break*. The weight break is the shipment size that equates the transportation charges for different rates and weight groups. That is,

LV rate × WB = HV rate × MW

where

$$
\begin{aligned}
\text{LV rate} &= \text{lesser-volume rate} \\
\text{WB} &= \text{weight break} \\
\text{HV rate} &= \text{higher-volume rate} \\
\text{MW} &= \text{minimum weight for higher-volume rate}
\end{aligned}
$$

Plugging in the numbers from the example used here, we find the weight break to be

$$
\begin{aligned}
\$2.33 \times \text{WB} &= \$1.77 \times 50 \text{ cwt} \\
\text{WB} &= 37.98 \text{ cwt}
\end{aligned}
$$

Next, we can establish a simple decision rule for shipping clerks to use to determine when it is economical to ship a shipment at a volume higher than the volume a firm is actually shipping. In this example, the decision rules are:

shipping decision rules

1. If the shipment weighs between 2,000 and 3,798 pounds, ship the actual weight at the 2,000-pound rate of $2.33/cwt.
2. If the shipment weighs between 3,798 and 5,000 pounds, ship at 5,000 pounds (minimum weight) at the 5,000-pound rate of $1.77/cwt.
3. If the shipment weighs more than 5,000 pounds but less than the truckload minimum weight, ship the actual weight at the 5,000-pound rate of $1.77/cwt. (*Note:* a weight break exists between the 5,000-pound rate and the truckload rate.)

Exception Ratings (Rates)

The classification and class rate system are the backbone of the transportation pricing system, but only about 10 percent of all volume (CL or TL) freight moves under this pricing system. The remaining 90 percent moves under either an exception rating (rate) or a commodity rate. These two rate types complicate the inherent simplification of the class rate structure.

Carriers publish exception ratings when the transportation characteristics of an item in a particular area differ from those of the same article in other areas. For example, large-volume movements or intensive competition in one area may require the publication of an exception rating; the exception rating supersedes the classification. The same procedures described earlier apply to determining the exception rate, except now we use the exception rating (class) instead of the classification rating. Table 10A–4 gives an example of an exception tariff.

TABLE 10A–4 Exception Tariff

Exceptions to National Motor Freight Classification				
	Classes (Ratings)			
Item	**Articles**	**LTL**	**TL**	**MW**
150110	Putty, in containers in steel-lined drum or tubs with metal or wooden covers	50	35	36

Continuing with the earlier example, an exception rating is available under item number 150110 of the exception tariff for the putty moving from Reading, Pennsylvania, to Washington, D.C. It lists a class rating for LTL quantities of 50. The exception rating of class 50 takes precedence and results in a rate of $2.14 for 2,000 to 5,000 pounds and $1.61 for 5,000 pounds to a truckload (see Table 10A–3).*

Using the exception rating, we find that the cost to ship 4,000 pounds of putty is 50 cwt @ $1.61 = $80.50. The exception rate produces a savings of $8.00, or 9.0 percent of the class rate.

Commodity Rates

Carriers can construct a commodity rate on a variety of bases. The most common is a specific rate concerning a specific commodity or related commodity group between specific points and generally by specific routes. Commodity rates are complete in themselves and are not part of the classification system. If the rate does not specifically state the commodity you are shipping, or if the origin-destination (O-D) is not one that the commodity rate specifically spells out, then the commodity rate does not apply for your particular movement. A published commodity rate takes precedence over the class rate or exception rate on the same article between the specific points.

commodity specific

direction specific

O-D (origin-destination) specific

Carriers offer this type of rate for commodities that firms move regularly and in large quantities. But such a pricing system, which completely undermines the attempts to simplify transportation pricing through the class rate structure, has caused transportation pricing to revert to the publishing of a multiplicity of rates and adds greatly to the pricing system complexity.

Table 10A–5 gives an example of a commodity tariff. Using the putty shipping example, we find that a commodity rate exists in item 493 in Table 10A–5. Item 493, which applies to classification items 149500 to 150230, includes putty, as shown in Table 10A–2. Note that the commodity rate specifies a route from Reading, Pennsylvania, to Washington, D.C., the example problem's origin and destination. However, Table 10A–5 lists only a TL rate with a minimum weight of 30,000 pounds.

---

*We find the exception rates for class 50 in Table 10A–3 at the intersection of class 50 and rate basis 92 to 99 for 2,000 LTL and 5,000 LTL.

TABLE 10A–5 Commodity Tariff

			Commodity Rates in Cents per 100 Pounds		
Item	Commodity	From	To	TL Rate	Min. Wt.
493	PAINTS GROUP, as described in NMFC Items 149500 to 150230, rated Class 35	Reading ... PA	Baltimore .... MD	79	23M
			Beltsville .... MD	82	30M
			Washington .... DC	82	30M

We can compare the class, exception, and commodity rates for the movement of putty from Reading, Pennsylvania, to Washington, D.C., in truckload quantities (36,000 pounds or more) as follows:

$$Class\ rate\ =\ \$1.01/cwt$$
$$Exception\ rate\ =\ \$1.01/cwt$$
$$Commodity\ rate\ =\ \$0.82/cwt$$

zip code

As we can see from this comparison, the commodity rate is the lowest, 18.8 percent less than the class rate and the exception rate.

Motor carriers have introduced a unique commodity rate that uses U.S. Postal Service zip codes to identify origins and destinations. The *zip code commodity rates* specify rates for named commodities from a specific origin to multiple destinations identified by a three-digit zip code prefix. Table 10A–6 contains an excerpt from a general commodity zip code tariff where the origin is zip code 430 (the Columbus, Ohio, area). The rates apply from the 430 zip code origin to multiple zip code destinations in the state of Indiana. The table gives rates for various shipment weights, subject to a minimum charge (the M/C column) of $20.00. The rate per cwt to ship 5,500 pounds from zip code 430 to zip code 464 is $4.46, and the total shipping charge is $245.30 (55 cwt @ $4.46/cwt).

Other Rates

In addition to class rates, exception rates, and commodity rates, many special rates have developed over the years to meet very specific situations. The most prevalent and most important of these special rates are all-commodity, released-value, actual-value, deferred, multiple-vehicle, incentive, and innovative rates.

All-Commodity Rates. All-commodity rates, also known as freight-all-kinds (FAK) rates, are a recent development in which the carrier specifies the rate per shipment either in dollars per hundredweight or in total dollars per shipment with a specified minimum weight. The shipped commodity or commodities are not important. These rates tend to price transportation services by cost rather than by

TABLE 10A–6   Zip Code Tariff

Dest. Zip Code	Rate Classifications									
	M/C	<500	500	1,000	2,000	5,000	10,000	20,000	30,000	40,000
460–462	20.00	10.59	8.49	6.15	5.01	3.57	3.31	1.96	1.58	1.42
463–464	20.00	12.39	9.95	7.37	6.07	4.46	4.12	2.43	1.95	1.74
465–466	20.00	11.35	9.13	6.72	5.45	3.99	3.68	2.19	1.75	1.57
467–468	20.00	10.19	8.24	5.94	4.78	3.39	3.14	1.79	1.43	1.30
469	20.00	10.59	8.49	6.15	5.01	3.57	3.31	1.96	1.58	1.42
470	20.00	10.08	8.08	5.74	4.68	3.32	3.07	1.77	1.41	1.28

Table spans "From OH Zip 430 (Columbus, OH, area) to Indiana"

SOURCE: ICC JTRC 5006 Tariff, Jones Transfer Company.

the value of service, and are used mostly by shippers who send mixed-commodity shipments to a single destination.

Value Rates. Of a whole host of value rates, released-value rates and actual-value rates are the most important. The degree of liability (commodity value) the carrier assumes determines these rates. Generally, a common carrier is liable for the actual value of any goods lost or damaged while in the carrier's custody. Carriers base a released-value rate on the assumption of a certain fixed liability, usually stated in cents per pound. Usually this fixed liability is considerably less than the actual value of the goods. As a result of this limited liability, the shipper receives a lower rate.

released value

actual value

Carriers use released-value rates extensively in the shipment of household goods and use actual-value rates when goods considered to be the same commodity—jewelry, for example—vary greatly in value. In these cases, a single rate is not desirable because some shipments have a high liability potential whereas other shipments have a low liability potential. The actual-value rates make allowances for this potential difference, and the rate the carriers charge reflects the liability difference. The 1980 deregulation acts reduced the ICC constraints on motor carrier and railroad use of value rates. Today, carriers may offer value rates without ICC approval.

Deferred Rates. Deferred rates are most common in air transportation. In general, they allow the carrier to charge a lower rate for the privilege of deferring a shipment's arrival time. For example, Federal Express offers a two-day two-pound package delivery rate that is 42 percent lower than the rate for priority, 10:00 A.M. next-day delivery. A deferred rate allows the carrier to move shipments at the carrier's convenience as long as the shipment arrives within a reasonable time or by the scheduled deferred delivery date. This allows the carrier to use the deferred-rate shipments as "filler freight" to more fully load its vehicles.

Multiple-Vehicle Rates. Carriers offer multiple-vehicle rates as a special incentive rate to firms shipping multiple vehicle loads of a particular commodity at one time to a single destination. Motor carriers first used these rates to overcome the fact that a railcar holds more than a truck. By publishing lower multiple-vehicle rates, the motor carriers competed more effectively with the railroads. Multiple-vehicle rates also reduce commodities' transportation costs, thus allowing those commodities to move to more distant markets. The savings that carriers achieve by economies of scale justify lower rates. The railroads can often demonstrate savings in multiple-vehicle pickups. Multiple-vehicle rates have progressed to the unit train rates that rail carriers give for whole trainloads of commodities such as coal, ore, and grain.

Incentive Rates. A carrier publishes incentive rates, or in-excess rates, to encourage heavier loading of individual vehicles so that the carrier can improve its equipment utilization. One rate covers all cargo up to a certain minimum weight, and a lower rate covers all cargo in excess of the minimum weight.

in-excess rates

Innovative Rates. Shippers commonly negotiate rates with carriers. The negotiated rate could take the form of (1) a discount from the prevailing rate, a situation common to shippers that ship small shipments under class rates; (2) a commodity rate for TL shipments that move in large volumes on a regular basis—for example, 40,000 pounds per day, seven days per week; and (3) a contract rate (rail) for very large freight volumes—for example, 800 carloads (80,000 tons) per year.

The following are examples of the rates that shippers and carriers have negotiated in recent years:

- *Density-based rating.* A lower rating (classification or exception) is possible when the shipper increases product density; the increased product density permits heavier loading of the carrier's vehicle, thus spreading the cost over a larger number of weight (pricing) units.
- *Specific description.* Shippers seek a specific commodity description for a commodity that does not fit an existing classification description; for example, defective goods being returned to the plant have a lower value, liability, and so forth than if perfect, and thus should receive a lower rating.
- *Loading and unloading allowance.* The carrier is responsible for loading and unloading LTL-size shipments. If the shipper and consignee perform this function, the carrier realizes a lower cost and passes it on to the shipper and consignee.
- *Aggregate tender rate.* The carrier gives a lower rate to the shipper who presents multiple shipments at one time. The carrier realizes a lower pickup cost per shipment, while the shipper delays delivery by aggregating shipments before dispatch.
- *Mileage rate.* This rate is quite common for truckload-type freight; carriers base it upon the number of miles the shipment moves, regardless of the commodity or the shipment's weight.
- *Contract rate.* Railroads may negotiate a specific rate with a shipper for moving a given commodity volume between specified points. These rates, which require large volumes, 600 cars or more per year, are appropriate for the movement of bulk commodities or manufactured products that move regularly between specific points in large volumes. The shipper may specify service constraints and penalties for noncompliance.

Ocean Freight Rates. Carriers set ocean freight rates at a level that will cover all the expenses of operating the ship, the ship's capital cost, and any charges specific to the voyage. The rates cover items such as fixed costs for crew, maintenance, repair, and insurance, and variable costs such as fuel, port fees, dockage, and cargo handling. The carrier and the shipper balance these factors against the cargo type, as well as the voyage's length and special requirements, to arrive at an agreeable price.

Ocean freight rates are typically quoted on a weight-ton or measurement-ton basis. There are three weight tons: short = 2,000 pounds; long = 2,240 pounds; and metric = 2,205 pounds. The measurement ton is 40 cubic feet. The carrier will use whichever ton generates the greatest revenue. For example, a 100-cubic-foot shipment weighing 3,500 pounds will be charged for 2.5 measurement tons (100 cubic feet divided by 40 cubic feet per measurement ton) rather than 1.563 metric tons (3,500 pounds divided by 2,205 pounds).

Container rates are quite common for shipping manufactured products. The container rate does not vary by the weight shipped in the container. Generally, container rates are quoted from port to port, not shipment origin to shipment destination. Land transportation costs are added to the container rate to get the through rate.

Finally, ocean carriers add numerous surcharges to the basic rate. Example surcharges include fuel, currency, port congestion, out-of-port differential, transshipment, and terminal handling.

As the following example indicates, the container rate for moving a container from Charleston, South Carolina, to Antwerp, Belgium, is only 54.8 percent of the total ocean freight charge.

Rate per 40-foot container	$1,201
Currency adjustment factor	408
Terminal handling charge	500
Fuel adjustment factor	80
Total container rate	$2,189

STUDY QUESTIONS

1. Determine the cost of shipping 8,500 pounds of blue, ultramarine, powdered paint in bulk in double bags to Newark, New York, from State College, Pennsylvania.

2. What is the freight cost to move 22,000 pounds of putty from Reading, Pennsylvania, to Baltimore, Maryland? The putty is in a container in a steel-lined tub with a wooden cover.

3. Calculate the shipping cost to move 1,500 pounds of aluminum powders in Package 2452 to Baltimore, Maryland, from Reading, Pennsylvania.

ORDER PROCESSING AND INFORMATION SYSTEMS

LEARNING OBJECTIVES

After reading this chapter, you should be able to do the following:

- Discuss the contemporary issues in information systems.

- Know how to build an information system and understand the varying types of expertise that are needed.

- Appreciate the importance of quality logistics information.

- Discuss currently used and innovative logistics information technologies.

- Understand the concept of the logistics information system and the important modules, or subsystems, that it comprises.

- Describe the order cycle and the overall order management process.

- Anticipate several challenges that must be understood and addressed when considering implementation of any of the new information technologies.

LOGISTICS PROFILE

KELLOGG COMPANY

Kellogg Co. was the first manufacturer to go live with LogiCNet, a logistics information system designed to link retailers' ordering and shipping with manufacturers' production. The chairman and CEO of LogiCNet said that the startup, which followed months of tests, marked a milestone in distribution resource planning for the consumer packaged-goods industry. "This is the first customer-driven continuous replenishment (CR) program in the world," he said. "There are a number of supplier-driven continuous programs, but ours is the first that is customer driven." Giant Food, a regional supermarket chain with 158 stores in Maryland, Virginia, and Washington, D.C., was the first grocery retailing company to work with manufacturers, in this instance Kellogg, using this information system.

In essence, a small number of firms are bidding to become the industry standard for a retailer-manufacturer information loop that will allow all parties to synchronize their planning and operations. The overall goal is a tighter supply chain, reduced inventory, lower costs, and improved efficiency. This is accomplished by having the retailer firms synchronize their inventory planning systems with the logistics and production operations of the participating manufacturers. The idea is to reduce costs by reducing unnecessary inventory. It is estimated that this synchronization of retailers' and manufacturers' information systems can potentially save the grocery industry as much as $50 billion in inventory, $12 billion in inventory carrying costs, and $6 billion in transportation, annually.

The industry's principal focus to date has been on the grocery supply chain, the participants in which are intensely involved in efforts to upgrade their inefficient distribution systems. If successful, the information system to be implemented by Kellogg and Giant will help to synchronize store sales with manufacturing and distribution. Today, it has been estimated that consumer packaged-goods inventory spends 90 percent of its time in a warehouse. One major cause is that manufacturers usually lack up-to-date data about what's being sold, so they typically forecast demand based on past experience and "push" goods down the supply chain.

LogiCNet's common database allows point-of-sale data to be fed daily to wholesalers/distributors, so they can tell manufacturers eight weeks in advance about what is selling—and what needs to be made and shipped. In essence, companies such as Giant and Kellogg who have access to and use appropriate database and decision support systems can monitor the inventory pipeline daily, aggregate demand by store or region, and determine the impact on transportation, warehousing, and manufacturing. Given the availability of better advance information, Kellogg should be able to anticipate marketplace needs and to improve in the areas of scheduling materials and production.

SOURCE: Joseph Bonney, "Kellogg Goes Live with LogiCNet," *American Shipper* (May 1994) 62, and Joseph Bonney, "LogiCNet Signs Giant Food Chain," *American Shipper* (February 1993): 28. Used with permission.

Many firms today view effective logistics management both as a prerequisite to overall cost efficiency and as a key to ensuring their ability to competitively price their products and services.[1] Many high-level corporate and marketing executives consider their firm's logistics strengths to be among the unique ways in which the firm can differentiate itself in the marketplace. An excellent example of this is the case of Becton Dickinson and Company, which was the subject of the Logistics Profile in Chapter 1. Numerous advances in the information technology field have led firms to consider the information systems area to be extremely important to the efficient conduct of business throughout the firm.[2]

leading edge technologies

Also, recent research completed at Michigan State University indicates that information technology is being used by leading edge firms to increase competitiveness and develop a sustainable competitive advantage.[3] Among the types of technology that are regarded as particularly useful today are electronic data interchange (EDI), enhanced order management and transportation control systems, and process automation such as bar coding and radio frequency (RF) capabilities. While each of these technologies has proven its ability to help reduce total cost and/or enhance service, the high-yield successes are associated with the development of integrated systems capable of providing information necessary to manage the overall supply chain process.[4]

According to author David Closs, "Logistics information systems combine hardware and software to manage, control, and measure logistics activities. These activities occur within specific firms as well as across the overall supply chain. Hardware includes computers, input and output devices, communications channels, ancillary technology such as bar code and RF devices, and storage media. Software includes system and applications programs used for logistics activities."[5]

customer needs

Effective information management can help to ensure that a firm meets the logistical needs of its customers. Studies have shown that firms should place priority on logistical elements such as on-time delivery, stockout levels, order status, shipment tracing and expediting, order convenience, completeness of orders, creation of customer pickup and backhaul opportunities, and production substitution.[6] These activities are within the logistics manager's domain, and their successful implementation depends heavily upon a timely and accurate flow of meaningful information. The logistics area can assist significantly in meeting customer needs, and a first-class information system can facilitate the logistics mission.

This chapter first identifies a number of contemporary issues that apply to information systems in general and then discusses the functional areas affected by significant corporate investments in information technology. Second, attention is directed toward the architecture and objectives of information systems, followed by a discussion of a number of topics relating to the quality of information. Following a brief coverage of several key information technologies in use today, the emphasis shifts toward a suggested concept for the logistics information system. This serves as a template for further discussion of the specific elements or modules that make up this system. The chapter concludes with a look toward the future and the ever-present task of adapting to new technologies.

CONTEMPORARY ISSUES IN INFORMATION SYSTEMS

The authors of the 1995 edition of the annual "Critical Issues of Information Systems Management" survey by Computer Sciences Corporation (CSC) cite "unrelenting competitive pressures and demands for better customer service" that are being experienced by firms of all types. As a result, businesses are increasing expenditures for information systems (I/S), replacing their I/S executives, and focusing more than ever on harnessing information technology to meet corporate goals."[7]

In its report, CSC identifies the top ten issues relating to information systems for 1995. These are listed in Table 11–1, along with the percentage of respondents indicating that each was of major concern. The area of greatest concern is that of "aligning I/S and corporate goals," with 57.5 percent of the respondents in agreement. The remainder of the top five are "instituting cross-functional systems," "organizing and utilizing data," "implementing business reengineering" (first in the 1994 study), and "improving the I/S human resource." Moving up significantly in rank from the 1994 study to the 1995 one were "connecting to customers/suppliers" (from sixteenth to seventh) and "educating management on information technology (I/T)" (eighteenth to eleventh).[8] With respect to the decline in the rankings for the issue of implementing reengineering, the chairman of CSC's Consulting & Systems Integration unit suggests that, "Despite the fact that reengineering is no longer first, it continues to be a popular business response to competitive pressures." He feels that while many of the reengineering processes are moving into the implementation phase, a logical next step is to place priority on instituting cross-functional systems to derive the full benefits of reengineering. It is suggested that this emphasis on cross-functional systems should continue for some time.[9]

Also reported in this study are responses to a question that asks respondents to identify the three businesses processes most critical to their businesses. The results are shown in Table 11–2, which indicates that the top three issues are all directly related to logistics and supply chain management (customer service, order processing, and delivery/logistics). In fact, the processes ranked fourth and fifth, respectively, sales and accounting/billing/finance, have significant areas of interaction with logistics. Thus, all of the top five critical business processes have at least some, and in most cases a very significant, relationship to logistics and supply chain management. These areas are all excellent candidates to be aggressively

key issues

critical business processes

TABLE 11–1   Top Information Systems Issues for 1995 (North American Responses)

Issue	Percentage of Respondents
1. Aligning I/S and corporate goals	57.5
2. Instituting cross-functional information systems	55.5
3. Organizing and utilizing data	54.9
4. Implementing business reengineering	52.3
5. Improving the I/S human resource	49.1
6. Enabling change and nimbleness	48.8
7. Connecting to customers or suppliers	46.2
8. Creating an information architecture	45.3
9. Updating obsolete systems	43.7
10. Improving the systems development process	43.1

SOURCE: Computer Sciences Corporation, *Critical Issues of Information Systems Management for 1995*, CSC News Release (Computer Sciences Corporation: Cambridge, MA, 1995), page 1H. Copyright © 1995 CSC. All rights reserved. Used with permission.

TABLE 11-2   Critical Business Processes (North American Responses)

Business Process	Percentage of Respondents
1. Customer service	48.4%
2. Order processing	38.8
3. Delivery/logistics	27.7
4. Sales	24.4
5. Accounting/billing/finance	22.6

SOURCE: Computer Sciences Corporation, *Critical Issues of Information Systems Management for 1995*, CSC News Release (Computer Sciences Corporation: Cambridge, MA, 1995), page 3H. Copyright © 1995 CSC. All rights reserved. Used with permission.

funded by companies in their future efforts to leverage I/S capabilities into greater profitability and improved service to customers.

ARCHITECTURE AND OBJECTIVES OF INFORMATION SYSTEMS[10]

designing information systems

IBM Corporation has expended significant resources to provide companies with a comprehensive direction for integrating information in a consistent, effective manner across the business enterprise and the logistics channel. The objectives are to utilize a CIL/IS (Computer Integrated Logistics/Information Systems) architecture to help design and implement systems to improve resource utilization, provide better customer service, and increase the effectiveness of inter-enterprise information flow. The objective of a CIL/IS is to integrate, manage, and provide access to the information associated with the positive control of end-to-end freight movement in order to ensure satisfaction of customer commitments consistent with desired levels of resource allocation.

Figure 11–1 illustrates the building process as it relates to the information system. The technique begins with a snapshot of a company or organization as it exists, an *enterprise model* (A). This indicates the overall organization and a general description of functions. Following determination of the organization's requirements, goals, objectives, and critical success factors, the *business process model* (B) shows what each area of the company does. The *data model* (C) shows the data and the data flow required to support these processes.

Following a decision as to the specific process(es) on which to focus attention, the detailed *process description* (D) and *data description* (E) steps must be completed. Either through the use of a programmer or a software engineering tool, the *application programs* (F) and *database descriptions* (G) are produced.

Finally, a systems programmer will look at the work to be done and build a *system platform* (H) that not only supports the operational system, but has tools, conveniences, and enablers to help the programmer do the job.

Overall, three key types of people are involved in the building process:

- *Architect.* Involved in designing the process and in specifying some standards and rules for certain processes, such as using EDI for communication. The

FIGURE 11–1   The Information System Building Process

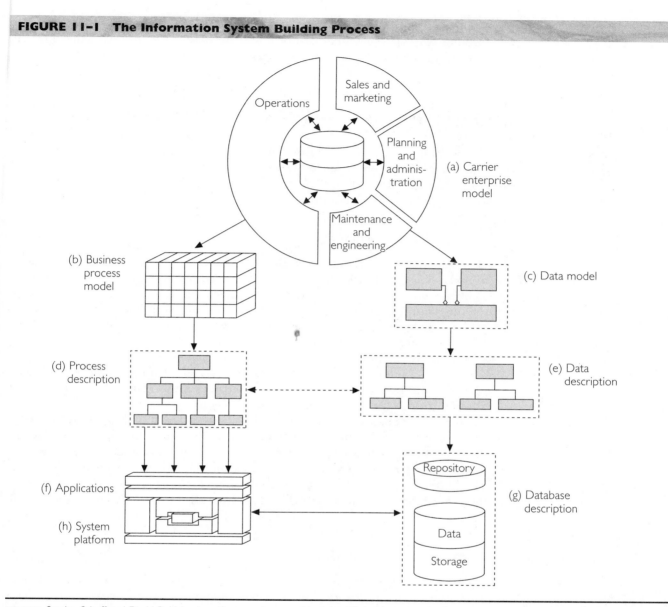

SOURCE: Stanley Scheff and David B. Livingston, *Computer Integrated Logistics: CIL Architecture in the Extended Enterprise* (Southbury, CT: IBM Corporation, U.S. Transportation Industry Marketing, 1991): 7.

architect specifies the size of the platforms (workstation or mainframe), physical data requirements, and the network to link users of the technology.

- *Systems programmer.* Assembles hardware and system software products.
- *Data manager.* Uses database products to build a directory or repository that describes what data exists, where it is stored, and how it will be used. The applications programmer uses this system platform and database to produce the operational application code.

Once an initial information system is complete, subsequent systems are easier to build because the system platform and database structure exist, the business process model and data model disciplines are understood, and the next business area information system will be integrated with the one previously developed.

QUALITY OF INFORMATION[11]

Three issues characterize information quality. The first is the availability of the information required to make the best possible decisions. The second is the accuracy of the information. The third is the effectiveness of the various means available to communicate information.

Availability of Information

relevance of information

Unfortunately, logistics managers do not always have the information they need to make effective decisions. Perhaps the most common reason is that many managers are uncertain of their information needs and thus have difficulty conceptualizing and verbalizing those needs. This is similar to the case of many customers who may not necessarily have a sound understanding of their needs or who have difficulty expressing them.

Another reason for not having the right information is that staff people charged with securing information give the logistics manager what they think is needed or what they find convenient or cost-effective to provide. Many times this is quite different from what the logistics manager truly needs.

Logistics managers need to know more about information systems, technology, and management. In addition, many information systems managers (such as the director of corporate MIS, the chief information officer, and so on) could benefit from a better understanding of logistics management and business in general. This indicates a need for a two-way educational process in which managers in these areas become far more aware of and sensitive to one another's needs and capabilities.

Accuracy of Information

Information available to logistics managers often leaves much to be desired, and as a result tends to cause suboptimal management decision making. This sometimes occurs because many companies use cost accounting and management control systems developed years ago in very different corporate and competitive environments. Many of these systems distort product-cost information and do not produce the information that logistics managers need to make the best decisions.

For example, many logistics managers have approved capital investments in equipment and systems to facilitate operations in areas such as warehousing, transportation, and inventory control. As a result, some have seen dramatic decreases in the labor component of total logistics cost. If firms continue to allocate overhead expenses on the basis of direct labor hours, as is the case in many standard cost accounting systems, the cost figures produced will not be very helpful for management decision making.[12] The information needs of the whole company, its functional areas and key processes, not the external reporting requirements of various industry and regulatory groups, need to drive each company's internal accounting practices.

Data accuracy sometimes proves to be a critical concern for retailers, who levy fines on suppliers who routinely provide inaccurate data. One of these retailers has instituted a "three strikes and you're out" program: any supplier providing inaccurate data on three or more occasions loses its "preferred supplier" status. Another example illustrating the need for accurate data is that of the mass merchant in a do-it-yourself chain. Because a case of padlocks was incorrectly labeled by the manufacturer, the merchant's computer charged for a single lock when an entire case was purchased. The inaccurate data was also responsible for erroneous inventory counts and costly stock outages.[13]

The logistics literature has raised the need for customization of accounting practices to accommodate logistics needs.[14] We are beginning to see significant progress in this area. The movement toward activity-based costing (ABC) is evidence of considerable attention being directed to this issue.

Effectiveness of Communication

To be useful to managers, information needs to be communicated effectively.[15] This in turn requires that it be communicated in the language of the intended recipient. Otherwise, perceiving the information will be difficult for him or her. Also, communication is sometimes thwarted when people ignore unexpected information. This is sometimes referred to as selective perception. Finally, communication takes place only if information keys into a person's values and pertains directly to the management decisions the recipient needs to make. In short, effective communication requires knowledge of what the recipient can perceive, what he or she expects to perceive, and what he or she intends to do with what is perceived. If the communicator misses any of these targets, communication will be more difficult.

POSITIONING INFORMATION IN LOGISTICS

critical information flows

According to Closs, logistics information systems include two types of flows, incorporating coordination and operational activities.[16] The key activities within each type of flow are indicated in Figure 11–2. The activities that make up the coordination flow include those related to scheduling and requirements planning throughout the firm. Operational flow activities relate to the initiation and tracking of receipts, inventory assignment, and shipment of replenishment and customer orders. Replenishment orders are those that resupply distribution centers from manufacturing facilities; customer orders relate to the movement of product from distribution facilities to customer locations. In either instance, order fulfillment requires a series of activities such as order placement, order processing, order preparation, and order shipment. These will be discussed in greater detail later in this chapter. The role of the inventory management component as it appears in Figure 11–2 is to assure that the operational activities are conducted in a manner consistent with the coordination activities. This involves synchronization of product and information flow both upstream and downstream in the order fulfillment process.

FIGURE 11-2   Logistics Information Flow

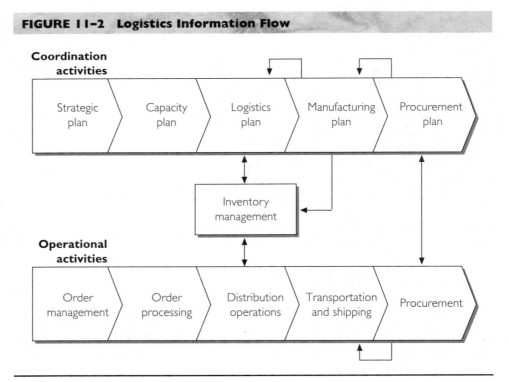

SOURCE: David J. Closs, "Positioning Information in Logistics," Chapter 31 in *The Logistics Handbook* (New York: The Free Press, 1994): 700. Reprinted with the permission of The Free Press, an imprint of Simon & Schuster from THE LOGISTICS HANDBOOK, James F. Robeson and William C. Copacino, Editors-in-Chief. Copyright © 1994 by James F. Robeson and William C. Copacino.

While it is essential to recognize the role to be played by both of these flows, Closs suggests three types of change that are needed in the future:[17] The first is to make sure that there is a significant interchange of data between the two flows. At present, it is not unusual for different data to be used for planning and operations activities. The second is the need to integrate coordination activities into operational modules. An example of this would be to assign customer orders to alternate distribution facilities when an out-of-stock situation exists at the primary shipping location. The third type of change is to think of these flows as flexible, not linear as depicted in Figure 11–2. This will provide added versatility and responsiveness to overall logistical needs.

Figure 11–3 shows an example of the logistics information flows that support the relationships among a shipper, a consignee, and suppliers of transportation service. To provide effective support for the functioning of this logistics channel, the overall information systems architecture must be capable of linking or coordinating the information systems of the individual parties into a cohesive whole.

proprietary versus shared data   In practice, each company's information system would support both proprietary and shared data.[18] Being needed to manage the company, the proprietary data would be accessible only to those employees having a legitimate internal business need. The shared data would be available through appropriate information interfaces to customers, logistics suppliers, or any other party having a need to know

FIGURE 11-3 Examples of Information Flows

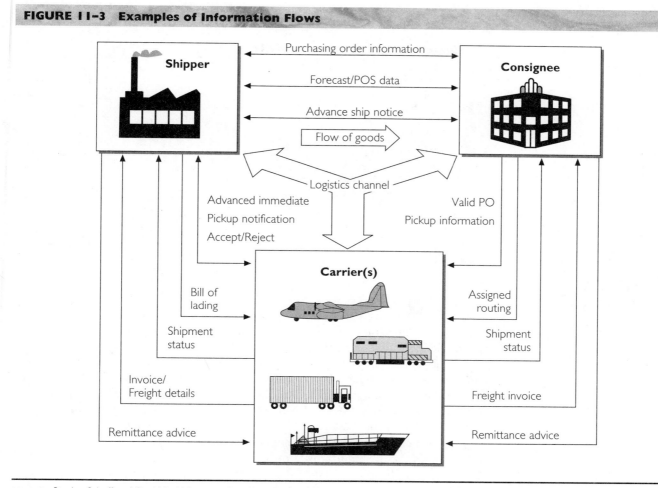

SOURCE: Stanley Scheff and David B. Livingston, *Computer Integrated Logistics: CIL Architecture in the Extended Enterprise* (Southbury, CT: IBM Corporation, U.S. Transportation Industry Marketing, 1991): 9.

through a contract or standard to which all parties agree. The data would physically be kept in the database of the individual company, but could be accessed when needed by other firms through the use of suitable database management technology.

CONTEMPORARY LOGISTICS INFORMATION TECHNOLOGIES

Table 11-3 lists several key information technologies and gives the results of a survey indicating the percentage of use by "logistically sensitive U.S. firms that benchmark," that is, search for the best practices that lead to superior performance.[19] Each of these technologies will be discussed individually in the following sections.

TABLE 11–3 Key Information Technologies

Technology	Percentage of U.S. Firms that Benchmark
Bar coding	59%
EDI	58
Handheld data entry	36
Optical scanning	34
CD-ROM storage	32
AI/expert systems	18
On-board computers	11
Radio frequency (RF) ID	NA

NA = not asked.

ADAPTED FROM: Dale S. Rogers and Richard L. Dawe, "Using Information Technology to Improve Logistics Competencies," *1994 Council of Logistics Management Annual Conference Proceedings* (Oak Brook, IL: Council of Logistics Management, 1994): 79–87.

Bar Coding

Discussed at length in Chapter 8, bar coding represents the most commonly used automatic-identification technology. Although there is considerable room for further implementation of this technology, it has become recognized as an essential component of a modern logistics information system. One of the more critical issues relating to bar coding is the fact that different bar code symbologies, or standards, are in use, not all of which are compatible. One of the most common such standards is the UCC/EAN-128. When the objective is to move product efficiently and effectively throughout an entire supply chain, consistency of bar code technologies, or the standardization of interfaces, is essential. This is a high priority today for those involved in the management of I/S activities.

Electronic Data Interchange (EDI)

According to Emmelhainz, EDI is "the organization-to-organization, computer-to-computer exchange of business data in a structured, machine-processable format. The purpose of EDI is to eliminate duplicate data entry and to improve the speed and accuracy of the information flow by linking computer applications between companies."[20] The contrast between EDI and more traditional, paper-based systems is shown in Figure 11–4. The use of EDI helps to improve the timely availability of logistics information, enhance the breadth and accuracy of data, and make the process less labor-intensive.

To utilize the full range of benefits offered by EDI, firms in a logistics channel must develop the capability to communicate with one another by computer. That is, effective implementation of EDI requires direct communication between the computer systems of both buyers and sellers of product. Figure 11–5 shows the major types of information flow linking buyers and sellers. The diagram indicates the relevance of planning, analysis, and transactional activity systems within each firm's logistics system. The diagram could be expanded as needed to include third-party suppliers of transportation, warehousing, and information systems services.

FIGURE 11–4 EDI versus Traditional Methods

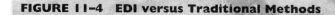

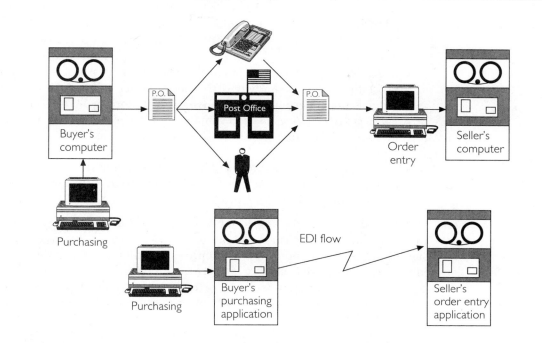

SOURCE: Margaret A. Emmelhainz, *Electronic Data Interchange: A Total Management Guide* (New York: Van Nostrand Reinhold, 1990): 5. Used with permission.

FIGURE 11–5 Major Logistics Information Flows Linking Companies

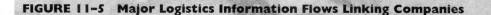

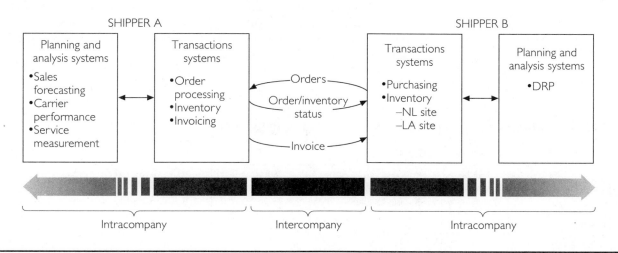

SOURCE: David L. Anderson, *Product Channel Management: The Next Revolution in Logistics?* (Lexington, MA: Temple, Barker & Sloane, Inc., 1987): 4. Used with permission.

successes
Among the notable successes of firms implementing EDI are the following:

- *Super-Valu Stores, Inc.* saved $5,000 to $6,000 per week by eliminating manual processing of invoices and other documents, and expected yearly savings of $600,000 by reducing the clerical staff that validates purchase orders against invoices.[21]
- *McKesson Corporation,* a major drug distributor, introduced customer order procedures triggered when EDI scans product bar code information. This reduces the ordering time for a typical drugstore by 50 to 75 percent.[22]
- *Volvo Transport AB of Sweden* estimates that it avoids carrying over $28 million in excess inventory stocks each year through its EDI-based information network.[23]
- *Warehouse Information Network System (WINS)* establishes a standard link between a company and its own or public warehouses through networks based on EDI applications.[24]

EDI standards
The EDI concept, moving forward quickly and effectively, has accelerated the move to paperless, electronic communication. While the progress to date has been significant, several important areas represent challenges. One is the current proliferation of standards, which generally are of two types, proprietary and generic. Just as there are numerous ways to develop bar codes, there are multiple EDI standards in use today. Perhaps the most commonly used standard in North America is ANSI X12. Figure 11–6 shows the difference between a traditional paper format and the ANSI X12 format. The current international standard of importance to logistics managers is UN/EDIFACT, which has been developed jointly by the United Nations and the International Standards Organization.[25]

The deregulation of national communications systems, the rapid growth in fiber optics as a transmission medium, and the development of artificial intelligence/expert systems (discussed later) should further reduce EDI costs and improve service diversity and quality over the years ahead. More incentives from cost and customer service should induce companies to introduce EDI systems into their operations.

Finally, many EDI applications can utilize third-party value-added networks, or VANs, to assist in transferring information from one party to another. This concept, proven successful in Europe and Japan, will become increasingly critical to successful information linkages among U.S.–based firms.

FIGURE 11–6   Comparison of Communications Formats: Paper versus ANSI X12

PAPER FORMAT					ANSI X12 FORMAT
Quantity	*Unit*	*No.*	*Description*	*Price*	
3	Cse	6900	Cellulose sponges	12.75	ITI • 3 • CA • 127500 • VC6900 N/L
12	Ea	P450	Plastic pails	.475	ITI • 12 • EA • 4750 • VC • P450 N/L
4	Ea	1640Y	Yellow dish drainer	.94	ITI • 4 • EA • 9400 • VC • 1640Y N/L
1	Dz	1507	6" plastic flower pots	3.40	ITI • 1 • DZ • 34000 • VC • 1507 N/L

Data Management

As was indicated in Table 11–3, several contemporary technologies are currently in use for data entry and storage. The use of handheld devices for data entry is popular today, as is the use of devices for optical scanning. Also, the use of CD-ROM technology is emerging as a significant factor in data management activity.

Another innovative technology is image processing, which allows a company to take electronic photographs of essential documents. The electronic photograph can then be stored in a computer and accessed or retrieved as needed. An optical disk is used to encode the thousands of bytes of data that make up a single document. This technology is used frequently by transportation firms who are asked to provide proof of delivery by many of their customers. By having a consignee sign an electronic pad, a facsimile of the signature is automatically digitized and stored for future reference. When necessary, a copy of the signature can easily be downloaded to provide proof of delivery.

image processing

Artificial Intelligence/Expert Systems

The use of artificial intelligence (AI) and expert systems is becoming increasingly prevalent in logistics today. Artificial intelligence has been described as the portion of computer science that is concerned with "making machines do things that would require intelligence if done by humans," [26] and also as the "development of computers that perform functions that people perform." [27] An expert system is "a computer program that mimics a human expert; using the methods and information acquired and developed by a human expert, an expert system can solve problems, make predictions, suggest possible treatments, and offer advice with a degree of accuracy equal to that of its human counterpart." [28]

The topic of expert systems in logistics will be covered in significant detail in the discussion of the decision support component of the logistics information system, later in this chapter.

Remote Access and Communications

There have been recent increases in the use of devices and systems for remote access and logistics communications. The use of radio frequency, or RF, for example, "allows users to relay information via electromagnetic energy waves from a terminal to a base station, which is linked in turn to a host computer. The terminals can be placed at a fixed station, mounted on a forklift truck, or carried in a worker's hand." [29] Communications with the remote terminals is accomplished via a transmitter and receiver that are contained in the base station. In essence, these systems can serve as "on-board computers" to assist the driver or operator in the accomplishment of his or her logistics duties.

RF technology

"RF systems use either narrow-band or spread-spectrum transmissions. Narrow-band transmissions move along a single limited radio frequency, while spread-spectrum transmissions move across several different frequencies. When combined with a bar code system for identifying inventory items, a radio-frequency system can relay data instantly, thus updating inventory records in so-called 'real time.'" [30] This results in significant improvement to the quality of order picking and shipping accuracy. The experience of Microsoft Corporation, in Redmond, Washing-

ON THE LINE

Computers Rank as Highly as Planes at Federal Express

Nearly 21 years after starting Federal Express Corp., Frederick W. Smith thinks the computer has become as important as his first love, the plane.

"Oh, absolutely, perhaps even more important," said Smith.

The company that invented airborne overnight shipping boasts of its computerized information services more than its transportation might these days.

The reason is that for hundreds of businesses, the information Federal Express provides about shipment and distribution has tremendous value. It allows them to cut costly inventory and accelerate business processes, efficiencies that can boost profits.

Smith said he recognized such possibilities before he started the company but didn't realize the role technology would play in reaching them....

The Federal Express computer system is now one of the busiest and most accessible in the business world. More than 20 million transactions are processed a day and 80,000 customers are plugged in. The location of each of the roughly 2 million packages and documents the company moves daily is recorded six times during shipping.

One reason Smith is still on top of the company is that he has kept up with technology.

"Airlines had to go from pistons to turbo props to jets and so forth down the line," said Smith, who was a decorated Marine pilot in Vietnam and remains an aviation buff.

His office is filled with models of Clipper ships, reflecting his belief that the company's 500+ jets are the "Clipper ships of the computer age." ...

Smith made his own tender computer skills the test for allowing the company's PowerShip 3 system to be sent to customers. PowerShip 3 is a desktop computer and printer for

offices to order pickups, print labels, and track shipments without an operator's assistance.

"There were people all over the building, saying, 'Has the old man put it together yet and turned it on?'" he said.

The system along with a predecessor, PowerShip 2 for mailrooms, and the recently advertised Tracking Software, represents a big effort to give more customers an electronic connection. All are offered free because the company has discovered they generally lead a customer to increase shipments.

Also, by summer the company hopes to offer software that may be used throughout a customer's computer system, not just on individual machines.

Auto manufacturers, clothing catalog merchants, and even makers of human joint replacements keep spare products in warehouses near Federal Express's chief hub at Memphis International Airport to handle late orders.

First Tennessee Bank has even set up a check sorting operation just across the street from the Memphis hub, claiming to be faster than the Federal Reserve Bank.

While the value of such logistics has become embedded in the business landscape, it is little understood by the world at large. But that's OK with Smith.

"If you go to the grocery store, you're not really concerned about how the eggs got there. But the people who sell the eggs are damn concerned," he said.

"So, if you go and talk to people that are running these new types of logistics solutions to add value to their product or service, they understand. And the people who don't understand, they're going to die."

ADAPTED FROM: Evan Ramstad (Associated Press), "Computer Ranking as Highly as Planes at Federal Express," *Knoxville News Sentinel* (January 25, 1995): C1–C4. Used with permission of Associated Press.

---

ton, for example, was that the implementation of an RF-based bar code system for tracking stored product improved inventory accuracy from 95 percent to well over 99 percent.[31]

satellite tracking   Another form of remote access involves the use of satellite tracking capabilities. The communications are actually "facilitated by two orbiting satellites. One serves as the communications link between driver and dispatcher, the other as the vehicle tracker. Two-way communications between the truck driver and dispatcher are routed through the first satellite. The second tracker satellite gives a fix on location. A truck dispatcher can determine a truck's location by measuring signal length from the tracker satellite to a communications terminal mounted in the truck cab."[32]

THE LOGISTICS INFORMATION SYSTEM CONCEPT

The logistics information system may be defined as follows:

An interacting structure of people, equipment, and procedures which together make relevant information available to the logistics manager for the purposes of planning, implementation, and control.[33]

Figure 11–7 highlights the relationship among the logistics information system (LIS), the elements of the logistics environments, and the logistics decision-making process. The diagram shows four principal subsystems, or modules, which constitute the logistics information system: order management, research and intelligence, decision support, and reports and outputs. Collectively, these systems should provide the logistics manager with timely and accurate information for the basic management functions of planning, implementation, and control.[34] Each of these modules is discussed in the major sections of this chapter that follow.

THE ORDER MANAGEMENT SYSTEM

The order management system represents the principal means by which buyers and sellers communicate information relating to individual orders of product. The order processing system, extremely significant to the firm's logistics area, is also one of the most important components of the firm's overall management

FIGURE 11–7   Logistics Information System

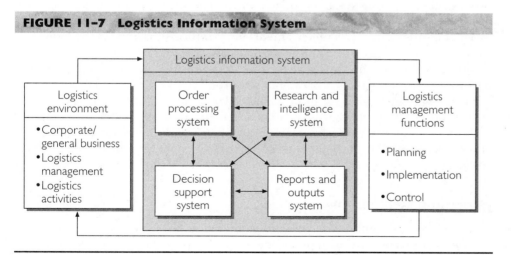

ADAPTED FROM: Framework for a marketing information system suggested by Philip Kotler, *Marketing Management: Analysis, Planning, and Control*, 5th ed. (Englewood Cliffs, NJ: Prentice-Hall, 1984): 189.

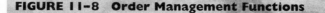

FIGURE 11-8 Order Management Functions

- Blanket order entry
- Credit checking
- Electronic order entry
- Inventory availability check
- Manual order entry
- Order acknowledgment
- Order editing
- Order modification

- Order pricing
- Order status inquiry
- Price and discount extensions
- Promotion checking
- Reassignment of order source
- Returns processing
- Service measurement

SOURCE: Margaret A. Emmelhainz, "Electronic Data Interchange in Logistics," *The Logistics Handbook* (New York: The Free Press, 1994): 704. Reprinted with the permission of The Free Press, an imprint of Simon & Schuster from THE LOGISTICS HANDBOOK, James F. Robeson and William C. Copacino, Editors-in-Chief. Copyright © 1994 by James F. Robeson and William C. Copacino.

information system. Recently, there has been considerable interest among companies in replacing and/or modernizing their overall order management systems. Among the various approaches that are commercially available, the order management systems available through SAP America, Inc., are used by many corporate customers.

Effective order management is a key to operational efficiency and customer satisfaction. Figure 11–8 provides a list of typical order management functions. To the extent that a firm conducts all activities relating to order management in a timely, accurate, and thorough manner, it follows that other areas of company activity can be similarly well-coordinated. In addition, both present and potential customers will take a positive view of consistent and predictable order cycle length and acceptable response times. By starting the process with an understanding of customer needs, firms can design order management systems that customers will view as superior to those of competitor firms. The firm's order management capabilities will contribute toward producing a competitive advantage.

The logistics area needs timely and accurate information relating to individual customer orders; thus, more and more firms are placing the corporate order processing function within the logistics area. The move is good not only from the perspective of the logistics process, but also from that of the overall organization.

order processing functions Figure 11–9 includes a list of principal order processing functions. The overall area of order processing has been a chief beneficiary of the enhanced computer and information systems technologies available today. In many firms, the area of order processing has become an innovator in exploiting new technological advances.

Order and Replenishment Cycles

order cycle When referring to outbound-to-customer shipments, we typically use the term order cycle; we use the term replenishment cycle more when referring to the acquisition of additional inventory, as in materials management. Basically, one firm's order cycle is another's replenishment cycle. For simplicity, we will use the term order cycle throughout the remainder of this discussion.

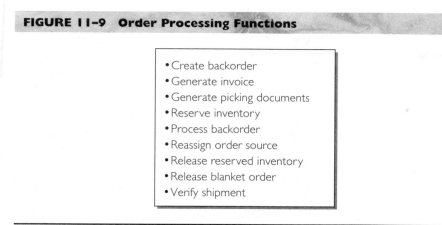

FIGURE 11–9   Order Processing Functions

- Create backorder
- Generate invoice
- Generate picking documents
- Reserve inventory
- Process backorder
- Reassign order source
- Release reserved inventory
- Release blanket order
- Verify shipment

SOURCE: Margaret A. Emmelhainz, "Electronic Data Interchange in Logistics," Chapter 33 in *The Logistics Handbook* (New York: The Free Press, 1994): 704. Reprinted with the permission of The Free Press, an imprint of Simon & Schuster from THE LOGISTICS HANDBOOK, James F. Robeson and William C. Copacino, Editors-in-Chief. Copyright © 1994 by James F. Robeson and William C. Copacino.

As was discussed earlier, four principal activities, or elements, constitute lead **lead time activities** time, or the order cycle: order placement, order processing, order preparation, and order shipment. These activities are shown in Figure 11–10, along with arrows indicating the principal directions in which information and product flow.

Traditionally, the order cycle includes only those activities that occur from the time an order is placed to the time that it is received by the customer. Special activities such as backordering and expediting will affect the overall length of the order cycle. Subsequent customer activities, such as product returns, claims processing, and freight bill handling, are not technically part of the order cycle.

Order Placement.   Order placement time can vary from days by mail to minutes by phone to instantaneously by EDI. Company experiences indicate that improvements in order placement systems and processes offer some of the greatest opportunities for significantly reducing the length and variability of the overall order cycle.[35]

Table 11–4 shows the results of a 1993 grocery industry study of how orders are **order placement** received from a number of different types of firms in the retail and wholesale **methods** food distribution business. As it indicates, approximately 40 percent of the orders placed by grocery retailers, wholesale grocers/distributors, and mass merchants/ club stores are placed through EDI. This represents an increase from a figure of 17 percent reported in a similar study in 1988. The more current figures might

FIGURE 11–10   Major Components of the Order Cycle

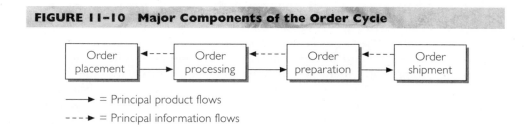

——► = Principal product flows

- - -► = Principal information flows

TABLE 11-4   Methods of Order Receipt in the U.S. Grocery Industry

	Telephone	Fax	Mail	EDI	Automatic Replenishment	Other
Grocery retail	20%	25%	5%	39%	3%	8%
Wholesale grocers/distributors	18	28	3	41	2	8
Mass merchants/club stores	15	29	3	40	3	10
Drug retail	16	33	8	29	0	14
Food service	22	57	3	12	0	6

NOTE: Figures shown indicate percentage of orders received using various methods of order receipt.

SOURCE: Data inferred from diagram appearing in Cleveland Consulting Associates, Inc., *1993 Logistics Benchmarking Survey Results* (Washington, DC: Grocery Manufacturers of America, Inc. and Cleveland Consulting Associates, 1993): 15. Used with permission.

have been higher had it not been for limits imposed by certain customers unable to justify EDI by head-count reduction.[36]

Based on the overall content of Table 11–4, there is significant opportunity for further use of contemporary approaches to assist with the order placement function. Drug retail and foodservice firms, in addition to having lower levels of EDI usage, have not been very involved to date with automatic replenishment systems such as CRP. These represent challenges for the future, as firms move toward more intense utilization of these proven technologies. The earlier discussion of Kellogg Company and its use of LogiCNet's logistics information system is an example of involvement with this type of concept.

A 1988 study of the Council of Logistics Management indicated that major industries involved with on-line electronic approaches to order placement technologies such as EDI included food, pharmaceutical, and auto. Industries evidencing lower levels of technology infusion included chemicals, paper, and clothing/textiles. Given the recent move to quick-response strategies in the clothing/textile industry, current figures for this sector would show increased usage of on-line electronic technologies.[37]

processing   ***Order Processing.***   The order processing function usually involves checking customer credit, transferring information to sales records, sending the order to the inventory area, and preparing shipping documents. Many of these functions can occur simultaneously through the effective use of electronic data processing equipment. Improvements in computer and information systems technologies have led to considerable reductions in the times necessary to accomplish these activities.

picking and packing   ***Order Preparation.***   Depending on the commodity being handled and other factors, the order preparation process may be very simple and done manually, or perhaps be complex and highly automated. In some instances, the time needed to prepare orders for shipment represents a significant bottleneck in the overall order cycle. Thus, a full understanding of the order preparation process and its strategies will prove to be useful.

Order Shipment. Order shipment time extends from the moment the order is placed upon the vehicle for movement until the moment it is received and unloaded at the buyer's destination. Measuring and controlling order shipment time can be difficult when using for-hire transportation services, depending on the capabilities of the carrier(s) being used. One way for receivers of product to increase the likelihood of timely delivery is to ask for advance shipment notification (ASN) from supplier firms. Alternatively, shippers may prefer to receive proof of delivery (POD) documentation from carriers to pinpoint the exact time and location of delivery. To improve service to customers, many transportation firms have utilized information technology to provide services such as these. In addition, carriers have made it easy for customers to trace shipments when needed, and provide these same customers with summary reports of shipment times, service levels, and so on.

transportation

One of the major U.S. automobile companies has established an integrated private/contract carriage system and a computerized parts locating and ordering system to produce prompt and dependable delivery service for small, less-than-truckload shipments. The system provides next-day delivery to most of its dealers from the company's eighteen distribution centers located throughout the United States. Approximately 80 percent of the parts deliveries are made at night through a passkey operation. Company drivers are given keys to the dealers' facilities and make deliveries to secured areas. The night deliveries reduce delays normally caused by daytime highway traffic and congestion at dealer facilities.

example

Because of the recent changes in the transportation environment, capable, time-sensitive logistics services are increasingly becoming available. While each of the modes of transport have evidenced considerable improvement in this area, there is opportunity to further enhance value-added services for customers. Also, the availability of real-time information has been identified as a priority by the growing number of third-party providers of logistics services. Companies such as FedEx Logistics Services, UPS Worldwide Logistics, and Roadway Package System have developed very innovative technologies of this type.

third-party services

Length and Variability of the Order Cycle. While interest has traditionally centered more on the overall length of the order/replenishment cycle, recent attention has been focused on the variability or consistency of this process. Consistent with the contemporary interest in meeting customer requirements, there is also a concern for making sure that the first priority is to deliver shipments at the time and location specified by the customer.

One landmark customer service study incorporated a series of questions pertaining to the time needed to complete the total order cycle as well as the relative time required to complete the individual elements of the order cycle.[38] One significant finding was that the greatest portion of total order cycle time occurred either before the manufacturer received the order from the customer or after the order was shipped. In other words, activities that are at least somewhat external to the manufacturer, and thus over which manufactures are likely to have less control, consumed more than one-half of the total order cycle time.

This phenomenon is supported by more recent data developed by Andersen Consulting, which is shown in Figure 11–11. In this example, the average total time for order transmission and transit to customer (7.0 days) exceeded the average time spent on the more internally focused activities such as order edit/entry,

example

FIGURE 11-11   Example of Order-Cycle Time Analysis

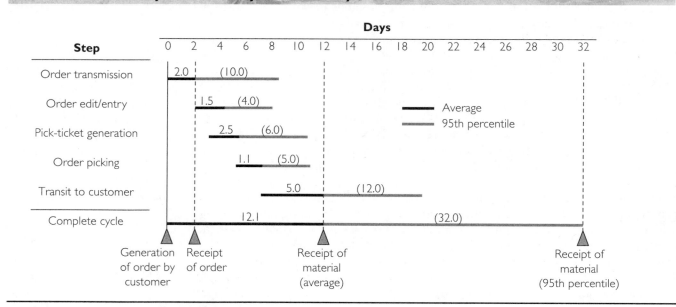

SOURCE: William C. Copacino, "Time to Review Order Management," *Traffic Management* (June, 1993): 32. Used with permission.

pick-ticket generation, and order picking (5.1 days). Also, there were significant differences between the average times for completing the various steps and the 95th percentile times. Realities such as this have caused many manufacturers to become more involved in the order placement function, by such means as taking steps to make it easier for customers to place orders via fax, toll-free number, or EDI, for example. Also, manufacturers have become more interested in seeing that shipments arrive at the customer's location in a timely manner.

Any reduction in the length of one or more order cycle components will provide either additional planning time for the manufacturer or a shortened order cycle for the buyer. If a manufacturing firm identifies an opportunity to reduce the length of one or more components of order cycle time, it can then choose to either absorb the extra time into its own system (perhaps as additional planning time) or share it with the customer by shortening the order cycle in a material fashion. In competitive markets, passing such time savings along to the customer whenever possible may be critical for the manufacturer.

safety stock impacts   Variability in order cycle length can also affect the levels of safety stock carried by purchasers of the firm's products. Specifically, as order cycle variability increases, needed safety stock levels also increase. Conversely, as firms reduce order cycle variability, customers may choose to carry less safety stock. In either instance, order cycle variability links directly to the levels of safety stock a customer must carry.

Ideally, improvement will take the form of shorter cycle lengths, coupled with improved consistency and reliability. Figure 11–12 illustrates a before-and-after situation in which a firm successfully reduced the length and variability of most of the activities constituting the order cycle. Aside from the improvement in each individual activity, the total order cycle time and variability have markedly decreased.

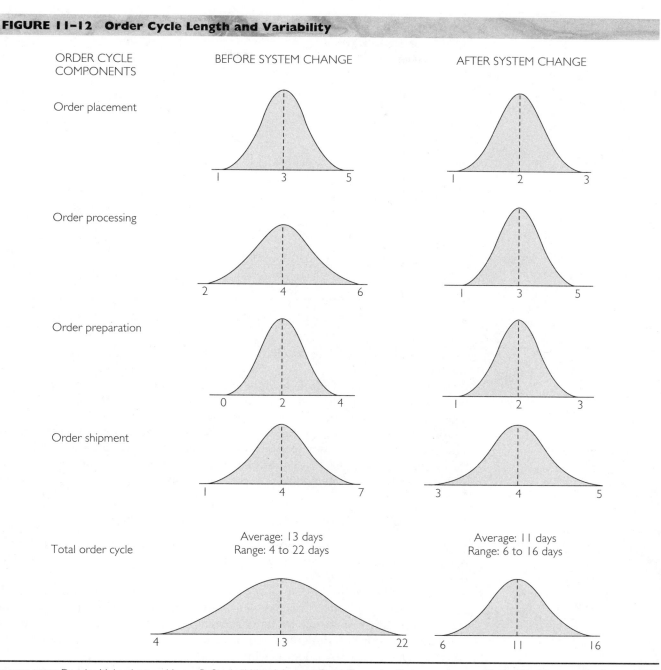

FIGURE 11-12 Order Cycle Length and Variability

ORDER CYCLE COMPONENTS · BEFORE SYSTEM CHANGE · AFTER SYSTEM CHANGE

Order placement

Order processing

Order preparation

Order shipment

Total order cycle — Before: Average: 13 days, Range: 4 to 22 days — After: Average: 11 days, Range: 6 to 16 days

ADAPTED FROM: Douglas M. Lambert and James R. Stock, "Using Advanced Order Processing Systems to Improve Profitability," *Business* (April–June 1982): 26.

Cost-Effectiveness of Order Processing Alternatives

Figure 11–13 shows how the cost of telecommunications alternatives may vary with increasing message volumes. At low volumes, for example, the least expensive alternative is to manually handle messages from customer to manufacturer through a mail-speed alternative. This form of message transfer is relatively inex-

cost of alternatives

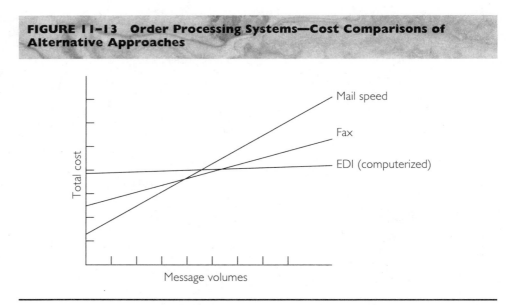

FIGURE 11-13 Order Processing Systems—Cost Comparisons of Alternative Approaches

pensive because it involves low fixed costs. Alternatively, when message volumes are high, the use of fax and/or EDI capabilities would be preferable. Although these approaches involve much higher levels of fixed costs, the incremental expense of handling individual message units makes them preferable at high message volumes. Also, the more manual systems would likely be slower, less consistent, and more prone to error than some of the more advanced systems. Thus, evaluating the cost-effectiveness of order processing alternatives involves thoroughly analyzing each available choice, the associated fixed and variable costs, and the levels of customer service that are likely to result.

Example of an Order Processing System

Figure 11–14, a flowchart of the order processing system used by a particular U.S. consumer goods manufacturing firm, provides an example of a more-or-less typical order processing system.

Although this company centralizes its information processing capabilities, the logistics vice president has considerable influence over this particular function. While not totally responsible for the firmwide information system, he or she provides ample input into designing and implementing systems related to order processing and other types of logistics information.

order cycle   In the figure, company sales representatives or members of a broker network send orders for the company's products directly to one of the company's twenty-two district sales offices, where they are keyed into a computer terminal linked to the general office. The mainframe computer at the company's corporate office then processes orders centrally. Following a credit check, the company sends shipment requests to plants, warehouses, and distribution centers. Product is then shipped to customers. The billing and invoicing cycle begins with information keying at the shipping points, which occurs immediately following order shipment.

FIGURE 11-14   Example of an Order Processing System

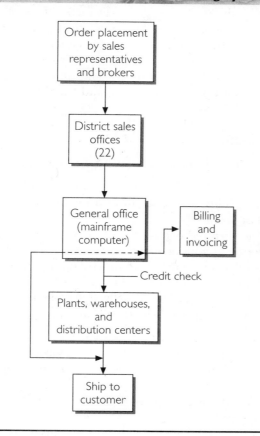

This particular company does not commit inventory to specific customer orders at the time of order placement. Rather, the company commits inventory when orders are picked and shipments made. As a result, the company assures its ability to allocate inventory consistently to specific customer orders according to a priority level assigned to each customer account.

While pleased with the current efficiency of its order processing system, this company foresees providing handheld data entry units for in-store use by company sales representatives. This kind of innovation would likely produce additional benefits to a system that is already running smoothly. In addition, this company would be able to benefit from an improved ability to anticipate customers' needs and to make inventory allocation decisions as customer orders are received. A move to a more proactive stance with regard to inventory management and order fulfillment would be advantageous to this firm and its customers. Ultimately, a move to an information-based replenishment system such as the one adopted by Kellogg Company would be desirable.

proactive stance

The Research and Intelligence System

As was discussed earlier in this text, three distinct, yet related, environments should interest the logistics manager. These include (1) the macro, or external, environment; (2) the interfirm environment, as characterized by a firm's distribution channels; and (3) the micro, or intrafirm, environment. The LIS research and intelligence system scans the environment and makes observations and conclusions available throughout the logistics area and the whole firm.

Environmental Scanning

approaches

The logistics manager may properly scan the environment in four recognized ways:[39]

- *Undirected viewing:* general exposure to information where the manager has no specific purpose in mind
- *Conditioned viewing:* directed exposure, not involving active search, to a more or less clearly identified area or information type
- *Informal search:* a relatively limited and unstructured effort to obtain specific information or information for a specific purpose
- *Formal search:* a deliberate effort—usually following a preestablished plan, procedure, or methodology—to secure specific information or information relating to a specific issue

We can also consider the environmental scanning process to be *irregular* (focusing on historical events and basically reactive), *regular* (basically anticipatory, including approaches such as customer surveys), or *continuous* (generally longer lasting and representing an ongoing process, such as the use of customer advisory boards).[40]

monitoring the environment

To maximize environmental scanning results, the logistics manager should include several key information sources in a comprehensive monitoring system. First are logistics employees, as well as other people employed throughout the firm. Account executives, for example, are in an excellent position to gather strategically valuable customer-related and competitive information, once the logistics manager tells them exactly what he or she desires. Similarly, fleet drivers can frequently gather valuable information on the loading dock, if they simply know what to look for. Second, channel partners such as vendors, customers, carriers, and warehouse managers represent a valuable source of additional environmental information. These firms are usually very willing to share their environmental observations and perceptions, once asked to do so. Third, either an internal function or an outside consultant or advisory firm should perform some form of ongoing environmental monitoring and evaluation. Many firms find that selectively using outside firms to assist in this process provides an extremely objective and thorough environmental scanning and evaluation.

Forecasting

integration with production scheduling

Firms frequently place responsibility for demand forecasting with the logistics area. Figure 11–15 outlines one firm's approach to sales forecasting and its integration with production scheduling activities.

FIGURE 11-15 Integration of Sales Forecasting and Production Scheduling

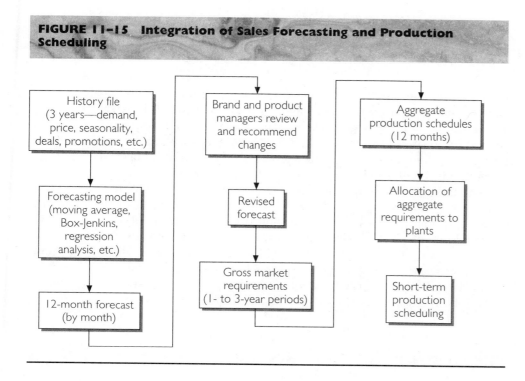

The first step is to develop a twelve-month forecast of demand by month by applying traditional approaches (moving average, Box-Jenkins, regression analysis, and so on) to a three-year history file of data on such factors as demand, price, seasonality, availability, deals, and promotions. In the second step, brand and product managers review this forecast and recommend relevant changes. The result is an agreed-upon statement of gross market requirements for the succeeding one- to three-year periods. The third step involves developing aggregate production schedules for the next twelve-month period and allocating specific production requirements to various manufacturing facilities. Finally, the logistics function commonly assumes responsibility for scheduling production on a short-term basis, in order to coordinate demand for finished product with the timing and availability of needed production inputs.

Actually, different approaches to forecasting serve different purposes:

- *Long-term forecasts* usually cover more than three years and are used for long-range planning and strategic issues. These will naturally be done in broad terms—sales by product line or division, throughput capacity by ton per period or dollars per period, and so on. These forecasts might go beyond customer demand to other key corporate resources such as production capacity and desired inventory asset levels.

- *Mid-range forecasts*—in the one- to three-year range—address budgeting issues and sales plans. Again, these might predict more than demand. The demand forecasts will very likely still be in dollars and now, perhaps, at a product family or product line level. The first year in a multiyear forecast might be by month while the following years might be by quarter.

• *Short-term forecasts* are most important for the operational logistics planning process. They project demands into the next several months and, in some cases, more than a year out. These forecasts are needed in units, by actual items to be shipped, and for finite periods of time." [41]

Given the extensive involvement of logistics in the order fulfillment process, there is a pressing need for timely and accurate forecasts of usage or demand at the individual item or unit level. As Ayers suggests, "it is important to have a method of overriding statistically over-rated projections with other intelligence." [42] This places added emphasis on the successful execution of other elements of the research and intelligence component of the logistics information system. It also suggests the need to supplement forecast-based information with timely point-of-sale data. The example of the Kellogg Company, discussed in this chapter's Logistics Profile, provides details as to how this may be accomplished.

Overall, much of the activity related to gathering information for forecasting purposes is part of the research and intelligence system. Conversely, the need for forecasting models and alternative approaches to production scheduling would rely heavily upon the decision support capabilities of the LIS, which are discussed in the following section.

THE DECISION SUPPORT SYSTEM

"The third major LIS component is the decision support system (DSS), an interactive computer-based system that provides data and analytic models to help decision makers solve unstructured problems—those with many difficult-to-define variables." [43] Essentially, the DSS represents a comprehensive set of computer-oriented tools designed to help managers make better decisions. In addition to discussing the importance of the logistics database, this section provides information concerning modeling approaches, types of computer applications in logistics, and artificial intelligence/expert systems.

Importance of the Database

The need for a comprehensive database encompassing the types of information logistics managers most often need to make decisions underpins the DSS concept. Table 11–5 identifies some of the major trends in logistics data computerization between 1975 and 1993. Overall, this information suggests that computerization levels increased by about 1 percent per year from 1975 to 1987, and by a total of only 3 percent from 1987 to 1993. Also, it is apparent that some of the greatest increases in computerization occurred in the areas of transportation and warehousing, while the least progress was reported in the product area. [44]

Once priorities have been established for data acquisition, plans should be made so that the data files will be available for use in various types of analyses, as well as for manager inquiry. The database management approach used should first identify the logical relationships among individual data elements and then restructure these elements into a logical database. Thus, the term *relational database management* has become very popular and descriptive in the industry today.

TABLE 11-5 Trends in Logistics Data Computerization

Logistics Data Element	% Contained in Computerized Database			
	1975	1982	1987	1992/3
Transportation				
Shipping open order files	84	85	89	92 (2)
Shipped manifest/bill of lading	49	55	70	74 (2)
Carrier files	57	53	64	69 (2)
Freight bill payment	51	56	62	67 (2)
Freight rates	45	36	61	65 (2)
Shipment schedules	34	51	57	62 (2)
Transit times	35	30	35	40 (2)
Warehousing				
Handling costs	30	31	42	41 (2)
Storage costs	29	28	39	40 (2)
Inventory				
Inventory levels	84	93	94	93 (3)
Purchasing open order files	51	71	80	89 (2)
Deleted order files	41	69	71	80 (1)
Back orders	74	74	75	80 (2)
Forecasted sales	65	67	72	69
Carrying costs	29	38	43	43 (2)
Stockout costs	7	10	15	18 (2)
Customer				
Names and locations	92	97	97	97 (3)
Financial limits	60	72	77	79 (3)
External market data	28	25	33	32
Product				
Master order files	24	89	90	93 (3)
Product descriptions	83	94	94	92 (3)
Production costs	60	71	70	71
Packaging costs	34	41	45	48 (2)
Average computerization level	50	58	64	67

(1) Significant difference between 1992/3 and 1987 ($Z_{95\%} = 1.96$)
(2) Significant difference between 1992/3 and 1982 ($Z_{95\%} = 1.96$)
(3) Significant difference between 1992/3 and 1975 ($Z_{95\%} = 1.96$)

SOURCE: Craig M. Gustin, "Logistics Information Systems: Progress Made During the Last Decade," *1993 Council of Logistics Management Annual Conference Proceedings* (Oak Brook, IL: Council of Logistics Management, 1993): 166. Used with permission.

Types of Modeling Approaches

As Chapter 12 will discuss in greater detail, models can be classified generally as optimization, simulation, or heuristic. Simply stated, optimization approaches search for "best" solutions, simulation models replicate the functioning of the logistics network, and heuristic techniques are able to accommodate broad problem definitions but do not provide optimum solutions.

Table 11–6 arrays three logistics time horizons (strategic, tactical, and operational) against several functional areas of logistics. This diagram shows that virtually every logistics area requires significant decisions in each of the three time frames. Logistics modeling needs flexible, capable approaches. The approaches

TABLE 11–6 Logistics Decisions

Subjects of Decisions	Nature of Decisions		
	Strategic	*Tactical*	*Operational*
Forecasting	• Long range • New products • Demographic shifts	• 6–12 months • Seasonality • Marketing impacts	• 12–16 weeks • Promotions • Trends
Network design/analysis	• Plant and DC locations • Sourcing alternatives	• Public warehouses—usage and assignments • Inventory positioning	• Customer reassignments • Contingency planning
Production planning	• Production mix • Equipment required • Equipment location	• Production mix • Inventory vs. overtime • Crew planning	• Contingency planning
Materials planning	• Materials and technology alternatives	• Stockpiling & contracts • Shortage analyzer • Distribution plans	• Purchasing • Inventory levels • Material releases

Production scheduling	• Economic analyses—
	  dedicated lines vs.
	  multiproduct
		• 6–12 month production
		  schedules
			• Daily/weekly production
			  schedules

Dispatching	• Fleet sizing and
	  configuration
		• Carrier contracts
		• Equipment location
			• Daily/weekly loading and
			  delivery plans
			• Billing

SOURCE: Richard F. Powers, "Optimization Models for Logistics Decisions," *Journal of Business Logistics* 10, no. 1 (1989): 108. Used with permission.

discussed above can be effective in helping to analyze problems such as those identified in Table 11–6.

Computer Applications in Logistics

logistics activities As part of the 1993 Ohio State University Survey of Career Patterns in Logistics, respondents were asked about the median percentage of transactions that involved the use of "new information technology." Table 11–7 summarizes the results, which clearly suggest dramatic increases in the use of information technology. Among the areas expected to be most intensely involved by 1996 are warehousing, order entry, and inventory control. The responses suggest that for most of the activities listed, the number of transactions affected by the use of new technologies will approximately double from 1993 to 1996.

As firms move toward increased computerization in logistics, they tend first to automate activities that are more routine and repetitive. Order entry and inventory control are examples of this. Alternatively, tasks that involve greater elements of judgment or choice, such as shipment consolidation, carrier selection and evaluation, and international decisions, tend to be automated later.

Overall, modern computer technology is essential to the effective management of logistics information. Firms are intensively involved in integrating this technology with other logistics information system capabilities, as well as with the corporate management information system when possible. This integration will continue and accelerate.

TABLE 11-7   Median Percentage of Transactions Using New Information Technology

Function	1990	1993	1996
Traffic	11%	28%	57%
Warehousing	16	36	69
Purchasing	10	20	47
Order entry	24	40	67
Customer service	15	24	45
Inventory control	23	39	68
International communication	7	16	38

SOURCE: James M. Masters and Bernard J. LaLonde, *The 1993 Ohio State University Survey of Career Patterns in Logistics* (Columbus, OH: The Ohio State University, 1993). Used with permission.

Artificial Intelligence/Expert Systems

As was discussed earlier, considerable attention has recently been directed to the topics of artificial intelligence and expert systems. In fact, the AI discipline of expert systems is already present in a number of areas of logistics management practice. AI and expert systems are evaluated for use because of their alleged abilities to solve problems, make predictions, suggest possible treatments, and offer advice with a degree of accuracy equal to that of a human counterpart.[45] Figure 11–16 provides an example of how the use of an expert system might structure the response of a customer service representative to a telephone inquiry.

general approach

Expert systems offer an economical and practical way to capture, refine, and proliferate management skills. These systems provide a framework in which to document the questions and answers that experts use to solve analytical and operational problems. With such systems, a firm can put one expert's know-how in the hands of many workers, improving consistency, accuracy, and productivity throughout the network. These systems allow more effective management of the organization's most critical resource: knowledge.

In short, the development of expert systems involves understanding and computerizing the human thought process. Once developers of expert systems sufficiently understand the thought process, they instruct a computer to make the same types of decisions a person would make. By observing how people make decisions, it is possible to identify decision rules and heuristics that guide the actions of logistics managers.

inventory management

Inventory management and control has emerged as the area in which expert systems have received the greatest attention. For example, Federal-Mogul Corporation has implemented a comprehensive inventory/MRP interface expert system called LOGIX. This system supports diverse activities such as ordering, forecasting, packaging, order entry, and receiving prioritization.[46] An expert system was developed for the U.S. Air Force by the late Major Mary Kay Allen, after she identified 441 decision rules by which inventory was being managed at the Sacramento Air Logistics Center.[47] Implementation resulted in performance improvements in the range of 15.1 percent to 17.7 percent,[48] and in the pretesting exercise the expert system uncovered a $600,000 error in a single item.[49]

FIGURE 11-16 Example of an Expert System Applicable to a Customer Service Representative

> Welcome to the ABC Catalog Advisor
>
> What product type does the customer require?
> >>*light bulb*
>
> What is the light bulb used for?
> >>*a photo emitter*
>
> Who was the original manufacturer of the photo emitter?
> >>*Beckman Instruments*
>
> What is the model number of this Beckman photo emitter?
> >>*unknown*
>
> Is the light emitter a "professional" or "series 5000" unit?
> >>*unknown*
>
> Which is the unit, a floor model or a desktop model?
> >>*desktop*
>
> Advice: Model No. 4367 best meets the customer's needs.
>   Unit price is $1.67.
>   We have 450 in stock.
>
> Do you wish to see alternate light bulbs that can also satisfy this requirement?
> >>*no*
>
> Does the customer wish to place an order?
> >>■

SOURCE: Mary Kay Allen and Omar Keith Helferich, *Putting Expert Systems to Work in Logistics* (Oak Brook, IL: Council of Logistics Management, 1990): 22–24. Used with permission.

examples Other examples of successful experiences with expert systems include the following:[50]

- *Digital Equipment Corporation (DEC)* uses an expert system to track work-in-process (WIP) inventories. The system ensures that an available workstation is always processing WIP and that supply and component orders are placed as soon as the need arises. The system has enabled DEC to cut its WIP cycle from thirty-six days to five days. In addition, DEC uses another expert system to route carriers distributing its products throughout the United States. This system has reduced transportation costs by 20 percent.

- *Sea-Land Service, Inc.,* a subsidiary of CSX Corporation, developed an expert system to assist in the routing and scheduling of ships by providing more consistent decisions by customer service representatives. The system also facilitates automated tracking of each shipment, significantly reducing the chances of misrouted freight.

THE REPORTS AND OUTPUTS SYSTEM

The reports and outputs subsystem is the fourth major component of the logistics information system. Many logistics managers believe that most reports and other forms of output do not communicate effectively. As a result, many good ideas, many notable research results, and many managerial recommendations simply go unnoticed for lack of proper communication.

Reports may serve purposes such as planning, operations, and control. For example, *planning reports* may include information such as sales trends and forecasts, other market information, and economic projections of cost factors. Planning reports include both historic and future-based information.

Operating reports inform managers and supervisors about such things as current on-hand inventories, purchase and shipping orders, production scheduling and control, and transportation. Typically, these reports make information available to managers on a real-time basis.

Control reports may summarize cost and operating information over relevant time periods, compare budgeted and actual expenses, and provide direct transportation costs. They serve as a basis for strategically redirecting operating approaches and tactics.

Remember, communication occurs only if the communicated information keys into a person's values and responds directly to the decisions that management personnel need to make. In actual business practice, molding people's expectations about the information contained in reports and outputs is essential. Incorporating the time-honored features of effective business communications—brevity, exception reporting, and getting at the heart of the matter—is also important. People have neither the time nor the inclination to deal with ineffective communication. In the firm's logistics area, high-quality communication through appropriate reports and outputs should be the standard, not the exception.

Whether the underlying information relates to managerial planning, operations, or control, communication effectiveness will affect how the firm's logistics function successfully achieves its mission.

effectiveness of reports and outputs

ADAPTING TO NEW INFORMATION TECHNOLOGIES

A relentless search is underway at many firms for information technologies that will lead to efficiency, effectiveness, and differentiation. In addition to the many approaches discussed in this chapter, other technologies of interest include client servers, network integration, and groupware. The latter refers to a growing set of information technologies that enhance people's interactions. Examples of groupware are E-mail, videoconferencing, electronic bulletin board, LotusNotes, the Internet, and so on. These are a welcome addition to existing technologies such as fax and voice mail.

As is the case with the move to any innovative technology, there is no shortage of challenges and opportunities. The following considerations will be relevant to the process of adapting to new information technologies such as those identified above.

challenges and opportunities

- It is important to have a scientific as well as an intuitive understanding of *customer and supplier information requirements,* as well as those of the entire logistics channel. It will be necessary for the information technologies to be flexible and adaptable, depending on the specific set of needs being served. As was mentioned previously, the decision by Kellogg Company to go live with LogiCNet was based on the commitment to having a truly customer-driven continuous-replenishment program.

- It is necessary to recognize that implementation delays can result from a *lack of coordination and integration among key logistics activities.* Inconsistencies and lengthy order cycles can result, for example, from the failure to synchronize logistics operational versus coordination activities.
- It is important to see that the *logistics organizational strategies move from a functional to a process orientation.* Emphasis on the latter will assure more meaningful process measurement, process feedback, and process knowledge.
- Inevitably, early implementation efforts may suffer due to *poor data or the nonavailability or nonsharing of future data* pertaining, for example, to future orders, forecasts, and target production schedules.
- It is important that the organization have the *financial resources* needed to assure a smooth, full implementation. Also, a *willingness among employees to accept the use of new technologies* will be critical to this process. A recent trend among firms has been to develop business strategies designed to make employees more enthusiastic and less resistant to change.
- It is necessary for firms to create opportunities for *interaction and team efforts among logistics managers and those others most knowledgeable about information technologies.* Logistics managers need to know more about the art and science of information systems, and information systems specialists must develop greater insight into the types of problems faced on a daily basis by those involved in managing the logistics process.

Overall, firms must recognize the strategic value of having timely and accurate logistics information. Companies must consider the LIS strategically important to the whole firm, and they need to develop logistics information strategies, just as they would develop strategies relating to new products or capital expenditures.

SUMMARY

- The timely availability and use of logistics information has been recognized as a prerequisite to overall cost efficiency and to the ability of a firm to competitively price its products in the marketplace.
- Businesses are increasing expenditures for information systems, replacing their information systems executives, and leveraging information technology to help meet corporate and logistics goals.
- Following the steps in the information-system building process will enhance the likelihood that the resulting system will meet its intended goals.
- Several factors significantly affect the quality of information. These include having the right information available, having accurate information, and having information that is communicated effectively.
- Logistics information is essential to the synchronizing and integration of logistics coordination and operational activities.
- New and innovative information technologies are gaining popularity in the logistics process. Included are bar coding, EDI, data management, artificial intelligence/expert systems, and remote access and communications.
- The logistics information system consists of specific modules, or subsystems,

relating to order management, research and intelligence, decision support, and reports and outputs.

- A number of challenges, as well as opportunities, await those people and firms who have targeted the logistics process as an exciting opportunity to further leverage new information technologies.

STUDY QUESTIONS

1. What are some of the most prevalent issues involving information systems today? Which are of greatest concern to companies?

2. Discuss how an "information systems architecture" can be used to build an information system.

3. What is meant by the "quality" of logistics information?

4. Describe the difference between coordination and operational activities. Why is it important to integrate these two sets of activities?

5. What information technologies are recognized as being particularly useful and relevant to the logistics process?

6. What does electronic data interchange, or EDI, mean? In what specific ways can EDI benefit buyers and sellers in a logistics channel?

7. Define artificial intelligence and expert systems.

8. Discuss a logistics information system in terms of its purpose and its components.

9. What are the major alternatives for order placement? Which of these are more likely to prevail in the future?

10. What is the objective of the research and intelligence subsystem of the LIS? What activities are performed by this subsystem?

11. Define a decision support system. What general modeling applications are included in a decision support system?

12. What are the principal modeling approaches, and what are their differences?

13. What are some of the key challenges to be faced by those individuals and firms involved with implementing new and innovative logistics information technologies?

NOTES

1. Portions of this discussion have been adapted from C. John Langley Jr., "Information-Based Decision Making in Logistics Management," *International Journal of Physical Distribution and Materials Management* 15, no. 7 (1985): 41–42.

2. See F. Warren McFarlan, "Information Technology Changes the Way You Compete," *Harvard Business Review* 62, no. 3 (May–June 1984): 98–103.

3. Donald J. Bowersox, Patricia J. Daugherty, Cornelia L. Droge, Dale S. Rogers, and Dan-

iel L. Wardlow, *Leading Edge Logistics: Competitive Positioning for the 1990's* (Oak Brook, IL: Council of Logistics Management, 1989).

4. See David J. Closs, "Positioning Information in Logistics," Chapter 31 in *The Logistics Handbook* (New York: The Free Press, 1994): 699–713.

5. Closs, "Positioning Information in Logistics," 699.

6. For example, see Bernard J. LaLonde, Martha C. Cooper, and Thomas G. Noordewier, *Customer Service: A Management Perspective* (Oak Brook, IL: Council of Logistics Management, 1988): 37–70.

7. Computer Sciences Corporation, *Critical Issues of Information Systems Management for 1995* (Cambridge, MA: Computer Sciences Corporation, 1995).

8. Computer Sciences Corporation, "Linking Technology to Corporate Goals Replaces Reengineering as Top Concern in 1995 CSC Survey," *CSC News Release* (Cambridge, MA: Computer Sciences Corporation, March 27, 1995): 1.

9. Computer Sciences Corporation, "Linking Technology to Corporate Goals Replaces Reengineering as Top Concern in 1995 CSC Survey."

10. Major portions of this section are contained in IBM Corporation, *Computer Integrated Logistics: CIL Architecture in the Extended Enterprise* (Southbury, CT: IBM Corporation, U.S. Transportation Industry Marketing, 1991): 6–7.

11. This section has been adapted from Langley, "Information-Based Decision Making in Logistics Management," 41–42.

12. Robert S. Kaplan, "Yesterday's Accounting Undermines Production," *Harvard Business Review* 62, no. 4 (July–August 1984): 95–101.

13. For example, see the following: Douglas M. Lambert and Howard M. Armitage, "Distribution Costs—The Challenge," *Management Accounting* (May 1979): 33–38; John L. Boros and R. E. Thompson, "Distribution Cost Accounting at PPG Industries," *Management Accounting* (January 1983): 54–60; and Howard M. Armitage, "The Use of Management Accounting Techniques to Improve Productivity Analysis in Distribution Operations," *International Journal of Physical Distribution and Materials Management* 14, no. 1 (1984): 41–51. Although not specifically oriented to logistics, see also Robin Cooper and Robert S. Kaplan, "Measure Costs Right: Make the Right Decisions," *Harvard Business Review* 66, no. 5 (September–October 1988): 96–103.

14. Joseph Bonney, "More Logistics Tools Than They Can Use," *American Shipper* (October 1994): 58.

15. The issue of managerial communication in general is dealt with effectively in Peter F. Drucker, *Management: Tasks, Responsibilities, Practices* (New York: Harper & Row, 1974). This paragraph draws particularly upon the content of Chapter 38, "Managerial Communications," 481–493.

16. Portions of this section have been adapted from Closs, "Positioning Information in Logistics," 699–707.

17. Closs, "Positioning Information in Logistics," 706–7.

18. For additional detail, see IBM Corporation, *Computer Integrated Logistics: CIL Architecture in the Extended Enterprise* (Southbury, CT: IBM Corporation, U.S. Transportation Industry Marketing, 1991): 9–11.

19. Richard L. Dawe and Dale S. Rogers, "Using Information Technology to Improve Logistics Competencies, *1994 Council of Logistics Management Annual Conference Proceedings* (Oak Brook, IL: Council of Logistics Management, 1994): 84.

20. Margaret A. Emmelhainz, "Electronic Data Interchange in Logistics," Chapter 33 in *The Logistics Handbook* (New York: The Free Press, 1994): 737.

21. See *The Wall Street Journal*, March 6, 1987.

22. *Logistics Data Interchange: An Emerging Competitive Weapon for Shippers* (Lexington, MA: Mercer Management Consulting, 1987): II–10.

23. *Logistics Data Interchange*, II–5.

24. *Logistics Data Interchange*, II–7.

25. Emmelhainz, "Electronic Data Interchange in Logistics," 740–41.

26. Digital Equipment Corporation, Systems Manufacturing Technology Group, "What is AI Anyway?" working paper (May 1982): 1.

27. James M. Masters and Bernard J. LaLonde, "The Role of New Information Technology in the Practice of Traffic Management," *The Logistics Handbook* (New York: The Free Press, 1994): 490.

28. Michael Ham, "Playing by the Rules," *PC World* (January 1984): 34.

29. James Aaron Cooke, "Technology Ups the Ante in the Technology Game," *Traffic Management* (April 1994): 66.

30. Cooke, "Technology Ups the Ante in the Technology Game," 66.

31. Cooke, "Technology Ups the Ante in the Technology Game," 65–66.

32. Cooke, "Technology Ups the Ante in the Technology Game," 66.

33. This definition has been adapted from a definition of a marketing information system suggested in Philip Kotler, *Principles of Marketing*, 3rd ed. (Englewood Cliffs, NJ: Prentice-Hall, 1986): 87.

34. For an interesting discussion of logistics information systems, see Alan J. Stenger, "Information Systems in Logistics Management: Past, Present, and Future," *Transportation Journal* 26, no. 1 (Fall 1986): 65–82. In this discussion, logistics information consists of four groups: transaction systems, short-term scheduling and inventory replenishment systems, flow planning systems, and network planning systems.

35. See Roy Dale Voorhees, John C. Coppett, and Eileen M. Kelley, "Telelogistics: A Management Tool for the Logistics Problems of the 1980s," *Transportation Journal* 23, no. 4 (Summer 1984): 62–70.

36. Cleveland Consulting Associates, Inc., *1993 Logistics Benchmarking Survey Results* (Washington, DC: Grocery Manufacturers of America, Inc. and Cleveland Consulting Associates, 1993): 14.

37. Bernard J. LaLonde, Martha C. Cooper, and Thomas G. Noordewier, *Customer Service: A Management Perspective* (Oak Brook, IL: Council of Logistics Management, 1988).

38. Bernard J. LaLonde and Paul H. Zinszer, *Customer Service: Meaning and Measurement* (Oak Brook, IL: Council of Logistics Management, 1976): 119.

39. Philip Kotler, *Marketing Management: Analysis, Planning, and Control*, 5th ed. (Englewood Cliffs, NJ: Prentice-Hall, 1984): 192.

40. Liam Fahey and William R. King, "Environmental Scanning for Corporate Planning," *Business Horizons* 20, no. 4 (August 1977): 61–71.

41. These descriptions appear in Allan F. Ayers, "Forecasting: Art or Reality," *Transportation & Distribution* (June 1994): 29–34.

42. Ayers, "Forecasting: Art or Reality," 30.

43. Omar Keith Helferich, "Logistics Decision Support Systems," *Computers in Manufacturing: Distribution Management* (Pennsauken, NJ: Auerbach, 1983): 1.

44. Craig M. Gustin, "Logistics Information Systems: Progress Made During the Last Decade," *1993 Council of Logistics Management Annual Conference Proceedings* (Oak Brook, IL: Council of Logistics Management, 1993): 166–67.

45. Ham, "Playing by the Rules," 34.

46. Mary Kay Allen and Omar Keith Helferich, *Putting Expert Systems to Work in Logistics* (Oak Brook, IL: Council of Logistics Management, 1990): 47–62.

47. Mary Kay Allen, *The Development of an Artificial Intelligence System for Inventory Management* (Oak Brook, IL: Council of Logistics Management, 1986).

48. Allen, *The Development of an Artificial Intelligence System for Inventory Management*, 185.

49. Allen, *The Development of an Artificial Intelligence System for Inventory Management*, 128.

50. These summaries have been taken directly from Allen and Helferich, *Putting Expert Systems to Work in Logistics*, xvi–xviii.

Case 11-1

PENINSULA POINT, INC.

In recent years, Peninsula Point, Inc. has become a very successful merchandiser of contemporary fashion apparel for men and women. The company publishes a high-quality catalog, which it sends to prospective customers. Customers place their orders by mail or by using a toll-free telephone number. The customer base consists principally of young couples with two incomes and no children. These customers typically receive other catalogs from competitor firms such as Land's End, Orvis, and L. L. Bean.

Although the apparel industry is fiercely competitive, the catalog business is growing. People who are "just too busy" to shop in retail stores regard it as an appealing alternative. Purchasing apparel merchandise by catalog also seems to have a certain prestige in some social circles.

Among companies of its kind, Peninsula Point is thought to offer the best product assortment, product quality, and customer service. Two critical customer service elements at Peninsula Point are that the company receives, packs, and ships orders in a timely manner and that product return procedures are "customer friendly." Although the company accommodates product returns with little or no bother to the customer, this practice is expensive and is of growing concern to upper-level management.

Peninsula Point does not produce any of the merchandise it sells. Instead, it contracts with manufacturers in Korea, Hong Kong, Taiwan, and Singapore to meet its largely seasonal product line needs. The company ships container loads of labeled and pretagged merchandise by a combination of ocean transportation and domestic inland motor freight to a centralized distribution center in Nashville, Tennessee. Subsequently, UPS makes all individual customer shipments.

Peninsula Point executives consider themselves to be in the "logistics business." They feel that the company's logistical capabilities are a key to its excellent reputation in the marketplace. An area of nagging concern to the managers, however, is that consumer tastes and company product preferences are beginning to change very quickly, sometimes in the middle of a selling season. Only a continued ability to react quickly to changing marketplace needs will separate market leaders from the others.

Case Questions

1. In what ways should we consider the components of the logistics information system (as discussed in this chapter) important to Peninsula Point? What suggestions do you have for improving the company's logistics information system?
2. What macroenvironmental factors will be critical to Peninsula Point's future success? In what specific ways can the company develop logistics capabilities to address these factors?

Case 11-2

SEA-TAC DISTRIBUTING COMPANY

Profit margins are being squeezed in the wholesale grocery business, and Michael McBee, logistics vice president for Sea-Tac Distributing Company, is under pressure to reduce unit costs and to improve customer service. Although in business for only four years, Sea-Tac enjoys an estimated 11 percent share of the Seattle-Tacoma-area wholesale grocery market and ranks fourth in total revenues among firms of its type. Sea-Tac is an aggressive marketplace competitor and is thought to be very progressive in its willingness to implement the latest available technologies.

The logistics vice president is responsible for all activities relating to product receipt, storage, and distribution, and has direct authority over the company's centralized computer system. Sea-Tac receives all of the grocery products it sells at either of its two distribution centers and makes deliveries directly from those facilities to customers' warehouses or stores. The company maintains a fleet of twelve trucks, which it uses exclusively to deliver products to customers.

All buying activities at Sea-Tac are the responsibility of the purchasing vice president, who depends on a team of eight qualified buyers, each of whom concentrates on a specific class of food and grocery items. In effect, each buyer has full authority to negotiate all sale terms (price, credit terms, and logistical responsibilities) with individual vendors. Given that the number of SKUs in the Sea-Tac product line exceeds 3,000, the buying function is extremely critical to the firm.

Although Sea-Tac does not integrate the purchasing and logistics functions divisions, both vice presidents feel that a high degree of coordination occurs between the two areas. Other Sea-Tac vice presidents control marketing and finance, respectively. The marketing vice president promotes and sells the company's product line, accomplishing this largely through Sea-Tac's effective advertising program and through the efforts of ten account executives. These people call on individual customers either once or twice weekly, depending on the account's importance. Customers place all orders through direct telephone contact with Sea-Tac's order entry clerks. The finance vice president provides the logistics vice president with a variety of cost-related information. Unfortunately, McBee feels uncomfortable making logistics decisions based on the average cost data provided.

Case Questions

1. Based on the content of this chapter, what suggestions would you offer the logistics vice president to help reduce unit costs and improve service?
2. What additional information would you like to have before finalizing your recommendations?

SUGGESTED READINGS FOR PART II

INVENTORY IN THE LOGISTICS SYSTEM AND INVENTORY DECISION MAKING

"A Close Look at How Distributors Manage Their Inventories," *The Distributor's & Wholesaler's Advisor* 6, no. 6 (March 15, 1994): 1–7.

Ansari, A., and Jim Heckel. "JIT Purchasing: Impact of Freight and Inventory Costs," *Journal of Purchasing and Materials Management* (Summer 1987): 24–28.

Bagchi, Prabir K. "Management of Materials Under Just-in-Time Inventory System: A New Look," *Journal of Business Logistics* 9, no. 2 (1988): 89–102.

Bagchi, Prabir K., and Frank W. Davis. "Some Insights into Inbound Freight Consolidation," in *Application of New Technologies, Methods and Approaches to Logistics* (James M. Stock, ed.), special issue of the *International Journal of Physical Distribution & Materials Management* 18, no. 6 (1988): 27–33.

Bregman, Robert L. "Enhanced Distribution Requirements Planning," *Journal of Business Logistics* 11, no. 2 (1990): 49–68.

Closs, David J. "Inventory Management: A Comparison of a Traditional vs. Systems View," *Journal of Business Logistics* 10, no. 2: 90–105.

Daugherty, Patricia J.; Dale S. Rogers; and Michael S. Spencer. "Just-in-Time Functional Model: Empirical Test and Validation," *International Journal of Physical Distribution & Logistics Management* 24, no. 6 (1994): 20–26.

Eppen, Gary D., and R. Kipp Martin. "Determining Safety Stock in the Presence of Stochastic Lead Time and Demand," *Management Science* 34, no. 11 (November 1988): 1380–91.

Evers, Philip T., and Frederick J. Beier. "The Portfolio Effect and Multiple Consolidation Points: A Critical Assessment of the Square Root Law," *Journal of Business Logistics* 14, no. 2 (1993): 109–25.

Forger, Gary. "We Now Manage More Inventory Better with Automation," *Modern Materials Handling* 48, no. 6 (May 1993): 46–48.

Harper, Donald V. "Characteristics and Transportation Practices of Just-in-Time Manufacturers," *Transportation Practitioners* 59, no. 3 (Spring 1992): 263–78.

Ho, Chrwan-jyh, and Philip L. Carter. "Adopting Rescheduling Capability in DRP to Deal with Operational Uncertainty in Logistics Systems," *International Journal of Logistics Management* 5, no. 1 (1994): 33–42.

Masters, James M. "Determination Stock Levels for Multi-Echelon Distribution Inventories," *Journal of Business Logistics* 14, no. 2 (1993): 165–95.

McLean, John M., and Alan L. Saipe. "Managing Inventory in Turbulent Times," *Council of Logistics Management Proceedings* (1992): 1–16.

Ronen, David. "Inventory Centralization/Decentralization—The Square Root Law Revisited Again," *Journal of Business Logistics* 11, no. 2 (1990): 129–38.

Tallon, William J. "The Impact of Inventory Centralization on Aggregate Safety Stock: The Variable Supply Lead Time Case," *Journal of Business Logistics* 14, no. 1 (1993): 185–204.

Tyworth, John E. "Modeling Transportation-Inventory Trade-Offs in a Stochastic Setting," *Journal of Business Logistics* 13, no. 2 (1992): 97–124.

van der Duyn Schouten, Frank A.; Marc J. G. van Eijs; and Ruud M. J. Heuts. "The Value of Supplier Information to Improve Management of Retailer's Inventory," *Decision Sciences Journal* 25, no. 1 (January/February 1994): 1–14.

Walter, Clyde Kenneth. "The Inventory Carrying Cost Methodology," *Logistics Spectrum* 22, Issue 2 (Summer 1988): 25–32.

Zemke, Douglas E., and Douglas M. Lambert. "Utilizing Information Technology to Manage Inventory," *1987 Council of Logistics Management Annual Conference Proceedings* (Oak Brook, IL: Council of Logistics Management, 1987): 119–40.

Zinn, Walter, and Howard Marmorstein. "Comparing Two Alternative Methods of Determining Safety Stock Levels: The Demand and the Forecast Systems," *Journal of Business Logistics* 11, no. 2 (1990): 95–110.

Zinn, Walter; Michael Levy; and Donald J. Bowersox. "On Assumed Assumptions and the Inventory Centralization/Decentralization Issue," *Journal of Business Logistics* 11, no. 2 (1990): 138.

WAREHOUSING DECISIONS

Ackerman, Kenneth B. "The Changing Role of Warehousing," *Warehousing Forum* 8, no. 12 (November 1993): 1–4.

Andel, Tom. "Inside Warehousing & Distribution," *Transportation & Distribution* 34, no. 3 (March 1993): 61–80.

Contract Warehousing: How It Works and How To Make It Work Effectively. (Oak Brook, IL: Warehousing Education and Research Council, 1993).

Cooke, James Aaron. "How Canada Makes a Pallet Co-Op Work," *Traffic Management—Warehousing and Distribution Supplement* (November 1993): 12S–16S.

Daly, Frank. "Warehousing: The Strategic Weapon for Customer Service," *Industrial Engineering* 25, no. 5 (May 1993): 61–62.

Derewecki, Donald J.; Robert B. Silverman; and Alex Donnan. "Warehouse Planning: Computer Aided Design," *1988 Council of Logistics Management Annual Conference Proceedings* (Oak Brook, IL: Council of Logistics Management, 1988): 427–58.

Kirk, John A. "Maximizing Productivity Performance and Operational Effectiveness of the Warehouse," *Focus on Physical Distribution and Logistics Management* 8, no. 4 (May 1989): 36–40.

McGinnis, Michael A. *Basic Economic Analysis for Warehouse Decisions* (Oak Brook, IL: Warehousing Education and Research Council, 1989).

Muroff, Cindy H. "State of the Warehouse Industry: Traditional vs. Functional," *Warehousing Management* 1, no. 4 (July/August 1994): 6–16.

Murphy, Paul R., and Richard F. Poist. "In Search of Warehousing Excellence: A Multivariate Analysis of HRM Practices," *Journal of Business Logistics* 14, no. 2 (1993): 145–64.

"New Distribution Center Design Geared for Future Growth," *Grocery Distribution* 20, no. 1 (September/October 1994): 22–45.

Pfohl, Hans-Christian; Werner A. Zollner; and Norbert Weber. "Economies of Scale in Customer Warehouses: Theoretical and Empirical Analysis," *Journal of Business Logistics* 13, no. 1 (1991): 95–124.

Schafer, Scott M., and Ricardo Ernst. "Applying Group Technology Principles to Warehousing Operations," *International Journal of Purchasing and Materials Management* (Spring 1993): 38–42.

Sheehan, William G. "Contract Warehousing: The Evolution of an Industry," *Journal of Business Logistics* 10, no. 1 (1989): 31–49.

Tompkins, James A. "20 Strategies for Successful Warehousing," (four-part series) *Material Handling Engineering* 44, no. 3–6 (March–June 1989).

Tompkins, James A., and Dale A. Harmelink. "How to Create an Integrated Distribution Strategy," *Transportation & Distribution* 34, no. 3 (March 1993): 82–88.

Trunk, Christopher. "Using Bar Codes for Warehouse Control," *Material Handling Engineering* (September 1994): 48–52.

Various articles, *Warehousing Management,* vol. 1., no. 2 (March/April 1994): 1–63.

Warrender, Roger. "Warehousing Management: The Critical Application of the 1990s," *Industrial Engineering* 26, no. 6 (June 1994): 25–27.

MATERIALS HANDLING AND PACKAGING

Andel, Tom. "Integrated Warehousing & Distribution Pallet Management," *Transportation & Distribution* 35, no. 8 (August 1994): 65–70.

Auguston, Karen. "Returnable Containers: Why You Need Them Now," *Modern Materials Handling* 48, no. 13 (November 1993): 40–42.

Auguston, Karen A. "The Denver Airport: A Lesson in Coping with Complexity," *Modern Materials Handling* 49, no. 12 (October 1994): 40–45.

Bonney, Joseph. "Bar Codes and Logistics," *American Shipper* 36, no. 1 (January 1994): 62–64.

"Chain's Experience with Plastic Pallets Brings Multi-Benefits," *Grocery Distribution* 20, no. 1 (September/October 1994): 26–46.

Cooke, James Aaron. "Block vs. Stringer: Which Pallet Is Best?" *Traffic Management* 32, no. 2 (February 1993): 36–38.

"Designing Docks: 14 Tips for Top Productivity," *Modern Materials Handling* 44, no. 7 (July 1989): 64–66.

Feare, Tom. "Better Ergonomics: It's the Law!" *Modern Materials Handling* 49, no. 6 (June 1994): 47–49.

Forger, Gary. "How More Data + Less Handling = Smart Warehousing," *Modern Materials Handling* 49, no. 4 (April 1994): 42–45.

Forger, Gary. "Productivity Climbs with Real-Time Warehouse Control," *Modern Materials Handling* 49, no. 3 (March 1994): 38–40.

Giust, Louis. "Just-in-Time Manufacturing and Material Handling Trends," *International Journal of Physical Distribution & Logistics Management* 23, no. 7: 32–38.

"Industrial Truck Technology," *Grocery Distribution* 18, no. 6 (July/August 1993): 22–28.

Livingstone, Susan, and Leigh Sparks. "The New German Packaging Laws: Effects on Firms Exporting to Germany," *International Journal of Physical Distribution & Logistics Management* 24, no. 7 (1994): 15–25.

Okogbaa, O. Geoffrey; Richard L. Shell; and Gordon M. Clark. "Modeling, Simulation and Analysis of an Automated Materials Handling System," *International Journal of Physical Distribution & Logistics Management* 24, no. 8 (1994): 15–32.

Robertson, Candace. "Package Design Yields Logistics Savings," *Transportation & Distribution* 35, no. 10 (October 1994): 48–50.

Schwind, Gene F. "Voice Recognition Deserves a Second Listen," *Material Handling Engineering* (February 1994): 63–67.

Witt, Clyde E. "Smart Scanners Verify Just What the Customer Ordered," *Material Handling Engineering* (January 1994): 44–46.

THE TRANSPORTATION SYSTEM

Arthur D. Little, Inc. *Direct Store Delivery: Store-Level Study* (Cambridge, MA: Arthur D. Little, Inc., 1987).

Chow, Garland, and Richard F. Poist. "The Measurement of Quality of Service and the Transportation Purchase Decision," *Logistics and Transportation Review* 20, no. 1 (1984): 25–44.

Coyle, John J.; Edward J. Bardi; and Robert A. Novack. *Transportation,* 4th ed. (St. Paul, MN: West Publishing, 1994)

Crum, Michael R., and Benjamin J. Allen. "Shipper EDI, Carrier Reduction, and Contracting Strategies: Impacts on the Motor Carrier Industry," *Transportation Journal* 29, no. 4 (Summer 1990): 18–31.

Cunningham, William A., and Grant M. Davis. "Public Policy Implications of Motor Carrier Restructuring: A Decade of Experience," *Transportation Practitioners Journal* 60, no. 3 (Spring 1993): 286–305.

De Salvo, Joseph S. "Measuring the Direct Impacts of a Port," *Transportation Journal* 33, no. 4 (Summer 1994): 33–42.

Glaskowsky, Nicholas A. *Effects of Deregulation on Motor Carriers* (Westport, CT: Eno Foundation for Transportation, 1986).

Grimm, Curtis M.; Thomas M. Corsi; and Judith J. Jarrell. "U.S. Motor Carrier Cost Structure under Deregulation," *Logistics and Transportation Review* 25, no. 3 (September 1989): 231–49.

Grimm, Curtis M.; Thomas M. Corsi; and Raymond D. Smith. "Determinants of Strategic Change in the LTL Motor Carrier Industry: A Discrete Choice Analysis," *Transportation Journal* 32, no. 4 (Summer 1993): 56–62.

Harper, Donald V., and Philip T. Evers. "Competitive Issues in Intermodal Railroad-Truck Service," *Transportation Journal* 32, no. 3 (Spring 1993): 31–45.

Higginson, James K., and James H. Bookbinder. "Implications of Just-in-Time Production on Rail Freight Systems," *Transportation Journal* 29, no. 3 (Spring 1990): 29–35.

Laine, Jouni T., and Ari P. J. Vepsalainen. "Economics of Speed in Sea Transportation," *International Journal of Physical Distribution & Logistics Management* 24, no. 8 (1994): 33–41.

Leeper, John H. "Collective Pricing in the U.S. Port Industry," *Transportation Practitioners Journal* 60, no. 3 (Spring 1993): 249–256.

LeMay, Stephen A.; G. Stephen Taylor; and Gregory B. Turner. "Driver Turnover and Management Policy: A Survey of Truckload Irregular Route Motor Carriers," *Transportation Journal* 33, no 2 (Winter 1993): 15–21.

Lieb, Robert C., and Robert A. Millen. "The Responses of General Commodity Motor Carriers to Just in Time Manufacturing Programs," *Transportation Journal* 30, no. 1 (Fall 1990): 5–11.

Murphy, Paul R., and James M. Daley. "A Comparative Analysis of Port Selection Factors," *Transportation Journal* 34, no. 1 (Fall 1994): 15–21.

Oum, Tae Hoom; Allison J. Taylor; and Anming Zhang. "Strategic Airline Policy in the Globalizing Airline Networks," *Transportation Journal* 32, no. 3 (Spring 1993): 14–30.

Rakowski, James P. "The Continuing Structural Transformation of the U.S. Less-Than-Truckload Motor Carrier Industry," *Transportation Journal* 34, no. 1 (Fall 1994): 5–14.

Smith, David G. "Resolving Schedule Failures in Multi-Modal Networks for Movement of Time-Sensitive Shipments," *Journal of Marketing Theory and Practice* 2, no. 2 (Spring 1994): 28–44.

Stephenson, Frederick J., and Theodore P. Stank. "Truckload Motor Carrier Profitability Strategies," *Transportation Journal* 34, no. 2 (Winter 1994): 5–17.

Stone, Richard D. "Administrative Deregulation of the Railroads," *Transportation Practitioners Journal* 61, no. 4 (Spring 1994): 278–88.

Valder, Rafael J., and Michael R. Crum. "U.S. Motor Carrier Perspectives on Trucking to Mexico," *Transportation Journal* 33, no. 4 (Summer 1994): 5–20.

Wong, Harry. "Intermodal Growth and Logistics Management," *Industrial Engineering* 26, no. 6 (June 1994): 20–22.

TRANSPORTATION MANAGEMENT

Andel, Tom. "Does Your Small-Shipment Plan Fit?" *Transportation & Distribution* 34, no. 3 (March 1993): 22–27.

Aron, Laurie Joan. "Taking Charge of Small-Package Deliveries," *Inbound Logistics* 14, no. 4 (April 1994): 18–23.

Augello, William J. *Freight Claims in Plain English*, 1982 rev. ed. (Huntington, NY: Shippers National Freight Claim Council, 1982).

Ballou, Ronald H., and Daniel W. DeHayes Jr. "Transport Selection by Interfirm Analysis," *Transportation and Distribution Management* 7, no. 6 (June 1967): 33–37.

Bardi, Edward J.; Prabir K. Bagchi; and T. S. Raghunathan. "Motor Carrier Selection in a Deregulated Environment," *Transportation Journal* 29, no. 1 (Fall 1989): 4–11.

Bardi, Edward J., and Michael Tracey. "Transportation Outsourcing: A Survey of U.S. Practices," *International Journal of Physical Distribution & Logistics Management* 15, no. 1 (1991): 15–21.

Beier, Frederick J. "Transportation Contracts and the Experience Effect: A Framework for Future Research," *Journal of Business Logistics* 10, no. 2 (1989): 73–89.

Bowersox, Donald J. "The Strategic Benefits of Logistics Alliances," *Harvard Business Review* (July/August 1990), 36–47.

Bowman, Robert. "Rookie Transportation Buyers," *Distribution* 93, no. 4 (April 1994): 30–34.

Brown, T. A. "Shippers' Agents and the Marketing of Rail Intermodal Service," *Transportation Journal* (Spring 1984): 44–52.

Forsythe, Kenneth H.; James C. Johnson; and Kenneth C. Schneider. "Traffic Managers: Do They Get Any Respect?" *Journal of Business Logistics* 11, no. 2 (1990), 87–100.

Husveth, John M. "The Legal Distinction between ICC Regulated Motor Common and Contract Carriage," *Transportation Journal* 33, no. 3 (Spring 1994): 26–35.

Jackson, George. "A Survey of Freight Consolidation Practices," *Journal of Business Logistics* 6, no. 1 (1985): 13–34.

LaLonde, Bernard J.; James M. Masters; Arnold B. Maltz; and Lisa R. Williams. *Evolution Status and Future of the Corporate Transportation Function* (Louisville, KY: American Society of Transportation and Logistics, 1991).

Lambert, Douglas M.; M. Christine Lewis; and James R. Stock. "How Shippers Select and Evaluate General Commodities LTL Motor Carriers," *Journal of Business Logistics* 14, no. 1 (1993): 131–44.

Matear, Sheelagh, and Richard Gray. "Factors Influencing Freight Service Choice for Shippers and Freight Suppliers," *International Journal of Physical Distribution & Logistics Management* 23, no. 2 (1993): 25–36.

Raghunathan, T. S.; Prabir K. Bagchi; and Edward J. Bardi. "Motor Carrier Services: The U.S. Experience," *International Journal of Physical Distribution & Materials Management* 18, no. 5 (1988): 3–7.

Rao, Kant, and Richard R. Young. "Global Supply Chains: Factors Influencing Outsourcing of Logistics Functions," *International Journal of Physical Distribution & Logistics Management* 24, no. 6 (1994): 11–19.

Richardson, Helen L. "Intangibles: New Role in Carrier Selection," *Transportation & Distribution* 35, no. 4 (April 1994): 41–42.

Tyworth, J. E.; J. L. Cavinato; and C. J. Langley Jr. *Traffic Management* (Prospect Heights, IL: Waveland Press, 1987).

Tyworth, John E.; Pat Lemons; and Bruce Ferrin. "Improving LTL Delivery Service with Statistical Process Control," *Transportation Journal* 28, no. 3 (Spring 1989): 4–12.

United States Code Annotated, Title 49, Transportation (St. Paul, MN: West Publishing, 1982).

Whyte, James L. "The Freight Transport Market: Buyer-Seller Relationships and Selection Criteria," *International Journal of Physical Distribution & Logistics Management* 23, no. 3 (1993): 29–37.

ORDER PROCESSING AND INFORMATION SYSTEMS

Allen, Benjamin J.; Michael R. Crum; and Charles D. Braunschweig. "The U.S. Motor Carrier Industry: The Extent and Nature of EDI Use," *International Journal of Physical Distribution and Logistics Management* 22, no. 8 (1992): 27–34.

Allen, Mary K. *The Development of an Artificial Intelligence System for Inventory Management* (Oak Brook, IL: Council of Logistics Management, 1986).

Andersen Consulting. *Survey of Logistics Software* (Oak Brook, IL: Council of Logistics Management, 1995).

Ayers, Allan F. "Forecasting: Art or Reality?" *Transportation and Distribution* 35, no. 6 (June 1994): 29–34.

Ballou, Ronald H. "Heuristics: Rules of Thumb for Logistics Decision Making," *Journal of Business Logistics* 10, no. 1 (1989): 122–32.

Bardi, Edward J.; T. S. Raghunathan; and Prabir K. Bagchi. "Logistics Information Systems: The Strategic Role of Top Management," *Journal of Business Logistics* 15, no. 1 (1994): 71–85.

Bausch, Dan O.; Gerald G. Brown; and David Ronen. "Dispatching Shipments at Minimal Cost with Multiple Mode Alternatives," *Journal of Business Logistics* 15, no. 1 (1994): 287–303.

Bookbinder, James H., and David M. Dilts. "Logistics Information Systems in a Just-in-Time Environment," *Journal of Business Logistics* 10, no. 1 (1989): 50–67.

Bowersox, Donald J., and David J. Closs. "Simulation in Logistics: A Review of Present Practice and a Look to the Future," *Journal of Business Logistics* 10, no. 1 (1989), 133–47.

Brickell, Geoff. "Logistics and the Single Market," *Logistics Information Management* 3, no. 2 (June 1990): 79–82.

Burbridge, John J. "Strategic Implications of Logistics Information Systems," *Logistics and Transportation Review* 24, no. 4 (December 1988): 368–83.

Byrne, Stephen M., and Shariar Javad. "Integrated Logistics Information Systems (ILIS): Competitive Advantage or Increased Cost?" in *1992 Council of Logistics Management Annual Conference Proceedings* (Oak Brook, IL: Council of Logistics Management 1992): 55–74.

Carter, Joseph; Robert Monczka; Keith Clauson; and Thomas Zelinski. "Education and Training for Successful EDI Implementation," *Journal of Purchasing and Materials Management* (Summer 1987): 13–20.

Cook, Robert L. "Expert Systems in Purchasing: Applications and Development," *International Journal of Purchasing and Materials Management* (Fall 1992): 20–27.

Dawe, Richard L. "An Investigation of the Pace and Determination of Information Technology Use in the Manufacturing Materials Logistics System," *Journal of Business Logistics* 15, no. 1 (1994): 229–59.

Gustin, Craig M.; Theodore P. Stank; and Patricia J. Daugherty. "Computerization: Supporting Integration," *International Journal of Physical Distribution & Logistics Management* 24, no. 1 (1994): 11–16.

Harrington, Lisa H. "The ABCs of EDI," *Traffic Management* 29, no. 8 (August 1990): 49–52.

Henderson, John C. "Plugging into Strategic Partnerships: The Critical IS Connection," *Sloan Management Review* 31, no. 3 (Spring 1990): 7–18.

Langley, C. John. "Information-Based Decision Making in Logistics Management," *International Journal of Physical Distribution and Materials Management* 15, no. 7 (1985): 41–55.

Langley, C. John. "Microcomputers as a Logistics Information Strategy," *Applications of New Technologies, Methods and Approaches to Logistics* (James M. Stock, ed.), special issue of the *International Journal of Physical Distribution & Materials Management* 18, no. 6 (1988): 11–17.

Langley, C. John; Stephen B. Probst; and Roy E. Cail. "Microcomputers in Logistics: 1987," *1987 Council of Logistics Management Annual Conference Proceedings* (Oak Brook, IL: Council of Logistics Management, 1987): 423–28.

Lavery, Hank, and G. A. Long. "EDI in Transportation," *1989 Council of Logistics Management Annual Conference Proceedings* (Oak Brook, IL: Council of Logistics Management, 1989): 261–77.

LeMay, Stephen A., and Wallace R. Wood. "Developing Logistics Decision Support Systems," *Journal of Business Logistics* 10, no. 2 (1989): 1–23.

Manheim, Marvin L. "Global Information Technology: Issues and Opportunities," in *Proceedings of the 24th Hawaii International Conference on System Sciences,* ed. Ralph Sprague (Los Alamitos, CA: IEEE Press, 1991).

Mentzer, John T., and Jon Schroeter. "Integrating Logistics Forecasting Techniques, Systems, and Administration: The Multiple Forecasting System," *Journal of Business Logistics* 15, no. 2 (1994): 205–25.

Mentzer, John T., and Nimish Gandhi. "Microcomputers versus Mainframes: Use among Logistics and Marketing Professionals," *International Journal of Physical Distribution and Logistics Management* 23, no. 3 (1993): 3–10.

Mentzer, John T.; Camille P. Schuster; and David J. Roberts. "Microcomputer versus Mainframe Usage in Logistics," *Logistics and Transportation Review* 26, no. 2 (June 1990): 115–32.

Monczka, Robert M., and Joseph R. Carter. "Implementing Electronic Data Interchange," *Journal of Purchasing and Materials Management* (Spring 1989): 26–33.

Powers, Richard F. "Optimization Models for Logistics Decisions," *Journal of Business Logistics* 10, no. 1 (1989): 106–21.

Rao, Kant; Alan J. Stenger; and Haw-Jan Wu. "Integrating the Use of Computers in Logistics Education," *International Journal of Physical Distribution and Logistics Management* 22, no. 2 (1992): 3–15.

Rogers, Dale S.; Patricia J. Daugherty; and Theodore P. Stank. "Enhancing Service Responsiveness: The Strategic Potential of EDI," *International Journal of Physical Distribution and Logistics Management* 22, no. 8 (1992): 15–20.

Stenger, Alan J. "Information Systems in Logistics Management: Past, Present, and Future," *Transportation Journal* 26, no. 1 (Fall 1986): 65–82.

Stenger, Alan J.; Steven C. Dunn; and Richard R. Young. "Commercially Available Software for Integrated Logistics Management," *The International Journal of Logistics Management* 4, no. 2 (1993): 61–74.

Temple, Barker & Sloane, Inc. *Logistics Data Interchange: An Emerging Competitive Weapon for Shippers* (Lexington, MA: Temple, Barker & Sloane, Inc., 1987).

Williams, Lisa R. "Understanding Distribution Channels: An Interorganizational Study of EDI Adoption," *Journal of Business Logistics* 15, no. 2 (1994): 173–203.

STRATEGIC ISSUES FOR LOGISTICS

The successful implementation of a logistics supply chain is a challenging and formidable task for any logistics manager. The complexity and intensity of today's marketplace creates an environment that is both stimulating and somewhat overwhelming. However, the successful manager recognizes that there are some "anchors" and areas of focus that help him or her "do it the right way."

The purpose of Part III is to help the logistics manager with resolving the thornier, more long-run issues he or she faces. Chapter 12 examines a critical long-run issue for efficient and effective logistics systems, *viz.*, logistics network design and facility location.

Chapter 13 provides an overview of and framework for discussing the special challenges of global logistics. Supply chains are typically global in today's marketplace. Companies procure supplies in foreign countries, manufacture in multiple locations worldwide, and sell in many international markets. Logistics is the link to all of these geographically dispersed activities.

Chapter 14 discusses the organization of the logistics process. Organizational issues in logistics have taken on increasing importance. Many companies are enhancing their logistics function by utilizing third-party logistics providers. This choice of inside versus outside services has added a new element to the decision making related to organizations. Using third-party companies can be an effective way to reduce costs, but it also has the potential to create additional problems.

Chapter 15, the book's final chapter, addresses the leading edge strategies that companies have utilized successfully to gain a competitive advantage. Discussing such strategies in the final chapter is a way to summarize many of the ideas that have been presented in this book.

CHAPTER 12

NETWORK DESIGN AND FACILITY LOCATION

LEARNING OBJECTIVES

After reading this chapter, you should be able to do the following:

- Identify factors that may suggest a need to redesign a logistics network.

- Structure an effective process for logistics network design.

- Be aware of key locational determinants and the impact they may have on prospective locational alternatives.

- Understand the different types of modeling approaches that may be used to gain insight into logistics network design and facility location.

- Apply the simple "grid" or center-of-gravity approach to facility location.

- Have knowledge of certain ways in which transportation and transportation costs affect the location decision.

- Be knowledgeable about several of the classical theories of location.

LOGISTICS PROFILE

STRIDE RITE CORPORATION

The "speed-to-market" retailing philosophy drives customer service in many American businesses today. In a fiercely competitive market, getting the right product to the right customer at the right time contributes handsomely to success.

As part of an effort to implement that philosophy in its logistics operations, Stride Rite Corporation recently relocated its distribution center to Louisville, Kentucky, a move that allowed the footwear maker to bring state-of-the-art technology to its warehouse function. "We wanted to improve speed to market on the inbound side and on the shipping side," says Stride Rite's vice president of logistics. "We looked at doing this through improvements in our operations."

One of America's leading sellers of adult and children's footwear, Stride Rite had outgrown its two distribution facilities in Massachusetts. The company, which recorded sales of $584 million in 1993, was having difficulty getting product shipped quickly enough to meet a two-day order turnaround commitment to customers. Stride Rite realized that, if it aspired to one-day order turnaround, a new, modern, paperless facility would be needed.

Actually, the management team looking into the issue hired a distribution consultant to conduct a site survey to determine the best location for a warehouse to serve Stride Rite's U.S. customers. After completing this study, the consultant proposed that the company situate its new distribution center somewhere in Ohio, Kentucky, or Tennessee.

Because the company had a long-standing commitment to Massachusetts, Stride Rite's executive board applied to the Commonwealth for some tax relief or incentives for the company to maintain distribution operations there before going ahead with the relocation plan. Based on a sound economic analysis indicating that the costs of transportation, labor, and land all pointed toward relocation out of Massachusetts, and the failure of the Commonwealth to come up with a plan to retain Stride Rite, the decision to move was made. According to the vice president of logistics, "When you added the customer service advantage to the costs, there was no way for us to justify staying."

After weighing the pros and cons of moving, Stride Rite opted to relocate to a facility that would take advantage of existing, proven technology to expedite receipt, storage, and shipment. The company spent $30 million on the entire project, which involved both closing down its old facilities and building a new distribution center. Despite the high price tag, Stride Rite officials consider it money well spent. The new facility is designed to ship 65 million pairs of shoes annually in a two-shift operation, nearly double the 35 million pairs handled in the three-shift operation back in Massachusetts.

ADAPTED FROM: James Aaron Cooke, "Stride Rite Steps Up the Pace," *Traffic Management* (June, 1994): 28–31. Reprinted by permission from *Traffic Management.*

---

strategic importance

As firms search for new ways to lower costs and improve service to their customers, the issue of where to locate logistics and manufacturing facilities has never been more complex or critical. In addition to enhancing the efficiency and effectiveness of a logistics operation, the redesign of a firm's logistics network can help to differentiate a firm in the marketplace. Several examples illustrate this type of success:[1]

- A leading pharmaceutical distributor with nationwide service recently reduced its logistics network from more than 60 to 20 distribution centers, while offering its customers a selection of service responses from which to choose (for example, same-day delivery, regular service, and so on).

- A prominent office products company reduced its network of distribution facilities from 11 to 3, while substantially increasing the level of cross-docking activity with its customers and significantly improving logistical customer service.
- A direct-selling company with a national distribution capability reengineered its customer service operation and eliminated a major distribution point, which resulted in significant reductions to its fixed assets and operating expenses, at the same time differentiating its services to meet a recognized range of customer requirements.
- A major manufacturer of semiconductor products recently consolidated its logistics network into a single, global distribution center in Singapore, and engaged a third-party supplier of express logistics services to manage its overall distribution activity. The end results included lower cost, improved service, and a new way for the firm to differentiate itself in the marketplace.

While there are also examples of the opposite situation, in which firms have justifiably expanded their logistics networks and increased the number of distribution facilities, the move to consolidate existing systems is far more common. Assuming that a firm considers the impact of such a decision on total logistics cost, it is not unusual for the inventory cost savings associated with consolidating facilities to outweigh any additional transportation expense involved with moving product to the customer. Also, the use of currently available information technology, coupled with the time-sensitive capabilities of many suppliers of transportation service, can mean that such a move enhances responsiveness and the levels of service experienced by customers.

change process This chapter first looks at several strategic aspects of logistics network design. While it may sometimes be that "change for the sake of change" is needed, a number of prominent factors may suggest that a redesign of the logistics network may be appropriate. Next, the process of logistics network redesign is examined in detail. This content will provide a useful framework for understanding the key steps that must be included in a comprehensive approach to logistics network design and facility location.

locational determinants Following these discussions, attention will shift to several major locational determinants. These factors may be either regionally focused or site-specific. Also included is a summary of current trends governing site selection. The chapter concludes with coverage of several modeling approaches that can be used to provide insight into the issues of logistics network design and facility location. Several examples of transportation-specific factors are also included. Appendix 12A provides a perspective on some of the classical theories of location.

THE NEED FOR LONG-RANGE PLANNING

In the short run, a firm's logistics network and the locations of its key facilities are givens, and the logistics manager must operate within the constraints imposed by the facility locations. Site availability, leases, contracts, and investments make changing facility locations impractical in the short run. In the long run, however, the design of the logistics network must be thought of as variable. Management decisions can and should be made to change the network to meet the logistics requirements imposed by customers, suppliers, and competitive changes.

In addition, the decisions as to network design and facility location that are made today will have implications far into the future. A facility properly located under today's economic, competitive, and technological conditions may not be at an optimum location under future conditions. Today's facility location decision will have a significant effect on future costs in such areas as logistics, marketing, manufacturing, and finance. Thus, the facility location decision must seriously consider anticipated business conditions and acknowledge a critical need to be flexible and responsive to customer needs as they may change in the future. This latter concern heightens the attractiveness of the third-party logistics option for many logistics operations today.

future implications

THE STRATEGIC IMPORTANCE OF LOGISTICS NETWORK DESIGN

Why analyze the logistics network? In essence, the answer lies in the fact that all businesses operate in a very dynamic environment in which change is the only constant. Characteristics of consumer and industrial-buyer demand, technology, competition, markets, and suppliers are constantly changing. As a result, business must redeploy its resources in response to and in anticipation of this ever-changing environment.

Considering the rate at which change is occurring, it is questionable whether any existing logistics network can be truly current or up to date. Any logistics network that has been in existence for a number of years is certainly a candidate for reevaluation and potential redesign. Even if the existing system is not functionally obsolete, an analysis of the existing network will probably uncover new opportunities to reduce cost and/or improve service.

network redesign

This section focuses attention on several types of change that may suggest a need to reevaluate and/or redesign a firm's logistics network. While not all of these factors will affect any single firm at the same time, they represent some of the more frequently changing elements of the business environment that affect logistics and supply chain management.

Changing Customer Service Requirements

As was discussed in Chapters 1 through 4, the logistical requirements of customers are changing in numerous ways. As a result, the need to reevaluate and redesign logistics networks is of great contemporary interest. While some customers have intensified their demands for more efficient and more effective logistics services, others are seeking relationships with suppliers who can take logistical capabilities and performance to new, unprecedented levels.

changing requirements

While customer service requirements may experience change, the types of customers served may also evolve over time. Consider, for example, the case of food manufacturers who have distributed their product to independent stores and regional retail chains for many years and who have recently added mass merchants to their list of customers.[2] Another example is manufacturers of stationery who

examples

traditionally served a multitude of customers, from small retail to club stores, but who now focus primarily on distributors of office supply products. In both of these examples, change has occurred at both the customer and supply chain level, with significant impacts on lead times, order size and frequency, and associated activities such as shipment notification, marking and tagging, and packaging.

Shifting Locations of Customer and/or Supply Markets

dynamic marketplace Considering that manufacturing and logistics facilities are positioned in the supply chain between customer and supply markets, any changes in these markets should cause a firm to reevaluate its logistics network. When the U.S. population shifted to the Southeast and Southwest, for example, new warehouses and distribution facilities followed the changing geo-location trends. As a result, cities such as Atlanta, Houston, and Reno/Sparks have become popular distribution center locations for companies serving these increasing population centers.

On the supply side, the service and cost requirements of the automobile industry's movement to JIT-based manufacturing have forced companies to examine the locations of logistics facilities. Many suppliers to Saturn Corporation in Spring Hill, Tennessee, for example, have selected nearby points for manufacturing and/or parts distribution facilities.

global examples On the global scene, the collapse of economic and political walls in Eastern Europe, plus the unification initiatives of the European Union, have forced many U.S. companies to examine facility locations in terms of their suitability for competition in these rapidly developing markets. In addition to reconfiguring their logistics networks, firms facing these challenges have taken steps such as establishing European branch operations and entering into joint agreements with European-based companies to gain a presence in this potentially significant marketplace.

Sourcing of raw materials from offshore suppliers is another reason to analyze the location of existing facilities. Using Pacific Rim suppliers makes the western United States a desirable location for a distribution center, whereas an East Coast location would be more desirable for a company receiving similar materials from Europe. As world economies become more interdependent, these facility location decisions will become more common.

Change in Corporate Ownership

A relatively common occurrence today is for a firm to experience an ownership-related change associated with a merger, acquisition, or divestiture. In such instances, many companies choose to be proactive and to conduct a formal evaluation of new versus previous logistics networks in advance of such a change. This is very helpful in terms of making sure that the newly merged or newly independent firm will have fully anticipated the logistics impacts of the change in corporate ownership. In other instances, the logistics manager may be the last one to find out about the impending change, and the role of logistics network design immediately takes on a defensive posture.

Even if the logistics impacts are not part of the planning process, it is critical for firms to reassess their logistics networks following ownership-related changes such as those identified above. Such changes increase the likelihood that the new operation is duplicating effort and incurring unnecessary logistics expense.

Cost Pressures

A major priority for many firms today is to figure out new and innovative ways to take cost out of their key business processes, including these relating to logistics. In such instances, a reevaluation of the logistics network and the functioning of the overall supply chain can frequently help to uncover new sources of such savings. Whether the answer lies in reducing cost in transportation, inventory, warehousing, or another area, a detailed examination of the current system versus alternative approaches can be exceptionally useful.

sources of cost savings

For example, labor issues have caused many firms to analyze a facility's location. High labor costs or restrictive union work rules have caused companies to move production and logistics facilities from the Northeast to the South, as well as to Mexico and the Pacific Rim countries. Companies balance the lower labor costs in these areas against what may be higher costs for transportation, inventory, and communications.

Companies considering plant modernization needs also sometimes benefit from a comprehensive cost analysis, which might accompany a reevaluation of the logistics network. A firm considering an investment of millions of dollars in an existing plant must ask, "Is this the proper location for a plant, given the current and future customer and vendor locations?"

Competitive Capabilities

Another factor relates to competitive pressures that may force a company to examine its logistics service levels and the costs generated by its network of logistics facilities. To remain competitive in the marketplace or to develop a competitive advantage, a company should frequently examine the relative locations of its facilities toward the goal of improving service and/or lowering costs. Companies often conduct this network review in light of newly developed transport alternatives.

For example, FedEx Logistics Services has established its PartsBank® operations near several of its major airport locations. The FedEx PartsBank maintains an inventory of its clients' high-value, time-sensitive products and fills and ships orders at the client's instruction. The resulting service level is higher, and the total cost of the comprehensive, express logistics services is lower than the total cost of warehousing the needed inventories at various locations in the client's logistics network. This innovative third-party logistics offering has been met with enthusiasm in the marketplace, as firms replace their own higher-cost logistics network with one that operates at lower cost and higher service levels.

FedEx PartsBank

Corporate Organizational Change

It is not unusual for logistics network design to become a topic of discussion at the same time that a firm considers any major corporate organizational change, such as downsizing. In such instances, the strategic functioning of the firm's logistics network is viewed as something that must be protected and even enhanced through the process of organizational change.

downsizing

reengineering   Considering the current popularity of corporate reengineering efforts, the logistics process is frequently a prime candidate for attention. For example, many firms today have become involved in the reengineering of their order fulfillment process, which has significant implications for the firm's logistics function. An important component of the overall effort will include a systematic evaluation of and recommendations for change to the firm's logistics network.

LOGISTICS NETWORK DESIGN

complex process   A firm must consider many factors as it approaches the task of determining the optimum design of its logistics network. These factors will be identified and discussed at a later point in this chapter. At the outset, however, it is important to realize that the task of designing an appropriate logistics network should be coordinated closely with the identification and implementation of key corporate and overall business strategies. Since the process of designing or redesigning a firm's logistics network can be complex, it will be discussed in the context of a major corporate reengineering process.

    Figure 12–1 identifies the six major steps that are recommended for a comprehensive logistics network design process. Each of these steps is discussed in detail below.

Step 1: Define the Logistics Network Design Process

logistics network reengineering team   Of initial importance is the formation of a logistics network reengineering team to be responsible for all elements of the logistics network design process. This team will first need to become aware of overall corporate and business strategies and the underlying business needs of the firm and the supply chains in which it is a participant.

design process objectives   Also in this step it will be important to establish the parameters and objectives of the logistics network design or redesign process itself. An awareness of the expectations of senior management, for example, will be essential to the effective progress of the overall reengineering process. Issues pertaining to the availability of needed resources in the areas of funding, people, and systems must be understood at an early stage in the process.

third-party suppliers   An additional topic to be addressed early on is the potential involvement of third-party suppliers of logistics services as a means of achieving the firm's logistics objectives. This consideration is critical, since it will expand the mind-set of the network design team to include a consideration of logistics network solutions that may involve externally provided as well as proprietary logistics resources.

Step 2: Perform a Logistics Audit

audit steps   The logistics audit provides members of the reengineering team with a comprehensive perspective on the firm's logistics process. In addition, it will help to gather essential types of information that will be useful throughout future steps in the redesign process. Figure 12–2 indicates a number of key steps that should be included in a logistics audit. Listed here are examples of the types of information that should become available as a result of this audit:

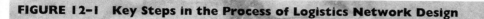

FIGURE 12–1   Key Steps in the Process of Logistics Network Design

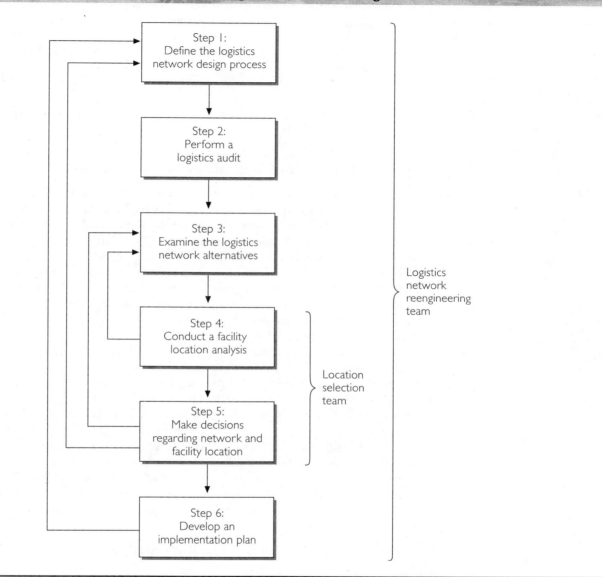

FIGURE 12-2   Key Steps in a Logistics Audit

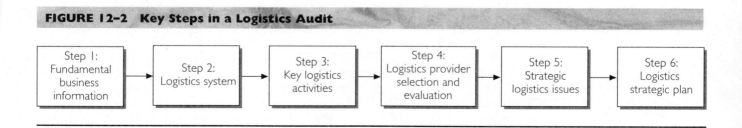

**important
information**

- Customer requirements and key environmental factors
- Key logistics goals and objectives
- Profile of the current logistics network and the firm's positioning in respective supply chain(s)
- Benchmark, or target, values for logistics costs and key performance measurements
- Identification of gaps between current and desired logistics performance (qualitative and quantitative)
- Key objectives for logistics network design, expressed in terms that will facilitate measurement

Step 3: Examine the Logistics Network Alternatives

**basic modeling
alternatives**

The next step is to examine the available alternatives for the logistics network. This involves applying suitable quantitative models to the current logistics system as well as to the alternative systems and approaches under consideration. The use of these models provides considerable insight into the functioning and cost/service effectiveness of the various possible networks. The principal modeling approach will be optimization, simulation, or heuristic. These approaches will be explored in detail later in this chapter. Briefly, optimization approaches search for "best" solutions, simulation models replicate the functioning of the logistics network, and heuristic techniques are able to accommodate broad problem definitions but do not provide optimum solutions.

insight, not answers

Once an appropriate modeling procedure has been selected, it should be used to help identify a logistics network that is consistent with the key objectives identified during the logistics audit. Although at first reengineering teams often look to the model to suggest answers to the key questions that have been raised, they quickly realize that the modeling effort is likely to produce more insight than answers.

Once preliminary design solutions have been identified, subsequent "what if" types of analysis should be conducted to test the sensitivity of recommended network designs to changes in key logistics variables. The results of this step should provide a valuable set of recommendations for the number and general location of logistics facilities that will help to meet the desired objectives.

Step 4: Conduct a Facility Location Analysis

**qualitative and
quantitative**

Once a general configuration of the desired logistics network has been recommended, the next task is to carefully analyze the attributes of specific regions and cities that are candidates for sites of logistics facilities. These analyses will have both quantitative and qualitative aspects. Many of the quantitative elements have already been incorporated into step 3 of the modeling effort. The qualitative aspects, to be discussed in a later section of this chapter, include such considerations as labor climate, transportation issues, proximity to markets and customers, quality of life, taxes and industrial development incentives, supplier networks, land costs and utilities, and company preference.

**location selection
team**

The effort in this step will be facilitated by the formation of a location selection team, which will collect information on specific attributes such as those identified above. In addition, this team should be able to examine potential sites in terms of topography, geology, and facility design. To supplement internally available resources, the firm may wish to engage the services of a consulting firm that specializes in assisting clients with the process of selecting a location.

The first screening by the location selection team will usually eliminate areas that are uneconomical from a logistics perspective, thereby reducing the number of alternatives. For example, consider the number of potential distribution center sites in the southeastern United States. Applying the logistics location determinant, the team may find that the logistically optimum location is in the Tennessee/ Georgia area. This definitely reduces the number of potential sites and enables the team to direct the location analysis toward a specific area.

initial screening

Step 5: Make Decisions Regarding Network and Facility Location

Next, the network and specific sites for logistics facilities recommended in steps 3 and 4 should be evaluated for consistency with the design criteria that were identified in step 1. This step should confirm the types of change that are needed to the firm's logistics network and should do so in the context of overall supply chain positioning. Although the feasibility of involving third-party suppliers should have been incorporated into the alternatives that were evaluated in the two preceding steps, the decision to involve external suppliers will have cost and service implications as well as strategic ones.

compare recommendations with criteria

Step 6: Develop an Implementation Plan

Once the overall direction has been established, the development of an effective implementation plan, or "blueprint for change," is critical. This plan should serve as a useful road map for moving from the current logistics network to the desired one. Since it was known from the beginning that this reengineering process was likely to produce recommendations for significant change, it is important that the firm commit the resources necessary to assure a smooth, timely implementation.

strategic implementation

MAJOR LOCATIONAL DETERMINANTS

The focus of step 4 in the logistics network redesign process is on analyzing the attributes of specific regions and areas that are candidates for sites of logistics facilities. Table 12–1 lists a number of major locational determinants for both regional and site-specific locations. While these factors are listed in general order of importance, the relative weighting applied to each will depend on the details of the specific location decision under consideration.

The importance of major locational determinants will vary among industries and among individual companies within specific industries. For example, labor-intensive industries such as textiles, furniture, and household appliances will place significant emphasis on the availability and cost of labor in both regional and local market areas. Alternatively, manufacturers of high tech products such as computers and peripherals, semiconductors, and engineering and scientific instruments will place great emphasis on assuring the availability of a highly qualified workforce with very specific technical skills. For industries such as drugs, beverages,

variation by industry and company

TABLE 12–1 Major Locational Determinants

Regional Determinants	Site-Specific Determinants
Labor climate	Transportation access
Availability of transportation	• Truck
Proximity to markets and customers	• Air
Quality of life	• Rail
Taxes and industrial development incentives	• Water
Supplier networks	Inside/outside metropolitan area
Land costs and utilities	Availability of workforce
Company preference	Land costs and taxes
	Utilities

and printing and publishing, in which competition or logistics costs are significant, other logistics variables will be very important.

Key Factors for Consideration

This discussion will focus attention on the regional determinants shown in Table 12–1. Because the site-specific determinants cannot be generalized as readily, this level of detail should be acquired through the efforts of the location selection team.

Labor Climate.   Location decision makers consider a number of factors in determining an area's labor climate. Given the typically labor-intensive nature of many logistics operations, labor cost and availability will prove to be major issues of concern. Other factors to be considered include the workforce's degree of unionization, skill level, work ethic, productivity, and the enthusiasm of local public officials. The existence of state right-to-work laws (which prohibit union membership as a condition of employment), and the unionization of major area employers reveal the area work force's degree of unionization. Government information regarding work stoppages, productivity (value added per employee), and skill levels is available for most areas. Data regarding hourly earnings by industry and occupation are available from governmental agencies.

Another labor-related factor to be considered is the rate of unemployment in the local areas under consideration. While many other factors may seem to be quite acceptable, low levels of unemployment may require a firm to significantly increase its projected hourly wage scales to attract qualified workers. This sometimes unexpected increase may affect the overall attractiveness of a particular local area under consideration. The location study team will need to visit areas of potential interest to gather impressions and study attitudes regarding work ethic, absenteeism, potential labor-management issues, and the cooperativeness of state and local public officials.

transport services and cost *Availability of Transportation.*   Given the need by many firms for high-quality, capable transportation services, this factor is of great significance in many location decisions. Depending on the product type and industry to be served, a suitable location may require one or more of the following features: interstate highway access, availability of intermodal or local rail facilities, convenience of a major airport facility, proximity to inland or ocean port facilities, and so on. The number of serving carriers, as well as the breadth of overall transport capabilities, are factors that may need to be evaluated.

Considering the significant service improvements that have been made in recent years by many transportation firms, most regional and local areas will be strong in at least one or more areas related to transportation. For certain high-value, low-weight products, such as computers, semiconductors, and electronic equipment, it may be that the location decision will focus on identifying a single national or international geographical area from which to distribute the company's entire manufactured output. Given the time-sensitive logistics services available today from firms such as FedEx, UPS, RPS, DHL, and Airborne, this strategy is becoming more prevalent.

Proximity to Markets and Customers. The nearness-to-market factor usually considers both logistics and competitive variables. Logistics variables include the availability of transportation, the freight cost, and the geographical market size that can be served, for example, on a same-day or next-morning basis. The greater the number of customer firms within the market area, the greater the competitive advantage offered by the proposed location. **market oriented**

Although many companies place a high priority on locating logistics facilities near markets and customers, an overly complex logistics network can be disadvantageous from a cost perspective. Also, the availability of high-quality transportation services and capable information technologies have resulted in an expansion of the geographical areas that can be served in a timely manner from key logistics facilities.

Quality of Life. A particular region's or area's quality of life is difficult to quantify, but it does affect the well-being of employees and the quality of the work they are expected to perform. The quality of life factor is more important to companies that must attract and retain a mobile professional and technical workforce capable of moving to any location. Such a situation is common in the high tech industry, especially in a company's research and development operations. The *Places Rated Almanac*[3] rates the quality of life in metropolitan areas in terms of climate, housing costs, health care and environment, crime, passenger transportation, education, recreation, the arts, and economic opportunities.

Taxes and Industrial Development Incentives. It is important to have advance knowledge of state and local taxes that apply to businesses and individuals. Prevailing business taxes, including revenue or income taxes, inventory taxes, property taxes, and so on will have a significant impact on the cost of operating a business in the area under consideration. Personal taxes that may affect the attractiveness of a particular region or local area include taxes on income and property, as well as applicable sales taxes, excise taxes, and so forth. **financial considerations**

Another significant factor is the availability of industrial development incentives, which are used by some states and communities to entice companies to locate in their area. Examples include tax incentives (reduced rates or tax abatements on things such as property, inventory, or sales), financing arrangements (state loans or state-guaranteed loans), reduced water and sewage rates, and rent-free buildings that are built by the community to the company's specifications. Most states have an industrial development commission that provides information about state and local inducements. In addition, early contact and discussions with representatives of the state and local-area banking institutions and financial communities will provide a wide range of useful information, as well as commitments regarding financing and other services.

Mercedes-Benz example   As an example, in 1993 the State of Alabama offered numerous incentives in its successful effort to be selected as the site for Mercedes-Benz AG's first U.S. car plant.[4] Among the incentives offered were agreement to build a $35 million training center at the company's plant and to pay employees' salaries while they studied; willingness to purchase more than 2,500 Mercedes vehicles for state use; and prominent placement of the distinctive Mercedes emblem in a football stadium in which the big, televised Alabama-Tennessee football game was scheduled to be played. Overall, it was estimated that Alabama would provide Mercedes with well over $300 million in industrial development incentives in return for being selected as the site for the new facility.

supply oriented   *Supplier Networks.*   In the case of a manufacturing facility, the availability and cost of raw materials and component parts, and the cost of transporting these materials to the proposed plant site, will be of significance. For a distribution center, it will be important to know how the proposed facility sites will fit with the geographic locations of key supplier facilities. In either instance, the cost and service sensitivity of the inbound movements from suppliers will be important to consider.

Land Costs and Utilities.   Depending on the type of facility under consideration, issues relating to the cost of land and the availability of needed utilities will be more or less critical. In the case of a manufacturing plant or distribution center, for example, it may be that a certain minimum acreage or parcel size will be needed for current use as well as future expansion. This represents a potentially significant expense. Factors such as local building codes and cost of construction will be important to consider. Also, the availability and expense of utilities such as electrical power, sewage, and industrial waste disposal will need to be factored into the decision-making process.

Company Preference.   Aside from all of the preceding types of factors, it may be that a company, or its CEO for that matter, prefers a certain region and/or local area for the location of a logistics facility. For example, a company may prefer to locate all new facilities in rural areas within fifty miles of a major metropolitan area. Or a company may wish to locate its facilities in areas where competitors already have a presence. In other instances, a firm may wish to locate facilities in an area where it may enjoy common access with other firms to benefits such as a skilled labor supply, excellent marketing resources, or proximity to key supplier industries. This determinant is referred to as "agglomeration," a topic that will be referred to again in the appendix to this chapter.

Current Trends Governing Site Selection

There are a number of trends in today's logistics environment that may have significant effects on decisions involving logistics facility location. Included among these are the following:[5]

- Direct, plant-to-customer shipments, which, if economical and practical, can diminish the need for field warehouses or distribution centers.
- "Drop" shipments that arrive directly from suppliers and bypass intermediate distribution facilities.
- Cross-docking operations that may involve the consolidation of multiple-vendor loads into full trailerloads being shipped to retail stores or points of use. Applied to inbound movements, this concept can eliminate the need for inbound consolidation facilities.
- Strategic use of centralized as well as regionally focused distribution facilities, typically in conjunction with the use of an inventory segmentation strategy.
- Use of third-party suppliers of logistics services to assume all responsibility for the warehousing and distribution of all or a portion of a company's products.

MODELING APPROACHES

As Appendix 12A indicates, the classical location theories concentrate attention on transportation cost as the major locational determinant. These theories emphasize selecting the location that minimizes total transportation costs and, by implicit assumption, maximizes profits. While these approaches are valid, they are narrow in scope. Considering the other issues relating to cost and to logistical customer service that need to be addressed, it is important to look at a broader set of techniques that apply to the location decision.

This section focuses broadly on the topic of modeling approaches that can provide insight into the choice of a logistics network design. As such, the techniques discussed here are applicable to a wide range of issues pertaining to the locations of plants, distribution centers, customers, and to the flows of product and information to support the functioning of the logistics network. The principal modeling approaches to be covered are optimization, simulation, and heuristic models. Detailed coverage of the grid method for facility location is included as part of the discussion of heuristic modeling approaches.

As was indicated previously, the use of appropriate modeling techniques will facilitate a comparison of the functioning and cost/service effectiveness of current versus proposed logistics networks. Once an appropriate modeling procedure has been selected, it should be used to help identify a logistics network that is consistent with the key objectives identified earlier in the logistics network redesign process. After preliminary solutions have been identified, subsequent "what if" types of analyses should be conducted to test the sensitivity of the recommended network designs to changes in key logistics variables. *use of techniques*

Optimization Models

The optimization model is based on precise mathematical procedures that are guaranteed to find the "best," or optimum, solution, given the mathematical definition of the problem under evaluation. This means that it can be proved mathematically that the resulting solution is the best. The simple EOQ model, discussed in Chapter 6, produces an optimum solution. *search for optimum solutions*

While recognizing relevant constraints, optimization approaches essentially select an optimal course of action from a number of feasible alternatives. The op-

TABLE 12-2   Examples of Vendors of Facility Location Optimization Modeling Software

Company	Model Name
Arthur D. Little	ADLnet
Chesapeake Decision Sciences, Inc.	MIMI
Cleveland Consulting Associates	LOCATE/SP
Haverly Systems, Inc.	OMNI HS/LP
Herbert W. Davis and Company	ASSIGN
Insight, Inc.	SAILS
J. F. Shapiro Associates	SLIM
Ketron Management Science	LOPTIS
Mercer Management Consulting	LPS
Metron	TERRALIGN
Microanalytics, Inc.	OPTISITE
R. H. Ballou	NETWORK
Simplex Consulting	DCSITE
SRI International	POFL

SOURCE: Tan Miller, "Learning about Facility Location Models," *Distribution* (May 1993): 50. Used with permission.

timization models in use today incorporate such techniques as mathematical programming (linear, integer, dynamic, mixed-integer linear, etc.), enumeration, sequencing, and the use of calculus.[6] Many of these have been incorporated into software packages for mainframe, minicomputer, and microcomputer use. Table 12–2 identifies several capable software packages that are useful for logistics network design.

key issues
Figure 12–3 lists the types of issues that may be addressed through the use of optimization techniques. Several advantages of this overall type of approach are as follows:

- The user is guaranteed to have the best solution possible for a given set of assumptions and data.
- Many complex model structures can be handled correctly.
- The analysis and evaluation of all alternatives that are generated result in a more efficient analysis.
- Reliable run-to-run comparisons can be made, since the "best" solution is guaranteed for each run.
- Cost or profit savings between the optimum and heuristic solution can be significant.[7]

linear programming
One of the optimization techniques that has traditionally received significant attention is linear programming, or LP. This approach is most useful for linking facilities in a network where supply and demand limitations at plants, distribution centers, or market areas must be treated as constraints. Given an objective function that focuses attention on, for example, minimizing total cost, LP defines the optimum facility distribution pattern consistent with the problem's demand-supply constraints. Although this technique is actually quite useful, its applicability is limited due to the need for the problem formulation to be deterministic and capable of linear approximation. Also, the use of LP itself does not allow for consideration of fixed as well as variable costs of operating logistics facilities.

FIGURE 12–3 Strategic Issues Relevant to Logistics Network Modeling

NETWORK RATIONALIZATION ISSUES

- Customer service levels to be maintained
- Assignments of customers to distribution centers (DCs)
- Number and locations of DCs
- DC operation—proprietary versus third party
- SKUs to be stocked at each DC; full-line versus segmented
- Assignments of DCs to plants by product
- Number and locations of plants
- How much and what to produce at each plant
- Supplier network analysis; need for inbound to manufacturing consolidation centers
- Transportation modal alternatives to be considered

"WHAT IF" QUESTIONS

- Environmental issues
  - Market shifts
  - Strikes, natural disasters, energy shortages
  - Global economic conditions
- Business decision and policy issues
  - Plant capacity expansion
  - New product introduction
  - Shipment planning policy analysis
  - DC capacity expansion or elimination
  - Multidivision distribution system merger

COST AND SERVICE SENSITIVITY ISSUES

- Distribution cost versus customer service
- Distribution cost as a function of number of DCs
- Demand forecasts

ADAPTED FROM: *SAILS™ (Strategic Analysis for Integrated Logistics Systems)*, (Alexandria, VA: Insight, Inc., 1994). Used with permission.

The use of mixed-integer linear programming permits the model to deal with issues such as fixed and variable costs, capacity constraints, economies of scale, cross-product limitations, and unique sourcing requirements. One of the leading models of this type is SAILS™ (Strategic Analysis for Integrated Logistics Systems), developed by Insight, Inc., which is available for use on a personal computer, as well as on mainframes and client-servers. In brief, SAILS answers the question "Given demand for a set of products, either historical or forecast, what is the optimal configuration of the production/distribution network to satisfy that demand at specified service levels and lowest cost?"

Once a modeling database, either simple or complex, has been created, the use of SAILS facilitates the rapid generation and evaluation of many alternate scenarios for analysis.[8] There are also numerous shipment planning controls that permit the user to evaluate the network impact of various shipment planning options such as pooling, stop-offs, pickups, and direct plant shipments. SAILS is a highly flexible logistics modeling tool that can be used for a range of problems from the very simple to ones in which data may exist in the form of millions of shipment transactions. When a given modeling scenario has been generated,

SAILS™

SAILS utilizes mixed-integer linear programming, along with an advanced technique called network factorization, to produce an optimum solution.

Although optimization approaches typically require significant computer resources, the availability of capable mainframe, minicomputer, and microcomputer systems today has greatly facilitated their ease of use. Along with improvements in model design and solver technologies, future approaches should be even more convenient for general use by those involved with the design and analysis of logistics networks.

Simulation Models

The second approach to logistics network design includes the development and use of simulation models. Simulation is defined as "the process of designing a model of a real system and conducting experiments with this model for the purpose either of understanding the behavior of the system or of evaluating various strategies within the limits imposed by a criterion or set of criteria for the operation of the system."[9] Network simulation involves developing a computer representation of the logistics network and then observing the cost and service characteristics of the network as cost structures, constraints, and other factors are varied. It has been stated that the process of simulation is "nothing more or less than the technique of performing *sampling experiments* on the model of the system."[10]

sensitivity analysis
For location analysis, the use of simulation allows the decision maker to test the effect of alternative locations upon costs and service levels. The modeling requires extensive data collection and analysis to determine how system factors such as transportation, warehousing, inventory, materials handling, and labor costs interact. The simulation process evaluates the decision maker's selected sites to determine respective costs. Simulation does not guarantee an optimum solution but simply evaluates the alternatives that are fed into it.[11]

static versus dynamic
A critical characteristic of a simulation tool is whether it is static or dynamic in nature. A dynamic tool will not only incorporate a multiperiod time perspective, but also will update system status for each time period based on the results of the previous time periods. Although many simulations are uniquely developed for a particular network design scenario, there are a number of simulators that specifically respond to logistics problems. As identified by Ronald H. Ballou,[12] some of these include LREPS,[13] PIPELINE MANAGER,[14] LSD,[15] LOCATE,[16] and SPSF.[17] When appropriate, other software has been written using the capabilities of general simulation languages such as SIMSCRIPT, GPSS, DYNAMO, and SLAM.[18]

Although simulation models are not designed to produce optimum solutions, they are very capable in terms of their ability to incorporate relatively comprehensive and detailed problem descriptions. Sometimes an optimization approach is used first to identify and evaluate feasible network design alternatives, and then highly customized simulation models are used to focus on the exact logistics network that will best meet the desired objectives.

Heuristic Models

Heuristic models are able to accommodate broad problem definitions, but they do not provide an optimum solution. The use of a heuristic approach can help to reduce a problem to a manageable size and search automatically through various alternatives in an attempt to find a better solution. As will be indicated in the discussion of the grid technique that follows, heuristic approaches can provide a good approximation to the least-cost location in a complex decision problem. To reduce the number of location alternatives, the decision maker should incorporate into the heuristic program site characteristics considered to be optimal.

For example, the location team may consider an optimum warehouse site to be (1) within 20 miles of a major market area, (2) at least 250 miles from other company distribution centers, (3) within 3 miles of an interstate highway, and (4) within 40 miles of a major airport facility. The heuristic model searches for sites with these characteristics, thus reducing the number of alternative sites to those the decision maker considers practical.

Additionally, heuristic decision rules are sometimes incorporated into the decision-making process in what may appear to be "rules of thumb." Examples might include requirements to locate distribution centers at or near points of demand, to supply customers from the nearest distribution facility, to choose as the next distribution site the one that will produce the greatest cost savings, or to serve all customers within a 24-hour delivery time.[19]

Example of a Heuristic Modeling Approach: The Grid Technique

Although other factors are also important, the availability and expense of transportation service is one that is commonly included in location analyses. While transportation itself can represent a significant cost, decision makers should strive to make the final decision on the basis of the full range of relevant cost factors, as well as on the customer service implications of the network alternative being evaluated.

grid technique

The grid technique is a well-known, heuristic approach to help companies with multiple markets and multiple supply points determine a least-cost facility location. Essentially, the grid technique attempts to determine a fixed facility (such as a plant or distribution center) location that represents the least-cost center for moving inbound materials and outbound product within a geographic grid. The technique determines the low-cost "center of gravity" for moving raw materials and finished goods.

approach

This technique assumes that the raw materials sources and finished goods markets are fixed and that a company knows the amount of each product it consumes or sells. The technique then superimposes a grid upon the geographic area containing the raw materials sources and finished goods markets. The grid's zero point corresponds to an exact geographic location, as do the grid's other points. Thus, the company can identify each source and market by its grid coordinates.

Figure 12–4 is an example of a supply source and market environment for a company that is deciding where to locate a plant. The company, which has located supply sources and markets on the map and has superimposed a grid system over the source-market area, purchases raw materials from sources in Buffalo, Memphis, and St. Louis—S_1, S_2 and S_3, respectively. The new plant will serve five markets: Atlanta, Boston, Jacksonville, Philadelphia, and New York—M_1, M_2, M_3, M_4, and M_5, respectively.

grid location

The technique defines each source and market location in terms of its horizontal and vertical grid coordinates. For example, the Jacksonville market (M_3)

FIGURE 12–4 Grid Locations of Sources and Markets

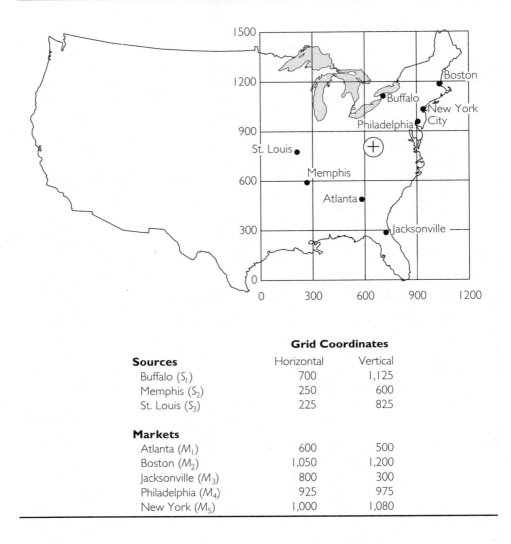

	Grid Coordinates	
Sources	Horizontal	Vertical
Buffalo (S_1)	700	1,125
Memphis (S_2)	250	600
St. Louis (S_3)	225	825
Markets		
Atlanta (M_1)	600	500
Boston (M_2)	1,050	1,200
Jacksonville (M_3)	800	300
Philadelphia (M_4)	925	975
New York (M_5)	1,000	1,080

has a horizontal grid coordinate of 800 and a vertical grid coordinate of 300. The Buffalo source is located at grid coordinates 700 horizontal and 1,125 vertical.

strings, weights, and knot We can visualize this technique's underlying concept as a series of strings to which are attached weights corresponding to the weight of raw materials the company consumes at each source and of finished goods the company sells at each market. The strings are threaded through holes in a flat plane; the holes correspond to the source and market locations. The strings' other ends are tied together, and the weights exert their respective pulls on the knot. The strings' knotted ends will finally reach an equilibrium; this equilibrium will be the center of mass, or the ton-mile center.

ton-mile center We can compute this concept mathematically, finding the ton-mile center, or center of mass, as follows:

$$C = \frac{\sum_{1}^{m} d_i S_i + \sum_{1}^{n} D_i M_i}{\sum_{1}^{m} S_i + \sum_{1}^{n} M_i}$$

where

C = center of mass, or ton-mile center

D_i = distance from 0 point on grid to the grid location of finished good i

d_i = distance from 0 point on grid to the grid location of raw material i

M_i = weight (volume) of finished goods sold in market i

S_i = weight of raw material purchased at source i

This equation will generate the least-cost location if transportation rates for raw materials and finished goods are the same. But transportation rates vary among commodities, and the ton-mile center equation does not reflect differences in the costs of moving commodities. The transportation rate pulls the location toward the location of the commodity with the higher rate. Thus, the higher rates of finished goods will draw the least-cost location toward the finished goods market and thereby reduce the distance the company moves these higher-rated goods. This will increase the distance the company transports lower-rated raw materials.

location and transportation rate

Thus, we must incorporate into our analysis the transportation rates of different products. This modification is as follows:

$$C = \frac{\sum_{1}^{m} r_i d_i S_i + \sum_{1}^{n} R_i D_i M_i}{\sum_{1}^{m} r_i S_i + \sum_{1}^{n} R_i M_i}$$

where

R_i = finished good transportation rate/distance unit for finished good i

r_i = raw material rate/distance unit for raw material i

R_i and r_i are the transportation rates per distance unit, and we assume them to be linear with respect to distance. This assumption does not correspond to the tapering principle of rates (to be discussed later), but it simplifies the analysis.

linear rates

Plant Location Example. Table 12–3 presents relevant data for a plant location example, as well as the grid technique solution using a computer spreadsheet program. The grid coordinates of the raw materials sources and markets correspond to their locations on the grid in Figure 12–4. For simplicity, we will assume that this company produces only one type of finished good, so that each finished good's transportation rate is the same.

To determine the least-cost center on the grid, we must compute two grid coordinates, one for moving the commodities along the horizontal axis and one for moving them along the vertical axis. We compute the two coordinates by using the grid technique formula for each direction.

compute two coordinates

TABLE 12-3 Grid Technique Analysis of Plant Location Example

Sources/Markets	Rate $/Ton-Mile (A)	Tons (B)	Grid Coordinates Hor.	Vert.	Calculations (A) * (B) * Hor.	(A) * (B) * Vert.
Buffalo (S_1)	$0.90	500	700	1,125	315,000	506,250
Memphis (S_2)	$0.95	300	250	600	71,250	171,000
St. Louis (S_3)	$0.85	700	225	825	133,875	490,875
		1,500			520,125	1,168,125
Atlanta (M_1)	$1.50	225	600	500	202,500	168,750
Boston (M_2)	$1.50	150	1,050	1,200	236,250	270,000
Jacksonville (M_3)	$1.50	250	800	300	300,000	112,500
Philadelphia (M_4)	$1.50	175	925	975	242,813	255,938
New York (M_5)	$1.50	300	1,000	1,080	450,000	486,000
	TOTALS	1,100			1,431,563	1,293,188
					Horizontal	**Vertical**
Numerator: $\Sigma (r * d * S) =$					520,125	1,168,125
$+ \Sigma (R * D * M) =$					1,431,563	1,293,188
Sum					1,951,688	2,461,313
Denominator: $\Sigma (r * S) =$					1,330	1,330
$+ \Sigma (R * M) =$					1,650	1,650
Sum					2,980	2,980
Grid center					655	826

Table 12–3 provides this example's computations. The two columns at the far right contain the calculations that the grid technique equation indicates. The first calculations column contains the calculations for the horizontal numerator, or the sum of the rate times the horizontal grid coordinate times the tonnage for each raw material source and market. The calculations at the bottom of Table 12–3 indicate the numerator and denominator of the grid technique equation.

As Table 12–3 indicates, the plant location's least-cost center in this example is 655 in the horizontal direction and 826 in the vertical direction. We measure both distances from the grid's zero point. Figure 12–4 indicates the least-cost center as point +. The least-cost location for the plant is in southeastern Ohio or northwestern West Virginia in the Wheeling-Parkersburg area.

warehouse application   The preceding example applied the grid technique to a plant location. Companies can use the technique to solve warehousing location problems as well. The company follows the same procedure, but the company's plants are the raw material sources.

simplicity   *Advantages.*   The grid technique's strengths are in its simplicity and its ability to provide a starting point for location analysis. Computationally, the technique is relatively easy to use. A company can generate the necessary data from sales figures, purchase records, and transportation documents (either the bill of lading or the freight bill). More exact market and source location coding is possible, as is modifying the rate-distance relationship quantification. A computer can easily handle such refinements.

The grid technique also provides a starting point for making a location decision. As we suggested earlier, transportation cost is not the only locational determinant. Using the grid technique can eliminate certain areas, permitting the decision maker to focus on an area that is logistically advantageous. For example, the grid technique may suggest Toledo, Ohio, as the least-cost location for a plant to serve the Ohio, Michigan, Indiana, and Illinois market area. This eliminates consideration of Chicago, Indianapolis, and other regional cities, and permits the decision maker to concentrate the location analysis in northwestern Ohio and southeastern Michigan. This is a tremendous step forward in the location decision process.

starting point

eliminates sites

Limitations. The grid technique has limitations that the decision maker must recognize. First, it is a static approach, and the solution is optimum for only one point in time. Changes in the volumes a company purchases or sells, changes in transportation rates, or changes in raw materials sources or market locations will shift the least-cost location. Second, the technique assumes linear transportation rates, whereas actual transportation rates increase with distance, but less than proportionally. Third, the technique does not consider the topographic conditions existing at the optimum location; for example, the recommended site may be in the middle of a lake. Fourth, it does not consider the proper direction of movement; most moves occur along a straight line between two points, not "vertically" and then "horizontally."

static

linear rates

topography

direction

Sensitivity Analysis. As mentioned above, the grid technique is a static approach; the computed location is valid only for the situation analyzed. If the transportation rates, market and source locations, and volumes change, the least-cost location changes.

Sensitivity analysis enables the decision maker to ask "what if" questions and measure the resultant impact on the least-cost location. For example, the decision maker may examine the least-cost location in light of a five-year sales projection by inserting the estimated market sales volumes into the grid technique equation and determining the least-cost location. Other "what if" scenarios could include adding new markets and/or sources, eliminating markets and/or sources, and switching transportation modes, thereby changing rates.

"what if"

Tables 12–4 and 12–5 perform two sensitivity analyses for the original problem in Table 12–3. The first "what if" scenario considers switching from rail to truck to serve the Jacksonville market; the switch entails a 50 percent rate increase. The data in Table 12–4 shows that the rate increase shifts the least-cost location toward Jacksonville; that is, the new location grid coordinates are 664 and 795, or east and south of the original location (655,826). Therefore, a rate increase will pull the least-cost location toward the market or supply source experiencing the increase.

rate increase

The second "what if" sensitivity analysis considers the elimination of a Buffalo supply source and increasing by 500 tons the amount the example company purchases from Memphis. Table 12–5 shows the effect of this sourcing change. With Memphis supplying all the material the company formerly purchased from Buffalo, the new least-cost location moves toward Memphis, or south and west of the original location. Similarly, a new market or a market experiencing a sales volume increase will draw the least-cost location.

sourcing change

TABLE 12–4 Impact of Rate Change on Least-Cost Location

Sources/Markets	Rate $/Ton-Mile (A)	Tons (B)	Grid Coordinates Hor.	Vert.	Calculations (A) * (B) * Hor.	(A) * (B) * Vert.
Buffalo (S_1)	$0.90	500	700	1,125	315,000	506,250
Memphis (S_2)	$0.95	300	250	600	71,250	171,000
St. Louis (S_3)	$0.85	700	225	825	133,875	490,875
		1,500			520,125	1,168,125
Atlanta (M_1)	$1.50	225	600	500	202,500	168,750
Boston (M_2)	$1.50	150	1,050	1,200	236,250	270,000
Jacksonville (M_3)	$2.25	250	800	300	450,000	168,750
Philadelphia (M_4)	$1.50	175	925	975	242,813	255,938
New York (M_5)	$1.50	300	1,000	1,080	450,000	486,000
	TOTALS	1,100			1,581,563	1,349,438
					Horizontal	**Vertical**
	Numerator: $\Sigma\,(r * d * S) =$				520,125	1,168,125
	$+ \Sigma\,(R * D * M) =$				1,581,563	1,349,438
	Sum				2,101,688	2,517,563
	Denominator: $\Sigma\,(r * S) =$				1,330	1,330
	$+ \Sigma\,(R * M) =$				1,838	1,838
	Sum				3,168	3,168
	Grid center				664	795

TABLE 12–5 Impact of Supply Source Change on Least-Cost Location

Sources/Markets	Rate $/Ton-Mile (A)	Tons (B)	Grid Coordinates Hor.	Vert.	Calculations (A) * (B) * Hor.	(A) * (B) * Vert.
Buffalo (S_1)	$0.90	0	700	1,125	0	0
Memphis (S_2)	$0.95	800	250	600	190,000	456,000
St. Louis (S_3)	$0.85	700	225	825	133,875	490,875
		1,500			323,875	946,875
Atlanta (M_1)	$1.50	225	600	500	202,500	168,750
Boston (M_2)	$1.50	150	1,050	1,200	236,250	270,000
Jacksonville (M_3)	$2.25	250	800	300	450,000	168,750
Philadelphia (M_4)	$1.50	175	925	975	242,813	255,938
New York (M_5)	$1.50	300	1,000	1,080	450,000	486,000
	TOTALS	1,100			1,581,563	1,349,438
					Horizontal	**Vertical**
	Numerator: $\Sigma\,(r * d * S) =$				323,875	946,875
	$+ \Sigma\,(R * D * M) =$				1,581,563	1,349,438
	Sum				1,905,438	2,296,313
	Denominator: $\Sigma\,(r * S) =$				1,355	1,355
	$+ \Sigma\,(R * M) =$				1,838	1,838
	Sum				3,193	3,193
	Grid center				597	719

We can conclude from these sensitivity analyses that the rates, product volumes, and source/market locations do affect a plant's least-cost location. The least-cost location moves toward a market or source experiencing a rate or volume increase, and away from the market or source experiencing a decrease. Introducing a new market or source pulls the location toward the additional market or source.

conclusions

Application to Warehouse Location in a City.   A special case exists for applying the grid technique to the location of a warehouse in a city. The situation's uniqueness comes from the blanket rate structure, which applies the same rate from an origin to any point within the city or commercial zone. Thus, any location within a city's commercial zone will incur the same inbound transportation cost from a company's mix of suppliers used; that is, the cost of moving supplies to a warehouse within the same city will not affect the location decision.

Since the supply volumes moving into the warehouse do not affect the location decision, the least-cost warehouse location within a city considers the cost of moving finished goods from the warehouse to the customers. We modify the grid technique equation as follows:

$$C = \frac{\sum\limits_{1}^{n} R_i D_i M_i}{\sum\limits_{1}^{n} R_i M_i}$$

If we assume that the cost of distributing (R) the commodity throughout the city will be the same, R cancels out, reducing the equation to a ton-mile center as follows:

$$C = \frac{\sum\limits_{1}^{n} D_i M_i}{\sum\limits_{1}^{n} M_i}$$

As before, this modified grid technique will enable the decision maker to eliminate certain areas of the city and to concentrate the analysis upon sites in the general vicinity of the least-cost location's grid coordinates. To determine a specific site for the warehouse, the decision maker must consider land and facility availability, expressway systems, and highway access in this general vicinity.

Transportation Pragmatics*

The previous discussion showed the importance of the transportation factor in the facility location decision. We simplified the rate structure focus on the transportation factor's locational pull. In this section, we will examine how dropping these transportation simplifications affects facility location, directing attention specifically toward tapering rates, blanket rates, commercial zones, and in-transit privileges.

*Adapted from Edward J. Taaffe and Howard L. Gauthier, Jr., *Geography of Transportation* (Englewood Cliffs, NJ: Prentice-Hall, 1973): 41–43.

TABLE 12-6 Locational Effects of Tapering Rates with Constant Rate Assumption

Distance from S (miles)	Transport Rate from S	Distance to M (miles)	Transport Rate to M	Total Transport Rate
0	$0.00	200	$3.70	$3.70
50	$2.00	150	$3.50	$5.50
100	$3.00	100	$3.00	$6.00
150	$3.50	50	$2.00	$5.50
200	$3.70	0	$0.00	$3.70

Tapering Rates. As we pointed out earlier, transportation rates increase with distance but not in direct proportion to distance. This tapering rate principle results from the carrier's ability to spread certain fixed shipment costs, such as loading, billing, and handling, over a greater number of miles. As Edgar M. Hoover noted (see Appendix 12A), a tapering rate in one-source, one-market situations pulls the location to either the source or the market, but not to a point in between.

To illustrate this effect, consider the data in Table 12–6 and Figure 12–5. In this example, we assume the rates to be constant (the same) for raw materials supplied at S and finished products sold at M. The rates in Table 12–6 increase with distance, but not proportionally. For example, the shipping rate from S is $2.00 for 50 miles and $3.00 for 100 miles, a distance increase of 100 percent but a rate increase of only 50 percent.

Table 12–6 and Figure 12–5 indicate that a location at either S or M will result in a total rate of $3.70. At any other location the total rate is higher. Thus, the tapering rate pulls the location toward the source or the market.

Dropping rate constancy between raw materials and finished goods draws the location toward M, the market. In Table 12–7 and Figure 12–6, the rates for moving the finished product into the market are higher than those for moving raw materials. The location having the least total transportation cost is at M, where the total transportation rate is $3.70.

Blanket Rates. A noted exception to the preceding rate structure is the blanket rate. The blanket rate does not increase with distance; it remains the same from one origin to all points in the blanket area. The carriers establish such rates to ensure a competitive price for a product in a given area, thereby ensuring demand for the product and its transportation. An example of a blanket rate would be the same rate on wine traveling from the West Coast to all points east of the Rocky Mountains, enabling the West Coast wine to compete with imported wines entering the East Coast.

eliminate transportation factor

The blanket rate eliminates any transportation cost advantage or disadvantage that companies associate with a given location. In the case of the wine blanket rates, the West Coast wine producers can effectively compete in the East Coast market area with East Coast and foreign producers. The blanket rate, then, is a

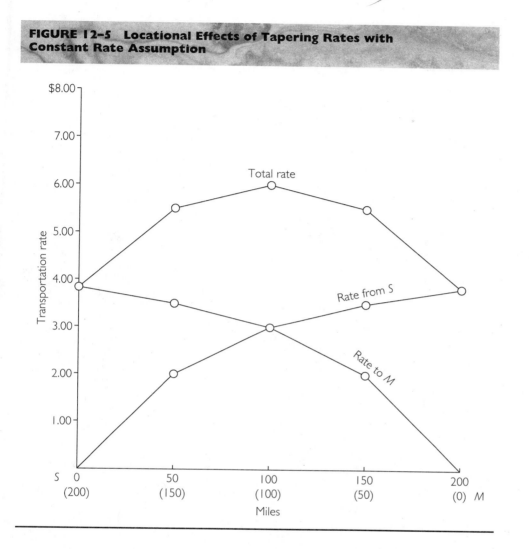

FIGURE 12–5 Locational Effects of Tapering Rates with Constant Rate Assumption

mutation of the basic rate-distance relationship that eliminates the transportation rate as a locational determinant; it is the exception rather than the rule in transportation rates.

TABLE 12–7 Locational Effects of Tapering Rates without Constant Rate Assumption

Distance from S (miles)	Transport Rate from S	Distance to M (miles)	Transport Rate to M	Total Transport Rate
0	$0.00	200	$5.20	$5.20
50	$2.00	150	$5.00	$7.00
100	$3.00	100	$4.50	$7.50
150	$3.50	50	$3.50	$7.00
200	$3.70	0	$0.00	$3.70

FIGURE 12–6 Locational Effects of Tapering Rates without Constant Rate Assumption

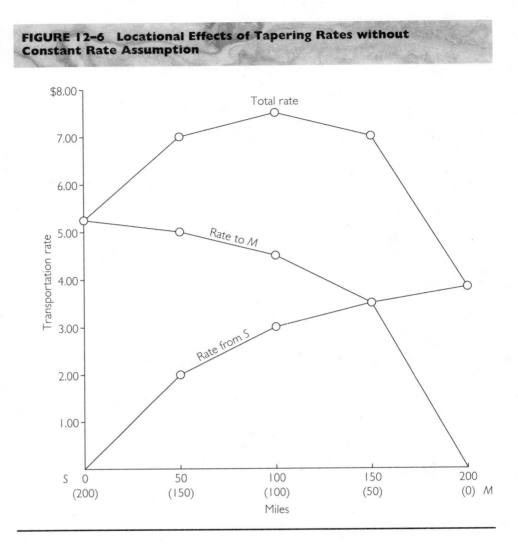

Commercial Zones.   A specific blanket area is the commercial zone, the transportation definition of a particular city or town. It includes the municipality itself plus various surrounding areas. The commercial zone rates that carriers quote to a particular town or city also apply to points in the surrounding area within the commercial zone.

The commercial zone's locational impact appears near the end of the location decision process when a company selects a specific site. If the specific site is beyond the limits of a municipality's commercial zone, rates that apply to the city will not apply to the site. Also, a site outside the commercial zone reduces carrier availability, especially the availability of motor carriers that define their operating scopes in terms of point-to-point operations.

[margin notes]

transportation definition of a city

rates

carrier availability

Maxwell House Picks Jacksonville: To Close Hoboken

David beat Goliath. At least that's how some people are looking at it. In the battle between Jacksonville, Florida, and Hoboken, New Jersey, to keep each city's Maxwell House processing plant open, Jacksonville has to come out the winner.

Americans' changing lifestyles prompted the need to eliminate one of the two plants.

"People aren't drinking coffee like they used to. There has been 24 percent decrease in coffee consumption in the United States since 1963," explained Frank Meegan, operations manager for Maxwell House. "Yet, we are still operating the same four plants we operated then, even though we use only 55 percent of their production capacity. Therefore, we must eliminate this excess."

And, in eighteen months, that's exactly what they will have done.

Maxwell House will expand the Jacksonville plant to process 40 percent more coffee. Meegan indicated that little additional construction would occur outside the existing Maxwell House structure, located across the street from the site of Jacksonville Shipyards, Inc.

The City of Jacksonville, the Jacksonville Port Authority, and numerous business groups lobbied to "Keep Max in Jax." The city offered Maxwell House a $4.8 million incentive package to keep its plant open. Hoboken reportedly offered $7.1 million.

But the economics were clear. "It's cheaper to do business in Jacksonville," Meegan said. "We decided to stay in Jacksonville because our total costs were less here, and our assessment is that they will continue to be less in the future.

"Here, we are closer to important supply plants: the Houston plant, which provides decaffeinated beans; our lithography plant in Tarrant City, Alabama, which provides coffee cans; and Central America, which of course is an important source of coffee beans."

In 1988, just over 90,000 tons of coffee moved over Jacksonville's docks. Though that total is only a drop in an annual 4.5 million-ton cargo bucket, the port feels that the coffee trade is important because of the liner trade it represents.

It's too early to tell exactly what effects a bigger coffee processing plant will have on the city and the state, but if the early economic ripples are any indication, it may well mean millions of dollars in increased business for a variety of maritime and transportation-related firms.

ADAPTED FROM: James Lida, "Maxwell House Picks Jacksonville: To Close Hoboken," *American Shipper* 32, no. 8 (August 1990): 74. Reprinted with permission from the August 1990 issue of *American Shipper*.

Transit Privileges.   Basically, the transit privilege permits the shipper to stop a shipment in transit and to perform some function that physically changes the product's characteristic. The lower through rate from origin to final destination (the tapering rate principle) applies, rather than the higher combination of rates from origin to transit point and from transit point to final destination.

stop shipment to perform processing

The transit privilege essentially makes intermediate locations, rather than just origins or destinations, optimum. The transit privilege eliminates any geographic disadvantage that companies associate with a producer's location. The intermediate point the carrier designates as a transit point enjoys the lower, long-distance through rate that applies at either the origin or the destination.

Like the blanket rate, the transit privilege is not available at all locations or for all commodities—only those sites and commodities the carrier specifies. If a commodity benefits from the availability of a transit privilege, the limited points specified by the carrier will be prime facility location alternatives.

SUMMARY

- The logistics network design decision is of great strategic importance to logistics, the firm as a whole, and the supply chain.
- There are a number of factors that may suggest the need to redesign the logistics network.
- A formal, structured process for logistics network design is preferable; the potential impacts on cost and service justify a significant effort toward following a sound process.
- Numerous factors may affect the design of a logistics network and the location of specific facilities within the context of the network.
- Principal modeling approaches to gain insight into the topic of logistics network design include optimization, simulation, and heuristic models.
- The availability and cost of transportation affect the location decision in a number of significant and unique ways.
- An understanding of the classical theories of location should help one to understand the factors that influence the locational priorities of firms, industries, and supply chains.

STUDY QUESTIONS

1. In what ways can the design of a firm's logistics network affect its ability to create value for customers through efficiency, effectiveness, and differentiation?

2. Discuss the factors that cause a company to analyze the design of a logistics network or to reconsider the location of a particular facility.

3. Why are most location decisions analyzed by a team of managers instead of a single person? What types of teams are suggested as being helpful to the task of logistics network redesign?

4. What are the major locational determinants, and how does each affect the location decision?

5. Discuss the role of the logistics variable in the decision as to where to locate a plant or warehouse.

6. Once you have gathered information concerning a variety of factors of relevance to the facility location decision, how would you determine what alternative is best?

7. What are the principal types of modeling techniques that apply to the task of logistics network design and facility location? What are the strengths and limitations of each?

8. Describe the grid technique. What is its purpose, and how does it lead to the making of a decision? What are its strengths and limitations?

9. Using the grid technique, determine the least-cost location for the following problems:

(a)

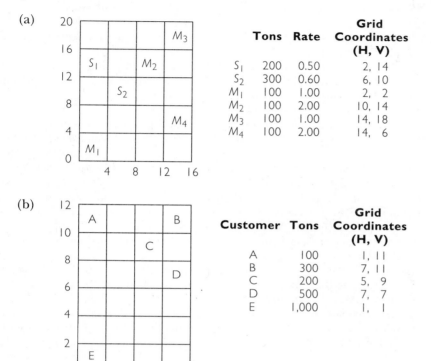

	Tons	Rate	Grid Coordinates (H, V)
S_1	200	0.50	2, 14
S_2	300	0.60	6, 10
M_1	100	1.00	2, 2
M_2	100	2.00	10, 14
M_3	100	1.00	14, 18
M_4	100	2.00	14, 6

(b)

Customer	Tons	Grid Coordinates (H, V)
A	100	1, 11
B	300	7, 11
C	200	5, 9
D	500	7, 7
E	1,000	1, 1

10. Explain how tapering rates, blanket rates, commercial zones, and in-transit privileges affect the facility location decision.

NOTES

1. The first three of these examples are adapted from Robin Pano, "Pull Out the Stops in Your Network," *Transportation & Distribution* (August 1994): 38–40.

2. Coopers & Lybrand, SysteCon Division, "Is It Time to Redesign?," *Total Logistics Forum* 1, no. 2 (November 1994): 1.

3. Richard Boyer and David Savageau, *Places Rated Almanac* (Chicago: Rand McNally, 1989).

4. E. S. Browning and Helene Cooper, "States' Bidding War over Mercedes Plant Made for Costly Chase," *The Wall Street Journal* (November 24, 1993).

5. This discussion is adapted from Peter Crosby, "Trends Governing Site Selection," *Transportation & Distribution* (August 1994): 38–39.

6. Ronald H. Ballou, *Business Logistics Management,* 3rd ed. (Englewood Cliffs, NJ: Prentice-Hall, 1992): 297.

7. Richard F. Powers, "Optimization Models for Logistics Decisions," *Journal of Business Logistics* 10, no. 1 (1989): 106.

8. *SAILS (Strategic Analysis of Integrated Logistics Systems),* (Alexandria, VA: Insight, Inc., 1994).

9. Robert E. Shannon, *Systems Simulation: The Art and Science* (Englewood Cliffs, NJ: Prentice-Hall, 1975): 1.

10. Frederick S. Hillier and Gerald J. Lieberman, *Introduction to Operations Research,* 3rd ed. (San Francisco: Holden-Day, Inc., 1980): 643.

11. For an excellent overview of simulation modeling, see Donald J. Bowersox and David J. Closs, "Simulation in Logistics: A Review of Present Practice and a Look to the Future," *Journal of Business Logistics* 10, no. 1 (1989): 133–48.

12. Ballou, *Business Logistics Management,* 295.

13. Donald J. Bowersox, Omar Keith Helferich, and Edward J. Marien, "Physical Distribution Planning with Simulation," *International Journal of Physical Distribution* (October 1971): 38–42.

14. PIPELINE MANAGER is a proprietary computer simulation software package developed by Andersen Consulting, Chicago, Illinois.

15. David Ronen, "LSD—Logistics System Design Simulation Model," *Proceedings of the Eighteenth Annual Transportation and Logistics Educators Conference,* The Ohio State University, Columbus, OH (Boston, MA: October 9, 1988): 35–47.

16. LOCATE is a simulator for facility location developed by Cleveland Consulting Associates, Cleveland, Ohio.

17. Donald J. Bowersox, David J. Closs, John T. Mentzer Jr., and Jeffrey R. Sims, *Simulated Product Sales Forecasting* (East Lansing, MI: Michigan State University Press, 1979).

18. Ballou, *Business Logistics Management,* 295.

19. For additional examples and a comprehensive perspective on heuristic modeling, see Ronald H. Ballou, "Heuristics: Rules of Thumb for Logistics Making," *Journal of Business Logistics* 10, no. 1 (1989): 122–32.

Case 12-1

ROLL FREE TIRE COMPANY

Roll Free Tire Company, a manufacturer of radial tires, sells its tires in the auto aftermarket and distributes them nationwide. It has three plants, located in Allentown, Pennsylvania; Toledo, Ohio; and Macomb, Illinois. The company divides the U.S. market into regions and each region has a distribution center. Normally, Roll Free ships tires to each distribution center from the plants, but the company typically sends truckload shipments directly to customers. All shipments to a region move under truckload rates applying to a minimum weight of 400 cwt, or 40,000 pounds.

Roll Free management is concerned about the most economical location for a distribution center to serve its southeastern region (North Carolina, South Carolina, Georgia, Florida, Mississippi, Alabama, and southeastern Tennessee; see map). Currently, an Atlanta warehouse serves this region. Roll Free management believes that the Atlanta location is not the most logistically economical location:

To help the logistics department conduct a grid analysis of this region's warehouse location, Roll Free's traffic department developed the following data:

1995 Shipments to Atlanta				Grid Coordinates	
From	cwt	Rate/cwt	Mileage	Horizontal	Vertical
Toledo	15,000	$2.20	640	1,360	1,160
Macomb	5,000	2.43	735	980	1,070
Allentown	11,000	2.52	780	1,840	1,150

1995 Shipments from Atlanta		Grid Coordinates	
To	cwt	Horizontal	Vertical
Chattanooga	2,700	1,350	650
Atlanta	3,500	1,400	600
Tampa	4,300	1,570	220
Birmingham	2,800	1,260	580
Miami	5,300	1,740	90
Jacksonville	5,100	1,600	450
Columbia	2,200	1,600	650
Charlotte	2,900	1,590	740
Raleigh/Durham	2,200	1,700	800

The traffic department also determined that total freight expenditures from the Atlanta warehouse during 1995 were $217,000 and that the average shipment distance was 330 miles.

Case Questions

1. Based upon the preceding information, is Atlanta the best location for a distribution center to serve the southeastern region?
2. The traffic department projects a 25 percent rate increase from all sources in 1996. How will this affect the Atlanta location?
3. Marketing anticipates that the Raleigh/Durham market will grow by 3,000 cwt in 1997. Roll Free will serve the growth from Allentown. How will this affect Atlanta as a location?

CLASSICAL THEORIES OF LOCATION

T his appendix describes the development of location theory and discusses the importance of transportation factors in this theoretical development. This discussion, which provides the basis of the transportation location decision, covers the theories of von Thunen, Weber, Hoover, and Greenhut.

J. H. VON THUNEN[1]

One of the first writers to theorize the production factors with respect to facility location was Johann Heinrich von Thunen. A German agriculturist, von Thunen was concerned with the location of agricultural production. In his theory, cost minimization (transportation cost) was the locational determinant.

The assumptions von Thunen utilized reduced the problem's complexity and allowed concentration upon the transportation variable. First, he assumed an isolated city-state that was surrounded by a plain of equal fertility. The plain ended in wilderness, and the city was the only market for the agricultural products. Production of any product could occur anywhere in the plain at the same cost. Von Thunen assumed equally accessible transportation to all locations in the plain, and transportation costs were a function of weight and distance; that is, transportation cost was a constant rate per ton-mile for all commodities.

Agricultural production would take place where the farmer would maximize profits. Von Thunen determined profits as follows: profits equal market price minus production costs and transportation costs. With a given product's market price and production costs the same at any production location, the transportation cost factor was the major locational determinant.

According to von Thunen, locations farther from the city (market) would incur a greater transportation cost. Such locations would not be economically feasible for producing low-value, high-weight products, which would incur very high transportation costs that they could not bear because of their low value-to-weight relationships. Thus, von Thunen concluded, those products should be produced near the city to minimize transport cost.

Another transport attribute recognized by von Thunen as a locational determinant was transit time. Perishable products (fresh vegetables) would be produced near the city; the influential determinant was not transportation cost but the time producers required to move the goods to the markets.* Such perishable products could not sustain long transit times and thus had to be produced near the city.

Von Thunen continued the analysis for various agricultural products, ultimately developing a series of concentric rings about the city. The rings, von Thunen's *belts,* delineated the products that should be produced at various distances from the city. Perishable products and products of low value-to-weight ratios would be produced in the belts nearest the city. Products with high value-to-weight ratios would be produced in the rings farther from the city.

The simplifying assumptions and concentration upon agricultural production location make von Thunen's theory seem unrealistic for the modern business firm. But his work remains a major part of the foundation upon which we predicate current location theory and forms a threshold for delineating the relationships between transportation costs and location theory. We also find his general conclusions still valid today. For example, land close to urban areas is expensive, and companies must use it intensively, possibly by building multistoried warehouses or distribution centers.

ALFRED WEBER[2]

Alfred Weber, a German economist, developed a theory for the location of industrial production facilities. Unlike von Thunen, Weber started with a given industry and determined its best location. He assumed equally accessible transportation and constant transportation costs with respect to weight and distance. Raw materials points and consumption points are known, and labor is geographically fixed and available at a given dollar amount.

Like von Thunen's analysis, Weber's analysis defines the optimum location as the point that represents the least-cost location. More specifically, the least-cost site is the location that minimizes total transportation costs—the costs of transferring raw materials to the plant and finished goods to the market. Thus, total transportation cost is the criterion Weber used to evaluate alternative plant locations.

Weber recognized that raw materials were different from a logistics standpoint. Raw materials possess two characteristics that directly relate to the total transportation costs they incur: geographic availability and weight lost in processing. With regard to geographic availability, a raw material is either ubiquitous or localized. A *ubiquity* is a raw material that we find everywhere (for example, water and air). A *localized* material is one that we find only in certain locations (for example, coal or iron ore). In addition, a raw material can be either pure or weight losing. A *pure* raw material does not lose weight in processing (a pure raw material's entire weight enters into the finished product's weight). A *weight-losing* raw material loses weight during production. Therefore, a raw material may be ubiquitous and pure, ubiquitous and weight losing, localized and pure, or localized and weight losing.

---

*Mechanical refrigeration was nonexistent at this time, so this was a practical solution to the problem. Perishability is still a factor today, in spite of advanced technology.

Raw materials' ubiquitous and localized characteristics define their geographic fixity and the need to transport them to and from proposed plant locations. By definition, ubiquities occur everywhere and thus would not require transportation to the plant site. Thus, ubiquities place no constraints upon a production facility's location. However, ubiquities generally favor location in the market, as the following analysis shows.

A localized raw material does not occur everywhere and therefore necessitates transportation (and corresponding transportation costs) to any location other than its supply source. Usually, the greater the plant's distance from the localized material source, the greater the material's transportation costs. But we must recognize the weight lost in processing, since this affects the total transportation cost for localized raw materials and finished goods.

The pure and weight-losing characteristics directly affect the total amount of weight a company will transport and correspondingly affect total transportation costs (for raw material and finished goods) at various plant locations. Since localized pure raw materials lose no weight in processing, their entire weight enters into the weight of the finished product. Assuming only one material and one market, a localized pure raw material's total transported weight will be the same both to and from the plant. However, with a localized weight-losing material, a supply-source location can minimize the material's transported weight and consequently minimize transportation costs. That is, by having the location at the supply source of the weight-losing raw material, a company avoids transporting the weight the material loses in processing.

One Market, One Raw Materials Source

Now let us consider some examples of Weber's location theory. To accomplish this, we will utilize the situation in Figure 12A–1. We will determine the least-cost location for a production facility that utilizes raw materials of different characteristics in the production process. The transportation rate is $1.00 per ton-mile for moving both raw materials and finished goods.

First, if the one raw material the facility uses is ubiquitous, either pure or weight losing, the least-cost location is at *M*. At *M*, the raw material or its finished good incurs no movement cost. This location is possible because the ubiquity is available at *RM* as well as at *M*. One example of such a situation is the soft drink industry. With water being the primary raw material and a ubiquity, soft drink bottlers can locate in various local markets and can eliminate transporting water from, for example, New York to the Toledo market area. Since water is available in Toledo

FIGURE 12A–1   One Market, One Raw Material Source

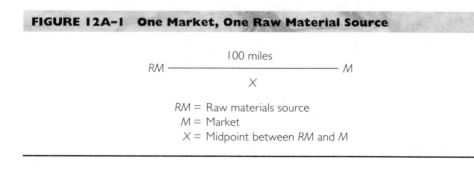

RM = Raw materials source
M = Market
X = Midpoint between RM and M

as well as in New York, the bottler can minimize total transportation costs simply by locating in Toledo.

Second, assume that a company uses a pure, localized raw material weighing 1 ton to produce one unit of finished good *(FG)* weighing 1 ton. To determine the least-cost location, we must analyze the total transportation cost at the plant's possible locations. If the plant is located at *RM*, the total transportation cost per unit is $100 (*RM* = 1 ton × 0 miles, or $0; *FG* = 1 ton × 100 miles, or $100); the total transportation cost per unit is also $100 for a plant located at *M* (*RM* = 1 ton × 100 miles, or $100; *FG* = 1 ton × 0 miles, or $0). If the plant is located at point X in Figure 12A–1, the total transportation cost per unit is also $100 (*RM* = 1 ton × 50 miles, or $50; *FG* = 1 ton × 50 miles, or $50). Thus, the least-cost location using a pure, localized raw material is *RM, M,* or anywhere in between on a straight line connecting the two. This led Weber to conclude that pure materials cannot bind production to their deposits.

Third, let us assume that a company uses a localized, weight-losing material weighing 1 ton to produce one unit of finished good weighing ½ ton. Again, we will analyze the alternative plant locations in terms of total transportation costs. A location at *RM* will result in a total per-unit transportation cost of $50 (*RM* = 1 ton × 0 miles, or $0; *FG* = ½ ton × 100 miles, or $50). The locations at *X* and *M* will result in total per-unit transportation costs of $75 and $100, respectively. The least-cost location for a localized, weight-losing raw material is the material's source; at this location, the company does not transport the weight lost in processing.

Considering a situation with one raw materials source and one market helps us to grasp the fundamental relationships between transportation costs and a production facility's location under varying raw material situations. However, an industrial firm rarely operates in such a simplified situation. Weber expanded his analysis to consider two sources and one market. We will consider this in the following section.

Two Raw Materials Sources, One Market

Weber approached the problem of two raw materials sources and one market by considering the advantage of locating the production facility in relation to this situation's three terminals. The two supply sources now complicate the effects of raw materials characteristics upon transportation costs.

Weber formalized the location influence of the relative product weights and resultant transportation costs at the various terminals into a *material index;* the ratio of the sum of the localized raw material weights to the finished product's weight. If greater than 1, the least-cost location gravitates away from the market toward the raw materials sources.

To determine which raw material source is the least-cost location when the material index is greater than 1, Weber considered the relative pull that the weight of the localized raw material exercised. He accomplished this through the location weight index (LWI), which he defined as the ratio of a material's weight at a terminal to the finished product's weight. The least-cost location is then the raw materials source at which the LWI is greater than the sum of the other LWIs. Envision a flat board with the market and raw materials sources arranged in a triangle. We drill a hole at each terminal and pass a string through each hole. To one end of each string we attach a weight corresponding to the localized raw material weight and finished good weight at the terminal. We tie the other ends of the strings together on top of the board. When we release the weights and they transfer their respective locational pulls to the knot, the knot's final resting point is the optimum location.

Consider the four situations in Figure 12A–2. We will attempt to determine the optimum plant location for each, again assuming a constant transportation rate per weight/distance.

In example A in Figure 12A–2, a company combines a ubiquitous raw material weighing 4 pounds with two localized materials weighing 4 pounds and 2 pounds. The material index is $(4 + 2) \div 8 = 3/4$, which is less than 1. This tells us that the least-cost location is the market. The influence of the ubiquity pulling the location toward the market is evident in this example, as it is in the previous one-source, one-market example. (Justify this example's conclusion, as well as those of the following examples, by assuming distances between each terminal pair and a transportation rate and then calculating total transportation costs for various locations.)

Example B in Figure 12A–2 offers a situation in which a company utilizes two pure raw materials in the production process. The material index is $(2 + 2) \div 4 = 1$, and we conclude that the optimum location is the market. Any other location would increase the commodities' transportation distance and therefore would be a higher-cost location.

In example C, both raw materials are weight losing. The material index is $(2 + 3) \div 1/2 = 10$, and we conclude that the location should not be at the market but nearer the deposit source. To determine the specific deposit location, we use the location weight index. The LWI for R_1 is $2 \div 1/2 = 4$, for R_2 is $3 \div 1/2 = 6$, and for M is $1/2 \div 1/2 = 1$. (The LWI for the market terminal is always 1.) Next, we compare the LWI for one terminal with the sum of the others and find that the LWI for R_2 is greater than the sum of the others ($6 > 4 + 1$). Our conclusion is that the location will gravitate toward the R_2 location.

FIGURE 12A–2 Two Raw Materials Sources, One Market

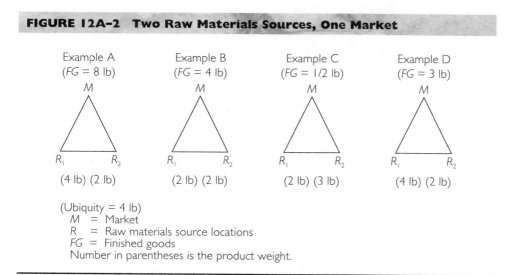

Example A
(FG = 8 lb)

M

R_1 R_2
(4 lb) (2 lb)

Example B
(FG = 4 lb)

M

R_1 R_2
(2 lb) (2 lb)

Example C
(FG = 1/2 lb)

M

R_1 R_2
(2 lb) (3 lb)

Example D
(FG = 3 lb)

M

R_1 R_2
(4 lb) (2 lb)

(Ubiquity = 4 lb)
M = Market
R = Raw materials source locations
FG = Finished goods
Number in parentheses is the product weight.

The last example, D, again involves two weight-losing raw materials, but the optimum location is not at any one of the three terminals. The material index of $(4 + 4) \div 3 = 2^{2/3}$ tells us to not locate at the market. The LWIs are as follows: $R_1 = {}^{4/3}$, $R_2 = {}^{2/3}$, and $M = 1$. No LWI is greater than the sum of the others, and the conclusion is not to locate at any one of the terminals. The optimum location will be somewhere inside the triangle.

We can determine the optimum location for example D by evaluating the total transportation costs our example company would incur at the many alternative sites inside the triangle. However, this involves a more complex mathematical process, as does the consideration of more than two sources. The grid technique, which basically expands the Weber approach, can facilitate many origins and many destinations in determining a facility's least-transportation-cost location.

Labor and Agglomeration Factors

Thus far, our discussion has concentrated upon how transportation affects the location decision. Weber then considered labor's locational pull by recognizing that labor costs vary at different locations. If labor costs less in a location other than the least-transportation-cost site, the firm will locate at the point with lower labor costs provided that the labor savings offset the increased transportation costs. In essence, a cost trade-off exists between labor and transportation costs.

We can use *isodapanes* to show the effect of the labor savings or other production cost savings. Isodapanes are lines of equal, though not minimal, transportation costs around the least-transportation-cost site. Figure 12A–3 shows a series of isodapanes drawn around a one-market, two-source situation. Point M (the market) is the location with the least transportation cost ($10). Any location on the isodapane labeled $12 will incur $12 total transportation costs. At point Y, which is on the $14 isodapane (where transportation costs are $4 greater than those of the least transportation cost point), if a company can purchase labor at a savings of $4 or more over that at M, the decision to locate at Y rather than M would be economically sound. The company would similarly investigate other alternative

FIGURE 12A–3 Example of Isodapanes

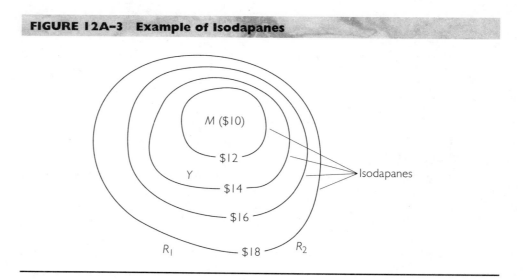

sites, analyzing the trade-offs between labor savings and increased transportation costs. Using isodapanes readily enables companies to examine these trade-offs.

In a similar trade-off analysis, Weber introduces another locational determinant that he calls *agglomeration,* a net advantage that a company gains through a common location with other firms. A common location offers benefits such as a skilled labor supply, better marketing outlets, and proximity to auxiliary industries. (We term a net common location disadvantage *deglomeration.*) Again utilizing Figure 12A–3, point *Y* will be a desirable location if the agglomeration benefits of $4 or more offset point *Y*'s higher transportation cost.

In summary, Weber's location analysis is a least-cost approach that emphasizes transportation costs. It is unrealistic to assume a constant, linear transportation rate, but we can eliminate the constant assumption by applying the actual rates for different raw materials or finished goods. Although Weber's theory is not adequate for handling more complex location decisions, its benefit lies in its easy application. In addition, it can provide the decision maker with a starting point for a location analysis, reducing the alternatives and bringing the decision maker one step closer to determining an exact location. Weber's emphasis upon transportation costs as a locational determinant for industrial facilities is the basis of many other locational works.

EDGAR M. HOOVER[3]

Edgar M. Hoover, an American theorist, investigated the optimum location of industrial facilities based upon cost factors. He also dealt with demand factors that von Thunen or Weber did not consider. His demand analysis relates to the definition of what the market area will be after a firm determines a location. His theories recognize distribution cost effects upon a product's price and resultant demand.

In terms of cost factors, Hoover greatly expanded the analysis of previous authors. He considered transportation costs, agglomerative forces, and industrial costs. In all three areas, Hoover's treatment is more inclusive than Weber's.

With regard to transportation costs, Hoover pointed out that rates are not linear with respect to distance. Most rates follow the tapering principle—rates increase with distance, but at a decreasing rate. This alters Weber's conclusions for localized pure raw materials in a one-market, one-source situation. Instead of requiring the decision maker to consider three location choices (market, raw material source, and anywhere in between), rate nonlinearity makes the location at either the market or the raw material source less expensive than one in between. Location in between would cause the rates of the two separate movements to be greater than the one rate from raw materials source to market.

Hoover also noted that transportation companies are not uniformly available throughout all areas. Companies desire locations in areas that have a high concentration of carriers, since they provide more alternative vendors to meet a logistics systems' varied link requirements.

Hoover pointed out that the importance of transportation costs as a locational determinant varies for different firms. Transportation costs may be less important to firms that can ship in carload or truckload quantities than they are to firms that ship in LCL or LTL quantities. Product characteristics also affect carrier rates and consequently influence the importance of transportation costs as a locational determinant.

Hoover's main contribution to location theory was his more-inclusive analysis of the cost factors affecting the location decision. Basically, he based his approach upon cost minimization.

MELVIN L. GREENHUT[4]

Melvin L. Greenhut, another American theorist, emphasized demand as a locational determinant. He pointed out that demand is a variable that enables a company to realize different profits at different locations; thus, the location that maximizes profits is the optimum site, which may not necessarily coincide with the least-cost definition.

Greenhut grouped his important locational determinants into demand, cost, and purely personal factors. Demand and cost factors influence all site selections. Companies should include personal considerations, which partially determine demand or production costs, with demand or product cost determinants.

At this point, you may be concerned with the location difference between the cost minimization and profit maximization criteria. If we assume constant demand, the two criteria will result in the same location. Given differing demand at different locations, a high-cost location may provide higher profits because of the ability to charge higher prices.

NOTES

1. C. M. Warnenburg, trans., and Peter Hall, ed., *von Thunen's Isolated State* (Oxford, England: Pergamon Press, 1966).
2. Carl J. Friedrich, trans., *Alfred Weber's Theory of the Location of Industries* (Chicago: University of Chicago Press, 1929).
3. Edgar M. Hoover, *The Location of Economic Activity* (New York: McGraw-Hill, 1948).
4. Melvin L. Greenhut, *Plant Location in Theory and in Practice* (Chapel Hill: University of North Carolina Press, 1956).

CHAPTER 13

GLOBAL LOGISTICS

LEARNING OBJECTIVES

After reading this chapter, you should be able to do the following:

- Discuss the reasons for the increase in global business activity.

- Define a global company.

- Explain Porter's dynamic diamond theory of global competitive advantage.

- Describe the critical changes affecting global logistics.

- Explain the effect of the changing legal and political environment in Europe, Asia, North America, and South America.

- Discuss the North American Free Trade Agreement and its effect on logistics.

- Define the nature and benefit of a Maquiladora.

- Explain the major transportation systems available for global logistics.

- Distinguish among the global logistics intermediaries: freight forwarders, customs house brokers, nonvessel-operating common carriers, and export management companies.

- Explain the criteria used to select a port for global shipments.

- Discuss warehousing and packaging requirements for global shipments.

- Define the role of customs duties and free trade zones.

TOYOTA'S GLOBAL CONVEYOR BELTS

Toyota Motor Company has extended the just-in-time (JIT) manufacturing concept halfway around the world. Typically, JIT systems are regional, that is, the suppliers are located within a close proximity to the assembly plant. Parts are produced and delivered on an as-needed basis. There are frequent shipments in relatively small lots timed for delivery to meet the plant's manufacturing schedule.

Toyota is applying the JIT concept between Japan and the United States. The company operates a JIT supply chain system to serve its Georgetown, Kentucky, and Fremont, California, assembly plants with parts produced in Japan. The plants receive parts from Japan five days per week, with deliveries timed to the minute. The frequent shipments of mixed loads in relatively small lots are synchronized with the U.S. plants' manufacturing schedules, which are based on sales data and forecasts.

Toyota and other Japanese auto manufacturers are producing more automobiles in domestic markets and are relying less on exporting finished cars. The strong yen, which makes Japanese exports more expensive, plus trade imbalances and resulting protectionist pressure are the primary reasons for establishing plants (transplants) in foreign countries. Toyota has 35 manufacturing plants in 25 countries outside of Japan.

The transplants obtain most of their parts from local sources. However, to assure quality and to reap the benefits from the huge investments in vehicle-component plants in Japan, Toyota supplies many vehicle parts from Japan. The North American transplants are now shipping some parts and components to Japan for use in the assembly plants there.

Moving thousands of parts and components around the globe on a JIT basis requires considerable rethinking of the global logistics components. Carriers are required to provide consistent, timely service over long distances while transferring cargo among a number of carriers. In addition, the transportation service must be economical to justify the long supply chain.

One key strategy making the global JIT system work effectively is the leveling of production. A steady production flow smooths out peaks and valleys in the logistics process and enables the carriers to optimize their capacity to meet the level volume. Toyota constantly shares information about future trends and volume outlooks to make sure there are no drastic fluctuations in volume.

The production schedule is developed from monthly forecasts of demand. The approximate average daily sales volume for each month is calculated, and daily production is adjusted to meet that figure. Shipments of components are scheduled accordingly.

Toyota uses four water carriers (American President Lines, Sea Land, Nipon Yusen Kaisha, and K Line) to provide daily service to North America for parts. One day's supply of components for each U.S. plant is loaded on a ship sailing each day from Japan to the West Coast of the United States. The lead time is five weeks from date of order to receipt of the shipment under a system of daily orders and daily shipments.

An example of how the global conveyor belt works is the Sea Land supply chain from Japan to the Georgetown plant. Containers of parts are loaded at Nagoya for shipment to Tacoma, Washington. The ocean voyage takes ten days and is scheduled for arrival at Tacoma on Sunday night. After reaching Tacoma, the containers are relayed to a stack train that arrives in Chicago late Wednesday. The stack train is handed off to the Norfolk Southern, which delivers it to the Georgetown plant on Friday morning at 12:30 A.M.

The tight schedules are essential to keep the Georgetown plant producing 1,000 Camry's per day. To facilitate efficiencies at the plant, the components are loaded in the container so that they can be unloaded in sequence to mesh with the assembly plant's needs.

Information flow is the key to tight supply chains. Leveled production is possible only by integrating all processes, from receipt of orders through production and transportation.

SOURCE: Joseph Bonney, "Toyota's Global Conveyor Belts," *American Shipper* (September 1994): 50–58. Used with permission.

GLOBAL BUSINESS LOGISTICS

In recent years, increasing numbers of companies have become aware that the marketplace encompasses the world, not just the United States. For example, many U.S. firms have found that evaluating offshore sourcing alternatives is essential to a well-run logistics and materials management organization. Alternatively, by developing export markets, U.S. firms have highlighted the need for effective logistics systems and networks throughout the world. Conversely, companies located in other countries have also broadened their sourcing and marketing considerations geographically; like U.S. firms, they look toward global logistics strategies and operations to provide *competitive advantage* through efficiency, effectiveness, and differentiation.

global sourcing

global distribution

As a practical matter, logistics managers are finding that they need to do much work in terms of conceptualizing, designing, and implementing logistics initiatives that may be effective globally. For this reason, this chapter addresses key issues and topics that are essential to the global aspects of business logistics. Logically, the development of global logistics approaches requires a high degree of coordination between logistics groups, marketing, and purchasing groups in individual companies.

key issues

This chapter deals first with the nature of global business and global logistics. Then, two successive sections deal with key global logistics trends and with changing political and legal environments. Finally, the chapter discusses transportation, channel strategies, storage and packaging, and governmental influences.

The Magnitude of Global Logistics Activity

World trade and world logistics expenditures are growing rapidly. World trade is growing nearly twice as fast as world output.

The growth of world trade is made possible by the planning of logistics companies all over the world. Countries are becoming closer and closer because of the success in logistics. Foreign trade has grown in tonnage and in value for the United States and most of the nations of the world. The world is becoming more and more competitive due to the growth in logistics activity. A firm will produce anywhere in the world where it is feasible and leave the transportation from country A to country B to the logistics professionals.

Figure 13–1 indicates historical and projected growth rates for various segments of world trade. Of particular interest is that regardless of trade lane (e.g. North America to the Far East, the Far East to North America, etc.) all of the recent and forecasted average annual growth rates are positive. This supports the observation that trade continues to grow between most or all major geographical trade areas.

world trade

Another interesting trend relates to worldwide logistics expenditures (see Figure 13–2). Worldwide logistics expenditures should rise to nearly $2.1 trillion by the year 1999. This amounts to approximately 16 percent of worldwide GNP.

logistics expenditures

Figures 13–3 and 13–4 present information about the percentages of freight tonnage imported to and exported from the United States. According to Figure 13–3, for example, the average percentage of U.S. freight tonnage represented by import shipments is expected to reach 16.0 percent in 1995. And Figure 13–4 reveals that U.S. exports as a percentage of U.S. freight tonnage should reach 15.7 percent in 1995.

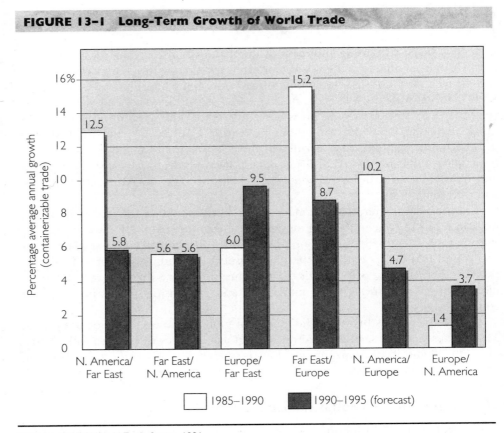

FIGURE 13-1   Long-Term Growth of World Trade

SOURCE: *TBS/DRI World Trade Service,* 1991.

Outsourcing, or purchasing materials for manufacture or sale from foreign suppliers, is a critical component of the logistics supply chain of companies. Managing the outsourcing decision may be complex, depending on the circumstances surrounding the specific acquisition.

Table 13–1 provides information about the foreign origins of outsourced goods. Europe and the Far East appear to be attractive sources for outsourced raw materials and finished products, while South America seems to be a popular source of component parts and subassemblies. Geographically, sources of component parts seem to be much more dispersed than sources of raw materials and/or finished products. Further data indicated that approximately 65 to 70 percent of the firms surveyed cited cost as a motive for outsourcing, 20 to 30 percent cited availability, and 5 to 20 percent cited quality.[1]

The major reason for outsourcing is lower cost. Lower labor costs in developing nations mean lower prices for materials. The trend today is to outsource from any part of the world that offers a cost advantage and to move it to any destination through the global logistics supply chain.

Global Markets and Global Corporations

global trade   Generally, the global business environment has seen many trade barriers fall over the past decade. Whether the case involves trade between the United States and

FIGURE 13-2 Worldwide Logistics Expenditures

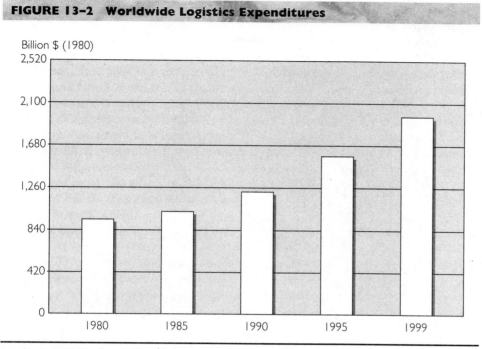

SOURCE: Temple, Barker, & Sloane, Inc., 1989.

FIGURE 13-3 Percent of Total U.S. Freight Tonnage Imported to the United States

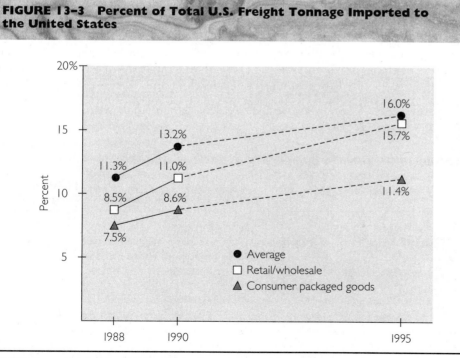

SOURCE: Bernard J. LaLonde, Ohio State University.

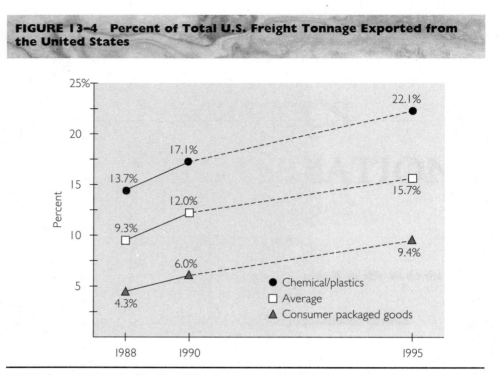

FIGURE 13-4 Percent of Total U.S. Freight Tonnage Exported from the United States

SOURCE: Bernard J. LaLonde, Ohio State University.

other countries or between two or more foreign countries, the trend toward facilitating, rather than constraining, global business activity is definitely accelerating. Thanks greatly to the growth and maturation of the ocean and air container shipping industries, distinct national and specific country-to-country international markets have been transformed into truly global businesses.

Global markets are a direct consequence of the acknowledgment and homogenization of global needs and wants.[2] Through new and extensive communications technologies, people throughout the world learn of and express the desire to have many of the same products. As a result, people have sacrificed traditional product

TABLE 13-1 Foreign Origins of Outsourced Goods

	Raw Materials (%)	Components (%)	Finished Products (%)
Europe	42	—	33
South America	5	40	4
Far East	29	18	35
Africa	—	15	—
Indian subcontinent	—	15	1
Middle East	1	12	1
Other	23	—	26

SOURCE: Temple, Barker, & Sloane, Inc., *International Logistics: Meeting the Challenges of Global Distribution Channels* (Lexington, MA: Temple, Barker, & Sloane, 1987): 2.

preferences for higher-quality, lower-priced products that are more highly standardized. This preference for nontraditional products is due to economic and cultural factors. The availability of high-quality merchandise at locally reasonable price levels is an attractor to people throughout the world. In addition, the opportunity to own or use products that are used in other countries helps people to feel that they enjoy standards of living that may be comparable to those of more prosperous nations.

We commonly see differences in promotion and in products themselves when manufacturers market their products to potential buyers in various parts of the world.[3] Canon's marketing of a new 35mm automatic camera served as a good example. As a result of extensive customer research conducted in markets worldwide, Canon decided to create a single "world camera" that would respond to the collective preferences of a wide variety of potential purchasers. In order to customize its appeal to buyers in individual countries, however, Canon positioned the camera differently in various market areas. In the United States, Canon described the camera as easy to use and slanted its appeal toward the growing market of nonprofessional photographers who nevertheless wanted a product of reasonable quality. Alternatively, in Japan, Canon designed the camera to appeal to the consumer as a state-of-the-art example of technological advancement in the photography field. This positioning was very effective, considering many Japanese buyers' strong desire for the latest, most advanced electronic equipment.

global product strategy

Global Competitive Strategy

An interesting distinction is that of a global company versus one whose operations are simply multidomestic. Essentially, global companies formulate strategy on a worldwide basis in order to exploit new market opportunities.[4] Such companies, which seek to influence their industries' competitive balance, implement global strategy effectively and efficiently. In comparison, multidomestic companies tend to operate within individual markets throughout the world, but do not emphasize coordinating individual strategies into a cohesive global strategy.

definition

Global companies tend to be more successful at developing strategies that help them to achieve their business objectives simultaneously at locations throughout the world. These companies are likely to strategically source materials and components worldwide, select global locations for key supply depots and distribution centers, use existing logistics networks when sourcing and distributing new products, and transfer existing logistics technologies to new markets. Examples of U.S.-based global companies include Xerox, IBM, DuPont, Kodak, Philips Consumer Electronics, Merck, Coca-Cola, Philip Morris, and McDonald's.

One key to achieving global success is to achieve global business volumes. This not only justifies entering markets and introducing new products in many areas of the world, but also provides business activity sufficient to absorb the significant cost outlays essential to this level of activity.

Global corporations typically design their operating strategy objectives around four components: technology, marketing, manufacturing, and logistics.[5] While initiatives in all four areas should function synchronously, the logistics system serves as the global infrastructure upon which the other systems operate. Also, firms have recognized that the global logistics system itself may provide a source of competitive advantage.

global operating strategies

For example, Toyota has developed the JIT concept for global operations as described in the Logistics Profile at the beginning of this chapter. By refining its information and planning systems, it is capable of outsourcing parts and components from many different nations for its plants in 25 countries. Instead of producing automobiles solely in Japan for export throughout the world, Toyota's strategy is to produce more automobiles within the national market and to outsource parts and components from Japan and other nations. The logistics system enables this strategy to operate effectively.

Customer Service Strategies for Global Markets

An interesting distinction exists between the meaning of the terms "global," and "international" or "multinational":

> Global marketing is as different from international or multi-national marketing as chalk is from cheese. Whereas the emphasis in multi-national marketing has been to tailor products and marketing strategies to meet perceived local needs, the thrust of global marketing is to seek to satisfy common demands worldwide. There has been a belated recognition that, for all the mythology, the customer in Bogota is little different from his counterpart in Birmingham.[6]

global competition Global competition has four prominent characteristics. First, companies competing globally seek to create standardized, yet customized, marketing. Second, product life cycles are shortening, sometimes lasting less than one year. This is true for certain high tech products such as computers and peripherals, photography items, and audio-visual equipment. Third, more companies are utilizing outsourcing and offshore manufacturing. Fourth, marketing and manufacturing activities and strategies tend to converge and be better coordinated in firms operating globally.[7]

As companies service global markets, logistics networks tend to become more expansive and complex. As a result, it is not unusual to see lead times increase and inventory levels rise. To successfully operate in a time-based competitive environment, firms emphasize managing logistics as a system, shortening lead times when possible, and moving toward the use of "focused" factories that produce limited product lines for geographically specific areas. In Europe, companies such as Unilever, Electrolux, and SKF have successfully practiced this latter strategy.

customer needs Perhaps the most important step in designing and implementing global logistics strategies is to understand the service needs of customers in locations dispersed throughout the world. This is a prerequisite to developing effective manufacturing, marketing, and logistics strategies to satisfy the needs of the global marketplace. The whole of the logistics operation should be based around the customers' needs.

CRITICAL FACTORS AND KEY TRENDS

This section first identifies significant factors that have affected the competitive positioning of companies in business environments throughout the world. It then briefly discusses several key logistics and transportation trends that have significantly affected the global business activity of U.S.-based firms and the activity of offshore firms doing business in the United States.

Importance of Competitive Environment

Based on a four-year study of ten countries, Michael Porter has concluded that "a nation's ability to upgrade its existing advantages to the next level of technology and productivity is the key to international (global) success." [8] He feels that a loss of global market share in advanced fields such as transportation and technology shows the United States slipping recently in international trade.

To explain his theories of what produces competitive advantage in a global business environment, Porter suggests a "dynamic diamond" containing four elements of competitive advantage that reinforce one another. These elements include:

Porter's "dynamic diamond"

- *Factor conditions:* A nation's ability to transform its basic factors (e.g., resources, education, or infrastructure) into competitive advantage
- *Demand conditions:* Examples include market size, buyer sophistication, and media exposure of available products
- *Related and supporting industries:* May include partners in the supply chain, co-packers and/or co-manufacturers, or marketing and distribution intermediaries
- *Company strategy, structure, and rivalry:* Market structures and the nature of domestic competition

Each element is necessary for success in domestic and global markets, and the presence of competition in domestic markets motivates individual firms to identify productive marketing, manufacturing, and logistics strategies. Creating more competitive business environments, stimulating demand for innovative new products (through the provision of tax credits, for example), placing greater emphasis on research and development, and refocusing trade policies on truly unfair subsidies and trade barriers are strategies for success in global markets.

Critical Changes in Logistics and Transportation

In this section, we will discuss briefly five major areas of change: deregulation of the U.S. ocean liner industry, shipment control, trade policies, and currency fluctuations.

Deregulation of the U.S. Ocean Liner Industry. Perhaps the most striking result of the Shipping Act of 1984 was that U.S. ocean liner companies received greater freedom to set rates, establish service, and share shipping activities. At the same time, this legislation included steps to guard against unfair practices by foreign-flag carriers toward U.S.-flag carriers.

market structure

Direct consequences of this shift to marketplace regulation included the use of service contracts, the right of ocean carriers to take independent action concerning rates and services, and the offering of intermodal through rates in conjunction with land carriers such as railroads and motor carriers. Chapter 9 fully discussed related issues.

intermodal transportation

Intermodalism. As discussed in Chapter 9, it is useful to introduce this topic as one critical area that has grown recently in usage and popularity. Intermodalism refers to the joint use of two or more transportation modes; moving highway trailers or containers on rail flatcars or in container ships is an example. Figure 13–5 shows intermodal options available to international shippers. Those options include all-water service, mini land bridge, land bridge, and microbridge operations.

As was seen in the Logistics Profile, Toyota uses a mini land bridge for the movement of parts and components from Japan to its two plants in the United States. The mini land bridge to Georgetown, Kentucky, has a lower cost than an all-water movement to an East or Gulf Coast port and then a land shipment by truck or rail to Georgetown. But more important, the cycle time is much lower by the mini land bridge.

Intermodal operations represent one of the fastest growing areas in the global logistics arena. By combining the resources of two or more transportation modes, logistics services suppliers can provide a service to the shipper-customer that appears to be seamless, despite the sometimes numerous and complex operations involved in moving the shipper's product. Among a number of firms that capably

FIGURE 13–5   International Distribution Shipping Options

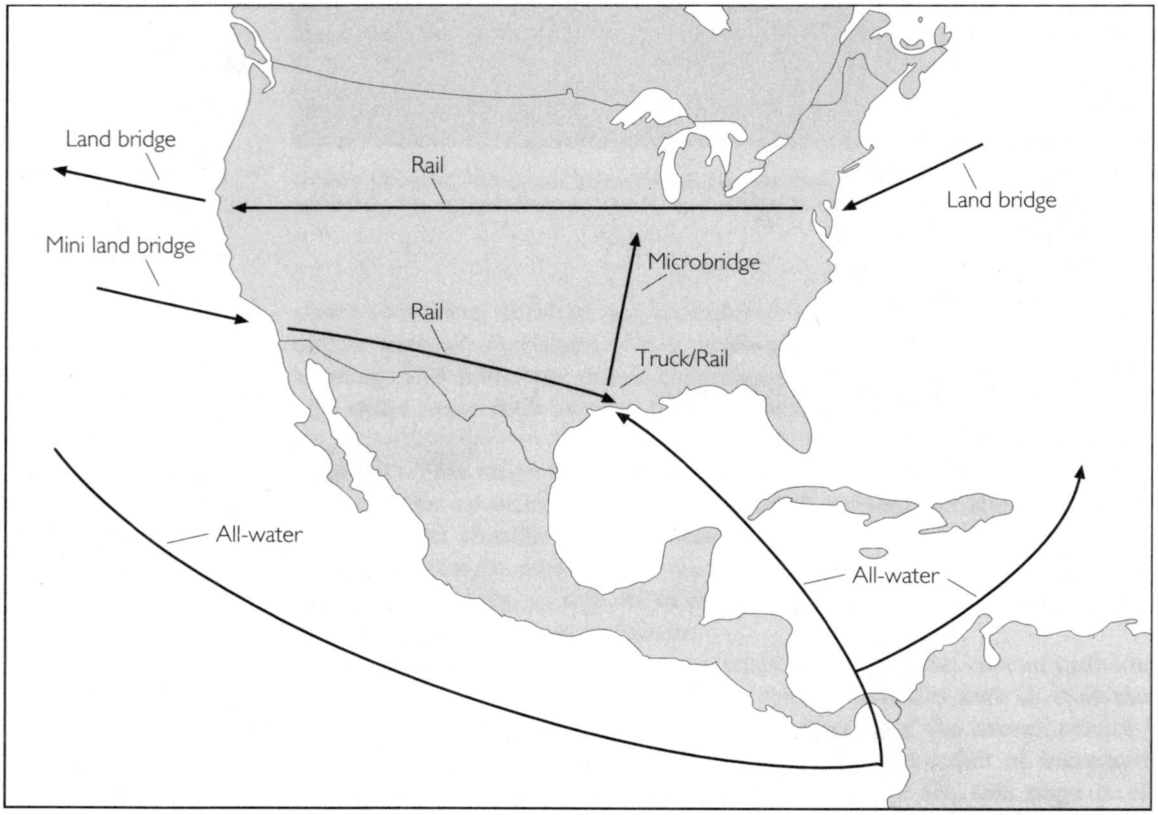

SOURCE: Temple, Barker, & Sloane, *International Logistics: Meeting the Challenges of Global Distribution Channels* (Lexington, MA: Temple, Barker & Sloane, 1987): 26.

provide comprehensive logistics and transportation services, CSX Corporation serves as an excellent example (see Figure 13–6).

In international shipping we have to understand three very fundamental concepts: port to port, port to point, and point to point. Port to port refers to moving cargo between two ports, for example, New York and Rotterdam, the Netherlands. Port to point refers to moving cargo between a port and final inland destination, for example, Kobe, Japan, and Chicago. Finally, point to point moves imply transportation between the shipper's door and the customer's door. The point-to-point movement is characteristic of intermodalism.

Shipment Control.   Effective communication and control systems are essential to a competitive global logistics capability. Issues concerning documentation, export-import management, and individual shipments' movements are critical to today's customers; and preferred suppliers are those who can meet these customer requirements.

communications and control

Most major international transportation companies, particularly the air carriers, have high tech communication systems that permit the tracking of the progress

FIGURE 13–6 CSX Corporation

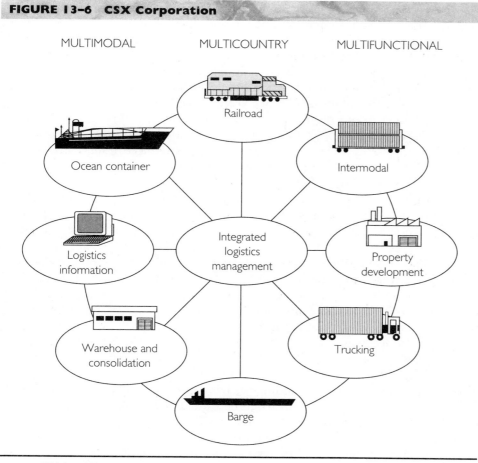

MULTIMODAL   MULTICOUNTRY   MULTIFUNCTIONAL

Railroad

Ocean container

Intermodal

Logistics information

Integrated logistics management

Property development

Warehouse and consolidation

Trucking

Barge

SOURCE: CSX, Inc., 1991.

of the shipment. Federal Express's tracking systems can locate an international shipment within seconds, indicate the time it is expected to be delivered, and the person who signed for delivery. Burlington Air provides shippers with publications describing the customs regulations of the countries it serves, and it provides assistance to shippers who have questions about shipping documentation.

free trade
agreements

Trade Policies.   Although a movement toward eliminating trade barriers worldwide characterized the years following World War II until about 1975, certain countries throughout the world have recently made selective changes in their trade policies. Many countries that are geographically close have negotiated free trade agreements. Europe has set the goal of becoming a Common Market under Europe 1992 guidelines. The United States, Canada, and Mexico have joined together to form the North American Free Trade Agreement (NAFTA), a free trade zone. (Both the European Common Market and NAFTA are discussed in more detail later in this chapter.) Even countries of the Asia-Pacific region that have historically set up protective barriers to restrict imports of goods into their home markets are starting to let down their guard. Australia, New Zealand, Japan, South Korea, Canada, and the United States have joined to found Asian Pacific Economic Cooperation (APEC).

However, we should keep in mind that official trade barriers and unofficial barriers such as customs delays still may impair the ability of logistics systems to function effectively in terms of product supply and/or distribution.

Another key element to remember is that countries have different cultures, customs, and business practices. Shipment delays are possible when these cultural differences are not understood. For example, in developing nations it is quite common for customs officials, who are not well paid, to accept a favor from the carrier or shipper to speed up processing of the documents. The offering of such favors is considered a bribe in the United States and is punishable by law.

The North American Free Trade Agreement has reduced trade barriers such as import duties on a wide number of products moving among the United States, Canada, and Mexico. But physical barriers still remain, especially into Mexico. One such physical barrier takes the form of prohibiting U.S. trucks and drivers from operating in Mexico, thus requiring all cargo to be handed off to a Mexican trucking company and driver.

Currency Fluctuations.   Both short- and long-term trends in the value of the U.S. dollar in comparison with the currencies of other nations may easily affect logistics decisions. When the dollar is strong, as it was during most of the 1980s, the United States tends to become a net importer of goods. This is logical, considering that when the dollar is rising in value it is less expensive for U.S. firms to buy other countries' products than it is for other countries to buy U.S. products. Conversely, when the dollar's value declines, as it did during the late 1980s and early 1990s, U.S. exports tend to rise and imports tend to fall.

A rise in exports and decline in imports has a direct link to ocean traffic. When exports are rising, outbound traffic from the United States increases. This, in turn, increases the price for outbound freight as the factors of demand and supply determine prices. At the same time, inbound traffic to the United States is declining due to a weak dollar, and ships traveling to the United States are carrying less freight; hence, shipping rates are lower for inbound traffic due to lower demand. This gives the shipper more power to negotiate rates on inbound shipments.

Fluctuations in world currency values can significantly affect logistics decisions such as inventory positioning, plant and distribution center location, and choice of transportation mode and carrier. Buyers and sellers of logistics services sometimes agree to currency adjustment factors, which help to equalize the effect of short-term changes in relative currency values. Currency adjustment is usually a percent of the basic price.

CHANGING POLITICAL AND LEGAL ENVIRONMENTS

trading partners

As we indicated earlier, fluctuating trade policies throughout the world can significantly affect global logistics activity. This section describes several instances wherein changing political and legal environments have enhanced opportunities for trade and logistics activity.

Before discussing examples of global logistics issues, we should note that the United States' top five trading partners are Canada, Japan, Mexico, the United Kingdom, and Germany. Table 13–2 shows the value of these countries' trade with the United States in billions of U.S. dollars.

A Single European Market

In one of the most far-reaching commercial efforts the world has ever seen, the twelve member nations of the European Economic Community (the EEC), formerly the Common Market, have agreed to a single, unified European market. The EEC is popularly called the European Union (EU). Instead of twelve fragmented markets in Belgium, Denmark, France, Greece, Ireland, Italy, Luxembourg, the Netherlands, Portugal, Spain, the United Kingdom, and Germany, the plan would create one integrated market of more than 320 million consumers and workers. The map in Figure 13–7 shows the locations of the EU member nations.

The Single European Act of 1987 eliminated trade barriers between EU member nations and facilitated the free movement of goods, services, capital, and people among them. To achieve these goals, the act identified three general barriers for elimination:

- *Physical barriers,* such as customs control and border formalities
- *Technical barriers,* for example, different health and safety standards
- *Fiscal barriers,* such as differences in value-added tax rates and excise duties

TABLE 13–2   U.S. Trading Partners

Country	Value of Trade ($ billion)
1. Canada	211.6
2. Japan	155.1
3. Mexico	81.5
4. United Kingdom	48.1
5. Germany	47.5

SOURCE: *U.S. Foreign Trade Highlights 1993* (U.S. Dept. of Commerce, July 1994): 29.

FIGURE 13-7 The Member States of the European Union (EU)

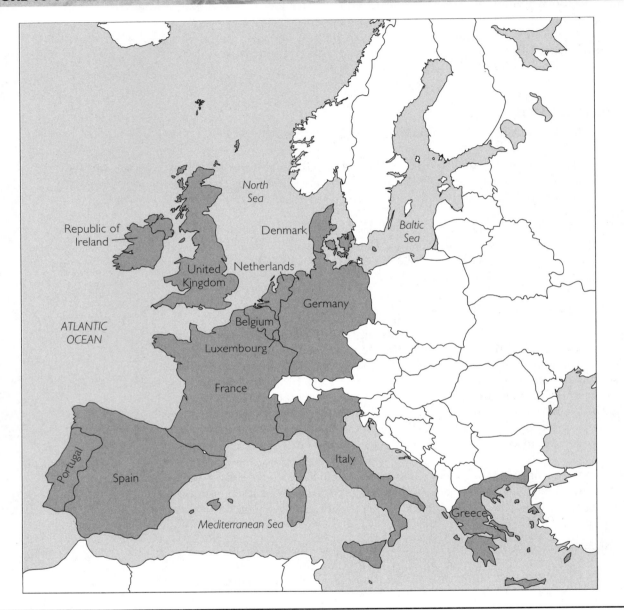

At first, these laws most benefited medium-sized companies who competed only with neighboring European Union countries. As the inspection of goods was eliminated between inland borders and free movement of goods was allowed, shorter transportation times resulted.

Other considerable changes have occurred in areas such as documentation and customs procedures, internal trade barriers, national brands and markets, and external trade barriers under the European Union. The area of patent protection has also been incorporated into the Common Market. At present when a European company wants patent protection, it has to register in each country individually. The Community Trade Mark (CTM) was established under the EU to simplify the process of protecting intellectual rights. Under the CTM, a trademark can be filed through one application to the CTM office to offer trademark protection in all of the EU. The office, located in Allocate, Spain, became fully functional in 1996 and should result in a large time and cost savings for all those who use it.

Of all the changes that the single European market concept encompasses, three affect logistics most directly.[9] The first is the facilitation of intercountry shipment procedures, most notably through the use of a single administrative document (SAD) to reduce border-crossing time. Second is the simplification of customs formalities for shipments simply "passing through" countries en route to others. This would reduce, for example, the time a container destined for Belgium would spend in customs activities at the entry port of Rotterdam, the Netherlands. Third is the introduction of common border posts, or "banalization." Essentially, this concept makes a border crossing from Spain to France, for example, a European customs entry, not a French one.

logistics effects

Generally, the facilitation of intercountry movements will concentrate European logistics networks of production and distribution into a more concise network of fewer facilities.

Overall, these initiatives will facilitate trade and the emergence of a more competitive business environment among EU member nations. This marketplace will likely attract new competitors, both from Europe and abroad. For example, many U.S. firms have been refining and implementing European market strategies even as this significant change has been occurring. Likewise, as the single European market concept grows and matures, EU member countries will find that they can be more competitive in other parts of the world.

In general, open-market relationships such as these will certainly facilitate trade and help to reduce the cost of doing business. Once again, this reduced cost of doing business would be due to improved efficiency of logistics operations focusing on ocean, rail, and trucking.

Eastern Europe

The countries of Eastern Europe and the Baltic states have broken away from their history of communist government and are fighting the uphill battle of restructuring their economies based on a capitalistic system. Presently the demand in these countries outweighs their capacity to produce. Most of these countries have old infrastructures, especially in the areas of roads and telecommunications, that need to be redesigned.

The Baltic states are working hard to restructure. Their level of reliability in service has recently risen to 80 percent, but it still not up to par with American standards. Russia seems to be one of the more problematic countries in the Baltic region. Since 1992, $1.6 billion of foreign capital has been invested there, yet there are still no rules governing commercial property or property guarantees. Other Eastern European governments have been selling off their assets in efforts to privatize their economies. At this time the Czech Republic has the most stable economy of that region.

The emergence of a capitalistic Eastern Europe means the probable expansion of the European Union. Already certain Eastern European countries have asked for membership but have been denied due to their poor economies. When and if the countries of Eastern Europe join the EU, the largest free trade zone in the world will be created.

The North American Free Trade Agreement (NAFTA)

The North American Free Trade Agreement (NAFTA), which became law on January 1, 1994, creates the world's richest trading block with the joining of the United States, Canada, and Mexico (and possibly Central and South American countries in the future). NAFTA encompasses 360 million people and a total market of $6.6 trillion. It will phase out tariffs on more than 10,000 commodities during the next 10 to 15 years. Almost half the tariffs on U.S. and Canadian exports to Mexico were eliminated.

One principal benefit of the removal of these trade barriers is that companies in the three countries should become more involved in cross-border business. As Table 13–2 indicates, Canada is the largest U.S. trading partner, and Mexico is the third largest. The eventual phaseout of tariffs on trade among the three countries will directly reduce the supplier and product discrimination that typically accompanies more insular, protected national business environments.

Since 1989, the United States and Canada have had in effect a Free Trade Agreement designed to open the border between these two countries by eliminating protective measures and tariffs. The result has been an increase in the flow of raw materials and components to manufacturing or processing facilities. Thus, the logistics for U.S./Canada trade is well developed.

Even though the U.S./Canada Free Trade Agreement has been in effect for some time, certain trade barriers still remain. For example, many U.S. companies have yet to recognize certain French/English requirements for packaging and ingredient labeling. Another sensitive issue is that of plant closings, particularly in Canada, as a result of the liberalized trade between the countries. Even though economic efficiency may justify this type of change, it does affect labor issues significant to the well-being of both countries.

Trade with Mexico poses many trade barriers that NAFTA did not eliminate. The logistics barriers include a poor transportation infrastructure, restrictive foreign capital rules, and customs rules. The Mexican highway system is poor when compared to that existing in the United States and Canada. There is only one railroad, which is owned and operated by the Mexican government. There are no national LTL (less-than-truckload) trucking companies, and air transportation is limited to the few airports.

Mexican law protects Mexican trucking companies. At present, U.S. and Canadian trucking companies are prohibited from operating in Mexico. By 1997, Mexico will grant U.S. and Canadian trucking companies permission to operate in the six states bordering the United States. Within ten years of the signing of NAFTA, U.S. and Canadian companies can have 100 percent ownership in Mexican trucking companies involved in international commerce (cross-border) only. Foreign trucking companies are restricted from hauling intracountry shipments in all three countries; these are known as cabatoge restrictions.

Figure 13–8 shows the procedure required to move a truck shipment from the United States into Mexico. The U.S. trucking company moves the shipment to the

FIGURE 13-8 A Typical Truck Shipment Crossing into Mexico

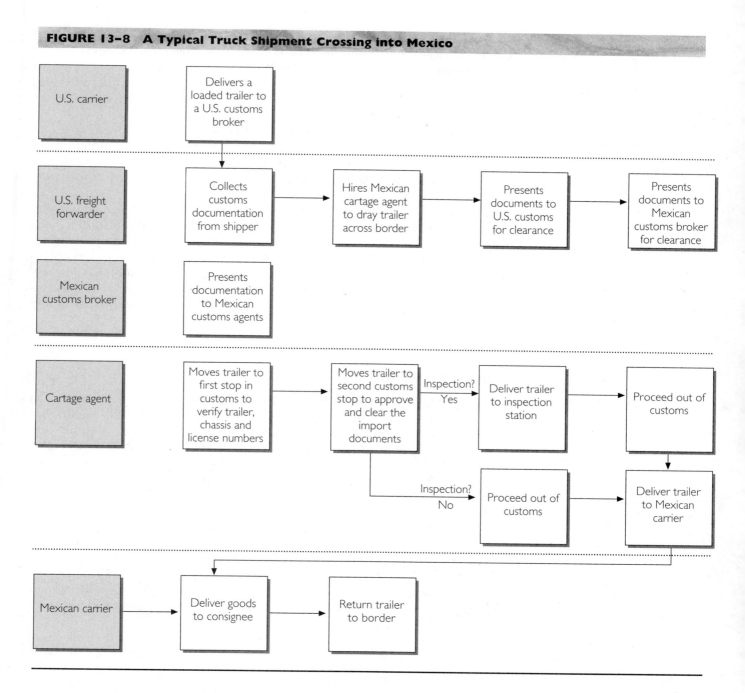

border, where a Mexican cartage carrier hauls the shipment across the border to Mexican customs and to the Mexican carrier after shipment clearance. The U.S. domestic freight forwarder submits shipment documents to the Mexican customs broker, who submits them to Mexican customs. Mexican customs inspects the documents, collects duties, inspects the goods, and clears the shipment. The Mexican cartage carrier delivers the shipment to a Mexican trucking company, who delivers it to the consignee.

Another logistics problem is Mexican labeling laws. Changes in labeling requirements are implemented with little notice given to shippers. For example, in early 1995 all imported retail goods were required to be individually labeled with the shipper's and buyer's tax identification numbers. This means that for a truckload shipment containing 30,000 bottles of wine, a label must be affixed to each of the 30,000 bottles before the shipment can clear customs.

Such logistics barriers will eventually be eliminated as NAFTA experience grows. Computerized customs information systems are currently operating in the United States and Canada, with Mexico a few years behind. The electronic transfer of information for NAFTA shipments into Mexico will speed the border crossing and improve logistics service.

In the long run, the goal of NAFTA is to create a better trading environment. But in the short run it has created much confusion due to the record keeping required to prove the origin of the product to obtain favorable tariff treatment. NAFTA's impact on logistics involves making the structural changes needed to operate a borderless logistics network in North America. Information systems, procedures, language, labels, and documentation are being redesigned. As new markets and supply sources develop, new transportation and storage facilities as well as intermediaries will be needed.

Maquiladora Operations

A concept that has become popular among U.S.-based firms is to use Mexican manufacturing/production facilities for subassembly or component manufacturing, or for final assembly of products such as electronic devices or television sets. While this has been occurring for some time, U.S. firms have only recently begun to include such Maquiladora operations (named for the region of Mexico in which many of these plant operations are located) as formal components of their manufacturing and logistics strategies.

Essentially, in a Maquiladora operation, a U.S. manufacturer either operates or subcontracts for a manufacturing, processing, or assembly activity to be performed in Mexico. Mexican production and labor costs are lower than those in the United States, and the operations involve no local content issues. U.S. firms often send semifinished product to Mexico for final assembly, for example, and then have the finished product shipped to the United States. This concept appeals to many companies: U.S. manufacturers operate more than 1,900 Maquiladora facilities in Mexico.

One feature that adds to the feasibility of such an approach is the concept of duty, which involves the importing, storing, manufacturing, and subsequent export of goods with virtually no net payment of customs duties or import charges. The duties are limited to the value-added portion of the goods, primarily labor, returning from Mexico. Effectively, this contributes to the economic efficiency of logistics alternatives such as Maquiladora operations.

Central America and South America

Generally, successful Mexican Maquiladora operations have served as role models for this concept's further exploitation in Central and South American countries. Coupled with the prospect of closer trade relations between the United States and Mexico, these alternatives offer considerable advantages to the firms utilizing them.

Asian Emergence

In perhaps the most significant trend of the past twenty-five years, Pacific Rim countries have emerged as key players in the global business environment. While Japan has achieved a dominant position in global financial markets, other Asian countries in general account for significant portions of global trade growth. Hong Kong, South Korea, Singapore, and Taiwan have all assumed leadership positions in certain markets and product types. This trend is likely to accelerate in the future.

Of the top 20 countries supplying manufactured goods to the United States in 1993, eight were Asian. Japan is the leading supplier of manufacturing imports to the United States, totaling $106.5 billion in manufactured goods. China is the fourth largest, followed by Taiwan (sixth), South Korea (eighth), Singapore (tenth), Malaysia (twelfth), Hong Kong (thirteenth), and Thailand (fourteenth).

Many Asian countries have become preferred sources for many raw materials and components. These countries have become trusted suppliers of finished goods such as apparel, furniture, consumer electronics, and automobiles. The advantage many of these countries offer is low labor cost and high quality.

New Directions

Aside from establishing product sources in other countries, offshore companies are beginning to locate plants and key logistics facilities in countries that use or consume their output. For example, Japanese-based firms such as Toyota (see the Logistics Profile) have located transplants in the United States. Similarly, U.S. automobile manufacturers such as Ford and General Motors have located transplants in other countries.

Many global manufacturers are using a strategy known as focus production in which a given plant produces one or two items of the company's total product line. The plants are typically located in different countries, requiring a global logistics system to tie the focused plant to the customer, who may be located within the producing country or a different country.

South America is making an economic resurgence in the 1990s. It is fighting against its old problems of high inflation, unstable governments, and corrupt leaders. The shift to free market policies has caused inflation to decrease and the total GNP to rise above 1991 levels. This new prosperity means a huge demand for U.S. goods and services and many new sourcing opportunities for U.S. firms.

Procter & Gamble, a producer of household cleaning and personal care products, opened operations in South America in the 1950s. Today, P&G's South American sales are $2 billion, and it has more than 11,000 employees who sell and maintain operations from Mexico southward. Most of the products are exported from the United States, but P&G is acquiring sources of production by building or acquiring manufacturing plants in a number of South American countries. These plants distribute to neighboring countries.

U.S. and global corporations are well advised to examine sourcing and distribution strategies involving countries other than the ones with which they have traditionally been involved. New business opportunities are available in Puerto Rico and Caribbean basin countries and in areas such as Australia and Africa. Trade with Russia and Eastern Europe represents opportunities for sourcing raw materials and components as well as fertile new market areas.

Benetton's Global Logistics

Benetton, headquartered in Ponzano, Italy, manufactures trend-setting apparel. It has set the world standard for apparel logistics and supply chain management for over ten years. Each year Benetton ships 80 million items directly to 7,000 stores in 100 countries. Most of these items are shipped from one automated warehouse near the headquarters and have an order cycle time of seven days.

The entire transportation and customs process is paperless. Benetton's 200 suppliers and 850 subcontractors are tied into the company's logistics, manufacturing, and information systems, as are its major carriers and its in-house forwarder. The results of this system are almost perfect levels of customer service and the best cycle time in the industry. There is no excess stock in process or in the distribution pipeline and no end stock that must be liquidated.

The high cost of lost sales is the reasoning behind Benetton's state-of-the art logistics system. Planning starts 10 months before each of the two annual fashion seasons, when each store commits to at least 80 percent of the season's order. Additional orders are shipped to the stores within eight days by airfreight.

Benetton uses reusable packaging for all goods in transit, unique product identifiers, bar coding on delivery orders, and EDI for all international shipments. This has reduced the total cost by 30 percent and greatly improved customer service. In the future, Benetton expects to double its $2 billion sales by increasing growth in developing countries and shifting a large part of production to China, Turkey, Egypt, India, and Mexico.

SOURCE: Thomas A. Foster, "Global Logistics Benetton Style," *Distribution* (October 1993): 62–66. Reprinted by permission of *Distribution Magazine.*

GLOBAL TRANSPORTATION OPTIONS*

Global transportation is much more complex than domestic U.S. transportation. The distances involved are greater, and the number of parties involved is typically more extensive. Because of the large expanses of water separating most regions of the world, the major modes of global transport are ocean and air. Land modes also carry significant amounts of freight between contiguous countries, particularly in Europe, where land routes are short. Each of these modes fills a specific niche in the worldwide distribution network.

Ocean

ocean shipping Transport by ship is by far the most pervasive and important global shipment method, accounting for two-thirds of all international movements. Table 13–3 provides an interesting perspective on the growth of oceangoing freight movements. In terms of millions of twenty-foot equivalent container units (TEU), the total volume increased from 8.5 to 36.2 million TEUs between 1974 and 1989, an increase of over 400 percent. In addition, Table 13–3 shows that 90 percent of today's liner trade is containerized and that the largest ships can accommodate nearly 5,000 TEUs, almost a doubling of capacity since 1974. Currently, 16 percent of U.S. rail intermodal shipments have either an offshore source or an offshore destination, or both. Table 13–4 contains a ranking of ship lines based on the number of TEUs moved to and from the U.S. in 1993.

---

*For an in-depth discussion of global transportation, see Chapters 9 and 10.

TABLE 13–3 Global Shipping Trends

	1974	1989
International container loads (TEUs in millions)	8.5	36.2
Containerized world liner trade (%)	40–50	90
Largest container ships (TEUs)	2,600	4,600
Container size (feet)	20/35/40	20/40/45/48/53
U.S. intermodal rail carloads (%)	6	16

SOURCE: Data from Temple, Barker, & Sloane, Inc., 1991.

The Structure of Ocean Shipping.   Ocean shipping comprises three major categories. One is *liner service,* which offers scheduled service on regular routes. Another is *charter vessels,* which firms usually hire on a contract basis and which travel no set routes. And finally are *private carriers,* which are part of a firm's own logistics system.

Liner carriers offer common carrier service, sailing on set schedules over specific sea routes. They also offer set tariffs and accept certain standards of liability. Liners usually carry break-bulk shipments of less-than-shipload size. Most container and RO-RO (roll-on, roll-off) ships are liners. **liner services**

Liners are the property of large steamship companies, many of which belong to shipping conferences. These conferences are voluntary associations of ocean carriers that operate over a common trade route and use a common tariff for setting rates on the commodities they handle. Conferences also work together to attract customers and to utilize member ships as effectively as possible.

In general, conferences provide excellent service with frequent and reliable schedules, published daily in the *Journal of Commerce.* Additionally, conferences help to standardize shipping on many routes by stabilizing prices and offering uniform contract rates.

Firms contract *charter ships* for specific voyages or for specified time periods. **charters** *Voyage charters* are contracts covering one voyage. The carrier agrees to carry a certain cargo from an origin port to a destination. The price the carrier quotes includes all of the expenses of the sea voyage. *Time charters* allow the use of a ship for an agreed-upon time period. The carrier usually supplies a crew as part of the contract. The charterer has exclusive use of the vessel to carry any cargo that the contract does not prohibit and assumes all expenses for the ship's operation dur-

TABLE 13–4 Top Container Ocean Carriers Serving the United States

Rank	Carrier	Rank	Carrier
1	Sea-Land Service	6	NYK Line
2	Evergreen Line	7	Hyundai Merchant Marine
3	Maersk Line	8	K Line
4	American President Line	9	Orient Overseas Container
5	Hanjin Shipping Co.	10	Mitsui OSK Line

SOURCE: Data from Peter Buxbaum, "Conference Controversies," *Distribution* (July 1994): 64.

ing the charter period. *Bareboat* or *demise charter* transfers full control of the vessel to the charterer. The charterer is then responsible for the ship and all expenses necessary for the vessel's operation, including hiring the crew.

Chartering usually takes place through *ship brokers,* who track the location and status of ships that are open for hire. When a shipper needs to contract for a ship, he or she contacts a broker, who then negotiates the price with the ship owner. The ship owner pays the broker a commission on the charter's cost.

private   In a logistics system, *private ocean carriers* play the same role as private carriage in general. In other words, companies utilize private ocean vessels to lower their overall costs and/or to improve their control over transportation service. The major differences between domestic and international private ocean transportation are the scale of investment, the complexity of regulations, and the greater risk international transport entails. In international operations, chartering often provides a very viable substitute for private carriage.

Air

low transit times   The low transit times that air transport provides have had a dramatic effect on international distribution. The tremendous speed of airplanes combined with a high frequency of scheduled flights has reduced some international transit times from as many as thirty days down to one or two days. Recently, these low transit times have spurred the development of international courier services. These couriers offer door-to-door, next-day services for documents and small packages between most large American cities and a growing number of overseas points.

Mostly, however, the world's air carriers have concentrated on passenger service. Air cargo presently accounts for only 1 percent of international freight by weight. This very small volume is misleading, however. The nature of the cargo, mostly high-value, low-density items, brings the total value of airfreight cargo up to nearly 20 percent of the world total. Air cargoes include high-valued items such as computers and electronic equipment; perishables such as cut flowers and live seafood; time-sensitive documents and spare parts; and even whole planeloads of cattle for breeding stock. Table 13–5 provides a list of quality international cargo air carriers.

Because airlines have traditionally concentrated on passenger carriage, airfreight has taken a secondary role. Most airfreight travels as *belly cargo* in the bag-

TABLE 13–5 Quality International Air Carriers for Cargo

Air Express Carriers	Airlines
Airborne Express	British Airways
Burlington Air Express	Japan Airlines
DHL Worldwide Express	KLM Royal Dutch Airlines
Emery Worldwide	Lufthansa
Federal Express	Scandinavian Airlines
TNT Express Worldwide	Singapore Airlines
United Parcel Service	Southwest Airlines

SOURCE: Data from *Distribution* (August 1994): 56, 58.

gage holds of scheduled passenger flights. Only a few major airlines have all-freight aircraft.

In addition to short transit time, air transportation offers an advantage in pack- **packaging**
aging. This mode requires less stringent packaging than ocean transport, since air transport will not expose the shipment to rough handling at a port, to a rough ride on the oceans, or to the weather. A firm using air transportation may also be able to use the same packaging for international shipping as for domestic shipping. In addition, shippers have developed special containers for air transport. These containers reduce handling costs and provide protection, but they also make intermodal shipments difficult. Their odd shapes usually require shippers to repack the shipment before transporting it by another mode. Recent container handling innovations have made it possible to load standard twenty-foot containers onto freight aircraft. For example, a carrier can now load a Boeing 747 with up to thirteen TEU containers in addition to any cargo in the belly holds.

A disadvantage of air carriage is high freight rates, which have prevented many shippers from transporting international shipments by air. Generally, only highly valuable, highly perishable, or urgently needed commodities can bear the higher cost of airfreight.

Motor

Companies most often use motor transport when shipping goods to an adjacent country—between the United States and Mexico or Canada, for example. It is also very common in Europe, where transport distances are relatively short. Motor also plays a large part in intermodal shipments.

The advantages of international motor transport are basically the same as those for domestic shipments: speed, safety, reliability, and accessibility to the delivery site. However, motor shipment across multiple national boundaries involves a number of different import regulations. To minimize paperwork, these shipments are often made *in bond;* the carrier seals the trailer at its origin and does not open it again until it reaches its destination country.

Rail

International railroad use is also highly similar to domestic rail use. Rail's accessibility is much more limited internationally, however, because border crossing points are scarce. Differing track gauges in various countries also prevent long-distance shipments.

Intermodal container shipments are where rail is proving its value. Various **land bridge**
maritime bridge concepts involve railroads both for transcontinental shipments and to and from inland points. For example, a shipper using a *land bridge* substitutes land transportation for part of a container's ocean voyage, taking several days off the transit time and saving in-transit inventory costs. A prime example of a land bridge occurs on the trade route between Japan and Europe. The all-water route takes anywhere from twenty-eight to thirty-one days. If the shipment travels by water from Japan to Seattle (ten days), then by rail to New York (five days), and by water from New York to Europe (seven days), we have a total shipping time of approximately 22 days.

STRATEGIC CHANNEL INTERMEDIARIES

As we indicated earlier, intermediaries play a much larger role in global logistics operations than in the domestic United States. To someone first exposed to global logistics, the scope of services that intermediaries offer is almost overwhelming. However, as the following sections will explain, intermediaries play a truly strategic role in helping new and established companies venture into the global arena. Companies are all too grateful for assistance in unraveling operations involving sources and destinations in other countries.

Foreign Freight Forwarders

For a company with little international shipping expertise, the *foreign freight forwarder* is the answer. The foreign freight forwarder, which employs individuals who are knowledgeable in all aspects of international shipping, supplies its experts to small international shippers who find employing such individuals in their shipping departments uneconomical. Foreign freight forwarders are regulated by the Federal Maritime Commission.

forwarder functions

Foreign freight forwarders, like their domestic counterparts, consolidate small shipments into more economical sizes. In the international arena, these larger sizes range from containers up to entire ships. Foreign freight forwarders also perform the routine actions that shipments require. The functions they perform include the following:

- Quoting water and foreign carrier rates
- Chartering vessels or booking vessel space
- Obtaining, preparing, and presenting all documents
- Obtaining cargo insurance
- Paying freight charges
- Collecting and submitting money for shipments
- Tracing and expediting shipments
- Providing language translation
- Arranging inland transportation service

Since no two international sales are exactly alike and since shippers have varying international traffic capabilities, the forwarder usually performs the export work that the shipper cannot handle. The logistics manager must weigh the forwarder's cost against the cost of hiring personnel to perform the same tasks.

income sources

The forwarder derives income from different sources. One source is the fees charged for preparing export documentation. Another source is the commissions the forwarder receives from carriers. These commissions are based on the amount of revenue the forwarder generates for the carrier. The third type of income comes from the price difference between the rate the forwarder charges a shipper and the lower rate per pound it pays for the consolidated shipments. The final two sources are from the provision of inland transportation and warehousing functions.

Airfreight Forwarders. Airfreight forwarders perform the same functions as foreign freight forwarders, but for air shipments only. They do not require a license from the federal government as foreign freight forwarders do. Airfreight forwarders primarily consolidate small shipments, which they present to the air carrier for movement to the destination. In addition, they perform the following functions:

- Obtain, prepare, and present documentation
- Coordinate ground transportation and warehousing
- Trace and expedite shipments
- Publish tariffs and issue air waybills
- Assume liability for damage to the shipment

There are two types of airfreight forwarders: consolidators and agents. The consolidator type is not aligned with a particular air carrier and will use the air carrier with the lowest rate. The agent type is aligned with a specific air carrier or carriers and markets cargo space for the carrier(s).

Like the foreign freight forwarder, the airfreight forwarder generates income from fees charged for services provided and the difference between the rate charged the shipper and that paid to the air carrier. The major competitors of airfreight forwarders are the air carriers, who can go directly to the shipper and eliminate the forwarder. For small shipments, the air express carriers, such as Federal Express, Emery, UPS Air, and DHL, compete directly with the forwarders.

Non-Vessel-Operating Common Carriers

The *non-vessel-operating common carrier* (NVOCC) consolidates and dispenses containers that originate at or are bound to inland points. The need for these firms arose from the inability of shippers to find outbound turnaround traffic after unloading inbound containers at inland points. Rail and truck carriers often charge the same rate to move containers, whether they are loaded or empty. NVOCC rates are regulated by the Federal Maritime Commission.

To reduce these costs, the NVOCC disperses inbound containers and then seeks outbound shipments in the same containers. It will consolidate many containers for multiple-piggyback-car or whole-train movement back to the port for export. They also provide scheduled container service to foreign destinations.

The shippers and receivers of international shipments gain from the shipping expertise NVOCCs possess and from the expanded and simplified import and export opportunities. The ocean carrier gains from the increased market area made possible by NVOCCs' solicitation services.

Export Management Companies

Often a firm wishes to sell its products in a foreign market but lacks the resources to conduct the foreign business itself. An *export management company* (EMC) can supply the expertise such firms need to operate in foreign environments.

EMCs act as agents for domestic firms in the international arena. Their primary function is to obtain orders for their clients' products by selecting appropriate markets, distribution channels, and promotional campaigns. The EMC collects and analyzes credit data for foreign customers and advises exporters on payment terms. It also usually collects payments from foreign customers. EMCs may also supply documentation, arrange transportation, provide warehouse facilities, maintain a foreign inventory, and handle break-bulk operations.

obtain orders

exclusive agent   A firm usually contracts an export management company to provide its exclusive representation in a defined territory. The EMC may either purchase the goods or sell them on commission. In order to present a complete product line to importers, an EMC will usually specialize in a particular product type or in complementary products.[10]

Using an export management company has several advantages. First, EMCs usually specialize in specific markets, so they understand in detail what an area requires. They will have up-to-date information on consumer preferences and will help the exporter to target its products most effectively. Second, EMCs will usually strive to maintain good relations with the governments of the importing countries. This enables them to receive favorable customs treatment when introducing new products. EMCs also remain current on documentation requirements. This helps the goods they are importing to enter with few holdups.

Export Trading Companies

An *export trading company* (ETC) exports goods and services. The ETC locates overseas buyers and handles most of the export arrangements, including documentation, inland and overseas transportation, and the meeting of foreign government requirements. The ETC may or may not take title to the goods.[11]

A trading company may also engage in other aspects of foreign trade, in which case it becomes a *general trading company*. One reason Japan has been successful in international trade is because of its large general trading companies, the *sogo shosha*. These firms, which consolidate all aspects of overseas trade into one entity, may include banks, steamship lines, warehouse facilities, insurance companies, sales forces, and communications networks.

advantages   A trading company allows small- to medium-size firms, which do not in themselves possess the resources, to engage in foreign trade. The trading company will purchase their goods and sell them on the international market, taking care of all the intermediate steps. Having all the functional areas under one control makes coordination easy and speeds response time when markets fluctuate.

Customs House Brokers

Customs house brokers oversee the movement of goods through customs and ensure that the documentation accompanying a shipment is complete and accurate for entry into the country. U.S. customs house brokers are licensed by the Department of the Treasury.

Customs house brokers operate under power of attorney from the shipper to pay all import duties due on the shipment. The importer is ultimately liable for any unpaid duties. The brokers keep abreast of the latest import regulations and of the specific requirements of individual products.

Today, customs house brokers use computers to transfer the information required to clear shipments for import. In the United States, the Automated Broker Interface system is used, and in Canada the system used is PARS (Pre-Arrival Review System). The use of computers has greatly reduced the time required for customs clearance and has reduced overall transit time for international shipments.

Ship Brokers

A ship broker acts as an intermediary for shippers desiring to charter a ship. The ship broker is a sales and marketing representative for ship owners and a purchasing representative for the shipper. The ship broker knows when ships will be or could be in port and coordinates this with the needs of the shipper.

Ship Agents

The ship agent is the local representative of the ship operator when the ship is in dock. The ship agent arranges for the ship's arrival, berthing, clearance, loading, and unloading, and for the payment of all fees while the ship is in port. Shippers can contact the ship agent for information regarding the arrival of the ship, the dock location, and arrangements for picking up or delivering the shipment.

Export Packers

Export packers supply export packaging services for shipments when the exporter lacks either the expertise or facilities. Having a specialist package the export has two distinct advantages. First, it helps the goods move through customs more easily. Many countries assess duties on the weight of the entire package, not just the contents. Export packagers, who know various countries' requirements, know what materials and methods to use in constructing the most economical crate or container.

    A second reason to use an export packager is to ensure adequate protection for the goods. International shipments must withstand the rigors of handling as well as climatic variations. Potential savings in time and reduced damage outweigh the cost of using an export packager.

rationale

Ports

One of the most important decisions in the global logistics arena is port selection. The port a firm selects for a global shipment must be appropriate to the cargo, since selecting the wrong port can add extra time and expense to the shipment's overall cost. The logistics manager must consider many factors simultaneously when selecting the best port for a particular shipment.

    The term "port authority" refers to any governmental unit or authority at any level that owns, operates, or otherwise provides wharf, dock, and other terminal facilities at port locations. These institutions, which provide access to the capital needed to develop and fund such operations, market the port to the shipping public and to other global logistics intermediaries.

port authority

    Figure 13–9 shows the factors that influence shippers' selection and evaluation of individual ports and port facilities. Over 90 percent of the shippers surveyed rated equipment availability as either important or very important. Factors such as cargo loss and damage frequency, and pickup and delivery times also received high rankings.

port evaluation study

    Another important aspect of port selection is the type of domestic transportation available between inland points and the port facility. As with domestic ship-

FIGURE 13–9   Port Evaluation Factors

Factor	Importance
Has equipment available	1
Provides low frequency of cargo loss/damage	2
Offers convenient pickup and delivery times	3
Allows large shipments	4
Offers flexibility in special handling needs	5
Has low freight handling charges	6
Provides information concerning shipments	7
Has loading/unloading facilities for large and/or odd-sized freight	8
Offers assistance in claims handling	9

SOURCE: Paul Murphy, James Daley, and Douglas Dalenberg, "Some Ports Lack Shipper Focus," *Transportation & Distribution* (February 1991): 48.

ments, the type of transportation a firm will use depends on factors such as the shipment's weight or quantity, the cargo's value, and the product's special handling requirements, if any. With a global/international shipment, a firm must decide whether or not to containerize the product for shipment.

After choosing the transport mode, the logistics manager must ensure that the inland carrier can get close enough to the overseas vessel to minimize handling and loading expenses. The manager must also consider these factors for the destination port. Such concerns particularly apply to less-developed areas, where advanced unloading equipment may be in short supply or even entirely absent.

Also important will be the identity of the specific ocean carriers serving the origin port and the desired destination port. Logically, the logistics manager will wish to select ocean carriers that serve the origin-destination pair(s) of greatest interest to the shipper.

Once the consignment reaches the destination port, the shipper should load it into the vessel as quickly and as inexpensively as possible. This is where the availability of proper equipment and an adequate labor supply will work to the customer's advantage. Containerized shipments will require specialized equipment. Extra-large or outsize cargoes may also require heavy-lift cranes. These specific equipment types may be available only at certain ports.

Finally, the person making the port selection decision should consider the facility's potential effects on overall "door-to-door" transit time and variability. Defined as the transit time from the shipment's initial origin to its ultimate destination, this door-to-door measure will certainly be longer than the ocean crossing, or port-to-port time. Ports that help to minimize the time and variability of door-to-door logistics service will be attractive to shippers who prefer a more comprehensive logistics approach.

Table 13–6 shows the ranking of U.S. ports based on the number of containers, tonnage, and value of commerce handled in 1993. The West Coast ports dominate in the number of containers and value of commerce handled because of the Pacific Rim trade. The Gulf and Atlantic Coast ports dominate in the tonnage handled.

TABLE 13-6   Ranking of U.S. Ports by Containers, Tons, and Cargo Value

By Containers	By Tons	By Cargo Value
Los Angeles	South Louisiana	Los Angeles
Long Beach	Houston	Long Beach
New York/New Jersey	Hampton Roads (VA)	New York/New Jersey
San Juan	New Orleans	Seattle
Oakland	New York/New Jersey	Oakland
Seattle	Baton Rouge	Houston
Tacoma	Corpus Christi	Tacoma

SOURCE: Data from *U.S. Public Port Facts* (Alexandria, VA: American Association of Port Authorities, September 1994).

STORAGE FACILITIES AND PACKAGING

Storage Facilities

containers

At several points during an international shipment, the goods being shipped may require storage. Storage may be necessary while the shipment waits for loading on an ocean vessel, after it has arrived at the destination port and is awaiting further transportation, or while customs clearance is being arranged for the merchandise. When packaged in a container, goods are protected from the weather, theft, and pilferage. A carrier or shipper can store containers outside between a journey's stages with little effect on the contents.

other options

Noncontainerized cargo, on the other hand, requires protection if it is to arrive in good order. Ports supply several types of storage facilities to fill this need. *Transit sheds*, located next to the piers or at the airport, provide temporary storage while the goods await the next portion of the journey. Usually, the port usage fee includes a fixed number of days of free storage. After this time expires, the user pays a daily charge. *In-transit storage areas* allow the shipper to perform some required operation on the cargo before embarkation. These actions may include carrier negotiations and waiting for documentation, packing, crating, and labeling to be completed. The carrier usually provides *hold-on-dock storage* free of charge until the vessel's next departure date, allowing the shipper to consolidate goods and to save storage costs.

When goods require long-term storage, the shipper uses a warehouse. *Public warehouses* are available for extended storage periods. The services and charges offered by these facilities are similar to those of public warehouses in the domestic sphere. *Bonded warehouses*, operated under customs supervision, are designated by the U.S. Secretary of the Treasury "for the purpose of storing imported merchandise entered for warehousing, or taken possession of by the collector of customs, or under seizure, or for the manufacture of merchandise in hand, or for repacking, sorting, or cleaning of imported merchandise." [12] Only bonded carriers may move goods into and out of bonded warehouses.

purpose   One purpose of bonded warehouses is to hold imported goods for reshipment out of the United States. The owner can store items in a bonded warehouse for up to three years, allowing him or her to decide on the goods' ultimate disposition without having to pay import duties or taxes on them. If the owner does not reexport the goods before the three years elapse, they are considered imports and are subject to all appropriate duties and taxes.

Packaging

importance   Export shipments moving by ocean transportation require more stringent packaging than domestic shipments normally do. An export shipment receives more handling: it is loaded at the origin, unloaded at the dock, loaded onto a ship, unloaded from the ship at port, loaded onto a delivery vehicle, and unloaded at the destination. This handling usually occurs under unfavorable conditions—in inclement weather or with antiquated handling equipment, for example. If storage facilities are inadequate, the goods may remain exposed to the elements for a long time.

protection   The shipper may find settling liability claims for damage to export goods very difficult. Usually, the freight handling involves many firms; and these firms are located in different countries. Stringent packaging is the key to claims prevention for export shipments.

higher cost Stockout costs justify more protective packaging (increased packaging cost) for export shipments. The export distance is often so great that the time (two to four months) required to receive a reordered shipment may cause the buyer and seller extremely high stockout costs. The buyer may resort to an alternative supply source, and the seller may lose business.

The package size—weight, length, width, height—must conform to the customer's instructions. Packaging dimensions usually reflect the physical constraints upon transportation in the buyer's country. For example, the 40 × 8 × 8-foot containers common in the United States may be nontransportable in certain foreign countries. The container may not be compatible with some countries' existing transportation equipment, or it may exceed the height and lateral clearance of highways, bridges, and overpasses. If the package cannot be transported, the shipper must repackage the shipment. This additional handling adds costs, causes delay, and increases the risk of loss or damage to the shipment.

containers   Sellers frequently use containers for international shipping. A containerized commodity receives considerably less handling. With reduced handling comes reduced risk of loss and damage as well as greater time efficiency in the transfer among modes. The decision to use containers must reflect the savings we noted earlier, as well as the container's added cost, return freight costs on it, and any additional handling and storing costs.

marking   The package marking requirements for international shipments also differ from those for domestic shipments. On domestic shipments, package markings provide detail concerning things such as the shipment content and consignee. On export shipments, the package provides little information about the shipment. Large geometric symbols, numbers, letters, and various codes (see Figure 13–10) provide handling instructions to foreign materials handlers who often cannot read English. Using codes conceals the identity of the shipper, the consignee, and the goods so as to reduce the possibility of pilferage.

FIGURE 13-10   Some Symbols Used for Packing Export Shipments

Keep away from heat

This way up

Keep dry

Do not use hooks

SOURCE: Courtesy of Air France.

GOVERNMENTAL INFLUENCES

As Figure 13–11 indicates, the export-import process can be quite complex in terms of the various intermediaries it may involve. In addition, export-import documentation is far more complicated than it is for domestic U.S. shipments. The topic of documentation was discussed in some detail in Chapter 10.

This section addresses issues relating to the role of government in international trade. As we discussed previously, an increasing number of governments are attempting to simplify international trade and to facilitate the flow of commerce.

role of government

There are several areas in which governments can exert power over the flow of international commerce. One method is through import tax and duties. Governments often set these at high rates to protect local firms from competition. Another approach is to place import quotas on certain goods. Quotas limit the physical amount of product that may be imported in a specific time period, usually

FIGURE 13-11 Export-Import Flowchart

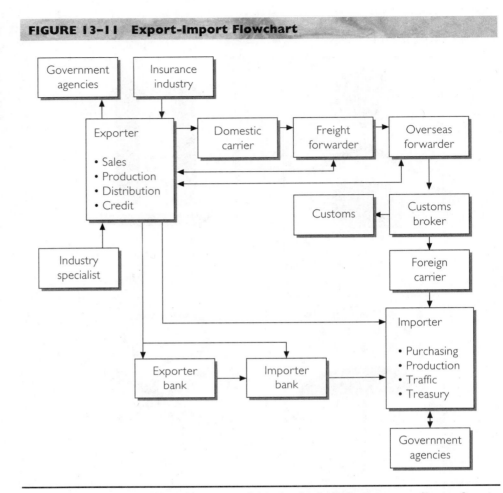

SOURCE: John E. Tyworth, Joseph L. Cavinato, and C. John Langley, Jr., *Traffic Management: Planning, Operations and Control* (Reading, MA: Addison-Wesley Publishing Company, 1987): 388.

a year. Individual nations may also enact regulations to prevent the import of dangerous items. For example, many nations restrict imports of animals and plants in order to prevent the spread of disease. The importing country may base still other restrictions on safety requirements.

A firm must take all possible restrictions into account before it can move goods internationally. Inadequate knowledge of current regulations may cause great losses in both time and money in terms of customer delays or extra import fees.

Customs Regulation

protection and revenue

National *customs regulations* have the greatest effect on the international movement of goods. Customs regulations fulfill two basic objectives: to protect domestic industry and to provide revenue.

Customs regulations protect national industries through high import duties, quotas, and restrictions on the items firms can import. If the companies involved research all of these factors before finalizing the sales contract, the shipment will encounter few problems at the actual time of entry.

Regulations raise revenue through the collection of *import duties*. These duties are set by national law and are determined in three different ways.

import duties

Ad valorem duties are the most common type of import duty. They are stated as a percentage of the value of the imported goods. For example, if a good has a value of $1,000 and is subject to an import duty of 15 percent, the amount customs collects is $150 ($1,000 × 0.15 = $150). The value used in computing the import duty is usually the merchandise's *transaction value,* the total price paid or payable for the good. It includes the good's price at its origin, the packing costs the buyer incurred, any selling commissions, any royalty or license fees, and the cost of any modifications necessary to allow the importation of the item.

The next major type of import duty is based on a cost per unit. For example, $5 per pound or $100 per unit could be a duty. If the shipment's weight or number of items is known, this *unit duty* is easy to calculate.

The third type is the *compound duty*. This method combines the ad valorem and unit duties. Suppose that a company wishes to import 100 items with a value of $200 each, and that applicable rates for this shipment are 12 percent of the value and $25 per unit. We would calculate the total import duty as follows:

Ad valorem rate: 100 × $200 × 0.12 = $2,400
Unit rate: 100 units × $25 = $2,500
Compound rate: $2,400 + $2,500 = $4,900

If the owner decides to reexport a good after importing it and the applicable duties have been paid, he or she may apply for a *drawback*. Drawbacks return 99 percent of the duty paid during import. The customs service retains the other 1 percent as an administrative fee. To receive a drawback, one must file an application within three years of re-export.

Other Customs Functions

As well as collecting import duties, the customs service also inspects imported merchandise. These inspections, conducted before the goods may enter the country, perform the following functions:

- Determine that the goods' value is the same as that stated on the shipment's documentation. This value is used to determine the import duties.
- Ensure that the items have the correct markings. They must have all appropriate safety labels, instructions, or special marks, as well as identification of the country of origin.
- Find any items that are excluded from entry. These items include illegal drugs and weapons, and articles that do not meet national standards.
- Ensure that the shipment is correctly invoiced and that the quantities stated are correct.
- Control quota amounts.

The customs service collects duties and performs inspections at *entry*. Entry includes all of the legal procedures a firm requires to secure possession of imported merchandise. Entry procedures must begin within five working days of a shipment's arrival. At entry, the customs service inspects the shipment's docu-

entry procedures

mentation for completeness and accuracy and inspects the items themselves to ascertain the value, to ensure that all import requirements are met, and to set the amount of any duties. The customs house broker is an essential intermediary for smooth flow through customs.

Customs procedures can be very time-consuming and expensive if a company does not conduct proper research before making a shipment. Knowing customs requirements beforehand is best. The U.S. Customs Service is striving to reduce import entry complications. The increasing use of electronic data transmission provides quicker entry times and improves the overall efficiency of customs procedures.

Foreign Trade Zones

Foreign trade zones (FTZs) are areas within a country that permit shippers to land, store, and process goods without incurring any import duties or domestic taxes. FTZs offer many advantages to parties engaged in international trade. Some of the major ones are as follows:

- Goods can be landed and stored without customs formalities, duty, or bond. FTZs offer excellent security for the merchandise because they are under customs control.
- Shippers can perform break-bulk operations on the goods before they are actually imported. Depending on the situation, this may lead to savings on duties and transportation costs.
- Imports can be processed, re-marked, or repackaged to meet local requirements before importation. This avoids any fines for importing improperly marked goods.
- FTZs can hold goods in excess of current quotas until the next quota period arrives.
- Buyers can test or sample products before import. This allows the buyer to ensure that the merchandise meets all contract stipulations before he or she accepts the goods and pays the import duties.
- The owner can reexport goods held in an FTZ at any time without having to pay any duties to the country where the FTZ is located.
- Goods can be stored indefinitely in an FTZ.

One very important aspect of a foreign trade zone is that a firm can use it for product manufacture. The manufacturer can purchase production process materials at the lowest price on the world market and bring them into the FTZ. The finished product can then be reexported or else imported using the duty on either the components or the final product, whichever is more advantageous to the importer. In addition, the manufacturer pays no duties on waste or by-products from the production process, realizing even more savings.

SUMMARY

- Global business activity and global logistics activity are increasing. Businesses are relying on foreign countries to provide a source of raw materials and markets for finished goods. Logistics ties together these geographically distant sources and markets.

- As global trade barriers fall, global competition increases. This has led to global companies that formulate strategies on a worldwide basis.
- The global company attempts to satisfy common demands worldwide.
- Porter's "dynamic diamond" theory suggests that a country's global competitive advantage is related to four elements: factor conditions, demand conditions, related and support industries, and company strategy, structure, and rivalry.
- The critical changes in global logistics are a result of deregulation of the U.S. ocean liner industry, intermodalism, shipment control, trade policies, and currency fluctuations.
- The largest U.S. trading partners are Canada, Japan, Mexico, the United Kingdom, and Germany.
- The European Union (EU) has unified twelve countries into a single trading block of 320 million consumers. The logistics impact of the EU is reduced documentation, simplified customs formalities, and common border posts.
- Eastern Europe, especially those countries that were once part of the USSR, represents a high-growth market potential for global companies.
- The North American Free Trade Agreement (NAFTA) joined the United States, Canada, and Mexico into the world's richest trading block. The logistics of moving products into and out of Canada poses minimal problems. But the logistics of trade with Mexico faces challenges in the areas of documentation, customs, transportation infrastructure, and labeling.
- A Maquiladora operation involves a U.S.-based company establishing a production or assembly facility in Mexico along the U.S.-Mexican border. The Maquiladora offers lower production (labor) costs, and U.S. import duties are limited to the value-added portion of the goods returning from Mexico.
- Asian and South American countries present sizable markets for goods and sources of raw materials and component parts.
- The primary global transportation system consists of ocean and air. For moves to bordering countries, rail and motor are used.
- The global logistics system relies heavily on intermediaries. The primary intermediaries are foreign freight forwarders, airfreight forwarders, non-vessel-operating common carriers, customs house brokers, and export management companies.
- The port used to exit and enter a country directly affects total logistics costs and service. Port authorities are governmental authorities that own, operate, or provide port facilities. Equipment availability is the most important port selection criterion.
- A bonded warehouse permits storage of an imported shipment without payment of duties on the goods until they are removed for sale or consumption.
- Packaging for global shipments is more stringent than for domestic.
- Customs regulations are designed to provide revenue to an importing country and to protect the country's industries.
- A foreign trade zone permits an importer to land, store, and process goods within the zone without incurring any import duties or domestic taxes.

STUDY QUESTIONS

1. What major trends do you see in world trade and in the significance of global logistics?

2. For global firms, describe the relationship between logistics strategy and other corporate strategies in the areas of technology, marketing, and manufacturing.

3. Discuss the importance of global logistics to both individual companies and to the United States as a whole.

4. What are the major elements of the "dynamic diamond" suggested by Michael Porter? Which do you feel are most important to the success of companies operating globally?

5. How have changes in the political, legal, and transportation environments affected global business and global logistics?

6. What is NAFTA? What impact has it had on global logistics systems for U.S. and European exporters?

7. Describe the role played by intermediaries in global logistics systems. Why are intermediaries not needed in domestic logistics systems?

8. What factors should be considered in selecting ports for global logistics operations?

9. What is a foreign trade zone, and what is its significance to global logistics operations?

10. What is the role of customs regulations, and how do they affect global logistics?

NOTES

1. Temple, Barker, & Sloane, Inc., *International Logistics: Meeting the Challenges of Global Distribution Channels* (Lexington, MA: Temple, Barker, & Sloane, 1987): 1–6.
2. David L. Anderson, "Logistics Strategies for Competing in Global Markets," in *1985 Council of Logistics Management Annual Conference Proceedings* (Oak Brook, IL: CLM, 1985): 414.
3. David L. Anderson, "Logistics Strategies for Competing in Global Markets," 415.
4. David L. Anderson, "Logistics Strategies for Competing in Global Markets," 415.
5. David L. Anderson, "Logistics Strategies for Competing in Global Markets," 416.
6. Martin Christopher, "Customer Service Strategies for International Markets," in *1989 Council of Logistics Management Annual Conference Proceedings* (Oak Brook, IL: CLM, 1989): 327.
7. Martin Christopher, "Customer Service Strategies," 327–28.
8. Michael Porter, "Why Nations Triumph," *Fortune* (12 March 1990): 54–60.
9. Richard R. Young, "Europe 1992: The Logistics Perspective of a European-Based Multinational," *Proceedings of the R. Hadly Waters Logistics and Transportation Symposium* (University Park, PA: Penn State University, 1990): 13–26.
10. John D. Daniels and Lee H. Radebaugh, *International Business* (Reading, MA: Addison-Wesley, 1986): 465–99.
11. Evelyn A. Thomchick and Lisa Rosenbaum, "The Role of U.S. Export Trading Companies in International Logistics," *Journal of Business Logistics* 5, no. 2: 86.
12. Paul S. Bender, "The International Dimension of Physical Distribution Management," in *The Distribution Handbook*, ed. James F. Robeson (New York: The Free Press, 1985): 801.

Case 13-1

SPORT SHOES, INC.

Sport Shoes, Inc. (SS) is a well-established U.S. sport shoe retailer. It sells a complete line of tennis shoes for all major sports as well as a top-of-the-line sport shoe that has become a fashion symbol with young professionals.

All of SS's shoes are manufactured in the Pacific Rim and are transported to the U.S. in containers by water carriers. The containers arrive at the port of Long Beach, where they are transferred to a stack train for movement to its distribution center in Indianapolis, Indiana. From its distribution center in Indianapolis, SS ships direct to its 250 stores in the U.S. and sixty stores in Mexico. The total cycle time from Pacific Rim manufacturers to U.S. stores is four weeks, and to Mexican stores it is seven weeks.

SS has been doing business in Mexico since 1990. It started with three stores and has expanded the business to a current total of sixty stores in Mexico's Golden Triangle. The Golden Triangle is the region bounded by Mexico City, Guadalajara, and Monterrey. This area contains over half of Mexico's population.

The logistics of shoes in Mexico reached a critical stage during the period of 1993 to 1994. Considerable growth in the Mexican economy, coupled with the increased importation of U.S. goods, caused an explosion in the demand for SS sport shoes. As SS increased the number of retail outlets in Mexico, it continued to logistically support these stores from its Indianapolis distribution center. With the increased flow of goods into Mexico from the United States, the congestion at the border crossing points created longer cycle times and increased stockouts.

The growth in the Mexican economy was not matched by an equal growth in its logistics infrastructure. The border crossing points became very congested, with two to three days being the normal customs clearance time during peak periods. The Mexican highway system consists mostly of dirt roads (about 55 percent) and secondary roads (about 25 percent). The Mexican trucking system is dominated by many small, local companies. No U.S. trucking companies operate in Mexico, because Mexican law prohibits foreign ownership of Mexican trucking companies. Some U.S. trucking companies have developed strategic alliances with Mexican trucking companies, and this has helped. In ten years, NAFTA will permit 100 percent ownership by foreign investors of Mexican trucking companies that are hauling foreign commerce.

Given the growing demand for SS shoes in Mexico, top management has made a strategic commitment to remain in Mexico. Also, top management has made it a high priority to solve the long cycle time for shoes going to the stores in Mexico.

Case Questions

1. Describe the logistics supply chain for shoes distributed in the United States and in Mexico. What are the major similarities and differences?
2. What changes would you recommend to the logistics system supporting the Mexican market?
3. In 1995 the Mexican government devalued the peso by 50 percent against the U.S. dollar. This devaluation had a very negative impact on the demand for U.S. goods in Mexico. How would this monetary action affect your recommended logistics system for shoes in Mexico?

CHAPTER 14

LOGISTICS ORGANIZATION

LEARNING OBJECTIVES

After reading this chapter, you should be able to do the following:

- Understand how logistics organizations develop.

- Know the characteristics of leading edge logistics organizations.

- Be aware of the fundamental ways in which logistics organizations differ.

- Evaluate the potential benefits of a centralized versus decentralized logistics network.

- Know how to measure logistics performance and the performance of logistics management.

- Understand how logistics creates customer value.

- Appreciate the value to be derived from a logistics quality process and understand some of the relevant quality issues and concepts.

- Structure a logistics quality process.

- Be aware of the contemporary interest in logistics process reengineering and in logistics value.

- Define what is meant by third-party logistics and describe the ways in which third parties create value for logistics customers.

- Understand the buying process used by firms in making the third-party decision.

- Know the differences between key types of third-party suppliers.

LOGISTICS PROFILE

NIKE

Nike represents a classic case of doing it right. The company continues to move ahead as its product lines proliferate and concept-to-cash cycles are squeezed to new levels.

James Brian Quinn, in his book *Intelligent Enterprise,* cites Nike, among others, such as Boeing and Apple, as intellectual organizations with the capabilities to sidestep the heavy investments involved in vertical integration and instead manage ideas and people.

Winning companies are not in the mouse trap business per se, but the service development and delivery business, suggests Quinn. From studying companies, Quinn has found that one component—service value—is the key to long-term success.

John Isbell, director of customer service, hopes that others in distribution recognize the bigger picture. "The whole logistics process needs to be placed on a horizontal process flow, which basically creates a seamless service delivery system where everyone on the continuum—be it sales, forecasting, production, transportation, customer service, credit, or distribution—sees him or herself as providing to the customer," says Isbell, who also oversees U.S. distribution at Nike.

Quinn suggests firms can move from being preoccupied with overseeing workers and machines to leveraging their real assets: knowledge bases as well as intellect and human skills. Extra risks and undesired costs are avoided when these companies—which are not "manufacturers"—become savvy marketers who typically perform their own R&D functions, outsource most of their production, and strike alliances with other companies, such as partnering with their carriers.

However, "The average manufacturing company today ain't" doing it, quipped management guru Tom Peters. For example, the only component on a Nike leather athletic shoe made by the company is the air-sole produced by its wholly/owned subsidiary Tetra Plastics of St. Louis.

Currently, Nike footwear production plants total some thirty-two across Asia, including China, Thailand, and Indonesia. About 40 percent of Nike apparel is manufactured within the United States, with additional production in Singapore, Malaysia, Sri Lanka, and Europe. The company is considering opening a footwear plant in Vietnam, while apparel production will expand to Central and South America.

Stateside, Nike distributes footwear from two DCs: a 500,000-square-foot facility in Wilsonville, Oregon, just south of its Beaverton, Oregon, "campus" and headquarters, and an 800,000-square-foot facility in Memphis, Tennessee.

The Memphis facility typically uses Federal Express to guarantee quick response for Nike's retailers. When a basketball player in Des Moines, Iowa, needs a pair of size 13 1/2 Air Jordans and his local store is out, the retailer can request next-day delivery by 10:30 A.M. "If they choose to use FedEx, we can take an order up to 7 P.M. CST because of our connection in Memphis and ship it that same evening," says Isbell.

Nike is also the embodiment of the "sneakerization" of society, a movement identified by Dr. Kenneth Preiss and fellow co-authors of the book *Agile Competitors and Virtual Organizations: Strategies for Enriching the Customer.*

"Sneakerizing," says the authors, is the transforming of commodity items to relatively high-priced specialty items. Today's technology allows such goods to be produced on a nearly customized scale. Air cargo and other refined distribution methods, combined with advances in information technology, enable speedy transference of goods to market.

Witness the proliferation of SKUs across any product line. The mind boggles at the thought of one manufacturer offering thousands of watch styles or hundreds of sunglasses. Nike produced 50 types of athletic shoes in 1977 for a relatively homogenized market, but by 1988, sharpened consumer demand and shortened product life spans multiplied products to 350.

ADAPTED FROM: Marcia Jedd, "Nike: Just Doing It Right," *Distribution* (January 1995): 36–40. Used with permission.

B usiness logistics management has grown in importance and complexity over the past two or three decades, and its strategic significance will accelerate in the years ahead. Although various factors have prompted companies to focus attention on the logistics process, the resulting awareness of and concern for logistics issues does not translate automatically into enhanced logistics efficiency and effectiveness. As firms search for new and innovative ways to accomplish their strategic missions, it is becoming increasingly apparent that the logistics area represents a significant opportunity for improvement.

need for organizational change

This chapter highlights a number of important considerations relating to the topic of logistics organization. While it would be reassuring to know that promising initiatives for organizational change would be met with enthusiasm, it is all too frequently the case that such opportunities are met with resistance. Rather than welcoming change, many traditional "departments" exhibit an extreme aversion to change and focus more attention on guarding their turf than on trying to identify and implement productive strategies that will lead to improvement.

If this challenge is not enough, managements today must acknowledge the inevitable conclusion that no single organizational approach will prove to be best under all circumstances. Today's business environment is constantly changing; therefore, the logistics organizational structure must be flexible, perhaps to the extent of being "virtual." Factors such as increased competitive pressures, global markets and supply sources, synchronous logistics and manufacturing systems, and movements toward pull-based logistics responsiveness all suggest the need for significant improvements in the ways we plan for and manage our logistics processes.

Logistics organizations that can deliver efficient and effective service will be critically important in the years ahead as companies compete more vigorously for the coveted preferred supplier status or strategic alliance. As Lee Iacocca, chairman of Chrysler Corporation, stated, "The company with the best distribution system and the best service will win all the marbles."[1]

To provide further insight into how to anticipate and address these issues, this chapter will introduce the available logistics alternatives and help the reader to appreciate the fundamental problems and opportunities faced by firms today. Following a discussion of the evolution of logistics organizations, the topic of corporate logistics organization is treated in detail. Subsequent sections focus on matters relating to the logistics quality process, logistics reengineering, and third-party logistics.

THE EVOLUTION OF LOGISTICS ORGANIZATION

logistics development

As we discussed in Chapter 1, logistics has, since the 1960s, become less fragmented and more integrated. As we approach the year 2000, the prevailing emphasis is on total integration. As a result, significant current attention is being directed toward integrated logistics management and integrated supply chain management. Table 1–1 in Chapter 1 provided a useful comparison of key characteristics of traditional systems with those of the more contemporary supply chain approach.

Traditionally, logistics activities were scattered throughout the organization. Figure 14–1 suggests examples of such activities, which may have been found in a

FIGURE 14-1   Traditional Locations of Logistics Activities in the Firm

	MARKETING	FINANCE/ ACCOUNTING	MANUFACTURING

Functional Areas and Activities	Customer service
	Demand forecasting
	Warehouse site selection
	Outbound traffic
	Warehousing
		Order processing
		Communications
		Procurement
		Inventory policy formulation
		Capital budgeting for
		   warehouses, plants, and
		   other logistics assets
			Inventory control
			Materials handling
			Parts and service support
			Plant site selection
			Packaging
			Inbound traffic
			Production planning

Objectives	High inventory levels Decentralized warehousing Frequent, short production runs ← Quick response On-line information processing	Lower inventory levels Less warehousing Concern for costs Most appropriate information- processing system	→ Long production runs

firm's marketing, finance/accounting, and manufacturing organizations. While it may have been the case that certain of these activities were managed effectively, there were no built-in mechanisms to assure their integration and coordination in order to make truly optimal logistics decisions. Compounded by the fact that many companies suffered from the "functional silo syndrome," in which firmwide decision making was stifled by the vertical flow of organizational authority, it was difficult to achieve any semblance of integrated logistics management. In the case of Nike, discussed in this chapter's Logistics Profile, the overall emphasis shifted from vertical integration to an emphasis on the effective management of ideas and people.

As the move toward formalizing the logistics organization took hold, companies began to think of logistics activities in terms of functional groupings. Table 14–1 lists a number of such activities and categorizes them into five function groupings: transportation, facility structure, inventory, materials handling, and communication and information. Although this step was strategically important at the time, a more recent emphasis on recognizing key logistics "processes" has suggested new and more innovative organizational alternatives. These will be discussed at a later point in this chapter.

functional groupings

Organizational Development[2]

According to research conducted by the Council of Logistics Management, the growth of logistics organizations occurs in three stages. These are indicated in Figure 14–2.

stages of development

Stage I.   In this first stage, the principal focus is on the effective management of finished goods transportation and warehousing. Thus, the overall orientation is operational and, with the exception of coordinating these two activities, there is little additional evidence of integration.

Stage II.   The objective here is to integrate finished goods distribution and to control inbound transportation. Characteristically, this is a managerial orientation,

TABLE 14–1   Functional Grouping of Logistics Activities

Activities	Functional Group
Inbound traffic Outbound traffic International traffic Carrier selection Mode selection Public versus private carriage	Transportation
Warehouse management Warehouse planning Distribution center management Distribution center planning Plant site selection	Facility structure
Purchasing Raw material inventory Work-in-process inventory Finished goods inventory Parts/service support Return goods handling	Inventory
Salvage/scrap disposal Materials handling Packaging	Materials handling
Order processing Demand forecasting Production scheduling	Communication and information

SOURCE: Kenneth C. Williamson, Daniel M. Spitzer Jr., and David J. Bloomberg, "Modern Logistics Systems: Theory and Practice," *Journal of Business Logistics* 11, no. 2 (1990): 72. Used with permission of *Journal of Business Logistics*.

where individual activities are considered to be part of an overall physical distribution process. Decisions reflect trade-offs, such as transportation versus warehousing, and inventory versus customer service, and are frequently coordinated with other areas such as marketing and manufacturing.

Stage III.   This stage suggests a priority on integrating the total logistics process and includes coordinating decision making throughout the activities associated with physical distribution and materials management. The overall orientation shifts to strategic issues such as the company's overall logistics/marketing/operations strategy, as well as to responding to and anticipating key changes in the external business environment.

strategic evolution   Essentially, Stage I initiates opportunities to lower the cost of individual activities but little else. Stage II explicitly integrates activities such as customer service and order processing and facilitates enhancement of the overall service offering. The end result may include increased revenues as a result of increased service. While these profit improvements increase in Stage III, this stage is of greater strategic benefit because it involves reductions in current assets such as inventory and accounts receivable, at the same time that asset productivity and utilization both increase. This has a positive impact on return on investment.

FIGURE 14–2 Evolution Occurs in Three Stages

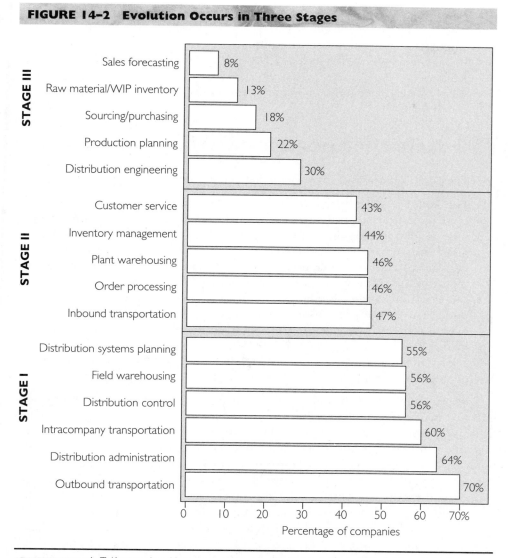

ADAPTED FROM: A. T. Kearney, Inc., *Measuring and Improving Productivity in Physical Distribution—1984* (Oak Brook, IL: Council of Logistics Management, 1984): 18. Used with permission of the Council of Logistics Management.

Contemporary Directions

In 1989, the Council of Logistics Management published a study describing the logistics organization, strategy, and behavior of companies on the "leading edge" of business.[3] These leading edge companies have a logistics competency superior to that of other firms, and they use logistics as a competitive weapon to gain and maintain customers.

leading edge firms

According to the results of this research, and other sources, the logistics organizations of leading edge companies have the following structures and characteristics:[4]

- Formal logistics organization
- Officer-level executive

- "Fluid" approach to logistics organization and encouragement for reorganization when appropriate
- Emphasis on centralized control of logistics
- Management scope that extends beyond traditional logistics line and staff activities
- Focus on customer satisfaction and creation of logistics value

CORPORATE LOGISTICS ORGANIZATION

Logistics organizations and logistics management consist of the following:[5]

- The senior logistics executive in the business unit.
- Line operations management personnel directly involved in the logistics process. This includes individuals responsible for purchasing, production planning, customer service operations, distribution centers, transportation activities, and private fleet operations, regardless of where these line organizations report in the corporation, and their respective line and staff organizations.
- The corporate and divisional logistics staff groups, which may or may not fall under one of the previously mentioned support service groups. These may exist as separate staff groups within the logistics organization, or they may be made up of changing groups of line personnel who devote only a portion of their time to staff projects (for example, planning a new distribution center, or designing a new information system).

management of logistics responsibilities

For any logistics organization to function effectively, a firm must ensure the effective management of logistics responsibilities at each level. Also, there are three requirements that a firm must meet to successfully staff its logistics function.[6] First, the firm must formulate accurate job descriptions. Each one should include the job's title, reporting relationships, scope of responsibility, and performance measures. Second, the firm should inventory the skills it needs in the logistics area and assess the extent to which available people meet the skill requirements of the various positions. Previous experience in the logistics area will often be helpful, but firms regard multifunctional backgrounds and experience as important qualifications for many senior logistics managers, who need a breadth of thinking and perspective as they attempt to successfully coordinate logistics activities and information flows across functions. A third requirement is that the firm should match people to jobs whenever possible, not vice versa. This will require interaction and flexibility in defining the job, inventorying skills, and adjusting jobs and titles to fit the skills and abilities of available personnel. A firm should consider relocating personnel or adding new personnel only when major gaps or duplications in abilities are obvious.

Organizational Dimensions

"structure follows strategy"

Structure.[7]   According to Thompson,[8] structure encompasses an organization's internal pattern of relationships, authority, and communication. The two critical components of structure, as suggested by Chandler,[9] are formal lines of authority and communication, and the information and data that flow along these lines. As a practical matter, however, many organizational structures serve to limit, rather than facilitate. Thus, the traditional wisdom that "structure follows strategy" has significant applicability.

Considering the rate of change in the business environment in general and in the aspects that affect logistics in particular, it is essential for an organization to be as flexible and responsive to change as possible. The fact that these attributes are ones in which third-party suppliers would be expected to have strength reinforces the potential role of this type of logistics supplier. This topic will be discussed in greater detail later in this chapter.

Overall Patterns. Based on the results from the *1994 Ohio State University Survey of Career Patterns in Logistics,*[10] Figure 14–3 indicates the activities over which logistics executives indicated they had authority (either by direct control or in an advisory capacity). Figure 14–4 identifies the name of the department within which the study's 208 respondents (an 18 percent response rate) were located. Although it is interesting to note that most of the executives work in an organization with the word "logistics" or "distribution" in its name, the 43 percent indicating "logistics" was up from 33 percent in the 1993 study.[11]

key logistics activities

Organizational Orientation[12]

The results of a multiphase research project conducted at Michigan State University suggest that there are three strategic alternatives for structuring a logistics

strategic organizational alternatives

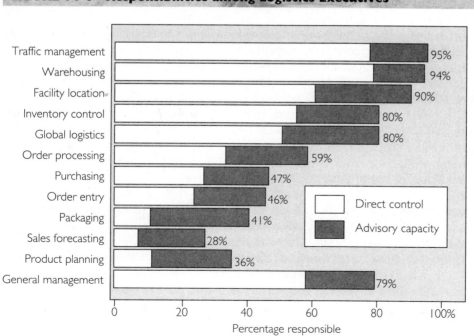

FIGURE 14–3 Responsibilities among Logistics Executives

Activity	Percentage responsible
Traffic management	95%
Warehousing	94%
Facility location	90%
Inventory control	80%
Global logistics	80%
Order processing	59%
Purchasing	47%
Order entry	46%
Packaging	41%
Sales forecasting	28%
Product planning	36%
General management	79%

Legend: Direct control / Advisory capacity

SOURCE: James M. Masters and Bernard J. LaLonde, *The 1994 Ohio State University Survey of Career Patterns in Logistics* (Columbus, OH: The Ohio State University, 1994), Figure 7. Used with permission.

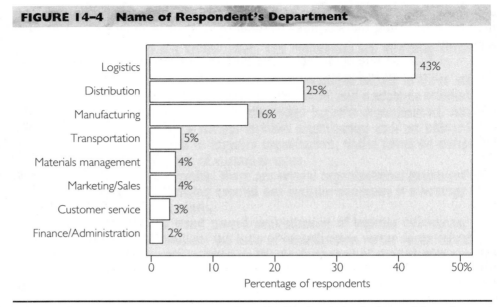

FIGURE 14–4 Name of Respondent's Department

Department	Percentage
Logistics	43%
Distribution	25%
Manufacturing	16%
Transportation	5%
Materials management	4%
Marketing/Sales	4%
Customer service	3%
Finance/Administration	2%

Percentage of respondents

SOURCE: James M. Masters and Bernard J. LaLonde, *The 1994 Ohio State University Survey of Career Patterns in Logistics* (Columbus, OH: The Ohio State University, 1994), Figure 5. Used with permission.

organization. The findings are based on an analysis of questionnaire responses from and personal interviews with corporate logistics officers.

Process Based.   The emphasis in a process-based structure is on managing a broad group of logistics activities as a "value-added chain." This strategy emphasizes the achievement of efficiency from logistics as an integrated system and was characteristic of approximately 60 percent of the respondents' organizations.

Market Based.   Priorities in a market-based structure include (1) making joint product shipments to customers on behalf of various business units or product groups and (2) coordinating sales and logistical efficiencies through the use of a single invoice. In this type of firm, there is likely to be organizational proximity between the logistics and sales areas. This strategy was in evidence in 30 percent of the firms represented by respondents.

Channel Based.   The emphasis in a channel-based structure is on the effective management of activities that are conducted jointly with customers, distributors, and suppliers. Firms exhibiting this strategy tend to have a significant interest in inventories at either downstream or upstream channel locations. This strategy was characteristic of about 10 percent of the respondents' firms.

Types of Logistics Organization

Logistics organization can be characterized in a number of ways. Some of these are functional versus divisional, centralized versus decentralized, activity versus process, staff versus line, large versus small, formal versus informal, and so on. In fact, there are so many potential ways to categorize logistics organizations that it is impossible to suggest that any single framework is best.

For the purposes of this section, the following major types of organization have been selected to serve as a template for discussion: functional organization, logistics service division, and process-oriented organization. Relevant issues and perspectives will be discussed within this overall approach. The issue of a centralized versus decentralized logistics organization will be treated separately.

Functional Organization.   Figure 14–5 shows an example of a functional logistics organization within the context of a single, functionally oriented corporate organization. Several directors of functional activities report to the vice president of logistics, and the vice president of logistics reports to the president/CEO. Although it is preferable for the chief logistics executive to report to the chief corporate executive, it is not unusual for a vice president of logistics to report to a vice president or senior vice president of operations or of marketing and sales.

Typically, directors and managers of both ''line'' and ''staff'' activities would report to the vice president of logistics. Line management involves making decisions about matters pertaining to daily logistics operations. Typical line activities might include transportation management, inventory control, order processing, warehousing, and packaging. Staff activities support line managers with advice and information to support decision making. Examples of staff activities include logistics network design and facility location, strategic planning, customer service strategies, and cost analysis. Regardless of how the line and staff activities are structured organizationally, it is essential to recognize that to sustain effectiveness, a line operation must have professional guidance and direction setting from a capable

FIGURE 14–5   A Functional Logistics Organization

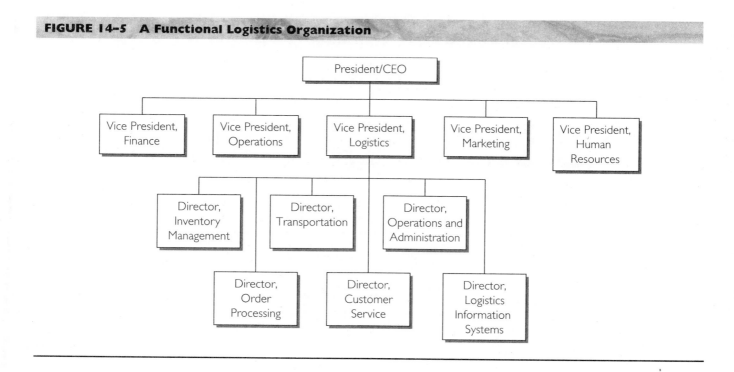

staff function. Similarly, the effectiveness of the staff function will be influenced by the quality of coordination with and information provided by line management.

divisionalized firms　　It may be that a firm is divisionalized, perhaps according to major product groupings, and that each division has its own logistics function. This example is illustrated in Figure 14–6, where separate logistics organizations support the needs of each of the product divisions. As one might expect, this approach quickly leads to duplication of logistics effort and motivates the firm to identify appropriate strategies for centralizing relevant logistics activities. The extent to which this centralization of logistics activity is occurring, along with an acknowledgment of the responsible factors, will be provided in a later section of this chapter.

Logistics Service Division.　　Properly implemented, the strategy of creating a separate logistics service division elevates logistics to an importance equal to that of major company product divisions. An excellent example of this is the Becton Dickinson Supply Chain Services (SCS) Division, which has been in place since 1995.[13] This division and its strategic significance were featured in the Logistics Profile included in Chapter 1. The firm's corporate organizational structure appears in Figure 14–7.

Becton Dickinson, a highly decentralized manufacturer of medical supplies, devices, and diagnostic systems, in 1989 formalized a corporate supply chain management organization that provided linkage of multidivisional supply chain activities with those offered individually by the company's fourteen product divisions. Because of the success of this effort, in February 1995 a new operating division was formed, BD Supply Chain Services, which has complete responsibility for all supply chain services, including distributor management and strategy, contract administration and rebate processing, order fulfillment, inventory management,

FIGURE 14–6　A Divisionalized Logistics Organization

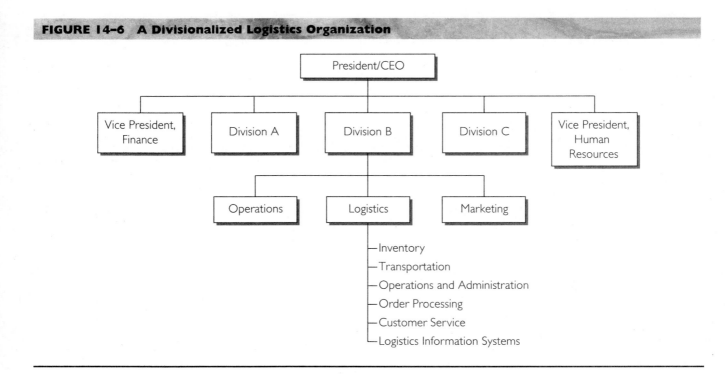

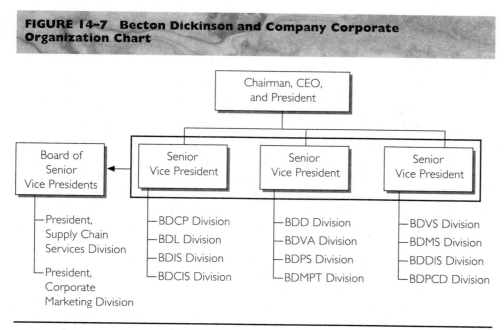

FIGURE 14–7 Becton Dickinson and Company Corporate Organization Chart

SOURCE: Becton Dickinson and Company, 1995.

physical distribution, international distribution services, transportation, invoicing, credit, and collection. These services are performed for the fourteen domestic and international divisions, providing a singular capability to the company's customers. This new operating division is responsible to a board of sector presidents whose divisions it supports.

Although it is not apparent from Figure 14–7, the BD Supply Chain Services Division is unique in several respects. First, while this division does perform a variety of traditional roles, it places emphasis on eliminating activities that are redundant or that do not add value at Becton Dickinson or its channel partners, thereby reducing the cost of logistics across the supply chain. The division's view of "price," for example, places less emphasis on what is charged and greater emphasis on the costs that can be reengineered out of the supply chain operation. Second, this division provides logistics, information technology, and financial services to both internal customers, and the external distributors and end customers of the firm. Third, the division includes the full range of companywide expertise needed to market and provide total channel services, and it is the service strategy provider just as the other divisions are the product/marketing strategy providers. Fourth, this division focuses attention on customer needs and on determining how those needs can be met through logistics or other supply chain services. Becton Dickinson believes that the same steps required to bring a product to market are applicable to the development of competent supply chain services.

Process-Oriented Organization. The overall movement to organizational structures based on key business processes is well documented. In essence, focusing attention on processes helps to avoid the myopic perspective associated with functional and activity-based approaches to organization. In addition, an emphasis on process makes it easier to truly move logistics organizations toward integrated logistics and integrated supply chain management. Just as the concept of the logistics service division helps to significantly upgrade the role and positioning of logistics, the attention directed toward process assists immensely in terms of moving toward the integration and coordination of logistics activities.

There are numerous ways to identify key logistics processes; Copacino suggests three that are significant: the order management process, the replenishment process, and the process of developing an integrated production and distribution strategy.[14] Figure 14–8 is an example of a logistics organization that focuses on processes relating to systems, planning, transportation, and operations. The diagram shows elements of each and the relationship to the firm's product groups (A through E) and to the customer needs/requirements to be met (customer satisfaction, logistics cost, on-time and complete delivery, and customer focus).

Movement to a process orientation requires rethinking and reconfiguring traditional organizations. According to Bowersox, Frayer, and Schmitz, most experts feel that traditional command and control systems have outlived their usefulness and are being replaced by flatter, more process-oriented structures. "They [traditional systems] simply are not the best way to operate in an information-based competitive environment."[15] Again, the Nike example cited in this chapter's Logistics Profile stresses the need for the logistics process to emphasize horizontal process flow, which basically creates a seamless service delivery system.

FIGURE 14–8   Example of a Process-Oriented Logistics Organization

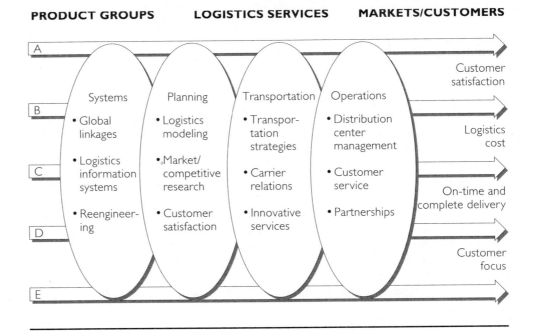

FIGURE 14–9 Structure of Logistics Organizations

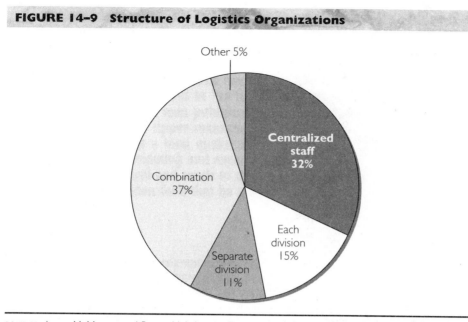

SOURCE: James M. Masters and Bernard J. LaLonde, *The 1994 Ohio State University Survey of Career Patterns in Logistics* (Columbus, OH: The Ohio State University, 1994), Figure 3. Used with permission.

Centralization versus Decentralization

trend toward centralization

Figure 14–9 summarizes the responses in the *1994 Ohio State University Career Patterns Study*[16] to a question regarding the logistics organizational strategies of respondent firms. Thirty-two percent indicated the existence of a centralized staff, 15 percent reported that each division of the firm had its own logistics department, and 37 percent indicated some combination of the two. According to the study results, the combined form of organization has been the one reported most frequently over the past several years. Also, 11 percent of the respondents indicated the existence of a separate logistics division.

Figure 14–10 provides details concerning the trend toward greater centralization of logistics operations in key activity areas. Clearly, the respondents perceived increased centralization in far more instances than they perceived decreased centralization.

Finally, Figure 14–11 identifies a number of factors cited as driving the move to centralization in a 1991 study conducted by The Ohio State University.[17] Among the principal factors mentioned were cost control (19 percent of respondents), management control (17 percent), negotiation leverage (12 percent), and economies of scale (10 percent). Responses in the same study to a similar question relating to decentralization of logistics indicated the chief reasons to be responsiveness (14 percent), customer differences (12 percent), need to be closer to customers (10 percent), and customer service (8 percent).

FIGURE 14-10   Centralization of Logistics Operations, 1993–1996

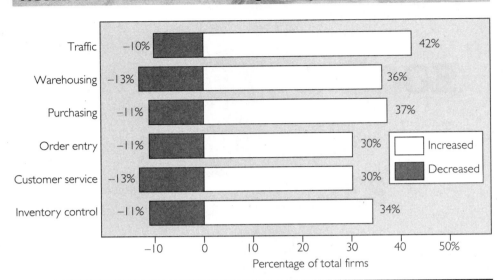

SOURCE: James M. Masters and Bernard J. LaLonde, *The 1993 Ohio State University Survey of Career Patterns in Logistics* (Columbus, OH: The Ohio State University, 1993), Figure 7. Used with permission.

FIGURE 14-11   Factors Driving the Centralization of Logistics Functions

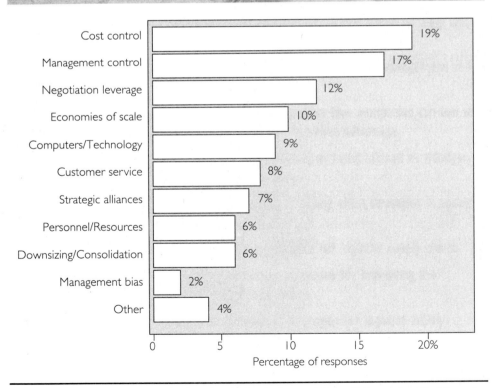

SOURCE: Bernard J. LaLonde, "The 1991 Ohio State University Survey of Career Patterns in Logistics," *Proceedings of the 1991 Annual Conference of the Council of Logistics Management* (Oak Brook, IL: CLM, 1991), 61. Copyright © The Ohio State University Career Patterns Study, 1994. Used with permission.

Structuring the Corporate Logistics Organization

When considering the alternatives for structuring the logistics organization, the principal objective should be to develop strategies for mobilizing and managing various resources to ensure that the logistical mission and corporate goals are achieved.

designing a logistics organization

Key Steps in the Process. While no single approach to the design of a logistics organization has proven to be universally appropriate, the following steps have been found to be useful.[18]

1. Research corporate strategies and goals
2. Organize functions to be compatible with corporate structure
3. Define functions for which you are accountable
4. Know your management style
5. Organize your flexibility
6. Know your support systems
7. Make plans to fit both individual and corporate objectives

The first step ensures that the logistics department's long-term direction is compatible with corporate goals. Organizing functions to parallel corporate structure will be useful, unless the overall corporate structure is in dire need of a major redesign. Defining accountability is necessary because of the confusion sometimes caused by the horizontal nature of logistics activities. The fourth step basically asks managers to be aware of how their attitudes and actions will affect subordinates' acceptance of change. Concern for flexibility ensures that the organization will be able to adapt to future changes. Knowing your support systems helps you to know exactly what your new system can and cannot accomplish. The last step ensures that the people who are to manage the new system accept it, because nothing can cause failure during implementation faster than user resistance.[19]

Measuring Logistics Performance

A company having implemented a logistics organization must continually monitor and evaluate its effectiveness. This feedback is essential for organizational changes that will increase the company's likelihood of achieving its desired goals.

A common misconception is that an organizational structure is a permanent fixture. In reality, change is the organization's only permanent trait. Business conditions change, new technologies develop, and firms modify strategic plans and goals, necessitating a structural change in logistics organization. The logistics manager must be aware of these changes and must modify the logistics organization accordingly to achieve corporate and logistics goals.

structural change

A company may utilize several different methods to measure the logistics organization's performance. In general, these performance measurements compare the logistics organization's output with the established objectives of the various logistics functions. Though these objectives may take different forms, they generally deal with cost, productivity, and service.

measuring logistics performance

Cost Criteria. Companies establish cost objectives for the performance of individual logistics functions. Examples include the cost per pound, per shipment, or per order. The company compares the logistics operation's cost with its established objectives and takes corrective actions if necessary.

cost output   Consider the example of a Cleveland department store that charged customers a preset cost of $25 for delivering furniture and appliances. The delivery cost became the objective against which the store measured the actual logistics delivery service cost. If the actual delivery cost exceeded the charge, the department incurred a loss on the delivery service. This excessive cost reduced the normal profit built into the product's price. A cost accounting report alerted the department store to such a situation. The report indicated that a problem existed in the delivery area. The logistics manager analyzed the delivery department's operation and productivity performance to locate the problem's cause and take corrective action.

output divided   *Productivity Criteria.* Productivity criteria measure the amount of output a firm
by input   produces per unit of input, or outputs divided by inputs. Examples of output measures are tons shipped, pounds loaded, orders filled, and shipments delivered. Inputs include labor hours, the number of employees or trucks, and warehouse space.

Upon analyzing the number of shipments delivered per delivery shift, the Cleveland department store logistics manager discovered that the current delivery rate equaled 4.7 per shift, down from 11.8 the previous year. The conclusion was obvious: increase the number of deliveries per shift, and the increased productivity would lower the cost per delivery.

The real question was why deliveries per shift had decreased from the previous year. To answer this question, the logistics manager established a quality circles program consisting of informational meetings between logistics management and the drivers and helpers. At these meetings, the logistics manager conveyed the problems low productivity and the fixed delivery charge generated; and the drivers and helpers presented reasons for and solutions to this low productivity. The logistics manager solved the problem by purchasing improved materials handling equipment for the delivery vehicles and improving delivery truck routing. (Not all productivity problems are resolved so easily.)

service quality   *Service Criteria.* Logistics service quality is becoming increasingly important in today's competitive global markets. Firms define service quality in terms of criteria such as time, accuracy, consistency, and damage. A seller's service level provides a competitive advantage (or disadvantage), and service is a criterion that buyers, especially industrial buyers, use in making the purchase decision.

stockouts   To continue with our Cleveland department store example, the store sold a line of women's clothing that it purchased from a plant in a Pacific Rim country. Because the clothing was very popular, the store experienced increasing numbers of stockouts at its retail outlets. When customers bought competing brands, the stockouts translated into lost profits. Sixty days elapsed between the time the store placed an order and the time it received the order in Cleveland.

Examining the international movement, the logistics manager found that the ocean voyage required 24 days and that the truck movement from Long Beach to Cleveland required eight days. During the remaining 28 days, the shipment was sitting in a warehouse at its origin or at Long Beach. Improved communication with the producer and the use of a new intermediate warehouse at Long Beach reduced the in-transit storage to four days and the total lead time to 36 days. Improved store sales monitoring enabled the logistics manager to anticipate demand for the clothing. These actions reduced both stockouts and lost profits.

Measuring Performance in Logistics Management

Firms evaluate logistics managers primarily on the basis of three factors: line man-   **three criteria**
agement ability, problem-solving ability, and project management ability.[20]

> **Line management ability.** This criterion considers the manager's ability to man-
> age logistics operations on a day-to-day basis and to meet goals that the firm
> has established for service quality, productivity, and all aspects of performance,
> including budget.

> **Problem-solving ability.** This deals with the ability to diagnose problems with
> the operation and to develop and apply innovative new ideas that result in cost
> savings, service improvement, or increased financial performance. Also in-
> cluded here is the logistics manager's ability to anticipate opportunities for
> improvement before they become problems that must be solved.

> **Project management ability.** This refers to the ability to structure and manage
> projects designed to correct problems and improve the logistics process.

Companies also frequently evaluate managers based on their ability to motivate
their subordinates and develop their technical and management skills. The company may measure the degree of success here according to individual employees'
productivity, utilization, and performance.

Figure 14–12 identifies responsibilities that would be typical for a vice president
of logistics. The following list sets specific standards against which a company

FIGURE 14–12   Sample Responsibilities of a Vice President of Logistics

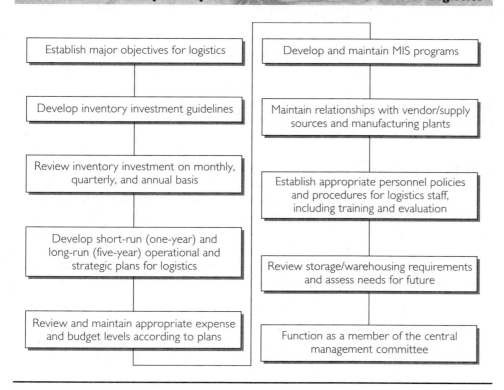

might evaluate performance. Together, these should illustrate the performance that companies expect of logistics managers, and ways of measuring the conformity between performance and expectations:

- Maintain inventory at four-month level during current year. Reduce to three-month level over the course of the next two years.
- Establish and maintain a customer service level of 92 percent product availability for all regular line items and have such items ready for shipment within five days of receipt of order.
- Develop procedures to maintain logistics operating expenses at 3.5 percent of sales during current year.
- Reduce transportation expenses, including private fleet, to 2.5 percent of sales during current year, and reduce them to 2.4 percent next year.
- Reduce freight shipment damage rate to 1 percent of total sales.
- Maintain 98 percent accuracy level in order filling.
- Maintain employee turnover rate at 12 percent per year.
- Achieve and/or exceed overall customer satisfaction objectives.

THE LOGISTICS QUALITY PROCESS AND LOGISTICS REENGINEERING

In their continuing quest for a competitive edge, companies are calling upon logistics managers to find innovative ways to reduce cost, enhance service, and increase customer satisfaction. As a result, many firms have taken significant steps toward identifying and implementing logistics quality improvement processes. While some of these processes are consistent with companywide quality initiatives, logistics frequently assumes a leadership role in terms of a firm's move toward a quality process.

Creating Customer Value through the Logistics Process

A growing number of firms serve as excellent role models in terms of the strategic impact of logistics management. At companies such as L.L. Bean, Xerox, Frito-Lay, and McDonalds, logistics helps to create customer value in three important ways: efficiency, effectiveness, and differentiation.

resource utilization

Efficiency. The efficiency component of customer value refers to the logistics organization's ability to provide the desired product/service mix at a level of cost the customer finds acceptable. This emphasizes the need for logistics to manage resources wisely and to leverage expenses into customer value whenever possible. Firms have achieved some of the most significant efficiencies by committing themselves to improving and "reengineering" logistics processes.[21] Enhanced efficiencies in a logistics operation translate directly into additional value for most firms' customers.

level of service

Effectiveness. The emphasis here is on performance and on whether the logistics function meets customer requirements. An excellent example of a company focusing on effectiveness is L.L. Bean, which has identified a number of customer service "key result areas" (KRAs). Included among these are product guarantee, in-stock availability, order fulfillment time, convenience, retail service, innovation, and market standing.[22]

Differentiation.   The differentiation element manifests itself logistically by creating value through unique logistical service. For example, The Limited—Distribution Services Company creates overall system value by marking and tagging all merchandise prior to store delivery. The FedEx PartsBank® operation also creates customer value by maintaining inventories of repair and emergency parts for immediate shipment to locations throughout the world.

    uniqueness

    The next section focuses first on several critical quality issues and concepts. A framework for the logistics quality process will be outlined and discussed, and a number of logistics quality successes will be described. The section concludes with a discussion of the results of a 1995 research study on logistics value conducted for the Council of Logistics Management.

Quality Issues and Concepts[23]

Formalization of the Quality Process.   One of the more popular trends in recent years has been for firms to commit themselves to a formal quality process. The evolution of a formal quality process has four distinct phases, as shown in Table 14–2. A greater emphasis on achieving customer satisfaction through customer-driven quality characterizes the shift from quality control (QC) to quality assurance (QA). Having management, employees, customers, and suppliers all working toward a common goal characterizes the evolution to total quality management (TQM). The fourth phase, customer value, reflects the need to do things that create the best comparative net value for the customer.[24]

    Although there are numerous ways to define the word "quality," the following was offered in a Council of Logistics Management (CLM) study on quality and productivity in the logistics process:[25]

    definition of quality

> Quality in logistics means meeting agreed-to customer requirements and expectations, including the following dimensions:
>
> - Ease of inquiry, order placement, and order transmission
> - Timely, reliable order delivery and communication
> - Accurate, complete, undamaged orders and error-free paperwork

TABLE 14–2   Implementation Stages in a Quality Process

Stage	Characteristics
Quality control (QC)	• Defect-free services • Management driven
Quality assurance (QA)	• 100% satisfied customer • Customer driven
Total quality management (TQM)	• Significant competitive advantage • Management, employees, customers, and vendors work toward a common goal
Customer value	• Emphasis on providing best comparative net value for the customer

- Timely and responsive post-sales support
- Accurate, timely generation and transmission of information among the functions of business and with external parties to support the planning, management, and execution of the above activities.

Common Characteristics of Successful Firms. According to the CLM study, companies such as Motorola, Xerox, Hewlett-Packard, and Federal Express, which have experienced significant quality successes, tend to have a number of common characteristics. The first is the belief that quality improvement must be a companywide effort, with the support and involvement of the CEO. The second is the creation of a cultural change that shifts the focus outward toward the customer and extends to relationships with suppliers as well. The third is a move away from traditional, vertical "functional silos" to an emphasis on cross-functional business processes. And the fourth characteristic is the tendency of these companies to view logistics quality and productivity improvement as integral to the success of the overall quality process.[26]

Firms having experience with implementing a formal quality process agree that quality efforts should strive for process integrity and should avoid measuring quality only by measuring output. Firms best serve the long-term interests of logistics management by emphasizing sound processes and by developing logistics systems that anticipate, meet, and exceed customer requirements.

Another common emphasis is on measuring and reducing the variability of key logistics processes such as order fulfillment, logistics information systems, and value creation and determination. The use of appropriate statistical tools, to be discussed later, can help to reduce variability and improve the consistency/reliability of logistics processes.

quality process drivers

Reasons for Initiating a Logistics Quality Process. Figure 14–13 identifies a number of reasons that firms decided to initiate a formal quality improvement process in logistics. For 72 percent of the CLM study respondents, the desire to gain an advantage over competitors was a key motivator. In 66 percent of the responses, the objective of reducing operating costs was cited as a major factor. Although the percentages continue to decline, other factors of interest were that logistics management identified the need (60 percent) and that the logistics quality process was part of an overall corporate or business-unit initiative (51 percent). Apparently, for 31 percent of the respondents, involvement in a formal quality process was simply required by customers.

Impact of Quality on Profitability

financial justification

An interesting finding of one of the widely cited PIMS (Profit Impact of Marketing Strategy) studies was that "companies with high quality and high market share generally tend to have profit margins five times greater than companies at the opposite extreme."[27] Figure 14–14, which charts firms' returns on sales and investment (ROS and ROI) along with the relative quality percentile in which their customers perceive them to be, supports this observation.

According to the study results, the achievement of superior quality yields two types of benefits. The first is that the lower cost of quality implies an overall cost lower than that of competitor organizations. The second is that quality is fre-

FIGURE 14–13 Major Factors in Decision to Initiate Logistics Improvement Process

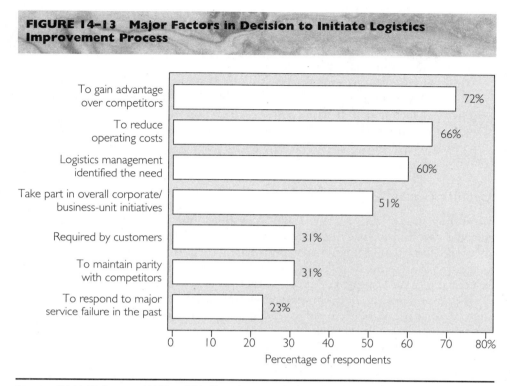

SOURCE: Patrick M. Byrne and William J. Markham, *Improving Quality and Productivity in the Logistics Process* (Oak Brook, IL: Council of Logistics Management, 1991): 238.

FIGURE 14–14 Relative Quality Boosts Rates of Return

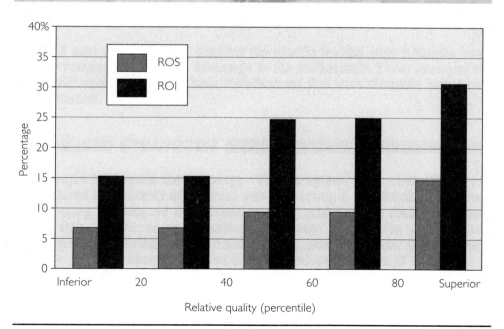

SOURCE: *Profit Impact of Marketing Studies*, The Strategic Planning Institute (Cambridge, Massachusetts, 1988).

quently a key attribute in the customer's purchase decision. The study also found that companies that ranked in the top third in terms of relative quality sold their products or services, on the average, at prices 5 to 6 percent higher than companies in the bottom half.

While these results are encouraging, the CLM study on quality and productivity indicated that many firms have not yet established a foundation of logistics excellence to facilitate a true customer satisfaction strategy.[28] Thus, the study suggests that attention at many firms needs to be directed toward further development and sophistication of the logistics process.

Quality Gurus[29]

Beginning in the early to mid-1980s, it became very popular for companies to become involved in formal efforts to move toward total quality management. Before and during this time, a number of experts and/or visionaries emerged to help lead the way as firms pursued established goals relating to quality and the structuring of an appropriate quality process.

Perhaps one of the best known of these quality "gurus," Dr. W. Edwards Deming was an advocate of the need to understand the customer and his or her needs. He placed great importance on the need to minimize the variability of the process under study and suggested that process variation was due either to "common" (i.e., systemic) or "special" causes. In addition, he was a strong proponent of the use of statistical techniques to gain insight into quality issues. One of Deming's contemporaries, Dr. Joseph M. Juran, had a pronounced interest in the managerial aspects of quality. He stressed seeking improvement on a "project-by-project" basis as well as the need for "breakthrough" improvements in quality processes. A third leader, Philip B. Crosby, established as his main theme "quality is conformance to requirements," and suggested that from a total quality perspective, "quality is free."

Numerous others have had a significant effect on United States and global businesses in the area of quality. Some of these include Genici Taguchi, who is best known for development of the quality function deployment (QFD) approach; Karou Ishikawa, who developed the cause and effect or "fishbone" diagram, as well as other statistically oriented tools; and Taiichi Ohno, who was instrumental in conceptualizing and implementing the Kanban system at Toyota.[30]

The Logistics Quality Process

While some firms have maintained an excellent reputation for product and service quality in their customers' eyes, adherence to a formal quality process makes long-term, sustainable improvement more likely. This observation applies to the entire firm as well as to the logistics process. Figure 14–15 indicates the six major steps in the development of a logistics quality process; each of these steps is discussed below.[31]

Step 1: Make an Organizational Commitment.   Top management must be the driving force behind the commitment to quality. This applies not only to corporate gen-

FIGURE 14-15   The Logistics Quality Process

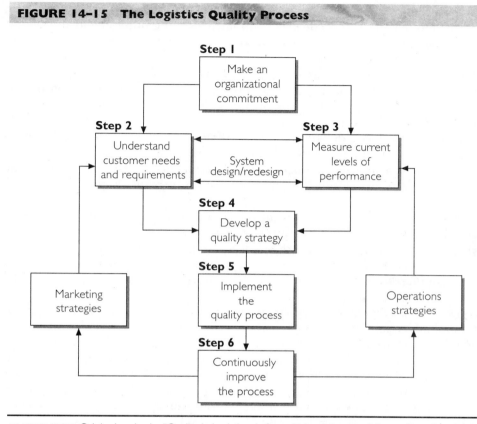

ADAPTED FROM: C. John Langley Jr., "Quality in Logistics: A Competitive Advantage," *Proceedings of the R. Hadly Waters Logistics and Transportation Symposium* (University Park, PA: Penn State University, 1990).

eral management, but also to the vice president or director of logistics. People at these levels must be fully dedicated to the objectives they must meet and the actions they must take. Also, these executives must provide the resources and encouragement their people need to produce tangible results from the commitment to quality.

Quality processes commonly fail due to a lack of commitment by top management. An unwillingness to sacrifice short-term financial results or productivity, for example, is a telltale sign that a manager may resist needed improvement efforts. Instead, a logistics process that is able to leverage managerial commitment can usually achieve "productivity through quality," and, by adhering to a formal quality process, can actually lower the cost of doing business.

At the outset of a formal quality process, the logistics organization should have **strategic direction** meaningful, well-developed statements of mission, goals, and objectives. This step helps logistics to assume leadership with regard to the quality area.

Step 2: Understand Customer Needs and Requirements.   The emphasis in this step is **customer** on specifically and scientifically understanding the needs and requirements of the **considerations** customers of the logistics process. While companies traditionally focus on the logistical needs of the firm's external customers, understanding the needs of the firm's internal customers is equally important. This recognition should also extend to associates in such areas as marketing, manufacturing/operations, and finance, as well as to logistics coworkers.

Identifying customer needs and requirements is not always straightforward and obvious. More often than not, this step requires a rigorous examination of customers and their needs, and the use of approaches such as customer studies, focus groups, and structured interviews.

Besides achieving a one-time understanding of customer needs and requirements, a firm should regularly monitor the marketplace's changing priorities. Although a firm may direct internal resources to such a task, this activity may justify the use of an outside consultant or service to regularly provide objective information.

Finally, firms desiring a successful quality process should think of their suppliers, vendors, and channel partners as "customers." Firms throughout a truly integrated supply chain must share significant coordination and singularity of purpose. A shortsighted firm's failure to view these other entities as customers will prove counterproductive to the total quality effort.

importance of measurement

Step 3: Measure Current Levels of Performance.   This step includes obtaining accurate and meaningful measures of current performance levels, in direct relation to the specific needs and requirements identified in step 2. For this information to be valid and useful, a firm must acquire it specifically and scientifically.[32] In addition to identifying suitable performance measures in key areas such as transportation, inventory, warehousing, information processing, and packaging, some form of logistics benchmarking will likely prove valuable to the logistics quality process.

gap analysis

Once steps 2 and 3 have been accomplished, there may be certain "gaps" between customer needs and requirements and current levels of performance. Among the factors that may contribute to such differences are supplier misunderstanding of logistics customer service requirements, the design of the service quality process not matching the requirements to be met, actual service levels differing from what was intended, and lack of effective supplier follow-up and reporting to the customer upon completion of the service delivery process. Alternatively, it may be that customers are not sufficiently aware of their "true" logistics needs and that their stated requirements are inconsistent with their needs. Also, the postservice measurement strategies and techniques used by customers may differ from those used by suppliers.

quality approaches

Step 4: Develop a Quality Strategy.   The term "quality strategy" refers to the specific initiatives selected for inclusion in the logistics quality process. Perhaps the first significant step is to study the teachings and philosophies of several of the quality "gurus" discussed previously. While the firm should consider many approaches, the ultimate priorities should focus on understanding the customer's needs, appropriate initiatives for education and training, measuring performance levels and monitoring variability, and overall organizational commitment.

quality tools and techniques

Figure 14–16 identifies the basic tools that should be considered as part of the quality strategy.[33] Each is categorized as more appropriate either for process analysis or for statistical analysis. The figure also indicates the appropriateness of each

FIGURE 14–16 Basic Quality Tools

	Plan/Do					Check/Act	
	Identify the problem	Understand the problem	Collect data	Analyze causes of the problem	Plan improvements	Measure results	Institutionalize results
PROCESS ANALYSIS							
Cause and effect diagram		✓		✓	✓		
Process flowchart	✓	✓			✓		✓
Brainstorming	✓	✓			✓		
STATISTICAL ANALYSIS							
Check sheets	✓	✓	✓	✓		✓	
Pareto charts	✓	✓		✓		✓	
Histograms		✓		✓		✓	
Scatter diagrams	✓			✓			
Run charts		✓	✓				
Control charts	✓	✓	✓			✓	✓

SOURCE: Patrick M. Byrne and William J. Markham, *Improving Quality and Productivity in the Logistics Process* (Oak Brook, IL: Council of Logistics Management, 1991): 116.

tool for various stages of the "plan/do" and "check/act" activities. In addition to those indicated in Figure 14–16, other tools such as customer research, advanced flowcharting, quality function deployment (QFD),[34] and benchmarking[35] should be considered. Table 14–3 identifies certain companies that have been regarded as role models in their benchmarking of the various activities indicated.

Step 5: Implement the Quality Process. As is the case with any formal quality process, smooth, effective implementation is essential for success. Thus, a firm should direct considerable attention to designing an overall quality strategy that will "roll out" productively and smoothly.   **implementation**

This step has significant logistical implications. Many of the more important people to include in the quality process are inventory control specialists, warehouse and dock workers, vehicle drivers, product packaging personnel, and order-entry clerks and staff. These people, any of whom can easily affect the service levels experienced by the firm's internal and external customers, are in a position to make a truly positive contribution to the overall quality process.

A meaningful implementation plan should include a timetable and a comprehensive list of necessary resources. These will help to assure the success of a well-conceived and well-executed quality process.

Step 6: Continually Improve the Process. The final major step is that of process improvement and the recognition that results should include both continuous as   **types of improvement**

TABLE 14–3   Companies That Exemplify Logistics Benchmarking

Benchmarking Aspect	Company
Automated inventory control	Westinghouse Apple Computer Federal Express
Billing and collection	American Express MCI
Customer service	Xerox Nordstrom, Inc. L.L. Bean
Manufacturing operations management	Hewlett-Packard Corning, Inc. Philip Morris
Purchasing	Honda Motor Xerox NCR
Quality process	Westinghouse Florida Power & Light Xerox
Warehousing and distribution	L.L. Bean Hershey Foods Mary Kay Cosmetics
Transportation	Japan National Railways Singapore Airlines Federal Express

ADAPTED FROM: Reprinted with permission of David Altany, "Copycats," *Industry Week* (November 5, 1990): 14. Copyright © Penton Publishing, Inc., Cleveland, Ohio.

well as breakthrough improvement. While the former should represent a daily pursuit for those involved in the logistics quality process, the accomplishment of breakthrough or "paradigm-shifting" improvement will be essential to maintain and grow a logistical competitive edge.

While this dedication to process improvement represents the sixth step in the quality process, the real benefit will accrue from modifying and enhancing the firm's marketing and operations strategies. Although we might think of this as the "last" step in the quality process, it is a reminder that the process should be a continuing one and that an effective, meaningful quality process really has no end as such. In terms of creating value for the customer, a formal commitment to quality represents another way for logistics to deliver the service quality essential to a firm competing in today's marketplace.

Improvements in Logistics Quality

logistics improvements

Table 14–4 provides results that indicate the types of improvements in logistics service levels experienced by firms participating in the recent study. Based on historical measurements at the time of the study, the respondents reported that service failures in five key service areas were reduced by 37 to 55 percent from 1985 to 1990. They also projected additional reductions in service failures ranging from 43 to 66 percent from 1990 to 1995. To provide an industry perspective,

TABLE 14–4 Improvements in Logistics Service Quality

Service Area	Service Level			Reduction in Error or Failure Rate	
	1985 Actual	1990 Actual	1995 Expected	1985–1990 Achieved	1990–1995 Expected
• On-time performance	81.4%	91.6%	97.0%	55%	66%
• Order completeness	83.1%	89.6%	95.0%	39%	52%
• Line-item fill rate	87.0%	92.8%	96.4%	45%	50%
• Invoice accuracy	90.3%	94.3%	97.9%	42%	64%
• Damage-free receipt	92.2%	95.1%	97.2%	37%	43%

SOURCE: Patrick M. Byrne and William J. Markham, *Improving Quality and Productivity in the Logistics Process* (Oak Brook, IL: Council of Logistics Management, 1991): 261. Used with permission.

Table 14–5 shows, by industry, actual levels of order completeness for 1985 and 1990 and projected levels for 1995. Also indicated are the percentages by which error or failure rates were reduced over these time periods.

Although there has been considerable improvement in recent years in traditional logistics areas such as product availability, order cycle time, invoice accuracy, on-time performance, and damage-free receipt of shipments, it is likely that many future improvements will come from nontraditional areas such as purchasing, materials planning and control, and information systems.[36] These types of activities will require increased cross-functional and cross-company coordination and will benefit significantly from integration of the total logistics process.

nontraditional areas for improvement

Figure 14–17 identifies several major impediments to quality and productivity improvement in logistics and indicates the percentages of surveyed firms which stated that the factors were significant. While each of the factors needs to be carefully considered, continual attention should be aimed at making sure that the

impediments to success

TABLE 14–5 Order Completeness by Industry

Industry Group	Service Level			Reduction in Error or Failure Rate	
	1985 Actual	1990 Actual	1995 Goal	1985–1990 Actual	1990–1995 Expected
Agricultural	85.0%	91.0%	95.3%	40%	48%
Automotive	81.4%	89.7%	97.0%	45%	71%
Chemicals and plastics	84.5%	91.1%	97.0%	43%	66%
Clothing and textiles	67.0%	81.6%	92.8%	44%	61%
Computer hardware	87.2%	93.2%	97.0%	47%	56%
Electrical machinery	61.3%	71.2%	87.3%	26%	56%
Electronics	91.7%	93.8%	98.7%	25%	79%
Food and beverage	89.0%	92.1%	96.6%	28%	57%
General merchandise	90.0%	95.9%	98.2%	59%	56%
Paper and related	93.7%	95.8%	98.1%	33%	55%
Pharmaceuticals and drugs	84.1%	90.3%	94.6%	39%	44%

SOURCE: Patrick M. Byrne and William J. Markham, *Improving Quality and Productivity in the Logistics Process* (Oak Brook, IL: Council of Logistics Management, 1991): 262. Used with permission.

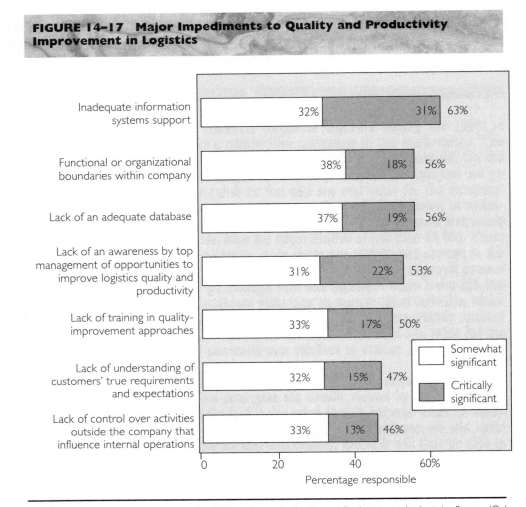

FIGURE 14–17 Major Impediments to Quality and Productivity Improvement in Logistics

SOURCE: Patrick M. Byrne and William J. Markham, *Improving Quality and Productivity in the Logistics Process* (Oak Brook, IL: Council of Logistics Management, 1991): 252. Used with permission.

quality issues being addressed are still current. If customer requirements happen to change, the time spent trying to perform well in areas of little significance will be wasted as a result.

To highlight actual company experiences, the following paragraphs describe the nature of the total quality effort at three major U.S.-based multinational corporations.

total commitment
to quality

Hewlett-Packard Company.[37] Quality has been a primary focus for Hewlett-Packard Company (HP), a leader in computers and information systems, since its beginnings in 1939. Although the philosophies of Dr. W. Edwards Deming have strongly influenced the company, it has also learned from other sources, essentially creating a unique quality process customized to HP's needs. The company bases its philosophy on a total commitment to quality and focuses directly on internal and external customer needs and expectations. HP has placed significant emphasis on the use of customer surveys and feedback systems to maintain a continual awareness of customer expectations and perceptions of logistics service quality.

DuPont Company.[38] Implementing total quality management for the complex multinational chemicals producer DuPont involves sensitizing the organization, setting direction and establishing a business mission, developing a quality management system, and institutionalizing a quality process and philosophy. DuPont believes that cultural change will accompany long-term, sustained gain.

DuPont's approach to quality represents a unique response to the collective directions suggested by several of the prominent quality philosophies. This approach reveals DuPont's priority on customizing a quality approach to meet its own needs and the needs and requirements of its external as well as internal customers. DuPont's logistics successes included improving supplier-customer coordination (which resulted in on-time delivery), finished product appearance, and product quality.

logistics quality successes

Federal Express Corporation.[39] The first service organization to receive the prestigious Malcolm Baldrige National Quality Award, FedEx is very much involved in the logistics business. A time-sensitive, global transportation service that has grown from handling seven packages on its first night in 1971 to a volume that sometimes exceeds more than two million packages per night, FedEx has become one of the best managed and operated companies in the world.

Central to the success of FedEx's quality process is the company's commitment to its People-Service-Profit philosophy. Addressing three specific aspects of customer service—fast delivery, time-definite delivery, and peace of mind—FedEx significantly affects customers not only through its high-quality service, but also through technological advances such as COSMOS (Customer Oriented Services and Management Operation System), VISTA (an integrated package of customer-responsive information services), and SuperTracker (for reading bar coded packages at origin and destination).

customer service

FedEx also credits the success of its quality process to its top management's commitment to change, its dedication to employee training and development, its belief that the company can use information strategically to differentiate itself from the competition, and a sincere desire to meet the needs of the customer.

Logistics Process Reengineering

Due largely to the significant impact of the book titled *Reengineering the Corporation,* there has been intense recent interest in the topic of business process reengineering. According to Hammer and Champy, the book's authors, reengineering is "the fundamental rethinking and radical redesign of businesses processes to achieve dramatic improvements in critical, contemporary measures of performance, such as cost, quality, service, and speed."[40] While the development of a logistics quality process can be a very complex and time-consuming effort, most reengineering processes actually go much further in terms of impact and degree of change. By definition alone, a reengineering process can and should result in very significant changes to a firm's logistics process and the structure of its supply chain. Firms involved in true reengineering processes fully expect that major alterations to their existing logistics networks and other structures may result.

The idea of reengineering logistics processes has become quite popular. For example, considerable attention has been directed by many corporate general managers to reengineering the order fulfillment process. Order fulfillment is a key logistics process, but it is also one that touches and interfaces with numerous other processes and activities throughout the firm. Thus, any attention directed toward this area will provide significant visibility and prominence for a whole host of logistics issues.

Logistics Value[41]

creating value
As was suggested earlier in this section, the fourth stage in the evolution of a formal quality process is customer value. It was also suggested that efficiency, effectiveness, and differentiation represent three important ways in which logistics creates customer value. An important consideration is that value must be viewed from the customer's perspective, because it is value to the customer that is most important. Most contemporary writing on the topic of customer value stresses this concern for the viewpoint of the customer.

CLM study
As part of a continuing stream of inquiry into logistics quality, satisfaction, and value, researchers at Penn State University, the University of Tennessee, and Michigan State University completed in 1995 a comprehensive study titled *Creating Logistics Value: Themes for the Future.* Sponsored and published by the Council of Logistics Management, the objectives of this study were to (1) offer multiple perspectives on the process of creating logistics value; (2) identify examples of value quantification and the impacts of value quantification on strategic and operational decision making; and (3) enhance knowledge of value creation by examining companies and their experiences and priorities in this area.

Study Design and Methodology. Based on the exploratory as well as "best practice" nature of the research objectives, the research design incorporated case study and mail survey elements. In both instances, participants were asked to discuss the topic of value in relation to the following types of logistics service outputs: product availability, order cycle time, logistics operations responsiveness, logistics system information, and postsale customer support. The study incorporated ten on-site case study visits with firms reputed to have made progress on the topic of logistics value, and a total of 396 responses (a 25 percent response rate) to a mail study of logistics executives at firms represented by individuals holding membership in the Council of Logistics Management.

common themes
Results and Findings. Overall, the study uncovered a number of excellent examples of logistics value quantification, seventeen of which are described in detail in the study. While these examples provided a useful basis for discussion with case study firms, it was also apparent that there were many instances in which value was not being quantified or, for that matter, understood. Thus, the study suggested that there is considerable progress to be made in terms of understanding, measuring, and quantifying logistics value.

Among the common themes exhibited among firms that had made progress were the following:

- Logistics value is enhanced through strong corporate leadership focusing on logistics efficiency, effectiveness, and differentiation.

- Value realization requires that logistics capabilities be "marketed" to customers both internal and external to the firm.
- Firms are beginning to place greater emphasis on the quantification of logistics value, although less progress has been made to date than might be expected.
- Logistics value is enhanced through the capability to integrate product, information, and cash flows for decision-making purposes that link both internal and external processes.
- Logistics value is enhanced through ownership of responsibility, both within the firm and outside it.
- Successful logistics organizations have as their single focus the creation of internal value for their organizations and external value for their suppliers and customers.

Aside from indicating the areas where future progress is needed, this study represented a key step in the process of better understanding the relationship between the value of logistics services and the concepts of customer satisfaction, service quality, and customer attitude toward the service supplier. Future, related research efforts should add clarity to issues such as these.

THIRD-PARTY LOGISTICS

As has been indicated throughout this book, firms have directed considerable attention toward working more closely with other channel members, including customers and suppliers, and with various types of logistics suppliers. In essence, this has resulted in the development of more meaningful "relationships" among the companies involved in overall supply chain activity. As a result, many companies have been in the process of "extending" logistics organizations into those of other supply chain participants and facilitators.

One way of extending the logistics organization beyond the boundaries of the company is through the use of a supplier of third-party or contract logistics services.[42] Ideas differ regarding how to define this type of logistics supplier and what services might be included; these issues will be dealt with next.

third-party services

Definition of Third-Party Logistics

Essentially, a third-party logistics firm may be defined as an external supplier that performs all or part of a company's logistics functions. This definition is purposefully broad and is intended to encompass suppliers of services such as transportation, warehousing, distribution, financial services, and so on. Recently, there have been significant increases in the number of firms offering such services, and this trend is expected to continue. While many of these firms are small, niche players, the industry has a number of large firms as well. Examples of the latter include FedEx Logistics Services, UPS Worldwide Logistics, Exel Logistics, GATX Logistics, Roadway Logistics Services, Menlo Logistics, Yellow Logistics Services, Schneider Logistics, and Caterpillar Logistics Services.

Depending on the firm and its positioning in the industry, the terms "contract logistics" and "outsourcing" are sometimes used in place of "third-party logistics." While some industry executives take care to distinguish among terms such as these, the terms all refer to the use of external suppliers of logistics services. Except for the fact that the use of contract logistics generally includes some form of contract, or formal agreement, this text will not suggest any unique definitional differences between these terms.

core and value-added activities   Table 14–6 identifies a number of services that might be included among the "core" activities of such suppliers, as well as potential "value-added" activities. While certain third-party relationships do involve a very comprehensive set of service offerings, most customer-supplier relationships begin with a more modest set of activities to be managed by the third party. Figure 14–18 provides one way of viewing the continuum of companies' involvement in the use of third-party services. As customers grow accustomed to using the services of a third party for certain activities such as transportation and warehousing, they become better candidates for a broader range of service offerings. Although a relatively limited number of companies have chosen to outsource their entire set of supply chain activities, the decision made in 1995 by Dell Computer to outsource all of its supply chain activities to Roadway Logistics Services (ROLS) was an important event for the industry.[43]

unique features   Generally, third-party operations differ from traditional, proprietary operations in several ways: (1) they integrate more than one logistics function; (2) third-party suppliers do not (ordinarily) take a position in inventory; (3) assets such as transportation equipment, warehouses, and so on are controlled by the third-party supplier, although they may be owned by either party; (4) total labor and man-

---

TABLE 14–6   Third-Party Logistics Activities

Examples of "Core" Capabilities

- Transportation
  - LTL and TL
  - Dedicated
  - Intermodal
  - Global sourcing/distribution
- Warehousing
- Inventory management and control
- Information systems
  - Order processing
  - Logistics systems
- Consolidation and distribution
- Freight management services
  - Carrier selection and rate negotiation
  - Freight bill auditing and control
- Consulting assistance

Examples of "Value-Added" Capabilities

- Pick and pack
- Marking, tagging, and labeling
- Product returns and reverse distribution
- Packaging and repackaging
- Salvage and scrap disposal
- Telemarketing

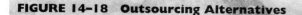

FIGURE 14–18 Outsourcing Alternatives

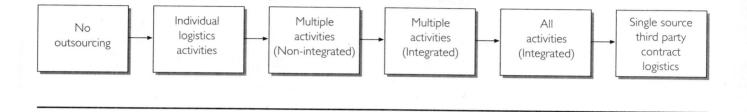

| No outsourcing | → | Individual logistics activities | → | Multiple activities (Non-integrated) | → | Multiple activities (Integrated) | → | All activities (Integrated) | → | Single source third party contract logistics |

agement services are available from the external supplier; and (5) specialty services (such as inventory management, product preparation, assembly/consolidation, and so on) are available.

Decision Drivers

Based on the results of a University of Tennessee study, Figure 14–19 identifies a number of benefits cited by users of third-party services. While both reduced operating costs and improved service levels were cited by users as being of interest, the opportunity to take cost out of the supply chain usually has the greatest impact in terms of importance. Following closely in importance were the ability to focus on core competencies, to reduce the employee base, and to reduce capital costs. Although not included in Figure 14–19, additional benefits that were cited in-

benefits

FIGURE 14–19 Benefits Resulting from Outsourcing Efforts

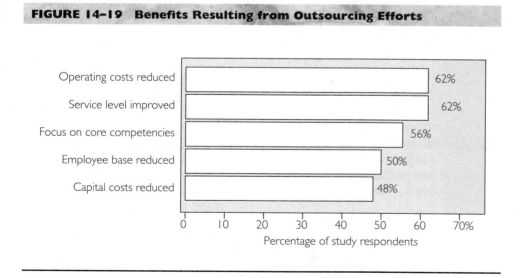

Percentage of study respondents

- Operating costs reduced — 62%
- Service level improved — 62%
- Focus on core competencies — 56%
- Employee base reduced — 50%
- Capital costs reduced — 48%

cluded access to greater or specialized logistics expertise, flexibility, and information technology.

Other research results have provided similar results. A 1994 study by Professor Robert Lieb, for example, lists a number of factors, including that the logistics function is becoming more complex. He cited globalization, SKU proliferation, channel fragmentation, and shorter product life cycles as evidence of this trend. Among the other factors cited were "unified point of contact" and a "simpler, more uniform supply chain."[44]

"trigger" events The University of Tennessee research also identified a number of "trigger" events that frequently were found to drive the decision to consider the use of third-party services. Included were the following: capacity/space constraints, lack of needed expertise, organizational change, labor issues, mergers and acquisitions, new products and markets, and changing customer requirements.[45]

The Buying Process

Figure 14–20 shows a representation of the buying process used by customers in relation to the third-party decision. Although the diagram suggests a linear flow from Stage I to Stage V, the buying process has been observed in many instances to be anything but linear. Each stage is discussed briefly in the paragraphs that follow.

Stage I: Diagnose and Conceptualize Needs. This first stage involves the process by which the customer becomes fully aware of his or her logistics needs and is able to articulate those needs in an understandable way. The needs must then be translated into the service requirements that potentially would be met by a third-party supplier. Given the significance of most third-party decisions and the potential complexity of the overall process, any time taken at the outset to gain an understanding of one's needs is well spent.

Stage II: Identify Alternatives. The first portion of this stage may be devoted to determining selection criteria for a third-party supplier. The statement of needs that emerged from the Stage I deliberations should make the process of identifying selection criteria manageable.

Although logistics executives and managers usually have significant involvement in the third-party decision, it is often the case that other executives are also in-

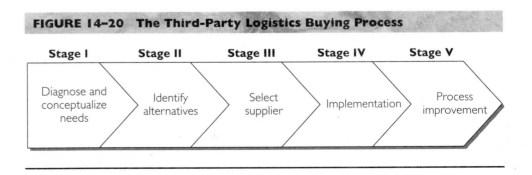

FIGURE 14–20 The Third-Party Logistics Buying Process

Stage I	Stage II	Stage III	Stage IV	Stage V
Diagnose and conceptualize needs	Identify alternatives	Select supplier	Implementation	Process improvement

volved. Table 14–7 shows the results to a question in the 1994 Lieb study that asked about the overall involvement of various nonlogistics executives in the third-party logistics buying process. As the table indicates, representatives from finance, manufacturing, and information systems were foremost among those included. It is also not unusual for the president/CEO to be involved with the third-party decision.[46]

The University of Tennessee study took a somewhat different approach, asking which executives were the key supporters, or drivers, of the decision to outsource. The survey results indicated the following executives, along with the percentage of study respondents characterizing each as a key supporter or driver: logistics/transportation (64 percent), finance (58 percent), president/CEO/owner (50 percent), manufacturing (24 percent), and marketing (20 percent).[47]

The process of identifying alternatives should include a request for proposals (RFP) from interested suppliers and then an initial screening to shorten the list of candidates to a manageable number. The task then involves detailed evaluation and consideration of those on the "short list."

request for proposals (RFP)

Stage III: Select a Supplier.   While this stage is of critical concern to the customer, the selection of a third-party supplier should be made only following very close consideration to the credentials of the most likely candidates. Also, it is highly advisable to interact with and get to know the final candidates on a professionally intimate basis.

As was indicated in the discussion of Stage II, it is likely that a number of executives will play key roles in the buying process. It is important to achieve consensus on the final selection decision, so as to encourage a significant degree of "buy-in" and agreement among those involved. Due to the strategic significance of the decision to use a third-party supplier, it will be essential to ensure that everyone has a consistent understanding of the decision that has been made and knows what to expect from the firm that has been selected.

Stage IV: Implement the Relationship.   Once the decision has been made to select a particular third-party supplier, it is important to recognize that the process of knowing and working with the winning firm has just begun. The fourth and fifth

TABLE 14–7   Nonlogistics Functions Most Frequently Involved in Third-Party Decision Making

Function	Percentage of Respondents
Finance	48%
Manufacturing	42
Marketing	29
Information systems	52
Human resource management	19

SOURCE: Robert C. Lieb and Hugh L. Randall, "Third Party Logistics: Surveys—Users and Service Provider CEO's," presented at the 1994 Annual Conference of the Council of Logistics Management, Cincinnati, Ohio, October, 1994. Used with permission.

ON THE LINE

Whirlpool Contracts Inbound Logistics to Ryder

Whirlpool Corporation has hired Ryder Dedicated Logistics to design and manage a logistics system for inbound materials and components to the appliance manufacturer's eleven U.S. plants.

"It's the largest non-automotive just-in-time business that Ryder has ever signed," said Larry S. Mulkey, president of Ryder Dedicated Logistics.

Terms of the five-year contract weren't disclosed, but Ryder executives said it was a multimillion-dollar deal that will rank among their ten largest accounts.

Whirlpool's hiring of a third party came after the company decided to centralize management of the $2-billion-plus worth of annual shipments to the plants, said Dan Prickett, director of inbound logistics.

There has been central coordination of outbound shipments for years, he said, but the flow of raw materials and components had been left to individual plants.

Whirlpool appointed a team to study the situation and sought outside advice from Cleveland Consulting Associates.

Prickett said the team quickly realized "that logistics was not a core competency at Whirlpool," and that the company's efforts were best focused on manufacturing and marketing.

Working with the consultants, Whirlpool asked thirty third-party logistics firms to supply information about themselves. Nineteen responded, and that number was culled to six.

The six were asked how they would run the business and were invited to study two plants—a dryer factory in Marion, Ohio, and Whirlpool's big refrigerator plant in Evansville, Indiana.

Dug Deeper

Prickett said Ryder went a step farther by asking to look at a third plant. Whirlpool obliged, taking Ryder representatives to a facility in Forth Smith, Arkansas.

Ryder was the only one of the six that made that request, and Prickett said Whirlpool was impressed by that attempt to learn more about its operation.

"We didn't want somebody who said, 'This works somewhere else and we know it will work for Whirlpool.' We were

looking for somebody to develop an innovative proposal for our business," Prickett said.

As the next step in this selection process, Whirlpool asked each of the six finalists to show a location that demonstrated "best practices" in logistics. Ryder used a Jeep Cherokee plant in Detroit.

The final step was a series of formal presentations in which the third-party candidates answered questions.

After that, the proposals of the six were evaluated. Prickett said Ryder emerged "the clear winner in a strong field."

Prickett said Whirlpool was seeking information technology and decision-support capabilities, commitment to continuous improvement, flexibility, creative and innovative solutions, reduced costs, and strategic commitment.

"We were looking for a company that not only is focused on it today, but is investing in it for the future," he said.

Prickett said that by hiring a third party for inbound logistics, Whirlpool expects "to reduce costs, improve quality, and reduce overall order-processing and manufacturing cycle time."

He said Ryder was the only one of the six third-party candidates to provide performance guarantees and a cooperative gain-sharing program.

Flexibility

Prickett said Whirlpool uses a "flexible manufacturing" system in which components are delivered to assembly lines that frequently are converted from production of one model to another.

Ryder will coordinate a just-in-time supply chain with the ability to "mix and match" loads bound for all 11 plants, Mulkey said.

For less time-sensitive freight, Ryder's LogiCorp division will recommend, manage, and monitor suppliers of inbound common carriage, Mulkey said.

Ryder will establish a Whirlpool logistics center at a site to be determined, Mulkey said. At that center, Ryder personnel will manage the supply chain, monitor performance, train workers, and share "best practices" among plants, he said.

SOURCE: Joseph Bonney, "Whirlpool Contracts Inbound Logistics to Ryder," *American Shipper* (April 1995): 52. Used with permission.

stages of the process will prove to be just as critical and intense as the first three stages.

Depending on the complexity of the new third-party relationship, the overall implementation process may be relatively short, or it may be extended over a

TABLE 14–8 Examples of Third-Party Relationships

Customer		Supplier
Inmac Corporation	◄──────►	Skyway Freight Systems
Whirlpool	◄──────►	Ryder Dedicated Logistics
Kodak	◄──────►	Bekins
Motorola	◄──────►	UPS Worldwide Logistics
Dell Computer	◄──────►	Roadway Logistics
Procter & Gamble	◄──────►	Exel Logistics
National Semiconductor	◄──────►	FedEx Logistics Services
Ford New Holland	◄──────►	Caterpillar Logistics Services

period of time. If the situation involves significant change to and restructuring of the customer's logistics network, for example, full implementation may take longer to accomplish. In an instance where the role of the third party will be relatively straightforward and uncomplicated, implementation may proceed very expeditiously.

Table 14–8 identifies several examples of third-party relationships. Note the relatively wide range of customer types and the variety of individual suppliers that have been included. Details concerning how the types of suppliers differ will be discussed in the following section.

Stage V: Process Improvement.   Many traditional models of the buying process conclude with the implementation stage. Regarding the involvement of third-party suppliers, it is essential to know what types of continuous and breakthrough improvements can be expected. While all suppliers should expect to be held accountable for the former type of improvement, the breakthrough or "paradigm-shift" type of improvement will also be necessary to enhance the firm's competitive advantage. Achieving this objective will require customer firms to encourage "out-of-the-box" thinking by the third-party supplier and to be creative and innovative as a result. While this inherently will involve a greater element of risk, it must be taken in order to enjoy the benefits of significant improvements to the logistics process.

Types of Relationships

Figure 14–21 shows one way of characterizing the various types of third-party suppliers. Included are transportation-based, warehouse/distribution-based, forwarder-based, shipper/management-based, and financial/information-based suppliers. Each type is discussed in the paragraphs that follow.

supplier types

Transportation Based.   Included among the transportation-based suppliers are firms such as Menlo Logistics (CF), Roadway Logistics Services (ROLS), Yellow Logistics Services, Schneider Logistics, J.B. Hunt Logistics, FedEx Logistics Services, UPS Worldwide Logistics, and Ryder Dedicated Logistics, all of which are subsidiaries or major divisions of large transportation firms. Some of the services provided by these firms are "leveraged" in that they utilize the assets of other

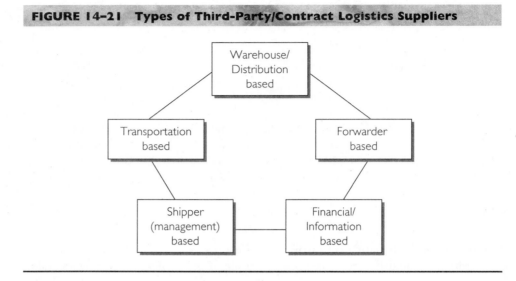

FIGURE 14–21   Types of Third-Party/Contract Logistics Suppliers

companies, and some are "nonleveraged," where the principal emphasis is on utilizing the transportation-based assets of the parent organization. In all instances, these firms extend beyond the transportation activity to provide a more comprehensive set of logistics offerings.

Warehouse/Distribution Based.   Traditionally, most warehouse/distribution logistics suppliers have been in the public or contract warehousing business and have expanded into a broader range of logistics services. Examples of such firms include Exel Logistics, GATX Logistics, DSC Logistics, and USCO. Based on their traditional orientation, these firms have already been involved in logistics activities such as inventory management, warehousing, distribution, and so on. Experience has indicated that these "facility-based" operators have found the transition to integrated logistics services to be less complex than have the transportation-based providers.

Forwarder Based.   The category of forwarder-based suppliers includes companies such as Kuehne & Nagel, Fritz, and C.H. Robinson, which have extended their current middleman roles as forwarders into the broader range of third-party logistics. These firms are essentially non-asset owners, are very independent, and deal with a wide range of suppliers of logistics services. They have proven quite capable at putting together packages of logistics services that meet customer needs.

Shipper/Management Based.   The shipper/management-based category is a very interesting type of supplier and includes third-party firms that have emerged from larger corporate logistics organizations. Prominent among these are Caterpillar Logistics Services (Caterpillar, Inc.), Intral (Gillette), IBM (IBM Corporation), and KLS (Kaiser Aluminum). Typically, logistics expertise and certain resources such as information technology are used to leverage the third-party operation. These

TABLE 14-9   Market Size for Third-Party Logistics, 1992-2000

	1992	1996 (est.)	2000 (est.)
Relevant services	374	421	474
Penetration rate	2.7%	6%	10%
Market size ($ billion)	$10	$25	$47–50

SOURCE: Robert V. Delaney, "Integrated Business Logistics: Doing What Is Right for the Country," presented at the Conference on the Transportation Industry of the Future, U.S. Department of Transportation, Washington, DC, January 9, 1995. Used with permission.

suppliers have significant current or previous experience in managing the logistics operations of the parent firm and, as a result, prove to be very capable suppliers of such services to external customers.

Financial/Information Based. The final category of third-party supplier, the financial/information-based category, includes firms such as Cass Information Systems (a division of Cass Commercial Corporation), GE Information Services (General Electric), and Encompass (a joint venture between CSX and AMR). These firms provide services such as freight payment and auditing, cost accounting and control, and logistics management tools for monitoring, booking, tracking, tracing, and inventory management.

Revenue/Growth Estimates

Table 14–9 gives estimates of the market size for third-party logistics in the 1990s as prepared by Robert V. Delaney of Cass Information Systems.[48] Overall, he estimates that manufacturers and distributors will spend $25 billion on third-party/contract logistics services by 1996 and $47–$50 billion by the year 2000. This latter figure is consistent with the market size of $50 billion projected for 2000 by a major logistics consulting firm.[49]

market potential

Overall Trends

Essentially, the third-party logistics industry is in the "growth" stage of its life cycle. Based on observations from the supplier and customer sides of this market, it is apparent that both types of firms are aggressively trying to figure out how best to organize and leverage the third-party resource. As more and more successes are reported and as firms become more comfortable with trusting significant elements of logistics responsibility to external suppliers, the involvement of third-party suppliers will continue to grow and gain acceptance.

Among the key issues for the future are leveraging the use of third parties into benefits for entire supply chains, strategic alliances between third parties and between third-party and customer firms, the cost/service realities of third-party relationships, and the development of globally capable information linkages that extend the third-party capabilities to logistics networks extending throughout the world.

SUMMARY

- Logistics organization is a critical issue, and companies are directing considerable attention toward how best to organize the logistics process.
- The growth and development of logistics organizations occurs in three stages: an operational orientation, a managerial orientation, and a strategic orientation.
- A number of factors characterize leading-edge logistics organizations. Among these are the existence of a formal logistics organization with an officer-level executive, a fluid approach to logistics organization, and a focus on customer satisfaction and the creation of customer value.
- As logistics organizations evolve, there are several organizational structures that may be considered. Organizing around key logistics processes is a strategy that seems to have significant merit.
- While there is a general trend toward centralization of logistics operations, it is important to objectively evaluate the issue of centralization versus decentralization.
- There are several key ways to measure the performance of the logistics process and of logistics management: through cost criteria, productivity criteria, and service criteria.
- Logistics creates customer value through efficiency, effectiveness, and differentiation.
- Adoption of a formal quality process can produce significant benefits.
- Current interest in logistics process reengineering will help to assure the continual evaluation and improvement of our logistics systems.
- An additional understanding of logistics value will help firms to realize benefit from the provision of logistics services.
- The third-party logistics industry is in its growth stage; users and suppliers are determining how best to structure and operate third-party relationships.
- There are several steps in the third-party logistics buying process, and each one is critical to the long-term success of the resulting supplier relationship.
- Various types of third-party suppliers have a presence in the market today.

STUDY QUESTIONS

1. Discuss the phases in the development of a logistics organization.

2. What activities are typically considered to be part of a firm's logistics organization?

3. What are some of the common patterns of logistics organizational structure? What are the advantages of logistics centralization versus decentralization?

4. What are the characteristics of leading-edge logistics organizations?

5. Identify the strategic alternatives that may influence the selection of a logistics organizational structure.

6. In what ways may logistics organizations differ? Evaluate the benefits of the functional, logistics service division, and process-oriented approaches to logistics organization.

7. What methods are available to measure the effectiveness of a logistics organization and the performance of logistics management?

8. How does the logistics process create customer value?

9. What are some of the common characteristics of successful logistics quality processes? What factors motivate companies to become involved in such processes?

10. Discuss the elements of a logistics quality process.

11. How does a logistics quality process relate to the objective of process improvement and to the topic of reengineering?

12. What key themes are associated with firms that have made progress in terms of understanding, measuring, and quantifying logistics value?

13. Describe third-party logistics and the role it plays in a company's logistics organization.

14. What factors drive a company's decision to use a third-party supplier? What key steps are included in the customer's buying process?

15. How do third-party supplier firms differ from one another?

16. At what stage of development is the third-party industry? What are the future prospects for the use of third-party suppliers by logistics users?

NOTES

1. "Organizing Logistics," *Distribution* (April 1989): 29.
2. A. T. Kearney, Inc., "Emerging Top Management Focus for the 1980s." (Chicago, IL: A.T. Kearney, Inc., 1994).
3. Donald J. Bowersox, Patricia J. Daugherty, Cornelia L. Droge, Dale S. Rogers, and Daniel L. Wardlow, *Leading-Edge Logistics: Competitive Positioning for the 1990s* (Chicago: Council of Logistics Management, 1989).
4. Adapted from Bowersox, et al., *Leading-Edge Logistics,* pp. i–vi.
5. Patrick M. Byrne and William J. Markham, *Improving Quality and Productivity in the Logistics Process* (Oak Brook, IL: Council of Logistics Management, 1991): 407.
6. James L. Heskett, "Organizing for Effective Distribution Management," Chapter 29 in *Distribution Handbook* (New York: The Free Press, 1985): 828–31.
7. Portions of this section are from Theodore P. Stank, Patricia J. Daugherty, and Craig M. Gustin, "Organizational Structure: Influence on Logistics Integration, Costs, and Information System Performance," *International Journal of Logistics Management* 5, no. 2 (1994): 41–42.
8. James D. Thompson, *Organizations in Action* (New York: McGraw-Hill, 1967).
9. Alfred D. Chandler, *Strategy and Structure* (Cambridge, MA: MIT Press, 1962).
10. James M. Masters and Bernard J. LaLonde, *The 1994 Ohio State University Survey of Career Patterns in Logistics* (Columbus, OH: The Ohio State University, 1994), Figure 5.
11. James M. Masters and Bernard J. LaLonde, *The 1993 Ohio State University Survey of Career Patterns in Logistics* (Columbus, OH: The Ohio State University, 1993), Figure 5.
12. Bowersox, et al., *Leading-Edge Logistics,* 34–35.
13. The details relating to the Becton Dickinson Supply Chain Services division appear in Robert A. Novack, C. John Langley Jr., and Lloyd M. Rinehart, *Creating Logistics Value: Themes for the Future* (Oak Brook, IL: Council of Logistics Management, 1995).
14. William C. Copacino, "Logistics Strategy: A New View of Logistics," *Traffic Management* (December 1993): 31.
15. Donald J. Bowersox, David J. Frayer, and Judith M. Schmitz, "Organizing for Effective

Logistics Management," Chapter 35 in *The Logistics Handbook* (New York: The Free Press, 1994): 777–79.

16. Masters and LaLonde, *The 1993 Ohio State University Survey of Career Patterns in Logistics,* Figure 7.

17. Bernard J. LaLonde, "The 1991 Ohio State University Survey of Career Patterns in Logistics," *Proceedings of the 1991 Annual Conference of the Council of Logistics Management* (Oak Brook, IL: CLM, 1991): 61.

18. James P. Falk, "Organizing for Effective Distribution," *Proceedings of the 1980 Annual Conference of the National Council of Physical Distribution Management* (Oak Brook, IL: NCPDM, 1980): 181–99.

19. "PDM Challenged at Seminar," *Handling and Shipping* (July 1973): 54.

20. Adapted from Byrne and Markham, *Improving Quality and Productivity in the Logistics Process,* 408.

21. For an excellent discussion of reengineering, see Michael Hammer and James Champy, *Reengineering the Corporation* (New York: HarperBusiness, 1993).

22. Bernard J. LaLonde, Martha C. Cooper, and Thomas G. Noordewier, *Customer Service: A Management Perspective* (Oak Brook, IL: Council of Logistics Management, 1988): 117–21.

23. For an overview of logistics quality principles and approaches, see C. John Langley Jr. and Mary C. Holcomb, "Total Quality Management in Logistics," Chapter 9 in *Distribution Handbook* (New York: The Free Press, 1985): 183–98.

24. R. Mohan Pisharodi and C. John Langley Jr., "A Perceptual Process Model of Customer Service Based on Cybernetic/Control Theory," *Journal of Business Logistics* 11, no. 1 (1990): 34–40.

25. Byrne and Markham, *Improving Quality and Productivity in the Logistics Process,* 2.

26. Byrne and Markham, *Improving Quality and Productivity in the Logistics Process,* 2–3.

27. The PIMS research program represents an extensive data bank relating to business performance and related factors. The program is conducted by the Strategic Planning Institute, Cambridge, Massachusetts.

28. Byrne and Markham, *Improving Quality and Productivity in the Logistics Process,* 4.

29. This section is based on an excellent discussion of the quality gurus found in Francis J. Quinn, "The Gurus of Quality," *Traffic Management* (July 1990): 34–39.

30. Yasuhiro Monden, *Toyota Production System* (Norcross, GA: Institute of Industrial Engineers, 1983).

31. These steps are described in detail in C. John Langley Jr., "Quality in Logistics: A Competitive Advantage," *Proceedings, R. Hadly Waters Logistics and Transportation Symposium* (University Park, PA: Penn State University, Center for Logistics Research, 1990): 28.

32. Langley, "Quality in Logistics: A Competitive Advantage," 30.

33. Excellent sources on these topics include Donald J. Wheeler and David S. Chambers, *Understanding Statistical Process Control* (Knoxville, TN: Statistical Process Controls, Inc., 1986); and Kaoru Ishikawa, *Guide to Quality Control* (Tokyo: Asian Productivity Organization, 1982).

34. The American Supplier Institute has helped to popularize this approach. Although it applies to many industrial situations, much of its United States experience to date has been in the automobile industry.

35. See Robert C. Camp, *Benchmarking* (Milwaukee, WI: ASQC Quality Press, 1989): 10. See also David Altany, "Copycats," *Industry Week* (November 5, 1990): 11–18.

36. Francis J. Quinn, "Quality: The Ante to Play the Game," *Traffic Management* (July 1990): 42–49.

37. C. John Langley Jr., Mary C. Holcomb, Joel Baudouin, Alexander Donnan, and Paul Caruso, "Approaches to Logistics Quality," *1989 Council of Logistics Management Annual Conference Proceedings* (Oak Brook, IL: Council of Logistics Management, 1989): 75–76.

38. Langley, et al., "Approaches to Logistics Quality," 82–88.

39. LaLonde, et al., *Customer Service: A Management Perspective,* 111–16.

40. Hammer and Champy, *Reengineering the Corporation,* 32.

41. Robert A. Novack, C. John Langley Jr., and Lloyd M. Rinehart, *Creating Logistics Value: Themes for the Future* (Oak Brook, IL: Council of Logistics Management, 1995).

42. For further information, see Robert C. Lieb, Robert A Millen, and Luk N. Van Wassenhove, "Third Party Logistics Services: A Comparison of American and European Manufacturers," *International Journal of Physical Distribution and Logistics Management* 23, 6 (1993): 35–44; Bernard J. LaLonde and Arnold B. Maltz, "Some Propositions about Outsourcing the Logistics Function," *International Journal of Logistics Management* 3, 1 (1992): 1–11; Lisa Harrington, "Quality and the Outsourcing Decision," *Private Carrier* (August, 1994): 16–21; Harry L. Sink, C. John Langley Jr., and Brian J. Gibson, "Buyer Observations of the U.S. Third Party Logistics Market," *International Journal of Physical Distribution and Logistics Management* (1996); and Donald J. Bowersox, "The Strategic Benefits of Logistics Alliances," *Harvard Business Review* 90, 4 (July-August 1990): 36–45.

43. Staff Report, "The Promise of Contract Logistics," *Outsourced Logistics* (Washington, DC: Logistics Publishing Group of Harrington-Harps Associates): 7.

44. Lieb and Randall, "Third Party Logistics: Surveys—Users and Service Provider CEOs," 26–27.

45. Harrington, "Quality and the Outsourcing Decision," 17.

46. Lieb and Randall, "Third Party Logistics: Surveys—Users and Service Provider CEOs," 5.

47. Harrington, "Quality and the Outsourcing Decision," 20.

48. Harrington, "Quality and the Outsourcing Decision," 16.

49. Tony Dollar, "Shaking Things Up," *Distribution* (July 1995): 90.

Case 14-1

SAVANNAH STEEL CORPORATION

Savannah Steel Corporation is one of a limited number of minimills specializing in the manufacture of custom products, specifically a high-quality line of steel joists used throughout the building industry. The product line is narrow, consisting primarily of angles, channels, and bars. Savannah produces these components and then assembles the joists according to the specifics of individual customer orders.

Mike Murray has recently been named vice president (VP) of logistics for Savannah Steel. With recent increased competitiveness in the custom-structure steel industry, Savannah Steel feels that an enhanced emphasis on the logistics systems concept will help to increase market share by improving customer service and lowering the unit cost of doing business.

The vice president of logistics reports directly to the executive vice president (EVP) of operations, who reports to the president of Savannah Steel. Other EVP positions are in the areas of sales and marketing, and finance. The position of VP of logistics is newly created, and an executive search firm identified Murray as a suitable person to accept the responsibility.

Murray's predecessor held the title of manager of transportation and distribution. He was basically responsible for the outbound-to-customer transportation of finished product and for managing activities on the shipping and receiving docks at Savannah Steel's single plant. The person holding this job reported to the director of manufacturing, who reported to the EVP of operations. It is common knowledge that he resigned because he felt that his responsibility was too limited and his contribution too "buried within the organization" to be meaningful.

When Murray took the job, he understood from the president of Savannah Steel that logistics was a top priority for the whole company. The president also made it clear that he expects to see results in terms of improved customer service and a reduced logistics unit cost in the near future.

Even though his tenure with Savannah Steel has been brief, Murray already has made several significant logistics changes. Logistics has acquired total responsibility for all finished goods transportation and inventory management, production planning, and operation of the company's small private truck fleet. The operations area houses the management of all purchasing activities, with the VP of purchasing also reporting to the EVP of operations. Savannah generally sells finished product to its customers on an F.O.B. delivered basis, and the company purchases most of its raw materials and supplies F.O.B. Savannah's dock.

The EVP of operations has given Murray his personal assurance that he will do whatever is necessary to help achieve the logistics organization's established goals. While he admits that he really does not know much about the logistics concept, he feels confident that Murray can achieve significant results without too much trouble.

Case Questions

1. How would you characterize the present status of the logistics organization at Savannah Steel? Specifically, at what phase is this company in the evolution of its logistics organization?
2. What activities should Murray add to the logistics area in order to maximize its likelihood for achieving its intended goals? What organizational issues and problems may surface if Murray decides to increase the comprehensiveness of the logistics function at Savannah Steel?
3. Is the logistics area positioned properly within the organization to achieve its intended goals? If not, what alternatives would you recommend? What obstacles to implementation would be relevant?
4. If you were Murray, in what way would you expect the company to measure your performance as VP of logistics? What specific programs would you implement to enhance this company's logistics productivity?
5. In general, what critical factors will determine whether Murray's performance will satisfy the president?

Case 14-2

HANOVER PHARMACEUTICALS, INC.

Like many American business executives, John Alden thinks he has seen it all. Strategic planning, management by objectives, cash cows, stars, budgeting, leadership . . . It just seems a matter of time before something else takes its place among the popular things for businesses to do. Having received his M.B.A. in the mid-1970s from a prestigious eastern university, Alden has been besieged with new approaches and new ways of doing business during his twenty-year career. He wonders if it is ever going to stop.

As vice president of logistics for Hanover Pharmaceuticals, Inc., Alden is very proud of the productivity program he has recently 'installed'' in the logistics area. Following the advice of a leading consultant, Alden has made sure that everything in the logistics area is measured, monitored, and controlled. The objective of the program is to see that each available resource performs to its maximum capability and that productivity measures in key logistics areas are at least equal to the industry averages Alden has seen published.

At a recent meeting, upper management informed Alden that the company would soon embark on a total quality management (TQM) process that would define quality as "anticipating and exceeding customer requirements." Although he is somewhat skeptical and tends to think of this new initiative as just another company program, Alden feels that he should respond meaningfully to this companywide priority.

Case Questions

1. Critique the productivity program Alden recently installed at Hanover Pharmaceuticals. What do you feel are key advantages and limitations of such a program?
2. What do you feel should be done in the logistics area to be consistent with the corporatewide commitment to TQM? Even though details about this process are sketchy at present, try to outline an approach you might recommend for Alden to consider.

CHAPTER 15

LEADING EDGE LOGISTICS STRATEGIES

LEARNING OBJECTIVES

After reading this chapter, you should be able to do the following:

- Discuss why companies are concerned about strategy and gaining strategic advantage.

- Understand the development of strategic management as it has evolved over time.

- Discuss basic types of strategies that companies can use to gain market share and competitive advantage.

- Understand the major strategies being utilized to manage supply chains effectively.

- Discuss the importance of supply chain strategies in today's global economy.

- Examine time-based strategies for logistics supply chains.

- Discuss asset utilization strategies for improving the efficiency of logistics systems.

- Understand value-added strategies for logistics supply chains.

KEEBLER COMPANY

Keebler Company is the second largest cookie and cracker maker in the United States and is probably best known for its advertisement that depicts elves baking cookies in a hollow tree. But Keebler is also well known in logistics circles for its world-class logistics operations—not what one would expect of a company run by elves. Keebler has very complex production and logistics requirements. Recently, the logistics organization of Keebler was given the objective of making and distributing in a week what is sold in a week. That challenge may seem simple, but in the complex environment in which Keebler operates, it is difficult to achieve.

The challenge to make and distribute in a week what is sold in a week required the reengineering of the logistics supply chain in Keebler. It necessitated changes in inventory management, production, and distribution. A system had to be put in place that would forecast weekly demand by SKU at each location. The net result also included a replacement of the management information system and just about every existing principle of how the company handled its products.

Keebler is one of the industry leaders in the sale of salty snacks and traditionally has relied heavily on national sales promotions. These promotions create tremendous spikes in demand and place a real strain on the logistics system to meet the peak demand requirements of the company's seventy distribution centers. It also should be noted that Keebler's sales representatives would draw from the distribution center stocks to build the large displays in the stores to attract consumer sales. Consequently, the baking plants would produce (push) products weeks in advance of demand to have adequate inventories to meet the sales demands at the stores.

The old system relied upon the sales representatives to predict weekly sales. As is usually the case in such situations, the margin of error was exceptionally high, resulting in too much stock of certain items and not enough of others—not exactly what is needed to provide high levels of customer service and to have efficient op-

erations in manufacturing and logistics. Also, as Keebler management was quick to point out, the company's products are not like wine; they do not improve with age. There was a tendency to carry too much safety stock to protect against stockouts, and some of that stock would become obsolete (read stale).

Essentially, Keebler felt that a quick-response system was necessary to reduce the cycle time from production to the distribution facilities to both meet the needs of the sales representatives and reduce inventory levels. The initial reengineering of the logistics supply chain was based on five interrelated modules:

- Improved plant execution
- Product rationalization
- Demand smoothing
- System balancing
- Sales forecasting

A key factor, in addition to better forecasting, was the ability of the manufacturing plants to be more demand-responsive, or to take more of a "pull" approach, rather than the traditional "push" approach that is so common in this industry. Manufacturing line changeovers are usually done after long production runs. The new approach requires more frequent changeovers and flexibility to respond to current demand. In other words, the logistics organization had to get the plants to produce more items more frequently in smaller lot sizes—not a popular idea with the manufacturing managers. But it was a necessary part of the new strategy to shorten cycle time and to lower inventory in the pipeline while giving high levels of customer service.

Another key element in the reengineering process was the effective utilization of point-of-sale information. The new forecasting models being developed require accurate and timely data. The efficient transfer of point-of-sale information will play an important part in improving the forecasts of SKUs by location.

Keebler operates six plants in its cookie/cracker division. In addition, the salty snack group operates two plants and a specialty bakery. The number of SKUs, while not large compared to some industries, is about

Continued

KEEBLER COMPANY—
Continued

550. These SKUs compete for production capacity at the various plant locations, which adds to the complexity of the new pull approach in manufacturing.

The next step in the process will be to rationalize the distribution facilities. Keebler feels that seventy distribution centers is too many in today's environment. It anticipates eliminating a number of these centers and converting some of the others to cross-docking operations, which will further reduce cycle times and inventory levels. Keebler is also changing its transportation management program. It is reducing the number of carriers, to gain leverage and improve transportation costs and delivery times.

Keebler is an excellent example of a company attempting to respond to today's competitive environment. It has established a goal of improving the efficiency and effectiveness of its manufacturing and distribution systems. Key strategies are the reduction of cycle times and a more flexible, demand-responsive manufacturing approach. Logistics-related tactics include utilizing point-of-sale information. Change is a part of the culture. In fact, the company states, "It is safe to say that anything that took place two years ago at Keebler Company will not be in place two years from now."

ADAPTED FROM: Gary Burrows, "Uncommon Logistics" *American Shipper* (May 1995): 72–76.

---

competitive environment

The terms *strategy, strategic, strategic management,* and *strategic advantage* have been used repeatedly in the previous fourteen chapters. The frequent use of these terms can be explained in part by the intensely competitive global environment that most companies are faced with today. That competitive global pressure brings constant change. It requires a management focus that is future oriented and a continuous analysis of the macro or external environment that drives many of the changes. (See Chapter 1 for a review of the major external factors driving the need for change.) The macro environment affects the micro (company) environment as a change agent, but more specifically, the external drivers of change present threats to the current company position.

survival

The macro environment also provides opportunities that can be taken advantage of if the company's management has the foresight to recognize them and protect itself against external competitive threats. The source of a firm's micro-level responses usually lies in how its internal strengths and weaknesses are recognized and whether they are used proactively and creatively in the face of the external environment. Economic success and viability are frequently measured in terms of profit, return on assets, return on investment, and other comparable performance barometers or metrics. Underlying all of these measures is essentially the issue of how "we" are going to survive as an organization, given the fast-paced rate of change and competitive threats and challenges, such as technological obsolescence.

It is no wonder that businesses talk strategy or reference strategic approaches. They must keep focused on a future course or direction and on positioning themselves to respond proactively. They must also achieve the necessary acumen to survive successfully, that is, to make a profit and have a sufficient return to add value for shareholders. Strategy is justifiably a part of our business lexicon.

Gaining some sort of strategic advantage over competitors is a key part of survival, and logistics has come to be recognized as having a role to play in helping to gain that competitive advantage. Understanding how we gain competitive advantage and how logistics can contribute is important. Initially, we will examine the background and development of strategy. Then we will discuss some generic or basic general strategies. Finally, we will examine the types of logistics strategies that companies are utilizing to help their organizations gain competitive advantage.

strategic advantage

OVERVIEW OF STRATEGIC PLANNING

As has been indicated in previous chapters, strategy and strategic advantage have become a meaningful part of the company culture in most successful corporations that operate globally or that are affected by global competition. Economic survival is closely related to having a vision and understanding the effect that major drivers of change will have upon the mission of an organization. Logistics supply chains should play an important role in the strategic plans of companies.

strategic vision

It is important to note at the outset that good planning is not a new phenomenon in successful companies. Rather, there have been several phases of evolutionary development with respect to planning. During the 1950s and 1960s, strategic planning typically meant investment planning. The prevailing doctrine was that diversity led to success and was a hedge against economic downturns. A broader array of products and/or services would, therefore, provide growth and stability.

stages of planning

During the 1970s, strategic planning began to focus on internal growth opportunities, with an emphasis upon marketing research, product development, and brand management. Also, cost reduction strategies were developed for expanded national and international sales.

During the 1980s, a combination of investment in other companies and internal growth opportunities were utilized. Strategic business units (SBUs) were developed; these were essentially components of the larger organization. The focus was upon predicting the impact of the forces of change and providing plans for the SBUs to become sources of growth in sales or sources of cash from profits to finance other SBUs that were moving up the growth curve.

During the 1990s, the emphasis has been refocused somewhat to the development of plans for gaining strategic advantage in the marketplace and for defending against competitors seeking greater market share. Strategic planning is more team oriented and more comprehensive in terms of participation by company personnel. The planners are less likely to be a remote group that does not actively participate in decision making. It is a much more challenging era both because of the dynamics of the changes that are occurring and also because more individuals in the company are getting an opportunity to provide input for changing existing practices and, perhaps, even to help change the direction of the organization.

team oriented

Before proceeding to discuss generic strategies, a discussion of the definition of strategy would be appropriate.

Definitions

The term *strategy* or *strategic* is a derivative of Greek word *strategos,* meaning "the art of the general," which is indicative of the word's military origins. In fact, strategy and tactics are a part of both the military and the business lexicon, and an appropriate definition should be provided of both terms.

strategy   *Strategy* can be defined as a course of action, a scheme, or a principal idea through which an organization or individual hopes to accomplish a specific objective or goal. In other words, a strategy is designed to determine how someone is going to achieve something that has been identified as being important to future success.

tactics   The word *tactics,* on the other hand, refers to the operational aspects that are necessary to support strategy. Tactics are more likely to involve daily short-run operations that help achieve the strategy that has been identified or agreed upon in the organization. An example may be useful to help clarify the essential differences between strategy and tactics.

Wal-Mart has been referred to on several occasions in previous chapters, and it provides a good example for this discussion of strategy. Wal-Mart's obvious goal as it was developing was to increase market share. The strategies that the company identified to accomplish this goal or objective were low prices to the consumer and high levels of customer service. Efficiency of logistics systems was critical to both strategies. A tactic that has been deployed on a continuing basis is cross-docking at the Wal-Mart warehouses. As was indicated previously, cross-docking means moving goods or freight through a storage facility in twenty-four hours or less, that is, in and out in less than a day, if possible.

cross-docking   The tactic of cross-docking plays an important part in the strategies to have low prices and excellent customer service. Products move through the warehouse to the shelf for consumers to purchase in a timely fashion. Cross-docking contributes to efficiency by helping to turn over inventory rapidly. That same speed of movement through the warehouse helps to achieve customer satisfaction by having stock available when the customer needs it.

Benetton is another well-known retailer that has used good logistics to achieve increased market share and higher levels of profit. Benetton's strategy was to develop a quick-response logistics system that would link manufacturing and the retail store, giving high levels of customer service by having the right stock available but with low in-store inventory. One of the tactics that the company uses is bar coded cartons that can be moved swiftly through the warehouse to be transported, often by airfreight, to the retail location needing that inventory (SKU). Other tactics, including postponement, are also utilized to achieve efficiency and high levels of customer satisfaction.

Both Wal-Mart and Benetton are good examples of companies that have increased market share through good logistics strategy or through strategies supported by good logistics tactics. Other examples that demonstrate the value of efficient and effective logistics strategies and tactics have been referred to in previous chapters, including Nabisco, Procter & Gamble, Becton Dickinson, Keebler, and so on. All of these organizations have logistics strategies and tactics to achieve corporate goals.

With strategy in mind, we turn to a review of basic or generic strategies that should shed some additional light on logistics strategy.

Strategy Classification

While there are several ways to classify strategy, one of the most popular is to use Porter's basic or generic strategies, namely, cost, differentiation, and focus. A strategy based upon cost essentially stresses offering a product or service in the market at a price or cost lower than that of other competitors. This frequently used strategy was used by many Japanese producers when they entered the U.S. market. Products such as autos, televisions, computers, copiers, stereos, and so on were usually priced lower than those of their U.S. competitors. U.S. companies such as Wal-Mart and McDonalds have also used this strategy to gain higher market share. The increased market share means higher volumes of output, with economies of scale that reinforce the low cost/low price strategy; that is, firms continue to lower prices as costs are lowered through economies of scale.

It should be noted that low price does not translate to low quality. Even low-priced products or services require an acceptable level of quality. There have been instances of companies utilizing the cost-based strategy, but the product or service offering was so inferior that customers soon ceased purchasing the product. The foreign-produced Yugo automobile is a good example of such a situation. In fact, companies such as Toyota, Honda, Wal-Mart, and so on have continually stressed quality because it too can lead to lower costs, if implemented in an effective manner. Quality is considered consistent with their low-cost strategy. High quality and low cost have become the hallmarks of companies such as Toyota.

The second type of basic strategy involves using differentiation to gain market share. The approach underlying differentiation is to make a product or service offering that is unique so that customers will be willing to pay a premium price. Typically that involves providing a bundle of attributes with the offering that makes it more valuable to the customer than some other offering available at a lower price. When a customer buys a higher-priced article of clothing, automobile, or stereo set, he or she perceives that this higher price is worth it because of better fit, higher quality, longer product life, better service, or some other perceived value associated with the higher-priced item.

You can probably think of examples from personal experience where you have paid for a higher-priced product because of its perceived extra value to you. From a strategic point of view, the differentiation approach requires good logistics to provide high-quality customer service. This may mean making deliveries on an appointment basis with a very tight window for delivery; being available twenty-four hours a day, seven days a week, to receive orders; or perhaps providing special pallet packs. Xerox Corporation, for example, in trying to compete against Canon, decided to differentiate its copiers by providing high levels of service for parts and repairs to minimize delay times when a machine needed repair. In some instances, that time frame for repair is fifteen hours or less. The company did not feel that it could match Canon's prices. Therefore, differentiation through excellent customer service became its strategy.

The third type of strategy is the focus strategy, which is based on identifying a smaller segment of the market or a market niche in which to utilize either the lower price or differentiation approach. Many small businesses are successful because they recognize the logic of this approach. It may be the local restaurant that offers home delivery or the laundry that is open twenty-four hours a day. Even large businesses can capitalize on this approach by providing product or service

[Margin notes: lower cost; cost versus quality; differentiation; niche]

offerings in different segments, with low cost in one or more market niches and differentiation in one or more others. Hotel chains are a good example of large companies using this approach. Marriott, for example, is a higher-priced set of hotels, but it also has Marriott Courtyards, which have lower prices. Marriott Suites cater to a different group of customers. And Fairfield Hotels, also owned by Marriott, offer low-end or budget-class rooms. Automobile companies are also good examples of large companies competing in different niches. General Motors, for example, produces Cadillacs at the high end of the market and Chevrolets at the low end.

The difficult task for some companies attempting to compete on price in some market niches and differentiation or value in others is to keep the systems that support the different market strategies separate. If, for example, a company is providing 24-hour delivery in the high-price market as a customer service tactic to help differentiate the product, it would be a problem if that same level of service was provided in the low-price segment. Using our hotel example, if customers perceived that the Fairfield Hotels were of the same quality as the Marriott Hotels, they would stay at Fairfield Hotels. Therefore, there has to be a clear and well-understood difference regarding what is being provided, or the distinction between the offerings will be blurred or lost.

value chain   In his discussion of these types of strategies, Porter presents the value chain (see Figure 15–1), which suggests that the corporation can be disaggregated into five primary activities and four support activities. The major point is that all of these activities have to be in sync in order for the value chain to operate effectively. It is important to note in this context that logistics is prominently displayed as two of the five primary activities, namely, inbound and outbound logistics. The obvious conclusion is that logistics activities can play an important role in helping to develop and/or sustain competitive advantage. Also, inbound and outbound logistics need to be coordinated with the other primary activities and the support activities.

FIGURE 15–1   The Generic Value Chain

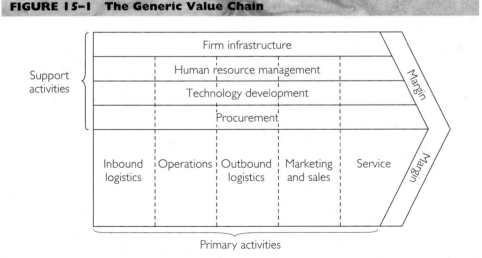

SOURCE: Reprinted with the permission of The Free Press, an imprint of Simon & Schuster from *Competitive Advantage: Creating and Sustaining Superior Performance* by Michael E. Porter. Copyright © 1985 Michael E. Porter.

ON THE LINE

Reengineering Logistics

Historically, logistics was not given much attention at Amdahl Corporation—it was not a "showstopper." When Amdahl's shiny new computers rolled off the assembly at its Hillsboro, Oregon, plant, they were usually shipped to a warehouse near Amdahl headquarters in Sunnyvale, California. Eventually, the computers would be shipped to customers around the world. This pattern seemed perfectly acceptable to the executives at Amdahl, who assumed that their approach was essentially what everyone else in the industry was doing. They rationalized that their customers wanted a high-quality product, and when their sales representatives sold a computer, they wanted to be sure that there was one available to ship (usually there were quite a number ready to ship).

In 1991, Amdahl's logistics costs were $150 million annually. For the $1.7 billion computer and information technology company, this was a significant portion of the cost of doing business. In 1993, Amdahl finally decided to do something about its logistics operation. What Amdahl discovered was that there were six vice presidents who had a piece of logistics and who essentially did their own thing when it came to logistics. Under the leadership of the company's new director of worldwide logistics, Amdahl took a big step in 1993 and put in place a process that allowed it to ship directly from the plant to the customer, eliminating the need for the expensive warehouse in California. In actuality, Amdahl was duplicating the asset reduction/cost-saving strategy used by the mail-order pioneers in the computer business, such as Dell and Gateway.

Another problem that Amdahl had faced was the lack of good cost information about its supply chain costs. Now the company has a clear global logistics strategy and much greater visibility of logistics supply chain costs. The net result of these efforts is that Amdahl's logistics costs have been reduced to 5 percent of sales from the previous high of 9 percent, but there is still a lot of work to do. The company really has not accounted for the inbound logistics system costs (the 5 percent applies only to outbound logistics). It is taking steps now to analyze the flow of materials into its several plants, with the goal of eliminating the non-value-adding activities from the inbound side as it did with the outbound side. If it is as successful at reengineering the inbound system as it was with the outbound side, the company will move closer to its overall goal of being the low-cost provider of quality computers. Logistics is now seen as playing a key role in establishing a competitive advantage for Amdahl.

ADAPTED FROM: "Putting It All Together," *CEO* (July 1995): 59–63.

In the next section, we will examine the specific leading edge strategies being used by companies to gain an advantage in the marketplace. These strategies will usually fall under one of the basic classifications that were discussed here—cost, differentiation, or niche.

TIME-BASED STRATEGIES

Most people have heard the old adage "Time is money." The value of time can be measured in a number of different ways. For example, the discussion in Chapter 6 of using the adapted EOQ model to make modal choice decisions demonstrated that a mode of transportation with faster transit times could reduce inventory and warehousing cost. Therefore, even though the faster mode of transportation may cost more, total costs could be reduced because of the savings in inventory and warehousing costs.

The obvious conclusion is that performing certain logistics-related strategies faster may produce efficiencies in other areas, resulting in cost reduction. As long as the cost of performing the selected processes faster does not offset the savings in other areas, faster is better or, more aptly stated, faster is cheaper. This rationale

cost reduction

is used, obviously, in investigating automation in a manufacturing or warehousing setting. If the savings in labor and related costs offset the investment in equipment under acceptable corporate "payback" periods, the thinking goes, then the investment in equipment for automation should be made.

In these examples, we are using the logic of the total cost model presented in Chapter 2 and its related trade-off framework. Time can be money if doing something faster means a lower total cost, and certainly transportation service should be evaluated as to the impact of faster times upon inventory-related costs, including stockout costs. Likewise, bar coding, electronic data interchange (EDI), and so on should be analyzed in the same way.

cash flow There is another aspect of time that has been receiving more attention in recent years, namely, cash flow. This concept was mentioned in Chapter 3. If we can move products through the supply chain faster, not only will there be savings in cost (inventory reductions) but there will also be faster payments. That is, cash flow will be improved, leading to higher returns for the firm. Companies have come to recognize the importance of improved cash flow to their financial viability. Since customers usually cannot be billed until they receive their order, logistics-related activities that shorten order cycle and material flow time play an important role in helping to improve cash flow. It should be noted that manufacturing and other areas can play a role in shortening the time to delivery of orders and therefore also improve cash flow.

Logistics-related strategies that shorten the length of the order and/or replenishment cycle have been the focus of much attention in recent years. Time-compression strategies have also received attention in the previous chapters in this text when inventory, transportation, warehousing, and so on were discussed. Before summarizing what has been stated in previous chapters, we will examine some more general aspects of time reduction.

Reducing Cycle Time

processes Reductions in cycle time are based upon three factors—processes, information, and decision making. The previous discussion mentioned performing logistics-related processes faster: faster transportation, faster order preparation, faster flow in a warehouse, and so on. If logistics is viewed as a series of processes, those processes being performed faster will reduce cycle time, with the associated benefits mentioned above. There is no question that performing logistics processes faster has been a continuous source of time and cost savings to companies. For example, overnight delivery by an air express company may reduce inventory cost significantly.

information Another important source of reductions in cycle time has been provided by faster provision of information. Transmitting orders through toll-free numbers, faxes, or EDI can have an important impact upon time reduction. The cost of providing information faster and more accurately has been declining at a geometric rate because of reductions in computer hardware and software costs and in communication costs. Timely, accurate information about sales, orders, inventory levels, transportation service, and so on leads to shorter cycle times and also reduces uncertainty about what is happening, which leads to lower inventory levels by reducing the need for safety stock. Information has become a source of significant savings to many companies.

The final factor in reducing cycle time is decision making. In some organizations this can be the most important of the three factors. The critical issue is to empower individuals at the action level to make decisions relevant to their areas of expertise. Too frequently, several layers of approval must be gone through before a decision can be made. One may refer to this as the approval process or, perhaps more unkindly, as red tape. The important point is that layers of approval slow down the decision-making process, which can in turn extend the order cycle. Delegation of decision-making authority downward in the organization is critical if companies want to be flexible and responsive. The flat, lean organizations that are becoming more common in today's environment are frequently characterized by delegated decision making, that is, decision making at the so-called action level, such as the customer service representative. While decision making at the lowest possible level in the company can lead to some mistakes being made, the experience of companies like Procter & Gamble and others suggest that the risk is worth it in terms of the time that is saved and the improvement that often takes place with respect to customer service response time. **decision making**

The combination of improved (faster) logistics processes, faster and more accurate flow of information, and quicker, more responsive decision making can lead to dramatic reductions in lead time or cycle time. We turn now to a more specific discussion of logistics initiatives that have led to reductions in cycle time.

Time-Reduction Logistics Initiatives

Logistics professionals have used a number of important time-reduction initiatives. One such initiative, featured in Chapters 4 and 7, is cross-docking. Recall that cross-docking involves the movement of freight through a warehouse in 24 hours or less if possible. This is in contrast to traditional warehouses, where goods are stored for considerable periods of time in some instances. Warehouses were often viewed as the buffer or decoupler between manufacturing and logistics. In that context, warehouses were used too frequently as storage facilities rather than as facilitators to speed up the distribution of goods to the customer. **cross-docking**

Just-in-time (JIT) systems are another example of time-related initiatives utilized from inbound logistics systems to reduce inventory and improve overall efficiency. Quick-response (QR) systems are being used on the outbound side of logistics, as was discussed in Chapter 6. While JIT and QR are often discussed in the context of inventory reduction strategies, there is no question that they both also have important implications for time reduction of the order cycle because they shorten the total time from vendor to delivery to customers. **JIT/QR**

Another technique, as discussed previously, is optical scanning and bar coding. Frequently, optical scanning of bar codes is used in conjunction with cross-docking. But there are many other applications of this technology in logistics systems involving such things as locating stock in a warehouse and placement and separation of orders. This technology is also being used by transportation companies to expedite and keep track of transportation equipment and shipments in general. **bar coding**

The use of EDI, faxes, and toll-free numbers to transmit orders is an additional example of a technology-based logistics initiative that reduces cycle time. EDI is being widely hailed in logistics circles as a means to improve efficiency and reduce time. The whole technology area as it is unfolding with computers, software, com- **technology** munications systems, cable operations, satellite transmission, and so on has done much to reduce the time needed to accomplish logistics-related tasks, but technology has even greater promise for the future as computer, cable, and communication technologies are combined to assimilate an information network or highway to transmit data and stimulate action.

ECR   The efficient consumer response (ECR) approach, discussed in Chapters 1 and 6, is another good example of a time-reduction strategy or initiative. The basic plan, as you will recall from Figure 6–20, is to reduce the length of time that grocery inventory spends in the pipeline, between the time it comes off the assembly line and when the final customer purchases the product. For a grocery chain, the average pipeline time was 104 days, and the goal was to reduce it to 61 days, which was quite an improvement. This initiative is obviously different from the others we have discussed in that it involves a whole group of companies that operate in the same supply chain.

Overall, leading edge companies have used a number of initiatives to improve their competitive position by reducing cycle time, producing significant benefits in terms of efficiency and effectiveness. Time-reduction strategies, because of the potential to reduce costs, improve cash flow, and enhance customer service have been the focus of much attention and have enabled companies to gain a competitive advantage.

ASSET PRODUCTIVITY STRATEGIES

ROA   As was indicated, companies are concerned about return on assets (ROA) as one of the barometers of successful operations. Companies can improve return on assets by increasing revenue earned or by earning the same level of revenue with a reduced investment in assets. Consequently, companies have been investigating approaches to improving asset productivity, or "doing more with less." Logistics is one of the important areas for improving asset productivity, and during the last ten to fifteen years many companies have been able to reduce logistics-related assets.

Inventory Reduction

VMI   One of the first assets to receive attention has been inventory, and there is much evidence to indicate that companies have been successful in reducing inventory levels or investment. (Chapter 2 presented macro-level data to substantiate this point.) Some of the initiatives that were discussed in the section on time reduction have the synergistic benefit of reducing investment in inventory, such as JIT, QR, and ECR, but there are others that are also important. One strategy that has been utilized in tandem with ECR is vendor managed inventories (VMI). Procter & Gamble and Wal-Mart have received the most press for this type of relationship. Essentially, P&G is managing the level of inventory of its products in Wal-Mart's stores and monitoring their movement through Wal-Mart's distribution cross-docking facilities. For each product, P&G decides when to ship and how much to ship to Wal-Mart. Other companies, such as Nabisco, have developed similar relations with some of their best customers. One of the major reasons for VMI is the reduction in inventory that both parties have been able to achieve.

Cross-docking, EDI, and optical scanning, which were discussed as part of the time-reduction initiatives, are also important for reducing inventory levels. Some of that improvement comes through increased inventory velocity, and some comes from the reduction in uncertainty because better information is available.

Facility Utilization

Logistics systems can be described in a number of ways, as indicated in Chapter 2. The logistics network, for example, can be viewed as being composed of a set of fixed facilities connected by links provided by transportation. The fixed facilities are plants and warehouses. The latter are typically controlled by logistics, and the inventory is stored in those facilities. Reducing the level of inventory obviously means that firms need less space for storage, which will reduce the level of investment in facilities. However, the current strategic initiatives have gone beyond merely reducing inventory.

Companies have learned to utilize their storage facilities more efficiently, that is, to increase throughput. "Doing more with less"—does that sound familiar? Again, some of the initiatives discussed previously have an important impact in improving facility utilization, including cross-docking, bar coding, and optical scanning. All have the impact of improving facility utilization by moving goods through faster.

In addition, there have been other initiatives that have improved facility utiliza- **DPS** tion or, more importantly, eliminated storage facilities altogether. One such initiative is direct plant shipments (DPS) and direct store shipments. Essentially, the idea is to ship products directly to their ultimate destination, rather than storing them in a warehouse. For example, a firm might ship products directly from its plant to the customer's warehouse without going through the firm's own warehouse, or it might ship directly from its own warehouse to the customer's store. The ideal would be to ship directly from the seller's plant to the customer's store. Direct shipments are becoming more difficult because orders are getting smaller. Therefore, in order to ship in truckload quantities, it is necessary to consolidate some shipments by, for example, combining smaller shipments. The Amdahl Corporation, featured in "On the Line" earlier in this chapter, is a good example of a company that has reduced the need for warehousing by direct plant shipments. Procter & Gamble is a good example of a large, Fortune 100 company that has achieved significant savings and asset productivity through DPS.

Equipment Utilization Strategies

Another area of asset investment for companies is logistics-related equipment such **materials handling** as materials handling equipment used in warehouses and transportation equip- **equipment** ment that is leased or owned by a company. Some reduction in the amount of this equipment has occurred because of the reduction in the number of privately owned warehouses, discussed in the previous section. Companies have rationalized their facilities and improved their throughput, utilizing the initiatives discussed previously. In other words, as companies have reduced the number of warehouse facilities that they operate, there has been a natural reduction in the materials handling equipment that is necessary.

Also, as companies have made greater use of public warehousing, for the rea- **technology** sons discussed in Chapter 7, the need for investment in materials handing equipment has declined. Even in instances where companies have retained privately owned warehousing facilities, they are utilizing their equipment more efficiently. Technology has played a big role in this improved use of equipment. The ability to communicate directly with operators while they are out in the warehouse and the use of optical scanning equipment have had a significant impact. The volume moved per person-hour and the unit cost of handling have both improved in most private warehouses as companies have taken advantage of computers and technology in general.

transportation equipment   In addition to materials handling equipment, transportation equipment is an important area in terms of asset investment. This has been another area of improvement for many companies. Since deregulation, many companies have reevaluated their position with respect to equipment ownership. Contract rates with railroads and motor carriers, more specialized service and equipment, lower rates, and so on have led companies to turn increasingly to for-hire carriers to provide their transportation service. As was explained in Chapters 9 and 10, transportation companies, particularly motor carriers, have become much more service oriented. Motor carriers frequently provide tailored service to large shippers in the current deregulated environment. With lower rates and better service, for-hire transportation service has become a much more attractive alternative for many shippers. These cost and/or service benefits, combined with a strategy to lower asset investment for increased productivity, can have a very synergistic impact that can result in an increased reliance upon the for-hire carrier system to provide transportation service.

private carriage   In addition to the improvements in productivity and efficiency made possible by the increased use of for-hire carriers, the companies that have continued to use private carriage in whole or in part to connect their nodes or fixed points have become more efficient in the utilization of their equipment. Many of them have duplicated the for-hire carriers, using software packages to schedule and dispatch their equipment more efficiently, installing direct communication links to drivers, consolidating shipments more effectively through load-planning software, and taking advantage of intermodal rail service for the line haul parts of their service needs. The net effect is similar to the observation that was made regarding warehouse facilities—companies have been able to do more with less.

In summary, there has been significant improvement in asset productivity with respect to transportation equipment. The improvement has been made possible by increased reliance upon for-hire carriers and better utilization of companies' own equipment through the use of technology, computer software, and better management planning.

THIRD-PARTY/CONTRACT LOGISTICS SERVICES

asset reduction   As was pointed out in Chapters 1 and 12, third-party or contract logistics companies have become an increasingly popular alternative. Even the so-called Fortune 100 companies like DuPont, Nabisco, Procter & Gamble, General Electric, and others are using third-party companies. The decision to utilize third-party or contract logistics companies has been fostered in part by the interest in reducing asset investment to improve asset productivity. Third-party companies that are asset based provide facilities such as warehouses and other needed fixed assets. Therefore, using third-party companies can lead to improved asset productivity.

However, the rationale for using third-party or contract logistics companies is **cost savings** more broad based than just the need to improve asset productivity. Companies have also turned to third-party companies to operate all or part of their logistics activities as a means of reducing costs. The third-party companies may be able to provide, for example, a combination of warehousing, inventory management, order preparation, and transportation at a lower cost. Because of economies of scale or volume leverage associated with providing the same services to other companies, the third-party company can operate with lower unit cost, at least theoretically.

The move to third-party or contract logistics companies is even more broad **core competencies** based than the two reasons offered above, however. Another rationale is the trend mentioned previously of focusing upon core competencies as a strategy to operate more effectively and efficiently. Essentially, a company may feel that its expertise or core competency may, for example, be producing and marketing cookies and crackers. While it is capable of providing the necessary inbound and outbound logistics services to support its products, the company may be even more effective if it focuses upon its two core competencies. The outsourcing of the logistics activities, in whole or part, is more attractive if it can also be demonstrated that there would be cost savings and/or improved asset productivity.

The decision to contract with a third-party provider is a very complex one. A **complex decision** number of companies have made mistakes in this area and have experienced higher costs and worse customer service than if they had provided the service themselves. Sometimes these situations were the fault of the third-party companies, who promised more than they could deliver. In other instances, the company that contracted for the service was at fault because it did not provide appropriate information or did not communicate its needs adequately. Sometimes both parties were at fault. The basic message is that the use of third-party providers does not automatically lead to lower cost and better service. Nevertheless, outsourcing some or all of a firm's logistics activities to third-party companies is an important strategic initiative in today's environment and one that has often resulted in lower costs and increased asset productivity.

A good example of a large company that has used third-party logistics to its advantage is Frito-Lay, a subsidiary of Pepsico. Frito-Lay is a $5 billion producer of snack foods, and it had traditionally relied upon its own fleet of trucks to ship products from its 38 plants to its 27 distribution centers. As the company expanded, the management decided that it was not economical to produce every product at every plant, and so the company started to specialize production at plants. However, it did not fully understand the impact of this new strategy upon the logistics system. Shipping distances grew increasingly longer from the specialized production facilities to the warehouses, and the company's private trucks usually had to return to their origin empty. Subsequently, Frito-Lay began to utilize an increasing number of common carriers to distribute its products to the distribution centers, but this did no go smoothly. Therefore, Frito-Lay decided to outsource the responsibility for managing its transportation operations to Menlo Logistics. Menlo has been able to pare the carrier base by 50 percent and to negotiate discount rates with the remainder of the carriers on a national basis. The routing of trucks is handled by Menlo Logistics, which has a staff member on site at Frito-Lay's headquarters in Plano, Texas. Frito-Lay's transportation savings exceeded 10 percent the first year, which was significant in this highly competitive market arena.

VALUE-ADDED STRATEGIES

internal aspect
Adding value has become a common corporate objective during the 1990s as companies have sought to gain a competitive advantage in the marketplace. The concept of adding value has both an internal and an external dimension. On the internal side, companies have recognized that frequently their employees are involved in transactional activities that do not add any real value for the company. For example, one of the largest insurance carriers in the United States, in reviewing its procurement organization, determined that its internal systems frequently required ten to fifteen approvals, even for expenditures of less than $5,000. These approvals were transactional in nature, since there was seldom any change to the original purchase order. The company decided to reengineer its approval process and allow a purchase order to go through with one signature when it was $25,000 or less. The net result was a significant reduction in transactional activities, which allowed the company to eliminate some personnel, but more importantly enabled the remaining personnel to focus more on activities that would add value for the company, such as negotiating contracts with vendors to reduce costs or improve service.

external aspect
It is fair to say that even though the internal ways in which companies add value are very important, the external strategies are usually viewed by management as being even more important. Why is this the case? Simply because external value-adding strategies focus upon customers; that is, they ask, how can we add value for customers? If companies can do that successfully, not only will they be able to retain those customers, but also they may be able to get more business, that is, build market share.

As was the case with time-compression strategies and asset productivity strategies, logistics can play an important role in value-adding strategies. Remember that logistics usually has the last contact with a customer after he or she decides to purchase a company's product. If customers do not receive the products that they order in the right quantity, at the right place, at the right time, and in the right condition, they will not be satisfied. At the lowest level, performing the basic logistics functions well will add value. But today's logistics managers have gone much further than the basics of providing reliable and timely service.

Stated simply, external value-added strategy aims to reduce costs and/or improve business results for customers. Other sections of this chapter, as well as previous chapters, discussed many of the strategic initiatives that contribute to either or both of these aims or objectives. The time-compression strategy and related initiatives, for example, can reduce costs for customers because the shorter cycle times will relate into lower inventory requirements for customers. The ECR initiative, which was discussed in some detail in Chapter 6, is a good example of how a shortened lead time can improve costs along the supply chain. The asset productivity strategy and related initiatives reduce internal costs, but these cost reductions can be passed along the supply chain in the form of lower prices to customers and therefore add value also.

The more specific value-added strategic initiatives include vendor-managed inventories such as the relationship described previously between Wal-Mart and Procter & Gamble. This is a significant undertaking on the part of P&G and requires the company to have marketing and logistics staff on location at Wal-Mart's headquarters in Arkansas. VMI, if implemented well, can add significant value through lower inventory costs and improved business results.

Another specific initiative is the quick-response approach discussed previously. QR programs have been particularly successful for certain types of companies and have enabled some customers to virtually eliminate their inventory. For example, American Hospital Supply provides QR systems to hospitals so that the hospitals essentially have zero inventory. This is also part of the strategy of Xerox in its quick-response service to customers. The automotive industry has been moving in this direction with its delivery of parts and supplies to dealers and parts stores. The availability of overnight service from a number of carriers such as Federal Express, UPS, RPS, DHL, and others has enabled companies to provide next-day delivery, especially from locations like Memphis (the major hub for Federal Express) to any place in the United States. A stockless or zero inventory resulting from a QR system can have important value for customers.

Other value-added initiatives include scheduled delivery to stores or warehouses, which adds a reliability factor that also leads to lower inventory requirements for customers. EDI and advanced shipment notices (ASN) are communication techniques that can add value for customers by providing information that helps to eliminate uncertainty, which can lead to reduced inventory requirements. Special pallet packs are also being used by companies to add value for their customers. Such arrangements allow customers to unpack products efficiently for stocking or use in their plants. The unique preparation of shipments to meet individual customer requirements can enhance and cement relationships between a buyer and seller, yielding a unique competitive advantage.

Many of the strategic initiatives just mentioned allow companies to offer tailored or customized logistics service to their best customers. This is an important trend that is developing among leading edge companies. These companies are developing a proactive, consultative approach to analyzing their customers' logistics requirements.

The consultative sales concept is one that has been used by transport carriers for many years to enable them to adapt their services to meet the special needs of the shippers that they serve. In other words, instead of offering a homogeneous, "plain vanilla" service to all of their customers, they identify the particular needs of their customers by consultation and analysis so that the service they offer will make their customers more efficient and/or effective. This same consultative concept can be applied to product companies and the relationship that they develop with their customers. This approach is synergistic with the supply chain concept and the related concept of a partnership or strategic alliance. Today's environment is much more conducive to developing a bundle of customized logistics services to meet the needs of individual customers. It provides the opportunity to extend and enhance business relationships and develop a competitive advantage in the market.

consultative sales concept

The consultative approach, and the development of tailored logistics systems, is not a panacea; it usually should not be implemented for all customers, nor should all companies adopt this concept. It requires a commitment of time and effort that can be expensive and may not always be successful. But there is no question that tailored or customized logistics services are being utilized successfully by such companies as P&G, Nabisco, Hershey Foods, and others to sustain and/ or improve their market share. The logistics manager has an arsenal of initiatives at his or her disposal that can be uniquely packaged to meet specific customer requirements.

PUSH TO PULL SYSTEMS

push systems   Several previous chapters have referred to push and pull systems. Traditionally, many manufacturing companies that made mass-produced rather than customized products would make use of long production runs. The underlying rationale for this approach was that it would lower unit costs. The net effect was that inventory was being pushed out into the system (usually some warehouse) in advance of demand. As was indicated previously, the push approach resulted in relatively large levels of inventory being accumulated, sometimes at several positions along the pipeline.

The push system has been described as the old culture for manufacturing. For example, Keebler Company, featured in the Logistics Profile at the beginning of this chapter, used a system that pushed inventory out well in advance of demand. Its push approach contributed to the excess inventory that it had in its logistics pipeline. As was indicated previously, inventory is used as a decoupler between manufacturing and marketing or logistics in such situations.

pull system   Increasingly, companies are changing from the traditional push approach to a pull approach, which is a demand-responsive system. The switch requires a major change in corporate culture that is frequently difficult to achieve. Not only does the change require a switch to a flexible, quick-change manufacturing environment, necessitating retraining of the manufacturing employees, it also requires that manufacturing operate at a less than optimal cost from time to time.

inventory impact   In its purest form, the pull approach requires that products be manufactured after an order is received. Obviously, this requires a fast manufacturing system. The ability to accomplish this feat essentially eliminates finished goods inventory, which can result in significant savings. Some very large companies are moving in this direction. Chrysler, for example, states that it can manufacture a car to order in fifteen days, which means that it fills a customer's order reasonably quickly. It is hoping to reduce that time to seven days by the end of the century. Chrysler's intent is to reduce dealer inventories. One of the Japanese auto manufacturers has a goal of being able to produce a car to order in three days. The achievement of these goals will significantly reduce the inventory of new cars.

Sears is moving to reduce the size of its retail furniture stores, which tend to be very large in terms of floor space. It will compensate by being able to produce furniture to order and deliver it within seven days after the order is received. Even some manufacturers of farm equipment, which is a seasonal product, are considering a change to a more demand-oriented manufacturing system. Pull systems are more challenging in such an environment because of the peak demand. These are just some of the many types of companies that have changed or are changing to a demand-responsive manufacturing and logistics system. It should also be noted that a pull system is consistent with the time-compression strategies discussed previously.

An additional aspect of pull systems that should be mentioned is that some companies use the concept of postponement to achieve a system that is close to a pure pull system. As was indicated, postponement involves not completely finishing products until an order is received. Recall the example in Chapter 3 of a food processor that adds labels to the "brights," or unlabeled canned goods, after the orders are received, enabling it to reduce inventory levels significantly. Even the auto industry is using a form of postponement by assembling basic component packages, for example, the wiring harnesses, in advance of orders and then assembling the auto to final specification.

postponement

Pull systems have been discussed at length here because they are so important in today's environment. Also, the impact such systems have upon manufacturing and the change in culture cannot be overemphasized. Many product companies have been dominated by a mentality in manufacturing that demands long production runs that push out vast quantities of inventory in advance of demand. This is not to say that long production runs are not economically viable in some situations, merely that the trade-offs should be examined. However, the push mentality is so deeply ingrained in some organizations that it is difficult for them to see the need to do an objective evaluation of a pull system.

importance of pull systems

Summary

- Today's competitive global environment, with the rapid changes that it engenders, has necessitated that companies utilize strategic planning to survive.
- Strategic planning has gone through several stages of development. Today, the planning process taken by many companies focuses on a team-oriented approach to gain competitive advantage in the marketplace.
- Strategic planning also involves understanding the difference between strategy and tactics. Strategy focuses on how a given goal is going to be achieved over the longer run, whereas tactics emphasize the short-run, operational aspects necessary to drive the strategy.
- There are three basic, generic strategies—cost, differentiation, and focus.
- One of the major strategies being implemented in today's environment is to reduce or compress order cycle time, which has the advantage of reducing inventory cost and improving customer service.
- Cycle time is affected by three components—processes, information, and decision making.
- There are numerous logistics-related initiatives that can improve cycle time, including cross-docking, JIT, quick response, bar coding and optical scanning, ECR, and other technology-related time improvements.
- Another major focus of logistics-related strategies is the improvement of asset productivity. For logistics, the major focus has been on improving the utilization of inventory, facilities, and equipment.
- Third-party or contract logistics service companies have also become a factor in logistics strategy because of the opportunities to reduce cost, improve asset productivity, and improve customer service if used appropriately.

- An additional area of focus for logistics-related strategies is to add value, which can be viewed internally or externally. There are many logistics initiatives that can add value externally, including ECR, quick response, special pallet packs, scheduled deliveries, advanced shipment notices, and EDI.
- A final area for logistics-related strategies is the development of pull systems, which involve both manufacturing and logistics in the effort to produce products after an order is received. Postponement is sometimes used as a method of helping to achieve a pull system.

STUDY QUESTIONS

1. As the principal consultant to Nantucket Enterprises, a medium-size electronics company operating primarily in the New England states, you have been requested to prepare a statement for the board of directors that points out the importance of strategic planning.

2. Your statement prepared in answer to the previous question was so well received by the board of Nantucket Enterprises that they have now asked you to prepare a statement that describes how strategic planning is implemented today and to compare today's practices to those used previously; that is, how has strategic planning developed to where it is today?

3. The third phase of your assignment for Nantucket Enterprises is to develop a statement explaining the difference between strategy and tactics, especially in terms of logistics.

4. The final phase of your consulting project for Nantucket Enterprises is to help the board understand the basic or generic types of strategies, again emphasizing logistics.

5. Increasingly, U.S. companies have turned to time-based or time-compression strategies to increase their efficiency and/or effectiveness. What is the rationale for the use of time-based strategies, and what are the processes that underlie the time reductions?

6. The success of your initial contract with Nantucket Enterprises has led to a new assignment. Now the president of the company wants you to present a brief report on the logistics-related initiatives that lead to reductions in cycle times.

7. Stockholders are very interested in financial indicators that provide information about the economic viability of companies in which they have invested. What role can logistics play in helping companies improve their return on assets?

8. Recently, *The Wall Street Journal* printed an article announcing that DuPont was going to outsource part of its logistics function to a third-party company. Why would a Fortune 100 company like DuPont turn to a third-party company, particularly when DuPont has traditionally been noted for having an effective logistics organization?

9. The concept of adding value is frequently referred to in business publications. Comment on the internal and external aspects of the value-added concept in logistics.

10. What is meant by customized or tailored logistics systems? How can companies use this concept to improve their market advantage?

Case 15–1

ROANI FOODS

Rosi Greaser, CEO and President of Roani Foods of Tipton, Pennsylvania, is exasperated, and she says, to no one in particular, "Thank God it's Friday. I can't take much more of this." She has had a bad week. She has just finished talking to Denny Jaworski, director of purchasing for Tyworth Stores in Sunbury, Pennsylvania. Jaworski was upset, and he vented his emotions on Greaser. The deliveries that he had been promised for that morning had not shown up at the Tyworth warehouse. It would not have been so bad if this had been the first time that this had happened, but late deliveries are getting to be a regular occurrence.

Rosi Greaser is frustrated but also worried. Tyworth Stores is Roani Foods' largest customer. Tyworth has more than 300 stores in Pennsylvania, Maryland, New York, and New Jersey. Jaworski is threatening to take his business elsewhere unless Greaser straightens out her logistics operation and provides the level of customer service that Tyworth is accustomed to receiving from its other vendors.

Something has to be done and relatively soon. Rosi pushes away from the desk and starts to reflect back over the years that she has been with Roani Foods. In fact, she knows the company intimately, since it was founded by her grandmother and grandfather. She has a lot to think about, and some action has to be taken. She cannot lose the Tyworth account. Roani has invested in a new plant and equipment based on the growth in the Tyworth account.

Background

Roani Foods was founded by Salvatore and Maria Roani. After immigrating to Tipton from Italy, they started a small Italian restaurant that soon became the rage of the area. People would drive from the many nearby communities of central Pennsylvania to eat at the restaurant. One of the attractions was the spaghetti sauce that Maria made from a recipe that she had brought from Italy. The sauce was so popular that Maria and Sal began to bottle small batches and sell it as a take-out item in the restaurant. The rest, as they say, is history. From this small beginning, Roani Foods was born.

It was not too long until the demand for Maria's spaghetti sauce was so great that Sal and Maria had to close down the restaurant and build a new facility to produce the sauce in its many varieties. The Roanis had two sons, and a daughter who was Rosi Greaser's mother. The two sons, Sal Jr. and Joe, expanded the business to the point that Roani is now the largest producer of spaghetti sauces in the

Middle Atlantic states. Their sauces are sold in several of the regional chain supermarkets and are distributed by brokers and wholesalers to smaller retail
establishments.

When Rosi Greaser took over the company, its sales were $80 million, and
under her leadership, sales have expanded to $125 million. The company has also
built a new manufacturing facility in Altoona, Pennsylvania. Greaser has focused
on improving quality in the manufacturing processes and expanding the variety
of sauces that Roani produces under its own label and under the private label of
some of its larger customers, such as Tyworth Stores. Roani also has its own warehouse in Tyrone, Pennsylvania, and a fleet of trucks for deliveries within 100 miles
of the warehouse.

Action Plan

When she arrives at the office on Monday morning, Greaser summons Jason Phillips, director of transportation, into her office. She explains the problem she is
faced with and the need to implement some type of action plan. The conclusion
that she has reached in her own mind is to upgrade Phillips' department into a
full-blown logistics department responsible for inbound and outbound logistics
systems. It would be a big step, but she knows that she could hire some top-notch
talent from Penn State's logistics program. In a recent telephone conversation, a
member of the Penn State business department informed her that they have an
outstanding class about to graduate, from which she could recruit one or two
individuals, and that the department could also help her to identify individuals
with several years of experience if she preferred.

Phillips listens to Greaser's explanation of the situation and agrees that Roani
needs a full-blown logistics effort. However, he counters with another alternative,
namely, to contract with a third-party logistics company. Phillips indicates that he
has been contacted by Skip Grenoble of CLSA Associates, a successful third-party
company, about the possibility of providing logistics services for Roani Foods.
CLSA, according to Phillips, can offer a comprehensive package of logistics
services.

Case Questions

Greaser decides that she really needs more information, and she instructs Phillips to develop
a report for her that addresses the following:

1. What is the role of third-party providers, and what type of services can they provide?
2. What are the advantages and disadvantages of using a third-party provider versus building
   an internal organization?
3. What should Phillips recommend if he had to make the decision, and why?

SUGGESTED READINGS FOR PART III

Andel, Tom, and Russ Cooper. "Network Planning: Plug into Powerful Resources," *Transportation and Distribution* 33, no. 5 (May 1992): 26–29.

Baker, Joanna R.; Edward R. Clayton; and Ajay K. Aggarwal. "An Attribute-Balancing Heuristic for the Design of Service Districts," *Journal of Business Logistics* 11, no. 2 (1990): 69–94.

Ballou, Ronald H. "Measuring Transport Costing Error in Customer Aggregation for Facility Location," *Transportation Journal* 33, no. 3 (Spring 1994): 49–59.

Ballou, Ronald H., and James M. Masters. "Commercial Software for Locating Warehouses and Other Facilities," *Journal of Business Logistics* 14, no. 2 (1993): 71–107.

Campbell, James F. "Designing Logistics Systems by Analyzing Transportation, Inventory and Terminal Cost Tradeoffs," *Journal of Business Logistics* 11, no. 2 (1990): 159–79.

Friedrich, Carl J. (trans.). *Alfred Weber's Theory of Location of Industries* (Chicago: University of Chicago Press, 1929).

Geoffrion, Arthur M. "A Guide to Computer-Assisted Methods for Distribution Planning," *Sloan Management Review* 16 (Winter 1975): 17–41.

Gold, Steven. "A New Approach to Site Selection," *Distribution* 90, no. 13 (December 1991): 29–33.

Greenhut, Melvin L. *Plant Location in Theory and Practice* (Chapel Hill: University of North Carolina Press, 1956).

Hoover, Edgar M. *The Location of Economic Activity* (New York: McGraw-Hill, 1948).

House, Robert G., and Jeffrey J. Karrenbauer. "Logistics System Modeling," *International Journal of Physical Distribution and Materials Management* 8, no. 4: 187–99.

MacCormack, Alan D.; Lawrence J. Newmann III; and Donald B. Rosenfield. "The New Dynamics of Global Manufacturing Site Location," *Sloan Management Review* 35, no. 4 (Summer 1994): 69–80.

Magrath, Allan J., and Kenneth G. Hardy. "Six Steps to Distribution Network Design," *Business Horizons* 34, no. 1 (January–February 1991): 48–52.

Mentzer, John T., and Allan D. Schuster. "Computer Modeling in Logistics: Existing Models and Future Outlook," special supplement to *Journal of Business Logistics* 3, no. 1 (1982).

Miller, Tan. "Learning about Facility Location Models," *Distribution* 92, no. 5 (May 1993): 47–50.

Robinson, E. Powell, Jr., and Ronald K. Satterfield. "Customer Service: Implications for Distribution System Design," *International Journal of Physical Distribution and Logistics Management* 20, no. 4: 22–30.

Ronen, David. "LSD—Logistic System Design Simulation Model," in *Proceedings of the 18th Annual Transportation and Logistics Educators Conference* (Columbus: The Ohio State University, 1988).

NETWORK DESIGN AND FACILITY LOCATION

Bowersox, Donald J. "Framing Global Logistics Requirements," in *1992 Council of Logistics Management Annual Conference Proceedings* (Oak Brook, IL: Council of Logistics Management, 1992): 267–78.

GLOBAL LOGISTICS

Buxbaum, Peter. "Timberland's New Spin on Global Logistics," *Distribution* 93, no. 5 (May 1994): 32–36.

Byrne, Patrick M.; John C. Taylor; and Stanley E. Fawcett. "Global Logistics," *Transportation and Distribution* 34, no. 6 (June 1993): 37–46.

Cooper, James C. "Logistics Strategies for Global Businesses," *International Journal of Physical Distribution and Logistics Management* 23, no. 4 (1993): 12–23.

Davies, G. J. "The International Logistics Concept," *International Journal of Physical Distribution and Materials Management* 17, no. 2 (1987): 20–27.

"Export/Import Terms You Need to Know," *Traffic Management* 29, no. 9 (September 1990): 37–41.

Fawcett, Stanley E., and David J. Closs. "Coordinated Global Manufacturing, the Logistics/ Manufacturing Interaction, and Firm Performance," *Journal of Business Logistics* 14, no. 1 (1993): 1–26.

Foster, Thomas A. "Global Logistics Benetton Style," *Distribution* (October, 1993): 62–66.

Garreau, Alain; Robert Lieb; and Robert Millen. "JIT and Corporate Transport: An International Comparison," *International Journal of Physical Distribution and Logistics Management* 21, no. 2 (1991): 42–47.

Gourdin, Kent N., and Richard L. Clarke. "Can U.S. Transportation Industries Meet the Global Challenge?" *International Journal of Physical Distribution and Logistics Management* 20, no. 4: 31–36.

Miller, Tan. "The International Modal Decision," *Distribution* 90, no. 11 (October 1991): 82–92.

Min, Hokey, and Sean B. Eom. "An Integrated Decision Support System for Global Logistics," *International Journal of Physical Distribution and Logistics Management* 24, no. 1 (1994): 29–39.

Murphy, Paul R.; James M. Daley; and Douglas R. Dalenberg. "Selecting Links and Nodes in International Transportation: An Intermediary's Perspective," *Transportation Journal* 31, no. 2 (Winter 1991): 33–40.

Porter, Michael E. "The Competitive Advantage of Nations," *Harvard Business Review* 68, no. 2 (March–April 1990): 73–93.

Rao, Kant, and Richard R. Young. "Global Supply Chains: Factors Influencing Outsourcing of Logistics Functions," *International Journal of Physical Distribution and Logistics Management* 24, no. 6 (1994): 11–19.

Rosenbloom, Bert. "Motivating Your International Channel Partners," *Business Horizons* 33, no. 2 (March–April 1990): 53–57.

Rydzkowski, Wlodzimierz, and H. Barry Spraggins. "Restructuring, Privatization and Deregulation of Transport in Poland: New Transport Policy Implications," *International Journal of Physical Distribution and Logistics Management* 24, no. 2 (1994): 23–29.

Taylor, John C., and David J. Closs. "Logistics Implications of an Integrated U.S.–Canada Market," *International Journal of Physical Distribution and Logistics Management* 23, no. 1 (1993): 3–13.

Thomchick, Evelyn A., and Lisa Rosenbaum. "The Role of U.S. Export Trading Companies in International Logistics," *Journal of Business Logistics* 5, no. 2: 86.

Trunick, Perry A.; C. W. Ebeling; and Patrick Byrne. "Global Logistics," *Transportation and Distribution* 34, no. 4 (April 1993): 51–62.

Van Der Hoop, Hans. "Is Europe Ready for the Single Market?" *Distribution* 91, no. 10 (October 1992): 66–70.

Voorhees, Roy Dale; Emerson L. Seim; and John I. Coppett. "Global Logistics and the Stateless Corporation," *Transportation Practitioners Journal* 59, no. 2 (Winter 1992): 144–51.

Zinn, Walter, and Robert E. Grosse. "Barriers to Globalization: Is Global Distribution Possible?" *International Journal of Logistics Management* 1, no. 1 (1990): 13–18.

Aron, Laurie Joan. "P&G's Logistics Strategy: Simplify and Standardize," *Inbound Logistics* 14, no. 4 (April 1994): 24–29.

Bowersox, Donald J., and Patricia J. Daugherty. "Emerging Patterns of Logistics Organization," *Journal of Business Logistics* 8, no. 1 (1987): 46–60.

Bowersox, Donald J.; David J. Frayer; and Judith M. Schmitz. "Organizing for Effective Logistics Management," Chapter 35 in *The Logistics Handbook*, ed. James F. Robeson and William C. Copacino (New York: The Free Press, 1994): 777–79.

Chandler, Alfred D. *Strategy and Structure* (Cambridge, MA: MIT Press, 1962).

Daugherty, Patricia J., and Cornelia Droge. "Organizational Structure in Divisionalised Manufacturers: The Potential for Outsourcing Logistical Services," *International Journal of Physical Distribution and Logistics Management* 21, no. 3: 22–29.

Falk, James P. "Organizing for Effective Distribution," in *Proceedings of the 1980 Annual Conference of the National Council of Physical Distribution Management* (Oak Brook, IL: National Council of Physical Distribution Management, 1980): 181–99.

Heskett, James L. "Leadership through Integration: The Special Challenge of Logistics Management," in 1988 *Council of Logistics Management Annual Conference Proceedings* (Oak Brook, IL: Council of Logistics Management, 1988): 13–22.

Heskett, James L. "Organizing for Effective Distribution Management," in *The Distribution Handbook* (New York: The Free Press, 1985): 828–31.

Kohn, Jonathon W.; Michael A. McGinnis; and Praveen K. Kesava. "Organizational Environment and Logistics Strategy: An Empirical Study," *International Journal of Physical Distribution and Logistics Management* 20, no. 2: 22–30.

Langley, John. "U.S. Logistics—The State of the Nation," *Focus on Physical Distribution and Logistics Management* 8, no. 6 (July/August 1989): 28–33.

Mentzer, John T., and John Firman. "Logistics Control Systems in the 21st Century," *Journal of Business Logistics* 15, no. 1 (1994): 215–27.

Novack, Robert A.; Lloyd M. Rinehart; and Michael V. Wells. "Rethinking Concept Foundations in Logistics Management," *Journal of Business Logistics* 13, no. 2 (1992): 233–68.

Pisharodi, R. Mohan, and C. John Langley, Jr. "A Perceptual Process Model of Customer Service Based on Cybernetic/Control Theory," *Journal of Business Logistics* 11, no. 2 (1990): 26–48.

Porter, Michael E. *Competitive Advantage: Creating and Sustaining Superior Performance* (New York: The Free Press, 1985).

Stank, Theodore P.; Patricia J. Daugherty; and Craig M. Gustin. "Organizational Structure: Influence on Logistics Integration, Costs and Information System Performance," *International Journal of Logistics Management* 5, no. 2 (1994): 41–42.

LOGISTICS ORGANIZATION

Andraski, Joseph C. "Foundations for Successful Continuous Replenishment Programs," *International Journal of Logistics Management* 5, no. 1 (1994): 1–8.

Byrne, Patrick M., and William J. Markham. *Improving Quality and Productivity in the Logistics Process* (Oak Brook, IL: Council of Logistics Management, 1991): 407.

Camp, Robert C. *Benchmarking* (Milwaukee, WI: ASQC Quality Press, 1989).

Crosby, Philip. *Quality Is Free* (New York: McGraw-Hill, 1979).

Daugherty, Patricia J.; Cornelia Droge; and Richard Germain. "Benchmarking Logistics in Manufacturing Firms," *International Journal of Logistics Management* 5, no. 1 (1994): 9–18.

Deming, W. Edwards. *Out of the Crisis* (Cambridge, MA: MIT Center for Advanced Engineering Technology, 1986).

Hall, Gene; Jim Rosenthal; and Judy Wade. "How to Make Reengineering Really Work," *Harvard Business Review* 71, no. 6 (November–December 1993): 119–31.

THE LOGISTICS QUALITY PROCESS AND LOGISTICS REENGINEERING

Hammer, Michael, and James Champy. *Reengineering the Corporation* (New York: Harper-Business, 1993).

Harrington, Lisa. "Quality and the Outsourcing Decision," *Private Carrier* (August 1994): 16–21.

Holcomb, Mary C. "Customer Service Measurement: A Methodology for Increasing Customer Value through Utilization of the Taguchi Strategy," *Journal of Business Logistics* 15, no. 1 (1994): 29–52.

Juran, Joseph M. *Juran on Planning for Quality* (New York: The Free Press, 1988).

Kearney, A. T. *Improving Quality and Productivity in the Logistics Process: Achieving Customer Satisfaction Breakthroughs* (Oak Brook, IL: Council of Logistics Management, 1991).

Kelly, Brian L. "Operating Performance Measures: The Critical Link to Strategic Management," in *1992 Council of Logistics Management Annual Conference Proceedings* (Oak Brook, IL: Council of Logistics Management, 1992): 513–18.

Langley, C. John, Jr. "Quality in Logistics: A Competitive Advantage," in *Proceedings of the R. Hadly Walters Logistics and Transportation Symposium* (University Park, PA: Penn State University, The Center for Logistics Research, 1990).

Langley, C. John, Jr., and Mary C. Holcomb. "Creating Logistics Customer Value," *Journal of Business Logistics* 13, no. 2 (1992): 1–28.

Langley, C. John, Jr., and Mary C. Holcomb. "Total Quality Management in Logistics," Chapter 9 in *The Logistics Handbook,* ed. James F. Robeson and William C. Copacino (New York: The Free Press, 1994): 183–98.

Larson, Paul D. "Business Logistics and the Quality Loss Function," *Journal of Business Logistics* 13, no. 1 (1992): 125–48.

Maltz, Arnold B. "The Relative Importance of Cost and Quality in the Outsourcing of Warehousing," *Journal of Business Logistics* 15, no. 2 (1994): 45–62.

Mentzer, John T., and John Firman. "Logistics Control Systems in the 21st Century," *Journal of Business Logistics* 15, no. 1 (1994): 215–27.

Novack, Robert A. "Logistics Control: An Approach to Quality," *Journal of Business Logistics* 10, no. 2 (1989): 24–43.

Novack, Robert A.; C. John Langley, Jr.; and Lloyd M. Rinehart. *Creating Logistics Value: Themes for the Future* (Oak Brook, IL: Council of Logistics Management, 1995).

Novack, Robert A.; Lloyd M. Rinehart; and C. John Langley, Jr. "An Internal Assessment of Logistics Value," *Journal of Business Logistics* 15, no. 1 (1994): 113–52.

Parasuraman, A.; Leonard L. Berry; and Valerie A. Zeithaml. "Understanding Customer Expectations of Service," *Sloan Management Review* 32, no. 3 (Spring 1991): 39–48.

"Quest for Quality," *Distribution* 94, no. 8 (August 1995): 28–56.

Short, James E., and N. Venkatraman. "Beyond Business Process Redesign: Redefining Baxter's Business Network," *Sloan Management Review* 34, no. 1 (Fall 1992): 7–21.

Sims, Arden C. "Does the Baldrige Award Really Work?" *Harvard Business Review* 70, no. 1 (January–February 1992): 126–47.

Stahl, Michael J., and Gregory M. Bounds, eds. *Competing Globally through Customer Value* (Westport, CT: Quorum Books, 1991). In particular, see Chapter 20, James H. Foggin, "Closing the Gaps in Service Marketing: Designing to Satisfy Customer Expectations," 510–30; and Chapter 22, C. John Langley, Jr., and Mary C. Holcomb, "Achieving Customer Value through Logistics Management," 547–65.

Steimer, Thomas E. "Activity-Based Accounting for Total Quality," *Management Accounting* 72, no. 4 (October 1990): 39–42.

Sterling, Jay U. "Measuring the Performance of Logistics Operations," Chapter 10 in *The Logistics Handbook,* ed. James F. Robeson and William C. Copacino (New York: The Free Press, 1994): 226–30.

Stock, James R., and Douglas M. Lambert. "Becoming a 'World Class' Company with Logistics Service Quality," *International Journal of Logistics Management* 3, no. 1 (1992): 73–81.

Wheeler, Donald J., and David S. Chambers. *Understanding Statistical Process Control* (Knoxville, TN: Statistical Process Controls, Inc., 1986); and Kaoru Ishikawa, *Guide to Quality Control.*

Ackerman, Kenneth B. "The Case against Third Party Warehousing," *Warehousing Forum* 9, no. 7 (June 1994): 1–2.

Aertsen, Freek. "Contracting Out the Physical Distribution Function: A Trade-off between Asset Specificity and Performance Measurement," *International Journal of Physical Distribution and Logistics Management* 23, no. 1 (1993): 23–29.

Bowersox, Donald J. "The Strategic Benefits of Logistics Alliances," *Harvard Business Review* 68, no. 4 (July–August 1990): 36–47.

Burke, Jack; John H. Perser; George Adcock; Marvin Meachum; and Michael Richman. "Contract Logistics Special Report," *Traffic World* 238, no. 9 (May 30, 1994): 21–33.

Delaney, Robert V. "Outsourcing Logistics Services—The Promises and Pitfalls," *Warehousing Forum* 9, no. 1 (December 1993): 1–2.

Ellram, Lisa M. "Partners in International Alliances," *Journal of Business Logistics* 13, no. 1 (1992): 1–26.

Gardner, John T.; Martha C. Cooper; and Tom Noordewier. "Understanding Shipper-Carrier and Shipper-Warehouser Relationships: Partnerships Revisited," *Journal of Business Logistics* 15, no. 2 (1994): 121–43.

Kanter, Rosabeth Moss. "Collaborative Advantage: The Art of Alliances," *Harvard Business Review* (July–August 1994): 96–108.

LaLonde, Bernard J., and Arnold Maltz. "Some Propositions about Outsourcing the Logistics Function," *International Journal of Logistics Management* 3, no. 1 (1992): 1–11 and 12–22.

Langley, C. John, Jr. "Business Processes in Third Party Relationships," in *Proceedings of the 1994 Annual Conference of the Warehousing Education and Research Council,* Orlando, Florida (May 1994).

Lei, David, and John W. Slocum, Jr. "Global Strategy, Competence-Building and Strategic Alliances," *California Management Review* 35, no. 1 (Fall 1992): 81–97.

Lieb, Robert C. "The Use of Third-Party Logistics Services by Large American Manufacturers," *Journal of Business Logistics* 13, no. 2 (1992): 29–42.

Lieb, Robert C.; Robert A. Millen; and Luk N. Van Wassenhove. "Third-Party Logistics Services: A Comparison of Experienced American and European Manufacturers," *International Journal of Physical Distribution and Logistics Management* 23, no. 6 (1993): 35–44.

MacDonald, Mitchell E. "Who's Who in Third Party Logistics," *Traffic Management* 32, no. 7 (July 1993): 34–46.

Quinn, James Brian, and Frederick G. Hilmer. "Strategic Outsourcing," *Sloan Management Review* 35, no. 4 (Summer 1994): 43–56.

Sarel, Dan, and Walter Zinn. "Customer and Non-Customer Perceptions of Third Party Service: Are They Similar?" *International Journal of Logistics Management* 3, no. 1 (1992): 12–13.

Sheffi, Yosef. "Third Party Logistics: Present and Future Prospects," *Journal of Business Logistics* 11, no. 2 (1990): 27–40.

Stuart, F. Ian. "Supplier Partnerships: Influencing Factors and Strategic Benefits," *International Journal of Purchasing and Materials Management* (Fall 1993): 21–28.

"1995 Logistics Annual Report," *Distribution* 94, no. 7 (July 1995).

Bowersox, Donald J.; Patricia J. Daugherty; Cornelia L. Droge; Richard N. Germain; and Dale S. Rogers. *Logistical Excellence: It's NOT Business as Usual* (Burlington, MA: Digital Press, 1992).

THIRD-PARTY LOGISTICS

THE INTEGRATED LOGISTICS CONCEPT

Bowersox, Donald J.; Patricia J. Daugherty; Cornelia L. Droge; Dale S. Rogers; and Daniel L. Wardlow. *Leading-Edge Logistics: Competitive Positioning for the 1990's* (Oak Brook, IL: Council of Logistics Management, 1989).

"A Compendium of Research in Logistics Strategy," *International Journal of Physical Distribution and Logistics Management* 23, no. 5 (1993).

Cooper, Martha C.; Innis, Daniel E.; and Peter R. Dickson. *Strategic Planning for Logistics* (Oak Brook, IL: Council of Logistics Management, 1992).

Copacino, William, and Donald B. Rosenfeld. "Analytic Tools for Strategic Planning," *International Journal of Physical Distribution and Materials Management* 15, no. 3 (1985): 47–61.

Davis, Frank W. Jr., and Karl B. Manrodt. "Service Logistics: An Introduction," *International Journal of Physical Distribution and Logistics Management* 21, no. 7 (1991): 4–13.

Fuller, J. B.; J. O'Conor; and R. Rawlinson. "Tailored Logistics: The Next Advantage," *Harvard Business Review* (May–June 1993): 87–98.

Henkoff, Ronald. "Delivering the Goods," *Fortune* 130, no. 11 (November 28, 1994): 64–78.

LaLonde, Bernard J., and James M. Masters. "Emerging Logistics Strategies: Blueprints for the Next Century," *International Journal of Physical Distribution and Logistics Management* 24, no. 7 (1994): 35–47.

LaLonde, Bernard J., and Richard F. Powers. "Disintegration and Reintegration: Logistics of the Twenty-First Century," *International Journal of Logistics Management* 4, no. 2 (1993): 1–12.

Langley, C. John, Jr., and William D. Morice. "Strategies for Logistics Management: Reactions to a Changing Environment," *Journal of Business Logistics* 3, no. 1 (1982): 1–18.

Masters, James M., and Bernard J. LaLonde. *The 1994 Ohio State University Survey of Career Patterns in Logistics* (Columbus: The Ohio State University, 1994).

Murphy, Paul R., and Richard F. Poist. "Educational Strategies for Succeeding in Logistics: A Comparative Analysis," *Transportation Journal* 33, no. 3 (Spring 1994): 36–48.

Neuschel, Robert P. "The New Logistics Challenge—Excellence in Management," *Journal of Business Logistics* 8, no. 1 (1987): 29–39.

Novack, Robert A.; Steven V. Dunn; and Richard R. Young. "Logistics Optimizing and Operational Plans and Systems and Their Role in the Achievement of Corporate Goals," *Transportation Journal* 32, no. 4 (Summer 1993): 29–40.

Sandelands, Eric. "The Logistics Challenge," *International Journal of Physical Distribution and Logistics Management* 24, no. 3 (1994): 5–16.

Sherman, Richard J. "The Process of Formulating Logistics Strategic Plans: Creating Customer Value for Competitive Advantage," *1992 Council of Logistics Management Annual Conference Proceedings* (Oak Brook, IL: Council of Logistics Management, 1992): 519–32.

Stock, James R., "Logistics Thought and Practice: A Perspective," *International Journal of Physical Distribution and Logistics Management* 20, no. 1 (1990): 3.

Williamson, Kenneth C.; Daniel M. Spitzer, Jr.; and David J. Bloomberg. "Modern Logistics Systems: Theory and Practice," *Journal of Business Logistics* 11, no. 2 (1990): 65–86.

SELECTED LOGISTICS PUBLICATIONS

Air Cargo World
6151 Powers Ferry Road NW
Atlanta, GA 30339-2941
Phone: (404) 955-2500   Fax: (404) 955-0400

Air Force Journal of Logistics
Air Force Logistics Management Center/JL
Maxwell AFB Gunter Annex, AL 36114-6693
Phone: (205) 416-4087

American Public Warehouse Register
P.O. Box 750
Sicklerville, NJ 08081
Phone: (609) 728-9745   Fax: (609) 728-5788

American Shipper International
P.O. Box 4728
Jacksonville, FL 32201
Phone: (904) 355-2601   Fax: (904) 791-8836

Containerization International
712 Broadwick Street
London W1V 2BP England
Phone: (44) 71 439-5602   Fax: (44) 71 439-5299

Council of Logistics Management Proceedings
Council of Logistics Management
2803 Butterfield Road, #380
Oak Brook, IL 60521
Phone: (708) 574-0985   Fax: (708) 574-0989

Customer Service Newsletter
Alexander Research & Communications
215 Park Avenue South, Suite 1301
New York, NY 10003
Phone: (212) 228-0246   Fax: (212) 228-0376

Distribution
Chilton Company, Inc.
One Chilton Way
Radnor, PA 19089
Phone: (610) 964-4386   Fax: (610) 964-4381

Distribution Center Management
Alexander Research & Communications
215 Park Avenue South, Suite 1301
New York, NY 10003
Phone: (212) 228-0246   Fax: (212) 228-0376

The Distributor's & Wholesaler's Advisor
Alexander Research & Communications, Inc.
215 Park Avenue South, Suite 1301
New York, NY 10003
Phone: (212) 228-0246   Fax: (212) 228-0376

Executive Report on Customer Satisfaction
Alexander Research & Communications
215 Park Avenue South, Suite 1301
New York, NY 10003
Phone: (212) 228-0246   Fax: (212) 228-0376

Grocery Distribution
Grocery Market Publications
455 South Frontage Road, #116
Burr Ridge, IL 60521
Phone: (708) 986-8767   Fax: (708) 986-0206

Inbound Logistics
Five Penn Plaza, 8th Floor
New York, NY 10001
Phone: (212) 629-1563   Fax: (212) 629-1565

Industrial Distribution
Cahners Publishing Company
275 Washington Street
Newton, MA 02158
Phone: (617) 964-3030

Intermodal Index
IANA/NITL and Mercer Management Consulting
33 Hayden Avenue
Lexington, MA 02173
Phone: (617) 861-7580   Fax: (617) 862-3935

International Journal of Logistics Management
International Logistics Research Institute, Inc.
P.O. Box 2166
Ponte Vedra Beach, FL 32004-2166
Phone: (904) 273-9063   Fax: (904) 273-5020

International Journal of Physical Distribution and Logistics Management
MCB University Press Limited
62 Toller Lane
Bradford, West Yorkshire BD8 9BY England
Phone: (44) 27 449-9821   Fax: (44) 27 454-1743

International Journal of Purchasing and Materials Management
National Association of Purchasing Management
2055 E. Centennial Circle
Tempe, AZ 85285

Journal of Business Logistics
Council of Logistics Management
2803 Butterfield Road
Oak Brook, IL 60521-1156
Phone: (708) 574-0985   Fax: (708) 574-0989

Journal of Transportation Management
621 Plainfield Road, Suite 308
Willowbrook, IL 60521

Journal of Transport Economics and Policy
London School of Economics and Political Science
and the University of Bath
Claverton Down, Bath BA2 7AY England

Logistics Focus
Institute of Logistics
Douglas House
Queens Square
Corby, Northants NN17 1PL England
Phone: (44) 53 620-5500   Fax: (44) 53 640-0979

Logistics and Transportation Review
Faculty of Commerce
University of British Columbia
Vancouver V6T 1W5 Canada
Phone: (604) 228-6707

Logistics Technology International
Sterling Publishing Group PLC
86-88 Edgware Road
London W2 2YW England

Material Handling Engineering
Penton Publishing
1100 Superior Avenue
Cleveland, OH 44114
Phone: (216) 696-7000   Fax: (216) 696-7658

Modern Bulk Transporter
Tunnell Publications, Inc.
4200 South Shepherd, Suite 200
Houston, TX 77098
Phone: (713) 523-8124   Fax: (713) 523-8384

Modern Materials Handling
Cahners Publishing Company, Inc.
275 Washington Street
Newton, MA 02158
Phone: (617) 964-3030

Operations & Fulfillment
Target Conference Corp.
535 Connecticut Avenue
Norwalk, CT 06854
Phone: (203) 857-5656

Progressive Railroading
Murphy-Richter Publishing Co.
230 West Monroe Street, Suite 2210
Chicago, IL 60606
Phone: (312) 629-1200   Fax: (312) 629-1304

Purchasing
Cahners Publishing Company, Inc.
275 Washington Street
Newton, MA 02158
Phone: (617) 558-4473   Fax: (617) 558-4327

Railway Age
Simmons-Boardman Publishing
345 Hudson Street
New York, NY 10014
Phone: (212) 620-7200   Fax: (212) 633-1165

The Staging Area
The Staging Area
P.O. Box 500
South Orleans, MA 02662
Phone: (508) 255-9099   Fax: (508) 255-9879

TR News
Transportation Research Board
National Research Council
2101 Constitution Avenue NW
Washington, DC 20418
Phone: (202) 334-2972   Fax: (202) 334-2519

Traffic Management
Cahners Publishing Company, Inc.
275 Washington Street
Newton, MA 02158
Phone: (617) 588-4473   Fax: (617) 558-4327

Traffic World
741 National Press Building
Washington, DC 20045
Phone: (202) 383-6140   Fax: (202) 737-3349

Transportation and Distribution
Penton Publishing, Inc.
1100 Superior Avenue
Cleveland, OH 44114
Phone: (216) 696-7000   Fax: (216) 696-4135

Transportation Journal
American Society of Transportation and Logistics
216 E. Church Street
Lock Haven, PA 17745
Phone: (717) 748-8515   Fax: (717) 748-9118

Transportation Practitioners Journal
Association of Transportation Practitioners
19564 Club House Road
Gaithersburg, MD 20879-3002
Phone: (301) 670-6733   Fax: (301) 670-6735

Warehouse Education and Research Council
1100 Jorie Boulevard, Suite 170
Oak Brook, IL 60521
Phone: (708) 990-0001

Warehousing Forum
The Ackerman Co.
1328 Dublin Road
Columbus, OH 43215
Phone: (614) 488-3165   Fax: (614) 488-9243

Warehousing Management
Chilton Company, Inc.
One Chilton Way
Radnor, PA 19089
Phone: (610) 964-4000

Waterways and Transportation Review
Waterways & Transportation Research Center
College of Business & Management Studies
University of Alabama
Mobile, AL 36688
Phone: (205) 460-7914

Worldwide Shipping
World Wide Shipping
77 Moehring Drive
Blauvelt, NY 10913-2093
Phone: (914) 359-1934   Fax: (914) 359-1938

DIRECTORY OF TRADE AND PROFESSIONAL ORGANIZATIONS IN LOGISTICS

Airforwarders Association, Inc.
P.O. Box 1602
Orange, CA 92668
Phone: (714) 634-9677   Fax: (714) 634-9678

Purpose: The Airforwarders Association is a not-for-profit organization formed in 1990 by three major forwarders who recognized that, in order to compete in today's sophisticated and competitive market, partnership needed more focus. The Airforwarders Association seeks to improve the systems and conditions under which member firms operate, to increase profits, to create marketing opportunities, to impact legislation that affects the industry, and to improve the level of service provided to customers.

Air Transport Association of America
1301 Pennsylvania Avenue NW
Washington, DC 20004
Phone: (202) 626-4000

Purpose: The Air Transport Association of America is the trade and service organization of the largest airlines of the United States.

American Marketing Association (AMA)
250 South Wacker Drive
Chicago, IL 60606-5819
Phone: (312) 648-0536   Fax: (312) 993-7542

Purpose: The AMA is an international professional society of individual members with an interest in the study, teaching, or practice of marketing. The AMA's principal roles are to urge and assist the professional development of members and to advance the science and practice of the marketing discipline.

American Production and Inventory Control Society (APICS)
500 West Annandale Road
Falls Church, VA 22046
Phone: (703) 237-8344   Fax: (703) 237-4316

Purpose: APICS's primary objectives are to develop professional efficiency in resource management through study, research, and application of scientific methods; to disseminate general and technical information on improved techniques and new developments; to further develop the professional body of knowledge; and, through the organized resources of the profession, thereby to advance the general welfare of the industrial economy.

American Productivity and Quality Center (APQC)
123 North Post Oak Lane
Houston, TX 77024
Phone: (713) 681-4020   Fax: (713) 681-8578

Purpose: The purpose of APQC is to increase productivity and quality through an approach that emphasizes total quality management. APQC has expertise in measurement, innovative pay systems, benchmarking, and employee involvement and has done action research in white collar, professional, and administrative areas. APQC issues a variety of publications and offers public seminars, conference information, and consulting services.

American Society of Transportation and Logistics, Inc. (AST&L)
216 East Church Street
Lock Haven, PA 17745
Phone: (717) 748-8515   Fax: (717) 748-9118

Purpose: The purpose of the AST&L is to establish, promote, and maintain high standards of knowledge and professional training; to formulate a code of ethics for the profession; to advance the professional interest of members of the organization; to serve as a source of information and guidance for the fields of traffic, transportation, logistics, and physical distribution management; and to serve the industry as a whole by fostering professional accomplishments.

American Trucking Associations, Inc. (ATA)
2200 Mill Road
Alexandria, VA 22314
Phone: (703) 838-1700

Purpose: The ATA is the national trade association of the trucking industry. ATA has 51 affiliated trucking associations located in every state and the District of Columbia, as well as 10 affiliated conferences. ATA represents every type and class of motor carrier in the country.

American Warehouse Association
1300 West Higgins Road, Suite 111
Park Ridge, IL 60068
Phone: (708) 292-1891   Fax: (708) 292-1896

Purpose: The goals of the American Warehouse Association are to promote the general interests of persons, firms, and corporations engaged in the public merchandise warehousing industry and to promote a high standard of business ethics therein, to collect and disseminate statistical and other information pertinent to the business of its members, to conduct research into ways and means of improving efficiency in the conduct of the business of its members, to advise its members of national legislation and regulations affecting them, and in general to engage in all activities for the benefit of its members.

Associacao Brasileira de Logistica (ASLOG)
Rual Gandavo, 41
Sao Paulo
Brazil 04023-000
Phone: (55) 11-570-9060   Fax: (55) 11-573-1902

Purpose: ASLOG works in cooperation with the private sector and various official organizations to further the understanding and development of the logistics concept. The organization sponsors formal activities, research, roundtables, and discussions designed to improve the theory and understanding of the logistics process and the science of managing logistics systems. It also offers courses, tours, and publications of interest to logistics personnel.

Association of American Railroads
50 F Street NW
Washington, DC 20001
Phone: (202) 639-2400   Fax: (202) 639-2286

Purpose: The Association of American Railroads serves two major purposes for its members. It provides industry support on matters that require cooperative handling to better enable the railroad to operate as a national system in the areas of operation, maintenance, safety, research, economics, finance, accounting, data systems, and public information. It also provides leadership for the industry, working with committees made up of representatives of member railroads on matters affecting the progress of the industry as a whole.

Association of Professional Material Handling Consultants (APMHC)
8720 Red Oak Boulevard
Charlotte, NC 28217
Phone: (704) 529-1725

Purpose: The APMHC promotes and coordinates the exchange of ideas and information among members; encourages the improvement of analysis, synthesis, installation, and training; advances the profession through the development of standards of performance; and aids and assists other groups in promoting material handling generally and the consulting profession specifically.

Association for Quality and Participation (AQP)
801-B West Eighth Street, Suite 501
Cincinnati, OH 45203
Phone: (513) 381-1959

Purpose: Founded in 1977, the AQP is a not-for-profit professional association dedicated to promoting quality through employee involvement and participation in the workplace. AQP promotes these concepts through education courses, national and regional conferences, resource materials, publications including *The Journal for Quality and Participation,* on-site training, a Professional Achievement Recognition System (PARS), and local chapters.

Association for Transportation Law, Logistics and Policy (formerly the Association of Transportation Practitioners)
19564 Club House Road
Gaithersburg, MD 20879-3002
Phone: (301) 670-6733   Fax: (301) 670-6735

Purpose: To promote the proper administration of the Revised Interstate Commerce Act, related acts, and other laws regulating transportation; to uphold the honor of practice before the Interstate Commerce Commission and other agencies regulating transportation; to cooperate in fostering educational opportunities; to maintain high standards of professional conduct; and to encourage cordial discourse among its members.

Bundesvereinigung Logistik E.V. (BVL)
Contrescarpe 45
28195 Bremen
Germany
Phone: (49) 421 335680   Fax: (49) 421 320369

Purpose: The BVL is the largest logistics association in Germany and is subdivided into 20 active regional logistics groups. The Deutsche Logistik-Kongress in Berlin is organized each year by BVL. The BVL operates a logistics data bank and a logistics education institute.

Canadian Association of Logistics Management (CALM)
610 Alden Road, Suite 201
Markham, Ontario L3R 9Z1
Canada
Phone: (416) 513-7300   Fax: (416) 513-0624

Purpose: The CALM is a not-for-profit organization of business professionals interested in improving their logistics and/or distribution management skills. It works in cooperation with the private sector and various organizations to further the understanding and development of the logistics concept. It does this through a continuing program of formal activities, research, and informal discussion designed to develop the theory and understanding of the logistics process; to promote the art and science of managing logistics systems; and to foster professional dialogue and development within the profession.

Canadian Industrial Transportation League (CITL)
1090 Don Mills Road
Don Mills, Ontario M3C 3R6
Canada
Phone: (416) 447-7766   Fax: (416) 447-7312

Purpose: The CITL aims to develop a thorough understanding of the transportation and distribution requirements of industry; and to promote, conserve, and protect commercial transportation interests.

Centro Espanol de Logistica (CEL)
Paseo de la Castellana
114-2a 4o Madrid
Spain 28046
Phone: (34) 1 411 67 53   Fax: (34) 1 564 09 10

Purpose: CEL is a not-for-profit organization of companies, academics, and others interested in the logistics field. By offering training courses, journeys, roundtables, visits, and publications, it seeks to improve the standard of individual and corporate skills in the area of logistics management.

Council of Consulting Organizations, Inc.
ACME
521 Fifth Avenue
New York, NY 10175
Phone: (212) 455-8221   Fax: (212) 949-6571

Purpose: The Council of Consulting Organizations is an umbrella organization with two divisions: ACME, representing management consulting firms; and IMC, representing individual consultants. Its purpose is to contribute to the development and better understanding of the art and science, practice, and role of management consulting; to conduct research for the development and improvement of the practice of management, and to disseminate the results of such research in the public interest.

Council of Logistics Management (CLM)
2803 Butterfield Road, Suite 380
Oak Brook, IL 60521-1156
Phone: (708) 574-0985   Fax: (708) 574-0989

Purpose: The mission of the CLM is to provide
- Leadership in defining and understanding the logistics process
- A forum for the exchange of ideas among logistics professionals

- Research that contributes to enhanced customer value and supply chain performance
- Awareness of career opportunities for logistics management

The CLM is an open organization that offers individual membership to persons in all industries, types of businesses, and job functions involved in the logistics process. In recognition of diversity, the CLM will give priority to actively involving individuals from currently underrepresented populations in its activities. The CLM operates on a not-for-profit, self-supporting basis, with emphasis on quality and in a cooperative manner with other organizations and institutions.

Delta Nu Alpha
530 Church Street, Suite 300
Nashville, TN 37219
Phone: (615) 251-0933   Fax: (615) 748-3030

Purpose: Delta Nu Alpha is a service organization providing educational opportunities to those having a professional interest in transportation, logistics, and related fields. Its goal is to serve as a sustaining resource for future needs of the industry.

Deutsche Gesselschaft fur Logistik E.V.
(Germany Society of Logistics)
Heinrich-Hertz-Strasse 4
Dortmund
Germany 44227
Phone: (49) 231 7 54 43-220
Fax: (49) 231 7 54 43-222

Purpose: The purpose of the Deutsche Gesellschaft fur Logistik is the promotion of scientific and practical research and development in the field of logistics, with particular consideration of industry, commerce and services, and educational programming.

Eno Transportation Foundation, Inc.
44211 Slatestone Court
Landsdowne, VA 22075
Phone: (703) 729-7200   Fax: (703) 729-7219

Purpose: The Eno Transportation Foundation provides a responsive and creditable institution and resource for transportation betterment that is facilitated through safe, efficient, and environmentally sound systems and services. In support of its role, the foundation (1) monitors transportation trends, developments, and related problem areas, with counsel from its board of advisors;

(2) maintains effective lines of communication with transportation leaders and their trade and professional organizations; (3) develops information for dissemination to all modal interests, the media, and the general public; (4) undertakes and manages selected research projects, studies, and seminars; (5) works to advance the development of transportation leadership; and (6) provides a forum for discussion of transportation public policy matters.

European Logistics Association (ELA)
Rue Archimed 5, 6th Floor
B-1040
Brussels
Belgium
Phone: (32) 2 230 0211   Fax: (32) 2 230 0211

Purpose: The mission of the ELA is to link the professional bodies in Europe into a functioning organization to service both industry and trade in Europe; to define the European logistics terminology on a multilingual basis to ensure ease and correctness of communication from country to country; to develop a "European" body of knowledge using information not only from within Europe but also by tracking new developments in other parts of the world and by acting as a focal point for logistics research in conjunction with academics, industry, and government; and to formulate a European Education Certification Program in order to have uniform standards within the European community.

Express Carriers Association
2200 Mill Road
Alexandria, VA 22314
Phone: (703) 838-1887   Fax: (703) 549-6196

Purpose: The main objectives of the Express Carriers Association are to:
- Build membership
- Improve member economics
- Provide a directory of express LTL and package express firms
- Publicize the industry and the association's members
- Conduct shipper-oriented events, such as annual meetings
- Provide services such as well-publicized surveys
- Improve the acceptance of the industry
- Help members and the public understand the developing initiatives that are changing transportation

- Promote awareness of the express industry as an important segment of the distribution and logistics profession

Food Marketing Institute (FMI)
800 Connecticut Avenue NW
Phone: (202) 452-8444   Fax: (202) 429-4519

Purpose: The FMI is a not-for-profit association that conducts research and facilitates education, industry relations, and public affairs on behalf of its 1,500 members, including their subsidiaries—food retailers and wholesalers and their customers in the United States and around the world.

French Association for Logistics (FAL)
119, rue Cardinet
75017 Paris
France
Phone: (3) 1 40 53 85 59   Fax: (33) 1 47 66 27 08

Purpose: The French Association for Logistics aims to promote logistics in companies through such activities as meetings, symposia, and special studies.

Grocery Manufacturers of America, Inc. (GMA)
1010 Wisconsin Avenue NW, Suite 900
Washington, DC 20007
Phone: (202) 337-9400   Fax: (202) 337-4508

Purpose: The GMA is a trade association of the leading manufacturers and processors of food and nonfood products sold in retail grocery outlets throughout the United States. GMA's objective is to solve for member companies those problems for which GMA group action is more effective than action by member companies working individually or through other associations.

Health and Personal Care Distribution Conference, Inc. (H&PCDC)
1090 12th Street
Vero Beach, FL 32960
Phone: (407) 778-7782   Fax: (407) 778-4111

Purpose: H&PCDC addresses concerns common to the shippers of drugs, medicines, toilet preparations, and health and personal care products. It represents their views in Washington and before state and federal agencies and courts. It provides seminars and educational speakers at its meetings.

Hungarian Association for Logistics, Purchasing, and Inventory Management (HALPIM)
Veres Palne u. 36
Budapest
Hungary 1053

Purpose: The main objectives of the HALPIM are to contribute to the increase of economic efficiency in the field and to develop the professional standard of the logistics profession within Hungarian trade, industry, and public administration. HALPIM helps establish contact between professionals in the field; supports the spread of new ideas; keeps in contact with other organizations at the international level; and publishes its own logistics newsletter.

Institute of Industrial Engineers (IIE)
25 Technology Park Atlanta
Norcross, GA 30092
Phone: (404) 449-0460   Fax: (404) 263-8532

Purpose: The purpose of the IIE is to advance the general welfare of mankind through the resources and creative abilities of the industrial engineering profession and to encourage and assist education and research in the art and science of industrial engineering.

Institute of Logistics
Douglas House, Queens Square
Corby, Northants
England NN17 1PL
Phone: (44) 536 205500   Fax: (44) 536 400979

Purpose: The objectives of the Institute of Logistics are to promote and develop the concepts and practice of logistics and to provide services to members, including library and information services, regional activities, career advice, and educational facilities.

Institute of Management Consultants, Inc. (IMC)
521 Fifth Avenue, 35th Floor
New York, NY 10175
Phone: (212) 697-9693   Fax: (212) 949-6571

Purpose: The IMC pursues professional certification (the CMC) to assure the public that members possess the ethical standards, the professional competence, and the independence required for membership, and are, therefore, qualified to practice.

Institute of Materials Handling, Transport, Packaging, and Storage Systems (IMADOS)
IMADOS, A.S.
Konevova 141
130 83 Praha 3
Czech Republic
Phone: (42) 2 6440560   Fax: (42) 2 2352993

Purpose: IMADOS has the following objectives:
- Research and development of project-engineered activities for technical and building equipment for the workplace in the spheres of production and physical distribution
- Research and development of special machines, devices, and equipment for materials handling, transportation, storage, and packaging engineering
- Technical standardization
- Information service systems for the Czech Republic, Slovakia, and foreign countries
- Publishing of professional monthly periodical, *Material Handling, Storage, and Packaging,* with summaries in English, German, and Russian
- Regular professional training, conferences, and symposia for experts in the spheres of materials management, storage, packaging, and logistics systems
- High tech commercial, technical, and marketing services for both capital investors and producers
- Delivery of the most effective handling and storage systems in the shortest terms
- Improved product quality for reasonable prices and terms

Institute of Packaging Professionals (IoPP)
481 Carlisle Drive
Herndon, VA 22070-4823
Phone: (703) 318-8970   Fax: (703) 318-0310

Purpose: IoPP's purpose is the professional development of packaging and handling professionals. The IoPP is an individual, professional membership organization of those who apply packaging design, engineering, production, and distribution principles and technologies and of those who manage these technologies and related production processes.

Institut International de Management pour la Logistique
IML-EPF-DGC
CH-1015 Lausanne
Switzerland

Purpose: The purpose of the institute is to:
- Promote the development and use of logistical organization methods through education and research
- Participate in the development of procedures concerning international trade
- Train high-level managers in the field of logistics
- Introduce young people to the methodological, instrumental, and practical foundations of the field of logistics

International Association of Refrigerated Warehouses
7315 Wisconsin Avenue, Suite 1200N
Bethesda, MD 20814
Phone: (301) 652-5674   Fax: (301) 652-7269

Purpose: The goals of the International Association of Refrigerated Warehouses are to advance the interests and welfare of the refrigerated warehousing, transportation, distribution, and logistics businesses; to elevate and improve industry standards; and to promote better understanding of its functions within the food distribution industry and among the general public.

International Customer Service Association (ICSA)
401 North Michigan Avenue
Chicago, IL 60611-4267
Phone: (312) 321-6800   Fax: (312) 527-6658

Purpose: ICSA is an organization dedicated to developing the theory and understanding of the total quality service process, advancing the art and science of managing that process, and encouraging professional dialogue in the achievement of customer satisfaction.

International Mass Retailing Association (IMRA)
1901 Pennsylvania Avenue NW
Washington, DC 20006
Phone: (202) 861-0774

Purpose: IMRA represents the nation's discount and variety general merchandise retail industry. IMRA's memberships include companies that operate more than 40,000 discount, variety, dollar, junior department, family center off-price, factory outlet, catalog showroom, and other general merchandise stores. Members range widely in size and include many of the nation's largest retail chains.

International Safe Transit Association (ISTA)
43 East Ohio Street, Suite 914
Chicago, IL 60611-2791
Phone: (312) 645-0083   Fax: (312) 645-1078

Purpose: The purpose of ISTA is to promote the reduction of physical distribution damage to packaged products through a cooperative framework of organizations by improvements in packaging technology, shipping, handling, and storage of products; to establish adequate testing methods and procedures; to certify and qualify testing agencies and laboratories; to promote safety in packaging and foster communication of up-to-date technical information among its membership; and to encourage and participate in the conservation of our natural environment, materials, and energy.

International Society for Inventory Research
Veres Palne u.36
Budapest
Hungary H-1053
Phone: (36) 1 117-2959

Purpose: The society, which is a professional, not-for-profit organization, provides those engaged in inventory research with an opportunity to exchange views and experiences on an international and interdisciplinary basis. The society's mission is to provide an appropriate and comprehensive framework for the dissemination of research results attained in the member's country and to take initiative in the development of research and higher education.

International Trade Facilitation Council (NCITD)
1800 Diagonal Road, Suite 220
Alexandria, VA 22314
Phone: (709) 519-0661   Fax: (709) 519-0664

Purpose: NCITD is a not-for-profit, industry-financed membership organization dedicated to simplifying and improving international trade documentation and procedures, including information exchange by either paper or electronic methods. Working through individuals and companies, members and nonmembers, United States and overseas governmental departments and agencies, and duly constituted national and international committees and organizations, NCITD serves as coordinator and as a central source of information and reference, and provides solutions to problems on international trade information exchange and procedures.

Japan Institute of Logistics Systems (JILS)
Shuwa No. 2 Shiba Park Building

2-12-7, Shiba Daimon Minajto-ku
Tokyo 105
Japan
Phone: (81) 3 3432-3291   Fax: (81) 3 3432-8681

Purpose: The objective of JILS is to contribute to the development of the national economy and to develop activities relating to the modernization of logistics; to promote logistics systems in the commercial field; to conduct seminars, workshops, and conferences; and to sponsor overseas tours that are of interest to logistics management personnel.

Korea Productivity Center (KPC)
CPO Box 834
Seoul
Korea 110-052
Phone: (82) 2 739-5868

Purpose: The major objectives of the KPC are to
- Stimulate interest in productivity and to promote productivity consciousness
- Render consultancy services to industries to increase their managerial and operational efficiency
- Train industrial personnel to improve their productivity
- Collect and disseminate information relating to productivity improvement
- Act as the integrated focal point of all organizations engaged in productivity improvement drives

Logistics Management Association of Australia (LMA)
P.O. Box 943
Auburn NSW
Australia 2144
Phone: (61) 2 649-1757   Fax: (61) 2 649-3794

Purpose: The LMA is an association representing the interests of those involved in logistics. This includes warehousing, distribution, purchasing, marketing, sales, customer service, and materials managers. The aim of increasing the professionalism of members is achieved by acting as the representative body for managers engaged in logistics functions; by providing opportunities for interaction and sharing of experiences with other professionals; by conducting monthly meetings to discuss topics and issues of interest; and by providing opportunities for learning through participation in seminars, site visits, and tertiary courses.

Logistics Management Association of New Zealand
P.O. Box 553
Manurewa
New Zealand
Phone: (64) 9 267-1106   Fax: (64) 9 267-9075

Material Handling Equipment Distributors Association
201 Route 45
Vernon Hills, IL 60061
Phone: (708) 680-3500   Fax: (708) 362-6989

Purpose: The purpose of the Material Handling Equipment Distributors Association is to educate distributor members in the methods and practices necessary for them to become the most efficient medium through which materials handling equipment manufacturers distribute their products, to educate manufacturers and suppliers on the value of distributors in the distribution of material handling products, and to enhance the professional image of the distributor and to endeavor in every way to make the material handling industry better tomorrow than it is today.

Material Handling Institute (MHI)
8720 Red Oak Boulevard, Suite 201
Charlotte, NC 28217-3992
Phone: (704) 522-8644   Fax: (704) 522-7826

Purpose: The Material Handling Institute is the not-for-profit umbrella organization of its two membership divisions—the Material Handling Institute (MHI) and the Material Handling Industry of America (MHIA). Since 1945, MHI has been the primary source of information on the industry. MHI aims to bring the nation's manufacturers, users, and educators together to provide lasting solutions to today's productivity challenges through better material handling. MHIA gives its member companies a greater voice in shaping the destiny of the industry, both nationally and internationally. MHIA sponsors trade events to showcase the products and services of its member companies and to provide material handling educational opportunities.

Materials Handling and Management Society (formerly International Materials Management Society)
8720 Red Oak Boulevard, Suite 224
Charlotte, NC 28217
Phone: (704) 525-4667   Fax: (704) 525-2880

Purpose: The Materials Handling and Management Society is a professional society dedicated to enhancing the professional stature of its members and their fields on all levels through promoting public recognition of material handling and material management as vital professional business activities, and providing members with activities and information that facilitate acquiring increased knowledge and skills in the areas of material handling and material management.

Mexican Association of Traffic and Distribution (SUEDYT)
Norte 59 No 860
Mexico City
Mexico
Phone: (52) 5 567-5001   Fax: (52) 5 587-2379

Purpose: The purpose of SUEDYT is to promote, develop, and maintain high standards of knowledge and professional training and to serve as a source of information for members, government, and other Mexican associations.

National American Wholesale Grocers' Association (NAWGA)
201 Park Washington Court
Falls Church, VA 22046
Phone: (703) 532-9400   Fax: (703) 538-4673

Purpose: The purpose of the NAWGA and its foodservice division is to improve the efficiency and increase the profitability of the wholesale grocery and foodservice distribution industry by
- Providing training and education in operations, management skills, and ways to improve productivity
- Effectively representing members' interests in Washington, DC

National Association of Chain Drug Stores
413 North Lee Street
Alexandria, VA 22313-1480
Phone: (703) 549-3001   Fax: (703) 836-4869

Purpose: Founded in 1933, the association's mission is to promote and preserve the general welfare of the chain drug industry and the consumers it serves; monitor activities of legislative, regulatory, pharmacy, and special interest groups; and initiate appropriate action that best serves the general welfare of the chain drug industry.

National Association of Manufacturers (NAM)
1331 Pennsylvania Avenue, Suite 1500N
Washington, DC 20004-1703
Phone: (202) 637-3000

Purpose: NAM's objectives are to promote America's economic health and productivity, particularly in the manufacturing sector, by developing and advocating sound industrial practices as well as effective domestic and international policies at the national government level; to make the American business community more aware of, and more involved in, the process of public policy formation, and to reinforce public understanding of the importance of the competitive market system in promoting national interest at home and abroad; and to serve NAM member companies and affiliated organizations with relevant, timely information on which to base their policy positions, and to help communicate those positions to the general public, employees, and shareholders of the company, as well as to the appropriate elements of government.

National Association of Purchasing Management, Inc. (NAPM)

P.O. Box 22160
Tempe, AZ 85285-2160
Phone: (602) 752-6276   Fax: (602) 752-7890

Purpose: The NAPM is committed to providing national and international leadership on purchasing and materials management. Through its 178 affiliated associations and over 37,000 members, the association provides opportunities for purchasing and materials management practitioners to expand their professional skill and knowledge, and works to foster a better understanding of purchasing and materials management concepts.

National Association of Wholesaler-Distributors (NAW)

1725 K Street NW
Washington, DC 20006
Phone: (202) 872-0885   Fax: (202) 785-0586

Purpose: The NAW represents the merchant wholesale distribution industry, which employs about 4.5 million workers. NAW's membership includes nearly 200 national and regional trade associations that specialize in the distribution of certain kinds of products and individual wholesale distribution firms. NAW's membership universe includes nearly 45,000 companies.

National Defense Transportation Association (NDTA)

50 South Pickett Street, Suite 220
Alexandria, VA 22304-3008
Phone: (703) 751-5011

Purpose: The NDTA is an educational, not-for-profit, worldwide organization that combines the transportation industry's manpower and skills with the expertise of those in government and the military to achieve the mutual objectives of a strong and responsive transportation capability. NDTA membership represents the transportation operators, users, mode carriers, manufacturers, traffic managers, and related industries, and military and government interests.

National Industrial Transportation League (NITL)

1700 North Moore Street, Suite 1900
Arlington, VA 22209-1904
Phone: (703) 524-5011   Fax: (703) 524-5017

Purpose: The NITL represents shippers in the legislative, judicial, and regulatory arenas. Among its specific benefits are designing and implementing transportation policy, fighting legal battles on behalf of shippers, providing networking opportunities, offering educational seminars as well as a domestic and international meeting and trade show, and producing informative publications.

National Perishable Logistics Association

P.O. Box 3021
Oak Park, IL 60301
Phone: (708) 524-1020   Fax: (708) 524-1064

Purpose: The purpose of the National Perishable Logistics Association is to provide a forum where shippers, carriers, receivers, and suppliers can meet to discuss the problems inherent in the distribution of perishable commodities. Legal counsel attends all meetings to preclude antitrust violations.

National Private Truck Council (NPTC)

66 Canal Center Plaza, Suite 600
Alexandria, VA 22314
Phone: (703) 683-1300   Fax: (703) 683-1217

Purpose: The NPTC represents the concerns and issues of corporate trucking—companies that use "in-house" or dedicated truck fleets to support distribution of their products and services. Members benefit from NPTC's work on a wide variety of issues, including federal and state taxes and regulations, safety, and environmental issues. NPTC counsels agencies on regulatory and rulemaking proceedings and, when appropriate, participates in court cases. NPTC publishes a monthly management journal, *Private Carrier,* and monthly newsletters, *The Private Line,* and *Safety & Compliance News.*

National Society of Professional Engineers (NSPE)
1420 King Street
Alexandria, VA 22314
Phone: (703) 684-2800   Fax: (703) 836-4875

Purpose: NSPE is dedicated to the protection and promotion of the profession of engineering as a social and economic influence vital to the affairs of society and the United States. It has actively promoted effective state registration laws for professional engineers to safeguard the public.

National Wholesale Druggists' Association (NWDA)
P.O. Box 2219
Reston, VA 22090
Phone: (703) 787-0000   Fax: (703) 787-6930

Purpose: The NWDA is a national trade association of full-service drug wholesalers. More than 300 manufacturers of pharmaceuticals, nonprescription drugs, and health and beauty aids are associate members. NWDA was founded in Indianapolis, Indiana, in 1876. Its primary purposes are to strengthen relations between wholesalers' suppliers and customers; to serve as a forum for major industry issues; to sponsor research and communicate information on new business systems, logistics technologies, and management practices for drug wholesalers; and to represent the industry on legislative and regulatory matters.

Norsk Forbund for Innkjop og Logistikk (NIMA)
(Norwegian Association of Purchasing and Logistics)
P.O. Box 6703 Rodelokka
0503 Oslo
Norway
Phone: (47) 2237 9710   Fax: (47) 2238 5323

Purpose: The aim of NIMA is to raise the professional standard of members and others engaged in the profession. For many years and in many ways NIMA has tried to get attention from official school authorities to get purchasing and logistics on the time table.

Office Furniture Distribution Association, Inc.
(OFDA)
P.O. Box 326
Petersham, MA 01366-0326
Phone: (508) 724-3267   Fax: (508) 724-3507

Purpose: OFDA is a not-for-profit office furniture shippers' association whose object, as stated in its con-

stitutions, is to promote the common interests of its members as to transportation and distribution management development through educational articles, seminars, programs, and presentations of views to regulatory agencies concerning these common interests. These common interests include rules, regulations, ratings, rates, and packing requirements of carriers as they related to the transportation of office furniture.

Society of Logistics Engineers (SOLE)
8100 Professional Place, Suite 211
New Carrollton, MD 20785
Phone: (301) 459-8446   Fax: (301) 459-1522

Purpose: SOLE is a not-for-profit, international organization devoted to scientific, educational, and literary endeavors to enhance the art and science of logistics technology, education, and management.

South African Institute of Materials Handling
P.O. Box 3656
Rivonia
South Africa 2128
Phone: (27) 883-0339   Fax: (27) 883-0716

Purpose: The South African Institute of Materials Handling is a not-for-profit organization that promotes, advances, and maintains technical competence in all aspects of materials handling and logistics through its members and worldwide affiliated bodies.

Swedish Materials Administration Forum (SMAF)
Bos 608 S-131 21
Nacka
Sweden
Phone: (46) 8 718-1280   Fax: (46) 8 718-0025

Purpose: The main objectives of SMAF are to
- Establish a bridge and unite common interests of different functions in the field of materials administration within a company and the society in general.
- Stimulate activities within the materials administration field and emphasize high-quality work.
- Support education and training of materials administration staff by presenting courses and arranging seminars and conferences in order to inform members of trends and current developments in materials and administration.
- Develop and support an integrated overall view of the concept of materials and administration.
- Present for the press and other groups of interest a wide picture of the development within the materials administration field and to stress the importance of

materials administration in the total economy of the society.

- Stimulate and support activities related to contacts with international organizations dealing with materials administration, logistics, and materials handling.

Swedish National Association of Purchasing and Logistics (SILF)

P.O. Box 1278
Kista
Sweden S-164 28
Phone: (46) 8 752-0470   Fax: (46) 8 750-6410

Purpose: SILF's objectives are to raise the professional standard of members and others engaged in the profession and to support training and education at the university and high school level.

Thai Logistics Society

Somkiat Leeratanakachorn
Administration Manager
Diethelm Company Limited
594 Luang Road Pomprab
Bangkok 10100
Thailand
Phone: (66) 541-9720   Fax: (66) 541-8581

Purpose: The purpose of the Thai Logistics Society is to promote the art and science of logistics, materials management, and physical distribution.

Transportation Claims and Prevention Council, Inc.

120 Main Street
Huntington, NY 11743
Phone: (516) 549-8984   Fax: (516) 549-8962

Purpose: The Transportation Claims & Prevention Council is an educational institution developing the latest teaching tools and techniques on carrier liability and claims administration through seminars and publications. The objective is to develop a greater degree of professionalism in claims management.

Transportation Research Board (TRB)

2101 Constitution Avenue NW
Washington, DC 20418
Phone: (202) 334-2934   Fax: (202) 334-2003

Purpose: TRB's goal is to advance knowledge concerning the nature and performance of transportation systems by stimulating research and disseminating the information derived from research.

Transportation Research Forum

11250 Roger Bacon Drive, Suite 8
Reston, VA 22090
Phone: (703) 437-4377

Purpose: The purpose of the Transportation Research Forum is to provide an impartial meeting ground for carriers, shippers, government officials, consultants, university researchers, suppliers, and others seeking an exchange of information and ideas related to both passengers and freight transportation.

Uniform Code Council, Inc.

8163 Old Yankee Road, Suite J
Dayton, OH 45458
Phone: (513) 435-3870   Fax: (513) 435-4749

Purpose: The mission of the Uniform Code Council is to take a global leadership role in establishing and promoting multi-industry standards and services that support product identification and electronic data interchange. The goal is to enhance transaction process and enable distribution channels to operate more efficiently and effectively while contributing added value to customers.

United States Chamber of Commerce

1615 H Street NW
Washington, DC 20062
Phone: (202) 659-6000   Fax: (202) 463-5636

Purpose: The United States Chamber of Commerce aims to advance human progress through a better economic, political, and social system based on individual freedom, incentive, opportunity, and responsibility. The Chamber develops positions on national, legislative, and economic issues through grassroots input and board action. Positions are then articulated to various constituencies, Chamber members, the press, the general public, the congress, and the Administration in order to produce public policy that will benefit the economy and business.

United States China Business Council

1818 N Street NW, Suite 500
Washington, DC 20036
Phone: (202) 429-0340   Fax: (202) 775-2476

Purpose: The United States China Business Council is the focal point for China trade and investment in the United States. American companies look to the council for representation in developing and continuing their trade and investment relations with the People's Republic of China.

VDI-Gesellschaft Foerdertechnik Materialflüss Logistik (VDI-FML), a division of Verein Deutscher Ingenierure (VDI)
Postfach 10 11 39
40002 Dusseldorf
Germany
Phone: (49) 211 6214-437　Fax: (49) 211 6214-155

Purpose: The purpose of VDI-FML is to promote research and development in the fields of material flow, transportation, and logistics; to exchange experience among members and with external experts; to cooperate with industry, commerce, and educational institutions; and to set and publish technical rules and standards.

Vereniging Logistiek Management
P.O. Box 444
Voorburg 2270 CK
Netherlands
Phone: (31) 70 387 3100　Fax: (31) 70 387 3005

Purpose: The purpose of Vereniging Logistiek Management is to promote the knowledge and dissemination of information about integral goods flow control. There is a wide variety of educational programs and a certification system that is under government supervision.

Warehousing Education and Research Council (WERC)
1100 Jorie Boulevard, Suite 170
Oak Brook, IL 60521
Phone: (708) 990-0001　Fax: (708) 990-0256

Purpose: WERC's purpose is to provide education and to conduct research concerning the warehousing process and to refine the art and science of managing warehouses. WERC fosters professionalism in warehouse management. It operates exclusively without profit and in cooperation with other organizations and institutions.

Women in Packaging, Inc.
4290 Bells Ferry Road, Suite 106-17
Kennesaw, GA 30144-1300
Phone: (404) 924-3563　Fax: (404) 928-2338

Purpose: Women in Packaging, Inc., is an international, not-for-profit professional organization established in January 1993. The group was formed to provide a forum for networking and education for the personal and professional development of women; to promote and encourage the growth and success of women in the packaging industry; to promote diversity across all levels in the industry; to educate the packaging industry about the contributions and potential of qualified women in packaging; and to help eliminate misconceptions, stereotypes, and discrimination against women in the profession.

GLOSSARY

ABC analysis The classification of items in an inventory according to importance defined in terms of criteria such as sales volume and purchase volume.

accessibility A carrier's ability to provide service between an origin and a destination.

accessorial charges A carrier's charge for accessorial services such as loading, unloading, pickup, and delivery.

action message An alert that an MRP or DRP system generates to inform the controller of a situation requiring his or her attention.

active stock Goods in active pick locations and ready for order filling.

advanced shipment notice (ASN) A list transmitted to a customer or consignor designating items shipped. May also include expected time of arrival.

agency tariff A rate bureau publication that contains rates for many carriers.

agglomeration A net advantage a company gains by sharing a common location with other companies.

aggregate tender rate A reduced rate offered to a shipper who tenders two or more class-related shipments at one time and one place.

air cargo Freight that is moved by air transportation.

Airport and Airway Trust Fund A federal fund that collects passenger ticket taxes and disburses those funds for airport facilities.

air taxi An exempt for-hire air carrier that will fly anywhere on demand; air taxis are restricted to a maximum payload and passenger capacity per plane.

Air Transport Association of America A U.S. airline industry association.

all-cargo carrier An air carrier that transports cargo only.

American Society of Transportation & Logistics A professional organization in the field of logistics.

American Trucking Association, Inc. A motor carrier industry association composed of subconferences representing various motor carrier industry sectors.

American Waterway Operators A domestic water carrier industry association representing barge operators on inland waterways.

Amtrak The National Railroad Passenger Corporation, a federally created corporation that operates most of the United States' intercity passenger rail service.

any-quantity (AQ) rate A rate that applies to any size shipment tendered to a carrier; no discount rate is available for large shipments.

artificial intelligence A field of research seeking to understand and computerize the human thought process.

Association of American Railroads A railroad industry association that represents the larger U.S. railroads.

auditing Determining the correct transportation charges due the carrier; auditing involves checking the freight bill for errors, correct rate, and weight.

automated guided vehicle system (AGVS) A computer-controlled materials handling system consisting of small vehicles (carts) that move along a guideway.

automated storage and retrieval system (ASRS) An

automated, mechanized system for moving merchandise into storage locations and retrieving it when needed.

average cost   Total cost, fixed plus variable, divided by total output.

backhaul   A vehicle's return movement from original destination to original origin.

back order   The process a company uses when a customer orders an item that is not in inventory; the company fills the order when the item becomes available.

backup   Making a duplicate copy of a computer file or a program on a disk or cassette so that the material will not be lost if the original is destroyed; a spare copy.

bar code   A series of lines of various widths and spacings that can be scanned electronically to identify a carton or individual item.

bar code scanner   A device to read bar codes and communicate data to computer systems.

barge   The cargo-carrying vehicle that inland water carriers primarily use. Basic barges have open tops, but there are covered barges for both dry and liquid cargoes.

basing-point pricing   A pricing system that includes a transportation cost from a particular city or town in a zone or region even though the shipment does not originate at the basing point.

batch picking   The picking of items from storage for more than one order at a time.

benchmarking   A management tool for comparing performance against an organization that is widely regarded as outstanding in one or more areas, in order to improve performance.

benefit-cost ratio   An analytical tool used in public planning; a ratio of total measurable benefits divided by the initial capital cost.

billing   A carrier terminal activity that determines the proper rate and total charges for a shipment and issues a freight bill.

bill of lading   A transportation document that is the contract of carriage between the shipper and carrier; it provides a receipt for the goods the shipper tenders to the carrier and, in some cases, shows certificate of title.

binder   A strip of cardboard, thin wood, burlap, or similar material placed between layers of containers to hold a stack together.

blanket rate   A rate that does not increase according to the distance a commodity is shipped.

bonded warehousing   A type of warehousing in which companies place goods in storage without paying taxes or tariffs. The warehouse manager bonds himself or herself to the tax or tariff collecting agency to ensure payment of the taxes before the warehouse releases the goods.

boxcar   An enclosed railcar, typically forty to fifty feet long, used for packaged freight and some bulk commodities.

bracing   To secure a shipment inside a carrier's vehicle to prevent damage.

break-bulk   The separation of a consolidated bulk load into smaller individual shipments for delivery to the ultimate consignee. The freight may be moved intact inside the trailer, or it may be interchanged and rehandled to connecting carriers.

broker   An intermediary between the shipper and the carrier. The broker arranges transportation for shippers and secures loads for carriers.

bulk area   A storage area for large items which at a minimum are most efficiently handled by the palletload.

business logistics   The process of planning, implementing, and controlling the efficient, effective flow and storage of goods, services, and related information from the point of origin to the point of consumption for the purpose of conforming to customer requirements. Note that this definition includes inbound, outbound, internal, and external movements.

cabotage   A federal law that requires coastal and intercoastal traffic to be carried in U.S.-built and -registered ships.

cage   (1) A secure enclosed area for storing highly valuable items, (2) a pallet-sized platform with sides that can be secured to the tines of a forklift and in which a person may ride to inventory items stored well above the warehouse floor.

capital   The resources, or money, available for investing in assets that produce output.

Carmack Amendment An Interstate Commerce Act amendment that delineates the liability of common carriers and the bill of lading provisions.

carousel A rotating system of layers of bins and/or drawers that can store many small items using relatively little floor space.

carrier liability A common carrier is liable for all shipment loss, damage, and delay with the exception of that caused by act of God, act of a public enemy, act of a public authority, act of the shipper, and the goods' inherent nature.

carton flow rack A storage rack consisting of multiple lines of gravity flow conveyors.

centralized authority The restriction of authority to make decisions to few managers.

central processing unit (CPU) The physical part of the computer that does the actual computing.

certificated carrier A for-hire air carrier that is subject to economic regulation and requires an operating certification to provide service.

certificate of origin An international business document that certifies the shipment's country of origin.

certificate of public convenience and necessity The grant of operating authority that common carriers receive. A carrier must prove that a public need exists and that the carrier is fit, willing, and able to provide the needed service. The certificate may specify the commodities the carrier may haul, the area it may serve, and the routes it may use.

charging area A warehouse area where a company maintains battery chargers and extra batteries to support a fleet of electrically powered materials handling equipment. The company must maintain this area in accordance with government safety regulations.

chock A wedge, usually made of hard rubber or steel, that is firmly placed under the wheel of a trailer, truck, or boxcar to stop it from rolling.

city driver A motor carrier driver who drives a local route as opposed to a long-distance, intercity route.

Civil Aeronautics Board A federal regulatory agency that implemented economic regulatory controls over air carriers.

CL Carload rail service requiring shipper to meet minimum weight.

claim A charge made against a carrier for loss, damage, delay, or overcharge.

Class I carrier A classification of regulated carriers based upon annual operating revenues—motor carriers of property; $\geq$ \$5 million; railroads; $\geq$ \$50 million; motor carriers of passengers; $\geq$ \$3 million.

Class II carrier A classification of regulated carriers based upon annual operating revenues—motor carriers of property: \$1–\$5 million; railroads: \$10–\$50 million; motor carriers of passengers: $\leq$ \$3 million.

Class III carrier A classification of regulated carriers based upon annual operating revenues—motor carriers of property: $\leq$ \$1 million; railroads; $\leq$ \$10 million.

classification An alphabetical listing of commodities, the class or rating into which the commodity is placed, and the minimum weight necessary for the rate discount; used in the class rate structure.

classification yard A railroad terminal area where railcars are grouped together to form train units.

class rate A rate constructed from a classification and a uniform distance system. A class rate is available for any product between any two points.

coastal carriers Water carriers that provide service along coasts serving ports on the Atlantic or Pacific Oceans or on the Gulf of Mexico.

commercial zone The area surrounding a city or town to which rate carriers quote for the city or town also apply; the ICC defines the area.

Committee of American Steamship Lines An industry association representing subsidized U.S. flag steamship firms.

commodities clause A clause that prohibits railroads from hauling commodities that they produced, mined, owned, or had an interest in.

commodity rate A rate for a specific commodity and its origin-destination.

common carrier A for-hire carrier that holds itself out to serve the general public at reasonable rates and without discrimination. To operate, the carrier must secure a certificate of public convenience and necessity.

common carrier duties   Common carriers must serve, deliver, charge reasonable rates, and not discriminate.

common cost   A cost that a company cannot directly assign to particular segments of the business; a cost that the company incurs for the business as a whole.

commuter   An exempt for-hire air carrier that publishes a time schedule on specific routes; a special type of air taxi.

comparative advantage   A principle based on the assumption that an area will specialize in producing goods for which it has the greatest advantage or the least comparative disadvantage.

Conrail   The Consolidated Rail Corporation established by the Regional Reorganization Act of 1973 to operate the bankrupt Penn Central Railroad and other bankrupt railroads in the Northeast; the 4-R Act of 1976 provided funding.

consignee   The receiver of a freight shipment, usually the buyer.

consignor   The sender of a freight shipment, usually the seller.

consolidation   Collecting smaller shipments to form a larger quantity in order to realize lower transportation rates.

container   A big box (ten to forty feet long) into which freight is loaded.

contingency planning   Preparing to deal with calamities (e.g., floods) and noncalamitous situations (e.g., strikes) before they occur.

continuous-flow, fixed-path equipment   Materials handling devices that include conveyors and drag lines.

continuous replenishment (CRP)   A system used to reduce customer inventories and improve service usually to large customers.

contract carrier   A for-hire carrier that does not serve the general public but serves shippers with whom the carrier has a continuing contract. The contract carrier must secure a permit to operate.

conveyor   A materials handling device that moves freight from one warehouse area to another. Roller conveyors utilize gravity, whereas belt conveyors use motors.

cooperative associations   Groups of firms or individuals having common interests; agricultural cooperative associations may haul up to 25 percent of their total interstate nonfarm, nonmember goods tonnage in movements incidental and necessary to their primary business.

coordinated transportation   Two or more carriers of different modes transporting a shipment.

cost of lost sales   The forgone profit companies associate with a stockout.

cost trade-off   The interrelationship among system variables in which a change in one variable affects other variables' costs. A cost reduction in one variable may increase costs for other variables, and vice versa.

Council of Logistics Management (CLM)   A professional organization in the logistics field that provides leadership in understanding the logistics process, awareness of career opportunities in logistics, and research that enhances customer value and supply chain performance.

courier service   A fast, door-to-door service for high-valued goods and documents; firms usually limit service to shipments weighing fifty pounds or less.

crane   A materials handling device that lifts heavy items. There are two types: bridge and stacker.

critical value analysis   A modified ABC analysis in which a company assigns a subjective critical value to each item in an inventory.

cross-docking   The movement of goods directly from receiving dock to shipping dock to eliminate storage expense.

currency adjustment factor (CAF)   An added charge assessed by water carriers for currency value changes.

customer service   Activities between the buyer and seller that enhance or facilitate the sale or use of the seller's products or services.

cycle inventory   An inventory system where counts are performed continuously, often eliminating the need for an annual overall inventory. It is usually set up so that A items are counted regularly (i.e., every month), B items are counted semi-regularly (every quarter or six months), and C items are counted perhaps only once a year.

decentralized authority A situation in which a company management gives decision-making authority to managers at many organizational levels.

decision support system (DSS) A set of computer-oriented tools designed to assist managers in making decisions.

defective goods inventory (DGI) Those items that have been returned, have been delivered damaged and have a freight claim outstanding, or have been damaged in some way during warehouse handling.

Delta Nu Alpha A professional association of transportation and traffic practitioners.

demurrage The charge a railroad assesses for a shipper or receiver holding a car beyond the free time the railroad allows for loading (twenty-four hours) or unloading (forty-eight hours).

density A physical characteristic measuring a commodity's mass per unit volume or pounds per cubic foot; an important factor in ratemaking, since density affects the utilization of a carrier's vehicle.

density rate A rate based upon the density and shipment weight.

deregulation Revisions or complete elimination of economic regulations controlling transportation. The Motor Carrier Act of 1980 and the Staggers Act of 1980 revised the economic controls over motor carriers and railroads, and the Airline Deregulation Act of 1978 eliminated economic controls over air carriers.

derived demand The demand for a product's transportation is derived from the product's demand at some location.

detention The charge a motor carrier assesses when a shipper or receiver holds a truck or trailer beyond the free time the carrier allows for loading or unloading.

differential A discount offered by a carrier that faces a service time disadvantage over a route.

direct product profitability (DPP) Calculation of the net profit contribution attributable to a specific product or product line.

direct store delivery (DSD) A logistics strategy to improve services and lower warehouse inventories.

dispatching The carrier activities involved with controlling equipment; involves arranging for fuel, drivers, crews, equipment, and terminal space.

distribution resource planning (DRP) A computer system that uses MRP techniques to manage the entire distribution network and to link it with manufacturing planning and control.

distribution warehouse A finished goods warehouse from which a company assembles customer orders.

diversion A carrier service that permits a shipper to change the consignee and/or destination while the shipment is en route and to still pay the through rate from origin to final destination.

dock receipt A receipt that indicates a domestic carrier has delivered an export shipment to a steamship company.

domestic trunk line carrier A classification for air carriers that operate between major population centers. These carriers are now classified as major carriers.

double bottoms A motor carrier operation that involves one tractor pulling two trailers.

double-pallet jack A mechanized device for transporting two standard pallets simultaneously.

download To merge temporary files containing a day's or week's worth of information with the main data base in order to update it.

drayage A motor carrier that operates locally, providing pickup and delivery service.

driving time regulations U.S. Department of Transportation rules that limit the maximum time a driver may drive in interstate commerce; the rules prescribe both daily and weekly maximums.

drop A situation in which an equipment operator deposits a trailer or boxcar at a facility at which it is to be loaded or unloaded.

dual operation A motor carrier that has both common and contract carrier operating authority.

dual rate system An international water carrier pricing system in which a shipper signing an exclusive use agreement with the conference pays a rate 10 to 15 percent lower than nonsigning shippers do for an identical shipment.

economic order quantity (EOQ)　An inventory model that determines how much to order by determining the amount that will minimize total ordering and holding costs.

economies of scale　The reduction in long-run average cost as the company's size (scale) increases.

efficient consumer response (ECR)　A customer-driven system where distributors and suppliers work together as business allies to maximize consumer satisfaction and minimize cost.

electronic data interchange (EDI)　Computer-to-computer communication between two or more companies that such companies can use to generate bills of lading, purchase orders, and invoices. It also enables firms to access the information systems of suppliers, customers, and carriers and to determine the up-to-the-minute status of inventory, orders, and shipments.

exception rate　A deviation from the class rate; changes (exceptions) made to the classification.

exclusive patronage agreements　A shipper agrees to use only a conference's member liner firms in return for a 10 to 15 percent rate reduction.

exclusive use　Vehicles that a carrier assigns to a specific shipper for its exclusive use.

exempt carrier　A for-hire carrier that is exempt from economic regulations.

expediting　Determining where an in-transit shipment is and attempting to speed up its delivery.

expert system　A computer program that mimics a human expert.

export declaration　A document required by the Department of Commerce that provides information about an export activity's nature and value.

export sales contract　The initial document in any international transaction; it details the specifics of the sales agreement between the buyer and seller.

fair return　A profit level that enables a carrier to realize a rate of return on investment or property value that the regulatory agencies deem acceptable for that level of risk.

fair value　The value of the carrier's property; the calculation basis has included original cost minus depreciation, replacement cost, and market value.

Federal Aviation Administration　The federal agency that administers federal safety regulations governing air transportation.

Federal Maritime Commission　A regulatory agency that controls services, practices, and agreements of international water common carriers and noncontiguous domestic water carriers.

FEU　Forty-foot equivalent unit, a standard size intermodal container.

field warehouse　A warehouse that stores goods on the goods' owner's property while the goods are under a bona fide public warehouse manager's custody. The owner uses the public warehouse receipts as collateral for a loan.

fill rate　The percentage of order items that the picking operation actually found.

finance lease　An equipment-leasing arrangement that provides the lessee with a means of financing for the leased equipment; a common method for leasing motor carrier trailers.

financial responsibility　Motor carriers must have bodily injury and property damage (not cargo) insurance of not less than $500,000 per incident per vehicle; higher financial responsibility limits apply for motor carriers transporting oil or hazardous materials.

finished goods inventory (FGI)　The products completely manufactured, packaged, stored, and ready for distribution.

firm planned order　In a DRP or MRP system, a planned order whose status has been updated to a fixed order.

fixed costs　Costs that do not fluctuate with the business volume in the short run.

fixed interval inventory model　A setup wherein a company orders inventory at fixed or regular time intervals.

fixed quantity inventory model　A setup wherein a company orders the same (fixed) quantity each time it places an order for an item.

flatbed　A trailer without sides used for hauling machinery or other bulky items.

flatcar　A railcar without sides, used for hauling machinery.

GLOSSARY

613

flexible-path equipment Materials handling devices that include hand trucks and forklifts.

F.O.B. A term of sale defining who is to incur transportation charges for the shipment, who is to control the shipment movement, or where title to the goods passes to the buyer; originally meant "free on board ship."

for-hire carrier A carrier that provides transportation service to the public on a fee basis.

forklift truck A machine-powered device used to raise and lower freight and to move freight to different warehouse locations.

flow rack A storage method where product is presented to picking operations at one end of a rack and replenished from the opposite end.

form utility The value the production process creates in a good by changing the item's form.

freight-all-kinds (FAK) An approach to rate making whereby the ante is based only upon the shipment weight and distance; widely used in TOFC service.

freight bill The carrier's invoice for a freight shipment's transportation charges.

freight forwarder A carrier that collects small shipments from shippers, consolidates the small shipments, and uses a basic mode to transport these consolidated shipments to a consignee destination.

Freight Forwarders Institute The freight forwarder industry association.

full-service leasing An equipment-leasing arrangement that includes a variety of services to support the leased equipment; a common method for leasing motor carrier tractors.

fully allocated cost The variable cost associated with a particular output unit plus a common cost allocation.

gathering lines Oil pipelines that bring oil from the oil well to storage areas.

general-commodities carrier A common motor carrier that has operating authority to transport general commodities, or all commodities not listed as special commodities.

general-merchandise warehouse A warehouse used to store goods that are readily handled, are packaged, and do not require a controlled environment.

going-concern value The value that a firm has as an entity, as opposed to the sum of the values of each of its parts taken separately; particularly important in determining a reasonable railroad rate.

gondola A railcar with a flat platform and sides three to five feet high, used for top loading long, heavy items.

grandfather clause A provision that enabled motor carriers engaged in lawful trucking operations before the passage of the Motor Carrier Act of 1935 to secure common carrier authority without proving public convenience and necessity; a similar provision exists for other modes.

granger laws State laws passed before 1870 in midwestern states to control rail transportation.

Great Lakes carriers Water carriers that operate on the five Great Lakes.

grid technique A quantitative technique to determine the least-cost center, given raw materials sources and markers, for locating a plant or warehouse.

Gross National Product (GNP) A measure of a nation's output; the total value of all final goods and services a nation produces during a time period.

gross weight The total weight of the vehicle and the payload of freight or passengers.

guaranteed loans Railroad loans that the federal government cosigns and guarantees.

hard copy Computer output printed on paper.

hazardous materials Materials that the Department of Transportation has determined to be a risk to health, safety, and property; includes items such as explosives, flammable liquids, poisons, corrosive liquids, and radioactive material.

Highway Trust Fund A fund into which highway users (carriers and automobile operators) pay; the fund pays for federal government's highway construction share.

highway use taxes Taxes that federal and state governments assess against highway users (the fuel tax is an example). The government uses the use tax money to pay for the construction, maintenance, and policing of highways.

hi-low Usually refers to a forklift truck on which the operator must stand rather than sit.

hopper cars Railcars that permit top loading and bottom unloading of bulk commodities; some hopper cars have permanent tops with hatches to provide protection against the elements.

household goods warehouse A warehouse that stores household goods.

hub airport An airport that serves as the focal point for the origin and termination of long-distance flights; flights from outlying areas meet connecting flights at the hub airport.

hundredweight (cwt) The pricing unit used in transportation; a hundredweight is equal to 100 pounds.

igloos Pallets and containers used in air transportation; the igloo shape fits the internal wall contours of a narrow-body airplane.

incentive rate A rate that induces the shipper to ship heavier volumes per shipment.

Incoterms International terms of sale developed by the International Chamber of Commerce.

independent action A carrier that is a rate bureau member may publish a rate that differs from the rate the rate bureau publishes.

information system (I/S) Managing the flow of data in an organization in a systematic, structured way to assist in planning, implementing, and controlling.

inherent advantage The cost and service benefits of one mode compared with other modes.

interchange The transfer of cargo and equipment from one carrier to another in a joint freight move.

intercoastal carriers Water carriers that transport freight between East and West Coast ports, usually by way of the Panama Canal.

intercorporate hauling A private carrier hauling a subsidiary's goods and charging the subsidiary a fee; this is legal if the subsidiary is wholly owned or if the private carrier has common carrier authority.

interline Two or more motor carriers working together to haul a shipment to a destination. Carriers may interchange equipment but usually they rehandle the shipment without transferring the equipment.

intermittent-flow, fixed-path equipment Materials handling devices that include bridge cranes, monorails, and stacker cranes.

intermodal marketing company (IMC) An intermediary that sells intermodal services to shippers.

intermodal transportation The use of two or more transportation modes to transport freight; for example, rail to ship to truck.

internal water carriers Water carriers that operate over internal, navigable rivers such as the Mississippi, Ohio, and Missouri.

International Air Transport Association An international air carrier rate bureau for passenger and freight movements.

International Civil Aeronautics Organization An international agency responsible for air safety and for standardizing air traffic control, airport design, and safety features worldwide.

interstate commerce The transportation of persons or property between states; in the course of the movement, the shipment crosses a state boundary.

Interstate Commerce Commission (ICC) An independent regulatory agency that implements federal economic regulations controlling railroads, motor carriers, pipelines, domestic water carriers, domestic surface freight forwarders, and brokers.

Interstate System The National System of Interstate and Defense Highways, 42,000 miles of four-lane, limited-access roads connecting major population centers.

intrastate commerce The transportation of persons or property between points within a state. A shipment between two points within a state may be interstate if the shipment had a prior or subsequent move outside of the state and the shipper intended an interstate shipment at the time of shipment.

inventory The number of units and/or value of the stock of goods a company holds.

inventory cost The cost of holding goods, usually expressed as a percentage of the inventory value; includes the cost of capital, warehousing, taxes, insurance, depreciation, and obsolescence.

inventory in transit Inventory in a carrier's possession, being transported to the buyer.

inventory management Inventory administration through planning, stock positioning, monitoring product age, and ensuring product availability.

irregular route carrier A motor carrier that may provide service utilizing any route.

joint cost A common cost in cases where a company produces products in fixed proportions and the cost the company incurs to produce one product entails producing another; the backhaul is an example.

joint rate A rate over a route that requires two or more carriers to transport the shipment.

just-in-time (JIT) inventory system An inventory control system that attempts to reduce inventory levels by coordinating demand and supply to the point where the desired item arrives just in time for use.

Kanban system A just-in-time inventory system used by Japanese manufacturers.

kitting The process by which individual items are grouped or packaged together to create a special single item.

lading The cargo carried in a transportation vehicle.

land bridge The movement of containers by ship-rail-ship on Japan-to-Europe moves; ships move containers to the U.S. Pacific Coast, rails move containers to an East Coast port, and ships deliver containers to Europe.

landed cost The total cost of a product delivered at a given location; the production cost plus the transportation cost to the customer's location.

land grants Grants of land given to railroads to build tracks during their development stage.

lash barges Covered barges that carriers load on board oceangoing ships for movement to foreign destinations.

LCL Less than carload rail service; less than container load.

lead time The total time that elapses between an order's placement and its receipt. It includes the time required for order transmittal, order processing, order preparation, and transit.

lessee A person or firm to whom a lessor grants a lease.

lessor A person or firm that grants a lease.

letter of credit An international business document that assures the seller that the bank issuing the letter of credit will make payment upon fulfillment of the sales agreement.

lighter A flat-bottomed boat designed for cross-harbor or inland waterway freight transfer.

line functions The decision-making areas companies associate with daily operations. Logistics line functions include traffic management, inventory control, order processing, warehousing, and packaging.

line-haul shipment A shipment that moves between cities and over distances more than 100 to 150 miles in length.

liner service International water carriers that ply fixed routes on published schedules.

link The transportation method a company uses to connect nodes (plants, warehouses) in a logistics system.

live A situation in which the equipment operator stays with the trailer or boxcar while it is being loaded or unloaded.

load factor A measure of operating efficiency used by air carriers to determine a plane's utilized capacity percentage or the number of passengers divided by the total number of seats.

loading allowance A reduced rate that carriers offer to shippers and/or consignees who load and/or unload LTL or AQ shipments.

localized raw material A raw material found only in certain locations.

local rate A rate published between two points served by one carrier.

local service carriers A classification of air carriers that operate between less-populated areas and major population centers. These carriers feed passengers into the major cities to connect with trunk (major) carriers. Local service carriers are now classified as national carriers.

locational determinant The factors that determine a

facility's location. For industrial facilities, the determinants include logistics.

logbook A daily record of the hours an interstate driver spends driving, off duty, sleeping in the berth, or on duty but not driving.

logistics channel The network of intermediaries engaged in transfer, storage, handling, and communications functions that contribute to the efficient flow of goods.

logistics data interchange (LDI) A computerized system that electronically transmits logistics information.

long ton 2,240 pounds.

lot size The quantity of goods a company purchases or produces in anticipation of use or sale in the future.

LTL shipment A less-than-truckload shipment, one weighing less than the minimum weight a company needs to use the lower truckload rate.

lumping The act of assisting a motor carrier owner-operator in the loading and unloading of property; quite commonly used in the food industry.

mainframe An organization's central computer system.

major carrier A for-hire certificated air carrier that has annual operating revenues of $1 billion or more; the carrier usually operates between major population centers.

marginal cost The cost to produce one additional unit of output; the change in total variable cost resulting from a one-unit change in output.

marine insurance Insurance to protect against cargo loss and damage when shipping by water transportation.

Maritime Administration A federal agency that promotes the merchant marine, determines ocean ship routes and services, and awards maritime subsidies.

market dominance The absence of effective competition for railroads from other carriers and modes for the traffic to which the rail rate applies. The Staggers Act stated that market dominance does not exist if the rate is below the revenue-to-variable-cost ratio of 160 percent in 1981 and 170 percent in 1983.

material index The ratio of the sum of the localized raw material weights to the weight of the finished product.

materials handling Short-distance movement of goods within a storage area.

materials management The movements and storage functions associated with supplying goods to a firm.

materials planning The materials management function that attempts to coordinate materials supply with materials demand.

materials requirements planning (MRP) A decision-making technique used to determine how much material to purchase and when to purchase it.

matrix organization An organizational structure that emphasizes the horizontal flow of authority; the company treats logistics as a project, with the logistics manager overseeing logistics costs but traditional departments controlling operations.

measurement ton Forty cubic feet; used in water transportation ratemaking.

merger The combination of two or more carriers into one company that will own, manage, and operate the properties that previously operated separately.

micro-land bridge An intermodal movement in which the shipment is moved from a foreign country to the U.S. by water and then moved across the U.S. by railroad to an interior, nonport city, or vice versa for exports from a nonport city.

mileage allowance An allowance, based upon distance, that railroads give to shippers using private railcars.

mileage rate A rate based upon the number of miles the commodity is shipped.

mini-land bridge An intermodal movement in which the shipment is moved from a foreign country to the U.S. by water and then moved across the U.S. by railroad to a destination that is a port city, or vice versa for exports from a U.S. port city.

minimum weight The shipment weight the carrier's tariff specifies as the minimum weight required to use the TL or CL rate; the rate discount volume.

mixed loads The movement of both regulated and exempt commodities in the same vehicle at the same time.

modal split The relative use that companies make of transportation modes; the statistics include ton-miles, passenger-miles, and revenue.

MRO items Maintenance, repair, and operating items—office supplies, for example.

multinational company A company that both produces and markets products in different countries.

multiple-car rate A railroad rate that is lower for shipping more than one carload at a time.

national carrier A for-hire certificated air carrier that has annual operating revenues of $75 million to $1 billion; the carrier usually operates between major population centers and areas of lesser population.

National Industrial Traffic League An association representing shippers' and receivers' interests in matters of transportation policy and regulation.

nationalization Public ownership, financing, and operation of a business entity.

National Motor Bus Operators Organization An industry association representing common and charter bus firms; now known as the American Bus Association.

National Railroad Corporation Also known as Amtrak, the corporation established by the Rail Passenger Service Act of 1970 to operate most of the United States' rail passenger service.

no location (No Loc) A received item for which the warehouse has no previously established storage slot.

node A fixed point in a firm's logistics system where goods come to rest; includes plants, warehouses, supply sources, and markets.

noncertificated carrier A for-hire air carrier that is exempt from economic regulation.

non-vessel-owning common carrier (NVOCC) A firm that consolidates and disperses international containers that originate at or are bound for inland ports.

on-line receiving A system in which computer terminals are available at each receiving bay and operators enter items into the system as they are unloaded.

operating ratio A measure of operating efficiency defined as

$$\frac{\text{Operating expenses}}{\text{Operating revenues}} \times 100$$

order cycle time The time that elapses from placement of order until receipt of order. This includes time for order transmittal, processing, preparation, and shipping.

ordering cost The cost of placing an inventory order with a supplier.

order picking Assembling a customer's order from items in storage.

order processing The activities associated with filling customer orders.

out-of-pocket cost The cost directly assignable to a particular unit of traffic and which a company would not have incurred if it had not performed the movement.

outsourcing Purchasing a logistics service from an outside firm, as opposed to performing it in-house.

over-the-road A motor carrier operation that reflects long-distance, intercity moves; the opposite of local operations.

owner-operator A trucking operation in which the truck's owner is also the driver.

pallet A platform device (about four feet square) used for moving and storing goods. A forklift truck is used to lift and move the loaded pallet.

pallet wrapping machine A machine that wraps a pallet's contents in stretch-wrap to ensure safe shipment.

passenger-mile A measure of output for passenger transportation that reflects the number of passengers transported and the distance traveled; a multiplication of passengers hauled and distance traveled.

P & D Pickup and delivery.

peak demand The time period during which customers demand the greatest quantity.

pegging A technique in which a DRP system traces demand for a product by date, quantity, and warehouse location.

per diem A payment rate one railroad makes to use another's cars.

permit A grant of authority to operate as a contract carrier.

personal computer (PC) An individual unit an operator uses for creating and maintaining programs and files; can often access the mainframe simultaneously.

personal discrimination Charging different rates to shippers with similar transportation characteristics, or, charging similar rates to shippers with differing transportation characteristics.

physical distribution The movement and storage of finished goods from manufacturing plants to warehouses to customers; used synonymously with business logistics.

physical supply The movement and storage of raw materials from supply sources to the manufacturing facility.

picking by aisle A method by which pickers pick all needed items in an aisle regardless of the items' ultimate destination; the items must be sorted later.

picking by source A method in which pickers successively pick all items going to a particular destination regardless of the aisle in which each item is located.

pick/pack Picking and packing immediately into shipment containers.

piggyback A rail-truck service. A shipper loads a highway trailer, and a carrier drives it to a rail terminal and loads it on a rail flatcar; the railroad moves the trailer-on-flatcar combination to the destination terminal, where the carrier offloads the trailer and delivers it to the consignee.

pin lock A hard piece of iron, formed to fit on a trailer's pin, that locks in place with a key to prevent an unauthorized person from moving the trailer.

place utility A value that logistics creates in a product by changing the product's location. Transportation creates place utility.

planned order In DRP and MRP systems, a future order the system plans in response to forecasted demand.

point of sale information (POS) Price and quantity data from the retail location as sales transactions occur.

police powers The United States' constitutionally granted right for the states to establish regulations to protect their citizens' health and welfare; truck weight; speed, length, and height laws are examples.

pooling An agreement among carriers to share the freight to be hauled or to share profits. The Interstate Commerce Act outlawed pooling agreements, but the Civil Aeronautics Board has approved profit pooling agreements for air carriers during strikes.

port authority A state or local government that owns, operates, or otherwise provides wharf, dock, and other terminal investments at ports.

possession utility The value created by marketing's effort to increase the desire to possess a good or benefit from a service.

primary-business test A test the ICC uses to determine if a trucking operation is bona fide private transportation; the private trucking operation must be incidental to and in the futherance of the firm's primary business.

private carrier A carrier that provides transportation service to the firm that owns or leases the vehicles and does not charge a fee. Private motor carriers may haul at a fee for wholly owned subsidiaries.

private warehousing The storage of goods in a warehouse owned by the company that has title to the goods.

production planning The decision-making area that determines when and where and in what quantity a manufacturer is to produce goods.

productivity A measure of resource utilization efficiency defined as the sum of the outputs divided by the sum of the inputs.

profit ratio The percentage of profit to sales—that is, profit divided by sales.

proportional rate A rate lower than the regular rate for shipments that have prior or subsequent moves; used to overcome combination rates' competitive disadvantages.

public warehouse receipt The basic document a public warehouse manager issues as a receipt for the goods a company gives to the warehouse manager. The receipt can be either negotiable or nonnegotiable.

public warehousing The storage of goods by a firm that offers storage service for a fee to the public.

pull ordering system A system in which each warehouse controls its own shipping requirements by placing individual orders for inventory with the central distribution center.

purchase price discount A pricing structure in which the seller offers a lower price if the buyer purchases a larger quantity.

purchasing The functions associated with buying the goods and services the firm requires.

pure raw material A raw material that does not lose weight in processing.

push ordering system A situation in which a firm makes inventory deployment decisions at the central distribution center and ships to its individual warehouses accordingly.

quality control The management function that attempts to ensure that the goods or services in a firm manufacturers or purchases meet the product or service specifications.

quick response A method of maximizing the efficiency of the supply chain by reducing inventory investment.

random access memory (RAM) Temporary memory on micro chips. Users can store data in RAM or take it out at high speeds. However, any information stored in RAM disappears when the computer is shut off.

rate basis number The distance between two rate basis points.

rate basis point The major shipping point in a local area; carriers consider all points in the local area to be the rate basis point.

rate bureau A carrier group that assembles to establish joint rates, to divide joint revenues and claim liabilities, and to publish tariffs. Rate bureaus have published single line rates, which were prohibited in 1984.

reasonable rate A rate that is high enough to cover the carrier's cost but not high enough to enable the carrier to realize monopolistic profits.

Recapture Clause A provision of the 1920 Transportation Act that provided for self-help financing for railroads. Railroads that earned more than the prescribed return contributed one-half of the excess to the fund from which the ICC made loans to less profitable railroads. The Recapture Clause was repealed in 1933.

reconsignment A carrier service that permits a ship-

the shipment has reached its originally billed destination and to still pay the through rate from origin to final destination.

Reed-Bulwinkle Act Legislation that legalized common carrier joint ratemaking through rate bureaus; extended antitrust immunity to carriers participating in a rate bureau.

reefer A refrigerated vehicle.

reengineering A fundamental rethinking and radical design of business processes to achieve dramatic improvements in performance.

refrigerated warehouse A warehouse that is used to store perishable items requiring controlled temperatures.

regional carrier A for-hire air carrier, usually certificated, that has annual operating revenues of less than $75 million; the carrier usually operates within a particular region of the country.

regular-route carrier A motor carrier that is authorized to provide service over designated routes.

relay terminal A motor carrier terminal that facilitates the substitution of one driver for another who has driven the maximum hours permitted.

released-value rates Rates based upon the shipment's value. The maximum carrier liability for damage is less than the full value, and in return the carrier offers a lower rate.

reliability A carrier selection criterion that considers the carrier transit time variation; the consistency of the transit time the carrier provides.

reorder point A predetermined inventory level that triggers the need to place an order. This minimum level provides inventory to meet the demand a firm anticipates during the time it takes to receive the order.

reparation A situation in which the ICC requires a railroad to repay users the difference between the rate the railroad charges and the maximum rate the ICC permits when the ICC finds a rate to be unreasonable or too high.

reverse logistics The process of collecting, moving, and storing used, damaged, or outdated products and/ or packaging from end users.

right of eminent domain   A concept that, in a court of law, permits a carrier to purchase land it needs for transportation right-of-way; used by railroads and pipelines.

roll-on-roll-off (RO-RO)   A type of ship designed to permit cargo to be driven on at origin and off at destination; used extensively for the movement of automobiles.

rule of eight   Before the Motor Carrier Act of 1980, the ICC restricted contract carriers requesting authority to eight shippers under contract. The number of shippers has been deleted as a consideration for granting a contract carrier permit.

rule of ratemaking   A regulatory provision directing the regulatory agencies to consider the earnings a carrier needs to provide adequate transportation.

safety stock   The inventory a company holds beyond normal needs as a buffer against delays in receipt of orders or changes in customer buying patterns.

salvage material   Unused material that has a market value and can be sold.

scrap material   Unusable material that has no market value.

separable cost   A cost that a company can directly assign to a particular segment of the business.

setup costs   The costs a manufacturer incurs in staging the production line to produce a different item.

ship agent   A liner company or tramp ship operator representative who facilitates ship arrival, clearance, loading and unloading, and fee payment while at a specific port.

ship broker   A firm that serves as a go-between for the tramp ship owner and the chartering consignor or consignee.

shipper's agent   A firm that primarily matches up small shipments, especially single-traffic piggyback loads, to permit shippers to use twin-trailer piggyback rates.

shippers association   A nonprofit, cooperative consolidator and distributor of shipments that member firms own or ship; acts in much the same way as a for-profit freight forwarder.

short-haul discrimination   Charging more for a shorter haul than for a longer haul over the same route, in the same direction, and for the same commodity.

short ton   2,000 pounds.

simulation   A computer model that represents a real-life logistics operation with mathematical symbols and runs it for a simulated length of time to determine how proposed changes will affect the operation.

sleeper team   Two drivers who operate a truck equipped with a sleeper berth; while one driver sleeps in the berth to accumulate mandatory off-duty time, the other driver operates the vehicle.

slip seat operation   A motor carrier relay terminal operation in which a carrier substitutes one driver for another who has accumulated the maximum driving time hours.

slip sheet   Similar to a pallet, the slip sheet, which is made of cardboard or plastic, is used to facilitate movement of unitized loads.

slurry   Dry commodities that are made into a liquid form by the addition of water or other fluids to permit movement by pipeline.

Society of Logistics Engineers   A professional association engaged in the advancement of logistics technology and management.

software   A computer term that describes the system design and programming that the computer's effective use requires.

special-commodities carrier   A common carrier trucking company that has authority to haul a special commodity; the sixteen special commodities include household goods, petroleum products, and hazardous materials.

special-commodity warehouses   A warehouse that is used to store products requiring unique facilities, such as grain (elevator), liquid (tank), and tobacco (barn).

spot   To move a trailer or boxcar into place for loading or unloading.

spur track   A railroad track that connects a company's plant or warehouse with the railroad's track; the user bears the cost of the spur track and its maintenance.

staff functions   The planning and analysis support activities a firm provides to assist line managers with daily operations. Logistics staff functions include location analysis, system design, cost analysis, and planning.

statistical process control (SPC)   A managerial control technique that examines a process's inherent variability.

steamship conferences   Collective ratemaking bodies for liner water carriers.

stock-keeping unit (SKU)   A single unit that has been completely assembled. In a DRP system, an item is not considered complete until it is where it can satisfy customer demand.

stockless purchasing   A practice whereby the buyer negotiates a purchase price for annual requirements of MRO items and the seller holds inventory until the buyer orders individual items.

stockout   A situation in which the items a customer orders are currently unavailable.

stockout cost   The opportunity cost that companies associate with not having supply sufficient to meet demand.

stores   The function associated with storing and issuing frequently used items.

strategic planning   Looking one to five years into the future and designing a logistical system (or systems) to meet the needs of the various businesses in which a company is involved.

strategic variables   The variables that effect change in the environment and logistics strategy. The major strategic variables include the economy, population, energy, and government.

strategy   A specific action to achieve an objective.

stretch-wrap   An elastic, thin plastic material that effectively adheres to itself, thereby containing product on a pallet when wrapped around the items.

substitutability   A buyer's ability to substitute different sellers' products.

supplemental carrier   A for-hire air carrier having no time schedule or designated route; the carrier provides service under a charter or contract per plane per trip.

supply chain management (SCM)   An approach to analyzing and/or managing logistics networks.

supply warehouse   A warehouse that stores raw materials; a company mixes goods from different suppliers at the warehouse and assembles plant orders.

surcharge   An add-on charge to the applicable charges; motor carriers have a fuel surcharge, and railroads can apply a surcharge to any joint rate that does not yield 110 percent of variable cost.

switch engine   A railroad engine that is used to move railcars short distances within a terminal and plant.

switching company   A railroad that moves railcars short distances; switching companies connect two mainline railroads to facilitate through movement of shipments.

system   A set of interacting elements, variable, parts, or objects that are functionally related to each other and form a coherent group.

systems concept   A decision-making strategy that emphasizes overall system efficiency rather than the efficiency of each part.

tally sheet   A printed form on which companies record, by making an appropriate mark, the number of items they receive or ship. In many operations, tally sheets become a part of the permanent inventory records.

tandem   A truck that has two drive axles or a trailer that has two axles.

tank cars   Railcars designed to haul bulk liquid or gas commodities.

tapering rate   A rate that increases with distance but not in direct proportion to the distance the commodity is shipped.

tare weight   The weight of the vehicle when it is empty.

tariff   A publication that contains a carrier's rates, accessorial charges, and rules.

temporary authority   Temporary operating authority as a common carrier granted by the ICC for up to 270 days.

TEU   Twenty-foot equivalent unit, a standard size intermodal container.

terminal delivery allowance A reduced rate that a carrier offers in return for the shipper or consignee tendering or picking up the freight at the carrier's terminal.

third party A firm that supplies logistics services to other companies.

three-layer framework A basic structure and operational activity of a company; the three layers include operational systems, control and administrative management, and master planning.

throughput A warehousing output measure that considers the volume (weight, number of units) of items stored during a given time period.

time/service rate A rail rate that is based upon transit time.

timetables Time schedules of departures and arrivals by origin and destination; typically used for passenger transportation by air, bus, and rail.

time utility A value created in a product by having the product available at the time desired. Transportation and warehousing create time utility.

TL (truckload) A shipment weighing the minimum weight or more. Carriers give a rate reduction for shipping a TL-size shipment.

TOFC (trailer-on-flatcar) Also known as piggyback.

ton-mile A freight transportation output measure that reflects the shipment's weight and the distance the carrier hauls it; a multiplication of tons hauled and distance traveled.

total cost analysis A decision-making approach that considers total system cost minimization and recognizes the interrelationship among system variables such as transportation, warehousing, inventory, and customer service.

total quality management (TQM) A management approach in which managers constantly communicate with organizational stakeholders to emphasize the importance of continuous quality improvement.

Toto authority A private motor carrier receiving operating authority as a common carrier to haul freight for the public over the private carrier's backhaul; the ICC granted this type of authority to the Toto Company in 1978.

tracing Determining a shipment's location during the course of a move.

traffic management The buying and controlling of transportation services for a shipper or consignee, or both.

tramp An international water carrier that has no fixed route or published schedule; a shipper charters a tramp ship for a particular voyage or a given time period.

transit privilege A carrier service that permits the shipper to stop the shipment in transit to perform a function that changes the commodity's physical characteristics, but to still pay the through rate.

transit time The total time that elapses between a shipment's delivery and its pickup.

Transportation Association of America An association that represents the entire U.S. transportation system—carriers, users, and the public; now defunct.

transportation method A linear programming technique that determines the least-cost means of shipping goods from plants to warehouses or from warehouses to customers.

transportation requirements planning (TRP) Utilizing computer technology and information already available in MRP and DRP databases to plan transportation needs based on field demand.

Transportation Research Board A division of the National Academy of Sciences which pertains to transportation research.

Transportation Research Forum A professional association that provides a forum for the discussion of transportation ideas and research techniques.

transshipment problem A variation of the linear programming transportation method that considers consolidating shipments to one destination and reshipping from that destination.

travel agent A firm that provides passenger travel information; air, rail, and steamship ticketing; and hotel reservations. The carrier and hotel pay the travel agent a commission.

trunk lines Oil pipelines used for the long-distance movements of crude oil, refined oil, or other liquid products.

two-bin system   An inventory ordering system in which the time to place an order for an item is indicated when the first bin is empty. The second bin contains supply sufficient to last until the company receives the order.

ubiquity   A raw material that is found at all locations.

umbrella rate   An ICC ratemaking practice that held rates to a particular level to protect another mode's traffic.

Uniform Warehouse Receipts Act   The act that sets forth the regulations governing public warehousing. The regulations define a warehouse manager's legal responsibility and define the types of receipts he or she issues.

United States Railway Association   The planning and funding agency for Conrail; created by the 3-R Act of 1973.

unitize   To consolidate several packages into one unit; carriers strap, band, or otherwise attach the several packages together.

unit train   An entire, uninterrupted locomotive, car, and caboose movement between an origin and destination.

Urban Mass Transportation Administration   A U.S. Department of Transportation agency that develops comprehensive mass transport systems for urban areas and for providing financial aid to transit systems.

value-of-service pricing   Pricing according to the value of the product the company is transporting; third-degree price discrimination; demand-oriented pricing; charging what the traffic will bear.

variable cost   A cost that fluctuates with the volume of business.

vendor   A firm or individual that supplies goods or services; the seller.

vendor managed inventories (VMI)   A customer service strategy used to manage inventory of customers to lower cost and improve service.

von Thunen's belts   A series of concentric rings around a city to identify where agricultural products would be produced according to von Thunen's theory.

warehousing   The storage (holding) of goods.

waterway use tax   A per-gallon tax assessed barge carriers for waterway use.

weight break   The shipment volume at which the LTL charges equal the TL charges at the minimum weight.

weight-losing raw material   A raw material that loses weight in processing.

work in process (WIP)   Parts and subassemblies in the process of becoming completed assembly components. These items, no longer part of the raw materials inventory and not yet part of the finished goods inventory, may constitute a large inventory by themselves and create extra expense for the firm.

zone of rate flexibility   Railroads may raise rates by a percentage increase in the railroad cost index that the ICC determines; the railroads could raise rates by 6 percent per year through 1984 and 4 percent thereafter.

zone of rate freedom   Motor carriers may raise or lower rates by 10 percent in one year without ICC interference; if the rate change is within the zone of freedom, the rate is presumed to be reasonable.

zone of reasonableness   A zone or limit within which air carriers may change rates without regulatory scrutiny; if the rate change is within the zone, the new rate is presumed to be reasonable.

zone price   The constant price of a product at all geographic locations within a zone.

Author Index

SUBJECT INDEX